Lecture Notes in Computer Science　　　10206

Commenced Publication in 1973
Founding and Former Series Editors:
Gerhard Goos, Juris Hartmanis, and Jan van Leeuwen

Advanced Research in Computing and Software Science
Subline of Lecture Notes in Computer Science

More information about this series at http://www.springer.com/series/7407

Axel Legay · Tiziana Margaria (Eds.)

Tools and Algorithms for the Construction and Analysis of Systems

23rd International Conference, TACAS 2017
Held as Part of the European Joint Conferences
on Theory and Practice of Software, ETAPS 2017
Uppsala, Sweden, April 22–29, 2017
Proceedings, Part II

 Springer

Editors
Axel Legay
Inria
Rennes Cedex
France

Tiziana Margaria
University of Limerick and Lero - The Irish
  Software Research Center
Limerick
Ireland

ISSN 0302-9743   ISSN 1611-3349 (electronic)
Lecture Notes in Computer Science
ISBN 978-3-662-54579-9   ISBN 978-3-662-54580-5 (eBook)
DOI 10.1007/978-3-662-54580-5

Library of Congress Control Number: 2017935566

LNCS Sublibrary: SL1 – Theoretical Computer Science and General Issues

Printed on acid-free paper

This Springer imprint is published by Springer Nature
The registered company is Springer-Verlag GmbH Germany
The registered company address is: Heidelberger Platz 3, 14197 Berlin, Germany

ETAPS Foreword

Welcome to the proceedings of ETAPS 2017, which was held in Uppsala! It was the first time ever that ETAPS took place in Scandinavia.

ETAPS 2017 was the 20th instance of the European Joint Conferences on Theory and Practice of Software. ETAPS is an annual federated conference established in 1998, and consists of five conferences: ESOP, FASE, FoSSaCS, TACAS, and POST. Each conference has its own Program Committee (PC) and its own Steering Committee. The conferences cover various aspects of software systems, ranging from theoretical computer science to foundations to programming language developments, analysis tools, formal approaches to software engineering, and security. Organizing these conferences in a coherent, highly synchronized conference program enables participation in an exciting event, offering the possibility to meet many researchers working in different directions in the field and to easily attend talks of different conferences. Before and after the main conference, numerous satellite workshops take place and attract many researchers from all over the globe.

ETAPS 2017 received 531 submissions in total, 159 of which were accepted, yielding an overall acceptance rate of 30%. I thank all authors for their interest in ETAPS, all reviewers for their peer reviewing efforts, the PC members for their contributions, and in particular the PC (co-)chairs for their hard work in running this entire intensive process. Last but not least, my congratulations to all authors of the accepted papers!

ETAPS 2017 was enriched by the unifying invited speakers Kim G. Larsen (Aalborg University, Denmark) and Michael Ernst (University of Washington, USA), as well as the conference-specific invited speakers (FoSSaCS) Joel Ouaknine (MPI-SWS, Germany, and University of Oxford, UK) and (TACAS) Dino Distefano (Facebook and Queen Mary University of London, UK). In addition, ETAPS 2017 featured a public lecture by Serge Abiteboul (Inria and ENS Cachan, France). Invited tutorials were offered by Véronique Cortier (CNRS research director at Loria, Nancy, France) on security and Ken McMillan (Microsoft Research Redmond, USA) on compositional testing. My sincere thanks to all these speakers for their inspiring and interesting talks!

ETAPS 2017 took place in Uppsala, Sweden, and was organized by the Department of Information Technology of Uppsala University. It was further supported by the following associations and societies: ETAPS e.V., EATCS (European Association for Theoretical Computer Science), EAPLS (European Association for Programming Languages and Systems), and EASST (European Association of Software Science and Technology). Facebook, Microsoft, Amazon, and the city of Uppsala financially supported ETAPS 2017. The local organization team consisted of Parosh Aziz Abdulla (general chair), Wang Yi, Björn Victor, Konstantinos Sagonas, Mohamed Faouzi Atig, Andreina Francisco, Kaj Lampka, Tjark Weber, Yunyun Zhu, and Philipp Rümmer.

The overall planning for ETAPS is the main responsibility of the Steering Committee, and in particular of its executive board. The ETAPS Steering Committee consists of an executive board, and representatives of the individual ETAPS conferences, as well as representatives of EATCS, EAPLS, and EASST. The executive board consists of Gilles Barthe (Madrid), Holger Hermanns (Saarbrücken), Joost-Pieter Katoen (chair, Aachen and Twente), Gerald Lüttgen (Bamberg), Vladimiro Sassone (Southampton), Tarmo Uustalu (Tallinn), and Lenore Zuck (Chicago). Other members of the Steering Committee are: Parosh Abdulla (Uppsala), Amal Ahmed (Boston), Christel Baier (Dresden), David Basin (Zurich), Lujo Bauer (Pittsburgh), Dirk Beyer (Munich), Giuseppe Castagna (Paris), Tom Crick (Cardiff), Javier Esparza (Munich), Jan Friso Groote (Eindhoven), Jurriaan Hage (Utrecht), Reiko Heckel (Leicester), Marieke Huisman (Twente), Panagotios Katsaros (Thessaloniki), Ralf Küsters (Trier), Ugo del Lago (Bologna), Kim G. Larsen (Aalborg), Axel Legay (Rennes), Matteo Maffei (Saarbrücken), Tiziana Margaria (Limerick), Andrzej Murawski (Warwick), Catuscia Palamidessi (Palaiseau), Julia Rubin (Vancouver), Alessandra Russo (London), Mark Ryan (Birmingham), Don Sannella (Edinburgh), Andy Schürr (Darmstadt), Gabriele Taentzer (Marburg), Igor Walukiewicz (Bordeaux), and Hongseok Yang (Oxford).

I would like to take this opportunity to thank all speakers, attendees, organizers of the satellite workshops, and Springer for their support. Finally, a big thanks to Parosh and his local organization team for all their enormous efforts enabling a fantastic ETAPS in Uppsala!

April 2017   Joost-Pieter Katoen

Preface

TACAS 2017 was the 23rd edition of the International Conference on Tools and Algorithms for the Construction and Analysis of Systems. The conference took place during April 2017, in the Uppsala Concert and Congress Hall as part of the 19th European Joint Conferences on Theory and Practice of Software (ETAPS 2017).

TACAS is a forum for researchers, developers, and users interested in rigorously based tools and algorithms for the construction and analysis of systems. The conference aims to bridge the gaps between different communities with this common interest and to support them in their quest to improve the utility, reliability, flexibility, and efficiency of tools and algorithms for building systems.

As in former years, TACAS 2017 solicited four types of submissions:

- Research papers, identifying and justifying a principled advance to the theoretical foundations for the construction and analysis of systems, where applicable supported by experimental validation
- Case-study papers, reporting on case studies and providing information about the system being studied, the goals of the study, the challenges the system poses to automated analysis, research methodologies and approaches used, the degree to which goals were attained, and how the results can be generalized to other problems and domains
- Regular tool papers, presenting a new tool, a new tool component, or novel extensions to an existing tool, with an emphasis on design and implementation concerns, including software architecture and core data structures, practical applicability, and experimental evaluation
- Short tool-demonstration papers, focusing on the usage aspects of tools

This year, 181 papers were submitted to TACAS, among which 167 were research, case study, or tool papers, and 14 were tool demonstration papers. After a rigorous review process followed by an online discussion, the Program Committee accepted 48 full papers and four tool demonstration papers. This volume also includes an invited paper by the ETAPS unifying speaker Kim. G. Larsen titled "Validation, Synthesis, and Optimization for Cyber-Physical Systems" and an invited paper by TACAS invited speaker Dino Distefano titled "The Facebook Infer Static Analyzer."

TACAS 2017 also hosted the 6th International Competition on Software Verification (SV-COMP), chaired and organized by Dirk Beyer. The competition again had a high participation: 32 verification tools from 12 countries were submitted for the systematic comparative evaluation, including two submissions from industry. This volume includes an overview of the competition results, and short papers describing 12 of the participating verification systems. These papers were reviewed by a separate Program Committee; each of the papers was assessed by four reviewers. One session in the TACAS program was reserved for the presentation of the results: the summary by the SV-COMP chair and the participating tools by the developer teams.

Many people worked hard and offered their valuable time generously to make TACAS 2017 successful. First, the chairs would like to thank the authors for submitting their papers to TACAS 2017. We are grateful to the reviewers who contributed to nearly 550 informed and detailed reports and discussions during the electronic Program Committee meeting. We also sincerely thank the Steering Committee for their advice. We also acknowledge the work of Parosh Aziz Abdulla and the local organizers for ETAPS 2017. Furthermore, we would like to express a special thanks to Joost-Pieter Katoen, who answered many of our questions during the preparation of TACAS 2017. Finally, we thank EasyChair for providing us with the infrastructure to manage the submissions, the reviewing process, the Program Committee discussion, and the preparation of the proceedings.

April 2017

Dirk Beyer
Axel Legay
Tiziana Margaria
Dave Parker

Organization

Program Committee

Gilles Barthe	IMDEA Software Institute, Spain
Dirk Beyer	LMU Munich, Germany
Armin Biere	Johannes Kepler University Linz, Austria
Radu Calinescu	University of York, UK
Franck Cassez	Macquarie University, Australia
Swarat Chaudhuri	Rice University, USA
Alessandro Cimatti	FBK-irst, Italy
Rance Cleaveland	University of Maryland, USA
Byron Cook	University College London, UK
Leonardo de Moura	Microsoft Research
Cezara Dragoi	IST Austria
Cindy Eisner	IBM Research, Haifa, Israel
Martin Fränzle	Carl von Ossietzky Universität Oldenburg, Germany
Sicun Gao	MIT CSAIL, USA
Susanne Graf	Universite Joseph Fourier, CNRS, VERIMAG, France
Orna Grumberg	Technion, Israel Institute of Technology, Israel
Kim Guldstrand Larsen	Aalborg University, Denmark
Klaus Havelund	Jet Propulsion Laboratory, California Institute of Technology, USA
Holger Hermanns	Saarland University, Germany
Falk Howar	TU Clausthal/IPSSE, Germany
Thomas Jensen	Inria, France
Jan Kretinsky	Masaryk University, Czech Republic
Salvatore La Torre	Università degli studi di Salerno, Italy
Axel Legay	IRISA/Inria, Rennes, France
P. Madhusudan	University of Illinois at Urbana-Champaign, USA
Pasquale Malacaria	Queen Mary University of London, UK
Tiziana Margaria	Lero, Ireland
Darko Marinov	University of Illinois at Urbana-Champaign, USA
Dejan Nickovic	Austrian Institute of Technology AIT, Austria
David Parker	University of Birmingham, UK
Charles Pecheur	Université catholique de Louvain, Belgium
Kristin Yvonne Rozier	University of Cincinnati, USA
Natasha Sharygina	Università della Svizzera italiana (USI Lugano, Switzerland), Switzerland
Bernhard Steffen	University of Dortmund, Germany
Stavros Tripakis	University of California, Berkeley, USA
Jaco van de Pol	University of Twente, The Netherlands
Thomas Wies	New York University, USA

Additional Reviewers

Adir, Allon
Aleksandrowicz, Gadi
Almagor, Shaull
Alt, Leonardo
Aniculaesei, Adina
Asadi, Sepideh
Ashok, Pranav
Bacci, Giorgio
Bacci, Giovanni
Bansal, Suguman
Barnat, Jiri
Barringer, Howard
Bartocci, Ezio
Bensalem, Saddek
Berthomieu, Bernard
Biewer, Sebastian
Bloemen, Vincent
Blom, Stefan
Bogomolov, Sergiy
Busard, Simon
Butkova, Yuliya
Ceska, Milan
Chadha, Rohit
Chothia, Tom
Clemente, Lorenzo
Courtieu, Pierre
Da Silva, Carlos Eduardo
Daca, Przemyslaw
Dang, Thao
Dangl, Matthias
Daniel, Jakub
Dantam, Neil
de Ruiter, Joeri
Della Monica, Dario
Delzanno, Giorgio
Demasi, Ramiro
Doyen, Laurent
Dräger, Klaus
Duedder, Boris
Dureja, Rohit
Echahed, Rachid
Ehlers, Rüdiger
Ellis, Kevin

Ellison, Martyn
Emmi, Michael
Faella, Marco
Fahrenberg, Uli
Falcone, Ylies
Fazekas, Katalin
Fedyukovich, Grigory
Ferrara, Anna Lisa
Finkbeiner, Bernd
Flores-Montoya, Antonio
Fogarty, Seth
Fontaine, Pascal
Fox, Gereon
Frehse, Goran
Freiberger, Felix
Frenkel, Hadar
Friedberger, Karlheinz
Frohme, Markus
Ganty, Pierre
Gao, Yang
Genet, Thomas
Gentilini, Raffaella
Gerasimou, Simos
Gerhold, Marcus
Gerwinn, Sebastian
Giacobbe, Mirco
Giantamidis, Georgios
Gillard, Xavier
Given-Wilson, Thomas
Gligoric, Milos
Graf-Brill, Alexander
Gregoire, Benjamin
Grigore, Radu
Gyori, Alex
Hadzi-Tanovic, Milica
Hahn, Ernst Moritz
Hartmanns, Arnd
Hashemi, Vahid
Hatefi, Hassan
Hyvärinen, Antti
Inverso, Omar
Islam, Md. Ariful
Ivrii, Alexander

Jabbour, Fadi
Jaeger, Manfred
Jaksic, Stefan
Jasper, Marc
Jensen, Peter Gjøl
Johnson, Kenneth
Kaminski, Benjamin Lucien
Kang, Eunsuk
Kauffman, Sean
Keefe, Ken
Keidar-Barner, Sharon
Khouzani, Arman Mhr
Kikuchi, Shinji
King, Tim
Konnov, Igor
Koskinen, Eric
Koukoutos, Manos
Krenn, Willibald
Kumar, Rahul
Kupferman, Orna
Lacerda, Bruno
Laporte, Vincent
Le Guernic, Colas
Leroux, Jérôme
Leue, Stefan
Limbrée, Christophe
Lipskoch, Kinga
Lorber, Florian
Mahmood, Muhammad Suleman
Marescotti, Matteo
Marin, Paolo
Martinelli Tabajara, Lucas
Maudoux, Guillaume
Mauritz, Malte
Meel, Kuldeep
Meggendorfer, Tobias
Meijer, Jeroen
Meller, Yael
Meyer, Philipp J.
Micheli, Andrea
Mikučionis, Marius
Miner, Andrew
Mogavero, Fabio
Muniz, Marco
Nevo, Ziv
Nies, Gilles

Norman, Gethin
O'Kelly, Matthew
Oliva, Paulo
Oortwijn, Wytse
Orni, Avigail
Palmskog, Karl
Paoletti, Nicola
Paterson, Colin
Peled, Doron
Peters, Henrik
Phan, Quoc-Sang
Pinisetty, Srinivas
Preiner, Mathias
Preoteasa, Viorel
Pulina, Luca
Quilbeuf, Jean
Rajhans, Akshay
Rasin, Dan
Ravanbakhsh, Hadi
Reger, Giles
Reynolds, Andrew
Rezine, Ahmed
Rival, Xavier
Rothenberg, Bat-Chen
Roveri, Marco
Rozier, Eric
Ruijters, Enno
Rüthing, Oliver
Sangnier, Arnaud
Sankur, Ocan
Schivo, Stefano
Schwarzentruber, Francois
Schwoon, Stefan
Sebastiani, Roberto
Sergey, Ilya
Shi, August
Shmarov, Fedor
Shudrak, Maksim
Sighireanu, Mihaela
Sinn, Moritz
Sosnovich, Adi
Sproston, Jeremy
Srba, Jiri
Strub, Pierre-Yves
Taankvist, Jakob Haahr
Tarrach, Thorsten

Tautschnig, Michael
Théry, Laurent
Tonetta, Stefano
Traonouez, Louis-Marie
Trostanetski, Anna
Tzevelekos, Nikos
Urbain, Xavier
Valero, Pedro
van der Berg, Freark
van Dijk, Tom
Vizel, Yakir

Wendler, Philipp
Westphal, Bernd
Widder, Josef
Xue, Bai
Xue, Bingtian
Yorav, Karen
Zhai, Ennan
Zhang, Lingming
Ziv, Avi
Zuliani, Paolo

Abstracts of Invited Talks

Validation, Synthesis and Optimization for Cyber-Physical Systems

Kim Guldstrand Larsen

Department of Computer Science, Aalborg University,
Selma Lagerlöfs Vej 300, 9220 Aalborg East, Denmark
kgl@cs.aau.dk

Abstract. The growing complexity of Cyber-Physical Systems increasingly challenges existing methods and techniques. What is needed is a new generation of scalable tools for model-based learning, analysis, synthesis and optimization based on a mathematical sound foundation, that enables trade-offs between functional safety and quantitative performance. In paper we illustrate how recent branches of the UPPAAL tool suit are making an effort in this direction.

This work is partly funded by the ERC Advanced Grant LASSO: Learning, Analysis, SynthesiS and Optimization of Cyber-Physical Systems as well as the Innovation Center DiCyPS: Data-Intensive Cyber Physical Systems.

The Facebook Infer Static Analyser

Dino Distefano

Facebook Inc., Menlo Park, USA

Abstract. Infer is an open-source static analyser developed at Facebook [1]. Originally based on Separation Logic [2, 3], Infer has lately evolved from a specific tool for heap-manipulating programs to a general framework which facilitates the implementation of new static analyses.

In this talk, I will report on the Infer team's experience of applying our tool to Facebook mobile code, each day helping thousands of engineers to build more reliable and secure software [4]. Moreover, I will discuss the team's current effort to turn Infer into a static analysis platform for research and development useful both to academic researchers and industrial practitioners.

References

1. http://fbinfer.com
2. Calcagno, C., Distefano, D., O'Hearn, P.W., Yang, H.: Compositional shape analysis by means of bi-abduction. In: POPL, pp. 289–300. ACM (2009)
3. Calcagno, C., Distefano, D.: Infer: an automatic program verifier for memory safety of C programs. In: Bobaru, M., Havelund. K., Holzmann, G.J., Joshi, R. (eds.) NFM 2011. LNCS, vol. 6617, pp. 459–465. Springer, Heidelberg (2011)
4. Calcagno, C., Distefano, D., Dubreil, J., Gabi, D., Hooimeijer, P., Luca, M., O'Hearn, P.W., Papakonstantinou, I., Purbrick, J., Rodriguez, D.: Moving Fast with Software Verification. In: Havelund, K., Holzmann, G., Joshi, R. (eds.) NFM 2015. LNCS, vol. 9058, pp. 3–11. Springer, Switzerland (2015)

Contents – Part II

Contents – Part I

Hybrid Systems

Security

Static Detection of DoS Vulnerabilities in Programs that Use Regular Expressions

Valentin Wüstholz[(✉)], Oswaldo Olivo[(✉)], Marijn J.H. Heule[(✉)],
and Isil Dillig[(✉)]

The University of Texas at Austin, Austin, USA
{valentin,olivo,marijn,isil}@cs.utexas.edu

Abstract. In an *algorithmic complexity attack*, a malicious party takes advantage of the worst-case behavior of an algorithm to cause denial-of-service. A prominent algorithmic complexity attack is *regular expression denial-of-service (ReDoS)*, in which the attacker exploits a vulnerable regular expression by providing a carefully-crafted input string that triggers worst-case behavior of the matching algorithm. This paper proposes a technique for automatically finding ReDoS vulnerabilities in programs. Specifically, our approach automatically identifies *vulnerable regular expressions* in the program and determines whether an "evil" input string can be matched against a vulnerable regular expression. We have implemented our proposed approach in a tool called REX-PLOITER and found 41 exploitable security vulnerabilities in Java web applications.

1 Introduction

Regular expressions provide a versatile mechanism for parsing and validating input data. Due to their flexibility, many developers use regular expressions to validate passwords or to extract substrings that match a given pattern. Hence, many languages provide extensive support for regular expression matching.

While there are several algorithms for determining membership in a regular language, a common technique is to construct a non-deterministic finite automaton (NFA) and perform backtracking search over all possible runs of this NFA. Although simple and flexible, this strategy has super-linear (in fact, exponential) complexity and is prone to a class of *algorithmic complexity attacks* [14]. For some regular expressions (e.g., (a|b)*(a|c)*), it is possible to craft input strings that could cause the matching algorithm to take quadratic time (or worse) in the size of the input. For some regular expressions (e.g., (a+)+), one can even generate input strings that could cause the matching algorithm to take exponential time. Hence, attackers exploit the presence of vulnerable regular expressions to launch so-called *regular expression denial-of-service (ReDoS)* attacks.

ReDoS attacks have been shown to severely impact the responsiveness and availability of applications. For example, the .NET framework was shown to be vulnerable to a ReDoS attack that paralyzed applications using .NET's default validation mechanism [2]. Furthermore, unlike other DoS attacks that require

© Springer-Verlag GmbH Germany 2017
A. Legay and T. Margaria (Eds.): TACAS 2017, Part II, LNCS 10206, pp. 3–20, 2017.
DOI: 10.1007/978-3-662-54580-5_1

thousands of machines to bring down critical infrastructure, ReDoS attacks can be triggered by a single malicious user input. Consequently, developers are responsible for protecting their code against such attacks, either by avoiding the use of vulnerable regular expressions or by *sanitizing* user input.

Unfortunately, protecting an application against ReDoS attacks can be non-trivial in practice. Often, developers do not know which regular expressions are vulnerable or how to rewrite them in a way that avoids super-linear complexity. In addition, it is difficult to implement a suitable sanitizer without understanding the class of input strings that trigger worst-case behavior. Even though some libraries (e.g., the .NET framework) allow developers to set a time limit for regular expression matching, existing solutions do not address the root cause of the problem. As a result, ReDoS vulnerabilities are still being uncovered in many important applications. For instance, according to the National Vulnerability Database (NVD), there are over 150 acknowledged ReDoS vulnerabilities, some of which are caused by exponential matching complexity (e.g., [2,3]) and some of which are characterized by super-linear behavior (e.g., [1,4,5]).

In this paper, we propose a static technique for automatically uncovering DoS vulnerabilities in programs that use regular expressions. There are two main technical challenges that make this problem difficult: First, given a regular expression $\mathcal{E}$, we need to statically determine the worst-case complexity of matching $\mathcal{E}$ against an arbitrary input string. Second, given an application A that contains a vulnerable regular expression $\mathcal{E}$, we must statically determine whether there can exist an execution of A in which $\mathcal{E}$ can be matched against an input string that could cause super-linear behavior.

We solve these challenges by developing a two-tier algorithm that combines (a) static analysis of regular expressions with (b) sanitization-aware taint analysis at the source code level. Our technique can identify both *vulnerable* regular expressions that have super-linear complexity (quadratic or worse), as well as *hyper-vulnerable* ones that have exponential complexity. In addition and, most importantly, our technique can also construct an *attack automaton* that captures all possible attack strings. The construction of attack automata is crucial for reasoning about input sanitization at the source-code level.

To summarize, this paper makes the following contributions:

- We present algorithms for reasoning about worst-case complexity of NFAs. Given an NFA $\mathcal{A}$, our algorithm can identify whether $\mathcal{A}$ has linear, super-linear, or exponential time complexity and can construct an *attack automaton* that accepts input strings that could cause worst-case behavior for $\mathcal{A}$.
- We describe a program analysis to automatically identify ReDoS vulnerabilities. Our technique uses the results of the regular expression analysis to identify *sinks* and reason about input sanitization using attack automata.
- We use these ideas to build an end-to-end tool called REXPLOITER for finding vulnerabilities in Java. In our evaluation, we find 41 security vulnerabilities in 150 Java programs collected from Github with a 11% false positive rate.

```
 1  public class RegExValidator {
 2    boolean validEmail(String t) { return t.matches(".+@.+\\.[a-z]+"); }
 3    boolean validComment(String t) {
 4      return !t.matches("(\\p{Blank}*(\\r?\\n)\\p{Blank}*)+"); }
 5    boolean safeComment(String t) { return t.matches("([^\\/<>])+"); }
 6    boolean validUrl(String t) {
 7      return t.matches("www\\.shoppers\\.com/.+/.+/.+/.+/"); }
 8  }
 9  public class CommentFormValidator implements Validator {
10    private Admin admin;
11    public void validate(CommentForm form, Errors errors) {
12      String senderEmail = form.getSenderEmail();
13      String productUrl = form.getProductUrl();
14      String comment = form.getComment();
15      if (!RegExValidator.validEmail(admin.getEmail())) return;
16      if (senderEmail.length() <= 254) {
17        if (RegExValidator.validEmail(senderEmail)) ... }
18      if (productUrl.split("/").length == 5) {
19        if (RegExValidator.validUrl(productUrl)) ... }
20      if (RegExValidator.safeComment(comment)) {
21        if (RegExValidator.validComment(comment)) ... }
22  }
```

Fig. 1. Motivating example containing ReDoS vulnerabilities

2 Overview

We illustrate our technique using the code snippet shown in Fig. 1, which shows two relevant classes, namely RegExValidator, that is used to validate that certain strings match a given regular expression, and CommentFormValidator, that checks the validity of a comment form filled out by a user. In particular, the comment form submitted by the user includes the user's email address, the URL of the product about which the user wishes to submit a comment[1], and the text containing the comment itself. We now explain how our technique can determine whether this program contains a denial-of-service vulnerability.

Regular Expression Analysis. For each regular expression in the program, we construct its corresponding NFA and statically analyze it to determine whether its worst-case complexity is linear, super-linear, or exponential. For our running example, the NFA complexity analysis finds instances of each category. In particular, the regular expression used at line 5 has linear matching complexity, while the one from line 4 has exponential complexity. The regular expressions from lines 2 and 7 have super-linear (but not exponential) complexity. Figure 2 plots input size against running time for the regular expressions from lines 2 and 4 respectively. For the super-linear and exponential regular expressions, our technique also constructs an attack automaton that recognizes all strings that cause worst-case behavior. In addition, for each regular expression, we determine a lower bound on the length of any possible attack string using dynamic analysis.

Program Analysis. The presence of a vulnerable regular expression does not necessarily mean that the program itself is vulnerable. For instance, the vulnerable

---

[1] Due to the store's organization, the URL is expected to be of the form
www.shoppers.com/Dept/Category/Subcategory/product-id/.

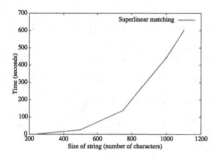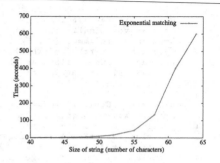

Fig. 2. Matching time against malicious string size for vulnerable (left) and hyper-vulnerable (right) regular expressions from Fig. 1.

regular expression may not be matched against an attacker-controlled string, or the program may take measures to prevent the user from supplying a string that is an instance of the attack pattern. Hence, we also perform static analysis at the source code level to determine if the program is actually vulnerable.

Going back to our example, the `validate` procedure (lines 11–22) calls `validEmail` to check whether the website administrator's email address is valid. Even though `validEmail` contains a super-linear regular expression, line 15 does not contain a vulnerability because the administrator's email is not supplied by the user. Since our analysis tracks taint information, it does not report line 15 as being vulnerable. Now, consider the second call to `validEmail` at line 17, which matches the vulnerable regular expression against user input. However, since the program bounds the size of the input string to be at most 254 (which is smaller than the lower bound identified by our analysis), line 17 is also not vulnerable.

Next, consider the call to `validUrl` at line 19, where `productUrl` is a user input. At first glance, this appears to be a vulnerability because the matching time of the regular expression from line 4 against a malicious input string grows quite rapidly with input size (see Fig. 2). However, the check at line 18 actually prevents calling `validUrl` with an attack string: Specifically, our analysis determines that attack strings must be of the form `www.shoppers.com·/`^{b}`·/`$^+$`·x`, where x denotes any character and b is a constant inferred by our analysis (in this case, much greater than 5). Since our program analysis also reasons about input sanitization, it can establish that line 19 is safe.

Finally, consider the call to `validComment` at line 21, where `comment` is again a user input and is matched against a regular expression with exponential complexity. Now, the question is whether the condition at line 20 prevents `comment` from conforming to the attack pattern `\n\t\n\t(\t\n\t)`^{k}`a`. Since this is not the case, line 21 actually contains a serious DoS vulnerability.

Summary of Challenges. This example illustrates several challenges we must address: First, given a regular expression $\mathcal{E}$, we must reason about the worst-case time complexity of its corresponding NFA. Second, given vulnerable regular expression $\mathcal{E}$, we must determine whether the program allows $\mathcal{E}$ to be matched against a string that is (a) controlled by the user, (b) is an instance of the attack pattern for regular expression $\mathcal{E}$, and (c) is large enough to cause the matching algorithm to take significant time.

Our approach solves these challenges by combining complexity analysis of NFAs with sanitization-aware taint analysis. The key idea that makes this combination possible is to produce an attack automaton for each vulnerable NFA. Without such an attack automaton, the program analyzer cannot effectively determine whether an input string can correspond to an attack string.

As shown in Fig. 3, the REX-PLOITER toolchain incorporates both static and dynamic regular expression analysis. The static analysis creates attack patterns $s_0 \cdot s^k \cdot s_1$ and dynamic analysis infers a lower bound b on the number of occurrences of s in order to exceed a minimum runtime threshold. The program analysis uses both the attack automaton and the lower bound b to reason about input sanitization.

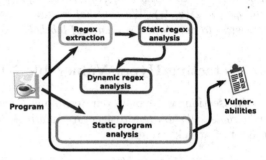

Fig. 3. Overview of our approach

3 Preliminaries

This section presents some useful background and terminology.

Definition 1. (NFA) *An NFA $\mathcal{A}$ is a 5-tuple $(Q, \Sigma, \Delta, q_0, F)$ where Q is a finite set of states, Σ is a finite alphabet of symbols, and $\Delta : Q \times \Sigma \to 2^Q$ is the transition function. Here, $q_0 \in Q$ is the initial state, and $F \subseteq Q$ is the set of accepting states. We say that (q, l, q') is a transition via label l if $q' \in \Delta(q, l)$.*

An NFA $\mathcal{A}$ accepts a string $s = a_0 a_1 \ldots a_n$ iff there exists a sequence of states $q_0, q_1, ..., q_n$ such that $q_n \in F$ and $q_{i+1} \in \Delta(q_i, a_i)$. The language of $\mathcal{A}$, denoted $\mathcal{L}(\mathcal{A})$, is the set of all strings that are accepted by $\mathcal{A}$. Conversion from a regular expression to an NFA is sometimes referred to as *compilation* and can be achieved using well-known techniques, such as Thompson's algorithm [25].

In this paper, we assume that membership in a regular language $\mathcal{L}(\mathcal{E})$ is decided through a worst-case exponential algorithm that performs backtracking search over possible runs of the NFA representing $\mathcal{E}$. While there exist linear-time matching algorithms (e.g., based on DFAs), many real-world libraries employ backtracking search for two key reasons: First, the compilation of a regular expression is much faster using NFAs and uses much less memory (DFA's can be exponentially larger). Second, the backtracking search approach can handle regular expressions containing extra features like backreferences and lookarounds. Thus, many widely-used libraries (e.g., `java.util.regex`, Python's standard library) employ backtracking search for regular expression matching.

In the remainder of this paper, we will use the notation $\mathcal{A}^*$ and $\mathcal{A}^\emptyset$ to denote the NFA that accepts Σ^* and the empty language respectively. Given two NFAs $\mathcal{A}_1$ and $\mathcal{A}_2$, we write $\mathcal{A}_1 \cap \mathcal{A}_2$, $\mathcal{A}_1 \cup \mathcal{A}_2$, and $\mathcal{A}_1 \cdot \mathcal{A}_2$ to denote automata intersection, union, and concatenation. Finally, given an automaton $\mathcal{A}$, we write $\overline{\mathcal{A}}$ to represent its complement, and we use the notation $\mathcal{A}^+$ to represent the NFA that recognizes exactly the language $\{s^k \mid k \geq 1 \wedge s \in \mathcal{L}(\mathcal{A})\}$.

Definition 2 (Path). *Given an NFA $\mathcal{A} = (Q, \Sigma, \Delta, q_0, F)$, a path π of $\mathcal{A}$ is a sequence of transitions $(q_1, \ell_1, q_2), \ldots, (q_{m-1}, \ell_{m-1}, q_m)$ where $q_i \in Q$, $\ell_i \in \Sigma$, and $q_{i+1} \in \Delta(q_i, \ell_i)$. We say that π starts in q_i and ends at q_m, and we write labels(π) to denote the sequence of labels $(\ell_1, \ldots, \ell_{m-1})$.*

4   Detecting Hyper-Vulnerable NFAs

In this section, we explain our technique for determining if an NFA is *hyper-vulnerable* and show how to generate an *attack automaton* that recognizes exactly the set of attack strings.

Definition 3 (Hyper-Vulnerable NFA). *An NFA $\mathcal{A} = (Q, \Sigma, \Delta, q_0, F)$ is hyper-vulnerable iff there exists a backtracking search algorithm MATCH over the paths of $\mathcal{A}$ such that the worst-case complexity of MATCH is exponential in the length of the input string.*

We will demonstrate that an NFA $\mathcal{A}$ is hyper-vulnerable by showing that there exists a string s such that the number of distinct matching paths π_i from state q_0 to a rejecting state q_r with labels$(\pi_i) = s$ is exponential in the length of s. Clearly, if s is rejected by $\mathcal{A}$, then MATCH will need to explore each of these exponentially many paths. Furthermore, even if s is accepted by $\mathcal{A}$, there exists a backtracking search algorithm (namely, the one that explores all rejecting paths first) that results in exponential worst-case behavior.

Theorem 1. *An NFA $\mathcal{A} = (Q, \Sigma, \Delta, q_0, F)$ is hyper-vulnerable iff there exists a pivot state $q \in Q$ and two distinct paths π_1, π_2 such that (i) both π_1, π_2 start and end at q, (ii) labels$(\pi_1) = $ labels(π_2), and (iii) there is a path π_p from initial state q_0 to q, and (iv) there is a path π_s from q to a state $q_r \notin F$.*

Proof. The sufficiency argument is laid out below, and the necessity argument can be found in the extended version of this paper [31].

To gain intuition about hyper-vulnerable NFAs, consider Fig. 4 illustrating the conditions of Theorem 1. First, a hyper-vulnerable NFA must contain a *pivot state* q, such that, starting at q, there are two different ways (namely, π_1, π_2) of getting back to q on the same

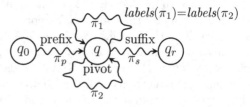

Fig. 4. Hyper-vulnerable NFA pattern

input string s (i.e., $labels(\pi_1)$). Second, the pivot state q should be reachable from the initial state q_0, and there must be a way of reaching a rejecting state q_r from q.

To understand why these conditions cause exponential behavior, consider a string of the form $s_0 \cdot s^k \cdot s_1$, where s_0 is the *attack prefix* given by $labels(\pi_p)$, s_1 is the *attack suffix* given by $labels(\pi_s)$, and s is the *attack core* given by $labels(\pi_1)$. Clearly, there is an execution path of $\mathcal{A}$ in which the string $s_0 \cdot s^k \cdot s_1$ will be rejected. For example, $\pi_p \cdot \pi_1^k \cdot \pi_s$ is exactly such a path.

Algorithm 1. Hyper-vulnerable NFA

```
 1: function ATTACKAUTOMATON(A)
 2:    assume A = (Q, Σ, Δ, q₀, F)
 3:    Aᵂ ← A∅
 4:    for qᵢ ∈ Q do
 5:       Aᵢᵂ ← ATTACKFORPIVOT(A, qᵢ)
 6:       Aᵂ ← Aᵂ ∪ Aᵢᵂ
 7:    return Aᵂ
 8: function ATTACKFORPIVOT(A, q)
 9:    assume A = (Q, Σ, Δ, q₀, F)
10:    Aᵂ ← A∅
11:    for (q, l, q₁), (q, l, q₂) ∈ Δ ∧ q₁ ≠ q₂ do
12:       A₁ ← LOOPBACK(A, q, l, q₁)
13:       A₂ ← LOOPBACK(A, q, l, q₂)
14:       Aₚ ← (Q, Σ, Δ, q₀, {q})
15:       Aₛ ← (Q, Σ, Δ, q, F)
16:       Aᵂ ← Aᵂ ∪ (Aₚ · (A₁ ∩ A₂)⁺ · Āₛ)
17:    return Aᵂ
18: function LOOPBACK(A, q, l, q′)
19:    assume A = (Q, Σ, Δ, q₀, F)
20:    q* ← NEWSTATE(Q)
21:    Q′ ← Q ∪ q*;   Δ′ ← Δ ∪ (q*, l, q′)
22:    return (Q′, Σ, Δ′, q*, {q})
```

Now, consider a string $s_0 \cdot s^{k+1} \cdot s_1$ that has an additional instance of the attack core s in the middle, and suppose that there are n possible executions of $\mathcal{A}$ on the prefix $s_0 \cdot s^k$ that end in q. Now, for each of these n executions, there are two ways to get back to q after reading s: one that takes path π_1 and another that takes path π_2. Therefore, there are $2n$ possible executions of $\mathcal{A}$ that end in q. Furthermore, the matching algorithm will (in the worst case) end up exploring all of these $2n$ executions since there is a way to reach the rejecting state q_r. Hence, we end up doubling the running time of the algorithm every time we add an instance of the attack core s to the middle of the input string.

Example 1. The NFA in Fig. 5 (left) is hyper-vulnerable because there exist two different paths $\pi_1 = (q, a, q), (q, a, q)$ and $\pi_2 = (q, a, q_0), (q_0, a, q)$ that contain the same labels and that start and end in q. Also, q is reachable from q_0, and the rejecting state q_r is reachable from q. Attack strings for this NFA are of the form $a \cdot (a \cdot a)^k \cdot b$, and the attack automaton is shown in Fig. 5 (right).

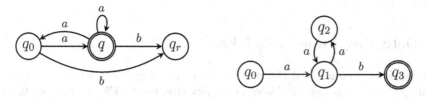

Fig. 5. A hyper-vulnerable NFA (left) and an attack automaton (right).

We now use Theorem 1 to devise Algorithm 1 for constructing the attack automaton $\mathcal{A}^\Psi$ for a given NFA. The key idea of our algorithm is to search for all possible pivot states q_i and construct the attack automaton $\mathcal{A}_i^\Psi$ for state q_i. The full attack automaton is then obtained as the union of all $\mathcal{A}_i^\Psi$. Note that Algorithm 1 can be used to determine if automaton $\mathcal{A}$ is vulnerable: $\mathcal{A}$ exhibits worst-case exponential behavior iff the language accepted by $\mathcal{A}^\Psi$ is non-empty.

In Algorithm 1, most of the real work is done by the ATTACKFORPIVOT procedure, which constructs the attack automaton for a specific state q: Given a pivot state q, we want to find two different paths π_1, π_2 that loop back to q and that have the same set of labels. Towards this goal, line 11 of Algorithm 1 considers all pairs of transitions from q that have the same label (since we must have $labels(\pi_1) = labels(\pi_2)$).

Now, let us consider a pair of transitions $\tau_1 = (q, l, q_1)$ and $\tau_2 = (q, l, q_2)$. For each q_i ($i \in \{1, 2\}$), we want to find all strings that start in q, take transition τ_i, and then loop back to q. In order to find all such strings $\mathcal{S}$, Algorithm 1 invokes the LOOPBACK function (lines 18–22), which constructs an automaton $\mathcal{A}'$ that recognizes exactly $\mathcal{S}$. Specifically, the final state of $\mathcal{A}'$ is q because we want to loop back to state q. Furthermore, $\mathcal{A}'$ contains a new initial state q^* (where $q^* \notin Q$) and a single outgoing transition (q^*, l, q_i) out of q^* because we only want to consider paths that take the transition to q_i first. Hence, each $\mathcal{A}_i$ in lines 12–13 of the ATTACKFORPIVOT procedure corresponds to a set of paths that loop back to q through state q_i. Observe that, if a string s is accepted by $\mathcal{A}_1 \cap \mathcal{A}_2$, then s is an attack core for pivot state q.

We now turn to the problem of computing the set of all attack prefixes and suffixes for pivot state q: In line 14 of Algorithm 1, $\mathcal{A}_p$ is the same as the original NFA $\mathcal{A}$ except that its only accepting state is q. Hence, $\mathcal{A}_p$ accepts all attack prefixes for pivot q. Similarly, A_s is the same as $\mathcal{A}$ except that its initial state is q instead of q_0; thus, $\overline{A_s}$ accepts all attack suffixes for q.

Finally, let us consider how to construct the full attack automaton $\mathcal{A}^\Psi$ for q. As explained earlier, all attack strings are of the form $s_1 \cdot s^k \cdot s_2$ where s_1 is the attack prefix, s is the attack core, and s_2 is the attack suffix. Since $\mathcal{A}_p$, $\mathcal{A}_1 \cap \mathcal{A}_2$, and $\overline{A_s}$ recognize attack prefixes, cores, and suffixes respectively, any string that is accepted by $\mathcal{A}_p \cdot (\mathcal{A}_1 \cap \mathcal{A}_2)^+ \cdot \overline{A_s}$ is an attack string for the original NFA $\mathcal{A}$.

Theorem 2 (Correctness of Algorithm 1)[2]. *Let $\mathcal{A}^\Psi$ be the result of calling* ATTACKAUTOMATON$(\mathcal{A})$ *for NFA* $\mathcal{A} = (Q, \Sigma, \Delta, q_0, F)$. *For every* $s \in \mathcal{L}(\mathcal{A}^\Psi)$, *there exists a rejecting state* $q_r \in Q \setminus F$ *s.t. the number of distinct paths* π_i *from* q_0 *to* q_r *with* $labels(\pi_i) = s$ *is exponential in the number of repetitions of the attack core in* s.

5   Detecting Vulnerable NFAs

So far, we only considered the problem of identifying NFAs whose worst-case running time is exponential. However, in practice, even NFAs with super-linear

---

[2] The proofs of Theorems 2 and 4 are given in the extended version of this paper [31].

complexity can cause catastrophic backtracking. In fact, many acknowledged ReDoS vulnerabilities (e.g., [1,4,5]) involve regular expressions whose matching complexity is "only" quadratic. Based on this observation, we extend the techniques from the previous section to statically detect NFAs with super-linear time complexity. Our solution builds on insights from Sect. 4 to construct an attack automaton for this larger class of vulnerable regular expressions.

5.1   Understanding Super-Linear NFAs

Before we present the algorithm for detecting super-linear NFAs, we provide a theorem that explains the correctness of our solution.

Definition 4 (Vulnerable NFA). *An NFA* $\mathcal{A} = (Q, \Sigma, \Delta, q_0, F)$ *is vulnerable iff there exists a backtracking search algorithm* MATCH *over the paths of* $\mathcal{A}$ *such that the worst-case complexity of* MATCH *is at least quadratic in the length of the input string.*

Theorem 3. *An NFA* $\mathcal{A} = (Q, \Sigma, \Delta, q_0, F)$ *is* vulnerable *iff there exist two states* $q \in Q$ *(the pivot),* $q' \in Q$, *and three paths* π_1, π_2, *and* π_3 *(where* $\pi_1 \neq \pi_2$*) such that (i)* π_1 *starts and ends at* q, *(ii)* π_2 *starts at* q *and ends at* q', *(iii)* π_3 *starts and ends at* q', *(iv)* labels(π_1) = labels(π_2) = labels(π_3), *and (v) there is a path* π_p *from* q_0 *to* q, *(vi) there is a path* π_s *from* q' *to a state* $q_r \notin F$.

Proof. The sufficiency argument is laid out below, and the necessity argument can be found in the extended version of this paper [31].

  Figure 6 illustrates the intuition behind the conditions above. The distinguishing characteristic of a super-linear NFA is that it contains two states q, q' such that q' is reachable from q on input string s, and it is possible to loop back from q and q' to the same state on string s. In addition, just like in Theorem 1, the pivot state q needs to be reachable from the initial state, and a rejecting state q_r must be reachable from q'. Observe that any automaton that is hyper-vulnerable according to Theorem 1 is also vulnerable according to Theorem 3. Specifically, consider an automaton $\mathcal{A}$ with two distinct paths π_1, π_2 that loop around q. In this case, if we take q' to be q and π_3 to be π_1, we immediately see that $\mathcal{A}$ also satisfies the conditions of Theorem 3.

  To understand why the conditions of Theorem 3 imply super-linear time complexity, let us consider a string of the form $s_0 \cdot s^k \cdot s_1$ where s_0 is the *attack prefix*

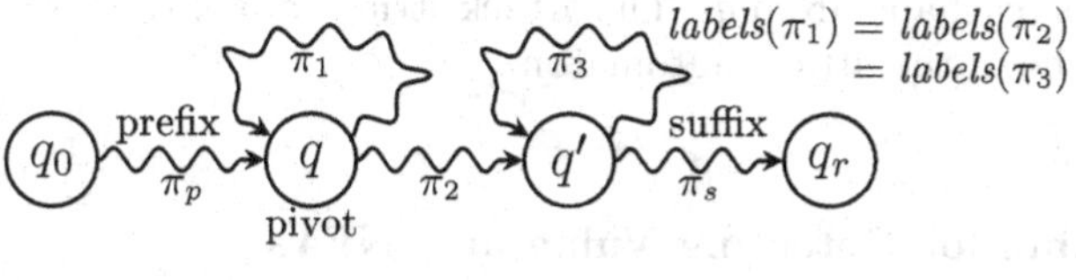

Fig. 6. General pattern characterizing vulnerable NFAs

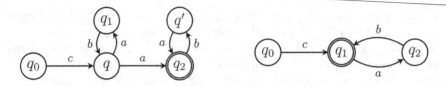

Fig. 7. A vulnerable NFA (left) and its attack automaton (right).

given by $labels(\pi_p)$, s_1 is the *attack suffix* given by $labels(\pi_s)$, and s is the *attack core* given by $labels(\pi_1)$. Just like in the previous section, the path $\pi_p \pi_1^k \pi_s$ describes an execution for rejecting the string $s_0 \cdot s^k \cdot s_1$ in automaton $\mathcal{A}$. Now, let $T_q(k)$ represent the running time of rejecting the string $s^k s_1$ starting from q, and suppose that it takes 1 unit of time to read string s. We can write the following recurrence relation for $T_q(k)$:

$$T_q(k) = (1 + T_q(k-1)) + (1 + T_{q'}(k-1))$$

To understand where this recurrence is coming from, observe that there are two ways to process the first occurence of s:

– Take path π_1 and come back to q, consuming 1 unit of time to process string s. Since we are back at q, we still have $T_q(k-1)$ units of work to perform.
– Take path π_2 and proceed to q', also consuming 1 unit of time to process string s. Since we are now at q', we have $T_{q'}(k-1)$ units of work to perform.

Now, observe that a lower bound on $T_{q'}(k)$ is k since one way to reach q_r is $\pi_3^k \pi_s$, which requires us to read the entire input string. This observation allows us to obtain the following recurrence relation:

$$T_q(k) \geq T_q(k-1) + k + 1$$

Thus, the running time of $\mathcal{A}$ on the input string $s_0 \cdot s^k \cdot s_1$ is at least k^2.

Example 2. The NFA shown in Fig. 7 (left) exhibits super-linear complexity because we can get from q to q' on input string ab, and for both q and q', we loop back to the same state when reading input string ab. Specifically, we have:

$$\pi_1 : (q, a, q_1), (q_1, b, q) \quad \pi_2 : (q, a, q_2), (q_2, b, q') \quad \pi_3 : (q', a, q_2), (q_2, b, q')$$

Furthermore, q is reachable from q_0, and there exists a rejecting state, namely q' itself, that is reachable from q'. The attack strings are of the form $c(ab)^k$, and Fig. 7 (right) shows the attack automaton.

5.2   Algorithm for Detecting Vulnerable NFAs

Based on the observations from the previous subsection, we can now formulate an algorithm that constructs an attack automaton $\mathcal{A}^\Psi$ for a given automaton $\mathcal{A}$.

Algorithm 2. Construct super-linear attack automaton $\mathcal{A}^{\psi}$ for $\mathcal{A}$ and pivot q

```
 1: function ANYLOOPBACK(A, q′)
 2:     assume A = (Q, Σ, Δ, q₀, F)
 3:     q* ← NEWSTATE(Q);   Q′ ← Q ∪ q*;   Δ′ ← Δ
 4:     for (q′, l, qᵢ) ∈ Δ do
 5:         Δ′ ← Δ′ ∪ (q*, l, qᵢ)
 6:     A′ ← (Q′, Σ, Δ′, q*, {q′})
 7:     return A′
 8: function ATTACKFORPIVOT(A, q)
 9:     assume A = (Q, Σ, Δ, q₀, F)
10:     A^ψ ← A^∅
11:     for (q, l, q₁) ∈ Δ ∧ (q, l, q₂) ∈ Δ ∧ q₁ ≠ q₂ do
12:         A₁ ← LOOPBACK(A, q, l, q₁)
13:         Aₚ ← (Q, Σ, Δ, q₀, {q})
14:         for q′ ∈ Q do
15:             qᵢ ← NEWSTATE(Q)
16:             A₂ ← (Q ∪ {qᵢ}, Σ, Δ ∪ {(qᵢ, l, q₂)}, qᵢ, {q′})
17:             A₃ ← ANYLOOPBACK(A, q′)
18:             Aₛ ← (Q, Σ, Δ, q′, F)
19:             A^ψ ← A^ψ ∪ (Aₚ · (A₁ ∩ A₂ ∩ A₃)⁺ · Āₛ)
20:     return A^ψ
```

Just like in Algorithm 1, we construct an attack automaton $\mathcal{A}_i^{\psi}$ for each state in $\mathcal{A}$ by invoking the ATTACKFORPIVOT procedure. We then take the union of all such $\mathcal{A}_i^{\psi}$'s to obtain an automaton $\mathcal{A}^{\psi}$ whose language consists of strings that cause super-linear running time for $\mathcal{A}$.

Algorithm 2 describes the ATTACKFORPIVOT procedure for the super-linear case. Just like in Algorithm 1, we consider all pairs of transitions from q with the same label (line 11). Furthermore, as in Algorithm 1, we construct an automaton $\mathcal{A}_p$ that recognizes attack prefixes for q (line 13) as well as an automaton $\mathcal{A}_1$ that recognizes non-empty strings that start and end at q (line 12).

The key difference of Algorithm 2 is that we also need to consider all states that could be instantiated as q' from Fig. 6 (lines 15–19). For each of these candidate q''s, we construct automata $\mathcal{A}_2, \mathcal{A}_3$ that correspond to paths π_2, π_3 from Fig. 6 (lines 16–17). Specifically, we construct $\mathcal{A}_2$ by introducing a new initial state q_i with transition (q_i, l, q_2) and making its accepting state q'. Hence, $\mathcal{A}_2$ accepts strings that start in q, transition to q_2, and end in q'.

The construction of automaton $\mathcal{A}_3$, which should accept all non-empty words that start and end in q', is described in the ANYLOOPBACK procedure. First, since we do not want $\mathcal{A}_3$ to accept empty strings, we introduce a new initial state q^* and add a transition from q^* to all successor states q_i of q'. Second, the final state of $\mathcal{A}'$ is q' since we want to consider paths that loop back to q'.

The final missing piece of the algorithm is the construction of $\mathcal{A}_s$ (line 19), whose complement accepts all attack suffixes for state q'. As expected, $\mathcal{A}_s$ is the same as the original automaton $\mathcal{A}$, except that its initial state is q'. Finally, similar to Algorithm 1, the attack automaton for states q, q' is obtained as $\mathcal{A}_p \cdot (\mathcal{A}_1 \cap \mathcal{A}_2 \cap \mathcal{A}_3)^+ \cdot \overline{\mathcal{A}_s}$.

Theorem 4 (Correctness of Algorithm 2). *Let NFA $\mathcal{A} = (Q, \Sigma, \Delta, q_0, F)$ and $\mathcal{A}^{\Psi}$ be the result of calling* ATTACKAUTOMATON($\mathcal{A}$). *For every $s \in \mathcal{L}(\mathcal{A}^{\Psi})$, there exists a rejecting state $q_r \in Q \setminus F$ s.t. the number of distinct paths π_i from q_0 to q_r with $labels(\pi_i) = s$ is super-linear in the number of repetitions of the attack core in s.*

6 Dynamic Regular Expression Analysis

Algorithms 1 and 2 allow us to determine whether a given NFA is vulnerable. Even though our static analyses are sound and complete at the NFA level, different regular expression matching algorithms construct NFAs in different ways and use different backtracking search algorithms. Furthermore, some matching algorithms may determinize the NFA (either lazily or eagerly) in order to guarantee linear complexity. Since our analysis does not perform such partial determinization of the NFA for a given regular expression, it can, in practice, generate false positives. In addition, even if a regular expression is indeed vulnerable, the input string must still exceed a certain minimum size to cause denial-of-service.

In order to overcome these challenges in practice, we also perform dynamic analysis to (a) confirm that a regular expression $\mathcal{E}$ is indeed vulnerable *for Java's matching algorithm*, and (b) infer a minimum bound on the size of the input string. Given the original regular expression $\mathcal{E}$, a user-provided time limit t, and the attack automaton $\mathcal{A}^{\Psi}$ (computed by static regular expression analysis), our dynamic analysis produces a refined attack automaton as well as a number b such that there exists an input string of length greater than b for which Java's matching algorithm takes more than t seconds. Note that, as usual, this dynamic analysis trades soundness for completeness to avoid too many false positives.

In more detail, given an attack automaton $\mathcal{A}^{\Psi}$ of the form $\mathcal{A}_p \cdot \mathcal{A}_c^+ \cdot \mathcal{A}_s$, the dynamic analysis finds the smallest k where the shortest string $s \in \mathcal{L}(\mathcal{A}_p \cdot \mathcal{A}_c^k \cdot \mathcal{A}_s)$ exceeds the time limit t. In practice, this process does not require more than a few iterations because we use the complexity of the NFA to predict the number of repetitions that should be necessary based on previous runs. The minimum required input length b is determined based on the length of the found string s. In addition, the value k is used to refine the attack automaton: in particular, given the original attack automaton $\mathcal{A}_p \cdot \mathcal{A}_c^+ \cdot \mathcal{A}_s$, the dynamic analysis refines it to be $\mathcal{A}_p \cdot \mathcal{A}_c^k \cdot \mathcal{A}_c^* \cdot \mathcal{A}_s$.

7 Static Program Analysis

As explained in Sect. 2, the presence of a vulnerable regular expression does not necessarily mean that the program is vulnerable. In particular, there are three necessary conditions for the program to contain a ReDoS vulnerability: First, a variable x that stores user input must be matched against a vulnerable regular expression $\mathcal{E}$. Second, it must be possible for x to store an attack string that triggers worst-case behavior for $\mathcal{E}$; and, third, the length of the string stored in x must exceed the minimum threshold determined using dynamic analysis.

To determine if the program actually contains a ReDoS vulnerability, our approach also performs static analysis of source code. Specifically, our program analysis employs the Cartesian product [7] of the following abstract domains:

- The *taint abstract domain* [6, 26] tracks taint information for each variable. In particular, a variable is considered *tainted* if it may store user input.
- The *automaton abstract domain* [12, 33, 34] overapproximates the contents of string variables using finite automata. In particular, if string s is in the language of automaton $\mathcal{A}$ representing x's contents, then x *may* store string s.
- The *interval domain* [13] is used to reason about string lengths. Specifically, we introduce a ghost variable l_x representing the length of string x and use the interval abstract domain to infer upper and lower bounds for each l_x.

Since these abstract domains are fairly standard, we only explain how to use this information to detect ReDoS vulnerabilities. Consider a statement $\mathrm{match}(x, \mathcal{E})$ that checks if string variable x matches regular expression $\mathcal{E}$, and suppose that the attack automaton for $\mathcal{E}$ is $\mathcal{A}^{\Psi}$. Now, our program analysis considers the statement $\mathrm{match}(x, \mathcal{E})$ to be vulnerable if the following three conditions hold:

1. $\mathcal{E}$ is vulnerable and variable x is tainted;
2. The intersection of $\mathcal{A}^{\Psi}$ and the automaton abstraction of x is non-empty;
3. The upper bound on ghost variable l_x representing x's length exceeds the minimum bound b computed using dynamic analysis for $\mathcal{A}^{\Psi}$ and a user-provided time limit t.

The extended version of this paper [31] offers a more rigorous formalization of the analysis.

8 Experimental Evaluation

To assess the usefulness of the techniques presented in this paper, we performed an evaluation in which our goal is to answer the following questions:

Q1: Do real-world Java web applications use vulnerable regular expressions?
Q2: Can REXPLOITER detect ReDoS vulnerabilities in web applications and how serious are these vulnerabilities?

Results for Q1. In order to assess if real-world Java programs contain vulnerabilities, we scraped the top 150 Java web applications (by number of stars) that contain at least one regular expression from GitHub repositories (all projects have between 10 and 2,000 stars and at least 50 commits) and collected a total of 2,864 regular expressions. In this pool of regular expressions, REXPLOITER found 37 that have worst-case exponential complexity and 522 that have super-linear (but not exponential) complexity. Thus, we observe that approximately 20% of the regular expressions in the analyzed programs are vulnerable. We believe this statistic highlights the need for more tools like REXPLOITER that can help programmers reason about the complexity of regular expression matching.

Results for Q2. To evaluate the effectiveness of REXPLOITER in finding ReDoS vulnerabilities, we used REXPLOITER to statically analyze all Java applications that contain at least one vulnerable regular expression. These programs include both web applications and frameworks, and cover a broad range of application domains. The average running time of REXPLOITER is approximately 14 min per program, including the time to dynamically analyze regular expressions. The average size of analyzed programs is about 58, 000 lines of code.

Our main result is that REXPLOITER found exploitable vulnerabilities in 27 applications (including from popular projects, such as the Google Web Toolkit and Apache Wicket) and reported a total of 46 warnings. We manually inspected each warning and confirmed that 41 out of the 46 vulnerabilities are exploitable, with 5 of the exploitable vulnerabilities involving hyper-vulnerable regular expressions and the rest being super-linear ones. *Furthermore, for each of these 41 vulnerabilities (including super-linear ones), we were able to come up with a full, end-to-end exploit that causes the server to hang for more than 10 min.*

In Fig. 8, we explore a subset of the vulnerabilities uncovered by REXPLOITER in more detail. Specifically, Fig. 8 (left) plots input size against running time for the exponential vulnerabilities, and Fig. 8 (right) shows the same information for a subset of the super-linear vulnerabilities.

Possible Fixes. We now briefly discuss some possible ways to fix the vulnerabilities uncovered by REXPLOITER. The most direct fix is to rewrite the regular expression so that it no longer exhibits super-linear complexity. Alternatively, the problem can also be fixed by ensuring that the user input cannot contain instances of the attack core. Since our technique provides the full attack automaton, we believe REXPLOITER can be helpful for implementing suitable

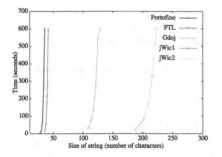
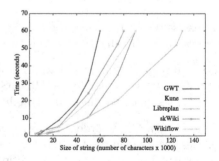

Fig. 8. Running times for exponential vulnerabilities (left) and super-linear vulnerabilities (right) for different input sizes.

sanitizers. Another possible fix (which typically only works for super-linear regular expressions) is to bound input size. However, for most vulnerabilities found by REXPLOITER, the input string can legitimately be very large (e.g., review). Hence, there may not be an obvious upper bound, or the bound may still be too large to prevent a ReDoS attack. For example, Amazon imposes an upper bound of 5000 words (~25,000 characters) on product reviews, but matching a super-linear regular expression against a string of that size may still take significant time.

9 Related Work

To the best of our knowledge, we are the first to present an end-to-end solution for detecting ReDoS vulnerabilities by combining regular expression and program analysis. However, there is prior work on static analysis of regular expressions and, separately, on program analysis for finding security vulnerabilities.

Static Analysis of Regular Expressions. Since vulnerable regular expressions are known to be a significant problem, previous work has studied static analysis techniques for identifying regular expressions with worst-case exponential complexity [9,18,22,24]. Recent work by Weideman et al. [30] has also proposed an analysis for identifying super-linear regular expressions. However, no previous technique can construct attack automata that capture all malicious strings. Since attack automata are crucial for reasoning about sanitization, the algorithms we propose in this paper are necessary for performing sanitization-aware program analysis. Furthermore, we believe that the attack automata produced by our tool can help programmers write suitable sanitizers (especially in cases where the regular expression is difficult to rewrite).

Program Analysis for Vulnerability Detection. There is a large body of work on statically detecting security vulnerabilities in programs. Many of these techniques focus on detecting cross-site scripting (XSS) or code injection vulnerabilities [8,11,12,15,17,19,20,23,27–29,32–35]. There has also been recent work on static detection of specific classes of denial-of-service vulnerabilities. For instance, Chang et al. [10] and Huang et al. [16] statically detect attacker-controlled loop bounds, and Olivo et al. [21] detect so-called *second-order DoS vulnerabilities*, in which the size of a database query result is controlled by the attacker. However, as far as we know, there is no prior work that uses program analysis for detecting DoS vulnerabilities due to regular expression matching.

Time-Outs to Prevent ReDoS. As mentioned earlier, some libraries (e.g., the .NET framework) allow developers to set a time-limit for regular expression matching. While such libraries may help *mitigate* the problem through a band-aid solution, they do not address the root cause of the problem. For instance, they neither prevent against stack overflows nor do they prevent DoS attacks in which the attacker triggers the regular expression matcher many times.

10   Conclusions and Future Work

We have presented an end-to-end solution for statically detecting regular expression denial-of-service vulnerabilities in programs. Our key idea is to combine complexity analysis of regular expressions with safety analysis of programs. Specifically, our regular expression analysis constructs an attack automaton that recognizes all strings that trigger worst-case super-linear or exponential behavior. The program analysis component takes this information as input and performs a combination of taint and string analysis to determine whether an attack string could be matched against a vulnerable regular expression.

We have used our tool to analyze thousands of regular expressions in the wild and we show that 20% of regular expressions in the analyzed programs are actually vulnerable. We also use REXPLOITER to analyze Java web applications collected from Github repositories and find 41 exploitable security vulnerabilities in 27 applications. Each of these vulnerabilities can be exploited to make the web server unresponsive for more than 10 min.

There are two main directions that we would like to explore in future work: First, we are interested in the problem of automatically *repairing* vulnerable regular expressions. Since it is often difficult for humans to reason about the complexity of regular expression matching, we believe there is a real need for techniques that can automatically synthesize equivalent regular expressions with linear complexity. Second, we also plan to investigate the problem of automatically generating sanitizers from the attack automata produced by our regular expression analysis.

Acknowledgments. This work is supported by AFRL Award FA8750-15-2-0096.

References

1. CVE-2013-2009. cve.mitre.org/cgi-bin/cvename.cgi?name=CVE-2013-2099
2. CVE-2015-2525. cve.mitre.org/cgi-bin/cvename.cgi?name=CVE-2015-2526
3. CVE-2015-2525. cve.mitre.org/cgi-bin/cvename.cgi?name=CVE-2009-3275
4. CVE-2016-2515. cve.mitre.org/cgi-bin/cvename.cgi?name=CVE-2016-2515
5. CVE-2016-2537. cve.mitre.org/cgi-bin/cvename.cgi?name=CVE-2016-2537
6. Arzt, S., Rasthofer, S., Fritz, C., Bodden, E., Bartel, A., Klein, J., Traon, Y.L., Octeau, D., McDaniel, P.: Flowdroid: precise context, flow, field, object-sensitive and lifecycle-aware taint analysis for Android apps. In: PLDI, pp. 259–269. ACM (2014)
7. Ball, T., Podelski, A., Rajamani, S.K.: Boolean and cartesian abstraction for model checking C programs. In: Margaria, T., Yi, W. (eds.) TACAS 2001. LNCS, vol. 2031, pp. 268–283. Springer, Heidelberg (2001). doi:10.1007/3-540-45319-9_19
8. Bandhakavi, S., Tiku, N., Pittman, W., King, S.T., Madhusudan, P., Winslett, M.: Vetting browser extensions for security vulnerabilities with VEX. Commun. ACM **54**(9), 91–99 (2011)
9. Berglund, M., Drewes, F., van der Merwe, B.: Analyzing catastrophic backtracking behavior in practical regular expression matching. In: AFL. EPTCS, vol. 151, pp. 109–123 (2014)

10. Chang, R.M., Jiang, G., Ivancic, F., Sankaranarayanan, S., Shmatikov, V.: Inputs of coma: static detection of denial-of-service vulnerabilities. In: CSF, pp. 186–199. IEEE Computer Society (2009)
11. Chaudhuri, A., Foster, J.S.: Symbolic security analysis of ruby-on-rails web applications. In: CCS, pp. 585–594. ACM (2010)
12. Christensen, A.S., Møller, A., Schwartzbach, M.I.: Precise analysis of string expressions. In: Cousot, R. (ed.) SAS 2003. LNCS, vol. 2694, pp. 1–18. Springer, Heidelberg (2003). doi:10.1007/3-540-44898-5_1
13. Cousot, P., Cousot, R.: Abstract interpretation: a unified lattice model for static analysis of programs by construction or approximation of fixpoints. In: POPL, pp. 238–252. ACM (1977)
14. Crosby, S.A., Wallach, D.S.: Denial of service via algorithmic complexity attacks. In: USENIX Security Symposium. USENIX Association (2003)
15. Dahse, J., Holz, T.: Static detection of second-order vulnerabilities in web applications. In: USENIX Security Symposium, pp. 989–1003. USENIX Association (2014)
16. Huang, H., Zhu, S., Chen, K., Liu, P.: From system services freezing to system server shutdown in Android: all you need is a loop in an app. In: CCS, pp. 1236–1247. ACM (2015)
17. Kiezun, A., Guo, P.J., Jayaraman, K., Ernst, M.D.: Automatic creation of SQL injection and cross-site scripting attacks. In: ICSE, pp. 199–209. IEEE (2009)
18. Kirrage, J., Rathnayake, A., Thielecke, H.: Static analysis for regular expression denial-of-service attacks. In: Lopez, J., Huang, X., Sandhu, R. (eds.) NSS 2013. LNCS, vol. 7873, pp. 135–148. Springer, Heidelberg (2013). doi:10.1007/978-3-642-38631-2_11
19. Livshits, V.B., Lam, M.S.: Finding security vulnerabilities in Java applications with static analysis. In: USENIX Security Symposium. USENIX Association (2005)
20. Martin, M.C., Livshits, V.B., Lam, M.S.: Finding application errors and security flaws using PQL: a program query language. In: OOPSLA, pp. 365–383. ACM (2005)
21. Olivo, O., Dillig, I., Lin, C.: Detecting and exploiting second order denial-of-service vulnerabilities in web applications. In: CCS, pp. 616–628. ACM (2015)
22. Rathnayake, A., Thielecke, H.: Static analysis for regular expression exponential runtime via substructural logics. CoRR abs/1405.7058 (2014)
23. Su, Z., Wassermann, G.: The essence of command injection attacks in web applications. In: POPL, pp. 372–382. ACM (2006)
24. Sugiyama, S., Minamide, Y.: Checking time linearity of regular expression matching based on backtracking. IPSJ Online Trans. **7**, 82–92 (2014)
25. Thompson, K.: Programming techniques: regular expression search algorithm. Commun. ACM **11**(6), 419–422 (1968)
26. Tripp, O., Pistoia, M., Fink, S.J., Sridharan, M., Weisman, O.: TAJ: effective taint analysis of web applications. In: PLDI, pp. 87–97. ACM (2009)
27. Wassermann, G., Su, Z.: Sound and precise analysis of web applications for injection vulnerabilities. In: PLDI, pp. 32–41. ACM (2007)
28. Wassermann, G., Su, Z.: Static detection of cross-site scripting vulnerabilities. In: ICSE, pp. 171–180. ACM (2008)
29. Wassermann, G., Yu, D., Chander, A., Dhurjati, D., Inamura, H., Su, Z.: Dynamic test input generation for web applications. In: ISSTA, pp. 249–260. ACM (2008)

30. Weideman, N., Merwe, B., Berglund, M., Watson, B.: Analyzing matching time behavior of backtracking regular expression matchers by using ambiguity of NFA. In: Han, Y.-S., Salomaa, K. (eds.) CIAA 2016. LNCS, vol. 9705, pp. 322–334. Springer, Cham (2016). doi:10.1007/978-3-319-40946-7_27
31. Wüstholz, V., Olivo, O., Heule, M.J.H., Dillig, I.: Static detection of DoS vulnerabilities in programs that use regular expressions (extended version). CoRR abs/1701.04045 (2017)
32. Xie, Y., Aiken, A.: Static detection of security vulnerabilities in scripting languages. In: USENIX Security Symposium. USENIX Association (2006)
33. Yu, F., Alkhalaf, M., Bultan, T.: STRANGER: an automata-based string analysis tool for PHP. In: Esparza, J., Majumdar, R. (eds.) TACAS 2010. LNCS, vol. 6015, pp. 154–157. Springer, Heidelberg (2010). doi:10.1007/978-3-642-12002-2_13
34. Yu, F., Alkhalaf, M., Bultan, T., Ibarra, O.H.: Automata-based symbolic string analysis for vulnerability detection. FMSD **44**(1), 44–70 (2014)
35. Yu, F., Bultan, T., Hardekopf, B.: String abstractions for string verification. In: Groce, A., Musuvathi, M. (eds.) SPIN 2011. LNCS, vol. 6823, pp. 20–37. Springer, Heidelberg (2011). doi:10.1007/978-3-642-22306-8_3

Discriminating Traces with Time

Saeid Tizpaz-Niari[✉], Pavol Černý, Bor-Yuh Evan Chang,
Sriram Sankaranarayanan, and Ashutosh Trivedi

University of Colorado Boulder, Boulder, USA
{saeid.tizpazniari,pavol.cerny,evan.chang,srirams,
ashutosh.trivedi}@colorado.edu

Abstract. What properties about the internals of a program explain the possible differences in its overall running time for different inputs? In this paper, we propose a formal framework for considering this question we dub *trace-set discrimination*. We show that even though the algorithmic problem of computing maximum likelihood discriminants is NP-hard, approaches based on integer linear programming (ILP) and decision tree learning can be useful in zeroing-in on the program internals. On a set of Java benchmarks, we find that compactly-represented decision trees scalably discriminate with high accuracy—more scalably than maximum likelihood discriminants and with comparable accuracy. We demonstrate on three larger case studies how decision-tree discriminants produced by our tool are useful for debugging timing side-channel vulnerabilities (i.e., where a malicious observer infers secrets simply from passively watching execution times) and availability vulnerabilities.

1 Introduction

Different control-flow paths in a program can have varying execution times. Such observable differences in execution times may be explainable by information about the program internals, such as whether or not a given function or functions were called. How can a software developer (or security analyst) determine what internals may or may not explain the varying execution times of the program? In this paper, we consider the problem of helping developers and analysts to identify such explanations.

We identify a core problem for this task—the *trace-set discrimination* problem. Given a set of execution traces with observable execution times binned (or clustered) into a finite set of labels, a *discriminant* (or classifier) is a map relating each label to a property (i.e., a Boolean formula) satisfied by the traces assigned to that label. Such a discriminant model can then be used, for example, to predict a property satisfied by some trace given the timing label of that trace.

This problem is, while related, different than the profiling problem. In performance profiling, the question is given an execution trace, how do the various parts of the program contribute to the overall execution time? The trace-set discrimination problem, in contrast, looks for distinguishing features among multiple traces that result in varying execution times.

This research was supported by DARPA under agreement FA8750-15-2-0096.

A. Legay and T. Margaria (Eds.): TACAS 2017, Part II, LNCS 10206, pp. 21–37, 2017.
DOI: 10.1007/978-3-662-54580-5_2

Crucially, once we can explain the timing differences in terms of properties of traces (e.g., what functions are called only in traces with long execution time), the analyst can use the explanation to diagnose the possible timing side-channel and potentially find a fix for the vulnerability. Section 2 shows on an example how a security analyst might use the tool for debugging information leaks.

In this paper, we consider the discriminating properties of traces to be Boolean combinations of a given set of atomic predicates. These atomic predicates correspond to actions that can be observed through instrumentation in a training set of execution traces. Examples of such predicates are as follows: (1) Does the trace have a call to the function f in the program? (2) Does the trace have a call to the **sort** function with an array of more than a 1000 numbers? In our case study, we consider atomic predicates corresponding to the number of times each function is called.

Concretely, our overall approach is to first obtain a set of execution traces with information recorded to determine the satisfiability of the given atomic predicates along with corresponding execution times. Then, we cluster these training traces based on their overall execution times to bin them into timing labels. Finally, we learn a trace-set discriminant model from these traces (using various techniques) to capture what is common amongst the traces with the same timing labels and what is different between traces with different labels.

In particular, we make the following contributions:

- We formalize the problem of *trace-set discrimination* with timing differences and show that the algorithmic problem of finding the maximum likelihood conjunctive discriminant is NP-hard (Sect. 3).
- We describe two methods for learning trace-set discriminants: (1) a direct method for inferring the maximum likelihood conjunctive discriminant using an encoding into integer linear programming (ILP) and (2) by applying decision tree learning that each offer different trade-offs (Sect. 4). For instance, decision tree algorithms are designed to tolerate noisy labels and work effectively on large data sets but do not have formal guarantees. On a set of microbenchmarks, we find that the methods have similar accuracy but decision tree learning appears more scalable.
- We present three case studies in identifying and debugging timing side-channel and availability vulnerabilities, armed with a prototype tool DISCRIMINER that performs label clustering and decision tree-discriminant learning (Sect. 5). These case studies were conducted on medium-sized Java applications, which range in size from approximately 300 to 3,000 methods and were developed by a third party vendor as challenge problems for identifying and debugging such side-channel vulnerabilities. We show that the decision trees produced by DISCRIMINER are useful for explaining the timing differences amongst trace sets and performing this debugging task.

In our approach, we need to execute both an instrumented and an uninstrumented version of the program of interest on the same inputs. This is because a trace of the instrumented program is needed to determine the satisfiability of the atomic predicates, while the execution time of interest is for the uninstrumented program. Therefore we need to assume that the program is deterministic. Since timing observations are noisy due to many sources of non-determinism, each trace is associated with a *distribution* over the labels. For instance, a trace may have a label ℓ_1 with probability 0.9 and label ℓ_2 with probability 0.1.

Like with profiling, we also assume the test inputs that drive the program of interest to expose interesting behavior are given. It is a separate problem to get such interesting inputs: whether the analyst has logged some suspicious inputs from a deployment or whether the developer generates tests using random or directed test-case generation.

2   Timing Side-Channel Debugging with DISCRIMINER

In this section, we demonstrate by example how DISCRIMINER can be useful in identifying timing side-channel vulnerabilities and suggesting ways to fix them. We use an application called SnapBuddy[1] as an example. SnapBuddy is a Java application with 3,071 methods, implementing a mock social network in which each user has their own page with a photograph.

Identifying a Timing Side-Channel with Clustering. The analyst interacts with the application by issuing download requests to the pages of various users to record execution times. Figure 1 shows a scatter plot of the running times of various traces with each trace represented by a point in the figure. The running times are clustered into 6 different clusters using a standard k-means clustering algorithm and shown using different colors. We see that for some users, the download times were roughly 15 s, whereas for some others they were roughly 7.5 s. This significant time differential suggests a potential timing side-channel if the difference can be correlated with sensitive program state and thus this differential should be investigated further with DISCRIMINER.

To see how such a time differential could be a timing side-channel, let us consider an attacker that (a) downloads the public profile pages of all users and learns each download time, and (b) can observe timing between packets by sniffing the network traffic between legitimate users. If the attacker observes user Alice downloading the page of another user whose identity is supposed to be a secret and sees that the download took approximately 7.5 s, the attacker can infer that Alice downloaded the page of one of the six users corresponding to the six squares (with time close to 7.5 s) in Fig. 1. The timing information leak thus helped the attacker narrow down the possibilities from hundreds of users to six.

Debugging Timing Side-Channels with Decision Tree Learning. How can the analyst go about debugging the SnapBuddy application to eliminate this timing side-channel? We show how DISCRIMINER can help. Recall that the analyst downloaded pages of all the users. Now the same download queries are executed over an instrumented version of the SnapBuddy server to record the

---

[1] From DARPA STAC (www.darpa.mil/program/space-time-analysis-for-cybersecurity).

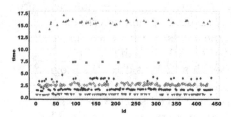

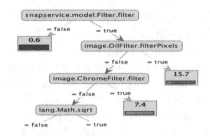

Fig. 1. Cluster running times from the SnapBuddy to produce labels. The scatter plot shows a differential corresponding to a possible timing side-channel.

Fig. 2. Snippet of a decision-tree discriminant learned from Snap-Buddy traces using the timing labels from Fig. 1.

number of times each method in the application is called by the trace. As a result, we obtain a set of traces with their (uninstrumented) overall running times and set of corresponding method calls.

Then DISCRIMINER uses the standard *CART* decision tree learning algorithm [5] to infer a decision tree that succinctly represents a discriminant using atomic predicates that characterize whether or not the trace invoked a particular method (shown in Fig. 2). For instance, the cluster representing the longest running time (around 15 s) is discriminated by the property `snapservice.model.Filter.filter` ∧ `image.OilFilter.filterPixels`, indicating that the two methods are both invoked by the trace. Likewise, the cluster representing the running time around 7.5 s is discriminated by the property `snapservice.model.Filter.filter` ∧ ¬`image.OilFilter.filterPixels` ∧ `image.ChromeFilter.filter`, indicating that `image.OilFilter.filterPixels` must not be invoked while the other two must be.

The analyst might now suspect what is going on: the timing differences are caused by the filters that each user chooses to apply to their picture. Note that the analyst running DISCRIMINER did not need to know that the filters are important for causing this time differential, or even that they existed. The tool discovers them simply because the trace contains all method calls, and the decision tree learning algorithm produces a useful discriminant.

A possible fix now suggests itself: make sure that the execution of each type of filter takes the same amount of time (though of course an implementation of such a fix still requires development effort). Overall, the example demonstrates how the decision tree produced by DISCRIMINER can be used to debug (and potentially fix) side-channel vulnerabilities.

3   Trace-Set Discrimination Problem

A *discrete probability distribution,* or just distribution, over a finite set L is a function $d : L \to [0, 1]$ such that $\sum_{\ell \in L} d(\ell) = 1$. Let $\mathcal{D}(L)$ denote the set of all discrete distributions over L.

Let $p_1, \ldots, p_m$ represent a set of *atomic predicates* over traces. Each predicate evaluates to a Boolean value over a given trace. Therefore, for simplicity, we represent a trace simply by the truth valuations of the predicates over the trace. In addition to atomic predicates, traces are associated with a distribution over labels. These distributions are generated by first measuring the execution time t of the trace. The execution time is obtained as the average over some fixed number of measurements $M > 0$. Therefore, the timing is taken to be a Gaussian random variable with mean t and a standard deviation σ_t. Using this information, we derive a discrete distribution $d \in \mathcal{D}(L)$ over the set of labels in L.

Definition 1 (Traces, Predicates and Label Distributions). *An execution trace T of the program is a tuple $\langle \tau, d \rangle$ wherein $\tau = \langle \rho_1, \ldots, \rho_m \rangle$ represents the truth valuations to the predicates $p_1, \ldots, p_m$, respectively and $d \in \mathcal{D}(L)$ is the associated label distribution over the finite set of labels L.*

We define a *trace discriminant* as a tuple of Boolean formulae that predict the labels of the traces given the truth valuations in the following fashion.

Definition 2. *Given a set of labels $L = \{\ell_1, \ldots, \ell_K\}$ and predicates $P = \{p_1, \ldots, p_m\}$, a **discriminant** Ψ is a tuple $\langle \varphi_1, \ldots, \varphi_K \rangle$ of Boolean formulae where each formula φ_i is over the predicates in P and corresponds to a label ℓ_i.*

A trace $\langle \tau, d \rangle$ receives a label ℓ_k under trace discriminant $\Psi = \langle \varphi_1, \ldots, \varphi_K \rangle$, and we write $\mathrm{LABEL}(\langle \tau, d \rangle, \Psi) = \ell_k$, if k is the smallest index $1 \leq i \leq K$ such that $\tau \models \varphi_i$, i.e. φ_i evaluates to **true** for the truth valuation τ. Formally,

$$
\mathrm{LABEL}(\langle \tau, d \rangle, \Psi) =
\begin{cases}
\ell_1 & \text{if } \tau \models \varphi_1, \text{ else} \\
\ell_2 & \text{if } \tau \models \varphi_2, \text{ else} \\
\vdots & \vdots \\
\ell_K & \text{if } \tau \models \varphi_K.
\end{cases}
$$

Definition 3. *Given a set of predicates $\{p_1, \ldots, p_m\}$, set of labels $\{\ell_1, \ldots, \ell_K\}$, and a set of traces $\{\langle \tau_1, d_1 \rangle, \ldots, \langle \tau_N, d_N \rangle\}$, the **trace set discriminant problem** (TDLP) is to learn a trace discriminant $\Psi = \langle \varphi_1, \ldots, \varphi_K \rangle$.*

In general, there are numerous possible discriminants that can be inferred for a given instance of the TDLP. We consider two approaches in this paper: (a) a *formal* maximum likelihood learning model over a structured set of discriminants and (b) an informal decision tree learning approach to maximize accuracy while minimizing the discriminant size.

3.1   Maximum Likelihood Learning

Given a discriminant and a set of traces, we define the likelihood of the discriminant as the probability that each trace $\langle \tau_i, d_i \rangle$ receives the label $\mathrm{LABEL}(\langle \tau_i, d_i \rangle, \Psi)$ dictated by the discriminant.

Definition 4. *The **likelihood** $\lambda(\Psi)$ of a discriminant Ψ over a set of traces $\{\langle \tau_1, d_1 \rangle, \ldots, \langle \tau_N, d_N \rangle\}$ is given by $\lambda(\Psi) = \prod_{i=1}^{N} d_i (\text{LABEL}(\langle \tau_i, d_i \rangle, \Psi)).$*

The *maximum likelihood* discriminant Ψ_{ml} is defined as the discriminant amongst all possible Boolean formulae that maximizes $\lambda(\Psi)$, i.e. $\Psi_{ml} = \text{argmax}_\Psi (\lambda(\Psi))$. This maximization runs over the all possible tuples of K Boolean formulae over m atomic predicates, i.e., a space of $(K!)\binom{2^{2^m}}{K}$ possible discriminants! In particular, Hyafil and Rivest [10] show that the problem of learning optimal decision trees is NP-hard. Therefore, for our formal approach, we consider the following simpler class of discriminants by restricting the form of the Boolean formulae φ_j that make up the discriminants to monotone conjunctive formulae.

Definition 5 (Conjunctive Discriminants). *A monotone* conjunctive *formula over predicates $P = \{p_1, \ldots, p_m\}$ is a finite conjunction of the form $\bigwedge_{j=1}^{r} p_{i_j}$ such that $1 \leq i_1, \ldots, i_r \leq m$. A discriminant $\Psi = \langle \varphi_1, \ldots, \varphi_K \rangle$ is a (monotone) conjunctive discriminant if each φ_i is a monotone conjunctive formula for $1 \leq i \leq K$. In order to make a traces discriminant exhaustive, we assume φ_K to be the formula* **true**.

The number of conjunctive discriminants is $(K-1)!\binom{2^m}{K-1}$. However, they can be easily represented and learned using SAT or ILP solvers, as shown subsequently. Moreover, working with simpler monotone conjunctive discriminants is preferable [7] in the presence of noisy data, as using formal maximum likelihood model to learn arbitrary complex Boolean function would lead to over-fitting. The problem of *maximum likelihood* conjunctive discriminant is then naturally defined. We refine the result of [10] in our context to show that the problem of learning (monotone) conjunctive discriminants is already NP-hard.

Theorem 1. *Given an instance of* TDLP, *the problem of finding the maximum likelihood conjunctive discriminant is* NP-hard.

Proof. We prove the NP-hardness of the problem of finding maximum likelihood conjunctive discriminant by giving a reduction from the *minimum weight monotone SAT problem* that is already known to be NP-hard. Recall that a monotone Boolean formula is propositional logic formula where all the literals are positive. Given a monotone instance of SAT $\phi = \bigwedge_{j=1}^{n} C_j$ over the set of variable $X = \{x_1, \ldots, x_m\}$, the minimum weight monotone SAT problem is to find a truth assignment satisfying ϕ with as few variables set to **true** as possible.

Consider the trace-set discrimination problem P_ϕ where there is one predicate p_i per variable $x_i \in X$ of ϕ, two labels ℓ_1 and ℓ_2, and the set of traces such that

- there is one trace $\langle \tau_j, d_j \rangle$ per clause C_j of ϕ such that predicate p_i evaluates to true in the trace τ_j if variable x_i *does not occur* in clause C_j, and the label distribution d_j is such that $d_j(\ell_1) = 0$ and $d_j(\ell_2) = 1$.
- there is one trace $\langle \tau^i, d^i \rangle$ per variable x_i of ϕ such that only the predicate p_i evaluates to false in the trace τ^i and the label distribution d^i is such that $d^i(\ell_1) = 1 - \varepsilon$ and $d^i(\ell_2) = \varepsilon$ where $0 < \varepsilon < \frac{1}{2}$.

Observe that for every truth assignment $(x_1^*, \ldots, x_m^*)$ to variables in X, there is a conjunctive discriminant $\wedge_{x_i^*=1} p_i$ such that if the clause C_j is satisfied then the trace $\langle \tau_j, d_j \rangle$ receives the label ℓ_2. This implies that the likelihood of the discriminant is non-zero only for the discriminant corresponding to satisfying valuations of ϕ. Moreover, for every variable x_i receiving a true assignment, the trace $\langle \tau^i, d^i \rangle$ receives the label ℓ_2 with ε contributed to the likelihood term and for every variable x_i receiving false assignment, the trace $\langle \tau^i, d^i \rangle$ receives the label ℓ_1 with $1 - \varepsilon$ being contributed to the likelihood. This construction implies that a maximum likelihood discriminant should give label ℓ_2 to all of the traces $\langle \tau_j, d_j \rangle$ and label ℓ_1 to as many traces in $\{\tau^i, d^i\}$ as possible. It is easy to verify that there exists a truth assignment of size k for ϕ if and only if there exists a conjunctive discriminant in P_ϕ with likelihood $\prod_{i=1}^{k} \varepsilon \cdot \prod_{i=1}^{m-k}(1 - \varepsilon)$. $\qquad \square$

3.2 Decision Tree Learning

As noted earlier, the max likelihood approach over structured Boolean formulae can be prohibitively expensive when the number of traces, predicates and labels are large. An efficient alternative is to consider decision tree learning approaches that can efficiently produce accurate discriminants while keeping the size of the discriminant as small as possible. The weighted accuracy of a discriminant Ψ over traces $\langle \tau_i, d_i \rangle, i = 1, \ldots, N$ is defined additively as $\alpha(\Psi) : \frac{1}{N} \sum_{i=1}^{N} d_i (\text{LABEL}(\langle \tau_i, d_i \rangle, \Psi))$. This accuracy is a fraction between $[0, 1]$ with higher accuracy representing a better discriminant.

A decision tree learning algorithm seeks to learn a discriminant as a decision tree over the predicates $p_1, \ldots, p_m$ and outcome labels $\ell_1, \ldots, \ell_K$. Typically, algorithms will maximize $\alpha(\Psi)$ while keeping the description length $|\Psi|$ as small as possible. A variety of efficient tree learning algorithms have been defined including ID3 [15], CART [5], CHAID [11] and many others [14,18]. These algorithms have been supported by popular machine learning tools such as Scikit-learn python library (http://scikit-learn.org/stable/) and RapidMiner [2].

4 Discriminant Analysis

In this section, we provide details of max likelihood and decision tree approaches, and compare their performances over a scalable set of micro-benchmarks.

4.1 Maximum Likelihood Approach

We now present an approach for inferring a conjunctive discriminant Ψ using integer linear programming (ILP) that maximizes the likelihood $\lambda(\Psi)$ for given predicates $p_1, \ldots, p_m$, labels $\ell_1, \ldots, \ell_K$ and traces $\langle \tau_1, d_1 \rangle, \ldots, \langle \tau_N, d_N \rangle$. This problem was already noted to be NP-hard in Theorem 1.

We first present our approach for the special case of $K = 2$ labels. Let ℓ_1, ℓ_2 be the two labels. Our goal is to learn a conjunctive formula φ_1 for ℓ_1. We use binary decision variables $x_1, \ldots, x_m$ wherein $x_i = 1$ denotes that φ_1 has the predicate

p_i as a conjunct, whereas $x_i = 0$ denotes that p_i is not a conjunct in φ_1. Also we add binary decision variables $w_1, \ldots, w_N$ corresponding to each of the N traces, respectively. The variable $w_i = 1$ denotes that the trace $\langle \tau_i, d_i \rangle$ receives label ℓ_2 under φ_1 and $w_i = 0$ indicates that the trace receives label ℓ_1. The likelihood of the discriminant Ψ can be given as $\lambda(\Psi) \overset{\text{def}}{=} \prod_{i=1}^{N} \begin{cases} d_i(\ell_1) \text{ if } w_i = 0 \\ d_i(\ell_2) \text{ if } w_i = 1 \end{cases}$. Rather than maximize $\lambda(\Psi)$, we equivalently maximize $\log(\lambda(\Psi))$

$$\log(\lambda(\Psi)) = \sum_{i=1}^{N} \begin{cases} \log(d_i(\ell_1)) \text{ if } w_i = 0 \\ \log(d_i(\ell_2)) \text{ if } w_i = 1 \end{cases}.$$

Let $r_i := d_i(\ell_1) = 1 - d_i(\ell_2)$, and simplify the expression for $\log(\lambda(\Psi))$ as $\sum_{i=1}^{N} (1 - w_i) \log(r_i) + w_i \log(1 - r_i)$.

Next, the constraints need to relate the values of x_i to each w_i. Specifically, let for each trace $\langle \tau_i, d_i \rangle$, $R_i \subseteq \{p_1, \ldots, p_m\}$ denote the predicates that are valued *false* in the trace. We can verify that if $w_i = 0$, then none of the predicates in R_i can be part of φ_1, and if $w_i = 1$, at least one of the predicates in R_i must be part of φ_1. This is expressed by the following inequality $\frac{1}{|R_i|}(\sum_{p_k \in R_i} x_k) \leq w_i \leq \sum_{p_k \in R_i} x_k$. If any of the $p_k \in R_i$ is included in the conjunction, then the LHS of the inequality is at least $\frac{1}{|R_i|}$, forcing $w_i = 1$. Otherwise, if all p_k are not included, the RHS of the inequality is 0, forcing $w_i = 0$.
The overall ILP is given by

$$\max \sum_{i=1}^{N} (1 - w_i) \log(r_i) + w_i \log(1 - r_i)$$
$$\text{s.t.} \quad \frac{1}{|R_i|}\left(\sum_{p_k \in R_i} x_k\right) \leq w_i \qquad i = 1, \ldots, N$$
$$w_i \leq \sum_{p_k \in R_i} x_k \qquad i = 1, \ldots, N$$
$$x_j \in \{0,1\}, \ w_i \in \{0,1\} \qquad i = 1, \ldots, N, \ j = 1, \ldots, m \quad (1)$$

Theorem 2. *Let $x_1^*, \ldots, x_m^*$ denote the solution for ILP* (1) *over a given TDLP instance with labels $\{\ell_1, \ell_2\}$. The discriminant $\Psi = \langle \varphi_1, \textbf{true} \rangle$ wherein $\varphi_1 = \bigwedge_{x_i^* = 1} p_i$ maximizes the likelihood $\lambda(\Psi)$ over all conjunctive discriminants.*

With the approach using the ILP in Eq. (1), we can tackle an instance with $K > 2$ labels by recursively applying the two label solution. First, we learn a formula φ_1 for ℓ_1 and $L \setminus \ell_1$. Next, we eliminate all traces that satisfy φ_1 and eliminate the label ℓ_1. We then recursively consider $\hat{L} : L \setminus \ell_1$ as the new label set. Doing so, we obtain a discriminant $\Psi : \langle \varphi_1, \varphi_2, \ldots, \varphi_{K-1}, \textbf{true} \rangle$.

In theory, the ILP in (1) has $N + m$ variables, which can be prohibitively large. However, for the problem instances considered, we drastically reduced the problem size through standard preprocessing/simplification steps that allowed us to resolve the values of x_i, w_j for many of the variables to constants.

4.2 Decision Tree Learning Appraoch

In order to discriminate traces, DISCRIMINER employs decision tree learning to learn classifiers that discriminate the traces. Given a set of N traces on a dependent variable (labels) L that takes finitely-many values in the domain $\{\ell_1, \ldots, \ell_K\}$ and m feature variables (predicates) $F = \{f_1, \ldots, f_m\}$, the goal of a classification algorithm is to produce a partition the space of the feature variables into K disjoint sets $A_1, \ldots, A_K$ such that the predicted value of L is i if the F-variables take value in A_i. Decision-tree methods yield rectangular sets A_i by recursively partitioning the data set one F variable at a time. CART (*Classification and Regression Trees*) is a popular and effective algorithm to learn decision-tree based classifiers. It constructs binary decision trees by iteratively exploring features and thresholds that yield the largest information gain (Gini index) at each node. For a detailed description of the CART, we refer to [5].

4.3   Performance Evaluation

We created a set of micro-benchmarks—containing a side-channel in time—to evaluate the performance of the decision-tree discriminator computed using *scikit-learn* implementation of CART and the maximum likelihood conjunctive discriminant using an ILP implementation from the GLPK library.

These micro-benchmarks consist of a set of programs that take as an input a sequence of binary digits (say a secret information), and perform some computation whose execution time (enforced using `sleep` commands) depends on some property of the secret information. For the micro-benchmark series LSB0 and MSB0, the execution time is a Gaussian-distributed random variable whose mean is proportional to the position of least significant 0 and most significant 0 in the secret, respectively. In addition, we have a micro-benchmark series Pat_d whose execution time is a random variable whose mean depends upon the position of the pattern d in the input. For instance, the micro-benchmark Pat_{101} takes a 20-bit input data and the leftmost occurrence i of the pattern 101 executes three methods F_i, F_{i+1}, F_{i+2} with mean exec. time of a method F_j being $10*j$ ms.

In our experiments with micro-benchmarks, we generate the dataset by randomly generating the input. For each input, we execute the benchmark programs 10 times to approximate the mean and the standard deviation of the observation, and log the list of method called for each such input. For a given set of execution traces, we cluster the execution time based on their mean and assign weighted labels to each trace according to Gaussian distribution. We defer the details of this data collection to Sect. 5. Our dataset consists of trace id, label, weight, and method calls for every execution trace. We use this common dataset to both the decision-tree and the maximum likelihood algorithms.

Table 1 shows the performance of the decision-tree classifiers and the max-likelihood approach for given micro-benchmarks. The table consists of benchmark scales (based on the number of methods and traces), the accuracy of approaches, time of computing decision tree and max-likelihood discriminant, the height of decision tree, and the maximum number of conjuncts among all learned discriminants in the max-likelihood approach. In order to compute the performance of both models and avoid overfitting, we train and test data sets using group k-fold cross-validation procedure with k set to 20.

Table 1. Micro-benchmark results for decision-tree discriminators learned using decision tree and the max-likelihood approach. Legend: #M: number of methods, #N: number of traces, T: computation time in seconds, A: accuracy, H: decision-tree height, M: max. discriminant size (Max. # of conjuncts in discriminants), $\epsilon < 0.1$ **sec.**

Benchmark ID	#M	#N	Decision tree			Max-likelihood		
			T	A	H	T	A	M
LSB0	10	188	ϵ	100%	7	ϵ	100 %	10
MSB0	10	188	ϵ	100%	7	ϵ	100 %	10
Pat_{101}	20	200	ϵ	100%	13	0.2	89.4%	20
Pat_{1010}	50	500	ϵ	98.4%	22	1.3	93.6%	50
Pat_{10111}	80	800	0.1	97.8%	37	8.1	94.8%	72
Pat_{10101}	100	1000	0.2	92.9%	43	9.8	87.9%	86
Pat_{10011}	150	1500	0.5	89.2%	44	45.0	91.5%	118
Pat_{101011}	200	2000	0.8	92.1%	50	60.2	90.9%	156
$Pat_{1010101}$	400	4000	4.2	88.6%	111	652.4	92.9%	294

Table 1 shows that both decision tree and max-likelihood approaches have decent accuracy in small and medium sized benchmarks. On the other hand, decision tree approach stands out as highly scalable: it takes only 4.2 s for the decision-tree approach to building a classifier for the benchmark $Pat_{1010101}$ with 400 methods and 4000 traces, while it takes 652.4 s for the max-likelihood approach to constructing the discriminants. Table 1 shows that the discriminants learned using decision tree approach are simpler than the ones learned using max-likelihood approach requiring a fewer number of tests.

5 Case Study: Understanding Traces with Decision Trees

The data on microbenchmarks suggest that the decision tree learning approach is more scalable and has comparable accuracy as the max-likelihood approach. Therefore, we consider three case studies to evaluate whether the decision tree approach produces useful artifacts for debugging program vulnerabilities.

Research Question. We consider the following question:

> Does the learned discriminant pinpoint code fragments that explain differences in the overall execution times?

We consider this question to be answered positively if we can identify an explanation for timing differences (which can help debug to side channel or availability vulnerabilities) through DISCRIMINER[2].

---

[2] https://github.com/cuplv/Discriminer.

Table 2. Parameters for trace set discriminant analysis, which predicts a class label based on attributes. Here, we wish to discriminate traces to predict the total execution time of the trace based on the methods called in the trace and the number of times each method is called. To consider a finite number of class labels, we fix a priori n possible time ranges based on choosing the best number of clustering.

Attributes	(1) the methods called in the trace (Boolean)
	(2) the number of times each method is called in a trace (integer)
Class label	A time range for the total execution time of the trace
Number of classes	6, 6, and 2 for SnapBuddy, GabFeed, and TextCrunchr

Methodology. We consider the discriminant analysis approach based on decision tree learning from Sect. 4. Table 2 summarizes the particular instantiations for the discriminant analysis that we consider here.

Attributes: Called Methods. For this case study, we are interested in seeing whether the key methods that explain the differences in execution time can be pinpointed. Thus, we consider attributes corresponding to the called methods in a trace. In order to collect information regarding the called methods, we instrumented Java bytecode applications using Javassist analysis framework (http://jboss-javassist.github.io/javassist/).

Class Label: Total Execution Time Ranges. To identify the most salient attributes, we fix a small number of possible labels, and cluster traces according to total execution time. Each cluster is defined by a corresponding time interval. The clusters and their intervals are learned using k-means clustering algorithm.

We consider the execution time for each trace to be a random variable and assume a normal distribution. We obtain the mean and variance through 10 repeated measurements. We apply clustering to the mean execution times of each trace to determine the class labels. Henceforth, when we speak of the execution time of a trace, we refer to the mean of the measurements for that trace.

A class label (or cluster) can be identified by the mean of all execution times belonging to that cluster. Then, considering the class labels sorted in increasing order, we define the lower boundary of a bucket for classifying new traces by averaging the maximum execution time in the previous bucket and the minimum execution time in this bucket (and analogously for the upper boundary).

Weighted Labeling of Traces. Given a set of time ranges (clusters), we define a weighted labeling of traces that permits a trace to be assigned to different clusters with different weights. For a given trace, the weights to clusters are determined by the probability mass that belongs to the time range of the cluster. For example, consider a sample trace whose execution-time distribution straddles the boundary of two clusters C_0 and C_1, with 22% area of the distribution intersecting with cluster C_0 and 78% with cluster C_1. In this case, we assign the trace to both clusters C_0 and C_1 with weights according to their probability mass in their respective regions. Note that this provides a smoother interpretation of the class labels rather than assigning the most likely label.

Decision Tree Learning. From a training set with this weighted labeling, we apply the weighted decision tree learning algorithm CART described in Sect. 4. We use DISCRIMINER both for clustering in the time domain as described above to determine the class labels and weights of each trace and for learning the classification model. We use group k-fold cross validation procedure to find accuracy.

Objects of Study. We consider three programs drawn from benchmarks provided by the DARPA STAC project. These medium-sized Java programs were developed to be realistic applications that may potentially have timing side-channel or availability security vulnerabilities.

Program	Total methods (num)	Total traces (num)	Observed methods (num)
SnapBuddy	3071	439	160
GabFeed	573	368	30
TextCrunchr	327	180	35
Total	3971	987	225

SnapBuddy is a web application for social image sharing. The profile page of a user includes their picture (with a filter). The profile page is publicly accessible. GabFeed is a web application for hosting community forums. Users and servers can mutually authenticate using public-key infrastructure. TextCrunchr is a text analysis program capable of performing standard text analysis including word frequency, word length, and so on. It uses sorting algorithms to perform the analysis.

In the inset table, we show the basic characteristics of these benchmarks. The benchmarks, in total, consist of 3,971 methods. From these programs, we generated 987 traces by using a component of each applications web API (scripted via `curl`). In these recorded traces, we observed 225 distinct methods called. Note that some methods are called thousands to millions of times.

Decision Trees Produced by DISCRIMINER. In Fig. 3(b)–(d)–(f), we show the decision tree learned from the SnapBuddy, GabFeed, and TextCrunchr traces, respectively. As a decision tree is interpreted by following a path from the root to a leaf where the leaf yields the class label and the conjunction of the internal nodes describes the discriminator, one can look for characteristics of discriminated trace sets by following different paths in the tree. The class labels at leaves are annotated with the bucket's mean time. For example, in (b), the label 15.7 shows that the path to this label which calls `image.OilFilter.filterPixels` takes 15.7 s to execute. The colors in bars in the leaves represent the actual labels of the training traces that would be classified in this bucket according to the learned discriminator. Multiple colors in the bars mean that a discriminator, while not perfectly accurate on the training traces, is also able to tolerate noise. The height of the bar gives an indication of the number of training traces following this discriminator. The scatter plots in (a)–(c)–(e) show the time of each trace, with the color indicating the corresponding cluster.

Findings for SnapBuddy. For SnapBuddy, the traces exercise downloading the public profile pages of all user from a mock database. We have explained in

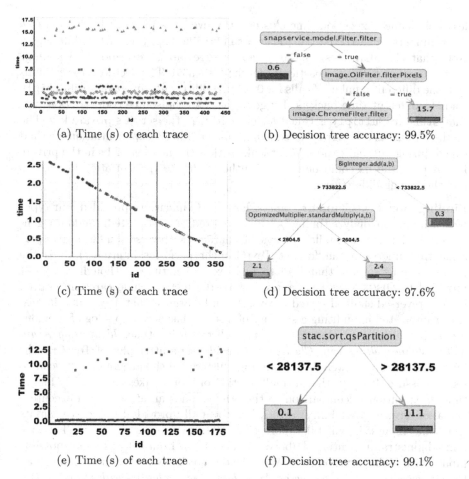

(a) Time (s) of each trace

(b) Decision tree accuracy: 99.5%

(c) Time (s) of each trace

(d) Decision tree accuracy: 97.6%

(e) Time (s) of each trace

(f) Decision tree accuracy: 99.1%

Fig. 3. Clustering in the time domain (a)-(c)-(e) to learn decision tree classification models (b)-(d)-(f). The upper row corresponds to SnapBuddy traces, the middle row corresponds GabFeed traces, while the bottom row corresponds to TextCrunchr traces. (Color figure online)

Sect. 2 how clustering (in Fig. 3(a)) helps to identify a timing side-channel, and how the decision tree (in Fig. 3b) helps in debugging the vulnerability.

Findings for GabFeed. *Inputs.* For GabFeed, the traces exercise the authentication web API by fixing the user public key and by sampling uniformly from the server private key space (3064-bit length keys). *Identifying a Timing Side-Channel with Clustering.* Considering scatter plot of GabFeed in Fig. 3c (boundaries show different clusters), we can see less definitive timing clusters. However, it shows timing differences that indicate a side channel. *Debugging Timing Side-Channels with Decision Tree Learning.* The (part of) decision tree for GabFeed in Fig. 3d is also less definitive than for SnapBuddy as we might expect given the less well-defined execution time clusters. However, the part of the decision tree discriminants `OptimizedMultiplier.standardMultiply` for time differences. Note that the attributes on the outgoing edge labels correspond to a range for the number of times a particular method is called. The decision tree explains that the different number of calls for `OptimizedMultiplier.standardMultiply` leads to different time buckets. By going back to the source code, we observed that `standardMultiply` is called for each 1-bit in the server's private key. The method `standardMultiply` is called from a modular exponentiation method called during authentication. What leaks is thus the number of 1s in the private key. A potential fix could be to rewrite the modular exponentiation method to pad the timing differences.

Findings for TextCrunchr. *Inputs.* For TextCrunchr, we provided four types of text inputs to analyze timing behaviors: sorted, reverse-sorted, randomly generated, and reversed-shuffled arrays of characters (reverse-shuffle is an operation that undoes a shuffle that TextCrunchr performs internally). It is the reverse shuffled inputs that lead to high execution time. Although the input provided to DISCRIMINER for analyzing TextCrunchr include carefully crafted inputs (reversed shuffled sorted array), it can be argued that a system administrator interested in auditing a security of a server has access to a log of previous inputs including some that resulted in high execution time. *Identifying Availability Vulnerabilities with Clustering.* Considering scatter plot of TextCrunchr in Fig. 3e we can see well-defined timing clusters which can potentially lead to security issues. It shows that a small fraction of inputs takes comparably higher time of execution in comparison to the others. Thus an attacker can execute a denial-of-service (availability) attack by repeatedly providing the costly inputs (for some inputs, it will take more than 600 s to process the text). The system administrator mentioned above probably knew from his logs about possible inputs with high execution time. What he did not know is why these inputs lead to high execution time. *Debugging Availability Vulnerabilities with Decision Tree Learning.* The decision tree for TextCrunchr in Fig. 3f shows that the number of calls on `stac.sort.qsPartition` as the explanation for time differences (out of 327 existing methods in the application). This can help identify the sorting algorithm (Quicksort) used as a source of the problem and leads to the realization that certain inputs trigger the worst-case execution time of Quicksort.

Threats to Validity. These case studies provide evidence that decision tree learning helps in identifying code fragments that correlate with differential execution time. Clearly, the most significant threat to validity is whether these programs are representative of other applications. To mitigate, we considered programs not created by us nor known to us prior to this study. These applications were designed to faithfully represent real-world Java programs—for example, using Java software engineering patterns and best practices. Another threat concerns the representativeness of the training sets. To mitigate this threat, we created sample traces directly using the web interface for the whole application, rather than interposing at any intermediate layer. This interface is for any user of these web applications and specifically the interface available to a potential attacker. A training set focuses on exercising a particular feature of the application, which also corresponds to the ability of an attacker to build training sets specific to different features of the application.

6 Related Work

Machine learning techniques have been used for *specification mining*, that is, for learning succinct representations of the set of all program traces. Furthermore, machine learning techniques have been applied to learn classifiers of programs for *malware detection* and for *software bug detection*.

Specification Mining. In [3], machine learning techniques are used to synthesize an NFA (nondeterministic finite automaton) that represents all the correct traces of a program. In our setting, this would correspond to learning a discriminant for one cluster (of correct traces). In contrast, our decision trees discriminate multiple clusters. However, the discriminants we considered in this paper are less expressive than NFAs. The survey [21] provides an overview of other specification mining approaches.

Malware and Bug Detection. In malware detection, machine learning techniques are used to learn classifiers that classify programs into benign and malicious [1,4,6,9,12,16,20]. In software bug detection, the task is to learn classifiers that classify programs behaviors into faulty and non-faulty [8,13,17,19]. In contrast, we consider more clusters of traces. In particular, Lo et al. [13] constructs a classifier to generalize known failures of software systems and to further detect (predict) other unknown failures. First, it mines iterative patterns from program traces of known normal and failing executions. Second, it applies a feature selection method to identify highly discriminative patterns which distinguish failing traces from normal ones.

In all these works, the training set is labeled: all the programs are labeled either benign or malicious (faulty or non-faulty). In contrast, we start with an unlabeled set of traces, and construct their labels by clustering in the time domain.

7 Conclusion

Summary. We introduced the trace set discrimination problem as a formalization of the practical problem of finding what can be inferred from limited run time observations of the system. We have shown that the problem is NP-hard, and have proposed two scalable techniques to solve it. The first is ILP-based, and it can give formal guarantees about the discriminant that was found but infers discriminants of a limited form. The second is based on decision trees, infers general discriminants, but does not give formal guarantees. For three realistic applications, our tool produces a decision tree useful for explaining timing differences between executions.

Future Work. There are several intriguing directions for future research. First, we will investigate the extension of our framework to reactive systems, by generalizing our notion of execution time observations to sequences of timed events. Second, we will build up the network traffic monitoring ability of our tool, to make it usable by security analysts for distributed architectures.

References

1. Aafer, Y., Du, W., Yin, H.: DroidAPIMiner: mining API-level features for robust malware detection in android. In: Zia, T., Zomaya, A., Varadharajan, V., Mao, M. (eds.) SecureComm 2013. LNICSSITE, vol. 127, pp. 86–103. Springer, Heidelberg (2013). doi:10.1007/978-3-319-04283-1_6
2. Akthar, F., Hahne, C.: Rapidminer 5 operator reference. Rapid-I GmbH (2012)
3. Ammons, G., Bodík, R., Larus, J.R.: Mining specifications. In: POPL, pp. 4–16 (2002)
4. Bailey, M., Oberheide, J., Andersen, J., Mao, Z.M., Jahanian, F., Nazario, J.: Automated classification and analysis of internet malware. In: Kruegel, C., Lippmann, R., Clark, A. (eds.) RAID 2007. LNCS, vol. 4637, pp. 178–197. Springer, Heidelberg (2007). doi:10.1007/978-3-540-74320-0_10
5. Breiman, L., Friedman, J., Olshen, R., Stone, C.: Classification and Regression Trees. Wadsworth, Belmont (1984)
6. Burguera, I., Zurutuza, U., Nadjm-Tehrani, S.: Crowdroid: behavior-based malware detection system for android. In: Workshop on Security and Privacy in Smartphones and Mobile devices, pp. 15–26 (2011)
7. Domingos, P.: The role of Occam's razor in knowledge discovery. Data Min. Knowl. Discov. **3**(4), 409–425 (1999). ISSN 1573–756X
8. Elish, K.O., Elish, M.O.: Predicting defect-prone software modules using support vector machines. J. Syst. Softw. **81**(5), 649–660 (2008)
9. Fredrikson, M., Jha, S., Christodorescu, M., Sailer, R., Yan, X.: Near-optimal malware specifications from suspicious behaviors. In: Security and Privacy (SP), pp. 45–60 (2010)
10. Hyafil, L., Rivest, R.L.: Constructing optimal binary decision trees is NP-complete. Inf. Process. Lett. **5**(1), 15–17 (1976)
11. Kass, G.V.: An exploratory technique for investigating large quantities of categorical data. J. R. Stat. Soc. Ser. C (Appl. Stat.) **29**(2), 119–127 (1980)
12. Kolbitsch, C., Comparetti, P.M., Kruegel, C., Kirda, E., Zhou, X., Wang, X.: Effective and efficient malware detection at the end host. In: USENIX Security, pp. 351–366 (2009)
13. Lo, D., Cheng, H., Han, J., Khoo, S.-C., Sun, C.: Classification of software behaviors for failure detection: a discriminative pattern mining approach. In: SIGKDD, pp. 557–566 (2009)
14. Mohri, M., Rostamizadeh, A., Talwalkar, A.: Foundations of Machine Learning. The MIT Press, Cambridge (2012). ISBN 026201825X, 9780262018258
15. Ross Quinlan, J.: Induction of decision trees. Mach. Learn. **1**, 81–106 (1986)
16. Rieck, K., Holz, T., Willems, C., Düssel, P., Laskov, P.: Learning and classification of malware behavior. In: Zamboni, D. (ed.) DIMVA 2008. LNCS, vol. 5137, pp. 108–125. Springer, Heidelberg (2008). doi:10.1007/978-3-540-70542-0_6
17. Sun, C., Lo, D., Wang, X., Jiang, J., Khoo, S.-C.: A discriminative model approach for accurate duplicate bug report retrieval. In: ICSE, pp. 45–54 (2010)

18. Tan, P.-N., Steinbach, M., Kumar, V., et al.: Introduction to Data Mining, vol. 1. Pearson Addison Wesley, Boston (2006)

19. Weimer, W., Necula, G.C.: Mining temporal specifications for error detection. In: Halbwachs, N., Zuck, L.D. (eds.) TACAS 2005. LNCS, vol. 3440, pp. 461–476. Springer, Heidelberg (2005). doi:10.1007/978-3-540-31980-1_30

20. Wu, D.-J., Mao, C.-H., Wei, T.-E., Lee, H.-M., Wu, K.-P.: Droidmat: android malware detection through manifest and API calls tracing. In: JCIS, pp. 62–69 (2012)

21. Zeller, A.: Specifications for free. In: Bobaru, M., Havelund, K., Holzmann, G.J., Joshi, R. (eds.) NFM 2011. LNCS, vol. 6617, pp. 2–12. Springer, Heidelberg (2011). doi:10.1007/978-3-642-20398-5_2

Directed Automated Memory Performance Testing

Sudipta Chattopadhyay[✉]

Singapore University of Technology and Design (SUTD), Singapore, Singapore
sudipta_chattopadhyay@sutd.edu.sg

Abstract. Understanding software non-functional properties (*e.g.* time, energy and security) requires deep understanding of the execution platform. The design of caches plays a crucial role in impacting software performance (for low latency of caches) and software security (for cache being used as a side channel). We present CATAPULT, a novel test generation framework to systematically explore the cache behaviour of an arbitrary program. Our framework leverages dynamic symbolic execution and satisfiability modulo theory (SMT) solvers for generating test inputs. We show the application of CATAPULT in testing timing-related properties and testing cache side-channel vulnerabilities in several open-source programs, including applications from OpenSSL and Linux GDK libraries.

1 Introduction

Program path captures an artifact of program behaviour in critical software validation process. For instance, in directed automated random testing (in short DART) [15], program paths are systematically explored to attempt path coverage and construct a test-suite for software validation. Several non-functional software properties (*e.g.* performance and security) critically depend on the execution platform and its interaction with the application software. For validating such properties, it is not sufficient to explore merely the program behaviour (*e.g.* program paths), it is crucial to explore *both* program behaviour and its interaction with the underlying hardware components (*e.g.* cache and communication bus). Hence, any technique that systematically explores both the program behaviour and the associated changes in the hardware, can be extremely useful for testing software non-functional properties.

In order to illustrate our observation, let us consider Fig. 1, which specifically records cache performance. We have generated Fig. 1 by executing an implementation of Advanced Encryption Standard (AES) [1]. We randomly generated 256000 different inputs to execute a single path of the respective implementation. Figure 1 captures the distribution of the number of inputs w.r.t. the number of observed cache misses [12]. We clearly observe a high variation on cache misses, hence the overall memory performance, even within the scope of a single program path. To solve the problem of systematically exploring cache behaviour

© Springer-Verlag GmbH Germany 2017
A. Legay and T. Margaria (Eds.): TACAS 2017, Part II, LNCS 10206, pp. 38–55, 2017.
DOI: 10.1007/978-3-662-54580-5_3

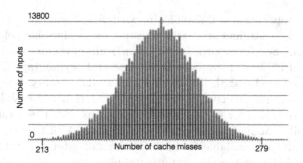

Fig. 1. Distribution of cache misses within a single program path [1]

and to expose the memory performance of a program, is the main contribution of our paper.

We present CATAPULT – a framework that leverages dynamic symbolic execution and satisfiability modulo theory (SMT) to explore both program behaviour and its associated cache behaviour. CATAPULT takes the binary code and a cache configuration as inputs, and produces a test suite as output. Each test in the test suite exposes a *unique* cache performance (*i.e.* the number of cache misses). Our framework does not generate *false positives*, meaning that the cache performance associated with each test indeed serves as an witness of an execution. Moreover, if our framework terminates, it guarantees to witness all possible cache behaviour in the respective program. Therefore, CATAPULT shares all the guarantees that come with classic approaches based on dynamic symbolic execution [15].

Our approach significantly differs from the techniques based on static cache analysis [20]. Unlike approaches based on static analysis, CATAPULT guarantees the absence of false positives. Moreover, unlike static analysis, CATAPULT generates a witness for each possible cache behaviour. To explore different cache behaviour of a program is, however, extremely involved. This is due to the complex interaction between program artifacts (*e.g.* memory-related instructions) and the design principle of caches. In order to solve this challenge, we have designed a novel symbolic model for the cache. Given a set of inputs, expressed via quantifier-free predicates, such a symbolic model encodes all possible cache behaviour observed for the respective set of inputs. As a result, this model can be integrated easily with the constraints explored and manipulated during dynamic symbolic execution. The size of our symbolic cache model is polynomial with respect to the number of memory-related instructions.

In summary, this paper makes the following contributions:

1. We present a test generator CATAPULT, leveraging on dynamic symbolic execution, to systematically explore the cache behaviour and hence, the memory performance of a program.
2. To show the generality of our approach, we instantiate our framework for two widely used cache replacement strategies – *least recently used* (LRU) and *first in first out* (FIFO).

3. We show the application of CATAPULT in two different contexts – *(i)* for testing timing-related constraints and *(ii)* for testing cache side-channel leakage.

4. We implement our framework on top of a *state-of-the-art* symbolic execution tool KLEE [2] and evaluate it with several cryptographic and device driver routines in OpenSSL library and Linux GDK library. For all the chosen subject programs, exhaustive test input generation is infeasible. However, CATAPULT terminates for all the subject programs and it generates *all tests* within a feasible timing-range from 10 s to 4.5 h. CATAPULT prototype and the obtained results are available for future usage and extension in the following URL: https://bitbucket.org/sudiptac/catapult/.

2   Background and Overview

Background on Caches. A cache is a fast memory employed between the CPU and the main memory (DRAM). For a given memory access, the cache is looked up first. A *cache configuration* can be defined by three parameters – cache line size (in bytes), number of cache sets, associativity and replacement policy. In an M-bit memory address, S bits are reserved to distinguish the cache set in which the respective address is mapped to and B bits are reserved to distinguish individual bytes within a cache line. For an arbitrary memory address $addr$, we say that it belongs to the *memory block* starting at address $\lfloor \frac{addr}{2^B} \rfloor$. If the content of $addr$ is not found in the cache, 2^B consecutive bytes are fetched from the memory address $\lfloor \frac{addr}{2^B} \rfloor$ and they are mapped into the cache set $\lfloor \frac{addr}{2^B} \rfloor \bmod 2^S$. Each cache set can only hold as many cache lines as the associativity of the cache. Therefore, if the associativity of the cache is A, the overall size of the cache is $(2^S \cdot 2^B \cdot A)$. Finally, since different memory blocks may map into the same cache set, caches store a *tag* in each cache line to distinguish different memory blocks. Since $(S + B)$ bits are used to identify cache sets and individual bytes in a cache line, the rest of the bits in the memory address are used as *tag*. For an A-way set-associative cache, a *cache state* is a set of ordered A-tuples, one for each cache set. Such a tuple captures the set of memory blocks contained in the respective set and the order in which these blocks would be replaced. For example, an ordered pair $\langle m_1, m_2 \rangle$ captures the cache state where m_2 would be replaced before m_1 in a 2-way set-associative cache.

Overview. In this section, we discuss the motivation behind our approach through the example in Fig. 2. For the sake of illustration, we use both assembly-level and source-level syntax in Fig. 2(a). However, our test generation is carried out directly on the binary. Let us assume the code shown in Fig. 2(a) runs on a platform having direct-mapped (*i.e.* associativity $A = 1$), 256 bytes cache. The mapping of different variables into the cache is shown in Fig. 2(b). We assume that the variable x is also allocated a register in the generated code. Therefore, reading variable x in the code fragment, as shown in Fig. 2(a), does not involve any cache access.

Let us assume that we want to check whether the code in Fig. 2(a) exhibits *more than two cache misses* when x is a program input. We first execute the

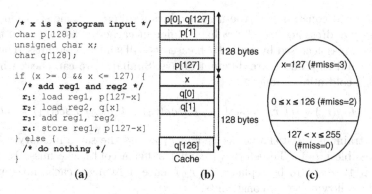

Fig. 2. (a) a program where cache performance exhibits variation within a program path, (b) mapping of variables in a 256 bytes cache, (c) cache performance with respect to different inputs

program with a random input $x = 0$. We also compute the path condition $x \geq 0 \wedge x \leq 127$ which symbolically encodes all inputs exercising the respective program path. We note that for $x = 0$, both r_1 and r_2 suffer cache misses. For $x = 0$, the store instruction r_4 is a cache hit, as p[127] is already loaded into the cache and it was not replaced by q[0].

Since dynamic symbolic execution aims to obtain path coverage, the next test input will be generated by manipulating the path condition and solving the following constraint: $\neg(x \geq 0 \wedge x \leq 127)$. This will result in inputs exercising the else branch in Fig. 2(a), which, in turn does not access memory.

It is worthwhile to note that classic symbolic execution may not reveal critical inputs related to cache performance. For instance, executing the code in Fig. 2(a), for $x = 127$, will access p[0], q[127] and p[0] in sequence. Since q[127] replaces p[0] from the cache, all accesses will be cache misses. Figure 2(c) shows the partitioning of the input space according to cache performance.

A classic symbolic-execution-based approach explores program paths instead of cache behaviour. The if branch in Fig. 2(a) encodes two different cache behaviors – one for inputs $0 \leq x \leq 126$ and another for input $x = 127$. Therefore, it is crucial to devise a methodology that can differentiate inputs based on cache behaviour, even though such inputs exercise the same program path.

How CATAPULT Works. For each explored program path, CATAPULT generates symbolic constraints to encode all possible cache behaviour. For instance, consider the program path captured by the path condition $x \geq 0 \wedge x \leq 127$. Assuming an empty cache, the first load instruction will suffer a cache miss. For instruction r_2, we check whether the memory block containing address &q[x] has been accessed for the first time as follows:

$$tag(r_2) \neq tag(r_1) \vee set(r_2) \neq set(r_1)$$

where tag (respectively, set) captures the cache-tag (respectively, cache set) for the memory address accessed by the respective instruction. Intuitively, the aforementioned constraint is true if r_2 accesses a different cache set than r_1 or the memory address accessed by r_2 has a different cache-tag as compared to the memory address accessed by r_1. In such cases r_2 will suffer a cold miss. The constraint is valid as p and q are different arrays. Similarly, we can check whether r_4 suffers a cold miss as follows:

$$(tag(r_4) \neq tag(r_1) \vee set(r_4) \neq set(r_1)) \wedge (tag(r_4) \neq tag(r_2) \vee set(r_4) \neq set(r_2))$$

This constraint is unsatisfiable, as r_1 and r_4 access the same memory address for all possible inputs. Therefore, r_4 cannot suffer a cold cache miss. To check whether p[127-x] can be replaced by r_2 (hence inducing a cache miss at r_4), we use the following set of constraints.

$$(tag(r_2) \neq tag(r_4) \wedge set(r_2) = set(r_4)) \Rightarrow (miss_4 = 1)$$

$$(tag(r_2) = tag(r_4) \vee set(r_2) \neq set(r_4)) \Rightarrow (miss_4 = 0)$$

The variable $miss_4$ indicates whether r_4 is a cache miss or not. CATAPULT explores different solutions of $miss_4$. In this example, $miss_4$ is 1 for $x = 127$ and $miss_4$ is 0 for $0 \leq x \leq 126$. Therefore, by systematically generating symbolic constraints and exploring the different solutions, CATAPULT can discover that r_4 suffers a cache miss only for input $x = 127$, leading to a total three cache misses in the respective execution.

3   Test Generation

Figure 3 and Algorithm 1 outline all the stages involved in CATAPULT. Algorithm 1 takes a program $\mathcal{P}$, the cache configuration $\mathcal{C}$ and an objective $\mathcal{O}$ as inputs. Informally, $\mathcal{O}$ captures dynamic properties related to cache performance. In Sect. 5, we show how $\mathcal{O}$ is formulated to check (i) timing-related properties and (ii) cache side-channel vulnerabilities. Given the inputs, Algorithm 1 leverages dynamic symbolic execution and computes all unique tests (in the given time budget) that satisfy $\mathcal{O}$.

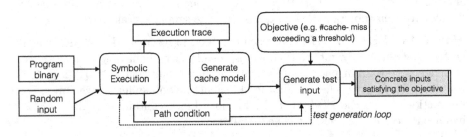

Fig. 3. Our test generation framework

Algorithm 1. Test Generation Algorithm

Input: Program $\mathcal{P}$, cache configuration $\mathcal{C}$, objective $\mathcal{O}$.
Output: A test suite $\mathcal{T}$, where each test $t \in \mathcal{T}$ satisfies $\mathcal{O}$

```
 1: AllPCs = UnchkdPCs = T = empty           24:   /* exclude current solutions */
 2: Select a random input I                   25:   /* this step ensures unique tests */
 3: Explore(P, C, I)                          26:   O_S := ExcludeCurTest(T, O_S)
 4: while UnchkdPCs ≠ empty do                27:   let Ω := Γ(Ψ_path) ∧ O_S ∧ Ψ_path
 5:     select φ ∈ UnchkdPCs                  28:   /* Generate relevant tests */
 6:     UnchkdPCs := UnchkdPCs \ {φ}          29:   /* See Sect. 5 */
 7:     let φ ← pc_1 ∧ pc_2 ∧ ... ∧ pc_{r-1} ∧ pc_r   30:   while Ω is satisfiable do
 8:     if φ is satisfiable then             31:       get k_θ satisfying Ω
 9:         t_θ ← concrete input satisfying φ 32:       T ∪ = {k_θ}
10:             Explore(P, C, t_θ)           33:       refine O_S to exclude solution k_θ
11:     end if                                34:       Ω := Γ(Ψ_path) ∧ O_S ∧ Ψ_path
12: end while                                 35:   end while
13: Report generated test suite T            36:   let Ψ_path ≡ pc_1 ∧ pc_2 ∧ ... ∧ pc_u
14:                                           37:   /* build partial path conditions */
15: procedure EXPLORE(P, C, t)               38:   for i ← 1, u do
16:     execute P on input t                  39:       φ_i := pc_1 ∧ pc_2 ∧ ... pc_{i-1} ∧ ¬pc_i
17:     let Ψ_path be the path condition     40:       if φ_i ∉ AllPCs then
18:     let S be the execution trace          41:           AllPCs ∪ = {φ_i}
19:     /* Generate the cache model */        42:           UnchkdPCs ∪ = {φ_i}
20:     /* See Sect. 5 */                     43:       end if
21:     Γ(Ψ_path) := CacheModel(C, Ψ_path, S) 44:   end for
22:     /* formulate objective (Sect. 5) */   45:   /* end exploration of Ψ_path */
23:     O_S := ObjectivePred(S)               46: end procedure
```

We first execute $\mathcal{P}$ with a random input $\mathcal{I}$ and compute the path condition Ψ_{path} as well as the execution trace $\mathbb{S}$. The trace $\mathbb{S}$ is captured via a sequence of pairs as follows:

$$\mathbb{S} \equiv \langle (r_1, \sigma_1), (r_2, \sigma_2), \ldots, (r_n, \sigma_n) \rangle \qquad (1)$$

Here r_i denotes the i-th memory-related instruction executed and σ_i symbolically captures the memory address accessed by r_i. For example, when we execute the code fragment of Fig. 2(a) with input $x = 0$, we obtain the following execution trace:

$$\mathbb{S} \equiv \langle (r_1, \&p + 127 - x), (r_2, \&q + x), (r_3, \&p + 127 - x) \rangle$$

We use the variable $miss_i$ to represent whether r_i is a cache miss (set to 1 if r_i was a cache miss and set to 0 otherwise) for inputs satisfying Ψ_{path}. The value of $miss_i$ depends on all symbolic memory addresses σ_k, where $k \in [0, i)$. Therefore, we bound the value of $miss_i$ through symbolic constraints. In particular, given the execution trace $\mathbb{S}$ and the path condition Ψ_{path}, the procedure $CacheModel$ computes $\Gamma(\Psi_{path})$ for cache configuration $\mathcal{C}$ (*cf.* line 21 in Algorithm 1). Such a model $\Gamma(\Psi_{path})$ encodes all possible values of $miss_i$ for all $i \in [1, n]$ and for any input satisfying Ψ_{path}. In Sect. 4, we describe the formulation of $\Gamma(\Psi_{path})$ in detail.

The cache model $\Gamma(\Psi_{path})$ and the path condition Ψ_{path} are used to generate test inputs that satisfy the objective $\mathcal{O}$ (*cf.* lines 31–34). We first extract a predicate $\mathcal{O}_\mathbb{S}$ from the execution trace $\mathbb{S}$ that captures such an objective (*cf.* line 23). For example, let us assume our objective is to generate test inputs that suffer at least 1000 cache misses. For an execution trace $\mathbb{S}$, we can simply extract $\mathcal{O}_{\mathbb{S}}$ as $\sum_1^n miss_i \geq 1000$. Subsequently, we can generate a test input that satisfies the following formula:

$$\Gamma\left(\Psi_{path}\right) \wedge \left(\sum_{i=1}^n miss_i \geq 1000\right) \wedge \Psi_{path} \tag{2}$$

The refinement of $\mathcal{O}_{\mathbb{S}}$ (line 33) depends on the context. For instance, let us assume that the designer needs to compute (at most) one test for each scenario exhibiting at least 1000 cache misses. In such a case, the following refinement is made to $\mathcal{O}_{\mathbb{S}}$:

$$\mathcal{O}_{\mathbb{S}} = \mathcal{O}_{\mathbb{S}} \wedge \left(\sum_{i=1}^n miss_i \neq \sum_{i=1}^n miss_i^{(c)}\right)$$

where $miss_i = miss_i^{(c)}$ (for $i \in [1, n]$) captures a satisfying solution of Constraint (2).

The procedure *ExcludeCurTest* ensures that the explored solutions in test suite $\mathcal{T}$ are unique (*cf.* line 26). In particular, once $\mathcal{O}_{\mathbb{S}}$ is constructed from the execution trace $\mathbb{S}$, it modifies $\mathcal{O}_{\mathbb{S}}$ to exclude the previous solutions. For instance, if $\mathcal{T}$ includes solutions of exhibiting 1000 and 2000 cache misses, *objtrace* is modified to $\mathcal{O}_{\mathbb{S}} \wedge \sum_{i=1}^n miss_i \neq 1000 \wedge \sum_{i=1}^n miss_i \neq 2000$. Subsequently, this modified $\mathcal{O}_{\mathbb{S}}$ is leveraged to explore different solutions of the predicate Ω (*cf.* lines 31–34).

When $\Gamma\left(\Psi_{path}\right) \wedge \mathcal{O}_{\mathbb{S}} \wedge \Psi_{path}$ becomes unsatisfiable, *UnchkdPCs* keeps track of all unexplored partial path conditions (*cf.* lines 39–42) to manifest the remaining cache behaviour. In particular, our test generation satisfies the following crucial property.

Theorem 1. *CATAPULT guarantees to discover all possible cache behaviour upon termination. Besides, each input generated by CATAPULT witnesses a unique cache behaviour.*

4   Generating $\Gamma\left(\Psi_{path}\right)$

Given a path condition Ψ_{path} and the execution trace $\mathbb{S}$ (*cf.* Eq. (1)), this section describes the formulation of $\Gamma\left(\Psi_{path}\right)$ – the set of all cache behaviour for inputs x satisfying Ψ_{path} (*cf.* line 21 in Algorithm 1). In order to explain the formulation of $\Gamma\left(\Psi_{path}\right)$, we assume the following notations throughout the paper:

- 2^S : The number of cache sets in the cache.
- 2^B : The size of a cache line (in bytes).
- $\mathcal{A}$: Associativity of cache.
- $set(r_i)$: Cache set accessed by memory-related instruction r_i.
- $tag(r_i)$: The tag stored in the cache for accessing address σ_i (*cf.* Eq. (1)).
- ζ_i : The cache state before r_i and after r_{i-1}.

The formulation of $\Gamma\left(\Psi_{path}\right)$ revolves around the concept of *cache conflict*. Formally, we define cache conflict as follows:

Definition 1 *(Cache Conflict):* r_j *generates a cache conflict to* r_i *only if* r_j *accesses a different memory block than* r_i *and executing* r_j *can influence the relative position of memory block* $\left\lfloor \frac{\sigma_i}{2^{\mathcal{B}}} \right\rfloor$ *within the cache state* ζ_i.

Clearly, r_j generates cache conflict to r_i only if $j < i$. In the next sections, we shall elaborate other crucial conditions required for the generation of cache conflicts. Subsequently, we build upon such conditions to formulate the number of cache misses.

4.1 Modeling Symbolic Cache Access

Recall from Eq. (1) that we record the address σ_i (σ_i can be symbolic or concrete) for each memory-related instruction r_i during the execution. From σ_i, we formulate the accessed cache set $set(r_i)$ and the respective cache tag $tag(r_i)$ as follows:

$$set(r_i) = (\sigma_i \gg \mathcal{B}) \ \& \ \left(2^{\mathcal{S}} - 1\right); \qquad tag(r_i) = (\sigma_i \gg (\mathcal{B} + \mathcal{S})) \qquad (3)$$

In Eq. (3), "&" captures a bitwise-and operation and "$\gg$" captures a right-shift operation. Since σ_i can be symbolic, both $set(r_i)$ and $tag(r_i)$, as captured via Eq. (3), can be symbolic expressions.

4.2 Modeling Symbolic Cache Constraints

In this section, we formulate constraints for the following two types of cache misses:

- *cold miss*: Cold miss occurs if a memory block is accessed for the *first time*.
- *eviction miss:* Any cache miss other than cold misses.

Conditions for Cold Misses. If r_i accesses a memory block for the first time, the following condition must hold:

$$\Theta_i^{cold} \equiv \bigwedge_{1 \leq k < i} \left((tag\,(r_k) \neq tag\,(r_i)) \vee (set\,(r_k) \neq set\,(r_i)) \right) \qquad (4)$$

Informally, Constraint (4) states that every memory access $r \in \{r_1, r_2, \ldots, r_{i-1}\}$ is either mapped to a different cache set than $set(r_i)$ or has a different tag compared to $tag(r_i)$. This leads to a cold cache miss at r_i.

In Constraint (4), for the sake of simplicity in the formulation, we assumed that initially, the cache is not loaded with any memory block used by the system under test. However, this condition can easily be relaxed via additional constraints that check the (un)availability of memory block $\left\lfloor \frac{\sigma_i}{2^{\mathcal{B}}} \right\rfloor$ in an arbitrary initial cache state.

Necessary Conditions for Cache Conflict. The basic design principle of cache dictates that every cache set is independent. Therefore, a necessary condition for cache conflict is that the accessed memory blocks are mapped to the same cache set. In particular, the following two conditions *must be satisfied* for a possible cache conflict from r_j to r_i:

1. $\psi_{cnf}(j, i)$: r_i and r_j access the same cache set. Therefore, we get the following:

$$\psi_{cnf}(j, i) \equiv (set(r_j) = set(r_i)) \tag{5}$$

2. $\psi_{dif}(j, i)$: r_i and r_j access different memory-block tags. Therefore, we have,

$$\psi_{dif}(j, i) \equiv (tag(r_j) \neq tag(r_i)) \tag{6}$$

The satisfiability of $\psi_{cnf}(j, i)$ and $\psi_{dif}(j, i)$ is necessary irrespective of the underlying cache replacement policy. However, these two constraints are not sufficient to guarantee that r_j can affect the cache state ζ_i ($i > j$). We need additional constraints that depend on the specific replacement policy. In the subsequent sections, we formulate these constraints for two widely used replacement policies – LRU and FIFO.

Constraints for LRU Caches. In this section, we formulate a set of constraints that precisely capture the cache conflict scenarios in LRU replacement policy.

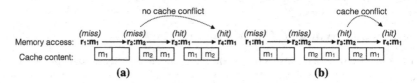

Fig. 4. Cache conflict scenarios for caches with LRU policy. $r_i:m_j$ captures memory-related instruction r_i accessing memory block m_j. The rightmost position in the cache denotes the memory block *accessed* in the cache the *earliest*. (a) r_2 does not generate any cache conflict to r_4, as $m1$ is reloaded between r_2 and r_4, (b) in order to count unique cache conflicts to r_4, we only record the cache conflict from r_3 and not from r_2, as both r_2 and r_3 access m_2.

Conditions for Eviction Misses. Let us check the conditions where instruction r_i will suffer a cache miss due to eviction. This might happen only due to instructions appearing before (in the program order) r_i. Consider one such instruction r_j, for $j \in [1, i)$. Informally, r_j generates a cache conflict to r_i, *only if* the following conditions hold:

1. $\psi_{eqv}^{lru}(j, i)$: There does not exist any instruction r_k where $k \in [j+1, i)$, such that r_k accesses the same memory block as r_i (*i.e.* $\lfloor \frac{\sigma_i}{2^B} \rfloor$). It is worthwhile to note that the execution of r_k will make the memory block $\lfloor \frac{\sigma_i}{2^B} \rfloor$ to be most recently used. For instance, in Fig. 4(a), r_3 accesses memory block m_1 and

therefore, r_2 cannot generate cache conflict to r_4. We capture $\psi_{eqv}(j, i)$ via the following constraints:

$$\psi_{eqv}^{lru}(j, i) \equiv \bigwedge_{k:\ j<k<i} ((tag(r_k) \neq tag(r_i)) \vee (set(r_k) \neq set(r_i))) \qquad (7)$$

2. $\psi_{unq}^{lru}(j, i)$: Secondly, we need to count cache conflicts from unique memory blocks. As an example, consider the example shown in Fig. 4(b). r_4 will still be a cache hit. This is because both r_2 and r_3 access the memory block m_2. In order to account unique cache conflicts, we only record the cache conflict from the *closest* access to different memory blocks. For instance, in Fig. 4(b), we only record cache conflict from r_3 to r_4. We use the constraint $\psi_{unq}(j, i)$ for such purpose. $\psi_{unq}(j, i)$ is satisfiable if and only if there does not exist any memory-related instruction between r_j (where $j \in [1, i)$) and r_i that accesses the same memory block as r_j. Therefore, $\psi_{unq}(j, i)$ is captured as follows:

$$\psi_{unq}^{lru}(j, i) \equiv \bigwedge_{k:\ j<k<i} ((tag(r_j) \neq tag(r_k)) \vee (set(r_j) \neq set(r_k))) \qquad (8)$$

Constraints to Formulate Cache Conflict. Constraints (5)–(8) accurately capture scenarios where r_j ($j \in [1, i)$) will create a unique cache conflict to r_i. Let us assume $\Psi_{i,j}^{evt}$ captures whether r_j creates a unique cache conflict to r_i. Using the intuition described in the preceding paragraph, we can now formulate the following constraints to set the value of $\Psi_{i,j}^{evt}$.

$$\Theta_{j,i}^{em,lru} \equiv \left(\psi_{cnf}(j, i) \wedge \psi_{dif}(j, i) \wedge \psi_{eqv}^{lru}(j, i) \wedge \psi_{unq}^{lru}(j, i) \right) \Rightarrow \left(\Psi_{j,i}^{evt} = 1 \right) \quad (9)$$

If any of the conditions in Constraints (5)–(8) is not satisfied between r_j and r_i, then r_j cannot influence the cache state immediately before r_i and therefore, r_j cannot create cache conflict to r_i, as captured by the following constraints:

$$\Theta_{j,i}^{eh,lru} \equiv \left(\neg\psi_{cnf}(j, i) \vee \neg\psi_{dif}(j, i) \vee \neg\psi_{eqv}^{lru}(j, i) \vee \neg\,\psi_{unq}^{lru}(j, i) \right) \Rightarrow \left(\Psi_{j,i}^{evt} = 0 \right)$$
$$(10)$$

Constraints for FIFO Caches. Unlike LRU replacement policy, for FIFO replacement policy, the cache state does not change for a cache hit. Therefore, r_j can generate a cache conflict to r_i (where $i > j$) only if r_j is a cache miss.

Conditions for Eviction Misses. In order to incorporate the changes in the formulation of $\Gamma(\Psi_{path})$, we need to modify Constraints (7)–(10) for FIFO replacement policy. In particular, instruction r_j can create a unique cache conflict to instruction r_i ($i > j$) only if r_j is a cache miss and the following conditions hold with $\psi_{cnf}(j, i)$ and $\psi_{dif}(j, i)$:

1. $\psi_{eqv}^{fifo}(j, i)$: There does not exist any instruction r_k, where $k \in [j+1, i)$, such that r_k is a cache miss and it accesses the same memory block as r_i. For

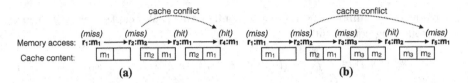

Fig. 5. Cache conflict scenarios in FIFO policy. $r_i:m_j$ captures memory-related instruction r_i accessing memory block m_j. The rightmost position in the cache denotes the memory block *inserted* in the cache the *earliest*. (a) r_2 generates cache conflict to r_4 even though m_1 is accessed at r_3. This is because r_3 is a cache hit. (b) We record cache conflict from r_2 to r_5 even though r_4 is closer to r_5 and r_5 accesses the same memory block as r_2. This is because r_4 is a cache hit.

instance, in Fig. 5(a), r_2 generates cache conflict to r_4 because r_3 was a cache hit. We capture $\psi_{eqv}^{fifo}(j,i)$ as follows:

$$\psi_{eqv}^{fifo}(j,i) \equiv \bigwedge_{k:\ j<k<i} ((tag(r_k) \neq tag(r_i)) \vee (set(r_k) \neq set(r_i)) \vee (miss_k = 0))$$

(11)

2. $\psi_{unq}^{fifo}(j,i)$: This constraint ensures that we only count unique cache conflicts. For LRU policy, we checked whether r_j was the closest instruction to r_i accessing memory block $\lfloor \frac{\sigma_j}{2^s} \rfloor$. For FIFO policy, we have a slightly different situation, as demonstrated in Fig. 5(b). Even though r_4 is the closest instruction to r_5 accessing m_2, r_4 cannot generate cache conflict to r_5. This is because r_4 is a cache hit. As a result, we record cache conflict from r_2 to r_5. It is worthwhile to mention that in LRU policy, we will discard the cache conflict from r_2 to r_5 due to the presence of r_4. Formally, we ensure there does not exist any instruction r_k, where $k \in [j+1, i)$, such that r_k is a cache miss and it accesses the same memory block as r_j. Therefore, $\psi_{unq}^{fifo}(j,i)$ can be formalized as follows:

$$\psi_{unq}^{fifo}(j,i) \equiv \bigwedge_{k:\ j<k<i} ((tag(r_j) \neq tag(r_k)) \vee (set(r_j) \neq set(r_k)) \vee (miss_k = 0))$$

(12)

Constraints to Formulate Cache Conflict. Let us assume $\Psi_{j,i}^{evt}$ captures whether r_j creates a cache conflict to r_i. For FIFO replacement policy, this is possible only if r_j is a cache miss (*i.e.* $miss_j = 1$). Using the intuition described in the preceding paragraphs, we can bound the value of $\Psi_{j,i}^{evt}$ as follows:

$$\Theta_{j,i}^{em,fifo} \equiv$$
$$\left(\psi_{cnf}(j,i) \wedge \psi_{dif}(j,i) \wedge \psi_{eqv}^{fifo}(j,i) \wedge \psi_{unq}^{fifo}(j,i) \wedge (miss_j = 1) \right) \Rightarrow \left(\Psi_{j,i}^{evt} = 1 \right)$$

(13)

$$\Theta_{j,i}^{eh,fifo} \equiv$$
$$\left(\neg\psi_{cnf}(j,i) \vee \neg\psi_{dif}(j,i) \vee \neg\psi_{eqv}^{fifo}(j,i) \vee \neg\psi_{unq}^{fifo}(j,i) \vee (miss_j = 0) \right) \Rightarrow \left(\Psi_{j,i}^{evt} = 0 \right)$$

(14)

Constraints to Formulate Cache Misses. Let us assume that $miss_i$ captures the cache behaviour of instruction r_i. Therefore, $miss_i$ is set to 1 if r_i is a cache miss, and is set to 0 otherwise. We can formulate the value of $miss_i$ using the following constraints:

$$\Theta_i^{mp} \equiv \left(\sum_{j \in [1,i)} \Psi_{j,i}^{evt} \geq \mathcal{A} \right) \vee \Theta_i^{cold} \qquad (15)$$

$$\Theta_i^m \equiv \Theta_i^{mp} \Rightarrow (miss_i = 1); \quad \Theta_i^h \equiv \neg\Theta_i^{mp} \Rightarrow (miss_i = 0) \qquad (16)$$

where $\mathcal{A}$ captures the associativity of the cache. Once a memory block is loaded into the cache, it requires at least $\mathcal{A}$ unique cache conflicts to evict the block. If $\Psi_{i,j}^{evt} \geq \mathcal{A}$, r_i has suffered at least $\mathcal{A}$ unique cache conflicts since the last access of the memory block referenced by r_i – resulting r_i to be a cache miss. If r_i is not a cold miss (*i.e.* $\neg\Theta_i^{cold}$ holds) and $\Psi_{i,j}^{evt} \geq \mathcal{A}$ does not hold, r_i will be a cache hit, as captured by Constraint (16).

Putting It All Together. To derive the symbolic cache behavior $\Gamma(\Psi_{path})$, we gather all constraints over $\{r_1, \ldots, r_n\}$ as follows:

$$\Gamma(\Psi_{path}) \equiv \bigwedge_{i \in [1,n]} \left(\Theta_i^m \wedge \Theta_i^h \wedge \bigwedge_{j \in [1,i)} \Theta_{j,i}^{em,repl} \wedge \bigwedge_{j \in [1,i)} \Theta_{j,i}^{eh,repl} \right) \qquad (17)$$

where $repl \in \{lru, fifo\}$ capturing the underlying replacement policy. Θ_i^m and Θ_i^h together bound the value of $miss_i$, which, in turn captures whether r_i is a cache miss. However, Θ_i^m and Θ_i^h are dependent on symbolic variables $\Psi_{j,i}^{evt}$ where $j \in [1,i)$. The bound on symbolic variables $\Psi_{j,i}^{evt}$ is captured via $\Theta_{j,i}^{em,repl}$ and $\Theta_{j,i}^{eh,repl}$ (Constraints (9)–(10) and Constraints (13)–(14)). Hence, the formulation of $\Gamma(\Psi_{path})$ includes both $\Theta_{j,i}^{em,repl}$ and $\Theta_{j,i}^{eh,repl}$ for $j \in [1,i)$.

Complexity of Constraints. The size of our constraint system is $O(n^3)$, where n is the number of memory accesses. The dominating factor in our constraint system is the set of constraints generated from Constraints (9)–(10) for LRU policy and from Constraints (13)–(14) for FIFO policy. In general, we generate constraints for each pair of memory accesses that may potentially conflict in the cache, leading to $O(n^2)$ pairs in total. For each such pair, the constraint may have a size $O(n)$ — making the size of overall constraint system to be $O(n^3)$. However, our evaluation reveals that such a bound is pessimistic and the constraint system can be solved efficiently for real-life programs.

5   Application

In this section, we instantiate Algorithm 1 to formulate the objective $\mathcal{O}_\mathbb{S}$ from the execution trace $\mathbb{S}$ and the refinement of $\mathcal{O}_\mathbb{S}$ (*cf.* line 23 and lines 31–34 in Algorithm 1).

Testing Timing-Related Properties. Embedded and real-time systems are often constrained via several timing-related properties. Given a timing deadline $\mathcal{D}$, Algorithm 1 can find a witness where such timing deadline is violated for program $\mathcal{P}$ or prove that no such witness exists.

In this paper, we assume that the timing of a given instruction may vary only due to the same incurring a cache hit or a cache miss. However, such a timing model can always be extended leveraging on the rich body of work in timing analysis [21].

Given the execution trace $\mathbb{S}$ (*cf.* Eq. (1)), we use the variable $miss_i$ to capture whether a memory-related instruction r_i suffered a cache miss. Let us assume $\mathbb{C}$ is the time taken to execute all instructions not accessing the memory subsystems. Given the preceding descriptions, we formulate the objective $\mathcal{O}_{\mathbb{S}}$ from $\mathbb{S}$ as follows:

$$\mathcal{O}_{\mathbb{S}} \equiv \left(\sum_{i=1}^{n} miss_i \right) * \mathcal{L} + \mathbb{C} > \mathcal{D} \tag{18}$$

where $\mathcal{L}$ is the latency incurred for a cache miss and n is the total number of memory-related instructions. If a solution is found for $\Gamma(\Psi_{path}) \wedge \mathcal{O}_{\mathbb{S}} \wedge \Psi_{path}$ using $\mathcal{O}_{\mathbb{S}}$ in Eq. (18), then we found witness of a violation of timing deadline $\mathcal{D}$. Such a witness can be used for further investigation and improve the timing behaviour of the system.

In our evaluation, we refine $\mathcal{O}_{\mathbb{S}}$ to find unique violations, meaning each test input capture a unique value of $\sum_{i=1}^{n} miss_i * \mathcal{L} + \mathbb{C}$. Therefore, if $\sum_{i=1}^{n} miss_i = N$ is true for a satisfying solution of $\Gamma(\Psi_{path}) \wedge \mathcal{O}_{\mathbb{S}} \wedge \Psi_{path}$, $\mathcal{O}_{\mathbb{S}}$ is refined as $\mathcal{O}_{\mathbb{S}} \wedge \sum_{i=1}^{n} miss_i \neq N$.

Testing Cache Side-Channel Vulnerabilities. The performance gap between cache and main memory (DRAM) can be exploited by an attacker to discover classified information (*e.g.* a secret key). Such attacks are often non-invasive and they can even be mounted over the network [8]. In this paper, we choose timing-related attacks, where the observer monitors the overall cache misses to discover secret information [8].

Let us assume the cache side channel to be a function $C : \mathbb{I} \to \mathbb{O}$, mapping a finite set of secret inputs to a finite set of observations. Since the attacker monitors the number of cache misses, in this scenario, an observation simply captures the number of cache misses in an execution. If we model the choice of a secret input via a random variable X and the respective observation by a random variable Y, the leakage through channel C is the reduction in uncertainty about X when Y is observed. In particular, the following result holds for any distribution of X [17].

$$ML(C) \leq \log_2 |C(\mathbb{I})| \tag{19}$$

where $ML(C)$ captures the maximal leakage of channel C. The equality holds in Eq. (19) when X is uniformly distributed.

CATAPULT can be tuned to compute each unique element in the set $C(\mathbb{I})$ and thereby, to derive an upper bound (exact bound when X is uniformly distributed) on the maximal leakage $ML(C)$. We accomplish this by setting and refining $\mathcal{O}_\mathbb{S}$ as follows:

$$\mathcal{O}_\mathbb{S} \equiv \left(\sum_{i=1}^{n} miss_i \geq 0 \right) \tag{20}$$

If $miss_i^{(c)}$ captures a satisfying solution of $miss_i$ (for $i \in [1,n]$) in $\Gamma\left(\Psi_{path}\right) \wedge \mathcal{O}_\mathbb{S} \wedge \Psi_{path}$, then we refine $\mathcal{O}_\mathbb{S}$ as follows: $\mathcal{O}_\mathbb{S} \wedge \left(\sum_{i=1}^{n} miss_i \neq \sum_{i=1}^{n} miss_i^{(c)} \right)$.

It is worthwhile to mention that the number of tests computed is directly correlated with the maximal leakage through the cache side channel (*cf.* Eq. (19)). As a result, our test generation method can be used as a metric to measure the information leak through cache side channel. Besides, since we also generate an witness for each possible observation (*i.e.* the number of cache misses), these witnesses can further be used for analyzing, quantifying and controlling the information leaked at runtime.

Due to the lack of space, we only show the instantiation for one type of attacker. However, our framework can model a variety of different attacking scenarios, as long as the observation by an attacker can be modeled via symbolic constraints over the set of variables $\{miss_1, miss_2, \ldots, miss_n\}$.

6   Evaluation

Experimental Setup. We build CATAPULT on top of KLEE symbolic execution engine [2]. We first decompile PISA [5] compliant binaries (a MIPS like architecture) into LLVM bitcode. It is worthwhile to note that compiling *source code* to LLVM bitcode will inaccurately capture the cache performance. This is because of the target-dependent compiler optimizations that take place while generating binary code. The decompiled LLVM bitcode is identical with the PISA binary in terms of functionality, memory placement and the number of memory-related instructions. This ensures that the translated LLVM code has exactly the same cache performance as the binary code. To use CATAPULT for a different architecture (*e.g.* ARM), we only need the translator that converts the binary code for the respective architecture to the LLVM bitcode. The rest of our test generation framework remains completely unchanged. The translated LLVM code is provided as an input to CATAPULT. All our experiments have been performed on an Intel I7 machine with 8 GB of RAM and running Debian operating system.

To evaluate CATAPULT, we choose cryptographic routines from OpenSSL and other libraries [1,3] and user-interface routines from Linux GDK library (*cf.* Table 1). Our choice is motivated by the importance of validating security and performance related properties in these programs. Moreover, these programs are memory intensive and in particular, the cryptographic routines exhibit complex memory access patterns. As a result, such programs are also appropriate for stress testing our framework.

Table 1. Evaluated subject programs (input sizes are unchanged from the original programs)

Program name	Input size	Lines of C code	Lines of LLVM code	Max. no. of memory accesses
AES [1]	16 bytes	800	4950	2134
AES [3]	16 bytes	1428	1800	420
DES [3]	8 bytes	552	3990	334
RC4 [3]	10 bytes	160	668	1538
RC5 [3]	16 bytes	256	1820	410
gdk_keyval_to_unicode	4 bytes	1300	268	114
gdk_keyval_name	4 bytes	1350	1408	12

Table 2. "#test" captures the total number of tests generated, where each test exhibits a unique cache performance (*cf.* Sect. 5). Testing time includes the total time to run Algorithm 1.

Program	Replacement policy	#tests	Time (in cycles) [min,max]	Maximum no. of constraints	Testing time
AES [1]	LRU	35	[3719,7619]	2397228	260 min
	FIFO	1	[5149,5149]	11578752	15 sec
AES [3]	LRU	37	[1796,4996]	26528	127 min
	FIFO	1	[1896,1896]	1205860	3 min
DES [3]	LRU	21	[3971,6071]	1501080	10 min
	FIFO	1	[7971,7971]	1947656	2 sec
RC4 [3]	LRU	1	[5553,5553]	337588	15 min
	FIFO	1	[3153,3153]	764208	15 sec
RC5 [3]	LRU	1	[6167,6167]	0	10 sec
	FIFO	1	[6367,6367]	0	10 sec
gdk_keyval_to_unicode	LRU	19	[652,2652]	10	13 sec
	FIFO	28	[652,4852]	10	12 sec
gdk_keyval_name	LRU	11	[126,1126]	11	18 sec
	FIFO	11	[126,1126]	11	18 sec

Basic Result. Table 2 captures the key result obtained from CATAPULT. For all experiments in Table 2, we used a two-way and 8 KB cache, with 32 bytes cache-line and a cache-miss latency of 10 cycles. We make the following crucial observations from Table 2. We observe that the number of tests generated for FIFO policy is significantly smaller than the number of tests obtained for LRU policy. Since each test is attached to a unique cache performance (*i.e.* the number of cache miss), the LRU policy suffers from significantly higher cache side-channel leakage (*cf.* Eq. (19)), as compared to FIFO policy. This happens due to the reason that cache states change more frequently in LRU policy as compared to FIFO policy (*e.g.* for every access in LRU policy and for every cache miss in FIFO policy). This potentially leads to more variation in cache performance across different inputs in LRU policy, resulting in more tests and higher cache side-channel leakage. This result indicates important trade-offs in system design, as LRU policy is, on average, superior compared to FIFO policy in terms of overall performance. For experiments in Table 2, we can also validate that the maximal leakage of a basic AES implementation [3] is comparable with the AES implementation in the OpenSSL library. The implementation of RC5 does not exhibit any input-dependent memory access or branch. Hence, the size of our constraint system is 0 and there is exactly one test generated for both replacement policies. As observed from Table 2, CATAPULT terminates within reasonable time for all the experiments. Therefore, our results guarantee both the exact number of test cases and the best/worst-case timing obtained over all inputs. Finally, it is worthwhile to note that an exhaustive enumeration (2^{128} possibilities for AES) of all test inputs is infeasible to provide such guarantees.

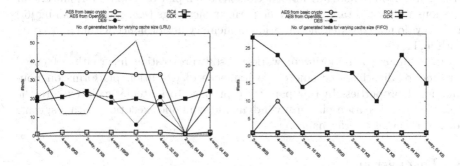

Fig. 6. Number of tests w.r.t. different cache configurations

Sensitivity Result. Figure 6 shows the sensitivity of CATAPULT with respect to cache configurations. Although increasing cache size usually improves performance, this may not be true for security. As an example, a smaller cache may result in cache misses for all possible inputs (*i.e.* one test), whereas a bigger cache may result in cache misses for a subset of inputs (*i.e.* more than one test). As a result, increasing the cache size may lead to increased number of tests and hence, increased likelihood of cache side-channel leakage (*cf.* Eq. (19)). For a huge cache, however, the dependency between inputs and the cache behaviour may disappear, resulting in reduced cache side-channel leakage. In Fig. 6, we observe both the increase and the decrease in the number of tests (and hence, the maximal leakage) with increased cache size. We also observe that FIFO policy on average outperforms LRU policy, in terms of side-channel resistant.

Summary. In summary, CATAPULT reveals useful information regarding the memory performance of programs. This includes the cache side-channel vulnerability of these programs as well as their worst-case memory performance. Concretely, we can show, for most of the chosen subjects, FIFO replacement policy is significantly more resistant to cache side channel as compared to LRU policy. We also show that increasing cache size may not necessarily lead to a more secure implementation (*cf.* Fig. 6).

7 Related Work

Works on worst-case execution time (WCET) analysis [20,21] compute an upper bound on the execution time of program. In addition, approaches based on program synthesis [9] aim to generate optimal software by construction. In contrast to these works, our approach has a significant flavor of testing and CATAPULT is used to generate witnesses violating certain non-functional properties. Our work is orthogonal to the efforts in statically analyzing cache side channels [7,14,17]. Specifically, CATAPULT generates test inputs that violate timing-related constraints and to quantify cache side-channel leakage. Our framework does not generate false positives, however, it is not aimed to verify the absence of cache side-channel leaks and timing-related violations.

Recent works on performance testing [16,18,19] consider performance purely at code level and ignore any influence of execution platform on performance. Our previous works had targeted specific performance bugs (*e.g.* cache thrashing [6]) and they do not consider the variation of memory performance within a program path [6,11,13].

In summary, a majority of works in software testing have either focused on functionality bugs or ignore the influence of execution platforms on non-functional properties. In this paper, we propose to systematically explore the behaviour of execution platform via dynamic symbolic execution, with a specific focus on memory performance.

8   Discussion

Extensions and Limitations. CATAPULT generates witnesses to show the evidence of side-channel leakage or timing-related faults. However, it does not debug these faults. Debugging faults related to software non-functional properties (*e.g.* timing and security) is a challenging research problem in its own right and CATAPULT provides the necessary foundation for debugging research in the context of timing or security-related faults. A limitation of our approach is the requirement of the knowledge of cache architecture (*e.g.* cache replacement policy). In the future, this limitation can be lifted via using some machine learning approach to approximately capture the cache replacement policy [4]. Subsequently, we can formulate the test generation problem via symbolic constraints in a similar fashion as in CATAPULT. The scalability of CATAPULT is primarily limited by the number of memory accesses in an execution. Since our symbolic constraints encode the cache conflict (and not the actual cache states), the scalability of CATAPULT is not affected by increased cache sizes and associativity [10].

Perspective. We have presented CATAPULT where the key insight is to express the platform-dependent software properties (*e.g.* performance and security) via logical constraints. Hence, our approach can be adapted easily within existing software testing methodologies based on symbolic execution. To show the generality of our approach, we have instantiated our framework for a variety of cache designs and shown its application in both performance and security testing via real-life case studies (*e.g.* including OpenSSL and Linux GDK applications). This makes the idea of CATAPULT quite appealing for further exploration in the future. Among others, techniques to improve the testing time and extension of CATAPULT for regression testing are worth exploring in the area of testing non-functional software properties.

References

1. Advanced Encryption Standard Implementation. https://github.com/B-Con/crypto-algorithms
2. KLEE LLVM execution engine. https://klee.github.io/
3. OpenSSL Library. https://github.com/openssl/openssl/tree/master/crypto
4. Abel, A., Reineke, J.: Measurement-based modeling of the cache replacement policy. In: RTAS, pp. 65–74 (2013)
5. Austin, T., Larson, E., Ernst, D.: Simplescalar: an infrastructure for computer system modeling. Computer **35**(2), 59–67 (2002)
6. Banerjee, A., Chattopadhyay, S., Roychoudhury, A.: Static analysis driven cache performance testing. In: RTSS, pp. 319–329 (2013)
7. Barthe, G., Betarte, G., Campo, J., Luna, C., Pichardie, D.: System-level non-interference for constant-time cryptography. In: CCS, pp. 1267–1279 (2014)
8. Bernstein, D.J.: Cache-timing attacks on AES (2005)
9. Černý, P., Chatterjee, K., Henzinger, T.A., Radhakrishna, A., Singh, R.: Quantitative synthesis for concurrent programs. In: Gopalakrishnan, G., Qadeer, S. (eds.) CAV 2011. LNCS, vol. 6806, pp. 243–259. Springer, Heidelberg (2011). doi:10.1007/978-3-642-22110-1_20
10. Chattopadhyay, S.: Directed Automated Memory Performance Testing. http://sudiptac.bitbucket.org/papers/catapult-TR.pdf
11. Chattopadhyay, S.: MESS: memory performance debugging on embedded multicore systems. In: Fischer, B., Geldenhuys, J. (eds.) SPIN 2015. LNCS, vol. 9232, pp. 105–125. Springer, Heidelberg (2015). doi:10.1007/978-3-319-23404-5_8
12. Chattopadhyay, S., Beck, M., Rezine, A., Zeller, A.: Quantifying the information leak in cache attacks through symbolic execution. CoRR, abs/1611.04426 (2016)
13. Chattopadhyay, S., Eles, P., Peng, Z.: Automated software testing of memory performance in embedded GPUs. In: EMSOFT, pp. 17:1–17:10 (2014)
14. Doychev, G., Köpf, B., Mauborgne, L., Reineke, J.: Cacheaudit: a tool for the static analysis of cache side channels. TISSEC **18**(1), 4 (2015)
15. Godefroid, P., Klarlund, N., Sen, K.: DART: directed automated random testing. In: PLDI (2005)
16. Jin, G., Song, L., Shi, X., Scherpelz, J., Lu, S.: Understanding and detecting real-world performance bugs. In: PLDI (2012)
17. Köpf, B., Mauborgne, L., Ochoa, M.: Automatic quantification of cache side-channels. In: Madhusudan, P., Seshia, S.A. (eds.) CAV 2012. LNCS, vol. 7358, pp. 564–580. Springer, Heidelberg (2012). doi:10.1007/978-3-642-31424-7_40
18. Nistor, A., Song, L., Marinov, D., Lu, S.: Toddler: detecting performance problems via similar memory-access patterns. In: ICSE, pp. 562–571 (2013)
19. Olivo, O., Dillig, I., Lin, C.: Static detection of asymptotic performance bugs in collection traversals. In: PLDI, pp. 369–378 (2015)
20. Theiling, H., Ferdinand, C., Wilhelm, R.: Fast and precise WCET prediction by separated cache and path analyses. Real-Time Syst. **18**(2–3), 157–179 (2000)
21. Wilhelm, R., Engblom, J., Ermedahl, A., Holsti, N., Thesing, S., Whalley, D.B., Bernat, G., Ferdinand, C., Heckmann, R., Mitra, T., Mueller, F., Puaut, I., Puschner, P.P., Staschulat, J., Stenström, P.: The worst-case execution-time problem - overview of methods and survey of tools. ACM Trans. Embed. Comput. Syst. **7**(3), 36 (2008)

Context-Bounded Analysis for POWER

Parosh Aziz Abdulla[1], Mohamed Faouzi Atig[1], Ahmed Bouajjani[2],
and Tuan Phong Ngo[1(✉)]

[1] Uppsala University, Uppsala, Sweden
{parosh,mohamed_faouzi.atig,tuan-phong.ngo}@it.uu.se
[2] IRIF, Université Paris Diderot, Paris, France
abou@irif.fr

Abstract. We propose an under-approximate reachability analysis algorithm for programs running under the POWER memory model, in the spirit of the work on context-bounded analysis intitiated by Qadeer et al. in 2005 for detecting bugs in concurrent programs (supposed to be running under the classical SC model). To that end, we first introduce a new notion of context-bounding that is suitable for reasoning about computations under POWER, which generalizes the one defined by Atig et al. in 2011 for the TSO memory model. Then, we provide a polynomial size reduction of the context-bounded state reachability problem under POWER to the same problem under SC: Given an input concurrent program $\mathcal{P}$, our method produces a concurrent program $\mathcal{P}'$ such that, for a fixed number of context switches, running $\mathcal{P}'$ under SC yields the same set of reachable states as running $\mathcal{P}$ under POWER. The generated program $\mathcal{P}'$ contains the same number of processes as $\mathcal{P}$, and operates on the same data domain. By leveraging the standard model checker CBMC, we have implemented a prototype tool and applied it on a set of benchmarks, showing the feasibility of our approach.

1 Introduction

For performance reasons, modern multi-processors may reorder memory access operations. This is due to complex buffering and caching mechanisms that make the response memory queries (load operations) faster, and allow to speed up computations by parallelizing independent operations and computation flows. Therefore, operations may not be visible to all processors at the same time, and they are not necessarily seen in the same order by different processors (when they concern different addresses/variables). The only model where all operations are visible immediately to all processors is the Sequential Consistency (SC) model [28] which corresponds to the standard interleaving semantics where the program order between operations of a same processor is preserved. Modern architectures adopt weaker models (in the sense that they allow more behaviours) due to the relaxation in various ways of the program order. Examples of such weak models are TSO adopted in Intel x86 machines for instance, POWER adopted in PowerPC machines, or the model adopted in ARM machines.

© Springer-Verlag GmbH Germany 2017
A. Legay and T. Margaria (Eds.): TACAS 2017, Part II, LNCS 10206, pp. 56–74, 2017.
DOI: 10.1007/978-3-662-54580-5_4

Apprehending the effects of all the relaxations allowed in such models is extremely hard. For instance, while TSO allows reordering stores past loads (of different addresses/variables) reflecting the use of store buffers, a model such as POWER allows reordering of all kinds of store and load operations under quite subtle conditions. A lot of work has been devoted to the definition of formal models that accurately capture the program semantics corresponding to models such as TSO and POWER [11,30,32,34,35]. Still, programming against weak memory models is a hard and error prone task. Therefore, developing formal verification approaches under weak memory models is of paramount importance. In particular, it is crucial in this context to have efficient algorithms for automatic bug detection. This paper addresses precisely this issue and presents an algorithmic approach for checking state reachability in concurrent programs running on the POWER semantics as defined in [21] (which is essentially the POWER model presented in [34] with small changes that have been introduced in order to increase the accuracy and the precision of the model).

The verification of concurrent programs under weak memory models is known to be complex. Indeed, encoding the buffering and storage mechanisms used in these models leads in general to complex, infinite-state formal operational models involving unbounded data structures like FIFO queues (or more generally unbounded partial order constraints). For the case of TSO, efficient, yet precise encodings of the effects of its storage mechanism have been designed recently [3,5]. It is not clear how to define such precise and practical encodings for POWER.

In this paper, we consider an alternative approach. We investigate the issue of defining approximate analysis. Our approach consists in introducing a parametric under-approximation schema in the spirit of context-bounding [12,25,27,31,33]. Context-bounding has been proposed in [33] as a suitable approach for efficient bug detection in multithreaded programs. Indeed, for concurrent programs, a bounding concept that provides both good coverage and scalability must be based on aspects related to the interactions between concurrent components. It has been shown experimentally that concurrency bugs usually show up after a small number of context switches [31].

In the context of weak memory models, context-bounded analysis has been extended in [12] to the case of programs running on TSO. The work we present here aims at extending this approach to the case of POWER. This extension is actually very challenging due to the complexity of POWER and requires developing new techniques that are different from, and much more involved than, the ones used for the case of TSO. First, we introduce a new concept of bounding that is suitable for POWER. Intuitively, the architecture of POWER is similar to a distributed system with a replicated memory, where each processor has its own replica, and where operations are propagated between replicas according to some specific protocol. Our bounding concept is based on this architecture. We consider that a computation is divided in a sequence of "contexts", where a context is a computation segment for which there is precisely one *active* processor. All actions within a context are either operations issued by the active processor, or propagation actions performed by its storage subsystem. Then, in our analysis, we consider only computations that have a number of contexts that is less or equal than some given bound. Notice that while we bound the number of contexts in a computation, we do not put any bound on the lengths of the contexts, nor on the size of the storage system.

We prove that for every bound $\mathbb{K}$, and for every concurrent program $Prog$, it is possible to construct, using code-to-code translation, another concurrent program $Prog^{\bullet}$ such that for every $\mathbb{K}$-bounded computation π in $Prog$ under the POWER semantics there is a corresponding $\mathbb{K}$-bounded computation $\pi^{\bullet}$ of $Prog^{\bullet}$ under the SC semantics that reaches the same set of states and vice-versa. Thus, the context-bounded state reachability problem for $Prog$ can be reduced to the context-bounded state reachability problem for $Prog^{\bullet}$ under SC. We show that the program $Prog^{\bullet}$ has the same number of processes as $Prog$, and only $O(|\mathcal{P}||\mathcal{X}|\mathbb{K} + |\mathcal{R}|)$ additional shared variables and local registers compared to $Prog$, where $|\mathcal{P}|$ is the number of processes, $|\mathcal{X}|$ is the number of shared variables and $|\mathcal{R}|$ is the number of local registers in $Prog$. Furthermore, the obtained program has the same type of data structures and variables as the original one. As a consequence, we obtain for instance that for finite-data programs, the context-bounded analysis of programs under POWER is decidable. Moreover, our code-to-code translation allows to leverage existing verification tools for concurrent programs to carry out verification of safety properties under POWER.

To show the applicability of our approach, we have implemented our reduction, and we have used cbmc version 5.1 [17] as the backend tool for solving SC reachability queries. We have carried out several experiments showing the efficiency of our approach. Our experimental results confirm the assumption that concurrency bugs manifest themselves within small bounds of context switches. They also confirm that our approach based on context-bounding is more efficient and scalable than approaches based on bounding sizes of computations and/or of storage systems.

Related work. There has been a lot of work on automatic program verification under weak memory models, based on precise, under-approximate, and abstract analyses, e.g., [2,5,8,10,12–16,18–20,23,24,26,29,36–40]. While most of these works concern TSO, only a few of them address the safety verification problem under POWER (e.g., [6,9–11,36]). The paper [21] addresses the different issue of checking robustness against POWER, i.e., whether a program has the same (trace) semantics for both POWER and SC.

The work in [9] extends the cbmc framework by taking into account weak memory models including TSO and POWER. While this approach uses reductions to SC analysis, it is conceptually and technically different from ours. The work in [10] develops a verification technique combining partial orders with bounded model checking, that is applicable to various weak memory models including TSO and POWER. However, these techniques are not anymore supported by the latest version of cbmc. The work in [6] develops stateless model-checking techniques under POWER. In Sect. 4, we compare the performances of our approach with those of [6,9]. The tool herd [11] operates on small litmus tests under various memory models. Our tool can handle in an efficient and precise way such litmus tests.

Recently, Tomasco et al. [36] presented a new verification approach, based on code-to-code translations, for programs running under TSO and PSO. They also discuss the extension of their approach to programs running under POWER (however the detailed formalization and the implementation of this extension are kept for future work). Our approach and the one proposed in [36] are orthogonal since we are using different bounding parameters: In this paper, we are bounding the number of contexts while Tomasco et al. [36] are bounding the number of write operations.

2   Concurrent Programs

In this section, we first introduce some notations and definitions. Then, we present the syntax we use for *concurrent programs* and its semantics under POWER as in [21,34].

Preliminaries. Consider sets A and B. We use $[A \mapsto B]$ to denote the set of functions from A to B, and write $f : A \mapsto B$ to indicate that $f \in [A \mapsto B]$. We write $f(a) = \bot$ to denote that f is undefined for a. We use $f[a \leftarrow b]$ to denote the function g such that $g(a) = b$ and $g(x) = f(x)$ if $x \neq a$. We will use a function **gen** which, for a given set A, returns an arbitrary element $\mathbf{gen}\,(A) \in A$. For integers i, j, we use $[i..j]$ to denote the set $\{i, i+1, \ldots, j\}$. We use A^* to denote the set of finite words over A. For words $w_1, w_2 \in A^*$, we use $w_1 \cdot w_2$ to denote the concatenation of w_1 and w_2.

Syntax. Figure 1 gives the grammar for a small but general assembly-like language that we use for defining concurrent programs. A program *Prog* first declares a set X of (shared) variables followed by the code of a set $\mathcal{P}$ of processes. Each process p has a finite $\mathcal{R}\,(p)$ of (local) *registers*. We assume w.l.o.g. that the sets of registers of the different processes are disjoint, and define $\mathcal{R} := \cup_p \mathcal{R}\,(p)$. The code of each process $p \in \mathcal{P}$ starts by declaring a set of registers followed by a sequence of instructions.

For the sake of simplicity, we assume that the data domain of both the shared variables and registers is a single set $\mathcal{D}$. We assume a special element $0 \in \mathcal{D}$ which is the initial value of each shared variable or register. Each instruction i is of the form $\lambda : \mathfrak{s}$ where λ is a unique label (across all processes) and $\mathfrak{s}$ is a statement. We

$$
\begin{aligned}
Prog &::= \mathbf{var}\,x^*\,(\mathbf{proc}\;p\;\mathbf{reg}\;\$r^*\;\mathsf{i}^*)^* \\
\mathsf{i} &::= \lambda : \mathfrak{s} \\
\mathfrak{s} &::= \$r \leftarrow x \mid x \leftarrow exp \mid \mathbf{assume}\;exp \\
&\quad \mid \mathbf{if}\;exp\;\mathbf{then}\;\mathsf{i}^*\;\mathbf{else}\;\mathsf{i}^* \\
&\quad \mid \mathbf{while}\;exp\;\mathbf{do}\;\mathsf{i}^* \mid \mathbf{term}
\end{aligned}
$$

Fig. 1. Syntax of concurrent programs.

define $\mathbf{lbl}\,(\mathsf{i}) := \lambda$ and $\mathbf{stmt}\,(\mathsf{i}) := \mathfrak{s}$. We define $\mathfrak{I}_p$ to be the set of instructions occurring in p, and define $\mathfrak{I} := \cup_{p \in \mathcal{P}} \mathfrak{I}_p$. We assume that $\mathfrak{I}_p$ contains a designated *initial* instruction i_p^{init} from which p starts its execution. A *read* instruction in a process $p \in \mathcal{P}$ has a statement of the form $\$r \leftarrow x$, where $\$r$ is a register in p and $x \in X$ is a variable. A *write* instruction has a statement of the form $x \leftarrow exp$ where $x \in X$ is a variable and exp is an *expression*. We will assume a set of expressions containing a set of operators applied to constants and registers, but not referring to the content of memory (i.e., the set of variables). Assume, conditional, and iterative instructions (collectively called *aci* instructions) can be explained in a similar manner. The statement **term** will cause the process to terminate its execution. We assume that term occurs only once in the code of a process p and that it has the label λ_p^{term}. For an expression exp, we use $\mathcal{R}(exp)$ to denote the set of registers that occur in exp. For a write or an aci instruction i, we define $\mathcal{R}(\text{i}) := \mathcal{R}(exp)$ where exp is the expression that occurs in stmt (i).

For an instruction $\text{i} \in \mathcal{I}_p$, we define next (i) to be the set of instructions that may follow i in a run of a process. Notice that this set contains two elements if i is an aci instruction (in the case of an assume instruction, we assume that if the condition evaluates to *false*, then the process moves to λ_p^{term} : term), no element if i is a terminating instruction, and a single element otherwise. We define Tnext (i) (resp. Fnext (i)) to be the (unique) instruction to which the process execution moves in case the condition in the statement of i evaluates to *true* (resp. *false*).

Configurations. We will assume an infinite set $\mathcal{E}$ of *events*, and will use an event to represent a single execution of an instruction in a process. A given instruction may be executed several times during a run of the program (for instance, when it is in the body of a loop). In such a case, the different executions are represented by different events. An event e is executed in several steps, namely it is *fetched*, *initialized*, and then *committed*. Furthermore, a write event may be propagated to the other processes. A *configuration* c is a tuple $\langle \mathbb{E}, \prec, \text{ins}, \text{status}, \text{rf}, \text{Prop}, \prec_{\text{co}} \rangle$, defined as follows.

Events. $\mathbb{E} \subseteq \mathcal{E}$ is a finite set of *events*, namely the events that have been created up to the current point in the execution of the program. ins : $\mathbb{E} \mapsto \mathcal{I}$ is a function that maps an event e to the instruction ins (e) that e is executing. We partition the set $\mathbb{E}$ into disjoint sets $\mathbb{E}_p$, for $p \in \mathcal{P}$, where $\mathbb{E}_p := \{ e \in \mathbb{E} \mid \text{ins} (e) \in \mathcal{I}_p \}$, i.e., for a process $p \in \mathcal{P}$, the set $\mathbb{E}_p$ contains the events whose instructions belong to p. For an event $e \in \mathbb{E}_p$, we define proc (e) := p. We say that e is a *write* event if ins (e) is a write instruction. We use $\mathbb{E}^{\text{W}}$ to denote the set of write events. Similarly, we define the set $\mathbb{E}^{\text{R}}$ of *read* events, and the set $\mathbb{E}^{\text{ACI}}$ of *aci* events whose instructions are either assume, conditional, or iterative. We define $\mathbb{E}_p^{\text{W}}$, $\mathbb{E}_p^{\text{R}}$, and $\mathbb{E}_p^{\text{ACI}}$, to be the restrictions of the above sets to $\mathbb{E}_p$. For an event e where stmt (ins (e)) is of the form $x \leftarrow exp$ or $\$r \leftarrow x$, we define var ($e$) := x. If e is neither a read nor a write event, then var (e) := $\perp$.

Program Order. The *program-order* relation $\prec \subseteq \mathbb{E} \times \mathbb{E}$ is an irreflexive partial order that describes, for a process $p \in \mathcal{P}$, the order in which events are fetched from the code of p. We require that (i) $e_1 \not\prec e_2$ if proc (e_1) $\neq$ proc (e_2), i.e., $\prec$ only relates events belonging to the same process, and that (ii) $\prec$ is a total order on $\mathbb{E}_p$.

Status. The function status : $\mathbb{E} \mapsto \{\text{fetch}, \text{init}, \text{com}\}$ defines, for an event e, the current *status* of e, i.e., whether it has been fetched, initialized, or committed.

Propagation. The function Prop : $\mathcal{P} \times X \mapsto \mathbb{E}^{\text{W}} \cup \mathcal{E}^{\text{init}}$ defines, for a process $p \in \mathcal{P}$ and variable $x \in X$, the latest write event on x that has been propagated to p. Here $\mathcal{E}^{\text{init}} := \{ e_x^{\text{init}} \mid x \in X \}$ is a set disjoint from the set of events $\mathcal{E}$, and will be used to define the initial values of the variables.

Read-From. The function $\mathtt{rf} : \mathbb{E}^{\mathtt{R}} \mapsto \mathbb{E}^{\mathtt{W}} \cup \mathcal{E}^{\mathtt{init}}$ defines, for a read event $e \in \mathbb{E}^{\mathtt{R}}$, the write event $\mathtt{rf}(e)$ from which e gets its value.

Coherence Order. All processes share a global view about the order in which write events are propagated. This is done through the *coherence order* $\prec_{\mathtt{co}}$ that is a partial order on $\mathbb{E}^{\mathtt{W}}$ s.t. $e_1 \prec_{\mathtt{co}} e_2$ only if $\mathtt{var}(e_1) = \mathtt{var}(e_2)$, i.e., it relates only events that write on identical variables. If a write event e_1 is propagated to a process before another write event e_2 and both events write on the same variable, then $e_1 \prec_{\mathtt{co}} e_2$ holds. Furthermore, the events cannot be propagated to any other process in the reverse order. However, it might be the case that a write event is never propagated to a given process.

Dependencies. We introduce a number of dependency orders on events that we will use in the definition of the semantics. We define the *per-location program-order* $\prec_{\mathtt{poloc}} \subseteq \mathbb{E} \times \mathbb{E}$ such that $e_1 \prec_{\mathtt{poloc}} e_2$ if $e_1 \prec e_2$ and $\mathtt{var}(e_1) = \mathtt{var}(e_2)$, i.e., it is the restriction of $\prec$ to events with identical variables. We define the *data dependency* order $\prec_{\mathtt{data}}$ s.t. $e_1 \prec_{\mathtt{data}} e_2$ if (i) $e_1 \in \mathbb{E}^{\mathtt{R}}$, i.e., e_1 is a read event; (ii) $e_2 \in \mathbb{E}^{\mathtt{W}} \cup \mathbb{E}^{\mathtt{ACI}}$, i.e., e_2 is either a write or an aci event; (iii) $e_1 \prec e_2$; (iv) $\mathtt{stmt}(\mathtt{ins}(e_1))$ is of the form $\$r \leftarrow x$; (v) $\$r \in \mathcal{R}(\mathtt{ins}(e_2))$; and (vi) there is no event $e_3 \in \mathbb{E}^{\mathtt{R}}$ such that $e_1 \prec e_3 \prec e_2$ and $\mathtt{stmt}(\mathtt{ins}(e_3))$ is of the form $\$r \leftarrow y$. Intuitively, the loaded value by e_1 is used to compute the value of the expression in the statement on the instruction of e_2. We define the *control dependency* order $\prec_{\mathtt{ctrl}}$ such that $e_1 \prec_{\mathtt{ctrl}} e_2$ if $e_1 \in \mathbb{E}^{\mathtt{ACI}}$ and $e_1 \prec e_2$.

We say that c is *committed* if $\mathtt{status}(e) = \mathtt{com}$ for all events $e \in \mathbb{E}$. The *initial configuration* $c_{\mathtt{init}}$ is defined by $\langle \emptyset, \emptyset, \lambda e.\bot, \lambda e.\bot, \lambda e.\bot, \lambda p.\lambda x.e_x^{\mathtt{init}}, \emptyset \rangle$. We use $\mathbb{C}$ to denote the set of all configurations.

Transition Relation. We define the transition relation as a relation $\rightarrow \subseteq \mathbb{C} \times \mathcal{P} \times \mathbb{C}$. For configurations $c_1, c_2 \in \mathbb{C}$ and a process $p \in \mathcal{P}$, we write $c_1 \xrightarrow{p} c_2$ to denote that $\langle c_1, p, c_2 \rangle \in \rightarrow$. Intuitively, this means that p moves from the current configuration c_1 to c_2. The relation $\rightarrow$ is defined through the set of inference rules shown in Fig. 2.

The rule `Fetch` chooses the next instruction to be executed in the code of a process $p \in \mathcal{P}$. This instruction should be a possible successor of the instruction that was last executed by p. To satisfy this condition, we define $\mathtt{MaxI}(c, p)$ to be the set of instructions as follows: (i) If $\mathbb{E}_p = \emptyset$ then define $\mathtt{MaxI}(c, p) := \{i_p^{\mathtt{init}}\}$, i.e., the first instruction fetched by p is $i_p^{\mathtt{init}}$. (ii) If $\mathbb{E}_p \neq \emptyset$, let e' be the maximal event of p (w.r.t. $\prec$) in the configuration c and then define $\mathtt{MaxI}(c, p) := \mathtt{next}(\mathtt{ins}(e'))$. In other words, we consider the instruction $i' = \mathtt{ins}(e') \in \mathcal{I}_p$, and take its possible successors. The possibility of choosing any of the (syntactically) possible successors corresponds to *speculatively* fetching statements. As seen below, whenever we commit an aci event, we check whether the made speculations are correct or not. We create a new event e, label it by $i \in \mathtt{MaxI}(c, p)$, and make it larger than all the other events of p w.r.t. $\prec$. In such a way, we maintain the property that the order on the events of p reflects the order in which they are fetched in the current run of the program.

There are two ways in which read events get their values, namely either from *local* write events that are performed by the process itself, or from write events that

$$\frac{e \notin \mathbb{E},\ \prec' = \prec \cup \{\langle e', e\rangle \mid e' \in \mathbb{E}_p\},\ i \in \mathsf{MaxI}\,(c, p)}{c \xrightarrow{p} \langle \mathbb{E} \cup \{e\},\prec',\mathsf{ins}[e \leftarrow i],\mathsf{status}[e \leftarrow \mathtt{fetch}],\mathsf{rf},\mathsf{Prop},\prec_{co}\rangle}\ \text{Fetch}$$

$$\frac{e \in \mathbb{E}_p^R,\ \mathsf{status}\,(e) = \mathtt{fetch},\ \mathsf{CW}\,(c, e) = e',\ \mathsf{status}\,(e') = \mathtt{init}}{c \xrightarrow{p} \langle \mathbb{E},\prec,\mathsf{ins},\mathsf{status}[e \leftarrow \mathtt{init}],\mathsf{rf}[e \leftarrow e'],\mathsf{Prop},\prec_{co}\rangle}\ \text{Local-Read}$$

$$\frac{e \in \mathbb{E}_p^R,\ \mathsf{status}\,(e) = \mathtt{fetch},\ (\mathsf{CW}\,(c, e) = \bot) \vee (\mathsf{CW}\,(c, e) = e' \wedge \mathsf{status}\,(e') = \mathtt{com})}{c \xrightarrow{p} \langle \mathbb{E},\prec,\mathsf{ins},\mathsf{status}[e \leftarrow \mathtt{init}],\mathsf{rf}[e \leftarrow \mathsf{Prop}\,(p, \mathsf{var}\,(e))],\mathsf{Prop},\prec_{co}\rangle}\ \text{Prop-Read}$$

$$\frac{e \in \mathbb{E}_p^R,\ \mathsf{status}\,(e) = \mathtt{init},\ \mathsf{ComCnd}\,(c, e),\ \mathsf{RdCnd}\,(c, e)}{c \xrightarrow{p} \langle \mathbb{E},\prec,\mathsf{ins},\mathsf{status}[e \leftarrow \mathtt{com}],\mathsf{rf},\mathsf{Prop},\prec_{co}\rangle}\ \text{Com-Read}$$

$$\frac{e \in \mathbb{E}_p^W,\ \mathsf{status}\,(e) = \mathtt{fetch},\ \mathsf{WrInitCnd}\,(c, e)}{c \xrightarrow{p} \langle \mathbb{E},\prec,\mathsf{ins},\mathsf{status}[e \leftarrow \mathtt{init}],\mathsf{rf},\mathsf{Prop},\prec_{co}\rangle}\ \text{Init-Write}$$

$$\frac{e \in \mathbb{E}_p^W,\ \mathsf{status}\,(e) = \mathtt{init},\ \mathsf{ComCnd}\,(c, e),\ \prec'_{co} = \prec_{co} \cup \{\langle e', e\rangle \mid e' \preceq_{co} \mathsf{Prop}\,(p, \mathsf{var}\,(e))\}}{c \xrightarrow{p} \langle \mathbb{E},\prec,\mathsf{ins},\mathsf{status}[e \leftarrow \mathtt{com}],\mathsf{rf},\mathsf{Prop}[\langle p, \mathsf{var}\,(e)\rangle \leftarrow e],\prec'_{co}\rangle}\ \text{Com-Write}$$

$$\frac{q \in \mathcal{P},\ e \in \mathbb{E}_p^W,\ \mathsf{status}\,(e) = \mathtt{com},\ \mathsf{Prop}\,(q, \mathsf{var}\,(e)) \prec_{co} e,\ \prec'_{co} = \prec_{co} \cup \{\langle e', e\rangle \mid e' \preceq_{co} \mathsf{Prop}\,(q, \mathsf{var}\,(e))\}}{c \xrightarrow{p} \langle \mathbb{E},\prec,\mathsf{ins},\mathsf{status},\mathsf{rf},\mathsf{Prop}[\langle q, \mathsf{var}\,(e)\rangle \leftarrow e],\prec'_{co}\rangle}\ \text{Prop}$$

$$\frac{e \in \mathbb{E}_p^{ACI},\ \mathsf{status}\,(e) = \mathtt{fetch},\ \mathsf{ComCnd}\,(c, e),\ \mathsf{ValidCnd}\,(c, e)}{c \xrightarrow{p} \langle \mathbb{E},\prec,\mathsf{ins},\mathsf{status}[e \leftarrow \mathtt{com}],\mathsf{rf},\mathsf{Prop},\prec_{co}\rangle}\ \text{Com-ACI}$$

Fig. 2. Inference rules defining the relation $\xrightarrow{p}$ where $p \in \mathcal{P}$.

are *propagated* to the process. The first case is covered by the rule Local-Read in which the process p initializes a read event $e \in \mathbb{E}^R$ on a variable (say x), where e has already been fetched. Here, the event e is made to read its value from a local write event $e' \in \mathbb{E}_p^W$ on x such that (i) e' has been initialized but not yet committed, and such that (ii) e' is the closest write event that precedes e in the order $\prec_{poloc}$. Notice that, by condition (ii), e' is unique if it exists. To formalize this, we define the *Closest Write* function $\mathsf{CW}\,(c, e) := e'$ where e' is the unique event such that (i) $e' \in \mathbb{E}^W$, (ii) $e' \prec_{poloc} e$, and (iii) there is no event e'' such that $e'' \in \mathbb{E}^W$ and $e' \prec_{poloc} e'' \prec_{poloc} e$. Notice that e' may not exist, i.e., it may be the case that $\mathsf{CW}\,(c, e) = \bot$. If e' exists and it has been inititialized but not commited, we initialize e and update the read-from relation appropriately. On the other hand, if such an event does not exist, i.e., if there is no write event on x before e by p, or if the closest write event on x before e by p has already been committed, then we use the rule Prop-Read to let e fetch its value from the latest write event on x that has been propagated to p. Notice this event is the value of $\mathsf{Prop}\,(p, x)$.

To commit an initialized read event $e \in \mathbb{E}_p^R$, we use the rule Com-Read. The rule can be performed if e satisfies two conditions in c. The first condition is defined as RdCnd $(c, e) := \forall e' \in \mathbb{E}^R : (e' \prec_{poloc} e) \implies (\text{rf}(e') \preceq_{co} \text{rf}(e))$. It states that for any read event e' such that e' precedes e in the order $\prec_{poloc}$, the write event from which e' reads its value is equal to or precedes the write event for e in the coherence order $\prec_{co}$. The second condition is defined by ComCnd $(c, e) := \forall e' \in \mathbb{E} : (e' \prec_{data} e) \lor (e' \prec_{ctrl} e) \lor (e' \prec_{poloc} e) \implies (\text{status}(e') = \text{com})$. It states that all events $e' \in \mathbb{E}$ that precede e in one of the orders $\prec_{data}$, $\prec_{ctrl}$, or $\prec_{poloc}$ should have already been committed.

To initialize a fetched write event $e \in \mathbb{E}_p^R$, we use the rule Init-Write that requires all events that precede e in the order $\prec_{data}$ should have already been initialized. This condition is formulated as WrInitCnd $(c, e) := \forall e' \in \mathbb{E}^R : (e' \prec_{data} e) \implies (\text{status}(e') = \text{init} \lor \text{status}(e') = \text{com})$. When a write event in a process $p \in \mathcal{P}$ is committed, it is also immediately propagated to p itself. To maintain the coherence order, the semantics keeps the invariant that the latest write event on a variable $x \in X$ that has been propagated to a process $p \in \mathcal{P}$ is the largest one in the coherence order among all write events on x that have been propagated to p up to now in the run. This invariant is maintained in Com-Write by requiring that the event e (that is being propagated) is strictly larger in the coherence order than the latest write event on the same variable as e that has been propagated to p.

Write events are propagated to other processes through the rule Prop. A write event e on a variable x is allowed to be propagated to a process q only if it has a coherence order that is strictly larger than the coherence of any event that has been to propagated to q up to now. Notice that this is given by coherence order of Prop (q, x) which is the latest write event on x that has been propagated to q.

When committing an aci event through the rule Com-ACI, we also require that we verify any potential speculation that have been made when fetching the subsequent events. We assume that we are given a function Val (c, e) that takes as input an aci event e and returns the value of the expression of the conditional statement in the instruction of e when evaluated in the configuration c. The Val (c, e) is only defined when all events that precede e in the order $\prec_{data}$ should have already been initialized.

To that end, we define predicate ValidCnd $(c, e) := (\exists e' \in \mathbb{E} : e \prec e' \land \nexists e'' \in \mathbb{E} : e \prec e'' \prec e') \implies ((\text{Val}(c, e) = true \land \text{ins}(e') = \text{Tnext}(\text{ins}(e))) \lor (\text{Val}(c, e) = false \land \text{ins}(e') = \text{Fnext}(\text{ins}(e))))$. The rule intuitively finds the event e' that was fetched immediately after e. Notice that such an event may not exist and it is unique if it exists. The predicate requires the choice of e' is consistent with the value Val (c, e) of the expression in the statement of the instruction of e.

Bounded Reachability. A *run* π is a sequence of transitions $c_0 \xrightarrow{p_1} c_1 \xrightarrow{p_2} c_2 \cdots c_{n-1} \xrightarrow{p_n} c_n$. In such a case, we write $c_0 \xrightarrow{\pi} c_n$. We define $\text{last}(\pi) := c_n$. We define $\pi \uparrow := p_1 p_2 \cdots p_n$, i.e., it is the sequence of processes performing the transitions in π. For a sequence $\sigma = p_1 p_2 \cdots p_n \in \mathcal{P}^*$, we say that σ is a *context* if there is a process $p \in \mathcal{P}$ such that $p_i = p$ for all $i : 1 \leq i \leq n$. We say that π is *committed* (resp. *k-bounded*) if $\text{last}(\pi)$ is committed (resp. if $\pi \uparrow = \sigma_1 \cdot \sigma_2 \cdots \sigma_k$ where σ_i is a context for all $i : 1 \leq i \leq k$).

For $c \in C$ and $p \in P$, we define the set of *reachable labels* of the configuration c as follows. (i) If $c = c_{init}$ then $\texttt{lbl}(c) := \{\bot\}$, i.e. process p does not reach to any label in the initial configuration. (ii) If $c \neq c_{init}$, let e be the maximal event of p (w.r.t. $\prec$) in c. We define $\texttt{lbl}(c) := \{\texttt{lbl}(\texttt{ins}(e))\}$, i.e. process p reaches to the label of the maximal event e of p (w.r.t. $\prec$) in the configuration c. In the *reachability problem*, we are given a label λ and asked whether there is a committed run π and a configuration c such that $c_{init} \xrightarrow{\pi} c$ where $\lambda \in \texttt{lbl}(c)$. For a natural number $\mathbb{K}$, the $\mathbb{K}$-*bounded reachability problem* is defined by requiring that the run π in the above definition is $\mathbb{K}$-bounded.

3 Translation

In this section, we introduce an algorithm that reduces, for a given number $\mathbb{K}$, the $\mathbb{K}$-bounded reachability problem for POWER to the corresponding problem for SC. Given an input concurrent program *Prog*, the algorithm constructs an output concurrent program *Prog*$^\bullet$ whose size is polynomial in *Prog* and $\mathbb{K}$, such that for each $\mathbb{K}$-bounded run π in *Prog* under the POWER semantics there is a corresponding $\mathbb{K}$-bounded run $\pi^\bullet$ of *Prog*$^\bullet$ under the SC semantics that reaches the same set of process labels. Below, we first present a scheme for the translation of *Prog*, and mention some of the challenges that arise due to the POWER semantics. Then, we give a detailed description of the data structures we use in *Prog*$^\bullet$. Finally, we describe the codes of the processes in *Prog*$^\bullet$.

Scheme. Our construction is based on code-to-code translation scheme that transforms the program *Prog* into the program *Prog*$^\bullet$ following the map function $[\![.]\!]_{\mathbb{K}}$ given in Fig. 3. Let P and X be the sets of processes and (shared) variables in *Prog*. The map $[\![.]\!]_{\mathbb{K}}$ *replaces* the variables of *Prog* by $(|P| \cdot (2\mathbb{K}+1))$ copies of the set X, in addition to a finite set of *finite-data* structures (which will be formally defined in the **Data Structures** paragraph). The map function then declares two additional processes iniProc and verProc that will be used to initialize the data structures and to check the reachability problem at the end of the run of *Prog*$^\bullet$. The formal definition of iniProc (resp. verProc) will be given in the **Initializing process** (resp. **Verifier**

$$[\![Prog]\!]_{\mathbb{K}} \overset{\text{def}}{=} \texttt{var} \bowtie \langle \texttt{addvars} \rangle_{\mathbb{K}}; \langle \texttt{iniProc} \rangle_{\mathbb{K}}$$
$$\langle \texttt{verProc} \rangle_{\mathbb{K}} (\![\texttt{proc } p \texttt{ reg } \$r^* \, i^*]\!]_{\mathbb{K}})^*$$

$$\langle \texttt{addvars} \rangle_{\mathbb{K}} \overset{\text{def}}{=} \mu(|P|,|X|,\mathbb{K}) \, \mu^{init}(|P|,|X|,\mathbb{K})$$
$$\alpha(|P|,|X|,\mathbb{K}) \, \alpha^{init}(|P|,|X|,\mathbb{K})$$
$$v(|P|,|X|) \, iR(|P|,|X|) \, cR(|P|,|X|)$$
$$iW(|P|,|X|) \, cW(|P|,|X|) \, iReg(|R|)$$
$$cReg(|R|) \, ctrl(|P|) \, active(\mathbb{K}) \, cntxt$$

$$\langle \texttt{iniProc} \rangle_{\mathbb{K}} \overset{\text{def}}{=} [\![\texttt{iniProc}]\!]_{\mathbb{K}}$$
$$\langle \texttt{verProc} \rangle_{\mathbb{K}} \overset{\text{def}}{=} [\![\texttt{verProc}]\!]_{\mathbb{K}}$$
$$[\![\texttt{proc } p \texttt{ reg } i^*]\!]_{\mathbb{K}} \overset{\text{def}}{=} \texttt{proc } p \texttt{ reg } \$r^* \, ([\![i]\!]_{\mathbb{K}}^p)^*$$
$$[\![i]\!]_{\mathbb{K}}^p \overset{\text{def}}{=} \lambda : \langle \texttt{activeCnt} \rangle_{\mathbb{K}}^p [\![s]\!]_{\mathbb{K}}^p \langle \texttt{closeCnt} \rangle_{\mathbb{K}}^p$$
$$\langle \texttt{activeCnt} \rangle_{\mathbb{K}}^p \overset{\text{def}}{=} \texttt{assume}(\texttt{active}(\texttt{cntxt}) = p)$$
$$\langle \texttt{closeCnt} \rangle_{\mathbb{K}}^p \overset{\text{def}}{=} \texttt{cntxt} \leftarrow \texttt{cntxt} + \texttt{gen}([0..\mathbb{K}-1]);$$
$$\texttt{assume}(\texttt{cntxt} \leq \mathbb{K})$$
$$[\![\$r \leftarrow x]\!]_{\mathbb{K}}^p \overset{\text{def}}{=} [\![\$r \leftarrow x]\!]_{\mathbb{K}}^{p,\text{Read}}$$
$$[\![x \leftarrow exp]\!]_{\mathbb{K}}^p \overset{\text{def}}{=} [\![x \leftarrow exp]\!]_{\mathbb{K}}^{p,\text{Write}}$$
$$[\![\texttt{assume } exp]\!]_{\mathbb{K}}^p \overset{\text{def}}{=} \texttt{assume } exp; \langle \texttt{control} \rangle_{\mathbb{K}}^p$$
$$[\![\texttt{if } exp \texttt{ then } i^* \overset{\text{def}}{=} \texttt{if } exp \texttt{ then } ([\![i]\!]_{\mathbb{K}}^p)^*$$
$$\texttt{else } i^*]\!]_{\mathbb{K}}^p \quad \texttt{else } ([\![i]\!]_{\mathbb{K}}^p)^*; \langle \texttt{control} \rangle_{\mathbb{K}}^p$$
$$[\![\texttt{while } exp \texttt{ do } i^*]\!]_{\mathbb{K}}^p \overset{\text{def}}{=} \texttt{while } exp \texttt{ do } ([\![i]\!]_{\mathbb{K}}^p)^*; \langle \texttt{control} \rangle_{\mathbb{K}}^p$$
$$\langle \texttt{control} \rangle_{\mathbb{K}}^p \overset{\text{def}}{=} \texttt{ctrl}(p) \leftarrow \texttt{ctrl}(p) + \texttt{gen}([0..\mathbb{K}-1]);$$
$$\texttt{assume}(\texttt{ctrl}(p) \leq \mathbb{K})$$
$$[\![\texttt{term}]\!]_{\mathbb{K}}^p \overset{\text{def}}{=} \texttt{term}$$

Fig. 3. Translation map $[\![.]\!]_{\mathbb{K}}$. We omit the label of an intermediary instruction when it is not relevant.

process) paragraph. Furthermore, the map function $[\![.]\!]_{\mathbb{K}}$ transforms the code of each process $p \in \mathcal{P}$ to a corresponding process $p^{\bullet}$ that will simulate the moves of p. The processes p and $p^{\bullet}$ will have the same set of registers. For each instruction i appearing in the code of the process p, the map $[\![i]\!]_{\mathbb{K}}^{p}$ transforms it to a sequence of instructions as follows: First, it adds the code defined by `activeCnt` to check if the process p is active during the current context, then it transforms the statement $\mathfrak{s}$ of the instruction i into a sequence of instructions following the map $[\![\mathfrak{s}]\!]_{\mathbb{K}}^{p}$, and finally it adds the sequence of instructions defined by `closeCnt` to guess the occurrence of a context switch. The translation of an aci statement keeps the same statements and adds `control` to guess the contexts when the corresponding event will be committed. The terminating statement remains identical by the map function $[\![\mathtt{term}]\!]_{\mathbb{K}}^{p}$. The translations of write and read statements will be described in the **Write Instructions** and **Read Instructions** paragraphs respectively.

Challenges. There are two *aspects* of the POWER semantics (cf. Sect. 2) that make it difficult to simulate the run π under the SC semantics, namely *non-atomicity* and *asynchrony*. First, events are not executed atomically. In fact, an event is first fetched and initialized before it is committed. In particular, an event may be fetched in one context and be initialized and committed only in later contexts. Since there is no bound on the number of events that may be fetched in a given context, our simulation should be able to handle unbounded numbers of pending events. Second, write events of one process are propagated in an *asynchronous* manner to the other processes. This implies that we may have unbounded numbers of "traveling" events that are committed in one context and propagated to other processes only in subsequent contexts. This creates two *challenges* in the simulation. On the one hand, we need to keep track of the coherence order among the different write events. On the other hand, since write events are not distributed to different processes at the same time, the processes may have different views of the values of a given variable at a given point of time.

Since it is not feasible to record the initializing, committing, and propagating contexts of an unbounded number of events in an SC run, our algorithm will instead predict the *summary* of effects of arbitrarily long sequences of events that may occur in a given context. This is implemented using an intricate scheme that first *guesses* and then *checks* these summaries. Concretely, each event e in the run π is simulated by a sequence of instructions in $\pi^{\bullet}$. This sequence of instructions will be executed atomically (without interruption from other processes and events). More precisely, if e is fetched in a context $k : 1 \leq k \leq \mathbb{K}$, then the corresponding sequence of instructions will be executed in the same context k in $\pi^{\bullet}$. Furthermore, we let $\pi^{\bullet}$ *guess* (*speculate*) (i) the contexts in which e will be initialized, committed, and propagated to other processes, and (ii) the values of variables that are seen by read operations. Then, we *check* whether the guesses made by $\pi^{\bullet}$ are valid w.r.t. the POWER semantics. As we will see below, these checks are done both on-the-fly during $\pi^{\bullet}$, as well as at the end of $\pi^{\bullet}$. To implement the guess-and-check scheme, we use a number of data structures, described below.

Data Structures. We will introduce the data structures used in our simulation in order to deal with the above asynchrony and non-atomicity challenging aspects.

Asynchrony. In order to keep track of the coherence order, we associate a *time stamp* with each write event. A time stamp τ is a mapping $\mathcal{P} \mapsto \mathbb{K}^{\otimes}$ where $\mathbb{K}^{\otimes} := \mathbb{K} \cup \{\otimes\}$. For a process $p \in \mathcal{P}$, the value of $\tau(p)$ represents the context in which the given event is propagated to p. In particular, if $\tau(p) = \otimes$ then the event is never propagated to p. We use $\mathbb{T}$ to denote the set of time stamps. We define an order $\sqsubseteq$ on $\mathbb{T}$ such that $\tau_1 \sqsubseteq \tau_2$ if, for all processes $p \in \mathcal{P}$, either $\tau_1(p) = \otimes$, or $\tau_2(p) = \otimes$, or $\tau_1(p) \leq \tau_2(p)$. Notice that if $\tau_1 \sqsubseteq \tau_2$ and there is a process $p \in \mathcal{P}$ such that $\tau_1(p) \neq \otimes$, $\tau_2(p) \neq \otimes$, and $\tau_1(p) < \tau_2(p)$ then $\tau_1(q) \leq \tau_2(q)$ whenever $\tau_1(q) \neq \otimes$ and $\tau_2(q) \neq \otimes$. In such a case, $\tau_1 \sqsubset \tau_2$. On the other hand, if either $\tau_1(p) = \otimes$ or $\tau_2(p) = \otimes$ for all $p \in \mathcal{P}$, then both $\tau_1 \sqsubseteq \tau_2$ and $\tau_2 \sqsubseteq \tau_1$. The coherence order $\prec_{co}$ on write events will be reflected in the order $\sqsubseteq$ on their time stamps. In particular, for events e_1 and e_2 with time stamps τ_1 and τ_2 respectively, if $\tau_1 \sqsubset \tau_2$ then e_1 precedes e_2 in coherence order. The reason is that there is at least one process p to which both e_1 and e_2 are propagated, and e_1 is propagated to p before e_2. However, if both $\tau_1 \sqsubseteq \tau_2$ and $\tau_2 \sqsubseteq \tau_1$ then the events are never propagated to the same process, and hence they need not to be related by the coherence order.

If $\tau_1 \sqsubseteq \tau_2$ then we define the *summary* of τ_1 and τ_2, denoted by $\tau_1 \oplus \tau_2$, to be the time stamp τ such that $\tau(p) = \tau_1(p)$ if $\tau_2(p) = \otimes$, and $\tau(p) = \tau_2(p)$ otherwise. For a sequence $\sigma = \tau_0 \sqsubseteq \tau_1 \sqsubseteq \cdots \sqsubseteq \tau_n$ of time stamps, we define the summary $\oplus \sigma := \tau'_n$ where τ'_i is defined inductively by $\tau'_0 := \tau_0$, and $\tau'_i := \tau'_{i-1} \oplus \tau_i$ for $i : 1 \leq i \leq n$. Notice that, for $p \in \mathcal{P}$, we have $\oplus \sigma(p) = \tau_i(p)$ where i is the largest $j : 1 \leq j \leq n$ s.t. $\tau_j(p) \neq \otimes$.

Our simulation observes the sequence of write events received by a process in each context. In fact, the simulation will initially *guess* and later *verify* the summaries of the time stamps of such a sequence. This is done using data structures α^{init} and α. The mapping $\alpha^{init} : \mathcal{P} \times X \times \mathbb{K} \mapsto [\mathcal{P} \mapsto \mathbb{K}^{\otimes}]$ stores, for a process $p \in \mathcal{P}$, a variable $x \in X$, and a context $k : 1 \leq k \leq \mathbb{K}$, an *initial guess* $\alpha^{init}(p, x, k)$ of the summary of the time stamps of the sequence of write events on x propagated to p up to the *start* of context k. Starting from a given initial guess for a given context k, the time stamp is updated successively using the sequence of write events on x propagated to p in k. The result is stored using the mapping $\alpha : \mathcal{P} \times X \times \mathbb{K} \mapsto [\mathcal{P} \mapsto \mathbb{K}^{\otimes}]$. More precisely, we initially set the value of α to α^{init}. Each time a new write event e on x is created by p in the context k, we guess the time stamp β of e, and then update $\alpha(p, x, k)$ by computing its summary with β. Thus, given a point in a context k, $\alpha(p, x, k)$ contains the summary of the time stamps of the whole sequence of write events on x that have been propagated to p up to that point. At the end of the simulation, we *verify*, for each context $k : 1 \leq k < \mathbb{K}$, that the value of α for a context k is equal to the value of α^{init} for the next context $k + 1$.

Furthermore, we use three data structures for storing the values of variables. The mapping $\mu^{init} : \mathcal{P} \times X \times \mathbb{K} \mapsto \mathcal{D}$ stores, for a process $p \in \mathcal{P}$, a variable $x \in X$, and a context $k : 1 \leq k \leq \mathbb{K}$, an *initial guess* $\mu^{init}(p, x, k)$ of the value of the latest write event on x propagated to p up to the *start* of the context k. The mapping $\mu : \mathcal{P} \times X \times \mathbb{K} \mapsto \mathcal{D}$ stores, for a process $p \in \mathcal{P}$, a variable $x \in X$, and a point in a context $k : 1 \leq k \leq \mathbb{K}$, the value $\mu(p, x, k)$ of the latest write event on x that has been propagated to p up to that point. Moreover, the mapping $\nu : \mathcal{P} \times \mathcal{X} \mapsto \mathcal{D}$ stores, for a process $p \in \mathcal{P}$ and a variable $x \in \mathcal{X}$, the latest value $\nu(p, x)$ that has been written on x by p.

Non-atomicity. In order to satisfy the different dependencies between events, we need to keep track of the contexts in which they are initialized and committed. One aspect of our translation is that it only needs to keep track of the *context* in which the *latest* read or write event on a given variable in a given process is initialized or committed. The mapping iW : $\mathcal{P} \times \mathcal{X} \mapsto \mathbb{K}$ defines, for $p \in \mathcal{P}$ and $x \in \mathcal{X}$, the context iW (p, x) in which the latest write event on x by p is initialized. The mapping cW : $\mathcal{P} \times \mathcal{X} \mapsto \mathbb{K}$ is defined in a similar manner for committing (rather than initializing) write events. Furthermore, we define similar mappings iR and cR for read events. The mapping iReg : $\mathcal{R} \mapsto \mathbb{K}$ gives, for a register $\$r \in \mathcal{R}$, the initializing context iReg $(\$r)$ of the latest read event loading a value to $\$r$. For an expression exp, we define iReg $(exp) := \max \{$ iReg $(\$r) \mid \$r \in \mathcal{R}(exp)\}$. The mapping cReg : $\mathcal{R} \mapsto \mathbb{K}$ gives the contexts for committing (rather than initializing) of the read events. We extend cReg from registers to expressions in a similar manner to iReg. Finally, the mapping ctrl : $\mathcal{P} \mapsto \mathbb{K}$ gives, for a process $p \in \mathcal{P}$, the committing context ctrl (p) of the latest aci event in p.

Initializing Process. Algorithm 1 shows the initialization process. The for-loop of lines 1, 3 and 5 define the values of the initializing and committing data structures for the variables and registers together with $\nu(p, x)$, $\mu(p, x, 1)$, $\alpha(p, x, 1)$ and ctrl (p) for all $p \in \mathcal{P}$ and $x \in \mathcal{X}$. The for-loop of line 7 defines the initial values of α and μ at the start of each context $k \geq 2$ (as described above). The for-loop of line 10 chooses an *active* process to execute in each context. The *current context* variable cntxt is initialized to 1.

Write Instructions. Consider a write instruction i in a process $p \in \mathcal{P}$ whose statement is of the form $x \leftarrow exp$. The translation of i is shown in Algorithm 3. The code simulates an event e executing i, by encoding the effects of the inference rules Init-Write, Com-Write and Prop that initialize, commit, and propagate a write event respectively. The translation consists of three parts, namely *guessing*, *checking* and *update*.

Guessing. We guess the initializing and committing contexts for the event e, together with its time stamp. In line 1, we guess the context in which the event e will be initialized, and store the guess in iW (p, x). Similarly, in line 3, we guess the context in which the event e will be committed, and store the guess in cW (p, x) (having stored its old value in the previous line). In the for-loop of line 4, we guess a time stamp for e and store it in β. This means that, for each process $q \in \mathcal{P}$, we guess the context in which the event e will be propagated to q and we store this guess in $\beta(q)$.

Checking. We perform sanity checks on the guessed values in order to verify that they are consistent with the POWER semantics. Lines 6–8 perform the sanity checks for iW (p, x). In lines 6–7, we verify that the initializing context of the event

Alg. 1: Translating $[\![\text{iniProc}]\!]_{\mathbb{K}}$.

1 **for** $p \in \mathcal{P} \wedge x \in X$ **do**
2 $\quad$ iR $(p, x) \leftarrow 1$; cR $(p, x) \leftarrow 1$;
$\quad\quad$ iW $(p, x) \leftarrow 1$; cW $(p, x) \leftarrow 1$;
$\quad\quad$ $\nu (p, x) \leftarrow 0$; $\mu (p, x, 1) \leftarrow 0$;
$\quad\quad$ $\alpha (p, x, 1) \leftarrow \otimes^{|\mathcal{P}|}$;

3 **for** $p \in \mathcal{P}$ **do**
4 $\quad$ ctrl $(p) \leftarrow 1$;

5 **for** $\$r \in \mathcal{R}$ **do**
6 $\quad$ iReg $(\$r) \leftarrow 1$; cReg $(\$r) \leftarrow 1$;

7 **for** $p \in \mathcal{P} \wedge x \in X \wedge k \in [2..\mathbb{K}]$ **do**
8 $\quad$ $\alpha (p, x, k) \leftarrow \alpha^{init} (p, x, k)$;
9 $\quad$ $\mu (p, x, k) \leftarrow \mu^{init} (p, x, k)$;

10 **for** $k \in [1..\mathbb{K}]$ **do**
11 $\quad$ active $(k) \leftarrow$ gen $(\mathcal{P})$;

12 cntxt $\leftarrow 1$;

Alg. 2: Translating $[\![\$r \leftarrow x]\!]_{\mathbb{K}}^{p,\text{Read}}$.

// Guess
1 old-iR $\leftarrow$ iR (p, x);
2 iReg $(\$r) \leftarrow$ iR $(p, x) \leftarrow$ gen $([1..\mathbb{K}])$;
3 old-cR $\leftarrow$ cR (p, x);
4 cReg $(\$r) \leftarrow$ cR $(p, x) \leftarrow$ gen $([1..\mathbb{K}])$;
// Check
5 assume (iR $(p, x) \geq$ cntxt);
6 assume (active (iR $(p, x)) = p$);
7 assume (iR $(p, x) \geq$ iW (p, x));
8 assume (iR $(p, x) \geq$ cW $(p, x) \implies$
$\quad\quad\quad$ iR $(p, x) \geq$
$\quad\quad\quad$ $\alpha (p, x, \text{old-iR}) (p)$);
9 assume (cR $(p, x) \geq$ iR (p, x));
10 assume (active (cR $(p, x)) = p$);
11 assume (cR $(p, x) \geq$
$\quad\quad\quad$ max $\{\text{ctrl} (p), \text{old-cR}, \text{cW} (p, x)\}$);

// Update
12 **if** iR $(p, x) <$ cW (p, x) **then**
$\quad\quad$ $\$r \leftarrow \nu (p, x)$;
13 **else** $\$r \leftarrow \mu (p, x, \text{iR} (p, x))$;

Alg. 3: Translating $[\![x \leftarrow exp]\!]_{\mathbb{K}}^{p,\text{Write}}$.

// Guess
1 iW $(p, x) \leftarrow$ gen $([1..\mathbb{K}])$;
2 old-cW $\leftarrow$ cW (p, x);
3 cW $(p, x) \leftarrow$ gen $([1..\mathbb{K}])$;
4 **for** $q \in \mathcal{P}$ **do**
5 $\quad$ $\beta (q) \leftarrow$ gen $(\mathbb{K}^{\otimes})$;

// Check
6 assume (iW $(p, x) \geq$ cntxt);
7 assume (active (iW $(p, x)) = p$);
8 assume (iW $(p, x) \geq$ iReg (exp));
9 assume (cW $(p, x) \geq$ iW (p, x));
10 assume (cW $(p, x) \geq$
$\quad\quad\quad$ max$\{\text{cReg} (exp), \text{ctrl} (p), \text{cR} (p, x), \text{old-cW}\}$);

11 **for** $q \in \mathcal{P}$ **do**
12 $\quad$ **if** $q = p$ **then**
13 $\quad\quad$ assume $(\beta (q) =$ cW $(p, x))$;
14 $\quad$ **if** $q \neq p$ **then**
15 $\quad\quad$ assume$(\beta (q) \neq \otimes \implies \beta (q) \geq$ cW $(p, x))$;
16 $\quad$ **if** $\beta (q) \neq \otimes$ **then**
17 $\quad\quad$ assume $(\alpha (q, x, \beta (q)) \sqsubseteq \beta)$;
18 $\quad\quad$ assume(active $(\beta (q)) = p)$;

// Update
19 **for** $q \in \mathcal{P}$ **do**
20 $\quad$ **if** $\beta (q) \neq \otimes$ **then**
21 $\quad\quad$ $\alpha (q, x, \beta (q)) \leftarrow \alpha (q, x, \beta (q)) \oplus \beta$;
22 $\quad\quad$ $\mu (q, x, \beta (q)) \leftarrow exp$;

23 $\nu (p, x) \leftarrow exp$;

Alg. 4: Translating $[\![\text{verProc}]\!]_{\mathbb{K}}$.

1 **for** $p \in \mathcal{P} \wedge x \in X \wedge k \in [1..\mathbb{K} - 1]$ **do**
2 $\quad$ assume $(\alpha (p, x, k) = \alpha^{init} (p, x, k + 1))$;
3 $\quad$ assume $(\mu (p, x, k) = \mu^{init} (p, x, k + 1))$;

4 **if** λ *is reachable* **then** *error* ;

---

e is not smaller than the current context. This captures the fact that initialization happens after fetching of e. It also verifies that initialization happens in a context in which p is active. In line 8, we check whether WrInitCnd in the rule **Init-Write** is satisfied. To do that, we verify that the data dependency order $\prec_{\text{data}}$ holds. More precisely, we find, for each register $\$r$ that occurs in exp, the initializing context of the latest read event loading to $\$r$. We make sure that the initializing context of e is later than the initializing contexts of all these read events. By definition, the largest of all these contexts is stored in iReg (exp).

Lines 9–10 perform the sanity checks for cW (p, x). In line 9, we check the committing context of the event e is at least as large as its initializing context. In line 10, we check that ComCnd in the rule **Com-Write** is satisfied. To do that, we check that the committing context is larger than (i) the committing context of all the read events from which the registers in the expression exp fetch their values (to satisfy the data dependency order $\prec_{\text{data}}$, in a similar manner to that described for initialization above), (ii) the committing contexts of the latest read and write events on x in p, i.e., $\text{cR}\,(p, x)$ and $\text{cW}\,(p, x)$ (to satisfy the per-location program order $\prec_{\text{poloc}}$), and (iii) the committing context of the latest aci event in p, i.e., $\text{ctrl}\,(p)$ (to satisfy the control order $\prec_{\text{ctrl}}$).

The for-loop of line 11 performs three sanity checks on the time stamp β. In line 12, we verify that the event e is propagated to p in the same context as the one in which it is committed. This is consistent with the rule Com-Write which requires that when a write event is committed then it is immediately propagated to the committing process. In line 14, we verify that if the event e is propagated to a process q (different from p), then the propagation takes place in a context later than or equal to the one in which e is committed. This is to be consistent with the fact that a write event is propagated to other processes only after it has been committed. In line 17, we check that guessed time stamp of the event e does not cause a violation of the coherence order $\prec_{\text{co}}$. To do that, we consider each process $q \in \mathcal{P}$ to which e will be propagated (i.e., $\beta\,(q) \neq \otimes$). The time stamp of e should be larger than the time stamp of any other write event e' on x that has been propagated to q up to the current point (since e should be larger in the coherence order than e'). Notice that by construction the time stamp of the largest such event e' is currently stored in $\alpha\,(q, x, \beta\,(q))$. Moreover, in line 18, we check that the event is propagated to q in a context in which p is active.

Updating. The for-loop of line 19 uses the values guessed above for updating the global data structure α. More precisely, if the event e is propagated to a process q, i.e., $\beta\,(q) \neq \otimes$, then we add β to the summary of the time stamps of the sequence of write operations on x propagated to q up to the current point in the context $\beta\,(q)$. Lines 22–23 assign the value exp to $\mu\,(p, x, \beta\,(q))$ and $\nu\,(p, x)$ respectively. Recall that the former stores the value defined by the latest write event on x propagated to q up to the current point in the context $\beta\,(q)$, and the latter stores the value defined by the latest write on x by p.

Read Instructions. Consider a read instruction i in a process $p \in \mathcal{P}$ whose statement is of the form $\$r \leftarrow x$. The translation of i is shown in Algorithm 2. The code simulates an event e running i by encoding the three inference rules Local-Read, Prop-Read, and Com-Read. In a similar manner to a write instruction, the translation scheme for a read instruction consists of guessing, checking and update parts. Notice however that the initialization of the read event is carried out through two different inference rules.

Guessing. In line 1, we store the old value of $\text{iR}\,(p, x)$. In line 2, we guess the context in which the event e will be initialized, and store the guessed context both in $\text{iR}\,(p, x)$ and $\text{iReg}\,(\$r)$. Recall that the latter records the initializing context of the latest read event loading a value to $\$r$. In lines 3–4, we execute similar instructions for committing (rather than initializing).

Checking. Lines 5–8 perform the sanity checks for $\text{iR}\,(p, x)$. Lines 5–6 check that the initializing context for the event e is not smaller than the current context and the initialization happens in a context in which p is active. Line 7 makes sure that at least one of the two inference rules Local-Read and Prop-Read is satisfied, by checking that the closest write event CW (c, e) (if it exists) has already been initialized. In line 8, we satisfy RdCnd in the rule Com-Read. Lines 9–11 perform the sanity checks for cR (p, x) in a similar manner to the corresponding instructions for write events (see above).

Updating. The purpose of the update part (the if-statement of line 12) is to ensure that the correct read-from relation is defined as described by the inference rules Local-Read and Prop-Read. If iR $(p, x) <$ cW (p, x), then this means that the latest write event e' on x by p is not committed and hence, according to Local-Read, the event e reads its value from that event. Recall that this value is stored in $v(p, x)$. On the other hand, if iR $(p, x) \geq$ cW (p, x) then the event e' has been committed and hence, according to Prop-Read, the event e reads its value from the latest write event on x propagated to p in the context where e is initialized. We notice that this value is stored in $\mu(p, x, \text{iR}(p, x))$.

Verifier Process. The verifier process makes sure that the updated value α of the time stamp at the end of a given context $k : 1 \leq k \leq \mathbb{K} - 1$ is equal to the corresponding guessed value α^{init} at the start of the next context. It also performs the corresponding checking for the values written on the variables (by comparing μ and μ^{init}). Finally, it checks whether we reach an error label λ or not.

4   Experimental Results

In order to evaluate the efficiency of our approach, we have implemented a context-bounded model checker for programs under POWER, called power2sc[1]. We use cbmc version 5.1 [17] as the backend tool. However, observe that our code-to-code translation can be implemented on the top of any backend tool that provides safety verification of concurrent programs running under the SC semantics. In the following, we present the evaluation of power2sc on 28 C/pthreads benchmarks collected from goto-instrument [9], nidhugg [6], memorax [5], and the SV-COMP17 bechmark suit [1]. These are widespread medium-sized benchmarks that are used by many tools for analyzing concurrent programs running under weak memory models (e.g. [2–4,7,8,10,12–15,22,24,37,40]). We divide our results in two sets. The first set concerns unsafe programs while the second set concerns safe ones. In both parts, we compare results obtained from power2sc to the ones obtained from goto-instrument and nidhugg, which are, to the best of our knowledge, the only two tools supporting C/pthreads programs under POWER[2]. All experiments were run on a machine equipped with a 2.4 GHz Intel x86-32 Core2 processor and 4 GB RAM.

Table 1a shows that power2sc performs well in detecting bugs compared to the other tools for most of the unsafe examples. We observe that power2sc manages to

---

[1] https://www.it.uu.se/katalog/tuang296/mguess.
[2] cbmc previously supported POWER [10], but has withdrawn support in later versions.

Table 1. Comparing ③ power2sc with ① goto-instrument and ② nidhugg on two sets of benchmarks: (a) unsafe and (b) safe (with manually inserted synchronizations). The LB column indicates whether the tools were instructed to unroll loops up to a certain bound. The CB column gives the context bound for power2sc. The program size is the number of code lines. A t/o entry means that the tool failed to complete within 1800 s. The best running time (in seconds) for each benchmark is given in bold font.

(a) Program/size	LB	① Time	② Time	③ Time	CB	(b) Program/size	LB	① Time	② Time	③ Time	CB
Bakery/76 [5]	8	226	t/o	**1**	3	Bakery/85 [5]	8	t/o	t/o	**70**	3
Burns/74 [5]	8	t/o	t/o	**1**	3	Burns/79 [5]	8	t/o	t/o	**1018**	3
Dekker/82 [1]	8	t/o	t/o	**1**	2	Dekker/88 [1]	8	t/o	t/o	**1158**	2
Sim Dekker/69 [5]	8	12	t/o	**1**	2	Sim Dekker/73 [5]	8	209	t/o	**14**	2
Dijkstra/82 [5]	8	t/o	t/o	**5**	3	Dijkstra/88 [5]	8	t/o	t/o	t/o	3
Szymanski/83 [1]	8	t/o	t/o	**1**	4	Szymanski/93 [1]	8	t/o	t/o	**89**	4
Fib_bench_0/36 [1]	-	**2**	1101	6	6	Fib_bench_1/36 [1]	-	9	t/o	**5**	6
Lamport/109 [1]	8	t/o	**1**	**1**	3	Lamport/119 [1]	8	928	t/o	t/o	3
Peterson/76 [1]	8	25	1056	**1**	3	Peterson/84 [1]	8	928	t/o	**7**	3
Peterson_3/96 [5]	8	t/o	**1**	3	4	Peterson_3/111 [5]	8	t/o	t/o	**348**	4
Pgsql/69 [9]	8	1079	**1**	**1**	2	Pgsql/73 [9]	8	1522	**2**	38	2
Pgsql_bnd/71 [6]	-	t/o	**1**	**1**	2	Pgsql_bnd/75 [6]	-	t/o	t/o	**10**	2
Tbar_2/75 [5]	8	16	**1**	**1**	3	Tbar_2/80 [5]	8	t/o	332	**29**	3
Tbar_3/94 [5]	8	104	**1**	**1**	3	Tbar_3/103 [5]	8	t/o	t/o	**138**	3

find all the errors using at most 6 contexts while nidhugg and goto-instrument time out to return the errors for several examples. This also confirms that few context switches are sufficient to find bugs. Table 1b demonstrates that our approach is also effective when we run safe programs. power2sc manages to run most of the examples (except Dijkstra and Lamport) using the same context bounds as in the case of their respective unsafe examples. While nidhugg and goto-instrument time out for several examples, they do not impose any bound on the number of context switches while power2sc does.

We have also tested the performance of power2sc with respect to the verification of small litmus tests. power2sc manages to successfully run all 913 litmus tests published in [34]. Furthermore, the output result returned by power2sc matches the ones returned by the tool herd [11] in all the litmus tests.

References

1. SV-COM17 benchmark suit (2017). https://sv-comp.sosy-lab.org/2017/benchmarks.php
2. Abdulla, P.A., Aronis, S., Atig, M.F., Jonsson, B., Leonardsson, C., Sagonas, K.: Stateless model checking for TSO and PSO. In: Baier, C., Tinelli, C. (eds.) TACAS 2015. LNCS, vol. 9035, pp. 353–367. Springer, Heidelberg (2015). doi:10.1007/978-3-662-46681-0_28

3. Abdulla, P.A., Atig, M.F., Bouajjani, A., Ngo, T.P.: The benefits of duality in verifying concurrent programs under TSO. In: CONCUR. LIPIcs, vol. 59, pp. 5:1–5:15. Schloss Dagstuhl-Leibniz-Zentrum fuer Informatik (2016)
4. Abdulla, P.A., Atig, M.F., Chen, Y.-F., Leonardsson, C., Rezine, A.: Automatic fence insertion in integer programs via predicate abstraction. In: Miné, A., Schmidt, D. (eds.) SAS 2012. LNCS, vol. 7460, pp. 164–180. Springer, Heidelberg (2012). doi:10.1007/978-3-642-33125-1_13
5. Abdulla, P.A., Atig, M.F., Chen, Y.-F., Leonardsson, C., Rezine, A.: Counterexample guided fence insertion under TSO. In: Flanagan, C., König, B. (eds.) TACAS 2012. LNCS, vol. 7214, pp. 204–219. Springer, Heidelberg (2012). doi:10.1007/978-3-642-28756-5_15
6. Abdulla, P.A., Atig, M.F., Jonsson, B., Leonardsson, C.: Stateless model checking for POWER. In: Chaudhuri, S., Farzan, A. (eds.) CAV 2016. LNCS, vol. 9780, pp. 134–156. Springer, Cham (2016). doi:10.1007/978-3-319-41540-6_8
7. Abdulla, P.A., Atig, M.F., Lång, M., Ngo, T.P.: Precise and sound automatic fence insertion procedure under PSO. In: Bouajjani, A., Fauconnier, H. (eds.) NETYS 2015. LNCS, vol. 9466, pp. 32–47. Springer, Cham (2015). doi:10.1007/978-3-319-26850-7_3
8. Abdulla, P.A., Atig, M.F., Ngo, T.-P.: The best of both worlds: trading efficiency and optimality in fence insertion for TSO. In: Vitek, J. (ed.) ESOP 2015. LNCS, vol. 9032, pp. 308–332. Springer, Heidelberg (2015). doi:10.1007/978-3-662-46669-8_13
9. Alglave, J., Kroening, D., Nimal, V., Tautschnig, M.: Software verification for weak memory via program transformation. In: Felleisen, M., Gardner, P. (eds.) ESOP 2013. LNCS, vol. 7792, pp. 512–532. Springer, Heidelberg (2013). doi:10.1007/978-3-642-37036-6_28
10. Alglave, J., Kroening, D., Tautschnig, M.: Partial orders for efficient bounded model checking of concurrent software. In: Sharygina, N., Veith, H. (eds.) CAV 2013. LNCS, vol. 8044, pp. 141–157. Springer, Heidelberg (2013). doi:10.1007/978-3-642-39799-8_9
11. Alglave, J., Maranget, L., Tautschnig, M.: Herding cats: modelling, simulation, testing, and data mining for weak memory. ACM TOPLAS **36**(2), 7:1–7:74 (2014)
12. Atig, M.F., Bouajjani, A., Parlato, G.: Getting rid of store-buffers in TSO analysis. In: Gopalakrishnan, G., Qadeer, S. (eds.) CAV 2011. LNCS, vol. 6806, pp. 99–115. Springer, Heidelberg (2011). doi:10.1007/978-3-642-22110-1_9
13. Bouajjani, A., Derevenetc, E., Meyer, R.: Checking and enforcing robustness against TSO. In: Felleisen, M., Gardner, P. (eds.) ESOP 2013. LNCS, vol. 7792, pp. 533–553. Springer, Heidelberg (2013). doi:10.1007/978-3-642-37036-6_29
14. Burckhardt, S., Alur, R., Martin, M.M.K.: CheckFence: checking consistency of concurrent data types on relaxed memory models. In: PLDI, pp. 12–21. ACM (2007)
15. Burckhardt, S., Musuvathi, M.: Effective program verification for relaxed memory models. In: Gupta, A., Malik, S. (eds.) CAV 2008. LNCS, vol. 5123, pp. 107–120. Springer, Heidelberg (2008). doi:10.1007/978-3-540-70545-1_12
16. Burnim, J., Sen, K., Stergiou, C.: Testing concurrent programs on relaxed memory models. In: ISSTA, pp. 122–132. ACM (2011)
17. Clarke, E., Kroening, D., Lerda, F.: A tool for checking ANSI-C programs. In: Jensen, K., Podelski, A. (eds.) TACAS 2004. LNCS, vol. 2988, pp. 168–176. Springer, Heidelberg (2004). doi:10.1007/978-3-540-24730-2_15
18. Dan, A.M., Meshman, Y., Vechev, M., Yahav, E.: Predicate abstraction for relaxed memory models. In: Logozzo, F., Fähndrich, M. (eds.) SAS 2013. LNCS, vol. 7935, pp. 84–104. Springer, Heidelberg (2013). doi:10.1007/978-3-642-38856-9_7

19. Dan, A., Meshman, Y., Vechev, M., Yahav, E.: Effective abstractions for verification under relaxed memory models. Comput. Lang. Syst. Struct. **47**(Part 1), 62–76 (2017)

20. Demsky, B., Lam, P.: Satcheck: sat-directed stateless model checking for SC and TSO. In: OOPSLA 2015, pp. 20–36. ACM (2015)

21. Derevenetc, E., Meyer, R.: Robustness against power is PSpace-complete. In: Esparza, J., Fraigniaud, P., Husfeldt, T., Koutsoupias, E. (eds.) ICALP 2014. LNCS, vol. 8573, pp. 158–170. Springer, Heidelberg (2014). doi:10.1007/978-3-662-43951-7_14

22. Huang, S., Huang, J.: Maximal causality reduction for TSO and PSO. In: OOPSLA 2016, pp. 447–461 (2016)

23. Kuperstein, M., Vechev, M.T., Yahav, E.: Automatic inference of memory fences. In: FMCAD, pp. 111–119. IEEE (2010)

24. Kuperstein, M., Vechev, M.T., Yahav, E.: Partial-coherence abstractions for relaxed memory models. In: PLDI, pp. 187–198. ACM (2011)

25. Torre, S., Madhusudan, P., Parlato, G.: Reducing context-bounded concurrent reachability to sequential reachability. In: Bouajjani, A., Maler, O. (eds.) CAV 2009. LNCS, vol. 5643, pp. 477–492. Springer, Heidelberg (2009). doi:10.1007/978-3-642-02658-4_36

26. Lahav, O., Vafeiadis, V.: Explaining relaxed memory models with program transformations. In: Fitzgerald, J., Heitmeyer, C., Gnesi, S., Philippou, A. (eds.) FM 2016. LNCS, vol. 9995, pp. 479–495. Springer, Cham (2016). doi:10.1007/978-3-319-48989-6_29

27. Lal, A., Reps, T.W.: Reducing concurrent analysis under a context bound to sequential analysis. FMSD **35**(1), 73–97 (2009)

28. Lamport, L.: How to make a multiprocessor computer that correctly executes multiprocess programs. IEEE Trans. Comput. **C–28**(9), 690–691 (1979)

29. Liu, F., Nedev, N., Prisadnikov, N., Vechev, M.T., Yahav, E.: Dynamic synthesis for relaxed memory models. In: PLDI 2012, pp. 429–440. ACM (2012)

30. Mador-Haim, S., Maranget, L., Sarkar, S., Memarian, K., Alglave, J., Owens, S., Alur, R., Martin, M.M.K., Sewell, P., Williams, D.: An axiomatic memory model for POWER multiprocessors. In: Madhusudan, P., Seshia, S.A. (eds.) CAV 2012. LNCS, vol. 7358, pp. 495–512. Springer, Heidelberg (2012). doi:10.1007/978-3-642-31424-7_36

31. Musuvathi, M., Qadeer, S.: Iterative context bounding for systematic testing of multithreaded programs. In: PLDI, pp. 446–455. ACM (2007)

32. Owens, S., Sarkar, S., Sewell, P.: A better x86 memory model: x86-TSO. In: Berghofer, S., Nipkow, T., Urban, C., Wenzel, M. (eds.) TPHOLs 2009. LNCS, vol. 5674, pp. 391–407. Springer, Heidelberg (2009). doi:10.1007/978-3-642-03359-9_27

33. Qadeer, S., Rehof, J.: Context-bounded model checking of concurrent software. In: Halbwachs, N., Zuck, L.D. (eds.) TACAS 2005. LNCS, vol. 3440, pp. 93–107. Springer, Heidelberg (2005). doi:10.1007/978-3-540-31980-1_7

34. Sarkar, S., Sewell, P., Alglave, J., Maranget, L., Williams, D.: Understanding POWER multiprocessors. In: PLDI, pp. 175–186. ACM (2011)

35. Sewell, P., Sarkar, S., Owens, S., Nardelli, F.Z., Myreen, M.O.: x86-TSO: a rigorous and usable programmer's model for x86 multiprocessors. CACM **53**, 89–97 (2010)

36. Tomasco, E., Lam, T.N., Fischer, B., La Torre, S., Parlato, G.: Embedding weak memory models within eager sequentialization (2016). http://eprints.soton.ac.uk/402285/

37. Tomasco, E., Lam, T.N., Inverso, O., Fischer, B., La Torre, S., Parlato, G.: Lazy sequentialization for TSO and PSO via shared memory abstractions. In: FMCAD 2016, pp. 193–200 (2016)

38. Travkin, O., Wehrheim, H.: Verification of concurrent programs on weak memory models. In: Sampaio, A., Wang, F. (eds.) ICTAC 2016. LNCS, vol. 9965, pp. 3–24. Springer, Cham (2016). doi:10.1007/978-3-319-46750-4_1

39. Yang, Y., Gopalakrishnan, G., Lindstrom, G., Slind, K.: Nemos: a framework for axiomatic and executable specifications of memory consistency models. In: IPDPS. IEEE (2004)

40. Zhang, N., Kusano, M., Wang, C.: Dynamic partial order reduction for relaxed memory models. In: PLDI, pp. 250–259. ACM (2015)

Run-Time Verification and Logic

Rewriting-Based Runtime Verification for Alternation-Free HyperLTL

Noel Brett, Umair Siddique, and Borzoo Bonakdarpour[✉]

Department of Computing and Software, McMaster University, Hamilton, Canada
borzoo@mcmaster.ca

Abstract. Analysis of complex security and privacy policies (e.g., information flow) involves reasoning about multiple execution traces. This stems from the fact that an external observer may gain knowledge about the system through observing and comparing several executions. Monitoring of such policies is in particular challenging because most existing monitoring techniques are limited to the analysis of a single trace at run time. In this paper, we present a rewriting-based technique for runtime verification of the full alternation-free fragment of HyperLTL, a temporal logic for specification of hyperproperties. The distinguishing feature of our proposed technique is its space complexity, which is independent of the number of trace quantifiers in a given HyperLTL formula.

1 Introduction

Dependability and reliability are two crucial aspects of any computing system that deals with *cybersecurity*. This is because even a short transient violation of security or privacy policies may result in leaking private or highly sensitive information, compromising safety, or lead to the interruption of vital public or social services. One approach to gain confidence about the well-being of such a system is to continuously monitor it with respect to a set of formally specified requirements that system should meet at all times. This approach is commonly known as *runtime verification* (RV).

We start with the premise that existing RV techniques cannot monitor a large but vital class of the security and privacy polices, e.g., information flow. Take, for instance, the *non-interference* policy [12], where a low user should not be able to acquire any information about the activities (if any) of the high user by observing independent execution traces. Monitoring this policy would require observing and reasoning about multiple execution traces, whereas existing RV techniques are limited to evaluating only one trace at run time.

In order to specify security and privacy policies, we focus on HyperLTL [8], a temporal logic for expressing *hyperproperties* [9]. A hyperproperty is a set of sets of execution traces. HyperLTL adds explicit and simultaneous quantification over multiple traces to the standard LTL. HyperLTL significantly extends the range of security policies under consideration, including complex

© Springer-Verlag GmbH Germany 2017
A. Legay and T. Margaria (Eds.): TACAS 2017, Part II, LNCS 10206, pp. 77–93, 2017.
DOI: 10.1007/978-3-662-54580-5_5

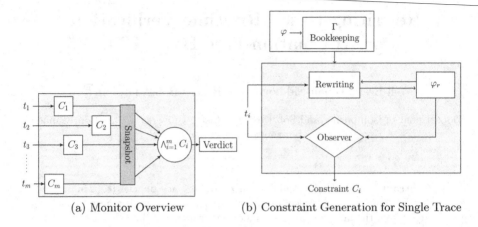

(a) Monitor Overview   (b) Constraint Generation for Single Trace

Fig. 1. RV framework for HyperLTL

information-flow properties like generalized non-interference, declassification, and quantitative non-interference. For example, the following is a HyperLTL formula:

$$\varphi = \forall\pi.\forall\pi'.\, a_\pi \;\rightarrow\; \mathbf{F} b_{\pi'}$$

It states that for any pair of traces π and π', if proposition a holds in the initial state of π, then proposition b should eventually hold in trace π'. To describe the challenges in monitoring HyperLTL specifications, consider formula φ and two traces $t = cde$ and $t' = acddb$. These traces individually (e.g., if π and π' are both instantiated by t), satisfy the formula, but collectively (e.g., if π is instantiated by t and π' by t') do not. If a monitor first observes trace t and then t', it has to somehow remember that b never occurred in t and declare violation as soon as it observes a in the initial state of t'. Thus, a HyperLTL monitor has to be memeoryful; i.e., the monitoring algorithm has to be able to memorize the status of propositions of interest in the past traces to be able to reason about current and future traces.

With this motivation, in this paper, we introduce a novel RV algorithm for monitoring the alternation-free fragment of (i.e., $\forall^*$ and $\exists^*$) HyperLTL (in Sect. 4, we will argue that alternating formulas cannot be monitored using a runtime technique only). Our algorithm takes as input a formula φ and a finite but unbounded-size set T of finite traces (see Fig. 1(a)). The traces in T can be produced by multiple sequential terminating or concurrent executions of a system under inspection. This means that the traces in T can grow in number and/or length at run time. The algorithm works as follows (see Fig. 1(b)):

- First, given φ, it identifies the propositions and possibly simple Boolean expressions that need bookkeeping using a function Γ.
- Then, for each trace $t_i \in T$, by incorporating the elements returned by Γ, the monitor generates a constraint C_i. This constraint basically encapsulates two things. It

1. encodes what the monitor has observed in t_i with respect to the elements returned by Γ, so it can reason about new incoming traces as well as existing traces growing in length, and
2. rewrites the inner LTL formula in φ using Havelund and Rosu's algorithm [13] and obtains a formula φ_r.

Hence, the resulting constraint C_i encodes the full memory of all relevant things that has occurred in t_i.

- At any point of time, the conjunction $\bigwedge_{i=1}^{m} C_i$ where m is the number of traces being monitored, determines the current RV verdict (see Fig. 1(a)). That is, the result of simplification of the conjunction shows whether φ has been satisfied, violated, or currently impossible to tell (i.e., it can go either way in the future).

Finally, we note that although the number and length of the generated constraints are theoretically unbounded, this can be prevented by making practical assumptions. One example is to incorporate a synchronization mechanism that ensures that the difference in length of traces do not grow over a certain bound. Furthermore, the complexity of our algorithm is detached from the number of trace quantifiers in a given HyperLTL formula.

Organization. The rest of the paper is organized as follows. Section 2 presents the syntax and semantics of HyperLTL. In Sect. 3, we introduce our finite semantics for HyperLTL. Section 4 discusses challenges in monitoring HyperLTL formulas. Subsequently, the components of our RV algorithm are presented in Sects. 5 and 6. Related work is discussed in Sect. 7. Finally, we make concluding remarks and discuss future work in Sect. 8.

2 Background

Let AP be a finite set of *atomic propositions* and $\Sigma = 2^{AP}$ be the finite *alphabet*. We call each element of Σ a *letter* (or an *event*). Throughout the paper, Σ^ω denotes the set of all infinite sequences (called *traces*) over Σ, and Σ^* denotes the set of all finite traces over Σ. For a trace $t \in \Sigma^\omega$ (or $t \in \Sigma^*$), $t[i]$ denotes the ith element of t, where $i \in \mathbb{Z}_{\geq 0}$. Also, $t[0, i]$ denotes the prefix of t up to and including i, and $t[i, \infty]$ is written to denote the infinite suffix of t beginning with element i. By, $|t|$ we mean the length of (finite or infinite) trace t.

Now, let u be a finite trace and v be a finite or infinite trace. We denote the concatenation of u and v by $\sigma = uv$. Also, $u \leq \sigma$ denotes the fact that u is a prefix of σ. Finally, if U is a set of finite traces and V is a finite or infinite set of traces, then the prefix relation $\leq$ on sets of traces is defined as:

$$U \leq V \equiv \forall u \in U. (\exists v \in V. u \leq v)$$

Note that V may contain traces that have no prefix in U.

2.1 HyperLTL

Clarkson and Schneider [9] proposed the notion of *hyperproperties* as a means to express security policies that cannot be expressed by traditional properties. A hyperproperty is a set of sets of execution traces. Thus, a hyperproperty essentially defines a set of systems that respect a policy. HyperLTL [8] is a logic for syntactic representation of hyperproperties. It generalizes LTL by allowing explicit quantification over multiple execution traces simultaneously.

Syntax. The set of HyperLTL formulas is inductively defined by the grammar as follows:

$$\varphi :: = \exists \pi . \varphi \mid \forall \pi . \varphi \mid \phi$$
$$\phi :: = a_\pi \mid \neg \phi \mid \phi \vee \phi \mid \phi \, \mathbf{U} \, \phi \mid \mathbf{X} \phi$$

where $a \in AP$ and π is a trace variable from an infinite supply of variables $\mathcal{V}$. Similar to LTL, $\mathbf{U}$ and $\mathbf{X}$ are the 'until' and 'next' operators, respectively. Other standard temporal connectives are defined as syntactic sugar as follows: $\varphi_1 \rightarrow \varphi_2 = \neg \varphi_1 \vee \varphi_2$, $\varphi_1 \wedge \varphi_2 = \neg(\neg \varphi_1 \vee \neg \varphi_2)$, $\mathtt{true} = a_\pi \vee \neg a_\pi$, $\mathtt{false} = \neg \mathtt{true}$, $\mathbf{F} \phi = \mathtt{true} \, \mathbf{U} \, \phi$, and $\mathbf{G} \phi = \neg \mathbf{F} \neg \phi$. Quantified formulas $\exists \pi$ and $\forall \pi$ are read as 'along some trace π' and 'along all traces π', respectively.

Semantics. A formula φ in HyperLTL satisfied by a set of traces T is written as $\Pi \models_T \varphi$, where trace assignment $\Pi : \mathcal{V} \rightarrow \Sigma^\omega$ is a partial function mapping trace variables to traces. $\Pi[\pi \rightarrow t]$ denotes the same function as Π, except that π is mapped to trace t. The validity judgment for HyperLTL is defined as follows:

$$
\begin{aligned}
\Pi &\models_T \exists \pi . \varphi & &\text{iff } \exists t \in T . \Pi[\pi \rightarrow t] \models_T \varphi \\
\Pi &\models_T \forall \pi . \varphi & &\text{iff } \forall t \in T . \Pi[\pi \rightarrow t] \models_T \varphi \\
\Pi &\models_T a_\pi & &\text{iff } a \in \Pi(\pi)[0] \\
\Pi &\models_T \neg \phi & &\text{iff } \Pi \not\models_T \phi \\
\Pi &\models_T \phi_1 \vee \phi_2 & &\text{iff } (\Pi \models_T \phi_1) \vee (\Pi \models_T \phi_2) \\
\Pi &\models_T \mathbf{X} \phi & &\text{iff } \Pi[1, \infty] \models_T \phi \\
\Pi &\models_T \phi_1 \mathbf{U} \phi_2 & &\text{iff } \exists i \geq 0 . (\Pi[i, \infty] \models_T \phi_2 \wedge \\
& & & \quad \forall j \in [0, i) . \Pi[j, \infty] \models_T \phi_1)
\end{aligned}
$$

where the trace assignment suffix $\Pi[i, \infty]$ denotes the trace assignment $\Pi' = \Pi(\pi)[i, \infty]$ for all π. If $\Pi \models_T \phi$ holds for the empty assignment Π, then T satisfies ϕ.

Example. Non-interference (NI) security policy requires any pair of traces with the same initial low observation to remain indistinguishable for low users, yet low inputs will be unaltered, irrespective of the the high inputs. This policy can be specified by the following HyperLTL formula:

$$\forall \pi . \forall \pi' . (\mathbf{G} \lambda_H(\pi') \wedge \mathbf{G} \neg (\bigwedge_{a \in H} a_\pi \leftrightarrow a_{\pi'})) \rightarrow \mathbf{G}(\bigwedge_{a \in L} a_\pi \leftrightarrow a_{\pi'})$$

Where $\mathbf{G} \lambda_H(\pi')$ denotes all the high variables in π' that hold the value λ, and H and L are the high and low variables in their respected security levels.

3 Finite Semantics for HyperLTL

In this section, we present our finite semantics for HyperLTL, inspired by the finite semantics of LTL [15]. For a finite trace t, let $t[i,j]$ denote the subtrace of t from position i up to and including position j:

$$t[i,j] \;=\; \begin{cases} \epsilon & \text{if} \quad i > |t| \\ t[i, \min(j, |t| - 1)] & \text{otherwise} \end{cases}$$

where ϵ is the empty trace. We let $t[i,..]$ denote $t[i, |t| - 1]$.

Let trace assignment $\Pi_F : \mathcal{V} \to \Sigma^*$ be a partial function mapping trace variables to *finite* traces. Similar to the infinite semantics, $\Pi_F[\pi \to t]$ denotes the same function as Π_F, except that π is mapped to finite trace t. We consider two truth values for the finite semantics: $\top$ and $\bot$. To distinguish finite from infinite semantics, we use $[\Pi_F \models_T \varphi]$ to denote the valuation of HyperLTL formula φ for a set T of finite traces. The finite semantics for Boolean operators '$\vee$' and '$\neg$' as well as for the trace quantifiers '$\forall$' and '$\exists$' are identical to those of infinite semantics. We define the finite semantics of HyperLTL for temporal operators as follows:

$$[\Pi_F \models_T \forall/\exists\pi.\varphi] = \begin{cases} \top & \text{if} \quad \forall/\exists t \in T.[\Pi_F[\pi \to t] \models_T \varphi] = \top \\ \bot & \text{otherwise} \end{cases}$$

$$[\Pi_F \models_T \phi_1 \vee \phi_2] = \begin{cases} \bot & \text{if} \quad [\Pi_F \models_T \phi_1] = \bot \wedge [\Pi_F \models_T \phi_2] = \bot \\ \top & \text{otherwise} \end{cases}$$

$$[\Pi_F \models_T \neg\phi] = \begin{cases} \bot & \text{if} \quad [\Pi_F \models_T \phi] = \top \\ \top & \text{otherwise} \end{cases}$$

$$[\Pi_F \models_T \mathbf{X}\,\varphi] = \begin{cases} [\Pi_F[1,..] \models_T \varphi] & \text{if} \quad \Pi[1,..] \neq \epsilon \\ \bot & \text{otherwise} \end{cases}$$

$$[\Pi_F \models_T \bar{\mathbf{X}}\,\varphi] = \begin{cases} [\Pi_F[1,..] \models_T \varphi] & \text{if} \quad \Pi[1,..] \neq \epsilon \\ \top & \text{otherwise} \end{cases}$$

$$[\Pi_F \models_T \varphi_1 \,\mathbf{U}\, \varphi_2] = \begin{cases} \top & \text{if} \quad \exists i \geq 0 : \Pi_F[i,..] \neq \epsilon \wedge [\Pi_F[i,..] \models_T \varphi_2] = \top \wedge \\ & \quad\quad \forall j \in [0,i) : [\Pi_F[j,..] \models_T \varphi_1] = \top \\ \bot & \text{otherwise} \end{cases}$$

where $\bar{X}$ denotes the 'weak next' operator.

Example. Consider formula $\phi = \forall \pi_1. \forall \pi_2.\ a_{\pi_1}\ \mathbf{U}\ b_{\pi_2}$ and $T = \{t_1 = aaab, t_2 = aab, t_3 = aab\}$. Although traces t_1, t_2, and t_3 individually satisfy the formula ϕ, we have $[\Pi_F \models_T \varphi] = \perp$, as there does not exist a position, where each pair of traces agree on the position of b. Now consider formula $\varphi' = \forall \pi_1. \forall \pi_2.\mathbf{F}a_{\pi_1} \wedge \mathbf{F}b_{\pi_2}$ and let $T' = \{**a*b,\ *b**a\}$. We have $[\Pi_F \models_{T'} \varphi'] = \top$.

4   Challenges in Monitoring HyperLTL Formulas

Let us assume we are to monitor a finite but unbounded-size set T of finite traces with respect to a HyperLTL formula φ. The traces in T can be produced by multiple sequential terminating or concurrent executions of a system under inspection. This means that traces in T can grow in number and/or length at run time. Unlike conventional runtime monitoring techniques, where verification decision only depends upon one current execution, monitoring T for φ may depend on the past, future, or concurrent evolution of the traces in T. Thus, a monitor for φ needs to bookkeep the occurrence (and even not occurrence) of certain events to be able to reason about φ at run time. In the following, we outline a set of challenges which need to be addressed in order to develop a monitoring algorithm.

Alternating Formulas. Let $\varphi = \forall \pi. \exists \pi'.\psi$. Verifying this formula requires us to show that *for all* traces in T, there exists a trace that satisfies ψ. However, since the number of traces in T may grow, a runtime monitor can never prove or disprove φ. This argument holds in general for $\forall^*\exists^*$ and $\exists^*\forall^*$ formulas. This is the main reason that in the remainder of this paper, we will only focus on the alternation-free fragment of HyperLTL. Observe that for $\forall^*$ (respectively, $\exists^*$) formulas, it is possible to compute verdict $\perp$ (respectively, $\top$) at run time.

Inter-trace Dependencies. Reasoning about φ by observing individual traces in T is clearly not sufficient. Progression through traces in T requires to keep information about the past or concurrent traces in T. One root cause of this is due to the existence of a disjunction in φ involving two distinct trace variables. For example, let $\phi = \forall \pi_1. \forall \pi_2.\ a_{\pi_1} \rightarrow \mathbf{F}b_{\pi_2}$. Now, consider two traces $t_1 = dcf$ and $t_2 = aeb$, where $AP = \{a, b, c, d, e, f\}$. Note that traces t_1 and t_2, individually satisfy φ, but they collectively violate φ, as event b does not occur in t_1.

Time of Occurrence of Events. Reasoning about some formulas requires bookkeeping the time of occurrence of some propositions in each trace. For example, consider formula $\varphi_1 = \forall \pi_1. \forall \pi_2.\ a_{\pi_1}\,\mathbf{U}\,b_{\pi_2}$ and traces $t_1 = aab$, $t_2 = ab$, and $t_3 = aaaab$. Although, each trace individually satisfies the formula, any pair of them violates the formula, as event b occurs at different times. This can become even more complex when the occurrence of some propositions needs to agree across multiple traces and multiple times. An example of such a formula is $\varphi_2 = \forall \pi_1. \forall \pi_2. \forall \pi_3.\ (a_{\pi_1}\ \mathbf{U}\ b_{\pi_2})\ \mathbf{U}\ c_{\pi_3}$, where the first occurrence of c and every occurrence of b need to be agreed across all traces in T. For example, for traces $t_1 = (ab)a(ac)(ac)b$, $t_2 = (ab)a(ac)(a)(b)$, and $t_3 = a(ac)(ac)b$, traces t_1 and t_2 agree on times of occurrence of b and c, but trace t_3 violates this agreement, thus violating formula φ_2. Yet other examples are formula $\varphi_3 = \forall\pi_1.\forall\pi_2.\ \mathbf{G}(a_{\pi_1} \to a_{\pi_2})$ (which requires all traces to agree on each occurrence of a) and the non-interference formula discussed in Sect. 2.

5   Identifying Propositions of Interest

The challenges and examples outlined in Sect. 4 suggest that monitoring a Hyper-LTL formula requires the identification of propositions which shape the trace agreement to be followed amongst distinct traces. We call this process *bookkeeping*, denote $\mathcal{BK}$ as a set of all elements which require bookkeeping, and Γ as the function that computes $\mathcal{BK}$.

We note that only the structure of the HyperLTL formula contributes to the elements of $\mathcal{BK}$. More precisely, the 'until' operator is the main contributor to $\mathcal{BK}$, as its semantics (in particular, the existential quantifier) may delineate the existence of an index for satisfaction of some propositions across multiple traces. Moreover, we may need to bookkeep Boolean expressions (and not just atomic propositions). We may prefix elements of $\mathcal{BK}$ by either # or $\mathbf{X}$. Prefixing an element by # means that only the first occurrence of the element needs to be bookkept. Prefixing by $\mathbf{X}$ means that bookkeeping starts from the next state.

Examples. In formula $\forall\pi_1.\forall\pi_2.\forall\pi_3.(a_{\pi_1}\ \mathbf{U}b_{\pi_2})\ \mathbf{U}c_{\pi_3}$, we will have $\mathcal{BK} = \{b, \#c\}$, meaning every occurrence of b and only the first occurrence of c should be memorized. For formula $\forall\pi_1.\forall\pi_2.a_{\pi_1}\ \mathbf{U}\ (b_{\pi_2} \vee c_{\pi_2})$, we have $\mathcal{BK} = \{\#(b \vee c)\}$. However, for formula $\forall\pi_1.\forall\pi_2.\forall\pi_3.a_{\pi_1}\ \mathbf{U}\ (b_{\pi_2} \vee c_{\pi_3})$, we have $\mathcal{BK} = \{\#b, \#c\}$. Finally, for formula $\forall\pi.\forall\pi'.\mathbf{X}(a_\pi\ \mathbf{U}b_{\pi'})$, we will have $\mathcal{BK} = \{\mathbf{X}\#b\}$.

Our bookkeeping recursive function Γ takes as input a HyperLTL formula, a set of trace variables $\mathcal{V}$ (initially empty), and a Boolean value (initially *false*), and it returns as output the set $\mathcal{BK}$, defined in Fig. 2. The function works as follows. The first three cases are straightforward, as a HyperLTL formula involving only a proposition requires bookkeeping if it is under the scope of an 'until' operator, whereas operators $\neg$ and $\mathbf{X}$ allow the recursive application of Γ function to the formula ϕ. The symbol $\odot$ denotes the application of unary operators ($\neg$, # and $\mathbf{X}$) to the elements of set $\mathcal{BK}$ (e.g., $\neg \odot \{a, b\} = \{\neg a, \neg b\}$).

The next case $\phi_1\mathbf{U}\phi_2$, we require further matching on the structure of both ϕ_1 and ϕ_2, as follows:

- **(Case 1: Both operands are propositions).** In this case, Γ returns $\{\#b\}$ if π and π' are bound by different quantifiers or removing π' from $\mathcal{V}$ does not result in an empty set. Otherwise, Γ returns the empty set. For example, consider two formulas $\forall\pi_1.a_{\pi_1}\ \mathbf{U}\ b_{\pi_1}$ and $\forall\pi_1.\forall\pi_2.a_{\pi_1}\ \mathbf{U}\ b_{\pi_2}$. The first formula does not require any trace agreement whereas the second does require a trace agreement due to the scope of the trace quantifiers.

$$\Gamma(a_\pi, \mathcal{V}, k) = \begin{cases} \{\#a\} & \text{if} \quad (k = true \wedge \mathcal{V} - \{\pi'\} \neq \emptyset) \\ \{\} & \text{otherwise} \end{cases}$$

$$\Gamma(\mathbf{X}\phi, \mathcal{V}, k) = \mathbf{X} \odot \Gamma(\phi, \mathcal{V}, k)$$
$$\Gamma(\neg\phi, \mathcal{V}, k) = \neg \odot \Gamma(\phi, \mathcal{V}, k)$$

$\Gamma(\phi_1 \mathbf{U} \phi_2, \mathcal{V}, k) =$
match ϕ_1 ϕ_2 **with**

$\quad | \ a_\pi \quad b'_\pi \quad \rightarrow \begin{cases} \{\#b\} & \text{if} \quad (\mathcal{V} - \{\pi'\} \neq \emptyset \vee \pi \neq \pi') \\ \{\} & \text{otherwise} \end{cases}$

$\quad | \ a_\pi \quad - \quad \rightarrow \Gamma(\phi_2, \mathcal{V} \cup \{\pi\}, k := true)$

$\quad | \ - \quad - \quad \rightarrow \begin{cases} \Gamma(\phi_2, \mathcal{V} \cup trace\_vars(\phi_1), k := true) \\ \qquad \text{if } \phi_1 \notin \text{HYPERLTL}_1(\mathbf{U}) \\ \#^{-1} \odot \Gamma(\phi_1, \mathcal{V}, k := true) \cup \\ \# \odot \Gamma(\phi_2, \mathcal{V} \cup trace\_vars(\phi_1), k := true) \quad \text{otherwise} \end{cases}$

$\Gamma(\phi_1 \vee \phi_2, \mathcal{V}, k) =$
match ϕ_1 ϕ_2 **with**

$\quad | \ a_\pi \quad b'_\pi \quad \rightarrow \begin{cases} \{a \vee b\} & \text{if} \quad k = true \wedge \pi = \pi' \\ \{a\} \cap \{b\} & \text{if} \quad k = true \wedge \pi \neq \pi' \\ \{\} & \text{otherwise} \end{cases}$

$\quad | \ a_\pi \quad - \quad \rightarrow \begin{cases} \{a\} \cup \Gamma(\phi_2, \mathcal{V}, k) & \text{if} \quad k = true \\ \Gamma(\phi_2, \mathcal{V}, k) & \text{otherwise} \end{cases}$

$\quad | \ - \quad b'_\pi \quad \rightarrow \begin{cases} \Gamma(\phi_1, \mathcal{V}, k) \cup \{b\} & \text{if} \quad k = true \\ \Gamma(\phi_1, \mathcal{V}, k) & \text{otherwise} \end{cases}$

$\quad | \ - \quad - \quad \rightarrow \Gamma(\phi_1, \mathcal{V}, k) \cup \Gamma(\phi_2, \mathcal{V}, k)$

Fig. 2. Bookkeeping function Γ

- **(Case 2: Only the left operand is a proposition).** In this case, we store the trace variable associated with a in set $\mathcal{V}$ and invoke Γ recursively to formula ϕ_2. We also set the value of Boolean variable k to $true$ which indicates that the original formula ϕ includes an 'until' operator. For example, for formula $\forall\pi.a_\pi \mathbf{U}(b_\pi \mathbf{U} c_\pi)$, recursing through Γ will result in an empty set since there were no variations in the trace variables, whereas for formula $\forall\pi_1.\forall\pi_2.a_{\pi_1} \mathbf{U}(b_{\pi_1} \mathbf{U} c_{\pi_2})$, the Γ function will simply return $\{\#c\}$.
- **(Case 3: None of the operands are propositions).** In this case, we recurse through ϕ_1 only if it contains an 'until' operator, where $trace\_vars(\phi)$ denotes the set of trace variables found in ϕ. Furthermore, we recurse through ϕ_2 and indicate that any elements produced need to be tracked only once (i.e., their first occurrence). Moreover, we prefix the recursion of Γ on ϕ_1 by symbol $\#^{-1}$, which helps to remove the prefix $\#$ for elements which require tracking more than once. The result will consist of the union of both produced sets. For example, for formula $\forall\pi_1.\forall\pi_2.\forall\pi_3.\forall\pi_4.(a_{\pi_1} \mathbf{U} b_{\pi_2})\mathbf{U}(c_{\pi_3} \mathbf{U} d_{\pi_4})$, we have

$\mathcal{BK} = \{b, \#d\}$. Note that expressions $\#^{-1}\#a$ and $\#\#b$ are equivalent to a and $\#b$, respectively.

The last inductive case includes an 'or' ($\vee$), which also requires further matching on the structure of formulas ϕ_1 and ϕ_2. Here, we consider the condition of k, which reflects the case when $\phi_1 \vee \phi_2$ is under the scope of an 'until' operator. For example, formula $\forall \pi_1.\forall \pi_2.a_{\pi_1} \mathbf{U} (b_{\pi_2} \vee c_{\pi_2})$. The application of Γ function will result in $\Gamma(b_{\pi_2} \vee c_{\pi_2}, \mathcal{V}, k := true)$, which further results in $\{\#(b \vee c)\}$. On the contrary, the case of formula $\forall \pi_1.\forall \pi_2.\forall \pi_3.a_{\pi_1} \mathbf{U} (b_{\pi_2} \vee c_{\pi_3})$, the Γ function will return $\{\#b, \#c\}$ due to the disparity of trace variables.

Theorem 1 (Soundness and optimality of Γ function). *Given a HyperLTL formula φ and assuming we have set T such that $[\Pi_F \models_T \varphi] = \top$ then*

– *Γ function returns all the propositions required for bookkeeping.*
– *Given the set $\mathcal{BK}$, every element $k \in \mathcal{BK}$ is included in some trace agreement described by φ.*

6 Monitoring Algorithm

6.1 Algorithm Sketch

Given an alternation-free HyperLTL formula φ of the form $\forall^*$, our algorithm consists of the following elements:

1. *Monitor:* In order to monitor φ, we begin by intaking an event for a particular trace and begin to generate the constraints. At any point of time, we can take a snapshot of our system and utilize our satisfaction function SAT to find the RV verdict (see Fig. 1(a)).
2. *Constraint Handler:* Next, we manipulate φ according to its structure. Disjunctions are divided and treated separately to detect which half prompted the satisfaction. Each sub-formula of the disjunction is then subject to ConstraintRewriting. Temporal formulas without disjunction do not undergo any manipulation before being sent to ConstraintRewriting.
3. *Constraint Rewriting:* Initially, φ is stripped of its quantifiers. This allows for rewriting using the technique in [22] to evaluate the altered formula φ_r. The events are examined against the propositions or Boolean expressions in $\mathcal{BK}$ and the satisfaction of φ_r to generate the corresponding constraints.
4. *Satisfaction of Function SAT:* On each invocation of the SAT function, we compute the conjunction of all the constraints collectively. If SAT returns false, then φ is violated. Otherwise, the constraints are further checked for possible refinement by checking the membership of other generated constraints.

Observe that a formula of the form $\forall^*$ cannot be evaluated to $\top$. This would require the full set of all possible system traces, which is not possible at run time. We note that monitoring a formula of the form $\exists^*$ can be achieved by simply monitoring its negation which would be of the form $\forall^*$.

6.2   Algorithm Details

We utilize the following HyperLTL formula as a running example to demonstrate the steps of our proposed algorithm.

$$\forall \pi_1.\forall \pi_2.\forall \pi_3.\forall \pi_4.\ ((a_{\pi_1} \vee b_{\pi_2})\, \mathbf{U}\, c_{\pi_3}) \vee d_{\pi_4}$$

where $AP = \{a, b, c, d\}$. We now describe the algorithm in detail which leads to the overview of Fig. 1.

Algorithm 1 (HyperLTL Monitor). This is our main monitoring algorithm which is comprised of a while loop. We continue to iterate as long as new events associated with a trace come in and until we find a violation. On Lines 2–3, we check for a new trace and then add it to our set of traces M. Given that the incoming event is associated with some trace t_j, at Line 4, we call ConstraintsHandler for t_j, which returns constraint C_j. Lines 5–6 deal with the process of taking a snapshot of our system to determine the RV verdict using function SAT. Finally, if the returned value from function SAT is false (Lines 7–9), then we have found a violation and return $\perp$ (Line 10). Otherwise, we continue to iterate through the while loop.

Algorithm 2 (Constraint Handler). In this algorithm, we treat the given HyperLTL formula according to its structure. The algorithm is recursively applied to the given formula based on different cases. The first block of the algorithm (Lines 1–10) handles the case ($\varphi = \phi_1 \vee \phi_2$), where the given (sub-) formula is a disjunction. In particular, we call ConstraintsHandler function for both ϕ_1 and ϕ_2 (Lines 2–3). We also need to pass the information about the elements of $\mathcal{BK}$ which are associated with ϕ_1 and ϕ_2 (as given by $\mathcal{BK}_{\phi_i}$). In our running example, we have $\phi_1 = ((a_{\pi_1} \vee b_{\pi_2})\, \mathbf{U}\, c_{\pi_3})$ and $\phi_2 = d_{\pi_4}$. In case both values from previous steps are false, then we have found a violation and the algorithm returns false (Lines 4–5). On the other hand, if one of the values from Lines 2 and 3 is a constraint, then we return the corresponding constraint (Lines 6–7). Moreover, if both values have generated constraints, we return them both (Lines 10) meaning that any one of them can influence the verdict in future.

Next block in the algorithm (Lines 12–22) handles the case when the input formula contains an 'until' operators with a disjunction on the left operand with a disparity in corresponding trace quantifiers. We invoke ConstraintsHandler function for both operands of '$\vee$'; i.e., ϕ_L and ϕ_R (Lines 13–14). In our running example, $\phi_1 = ((a_{\pi_1} \vee b_{\pi_2})\, \mathbf{U}\, c_{\pi_3})$ matches this case and a_{π_1} and b_{π_2} will go through ConstraintsHandler. If both values in Lines 13 and 14 result in false, then the formula has been violated and we return false.

However, if only one of the sides returns some constraints, then we return false and alternating constraint for further refinement (Lines 17–20). Finally, if both sides satisfy the formula, then we return a combination of the returned values of Lines 13 and 14. This allows us to refine the constraints from the function SAT in Algorithm 4.

Algorithm 1. HyperLTL Monitor

Input: HyperLTL formula ϕ, $\mathcal{BK}$, set of incoming traces M
Output: $\lambda = \{\bot, ?\}$
1 while getEvent(e_i, t_m) do
2   if newIncomingTrace(t_m) then
3        $M \leftarrow M \cup \{t_m\}$
4     $C_m \leftarrow$ ConstraintsHandler $(\phi, \mathcal{BK}, e_i)$
5   Take a snapshot for constraints $C = \{C_1, C_2, \cdots, C_m\}$ at time instant
6     $\beta \leftarrow$ SAT(C)
7   if $(\beta = false)$ then
8        $\lambda \leftarrow \bot$
9   break
10 return (λ)

Algorithm 3. ConstraintRewriting

Input: HyperLTL formula φ, $\mathcal{BK}$, e_i
Output: Constraints r
1 $r \leftarrow$ true
2 $\varphi_r \leftarrow$ quantifier-elimination(φ)
3 $\varphi_r \leftarrow$ REWRITE (e_i, φ_r)
4 if $(\varphi_r = false)$ then
5   return φ_r
6 for $(each\ a \in \mathcal{BK}\ s.t.\ e_i \models a)$ do
7     $r \leftarrow r \wedge \mathbf{X}^i a$
8   if $(a = \#a')$ then
9        $\mathcal{BK} \leftarrow \mathcal{BK} \setminus \{a\}$
10 for $(each\ a \in \mathcal{BK}\ s.t.\ a = \mathbf{X}a')$ do
11    $\mathcal{BK} \leftarrow (\mathcal{BK} \setminus \{a\}) \cup \{a'\}$
12 return r

Algorithm 2. ConstraintsHandler

Input: HyperLTL formula ϕ, $\mathcal{BK}$, event e_i
Output: {false, Set of Constraints}
1 if $(\phi = \phi_1 \vee \phi_2)$ then
2     $\psi_1 \leftarrow$ ConstraintsHandler $(\phi_1, \mathcal{BK}_{\phi_1}, e_i)$
3     $\psi_2 \leftarrow$ ConstraintsHandler $(\phi_2, \mathcal{BK}_{\phi_2}, e_i)$
4   if $(\psi_1 = false \wedge \psi_2 = false)$ then
5   return $(false)$
6   else if $(\psi_1 = false)$ then
7   return (ψ_2)
8   else if $(\psi_2 = false)$ then
9   return (ψ_1)
10   else
11   return (ψ_1, ψ_2)
12 else if $(\phi := \phi_1\ \mathbf{U}\ \phi_2 \wedge ((\phi_1 := \phi_L \vee \phi_R) \wedge \neg(\text{samequantifiers}(\phi_L, \phi_R))))$ then
13    $\psi_1 \leftarrow$ ConstraintsHandler $(\phi_L \mathbf{U}\ \phi_2, \mathcal{BK}, e_i)$
14    $\psi_2 \leftarrow$ ConstraintsHandler $(\phi_R \mathbf{U}\ \phi_2, \mathcal{BK}, e_i)$
15   if $(\psi_1 = false \wedge \psi_2 = false)$ then
16   return $(false)$
17   else if $(\psi_1 = false)$ then
18   return $(\psi_2, false)$
19   else if $(\psi_2 = false)$ then
20   return $(false, \psi_1)$
21   else
22   return (ψ_2, ψ_1)
23 else
24    $r \leftarrow$ ConstraintRewriting$(\phi, \mathcal{BK}, e_i)$
25   if $(r = false)$ then
26   return false
27   else
28   return r

The last part of the algorithm (Lines 24–28) invokes the ConstraintRewriting function which return the constraints for other types of formulas. For example, formula $\forall \pi_1.\forall \pi_2.\forall \pi_3.\forall \pi_4.(a_{\pi_1} \mathbf{U} b_{\pi_2})\ \mathbf{U}\ (c_{\pi_3}\ \mathbf{U}\ d_{\pi_4}))$ will directly undergo constraint generation.

Algorithm 3 (Constraints Rewriting). This algorithm generates the constraints (denoted by r) by utilizing the elements of $\mathcal{BK}$. We set the initial value of r to true as we have no violation in the start of the monitoring process. We strip off the quantifiers of our formula φ to convert into its corresponding LTL form φ_r (Line 2). For example, $\forall \pi_1.\forall \pi_2.(a_{\pi_1}\ \mathbf{U}\ b_{\pi_2})$ will be converted to $(a\ \mathbf{U}\ b)$. Then, we apply REWRITE function to formula φ_r with the given event e_i (Line 3).

This function is essentially the rewriting algorithm by Havelund and Rosu [13] (see Algorithm 5). If the event violates our formula then we immediately return the violation (Lines 4–5).

If ϕ is not violated and if the event satisfies any object $a \in \mathcal{BK}$, then a is considered for our constraints (Line 6). Given the position of the event is i in a trace, in Line 7 we administer $\mathbf{X}^i$ on a (i.e., $\mathbf{X}^i a$). The elements of $\mathcal{BK}$ which are prefixed by "#" are removed from $\mathcal{BK}$ as we have indicated that their first appearance is significant (Lines 8–9). In our running example, the invocation of ConstraintRewriting for $a_{\pi_1} \, \mathbf{U} \, c_{\pi_3}$ with set $\mathcal{BK} = \{\#c\}$ and consecutive events of traces $t_1 = (ab)(ab)a(ad)c$, $t_2 = a(abcd)$, $t_3 = c$ will result in $r_1 = \mathbf{X}^4 c$, $r_2 = \mathbf{X}c$ and $r_3 = c$, respectively.

The elements of $\mathcal{BK}$ with "$\mathbf{X}$" operators are considered for upcoming events by stripping one instance of "$\mathbf{X}$" on that element (Lines 10–11). Indeed, the presence of $\mathbf{X}$'s in the elements of $\mathcal{BK}$ delays the observation and expose the corresponding proposition to be observed for constraint generation in the subsequent rounds. Finally, we return our generated constraint r.

Algorithm 4. SAT

Input: Constraint Matrix $\mathcal{C}$
Output: $\lambda = \{\text{false}, ?\}$
1 **Function** SAT $(\mathcal{C})$
2   Initialize m'
3    $columns \leftarrow \max\{|x| \mid x \in \mathcal{C}\}$
4    $existsConstrains \leftarrow$ false
5   **for**
    $(j \leftarrow 0;\ j < columns;\ j{+}{+})$
    do
6      $\beta \leftarrow \bigwedge_{m=1}^{|M|} C_m[j]$
7   **if** $(\beta = \text{false})$ **then**
8       $dropColumn$
9   **else**
10       $m' \leftarrow$
       largest constraint of column j
11   **if** $(\exists t \in$
       $C_{(t,j)}.\neg memberof(t, m')$
       then
12        $dropColumn$
13   **else**
14        $existsConstrains \leftarrow$
        true
15   **if**
    $(existsConstraints = \text{false})$
    then
16   **return** (false)
17   **else**
18   **return** (?)

Algorithm 5. REWRITE

Input: φ_r, e
Output: $\{\text{true}, \text{false}, \phi\}$
1 **match** (φ_r) **with**
2 $\mid (a)$:
3   **if** $(a \in e)$ **then**
4   **return** (true)
5   **else if** $(a \notin e)$ **then**
6   **return** (false)
7 $\mid (\text{true})$:
8   **return** (true)
9 $\mid (\text{false})$:
10   **return** (false)
11 $\mid (\phi_1 \vee \phi_2)$:
12   **return**
    (REWRITE(ϕ_1, e) $\vee$
    REWRITE(ϕ_2, e))
13 $\mid (\phi_1 \, \mathbf{U} \, \phi_2)$:
14   **if** (lastevent (e)) **then**
15   **return**
     (REWRITE(ϕ_2, e))
16   **else**
17   **return**
     (REWRITE(ϕ_2, e) $\vee$
     (REWRITE(ϕ_1, e) $\wedge$
     $(\phi_1 \, \mathbf{U} \, \phi_2)$)))
18 $\mid (\mathbf{X}\phi)$:
19   **if** (lastevent (e)) **then**
20   **return** (false)
21   **else**
22   **return**
     (REWRITE(ϕ, e))

Algorithm 4 (Satisfaction Function). The input of the SAT function is a set consisting of the constraints associated with each trace, i.e., $\mathcal{C} = \{C_1, C_2, \ldots, C_m\}$. We can imagine all these constraints as rows of a matrix. For our running example, we will have $\mathcal{C}_i = [C_i^{(a_{\pi_1} \, \mathbf{U} \, c_{\pi_3})}, C_i^{(b_{\pi_2} \, \mathbf{U} \, c_{\pi_3})}, C_i^{d_{\pi_4}}]$ where i corresponds to i^{th} trace in M. We iterate through the columns for each of the traces and conjunct together their constraints. If they evaluate to `false`, then we can drop the column as traces have found a disagreement (Lines 3–8). If the conjunction is not `false`, we acquire the longest constraint m' of the corresponding column. We then check to see that no constraints associated by other traces disagree by confirming that they are members of m' (Lines 10–11). If one of the constraints disagrees, then we drop the column, or else we have found an agreement of constraints between the traces (Lines 12–14). Finally, we return a violation if we were unable to find any agreement within the constraints between traces (Lines 15–18).

Note that the process of dropping columns indeed results in a refined set of constraints. Since the incoming traces can progress at various speeds, we confirm that the constraints for "slower" traces are in-fact a member of the "fastest" trace's constraints. If no traces contradict the "fastest trace", then this suggests that no disagreement has yet emerged in the system. We resume taking snapshots of the system until a violation is detected.

Theorem 2 (Correctness of Algorithm 1). *Let φ be a HyperLTL formula. Algorithm 1 returns $\bot$ for an input set of traces T iff $[\Pi_F \models_T \varphi] = \bot$.*

6.3 Discussion

Our algorithms reflect that the decision of appropriate consideration for propositions or Boolean expressions, paired with the effective structural division of a HyperLTL formula, and provides an effective way to monitor complex HyperLTL formulas. Additionally, we encode only the minimum information to check that the agreement between traces is delineated according to the observed locations of propositions or Boolean expressions.

A potential drawback of our RV technique is its theoretical unbounded memory requirement. However, this requirement does not influence the cases where the verification is done offline. For online RV we can still use our algorithms for by making practical assumptions. For example, we can incorporate a synchronization mechanism amongst traces to ensure that the difference in length of traces is not beyond some bound. We note that the worst case complexity of Algorithm 1 is $\mathcal{O}(|t| \cdot |T|)$, where $|t|$ is the length of the longest trace in set T. Interestingly, this complexity is independent from the number of trace quantifiers in a given HyperLTL formula. Indeed, the set $\mathcal{BK}$ computed pre-runtime by Γ function provides the means to avoid dependence on the trace quantifiers, which otherwise is polynomial on the order of numbers of quantifiers. We believe that our proposed algorithm is efficient enough to be adopted for the monitoring of security policies in real-world applications.

Note that our proposed algorithm can only be used to monitor alternation-free fragment (i.e., $\forall^*$ and $\exists^*$) of HyperLTL, which can express a wide class of security policies including non-interference and declassification. However, specification of some security policies require alternation in the trace quantifiers. For example, *noninference* [17] specifies that the behavior of low-variables should not change when all high variables are replaced by an arbitrary variable λ, given as follows:

$$\forall \pi.\exists \pi'.(\mathbf{G}\lambda_H(\pi') \wedge \mathbf{G}(\bigwedge_{a \in L} a_\pi \leftrightarrow a_{\pi'})$$

Similarly, generalized non-interference (GNI) [16] also requires alternation in trace quantifiers as it allows non-determinism in the low variables of the system.

7 Related Work

Static Analysis. Sabelfeld and Myers [24] survey the literature focusing on static program analysis for enforcement of security policies. In some cases, with compilers using Just-in-time compilation techniques and dynamic inclusion of code at run time in web browsers, static analysis does not guarantee secure execution at run time. Type systems, frameworks for JavaScript [6] and ML [21] are some approaches to monitor information flow. Several tools [11,18,19] add extensions such as statically checked information flow annotations to Java language. Clark and Hunt [7] present verification of information flow for deterministic interactive programs. On the other hand, our approach is capable of monitoring the subset of hyperproperties described by alternation-free HyperLTL and not just information flow without assistance from static analyzers. In [2], the authors propose a technique for designing runtime monitors based abstract interpretation of the system under inspection.

Dynamic Analysis. Russo and Sabelfeld [23] concentrate on permissive techniques for the enforcement of information flow under flow-sensitivity. It has been shown that in the flow-insensitive case, a sound purely dynamic monitor is more permissive than static analysis. However, they show the impossibility of such a monitor in the flow-sensitive case. A framework for inlining dynamic information flow monitors has been presented by Magazinius et al. [14]. The approach by Chudnov and Naumann [5] uses hybrid analysis instead and argues that due to JIT compilation processes, it is no longer possible to mediate every data and control flow event of the native code. They leverage the results of Russo and Sabelfeld [23] by inlining the security monitors. Chudnov et al. [4] again use hybrid analysis of 2-safety hyperproperties in relational logic. In [1], the authors propose an automata-based RV technique for monitoring only a disjunctive fragment of alternation-free HyperLTL.

Austin and Flanagan [3] implement a purely dynamic monitor, however, restrictions such as "no-sensitive upgrade" were placed. Some techniques deploy taint tracking and labelling of data variables dynamically [20,26]. Zdancewic and Myers [25] verify information flow for concurrent programs. Most of the techniques cited above aim to monitor security policies described solely with two trace quantifiers (without alternation), on observing a single run, whereas, our work is for any hyperproperties that can be described with alternation-free HyperLTL, when multiple runs are observed.

SME. Secure multi-execution [10] is a technique to enforce non-interference. In SME, one executes a program multiple times, once for each security level, using special rules for I/O operations. Outputs are only produced in the execution linked to their security level. Inputs are replaced by default inputs except in executions linked to their security level or higher. Input side effects are supported by making higher-security-level executions reuse inputs obtained in lower-security-level threads. This approach is sound in a deterministic language.

While there are small similarities between SME and our work, there are fundamental differences. SME only focuses on non-interference and aims to enforce it, but there are many critical hyperproperties that differ from non-interference that our method is able to monitor. Thus, SME enforces a security policy at the cost of restricting what it can enforce, whereas our technique monitors a much larger set of policies.

8 Conclusion

In this paper, we introduced an algorithm for monitoring alternation-free fragment of HyperLTL [8], a temporal logic that allows for expressing complex information-flow properties like generalized non-interference, declassification, and quantitative non-interference. The main challenge in designing an RV algorithm for HyperLTL formulas is that reasoning about the formula involves analyzing multiple traces (as opposed to a single trace in traditional RV techniques). Our algorithm has three components: (1) a function that identifies propositions that have to be bookkept across multiple traces, (2) a constraint generator that encodes the occurrence of propositions of interest, and (3) a rewriting module based on the algorithm in [22] that incorporates formula progression with respect to incoming events for traces. In our view, our algorithm is a significant step forward in monitoring sophisticated information-flow security and privacy policies.

Our first step to extend this work will be to implement our algorithm and test it for real-world applications, e.g., in smartphones. For future work, one may consider RV algorithms based on monitor synthesis (as opposed to rewriting). We are also planning to develop techniques for monitoring alternating Hyper-LTL formulas. We believe dealing with such formulas is not possible without assistance from a static analyzer.

References

1. Agrawal, S., Bonakdarpour, B.: Runtime verification of k-safety hyperproperties in HyperLTL. In: Proceedings of the 29th IEEE Computer Security Foundations Symposium (CSF), pp. 239–252 (2016)
2. Assaf, M., Naumann, D.A.: Calculational design of information flow monitors. In: Proceedings of the 29th IEEE Computer Security Foundations Symposium (CSF), pp. 210–224 (2016)
3. Austin, T.H., Flanagan, C.: Efficient purely-dynamic information flow analysis. In: ACM Transactions on Programming Languages and Systems, pp. 113–124 (2009)

4. Chudnov, A., Kuan, G., Naumann, D.A.: Information flow monitoring as abstract interpretation for relational logic. In: IEEE 27th Computer Security Foundations Symposium, CSF 2014, Vienna, Austria, 19–22 July 2014, pp. 48–62 (2014)

5. Chudnov, A., Naumann, D.A.: Information flow monitor inlining. In: Proceedings of CSF, pp. 200–214 (2010)

6. Chugh, R., Meister, J.A., Jhala, R., Lerner, S.: Staged information flow for JavaScript. In: Proceedings of PLDI, pp. 50–62 (2009)

7. Clark, D., Hunt, S.: Non-interference for deterministic interactive programs. In: Degano, P., Guttman, J., Martinelli, F. (eds.) FAST 2008. LNCS, vol. 5491, pp. 50–66. Springer, Heidelberg (2009). doi:10.1007/978-3-642-01465-9_4

8. Clarkson, M.R., Finkbeiner, B., Koleini, M., Micinski, K.K., Rabe, M.N., Sánchez, C.: Temporal logics for hyperproperties. In: Abadi, M., Kremer, S. (eds.) POST 2014. LNCS, vol. 8414, pp. 265–284. Springer, Heidelberg (2014). doi:10.1007/978-3-642-54792-8_15

9. Clarkson, M.R., Schneider, F.B.: Hyperproperties. J. Comput. Secur. **18**(6), 1157–1210 (2010)

10. Devriese, D., Piessens, F.: Noninterference through secure multi-execution. In: 31st IEEE Symposium on Security and Privacy, S&P, pp. 109–124 (2010)

11. Enck, W., Gilbert, P., Chun, B.-G., Cox, L.P., Jung, J., McDaniel, P., Sheth, A.N.: TaintDroid: an information-flow tracking system for realtime privacy monitoring on smartphones. In: Proceedings of the 9th USENIX Conference on Operating Systems Design and Implementation, OSDI 2010, Vancouver, BC, Canada, pp. 393–407. USENIX Association, Berkeley (2010). http://dl.acm.org/citation.cfm?id=1924943.1924971

12. Goguen, J.A., Meseguer, J.: Security policies and security models. In: IEEE Symposium on Security and Privacy, pp. 11–20 (1982)

13. Havelund, K., Rosu, G.: Monitoring programs using rewriting. In: Automated Software Engineering (ASE), pp. 135–143 (2001)

14. Magazinius, J., Russo, A., Sabelfeld, A.: On-the-fly inlining of dynamic security monitors. Comput. Secur. **31**(7), 827–843 (2012)

15. Manna, Z., Pnueli, A.: Temporal Verification of Reactive Systems - Safety. Springer, Heidelberg (1995)

16. McCullough, D.: Noninterference and the composability of security properties. In: IEEE Symposium on Security and Privacy, pp. 177–186 (1988)

17. McLean, J.: A general theory of composition for trace sets closed under selective interleaving functions. In: IEEE Computer Society Symposium on Research in Security and Privacy, pp. 79–93 (1994)

18. Myers, A.C.: JFlow: practical mostly-static information flow control. In: Proceedings of Conference Record of the Annual ACM Symposium on Principles of Programming Languages, pp. 228–241 (1999)

19. Myers, A.C., Liskov, B.: Complete, safe information flow with decentralized labels (1998)

20. Nair, S., Simpson, P.N.D., Crispo, B., Tanenbaum, A.S.: A virtual machine based information flow control system for policy enforcement. Electron. Notes Theor. Comput. Sci. **197**(1), 3–16 (2008)

21. Pottier, F., Simonet, V.: Information flow inference for ML. In: Proceedings of Conference Record of the Annual ACM Symposium on Principles of Programming Languages, pp. 319–330 (2002)

22. Rosu, G., Havelund, K.: Rewriting-based techniques for runtime verification. Autom. Softw. Eng. **12**(2), 151–197 (2005)

23. Russo, A., Sabelfeld, A.: Dynamic vs. static flow-sensitive security analysis. In: Proceedings of the XXrd IEEE Computer Security Foundations Symposium (CSF), pp. 186–199 (2010)
24. Sabelfeld, A., Myers, A.C.: Language-based information-flow security. IEEE J. Sel. Areas Commun. **21**(1), 5–19 (2003)
25. Zdancewic, S., Myers, A.C.: Observational determinism for concurrent program security. In: Computer Security Foundations Workshop, p. 29 (2003)
26. Zhu, Y., Jung, J., Song, D., Kohno, T., Wetherall, D.: Privacy scope: a precise information flow tracking system for finding application leaks. Technical report, EECS Department, University of California, Berkeley, October 2009

Almost Event-Rate Independent Monitoring of Metric Temporal Logic

David Basin, Bhargav Nagaraja Bhatt[✉], and Dmitriy Traytel[✉]

Department of Computer Science, Institute of Information Security, ETH Zürich,
Zürich, Switzerland
{bhargav.bhatt,traytel}@inf.ethz.ch

Abstract. A monitoring algorithm is trace-length independent if its space consumption does not depend on the number of events processed. The analysis of many monitoring algorithms has aimed at establishing trace-length independence. But a trace-length independent monitor's space consumption can depend on characteristics of the trace other than its size.

We put forward the stronger notion of *event-rate independence*, where the monitor's space usage does not depend on the event rate. This property is critical for monitoring voluminous streams of events arriving at a varying rate. Some previously proposed algorithms for past-only temporal logics satisfy this new property. However, when dealing with future operators, the traditional approach of using a queue to wait for future obligations to be resolved is not event-rate independent. We propose a new algorithm that supports metric past and bounded future operators and is almost event-rate independent, where "almost" denotes a logarithmic dependence on the event rate: the algorithm must store the event rate as a number. We compare our algorithm with traditional ones, providing evidence that almost event-rate independence matters in practice.

1 Introduction

Rules are integral to society. Companies and administrations are highly regulated and subjected to rules, laws, and policies that they must comply to and demonstrate their compliance to. In many domains, the rules are sufficiently precise that automatic monitoring tools can be used to prove compliance or identify violations.

A monitoring tool should solve the standard (*online*) *monitoring problem*: Given a stream of time-stamped data, called events, and a policy formulated in a temporal logic, decide whether the policy is satisfied at every point in the stream [6,13,17]. Compared with other verification techniques, the monitoring problem is attractive because it can be solved in a scalable way. Monitoring algorithms usually have a modest time complexity per inspected event. In contrast, keeping the space requirements low for high-velocity event streams is more challenging; this is precisely the problem we tackle here.

© Springer-Verlag GmbH Germany 2017
A. Legay and T. Margaria (Eds.): TACAS 2017, Part II, LNCS 10206, pp. 94–112, 2017.
DOI: 10.1007/978-3-662-54580-5_6

Monitoring algorithms have been analyzed in the past with respect to their space requirements. The notion of *trace-length independence* requires a monitor's space complexity to be constant in the overall number of events. In some settings, only algorithms satisfying this property are considered worthy of being called monitors [5]. Trace-length independence aims at distinguishing monitors that can handle huge volumes of data from those that cannot. The classic 3 V characterization by volume, velocity, and variety [15], however, tells us that this is only one challenging aspect of big data. Here, we account for another aspect: velocity or event rate.

We propose a new notion, *event-rate independence*, which states that a monitor's space requirement does not depend on the number of events in a fixed time unit. We survey existing monitoring algorithms (Sect. 2) and identify several for past-only linear temporal logic (ptLTL) [10] and its extension with metric intervals (ptMTL) [19] that have this property. No such monitors exist, however, that support future operators.

We tackle this problem, focusing on *metric temporal logic (MTL)* [12] with bounded future operators interpreted over streams of time-stamped events (Sect. 3). This discrete semantics is based on integer time-stamps, which mirrors the imprecision of physical clocks. A finite number of consecutive events, each defining a *time-point*, might, however, carry the same time-stamp. The event rate is defined as the number of time-points per time-stamp. There are several trace-length independent monitoring algorithms for MTL on streams with a bounded event rate, but none that are event-rate independent or even trace-length independent on streams with an unbounded event rate.

From a traditional standpoint, event-rate independent monitors for MTL seem impossible: future operators require the monitor to wait before it can output a *Boolean verdict* on whether the formula holds. The sheer number of events that the monitor may need to wait for is larger than the event rate. Moreover, it is unclear if one could even achieve a slightly weaker notion, which we call *almost event-rate independence*, where the monitor's space complexity is upper bounded by a logarithm of the event rate (and hence the monitor can store indices or pointers).

As a way out of this dilemma, we propose a monitor that works differently from the traditional ones. Our monitor outputs two kinds of verdicts: standard Boolean verdicts expressing that a formula is true or false at a particular time-point and *equivalence verdicts*. The latter express that the monitor does not know the Boolean verdict at a given time-point, but it knows that the verdict will be equal to another one (presently also not known) at a different time-point. Additionally, our monitor will output verdicts out of order relative to the input stream. Thus, it must indicate in the output to which time-point a verdict belongs. Instead of storing (and outputting) a global time-point reference, we store the time-stamp and the time-point's relative *offset* denoting its position among the time-points labeled with the same time-stamp. We assume that time-stamps can be stored in constant space, which is realistic since 32 bits (as used for Unix time-stamps) will suffice to model seconds for the next twenty years.

Storing the offset, however, requires space logarithmic in the event rate.[1] Beyond this, our monitor's space requirement is independent of the event rate.

Although our monitor's output is nonstandard, we are convinced that it is useful. First, the output provides sufficient information to reconstruct all violations. Second, often the monitor's users are only interested in the existence of violations. In this case, they can safely ignore all equivalence verdicts. Third, users are generally interested in the first (earliest) violation. When outputting equivalences, we ensure that the equivalence is output for the later time-points, while the earliest time-point stays in the monitor's memory and is eventually output with a Boolean verdict. Thus, users will always see a truth value at the earliest violating event.

In summary, our work makes the following contributions. We propose the new notion of (almost) event-rate independence, which is crucial for the online monitoring of high-velocity event streams (Sect. 4). We provide an almost event-rate independent monitoring algorithm for MTL on integer time-stamps with bounded future operators (Sect. 5). Finally, we report on a prototype implementation of our algorithm (Sect. 5.4) together with an experimental evaluation (Sect. 6). Taken together, these contributions lay the foundations for online monitoring that scales both with respect to the volume and the velocity of the event stream.

2   Related Work

There is considerable related work on monitoring. We focus on those algorithms and techniques that are closely related to ours and we touch upon other related works.

Havelund and Roşu [10] propose a simple, yet efficient online monitor for past-time linear temporal logic (ptLTL) using dynamic programming. The satisfaction relation of ptLTL can be recursively defined on a trace by examining the truth-values of subformulas only at the previous time-point. They exploit this insight to develop an algorithm that stores the truth-values of subformulas only at the two latest time-points. The algorithm's space complexity is $\mathcal{O}(n)$, where n is the number of subformulas.

Thati and Roşu [19] extend the results by Havelund and Roşu [10] to provide a trace-length independent, dynamic programming monitoring algorithm for MTL based on derivatives of formulas. Their monitor's space complexity depends only on the size of the formula and the constants occurring in its intervals. Thus their monitor is event-rate independent. However, the algorithm outputs verdicts with respect to a non-standard semantics of MTL, truncated to finite traces. It immediately outputs a verdict at time-points without looking at future events

---

[1] One could argue that, if time-stamps model seconds, there is a physical bound on the number of events that fit into this fixed unit of time and the space to store this number can be considered constant. However, we envision applications where time-stamps model days, month, or even years, for which the number of events fitting into one time unit increases dramatically.

that could possibly alter the verdict. Computing verdicts this way defeats the purpose of (top-level) future operators: An *until* that is not satisfied at the current time-point, but only at the next one, is reported as a violation.

Our algorithm builds on these dynamic programming approaches [10,19] to handle past-time operators. Our technique for monitoring future formulas under the standard non-truncated semantics of MTL in an event-rate independent manner is new.

Basin et al. [3,4] introduce techniques to handle MTL and metric first-order temporal logic with bounded future operators, adhering to the standard non-truncated semantics for future formulas. Their monitor uses a queue to postpone evaluation until sufficient time has elapsed to determine the formula's satisfiability at a previous time-point. This requires the algorithm to store in the worst case all time-points during the time-interval it waits. Therefore the monitor's space complexity grows linearly with the event rate, as is confirmed by their empirical evaluation [3, Sect. 6.3]. Their monitor outputs verdicts in order with respect to time-points, while our algorithm may output verdicts out of order to achieve a better space complexity.

Researchers have developed *trace-length independent* monitoring algorithms for various temporal specification languages. Maler et al. [14] compare the expressive power of timed automata and MTL. They show that past formulas can be converted to deterministic timed automata (DTA) and there exist future formulas that cannot be represented by a DTA. Ho et al. [11] give a trace-length independent algorithm for MTL in the dense time domain. There exist trace-length independent monitors for timed regular expressions [20], ptLTL extended with counting quantifiers [7], and ptMTL extended with recursive definitions [9]. The underlying logics have different time domains and semantics. We leave the study of event-rate independence in these settings as future work.

3   Metric Temporal Logic

Metric temporal logic (MTL) [12] is a logic for specifying qualitative and quantitative temporal properties. We briefly describe the syntax and the point-based semantics of MTL over a discrete time domain. A more in-depth discussion of various flavors of MTL is given elsewhere [4].

Let $\mathbb{I}$ denote the set of non-empty intervals over $\mathbb{N}$. We write an interval in $\mathbb{I}$ as $[a, b]$, where $a \in \mathbb{N}, b \in \mathbb{N} \cup \{\infty\}, a \leq b$, and $[a, b] = \{x \in \mathbb{N} \mid a \leq x \leq b\}$. For a number $n \in \mathbb{N}, I - n$ denotes $\{x - n \mid x \in I\} \cap \mathbb{N}$. For an interval I, let $\max(I)$ denote the largest constant occurring at the endpoints of I, i.e. $\max([a, b]) = b$ if $b \neq \infty$, else a. We write r for the upper bound of the interval, i.e., $r([a, b]) = b$, which is possibly ∞.

The set of MTL formulas over a set of atomic propositions P is defined inductively:

$$\varphi = p \mid \neg\varphi \mid \varphi_1 \vee \varphi_2 \mid \bigcirc_I \varphi \mid \bullet_I \varphi \mid \varphi_1 \, \mathcal{S}_I \, \varphi_2 \mid \varphi_1 \, \mathcal{U}_I \, \varphi_2,$$

where $p \in P$ and $I \in \mathbb{I}$. Along with the standard Boolean operators, MTL includes the temporal operators $\bullet_I$ (*previous*), $\mathcal{S}_I$ (*since*), $\bigcirc_I$ (*next*), and $\mathcal{U}_I$

(*until*), which may be nested freely. We restrict the intervals attached to future operators to be bounded, i.e., we require $r(I) \neq \infty$, as we want the formulas to be both finitely satisfiable and falsifiable (see [3] for details). We omit the subscript I if $I = [0, \infty)$, and use the usual syntactic sugar for additional Boolean constants and operators $true = p \vee \neg p$, $false = \neg true$, $\varphi \wedge \psi = \neg(\neg\varphi \vee \neg\psi)$ and future temporal operators *eventually* $\Diamond_I \varphi \equiv true \, \mathcal{U}_I \, \varphi$ and *always* $\Box_I \varphi \equiv \neg \Diamond_I \neg \varphi$ as well as their *past* counterparts *once* $\blacklozenge_I$ and *historically* $\blacksquare_I$.

MTL formulas are interpreted over *streams*, which are infinite sequences of time-stamped events. A time-stamped event is of the form (π_i, τ_i), where $\pi_i \in 2^P$ and $\tau_i \in \mathbb{N}$. Given a stream $\rho = \langle (\pi_0, \tau_0), (\pi_1, \tau_1), (\pi_2, \tau_2), \ldots \rangle$, abbreviated by $\langle (\pi_i, \tau_i) \rangle_{i \in \mathbb{N}}$, we call the τ_i *time-stamps* and their indices i *time-points*. The sequence of time-stamps $\langle \tau_i \rangle_{i \in \mathbb{N}}$ is monotonically increasing, i.e., $\tau_i \leq \tau_{i+1}$ for all $i \geq 0$. Moreover, $\langle \tau_i \rangle_{i \in \mathbb{N}}$ makes progress, i.e., for every $\tau \in \mathbb{N}$, there is some index $i \geq 0$ such that $\tau_i > \tau$. Note that successive time-points can have identical time-stamps; for example, $\langle 5, 5, 5, 7, 8, \ldots \rangle$. Hence, time-stamps may stutter, but only for finitely many time-points. A finite prefix of an event stream is called *trace*.

The semantics of MTL formulas for a given stream $\rho = \langle (\pi_i, \tau_i) \rangle_{i \in \mathbb{N}}$ and a time-point i is defined inductively as follows.

$$
\begin{aligned}
(\rho, i) &\models p && \text{iff } p \in \pi_i \\
(\rho, i) &\models \neg\varphi && \text{iff } (\rho, i) \not\models \varphi \\
(\rho, i) &\models \varphi_1 \vee \varphi_2 && \text{iff } (\rho, i) \models \varphi_1 \text{ or } (\rho, i) \models \varphi_2 \\
(\rho, i) &\models \blacklozenge_I \varphi && \text{iff } i > 0 \text{ and } \tau_i - \tau_{i-1} \in I \text{ and } (\rho, i-1) \models \varphi \\
(\rho, i) &\models \bigcirc_I \varphi && \text{iff } \tau_{i+1} - \tau_i \in I \text{ and } (\rho, i+1) \models \varphi \\
(\rho, i) &\models \varphi_1 \, \mathcal{S}_I \, \varphi_2 && \text{iff } (\rho, j) \models \varphi_2 \text{ for some } j \leq i \text{ with } \tau_i - \tau_j \in I \\
& && \text{and } (\rho, k) \models \varphi_1 \text{ for all } j < k \leq i \\
(\rho, i) &\models \varphi_1 \, \mathcal{U}_I \, \varphi_2 && \text{iff } (\rho, j) \models \varphi_2 \text{ for some } j \geq i \text{ with } \tau_j - \tau_i \in I \\
& && \text{and } (\rho, k) \models \varphi_1 \text{ for all } i \leq k < j
\end{aligned}
$$

When the stream ρ is clear from the context, we also simply write $i \models \varphi$.

From the semantics of MTL, it is easy to derive an equivalent recursive definition for the *until* and *since* operators for a fixed stream ρ:

$$
\begin{aligned}
i \models \varphi_1 \, \mathcal{S}_I \, \varphi_2 \text{ iff } & 0 \in I \text{ and } i \models \varphi_2, \text{ or} \\
& i > 0, \, \tau_i - \tau_{i-1} \leq r(I), \, i \models \varphi_1, \text{ and } i-1 \models \varphi_1 \, \mathcal{S}_{I - (\tau_i - \tau_{i-1})} \, \varphi_2
\end{aligned}
$$

$$
\begin{aligned}
i \models \varphi_1 \, \mathcal{U}_I \, \varphi_2 \text{ iff } & 0 \in I \text{ and } i \models \varphi_2, \text{ or} \\
& \tau_{i+1} - \tau_i \leq r(I), \, i \models \varphi_1, \text{ and } i+1 \models \varphi_1 \, \mathcal{U}_{I - (\tau_{i+1} - \tau_i)} \, \varphi_2
\end{aligned}
$$

Note that the formula being "evaluated" on the right-hand side of these recursive equations has the same structure as the initial formula, except that the interval has been shifted by the difference between the current and the previous (or the next) time-stamps. Our algorithm, described in Sect. 5, uses these recursive equations to update the monitor's state by simultaneously monitoring the formulas arising from all possible interval shifts. We call such formulas *interval-skewed subformulas*. For an MTL formula φ, let $\mathsf{SF}(\varphi)$ denote the set of

i (time-point)	0	1	2	3	4	...
π_i (events)	$\{a\}$	$\{a\}$	$\{a\}$	$\{b\}$	$\{a,b\}$	...
τ_i (time-stamps)	1	2	2	3	4	...
$i \models a\,\mathcal{U}_{[0,1]}\,b$	$\bot$	$\top$	$\top$	$\top$	$\top$	...

Fig. 1. Evaluation of $a\,\mathcal{U}_{[0,1]}\,b$ on an example stream

its subformulas defined in the usual manner. Note that $\varphi \in \mathsf{SF}(\varphi)$. The set of interval-skewed subformulas of φ is defined as

$$\mathsf{ISF}(\varphi) = \mathsf{SF}(\varphi) \cup \{\varphi_1\,\mathcal{S}_{I-n}\,\varphi_2 \mid \varphi_1\,\mathcal{S}_I\,\varphi_2 \in \mathsf{SF}(\varphi) \text{ and } n \in [1, \max(I)]\}$$
$$\cup \{\varphi_1\,\mathcal{U}_{I-n}\,\varphi_2 \mid \varphi_1\,\mathcal{U}_I\,\varphi_2 \in \mathsf{SF}(\varphi) \text{ and } n \in [1, \max(I)]\}.$$

Clearly, the size of $\mathsf{ISF}(\varphi)$ is bounded by $\mathcal{O}(|\mathsf{SF}(\varphi)| \times c)$, where c is the largest integer constant occurring in the intervals of φ. We define a well-order $<$ over $\mathsf{ISF}(\varphi)$ that respects the following conditions:

– if φ_1 is a subformula of φ_2 and $\varphi_1 \neq \varphi_2$, then $\varphi_1 < \varphi_2$
– if $\varphi_1 = \alpha\,\mathcal{S}_I\,\beta$ and $\varphi_2 = \alpha\,\mathcal{S}_{I'}\,\beta$ and $I' = I - n$ for some $n > 0$, then $\varphi_1 < \varphi_2$.

We use this to order the elements of $\mathsf{ISF}(\varphi)$ into an array in Sect. 5.

We also define the *future reach* (FR) of an MTL formula following Ho et al. [11], which we subsequently use to analyze the complexity of our proposed algorithm.

$$\mathsf{FR}(p) = 0 \qquad \mathsf{FR}(\neg\varphi) = \mathsf{FR}(\varphi) \qquad \mathsf{FR}(\varphi_1 \vee \varphi_2) = \max(\mathsf{FR}(\varphi_1), \mathsf{FR}(\varphi_2))$$
$$\mathsf{FR}(\bullet_I\varphi) = \mathsf{FR}(\varphi) - \inf(I) \qquad\quad \mathsf{FR}(\bigcirc_I\varphi) = \sup(I) + \mathsf{FR}(\varphi)$$
$$\mathsf{FR}(\varphi_1\,\mathcal{S}_I\,\varphi_2) = \mathrm{maximum}(\mathsf{FR}(\varphi_1), \mathsf{FR}(\varphi_2) - \inf(I))$$
$$\mathsf{FR}(\varphi_1\,\mathcal{U}_I\,\varphi_2) = \sup(I) + \mathrm{maximum}(\mathsf{FR}(\varphi_1), \mathsf{FR}(\varphi_2))$$

Here maximum denotes the maximum of two integers and sup and inf denote the *supremum* and *infimum* of sets of integers, respectively. For a bounded future MTL formula φ, we have $\mathsf{FR}(\varphi) \neq \infty$. Intuitively, events that have a time-stamp larger than $\tau_i + \mathsf{FR}(\varphi)$ are irrelevant for determining φ's validity at a time-point i with time-stamp τ_i.

Example 1. Consider the formula $\varphi = a\,\mathcal{U}_{[0,1]}\,b$ and the event stream $\rho = \langle(\{a\}, 1), (\{a\}, 2), (\{a\}, 2), (\{b\}, 3), (\{a,b\}, 4), \ldots\rangle$. In Fig. 1, $\top$ and $\bot$ denote the satisfaction and violation of φ. Note that the verdict $\bot$ at time-point 0 is determined only after the event $(\{b\}, 3)$ has arrived. This observation would also apply, even if the event $(\{a\}, 2)$ was replicated arbitrarily often in the stream.

4   Almost Event-Rate Independence

The space complexity of monitoring algorithms has been previously analyzed with respect to two parameters: *formula size* and *trace length*. In most scenarios, the formula is much smaller than the trace and does not change during monitoring. Hence, an algorithm with a space complexity exponential in the formula size is usually tolerable, but a space complexity linear in the trace length is problematic since this corresponds to storing the entire trace. Recently, researchers have studied *trace-length independence* [5]. A monitor is trace-length independent if its efficiency does not decline as the number of events increases. In the setting of MTL, we call a monitoring algorithm $\mathcal{M}$ *trace-length independent on the stream* ρ if the space required by $\mathcal{M}$ to output the verdict at time-point i when monitoring ρ is independent of i. This property is critical for determining whether a monitor scales to large quantities of data. However, it does not yield insights into the monitor's performance regarding other aspects of the stream such as its velocity.

We propose the notion of event-rate independence, which not only guarantees the monitor's memory efficiency with respect to the number of events, but also with respect to the rate at which the events arrive. A varying event rate is a realistic concern in many practically relevant monitoring scenarios. For example, if the unit of time-stamps is on the order of days, there may be millions of time-points with the same time-stamp in a stream. An event-rate dependent algorithm may work well on days with a few thousand events, but fall short of memory when the number of events rises significantly. (Such a situation could be an indicator that something interesting happened, which in turn makes the monitor's output particularly valuable on that day.)

We first formally define a stream's *event rate*.

Definition 1. The *event rate* er of a stream $\rho = \langle (\pi_i, \tau_i) \rangle_{i \in \mathbb{N}}$ at time-stamp τ is defined as the number of time-points whose time-stamps are equal to τ, i.e., $\text{er}_\rho(\tau) = |\{i \mid \tau_i = \tau\}|$.

An online monitoring algorithm $\mathcal{M}$ for MTL is *event-rate independent on the stream* ρ if for all time-points i the monitor $\mathcal{M}$'s space complexity to compute the verdict at i is constant with respect to $\text{er}_\rho(\tau_j)$ for all $j \leq i$, i.e., the event rates in ρ at all time-stamps up to and including the current one. Ultimately, we are interested in monitors that are event-rate independent on all streams ρ. For example, the dynamic programming algorithms [10,19] are event-rate independent on all streams ρ for past-only MTL.

The trace length up to time-point i is greater than the sum of the event rates $\text{er}_\rho(\tau)$ for $\tau < \tau_i$ for all streams ρ. Hence, we obtain the following lemma by contraposition.

Lemma 1. *Fix a stream ρ. Let $\mathcal{M}$ be a monitoring algorithm for MTL. If $\mathcal{M}$ is event-rate independent on ρ, then $\mathcal{M}$ is trace-length independent on ρ.*

In general, event-rate independence is not strictly stronger than trace-length independence. To see this, consider the following stream where the event rate itself depends on the trace length: $\rho = \langle (\pi_0, 0), (\pi_1, 1), (\pi_1, 1), (\pi_2, 2), (\pi_2, 2), (\pi_2, 2), (\pi_2, 2), \ldots \rangle$, where (π_τ, τ) is repeated 2^τ times. Any event-rate dependent monitor for ρ is also trace-length dependent, since the event rate is roughly half of the trace length at each time-point.

In contrast to the above example, streams arising in practice have a bound on the event rate. For such an *(event-rate) bounded stream* ρ we have $\forall i.\ \text{er}_\rho(\tau_i) < b_\rho$

for some arbitrary but fixed b_ρ. In fact, the related *bounded variability* assumption [8,11,14] is deemed necessary for trace-length independence. The consideration of the event rate clarifies the need for this assumption: On bounded streams ρ, event-rate independence is strictly stronger than trace-length independence. For example, monitors using a waiting queue for future operators [3] are trace-length independent on ρ, but not event-rate independent on ρ. On unbounded streams, i.e., streams that are not event-rate bounded, the two notions coincide. This is in line with the fact that there are trace-length independent monitors for MTL (with future operators) on bounded streams [3,11], but none on unbounded streams.

Event-rate independence and trace-length independence for unbounded streams are indeed impossible if we adhere to the mode of operation of existing MTL monitors. Existing monitors output verdicts *monotonically*, i.e., for time-points i and j, if $i < j$ then the verdict at i is output before the verdict at j. Monotonicity makes any monitor handling future operators linearly event-rate dependent (and hence trace-length dependent for unbounded streams), as it must wait for and therefore store information associated to more than $\mathsf{er}_\rho(\tau)$-many events (for some τ) before being able to output a verdict. So event-rate independence seems to be too strong a condition for traditional monitors.

To overcome this problem, our monitor outputs verdicts differently. In addition to the standard Boolean verdicts $\top$ and $\bot$, it outputs *equivalence verdicts* $j \equiv i$ (with $i < j$) if it is certain that the verdict at time-point j will be equivalent to the verdict at a previous time-point i, even if the exact truth value is presently unknown at both points. This makes verdict outputs *non-monotonic with respect to time-points*, but it is still possible to ensure *monotonicity with respect to time-stamps* for time-stamps that are far enough apart. More precisely, a monitor that is monotonic with respect to time-stamps outputs the verdict at i before the verdict at j when monitoring φ, if $\tau_j - \tau_i > \mathsf{FR}(\varphi)$.

To output equivalence verdicts, the algorithm must refer to time-points. This requires non-constant space, e.g., logarithmic space for natural numbers. Time-points increase with the trace length, leading to a logarithmic dependence on the trace length. An alternative way to refer to time-points is to use time-stamps together with an offset pointing into a block of consecutive time-points labeled with the same time-stamp. (The size of such a block is bounded by the event rate.) The space requirement of an algorithm outputting such verdicts is therefore not event-rate independent. However, it is logarithmic in the event rate. These observations suggest the slightly weaker notion of almost event-rate independence, which is defined identically to event-rate independence except that the space complexity is upper bounded by a logarithm of the event rate.

Definition 2. An online monitoring algorithm $\mathcal{M}$ for MTL is *almost event-rate independent* if for all time-points i and streams ρ the space complexity of $\mathcal{M}$ for outputting the verdict at i is $\mathcal{O}(\log(\max_{j \leq i} \mathsf{er}_\rho(\tau_j)))$.

Our proposed monitor is almost event-rate independent. Moreover, it is the first almost trace-length independent monitor on unbounded streams.

5   Monitoring Algorithm

We describe the high-level design of our monitoring algorithm for MTL informally. Then we give a formal description using functional programming notation, prove its correctness and almost event-rate independence, and discuss implementation details.

5.1   Informal Account

The idea of outputting equivalence verdicts draws inspiration from a natural way to approach simultaneous suffix matching with automata. To decide which suffixes of a word are matched by an automaton, a naive approach is to start running the automaton at each position in the word. For a word of length n this requires storing n copies of the automaton. A more space-efficient approach is to store a single copy, and use markers (one marker for each position in the word) that are moved between states upon transitions. If n is larger than the number of states, then at some point two markers will necessarily mark the same state. At this point, it suffices to output their equivalence and track only one of them, since they would travel through the automaton together. Our algorithm follows a similar approach; however, we avoid explicitly constructing automata from formulas.

Our algorithm builds on Havelund and Roşu's dynamic programming algorithm for past-time LTL [10], where the monitor's state consists of an array of Boolean verdicts for all subformulas of the monitored formula at a given time-point. The array is dynamically updated when consuming the next event based on the recursive definition of satisfiability for LTL. To support intervals, we use the idea by Thati and Roşu [19] to store an array of verdicts for all interval-skewed subformulas instead of plain subformulas as in Havelund and Roşu. This accounts for possible interval changes when moving between different time-stamps according to the recursive definition of satisfiability for past-time MTL. This step crucially relies on the time-stamps being integer-valued, as otherwise the number of skewed subformulas would be infinite.

The problem with future operators is that they require us to wait until we are able to output a verdict. At first, we sidestep almost event-rate independence and formulate a dynamic programming algorithm that treats past operators as Havelund and Roşu's algorithm [10] but also supports future operators. The recursive equation for *until* reduces the satisfaction of a formula $\varphi_1 \, \mathcal{U}_I \, \varphi_2$ at the current time-point to a Boolean combination of the satisfaction of φ_1 and φ_2 at the current time-point and the satisfaction of $\varphi_1 \, \mathcal{U}_{I-n} \, \varphi_2$ (for some n) at the next time-point. While we can immediately resolve the dependencies on the current time-point, those on the next time-point force us to wait. This also means that we cannot store the verdict in an array (because we do not know it yet), but instead we will store the dependency in the form of pointers to some entries in the next array to be filled. In general, our dynamically updated array (of length $|\mathsf{ISF}(\varphi)|$), indexed by interval-skewed subformulas, will contain Boolean expressions instead of Booleans, in which the variables denote the dependencies on those next entries.

Additionally, we may only output verdicts when the Boolean expressions are resolved to a Boolean verdict. This will happen eventually, since in our setting time progresses and future intervals are bounded. But until this happens, the yet-to-be-output Boolean expressions must be stored, which affects the algorithm's space consumption. In the worst case, the monitor would store as many expressions as there are time-points in any interval of timespan d, where d is the future reach of the monitored formula.

Finally, to obtain almost event-rate independence, we refine our monitor's output by allowing it to output equivalence verdicts between different time-points. As soon as the monitor sees two semantically equivalent Boolean expressions, it may output such verdicts and discard one of the two expressions. Since there are only $\mathcal{O}(2^{2^{|\mathsf{ISF}(\varphi)|}})$ semantically different Boolean expressions in $\mathcal{O}(|\mathsf{ISF}(\varphi)|)$ variables (corresponding to the verdicts for interval-skewed subformulas at the next time-point), the space required to store them depends only on the monitored formula φ. However, for the equivalence verdicts to be understandable to users, the equivalences must refer to different time-points via indices. Storing those indices requires logarithmic space in the event rate. Hence, the overall algorithm is almost event-rate independent.

5.2   The Algorithm

We now give a more formal description of our algorithm. For the presentation, we use a functional programming-style pseudo code, with pattern matching, that resembles Standard ML. Type constructors, such as _ *list* or _ *array* for functional lists and arrays (lists of fixed length with constant time element access), are written postfix, with the exception of the product type $\times$ and the function space $\rightarrow$, which are written infix. We write $\mathbb{N}$ for the type of natural numbers and ⊛ for the type of time-stamps (although, in our case, these are again just natural numbers). Lists are either empty [] or constructed by prepending an element to a list $x::xs$. List concatenation is written infix as ⧺. Anonymous functions are introduced using λ-abstractions.

Our monitor for a fixed formula Φ operates on an input stream of time-stamped events I and writes verdicts to an output stream O. Additionally, it starts in some initial state init of type σ and can perform state transitions step : $\sigma \rightarrow \sigma$. The state consists of three parts: a list of time-stamped Boolean expressions for which the verdict depends on future events, a current time-stamp, and an array of Boolean expressions for all interval-skewed subformulas at the current time-point (similarly to the state of Havelund and Roşu's algorithm). Expressions for small subformulas are stored at low indices in this array, while the monitored formula Φ has index $|\mathsf{ISF}(\Phi)| - 1$. In other words, if we think of the array as being indexed by subformulas, then the array's indices are ordered by the well-order $<$. We formalize the state using a record type:

record $\sigma = \{$hist : (⊛ $\times \mathbb{N} \times$ *bexp*) *list*, now : ⊛ $\times \mathbb{N}$, arr : ⊛ $\rightarrow$ *bexp array*$\}$.

$$\begin{aligned}
&\text{init} = \{\text{hist} = [], \text{now} = (-1, 0), \text{arr} = \lambda\_. \perp^n\} \\
&\text{step} \{\text{hist} = h, \text{now} = (\tau, i), \text{arr} = fa\} = \\
&\quad \text{let } (\pi, \tau') \Leftarrow I \\
&\qquad a = fa\,\tau' \\
&\qquad h' = \text{fold (update } a) \text{ (rev } h) [] \\
&\qquad j = \text{if } \tau = \tau' \text{ then } i + 1 \text{ else } 0 \\
&\quad \text{in } \{\text{hist} = \text{add } (\tau, i, a[\Phi]) \, h', \text{now} = (\tau', j), \\
&\qquad \text{arr} = \text{progress } a\,\tau\,\pi\,\tau'\}
\end{aligned}$$

$$\begin{aligned}
&\text{update } a \, (\tau, i, b) \, h = \\
&\quad \text{let } c = \text{subst } (\lambda x.\, a[x]) \, b \\
&\quad \text{in if } c = \top \vee c = \perp \\
&\quad \text{then} \\
&\qquad \text{let if } \tau \geq 0 \text{ then } (\tau, i, c) \Rightarrow O \\
&\qquad \text{in } h \\
&\quad \text{else} \\
&\qquad \text{add } (\tau, i, c) \, h
\end{aligned}$$

Fig. 2. The transition system of the monitor: init and step

Two points are worth noting here. First, in addition to the time-stamp for each time-point, we store an *offset* of type $\mathbb{N}$, which stores the position of the time-point within a block of time-points with the same time-stamp. Using the time-stamp and the offset, each time-point can be uniquely identified. Second, the array in arr has a dependency on a future time-stamp because the recursive definition of satisfaction for *until* depends the time-stamp difference between the next and the current time-point. As a result, our monitor will output a verdict for a time-point only after having seen the time-stamp of the next time-point. We will revisit and rectify this limitation in Sect. 5.4.

Overloading notation, *(Boolean) expressions* can be defined inductively as follows:

$$bexp = \perp \mid \top \mid bexp \wedge bexp \mid bexp \vee bexp \mid \neg bexp \mid \text{var } \mathbb{N}.$$

Here, a variable should be thought of as a pointer into the arr array of the yet-to-be-computed next state, i.e., a natural number less than n, where n is the number of interval-skewed subformulas of Φ. To lighten the notation, we implicitly convert interval-skewed subformulas of Φ to natural numbers between 0 and $n - 1$, and vice versa. For example, we write var φ (or $a[\varphi]$) to denote a variable pointing to the array entry corresponding to the formula φ (or the array entry itself). We assume that all expressions of type $bexp$ are normalized using Boolean simplifications, e.g., $\perp \wedge x$ is rewritten to $\perp$. Thus, each expression is either a Boolean $\perp$ or $\top$ or does not contain $\perp$ or $\top$ as a subexpression. Furthermore, we will use the function subst : $(\mathbb{N} \to bexp) \to bexp \to bexp$ to replace variables with expressions according to the given function argument as well as a decision procedure $\equiv : bexp \to bexp \to \{\perp, \top\}$ for the semantic equivalence of Boolean expressions. We omit the definitions of those two functions.

The monitor's initial state init and its transition function step are shown in Fig. 2. The function step formalizes the transition from the current time-point to the next one. First, it retrieves the new event π and its time-stamp τ' from the input stream I (which we write as $(\pi, \tau') \Leftarrow I$). Using τ', the next step evaluates the future-dependent array fa to obtain an array of Boolean expressions a. Note that the expressions in a refer to the array of the next state, while all

$$\text{progress } a \, \tau \, \pi \, \tau' \, \tau'' =$$
$$\quad \text{let } b = \bot^n$$
$$\quad\quad \text{for } x = 0, \dots, n-1$$
$$\quad\quad\quad b[x] = \text{case } x \text{ of}$$
$$\quad\quad\quad\quad | \, p \quad\quad \Rightarrow p \in \pi$$
$$\quad\quad\quad\quad | \, \neg\varphi \quad\quad \Rightarrow \neg \, b[\varphi]$$
$$\quad\quad\quad\quad | \, \varphi \vee \psi \Rightarrow b[\varphi] \vee b[\psi]$$
$$\quad\quad\quad\quad | \, \bullet_I \varphi \Rightarrow \text{if } \tau' - \tau \in I \text{ then subst } (\lambda x.\, b[x]) \, a[\varphi] \text{ else } \bot$$
$$\quad\quad\quad\quad | \, \bigcirc_I \varphi \Rightarrow \text{if } \tau'' - \tau' \in I \text{ then var } \varphi \text{ else } \bot$$
$$\quad\quad\quad\quad | \, \varphi \, \mathcal{S}_I \, \psi \Rightarrow (\text{if } 0 \in I \text{ then } b[\psi] \text{ else } \bot) \vee$$
$$\quad\quad\quad\quad\quad (\text{if } \tau' - \tau \le \mathsf{r}(I) \text{ then } b[\varphi] \wedge \text{subst } (\lambda x.\, b[x]) \, a[\varphi \, \mathcal{S}_{I - (\tau' - \tau)} \, \psi] \text{ else } \bot)$$
$$\quad\quad\quad\quad | \, \varphi \, \mathcal{U}_I \, \psi \Rightarrow (\text{if } 0 \in I \text{ then } b[\psi] \text{ else } \bot) \vee$$
$$\quad\quad\quad\quad\quad (\text{if } \tau'' - \tau' \le \mathsf{r}(I) \text{ then } b[\varphi] \wedge \text{var } (\varphi \, \mathcal{S}_{I - (\tau'' - \tau')} \, \psi) \text{ else } \bot)$$
$$\quad \text{in } b$$

$$\text{go } loc \; done \; x \, [] = x :: \text{rev } done$$
$$\text{go } loc \; done \; (\tau, i, b) \, ((\tau', j, c) :: todo) =$$
$$\quad \text{if } loc \wedge \tau \neq \tau' \text{ then } (\tau, i, b) :: \text{rev } done \mathbin{+\!\!+} (\tau', j, c) :: todo$$
$$\quad \text{else if } c \equiv d \text{ then}$$
$$\quad\quad \text{let } (\tau, i) \equiv (\tau', j) \Rightarrow O \text{ in } \text{rev } done \mathbin{+\!\!+} (\tau', j, c) :: todo$$
$$\quad \text{else go } loc \; ((\tau', j, c) :: done) \; (\tau, i, b) \; todo$$

Fig. 3. Recursive formula progression and insertion modulo semantic expression equivalence

expressions in the history h refer to the current state, namely to a itself. To overcome this mismatch, the monitor iterates over the history using the standard fold combinator on lists and updates each of the Boolean expressions to refer to the next state using subst in the function update. This update may convert some of the expressions into Boolean verdicts, which are immediately output (written $\dots \Rightarrow O$) and removed from the history. Next, the monitor computes the new offset j depending on whether the time-stamp has increased. Finally, the last entry of the array a is added to the history (or output in case it is a Boolean verdict) using the function add and the new future-dependent array is produced by (a partial application of) the progress function and stored in the state. We describe these two core functions next.

We consider three different implementations of the add function:

$$\text{add } (x \text{ as } (\_, \_, c)) \; xs =$$
$$\quad \text{if } c = \bot \vee c = \top \text{ then } (\text{let } x \Rightarrow O \text{ in } xs) \text{ else } \begin{cases} x :: xs & \text{NAIVE} \\ \text{go } \bot \, [] \; x \; xs & \text{GLOBAL} \\ \text{go } \top \, [] \; x \; xs & \text{LOCAL} \end{cases}$$

The NAIVE version simply prepends the element to the history (which is kept in reversed order with respect to the input stream). This version is not almost event-rate independent. The GLOBAL version adds the new expression only if there is no semantically equivalent expression in the history. The LOCAL version adds the new expression only if there is no semantically equivalent expression labeled with the same time-point. Whenever an expression is *not* added to the history, an equivalence verdict is output. Both versions, LOCAL and GLOBAL, are implemented using the auxiliary function go shown in Fig. 3 and give rise to almost event-rate independent algorithms.

π		$\{a\}$	$\{a\}$	$\{a\}$	$\{b\}$	$\{a,b\}$
τ	$-$	1	2	2	3	4
i	0	0	0	1	0	0
h	$[]$	$[]$	$[(1,0,\mathrm{var}\,\varphi_0)]$	$[(2,0,\mathrm{var}\,\varphi_1),\ (1,0,\mathrm{var}\,\varphi_0)]$	$[(2,0,\mathrm{var}\,\varphi_0)]$	$[]$
	$fa\,1$	$fa\,2$	$fa\,2$	$fa\,3$	$fa\,4$	$\cdots$
a	$\bot$	$\top$	$\top$	$\top$	$\bot$	$\cdots$
b	$\bot$	$\bot$	$\bot$	$\bot$	$\top$	$\cdots$
$\varphi_0 = a\,\mathcal{U}_{[0,0]}\,b$	$\bot$	$\bot$	$\mathrm{var}\,\varphi_0$	$\bot$	$\top$	$\cdots$
$\varphi_1 = a\,\mathcal{U}_{[0,1]}\,b$	$\bot$	$\mathrm{var}\,\varphi_0$	$\mathrm{var}\,\varphi_1$	$\mathrm{var}\,\varphi_0$	$\top$	$\cdots$
verdicts					$(1,0)=\bot \quad (2,0)=\top$ $(2,1)=(2,0)\quad(3,0)=\top$	

Fig. 4. An execution of the monitoring algorithm on $a\,\mathcal{U}_{[0,1]}\,b$

The last missing piece is the update of the arr entry of the monitor's state. The function progress shown in Fig. 3 performs this update. It has access to the previous time-stamp τ, the current time-stamp τ', the next time-stamp τ'', the current event π, and the previous array of Boolean expressions a. Given these inputs, it fills the next array b starting from the smallest subformulas and progressing up to the formula Φ itself. Each array entry is filled following the recursive definition of satisfaction of the topmost operator of the formula it corresponds to. Moreover, whenever the previous array a is accessed for past operators, the retrieved expression's dependencies are updated using subst as before. In contrast, for future dependencies, the var constructor of expressions is used.

Example 1 (continued). Figure 4 shows the internal states of the GLOBAL version of our algorithm when monitoring the formula $a\ \mathcal{U}_{[0,1]}\ b$ on the stream $\rho = \langle(\{a\},\,1),\,(\{a\},\,2),\,(\{a\},\,2),\,(\{b\},\,3),\,(\{a,b\},\,4),\dots\rangle$. The first two rows show the incoming events and their time-stamps, the third the within-time-stamp offset, and the fourth the current history. The next four rows are dedicated to the Boolean expressions stored for each interval-skewed subformula. The last row displays the monitor's verdicts. At each time-point, the monitor's state consists (roughly) of one column from this table. Since it is hard to display the function fa, we show instead the result of applying fa to the time-stamp of the next state. This causes a delay of one time-point between the values in the arrays and the history updates and verdict outputs.

5.3   Correctness and Complexity Analysis

In this subsection, we fix a formula Φ and a stream ρ. To prove the soundness and completeness of our monitor and to establish its space complexity bounds, we formulate an invariant $\mathcal{I}$ that holds after processing the first event and all subsequent states.

$\mathcal{I} \{\text{hist} = h, \text{now} = (\tau, i), \text{arr} = fa)\} =$
  $(\mathcal{I}1) \quad (\forall(\tau', j, b) \in h. \ \tau'@j \models \Phi \leftrightarrow \tau@i \models_{bexp} b)$
  $\land (\mathcal{I}2) \quad (\forall \varphi \in \mathsf{ISF}(\Phi). \ \tau@i \models \varphi \leftrightarrow \tau@i + 1 \models_{bexp} fa \ (\tau_{\tau@i+1})[\varphi])$
  $\land (\mathcal{I}3) \quad (\forall \varphi \in \mathsf{ISF}(\Phi). \ \text{vars} \ (fa \ (\tau_{\tau@i+1})[\varphi]) \subseteq \mathsf{ISF}(\varphi))$
  $\land (\mathcal{I}4) \quad (\forall(\tau', j, b) \in h. \ b \neq \top \land b \neq \bot)$
  $\land (\mathcal{I}5) \quad h \text{ is sorted in strictly descending order by time-point}$
  $\land (\mathcal{I}6) \quad (\forall(\tau', j, b) \in h. \ \forall(\tau'', k, c) \in h. \ \tau'@j \neq \tau''@k \rightarrow \text{compact } \tau' \ \tau'' \ b \ c)$

We write $\tau@i$ to denote the time-point uniquely identified by the time-stamp τ and the within-time-stamp offset i. Moreover, vars is the set of vars in a Boolean expression, τ_k is the time-stamp from ρ at time-point k, and $\models_{bexp}$ is the lifting of MTL satisfaction to expressions. For the base case of this lifting, we have $k \models_{bexp} \text{var } \varphi \leftrightarrow k \models \varphi$.

The invariant consists of six predicates. $(\mathcal{I}1)$ and $(\mathcal{I}2)$ capture the semantics of the entries in the history and the expression array. $(\mathcal{I}3)$ expresses that future dependencies in any expression indexed by a subformula φ may only refer to φ's interval-skewed subformulas. $(\mathcal{I}4)$ and $(\mathcal{I}5)$ are important structural properties of the history. $(\mathcal{I}6)$ is crucial for our complexity analysis. It uses an auxiliary predicate compact, defined differently for each of the three versions of the monitoring algorithm we consider.

$$\text{compact } \tau' \ \tau'' \ b \ c = \begin{cases} \top & \text{NAIVE} \\ b \not\equiv c & \text{GLOBAL} \\ \tau' = \tau'' \rightarrow b \not\equiv c & \text{LOCAL} \end{cases}$$

We prove that $\mathcal{I}$ holds for every reachable state except the initial state itself. In the initial state $(\mathcal{I}2)$ is violated. The fa array of the initial state is accessed only for past-time operators at the first event. In this case, the stored values $\bot$ for all subformulas have exactly the right semantics: essentially they affirm that there is no previous time-point.

Lemma 2. $\mathcal{I}$ (step init) *and for any state s if $\mathcal{I}(s)$ then $\mathcal{I}$ (step s).*

Proof (core idea). The core of the proof is the preservation of $(\mathcal{I}2)$ by the progress function. We prove the following auxiliary lemma: *Fix a stream $\rho = \langle(\pi_i, \tau_i)\rangle_{i \in \mathbb{N}}$ and a time-point k. Assume* progress $a \ \tau_k \ \pi_{k+1} \ \tau_{k+1} \ \tau_{k+1} = b$ *and for all $\varphi \in$* $\mathsf{ISF}(\Phi)$ *we have* $k \models \varphi \leftrightarrow k + 1 \models_{bexp} a[\varphi]$. *Then* $k + 1 \models \varphi \leftrightarrow k + 2 \models_{bexp} b[\varphi]$ *holds for all* $\varphi \in \mathsf{ISF}(\Phi)$.

The lemma follows by well-founded induction on the lexicographic product of the natural number order on time-points and the order $<$ on formulas: Fix $\varphi \in \mathsf{ISF}(\Phi)$. The induction hypothesis allows us to assume $k + 1 \models \psi \leftrightarrow k + 2 \models_{bexp} b[\psi]$ for any $\psi < \varphi$. We continue by a case distinction on φ and present here only the case where $\varphi = \varphi_1 \ \mathcal{U}_I \ \varphi_2$. Let $\Delta = \tau'' - \tau'$ and $I' = I - \Delta$. We calculate

$$k + 1 \models \varphi_1 \, \mathcal{U}_I \, \varphi_2 \quad \overset{\text{recursive def. of} \models}{\longleftrightarrow} \quad \begin{aligned} &(0 \in I \wedge k + 1 \models \varphi_2) \vee \\ &(\varDelta \leq r(I) \wedge k + 1 \models \varphi_1 \wedge k + 2 \models \varphi_1 \, \mathcal{U}_{I'} \, \varphi_2) \end{aligned}$$

$$\overset{\text{twice IH + def. } \models_{bexp}}{\longleftrightarrow} \quad \begin{aligned} &(0 \in I \wedge k + 2 \models_{bexp} b[\varphi_2]) \vee \\ &(\varDelta \leq r(I) \wedge k + 2 \models_{bexp} b[\varphi_1] \wedge k + 2 \models_{bexp} \mathsf{var} \, (\varphi_1 \, \mathcal{U}_{I'} \, \varphi_2)) \end{aligned}$$

$$\overset{\text{def. of progress}}{\longleftrightarrow} \quad k + 2 \models_{bexp} b[\varphi_1 \, \mathcal{U}_I \, \varphi_2]$$

Other cases follow similarly. Past operators additionally use the assumption on a.
□

The step from the invariant to a correctness theorem is easy. For soundness, we calculate the expected semantic properties for verdicts output in a **step** taking $(\mathcal{I}1)$ and $(\mathcal{I}2)$ of the invariant into account. Completeness also holds: for each time-point either a verdict is output or an expression is inserted into the history. Each expression from the history is eventually output as time progresses and all future intervals are bounded.

Theorem 1 (Correctness). *The monitor for a formula Φ is sound: whenever it outputs the Boolean verdict (τ, i, b) we have $\tau@i \models \Phi \longleftrightarrow b$ and whenever it outputs the equivalence verdict $(\tau, i) \equiv (\tau', j)$ we have $\tau@i > \tau'@j$ and $\tau@i \models \Phi \longleftrightarrow \tau'@j \models \Phi$. For the LOCAL mode, we additionally have $\tau = \tau'$. Moreover, the monitor is complete.*

Finally, we establish complexity bounds. Let $n = |\mathsf{ISF}(\Phi)|$ and $d = \mathsf{FR}(\varphi)$. Note that $d \leq n$. The size of a Boolean expression in n variables can be bounded by 2^n assuming a normal form for expressions such as CNF. Then the size of the future-dependent array arr is $n \cdot 2^n$. The length of the history depends on the version of the algorithm used and (except for the NAIVE algorithm) dominates the size of arr.

Theorem 2 (Space Complexity). *The space complexity for storing all Boolean expressions used by the three versions of the algorithm at the time-stamp τ is*

NAIVE: $\mathcal{O}(2^n \cdot (n + \sum_{\tau'=\tau-d}^{\tau} \mathsf{er}(\tau')))$, GLOBAL: $\mathcal{O}(2^{2^n+n})$, *and* LOCAL: $\mathcal{O}(d \cdot 2^{2^n+n})$.

Time-stamps additionally require a constant and the offsets a logarithmic amount of space in the event rate. Hence, GLOBAL and LOCAL are almost event-rate independent.

Proof. Each stored Boolean expression requires $\mathcal{O}(2^n)$ space. The bound for NAIVE follows since, at time-stamp τ, we can output Boolean verdicts for all time-stamps that are at most $\tau - d$. Hence, the history needs to store only those expressions that fit into the interval $(\tau - d, \tau]$. For GLOBAL (or LOCAL) there are at most 2^{2^n} (or $d \cdot 2^{2^n}$) semantically different Boolean expressions that must be stored in the history. □

5.4   Implementation

We have implemented the presented algorithm using Standard ML. The implementation comprises just roughly 600 lines of code. It is available online [1].

Our implementation follows the pseudo-code in Sect. 5.2. In one aspect, it takes a more refined approach. The monitor's users would like violations to be reported as early as possible. The presented monitor does not do this as it delays the output of verdicts for one time-point, even if no future operators are involved. Our implementation improves this by refining the type of arr in the monitor's state from $\circledast \times \mathbb{N} \times (\circledast \to bexp\ array)$ to the more precise $\circledast \times \mathbb{N} \times bexp_f\ array$,, where the type of *potentially future expressions* $bexp_f$ is either an immediate Boolean expression or a future-dependent expression as before. Formally $bexp_f = \mathsf{Now}\ bexp\ |\ \mathsf{Later}\ (\circledast \to bexp)$.

This refined type makes it possible to output verdicts at the current time-point instead of the following one, provided that the computation of progress resulted in a Now constructor for the monitored formula Φ. Accordingly, the function progress must be refined to carefully assemble possibly future expressions to maximize the number of Now constructors in the array. To achieve this, all constructors (e.g., $\wedge$) of $bexp$ are lifted to functions (e.g., $\wedge_f$) on $bexp_f$ that try to produce as many Nows as possible by applying simplification rules such as $\mathsf{Now}\ \bot \wedge_f \mathsf{Later}\ f = \mathsf{Now}\ \bot$.

To implement the expression equivalence check, we use a simple BDD based algorithm that has been formally verified in the Isabelle proof assistant by Nipkow [16]. It would be interesting to explore working with BDDs instead of Boolean expressions all the time (and not only in the equivalence check) to potentially improve time complexity.

6   Evaluation

We compare the three versions of our tool with MonPoly [2,3], a state-of-the art monitor for *metric first-order temporal logic*. The experiments were run on a 3.1 GHz dual-core Intel Core-i7 processor and 16 GB RAM. We evaluate the memory consumption of all tools while monitoring four MTL formulas on pseudo-randomly generated event logs with varying average event rates. For the random generation, we used a different probability distribution for each event, depending on the formula. For example, for the formula $\Diamond_{[0,5]}p$, the probability of p occurring was very small. All our logs consist of 100 different time-stamps, with the number of time-points labeled with the same time-stamp ranging from 100 to 100 000 on average per log. Overall, the log files comprised 8 GB of data. Their generation required more time than the actual monitoring task (at least for the LOCAL and GLOBAL version of our algorithms). GNU Parallel [18] was invaluable for both generating the logs and running the four tools on them.

Figure 5 shows our evaluation results. Each data point in the graphs represents the average of the maximum memory consumption over 10 randomly generated logs of a fixed average event rate. (The standard deviation is omitted in the figure as it was far below 1 MB for most time-points.) For all formulas,

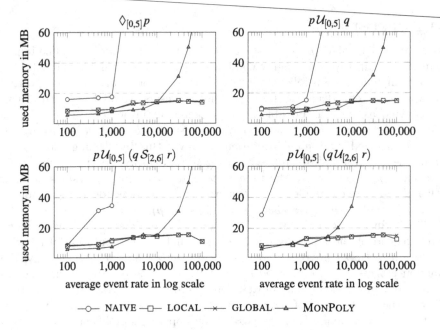

Fig. 5. Results of the experimental evaluation

the space consumption of both the NAIVE version of our tool and MONPOLY increases linearly in the event rate, while for LOCAL and GLOBAL it stays almost constant. This relationship between the memory usage and the average event rate is consistent with our theoretical analysis. Moreover, LOCAL and GLOBAL do not differ essentially in memory consumption. We therefore advise using the LOCAL version of the algorithm given its additional guarantee of outputting equivalence verdicts only for time-points labeled with the same time-stamp.

Although we were not measuring time, increasing the memory consumption to 60 MB results in a significant increase in processing time per event, which leads to a much lower throughput for monitors like NAIVE and MONPOLY. This is not the case for our almost event-rate independent monitors.

7   Conclusion

We introduced the notion event-rate independence for measuring the space complexity of monitoring algorithms. This notion is desirable for monitors processing event streams of varying velocity. We presented a novel algorithm for monitoring metric temporal logic with bounded future operators that is almost event-rate independent. Our algorithm is concise and efficient.

As future work, we plan to study which extensions of metric temporal logic permit almost event-rate independent algorithms. Moreover, we intend to parallelize our algorithm, using existing frameworks in the spirit of Spark [21], to obtain monitors for expressive temporal logics that scale to big data applications.

Acknowledgment. Jasmin Blanchette, Srdjan Krstic, and anonymous TACAS reviewers helped to improve the presentation of this work. Bhatt is supported by the Swiss National Science Foundation grant Big Data Monitoring (167162).

References

1. Aerial: An almost event-rate independent monitor for metric temporal logic (2016). https://bitbucket.org/traytel/aerial
2. Basin, D.A., Klaedtke, F., Müller, S., Pfitzmann, B.: Runtime monitoring of metric first-order temporal properties. In: FSTTCS 2008, pp. 49–60 (2008)
3. Basin, D.A., Klaedtke, F., Müller, S., Zalinescu, E.: Monitoring metric first-order temporal properties. J. ACM **62**(2), 15 (2015)
4. Basin, D., Klaedtke, F., Zălinescu, E.: Algorithms for monitoring real-time properties. In: Khurshid, S., Sen, K. (eds.) RV 2011. LNCS, vol. 7186, pp. 260–275. Springer, Heidelberg (2012). doi:10.1007/978-3-642-29860-8_20
5. Bauer, A., Küster, J.-C., Vegliach, G.: From propositional to first-order monitoring. In: Legay, A., Bensalem, S. (eds.) RV 2013. LNCS, vol. 8174, pp. 59–75. Springer, Heidelberg (2013). doi:10.1007/978-3-642-40787-1_4
6. Bauer, A., Leucker, M., Schallhart, C.: Comparing LTL semantics for runtime verification. J. Log. Comput. **20**(3), 651–674 (2010)
7. Du, X., Liu, Y., Tiu, A.: Trace-length independent runtime monitoring of quantitative policies in LTL. In: Bjørner, N., de Boer, F. (eds.) FM 2015. LNCS, vol. 9109, pp. 231–247. Springer, Heidelberg (2015). doi:10.1007/978-3-319-19249-9_15
8. Furia, C.A., Spoletini, P.: Bounded variability of metric temporal logic. In: Cesta, A., Combi, C., Laroussinie, F. (eds.) TIME 2014, pp. 155–163. IEEE Computer Society (2014)
9. Gunadi, H., Tiu, A.: Efficient runtime monitoring with metric temporal logic: a case study in the android operating system. In: Jones, C., Pihlajasaari, P., Sun, J. (eds.) FM 2014. LNCS, vol. 8442, pp. 296–311. Springer, Heidelberg (2014). doi:10.1007/978-3-319-06410-9_21
10. Havelund, K., Roşu, G.: Synthesizing monitors for safety properties. In: Katoen, J.-P., Stevens, P. (eds.) TACAS 2002. LNCS, vol. 2280, pp. 342–356. Springer, Heidelberg (2002). doi:10.1007/3-540-46002-0_24
11. Ho, H.-M., Ouaknine, J., Worrell, J.: Online monitoring of metric temporal logic. In: Bonakdarpour, B., Smolka, S.A. (eds.) RV 2014. LNCS, vol. 8734, pp. 178–192. Springer, Heidelberg (2014). doi:10.1007/978-3-319-11164-3_15
12. Koymans, R.: Specifying real-time properties with metric temporal logic. Real-Time Syst. **2**(4), 255–299 (1990)
13. Leucker, M., Schallhart, C.: A brief account of runtime verification. J. Log. Algebr. Program. **78**(5), 293–303 (2009)
14. Maler, O., Nickovic, D., Pnueli, A.: Real time temporal logic: past, present, future. In: Pettersson, P., Yi, W. (eds.) FORMATS 2005. LNCS, vol. 3829, pp. 2–16. Springer, Heidelberg (2005). doi:10.1007/11603009_2
15. McAfee, A., Brynjolfsson, E.: Big data: the management revolution. Harv. Bus. Rev. **90**(10), 61–67 (2012)
16. Nipkow, T.: Boolean expression checkers. Archive of Formal Proofs (2014). http://isa-afp.org/entries/Boolean_Expression_Checkers.shtml
17. Roşu, G., Havelund, K.: Rewriting-based techniques for runtime verification. Autom. Softw. Eng. **12**(2), 151–197 (2005)

18. Tange, O.: GNU parallel - the command-line power tool. login: USENIX Mag. **36**(1), 42–47 (2011). http://www.gnu.org/s/parallel

19. Thati, P., Roşu, G.: Monitoring algorithms for metric temporal logic specifications. Electr. Notes Theor. Comput. Sci. **113**, 145–162 (2005)

20. Ulus, D., Ferrère, T., Asarin, E., Maler, O.: Online timed pattern matching using derivatives. In: Chechik, M., Raskin, J.-F. (eds.) TACAS 2016. LNCS, vol. 9636, pp. 736–751. Springer, Heidelberg (2016). doi:10.1007/978-3-662-49674-9_47

21. Zaharia, M., Chowdhury, M., Franklin, M.J., Shenker, S., Stoica, I.: Spark: cluster computing with working sets. In: Nahum, E.M., Xu, D. (eds.) HotCloud 2010. USENIX Association (2010)

Optimal Translation of LTL to Limit Deterministic Automata

Dileep Kini$^{(\boxtimes)}$ and Mahesh Viswanathan

Department of Computer Science, University of Illinois at Urbana-Champaign,
Urbana, USA
kini2@illinois.edu

Abstract. A crucial step in model checking Markov Decision Processes (MDP) is to translate the LTL specification into automata. Efforts have been made in improving deterministic automata construction for LTL but such translations are double exponential in the worst case. For model checking MDPs though limit deterministic automata suffice. Recently it was shown how to translate the fragment LTL\$GU$ to exponential sized limit deterministic automata which speeds up the model checking problem by an exponential factor for that fragment. In this paper we show how to construct limit deterministic automata for full LTL. This translation is not only efficient for LTL\$GU$ but for a larger fragment LTL$_D$ which is provably more expressive. We show experimental results demonstrating that our construction yields smaller automata when compared to state of the art techniques that translate LTL to deterministic and limit deterministic automata.

1 Introduction

Markov Decision Processes (MDPs) [4,19,23] are the canonical model used to define the semantics of systems like concurrently running probabilistic programs that exhibit both stochastic and nondeterministic behavior. MDPs are interpreted with respect to a scheduler that resolves the nondeterminism. Such a scheduler chooses a probabilistic transition from a state based on the past sequence of states visited during the computation. When undesirable system behaviors are described by a formula φ in linear temporal logic (LTL), *qualitative verification* involves checking if there is some (adversarial) scheduler with respect to which the measure of paths satisfying φ is non-zero. Model checking algorithms [4] in this context proceed by translating the LTL requirement φ into an automaton $\mathcal{A}$, taking the synchronous cross-product of the MDP model M and the automaton $\mathcal{A}$ to construct a new MDP M', and finally, analyzing the MDP M' to check the desired property. The complexity of this procedure is polynomial in the size of the final MDP M', and hence critically depends on the size of automaton $\mathcal{A}$ that results from translating the LTL specification.

D. Kini and M. Viswanathan—Authors were supported by NSF grants CNS 1314485 and CCF 1422798.

© Springer-Verlag GmbH Germany 2017
A. Legay and T. Margaria (Eds.): TACAS 2017, Part II, LNCS 10206, pp. 113–129, 2017.
DOI: 10.1007/978-3-662-54580-5_7

MDP model checking algorithms based on the above idea require the translated automaton to be of a special form as general non-deterministic automata are not sufficient. The Büchi automaton has to be either deterministic or *deterministic in the limit* — a Büchi automaton is deterministic in the limit if every state reachable from an accepting state has deterministic transitions[1]. Limit-determinism is also sometimes referred to as semi-determinism. Deterministic or limit deterministic automata for LTL formulae can be constructed by first translating the formula into a nondeterministic Büchi automaton, and then either determinizing or "limit-determinizing" the machine. This results in an automaton that is doubly exponential in the size of the LTL formula, which gives a 2EXPTIME algorithm for model checking MDPs.

Direct translations of LTL (and fragments of LTL) to deterministic Rabin automata have been proposed [3,5,10,13,16,17]. However, any such translation, in the worst case, results in automata that are doubly exponential in size [2]; this holds for any fragment of LTL that contains the operators $\lor$, $\land$, and $\mathbf{F}$. Recently [8] a fragment of LTL called LTL\$GU$ [14] was translated into limit deterministic Büchi automata. LTL\$GU$ is a fragment of LTL where formulae are built from propositions and their negations using conjunction, disjunction, and the temporal operators $\mathbf{X}$ (next), $\mathbf{F}$ (eventually/finally), $\mathbf{G}$ (always/globally), and $\mathbf{U}$ (until), with the restriction that no $\mathbf{U}$ operator appears within the scope of a $\mathbf{G}$ operator. The most important feature of this translation from LTL\$GU$ to limit deterministic automata is the fact that the resulting automaton is only exponential in the size of the formula. Thus, this automata construction can be used to obtain an EXPTIME algorithm for model checking MDP against LTL\$GU$ formulas, as opposed to 2EXPTIME.

Recently, a translation from full LTL logic to limit deterministic automata has been proposed [20]. This translation is very similar to the translation to deterministic automata proposed in [5], with the use of nondeterminism being limited to simplifying the acceptance condition. Therefore, like the deterministic translations of LTL, it can be shown to construct doubly exponential sized automata even for very simple LTL fragments like those that contain $\lor$, $\land$, and $\mathbf{F}$. Thus, it does not achieve the optimal bounds for LTL\GU shown in [8]. However, one advantage of the construction in [20] is that it can be used in quantitative verification as well as qualitative verification of MDPs and has been implemented in [21]. Quantitative verification of MDPs can also be performed using nondeterministic automata that have the *good-for-games* (GFG) property [7,11], but translating a general NBA into a GFG automaton is known to result in an exponential blow-up. An alternate approach to quantitative verification using subset/breakpoint construction on a NBA is proposed in [6] but it also suffers from an exponential blow up.

---

[1] Limit deterministic automata are not the same as *unambiguous automata*. Unambiguous automata have at most one accepting run for any input. It is well known that every LTL formula can be translated into an unambiguous automaton of exponential size [22]. This has been shown to be not true for limit deterministic automata in [20].

In this paper we continue the line of work started in [8, 20], and present a new translation of the full LTL logic to limit deterministic Büchi automata. The new translation can be shown to be a generalization of the construction in [8] in that it constructs exponential sized automata for $LTL\backslash GU$. In fact, we show that this new translation yields exponential sized automata for a richer fragment of LTL that we call LTL_D (see Sect. 5 for a comparison between the expressive powers of LTL_D and $LTL\backslash GU$). This improves the complexity of qualitative MDP model checking against LTL_D to EXPTIME from 2EXPTIME.

Our automaton construction uses two main ideas. The first is an idea discovered in [8]. To achieve limit determinism, for certain subformulae ψ of φ, the automaton of φ tracks how often $\mathbf{F}\psi$ and $\mathbf{G}\psi$ formulae are true; this is in addition to tracking the truth (implicitly) of all subformulae ψ, as all translations from LTL to automata do. Second, for untils within the scope of $\mathbf{G}$, we do a form of subset construction that ensures that the state explores all the possible ways in which such formulae can be satisfied in the future, and for untils outside the scope of $\mathbf{G}$ we use non-determinism to check its truth.

We have implemented our translation from LTL to limit deterministic automata in a tool called Büchifier. We show experimental results demonstrating that in most cases our construction yields smaller automata when compared to state of the art techniques that translate LTL to deterministic and limit deterministic automata.

2   Preliminaries

First we introduce the notation we use throughout the paper. We use P to denote the set of propositions. We use w to denote infinite words over a finite alphabet. We use w_i to denote the ith (index starting at 0) symbol in the sequence w, and use $w[i]$ to denote the suffix $w_i w_{i+1} \ldots$ of w starting at i. We use $w[i, j]$ to denote the substring $w_i \ldots w_{j-1}$. We use $[n]$ to denote all non-negative integers less than n that is $\{0, 1, \ldots, n-1\}$. We begin by recalling the syntax of LTL:

Definition 1 (LTL Syntax). *Formulae in LTL are given by the following syntax:*

$$\varphi \quad ::= \quad p \mid \neg p \mid \varphi \wedge \varphi \mid \varphi \vee \varphi \mid \mathbf{X}\varphi \mid \mathbf{F}\varphi \mid \mathbf{G}\varphi \mid \varphi \mathbf{U} \varphi \qquad p \in P$$

Next, we look at the semantics of the various operators:

Definition 2 (Semantics). *LTL formulae over a set P are interpreted over words w in $(2^P)^\omega$. The semantics of the logic is given by the following rules*

$$
\begin{aligned}
&w \vDash p\,(\neg p) &&\iff p \in w_0\,(p \notin w_0) && w \vDash \mathbf{X}\varphi &&\iff w[1] \vDash \varphi \\
&w \vDash \varphi \vee \psi &&\iff w \vDash \varphi \text{ or } w \vDash \psi && w \vDash \mathbf{F}\varphi &&\iff \exists i : w[i] \vDash \varphi \\
&w \vDash \varphi \wedge \psi &&\iff w \vDash \varphi \text{ and } w \vDash \psi && w \vDash \mathbf{G}\varphi &&\iff \forall i : w[i] \vDash \varphi \\
&w \vDash \varphi \mathbf{U} \psi &&\iff \exists i : w[i] \vDash \psi,\, and \\
&&& \qquad \forall j < i : w[j] \vDash \varphi
\end{aligned}
$$

The semantics of φ, denoted by $\llbracket \varphi \rrbracket$, is defined as the set $\{w \in (2^P)^\omega \mid w \vDash \varphi\}$.

(Note that the release operator **R**, the dual of **U**, can be expressed using **U** and **G**, i.e. $\psi_1 \mathbf{R} \psi_2 \equiv (\psi_2 \mathbf{U} (\psi_1 \wedge \psi_2)) \vee \mathbf{G}\psi_2$. Hence we omit it from any of the logics we consider.)

In this paper the terminology *subformula of* φ is used to denote a node within the parse tree of φ. When we refer to the subformula as an LTL formula we will be referring to the formula at that node. Two subformulae that have the same formulae at their nodes need not be the same owing to the possibility of them being in different contexts. This distinction will be important as we treat formulae differently depending on their contexts. For the purposes of describing different subfragments we qualify subformulae as being either *internal* or *external*.

Definition 3. *A subformula ψ of φ is said to be* internal *if ψ is in the scope of some **G**-subformula of φ, otherwise it is said to be* external.

Many syntactic restrictions of LTL have been considered for the sake of obtaining smaller automata translations. LTL(F,G) (read "LTL F G") and LTL$\backslash GU$ (read "LTL set minus G U") are two such fragments which we recall in the next two definitions.

Definition 4 (LTL(F,G) Syntax). *The fragment* LTL(F,G) *over propositions P is described by the following syntax*

$$\varphi \quad ::= \quad p \mid \neg p \mid \varphi \wedge \varphi \mid \varphi \vee \varphi \mid \mathbf{X}\varphi \mid \mathbf{F}\varphi \mid \mathbf{G}\varphi \qquad p \in P$$

Definition 5 (LTL\GU Syntax). *The fragment* LTL$\backslash GU$ *is given by the syntax*

$$\psi \quad ::= \quad \varphi \mid \psi \wedge \psi \mid \psi \vee \psi \mid \mathbf{X}\psi \mid \psi \mathbf{U} \psi \qquad \varphi \in \mathrm{LTL}(F,G)$$

LTL(F,G) allows for **G** and **F** as the only temporal operators. The fragment LTL$\backslash GU$ additionally allows for external **U** but not internal ones. Also, we choose to represent an external **F** using **U**. In other words every **F** will be internal. Next, we introduce the fragment LTL$_D$ (read "LTL D")

Definition 6 (LTL$_D$ Syntax). *The formulae in the fragment* LTL$_D$ *are given by the syntax for ϑ:*

$$\psi \quad ::= \quad \varphi \mid \psi \vee \varphi \mid \varphi \vee \psi \mid \psi \wedge \psi \mid \psi \mathbf{U} \varphi \mid \mathbf{G}\psi \mid \mathbf{X}\psi \qquad \varphi \in \mathrm{LTL}(F,G)$$
$$\vartheta \quad ::= \quad \psi \mid \vartheta \vee \vartheta \mid \vartheta \wedge \vartheta \mid \vartheta \mathbf{U} \vartheta \mid \mathbf{X}\vartheta$$

Unlike LTL$\backslash GU$, LTL$_D$ allows for internal **U** but it is restricted. The following restrictions apply on LTL$_D$:

1. The second argument of every internal **U** formula is in LTL(F,G)
2. At least one argument of every internal $\vee$ is in LTL(F,G)

Note that LTL$_D$ is strictly larger than LTL$\backslash GU$ in the syntactic sense, as every LTL$\backslash GU$ formula is also an LTL$_D$ formula. We shall show in Sect. 5 that it is strictly richer in the semantic sense as well.

Next we define depth and height. A subformula ψ of φ is said to be at depth k if the number of $\mathbf{X}$ operators in φ within which ψ appears is exactly k. The height of a formula is the maximum depth of any of its subformulae.

Definition 7 (Büchi Automata). *A nondeterministic Büchi automaton (NBA) over input alphabet Σ is a tuple (Q, δ, I, F) where Q is a finite set of states; $\delta \subseteq Q \times \Sigma \times Q$ is a set of transitions; $I \subseteq Q$ is a set of initial states and $F \subseteq Q$ is a set of final states.*

A run of a word $w \in \Sigma^\omega$ over a NBA is an infinite sequence of states $q_0 q_1 q_2 \ldots$ such that $q_0 \in I$ and $\forall i \geq 0$ $(q_i, w_i, q_{i+1}) \in \delta$. A run is accepting if $q_i \in F$ for infinitely many i.

The language accepted by an NBA $\mathcal{A}$, denoted by $L(\mathcal{A})$ is the set of all words $w \in \Sigma^\omega$ which have an accepting run on $\mathcal{A}$.

Definition 8 (Limit Determinism). *A NBA (Q, δ, I, F) over input alphabet Σ is said to be* limit deterministic *if for every state q reachable from a final state, it is the case that $|\delta(q, \sigma)| \leq 1$ for every $\sigma \in \Sigma$.*

3   Construction

In this section we show our construction of limit deterministic automata for full LTL. First, let us look at an example that shows that the standard construction (Fischer-Ladner and its variants) is not limit deterministic. The standard construction involves guessing the set of subformulae that are true at each step and ensuring the guess is correct. For $\varphi = \mathbf{G}(a \vee \mathbf{F}b)$ this gives us the automaton (after pruning unreachable states and merging bisimilar ones. Here all 3 states are initial) in Fig. 1a which is not limit deterministic as the final state q_1 has non-deterministic choices enabled.

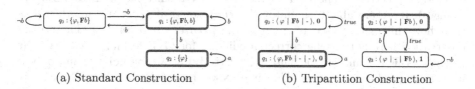

| (a) Standard Construction | (b) Tripartition Construction |

Fig. 1. Automata for $\mathbf{G}(a \vee \mathbf{F}b)$

Our construction builds upon the idea introduced in [8] of keeping track of how often $\mathbf{F},\mathbf{G}$-subformulae are true. Therefore, we will incrementally describe the features of our automaton: first by revisiting the technique required for LTL(F,G) without $\mathbf{X}$s, later by introducing the new ideas required to handle the untils and nexts.

Given an LTL(F,G) formula, for each of its $\mathbf{G}$-subformula we are going to predict whether it is: always true (α), true at some point but not always (β), never true (γ). Note that for any formula if we predict α/γ then the prediction should remain the same going forward. For a **G**-subformula, $\mathbf{G}\psi$, if we predict β it means we are asserting $\mathbf{FG}\psi \wedge \neg\mathbf{G}\psi$ and therefore the prediction should remain β until a certain point and then change to α. This prediction entails two kinds of non-deterministic choices: **(i)** the initial choice of assigning one of α, β, γ **(ii)** if assigned β initially then the choice of the time point at which to change it to α. The first choice needs to be made once at the beginning and the second choice has to be made eventually in a finite time. They together only constitute finitely many choices which is the source of the limit determinism. We similarly define predictions for **F**-subformulae as: never true (α), true at some point but not always (β), always true (γ). We flip the meaning of α and γ to ensure β becomes α eventually as for **G**-subformulae. An *FG-prediction* for a formula $\varphi \in \mathrm{LTL}(F,G)$, denoted by π, is a tri-partition $\langle \alpha(\pi), \beta(\pi), \gamma(\pi) \rangle$ of its **F**, **G**-subformulae. We drop π when it is clear from the context. The *prediction* for a subformula ψ made by π is said to be $\alpha/\beta/\gamma$ depending upon the partition of π in which ψ is present. The space of all FG-predictions for φ is denoted by $\Pi(\varphi)$.

Example 1. Consider the formula $\varphi = \mathbf{G}(a \vee \mathbf{F}b)$, and an FG-prediction $\pi = \langle \alpha, \beta, \gamma \rangle$ for φ where $\alpha = \{\varphi\}$, $\beta = \{\mathbf{F}b\}$ and $\gamma = \emptyset$. For the formula φ the prediction made is α. Since it is a **G**-formula this prediction says that φ is always true or simply φ is true. For the subformula $\mathbf{F}b$ the prediction made is β. This prediction says that $\mathbf{F}b$ is true at some point but not always which implies $\mathbf{F}b$ is true but not $\mathbf{GF}b$.

The automaton for $\mathrm{LTL}(F,G)$ essentially makes a non-deterministic choice for π initially and at each step makes a choice of whether to move some formula(e) from β to α. The correctness of predictions made by π is monitored inductively. Suppose our prediction for a formula $\mathbf{G}\psi$ is α at some instant: this implies we need to check that ψ is true at every time point there onwards (or equivalently check that ψ is true whenever α is predicted for $\mathbf{G}\psi$ since the prediction α never changes). If we are able to monitor the ***truth*** of ψ at every instant then it is clear how this can be used to monitor the ***prediction*** α for $\mathbf{G}\psi$. The crucial observation here is that the correct prediction for $\mathbf{G}/\mathbf{F}$ formula gives us their truth: a $\mathbf{G}/\mathbf{F}$ formula is true/false (respectively) at a time point if and only if its correct prediction is α at that time. Now the prediction α for $\mathbf{G}\psi$ can be checked by using the truths (derived from the predictions) of the subformulae of ψ (inductive step). If ψ is propositional then its truth is readily available from the input symbol being seen (base case of the induction). This inductive idea shall be used for all predictions. Note that since our formulae are in negation normal form we only need to verify a prediction is correct if it asserts the truth rather than falsehood of a subformula. Therefore the predictions β, γ for $\mathbf{G}\psi$ need not be checked. In case of $\mathbf{F}\psi$ the prediction α need not be checked (as it entails falsehood of $\mathbf{F}\psi$) but β, γ do need to be checked. If our prediction for $\mathbf{F}\psi$ is β then we are asserting ψ is true until a certain point in the future at which the prediction becomes α. Therefore we only need to check that ψ is true when the prediction for $\mathbf{F}\psi$ changes to α. Once again we can inductively obtain the truth of ψ at that instant from the predictions for the subformulae of ψ and from the next input. For checking a prediction γ about $\mathbf{F}\psi$ we need to check ψ is true infinitely often. For this purpose we use the Büchi acceptance where the final states are those where ψ is evaluated to be true, again inductively. When we are monitoring multiple $\mathbf{F}\psi$ for γ we will need a counter to cycle through all the $\mathbf{F}\psi$ in γ. Let m be the number of $\mathbf{F}\psi$ in γ. Observe that the set of formulae predicted to be γ never changes once fixed at the beginning and hence m is well defined. When the counter has value n, it is incremented cyclically to $n + 1(\mathrm{mod}\ m)$ whenever the ψ corresponding to the nth $\mathbf{F}\psi \in \gamma$ evaluates to true. The initial states are those in which the top formula evaluates to true given the predictions in that state. The final states are those where no formula is assigned β and the counter is 0. Summarizing, a state in our automata has two components: **(a)** an FG-prediction $\pi = \langle \alpha, \beta, \gamma \rangle$ (a tri-partition of the $\mathbf{F}, \mathbf{G}$-subformulae) and **(b)** a cyclic integer counter n. The transitions are determined by how the predictions and counters are allowed to change as described. We illustrate the construction using once again the formula $\varphi = \mathbf{G}(a \vee \mathbf{F}b)$ for which the automaton is presented in Fig. 1b and its details are completely described in the technical report [9].

3.1   Handling Untils and Nexts

Next we observe that the above technique does not lend itself to the $\mathbf{U}/\mathbf{X}$ operators. The crucial property used above about $\mathbf{F}, \mathbf{G}$-formulae is that they cannot be simultaneously infinitely often true and infinitely often false unlike $\mathbf{U}/\mathbf{X}$ formulae. So if we tried the above technique for $\mathbf{U}/\mathbf{X}$ we would not get limit determinism since the truth of the $\mathbf{U}/\mathbf{X}$ formulae would have to be guessed infinitely often.

The key idea we use in handling $\mathbf{U}/\mathbf{X}$s is to propagate their *obligation* along the states. Let us say the automaton needs to check if a formula φ holds for an input w, and it begins by making an FG-prediction π about w. The obligation when no input has been seen is φ. When the first symbol w_0 is seen it needs to update the obligation to reflect what "remains to be checked" for the rest of the input $w[1]$, in order for $w \vDash \varphi$ to hold, assuming π is correct for w. The automaton can keep updating the obligation as it sees each input symbol. The claim will be that the obligation is never falsified iff $w \vDash \varphi$, given that π is correct. This brings up some questions:

1. How are we exploiting opportunities for non-determinism?
2. How is the obligation computed at each step?
3. How is π checked to be correct in the presence of $\mathbf{U}/\mathbf{X}$s?

Exploiting Non-determinism. Being able to exploit non-determinism helps in reducing the size of the automaton we construct. So the question is: how are we exploiting any opportunities for non-determinism (albeit for finite time)? The answer is to update the obligation non-deterministically. Checking the formula $\psi_1 \mathbf{U} \psi_2$ presents us with two alternatives: either ψ_2 is true now or $\psi_1 \wedge \mathbf{X}(\psi_1 \mathbf{U} \psi_2)$ is true now. Similarly $\psi_1 \vee \psi_2$ brings up two alternatives. We can pick between the obligations of these two choices non-deterministically. But we should somehow

Fig. 2. Standard NBA construction for $\varphi = a\mathbf{U}(\mathbf{G}b)$.

ensure that we are only allowed to use this non-determinism finitely often. This is where we treat internal and external (Definition 3) $\mathbf{U}/\vee$ subformulae differently. The observation is that external $\mathbf{U}/\vee$ need to be checked for only a finite amount of time. Hence the disjunctive choice presented by them can be dispatched non-deterministically each time without worrying about violating limit determinism. To illustrate this point we show the standard NBA for the formula $\varphi = a\mathbf{U}(\mathbf{G}b)$ in Fig. 2 which turns out to be limit deterministic owing to the fact that the $\mathbf{U}$ is external. In Fig. 1a we saw that the standard construction for $\varphi = \mathbf{G}(a \vee \mathbf{F}b)$ resulted in a NBA that was not limit-deterministic, and one of the reasons is that the $\mathbf{F}$, which is a special form of $\mathbf{U}$, is internal. An internal $\mathbf{U}/\vee$ may need to be checked infinitely many times and hence the choice should not be resolved non-deterministically, but carried forward as a disjunction of the obligations of the choices. Passing the choice forward without resolving it comes at a cost of a bigger state space, this is akin to the subset construction where all the choices are being kept track of.

Now we begin to formalize the ideas. To exploit the non-determinism allowed by the external $\mathbf{U}/\vee$ we introduce the concept of *ex-choice*. We use Λ_φ to denote the set of all external $\mathbf{U}/\vee$ subformulae. Any subset of it $\lambda \subseteq \Lambda_\varphi$ is called an ex-choice. An ex-choice dictates how each external $\mathbf{U}/\vee$ should be satisfied if it needs to be satisfied. The interpretation associated with λ is the following: if $\psi_1\mathbf{U}\psi_2 \in \lambda$ then ψ_2 has to hold or if $\psi_1\mathbf{U}\psi_2 \in \Lambda_\varphi - \lambda$ then $\psi_1 \wedge \mathbf{X}(\psi_1\mathbf{U}\psi_2)$ has to hold. Similarly if $\psi_1 \vee \psi_2 \in \lambda$ then ψ_1 has to hold and if $\psi_1 \vee \psi_2 \in \Lambda_\varphi - \lambda$ then ψ_2 has to hold. The automaton we are going to construct is going to non-deterministically pick an ex-choice at each step and use it resolve the choices on external $\mathbf{U}/\vee$. After a finite time the ex-choice will not matter as the obligations will not consist of any external $\mathbf{U}/\vee$ that need to be checked (which will be enforced as a part of the acceptance condition), and hence limit determinism is ensured. The ex-choice picked along a transition is going to determine the obligation computed. Which leads us to the question of how the obligation is computed.

Computing Obligation. We define the *derivative* of a formula μ w.r.t an input symbol σ, FG-prediction π and ex-choice λ. The derivative should capture the obligation/requirement on any word ρ such that those obligations are able to imply that $\sigma\rho$ satisfies μ. This enables us to keep passing on the obligation forward as we see each symbol of the input by taking the derivative of the obligation so far. First, we need to ensure that the ex-choice λ picked when we are taking the transition dictates how a formula in Λ_φ should be satisfied if it needs to be. With that in mind we define $f(\lambda)$ as follows:

$$f(\lambda) = (\wedge_{(\phi\mathbf{U}\psi\in\lambda)}\phi \mathbf{U} \psi \Rightarrow \psi) \wedge (\wedge_{(\phi\mathbf{U}\psi\in(\Lambda_\varphi-\lambda))}\phi \mathbf{U} \psi \Rightarrow (\phi \wedge \mathbf{X}(\phi \mathbf{U} \psi)))$$
$$\wedge (\wedge_{(\phi\vee\psi\in\lambda)}\phi \vee \psi \Rightarrow \phi) \wedge (\wedge_{(\phi\vee\psi\in\Lambda_\varphi-\lambda)}\phi \vee \psi \Rightarrow \psi)$$

Since predictions made by π already tell us the truth of some of the subformulae, they need to be taken into account. Towards that we define the *substitution* of a formula ϕ w.r.t π, denoted by $[\phi]_\pi$ as the formula obtained from ϕ by substituting occurrences $\mathbf{G}\psi$ with $\mathbf{tt}$ if $\mathbf{G}\psi \in \alpha$ and $\mathbf{ff}$ otherwise, and similarly for $\mathbf{F}\psi$ with $\mathbf{ff}$ if $\mathbf{F}\psi \in \alpha$ and $\mathbf{tt}$ otherwise. The substitutions are done only for the maximal formulae in π that appear in ϕ, i.e., if ψ_1, ψ_2 are formulae in π such that ψ_1 is a subformula of ψ_2 then the substitution is not performed for ψ_1. Now we are ready to give a declarative definition of the derivative:

Definition 9. *Given an LTL formula μ over P, and a triple $\varepsilon = (\sigma, \pi, \lambda)$ where $\sigma \in 2^P$, $\pi \in \Pi(\varphi)$ and $\lambda \subseteq \Lambda_\varphi$: an LTL formula ψ is said to be a **derivative** of μ w.r.t to ε if*

$$\forall \rho \in \left(2^P\right)^\omega \quad \rho \vDash \psi \implies \sigma\rho \vDash [\mu \wedge f(\lambda)]_\pi$$

*The **weakest derivative** of μ w.r.t ε, denoted by $\nabla(\mu, \varepsilon)$, is a derivative such that $\psi \implies \nabla(\mu, \varepsilon)$ for any other derivative ψ.*

Since we will only be interested in the weakest derivative (as opposed to any other derivative) we shall refer to it as the derivative. The above definition is only declarative in the sense that it does not give us an explicit way to compute the derivative. We present this definition here for the sake of simplicity and ease of understanding for the reader. In the companion technical report [9] we provide a syntactic definition and all the necessary machinery that allows us to compute such a formula. The syntactic definition also restricts the representation of the obligations to $\mathcal{B}^+(\varphi)$ which is the set of all positive Boolean combinations of subformulae of φ.

The automaton now will have an extra component μ corresponding to the obligation along with (π, n) from before. In the initial state μ will be the given formula φ that needs to be checked. At each step, the automaton sees an input symbol σ and makes a non-deterministic ex-choice $\lambda \subseteq \Lambda_\varphi$. The obligation at the next state will then become $\nabla(\mu, \varepsilon)$ where $\varepsilon = (\sigma, \pi, \lambda)$. The process continues as long as the obligation is never falsified. In order to ensure that every external until is dispatched in finite time, we impose that the obligation μ in the final states is *ex-free*, i.e. free of any formulae in Λ_φ. When the obligation is ex-free the ex-choice does not play a role in determining its derivative and we shall drop λ whenever that is the case, and this eliminates any non-determinism once a final state is visited. In order to ensure that an internal until, say $\phi\,\mathbf{U}\,\psi$ is not delayed forever, we involve $\mathbf{F}\psi$ in the FG-prediction and enhance the definition of substitution to say that $\phi\,\mathbf{U}\,\psi$ is replaced with $\mathbf{ff}$ if $\mathbf{F}\psi \in \alpha$. This way the derivative will impose that $\mathbf{F}\psi$ is true whenever $\phi\,\mathbf{U}\,\psi$ is claimed to be true. With this in mind we define the closure of φ, denoted by $\mathcal{C}(\varphi)$, to be set of all $\mathbf{F}, \mathbf{G}$-subformulae of φ, along with all $\mathbf{F}\psi$ for every internal $\phi\mathbf{U}\psi$ subformula of φ. We re-define an FG-prediction π to be any tri-partition of $\mathcal{C}(\varphi)$. Note that for every $\mathbf{F}\psi$ or $\mathbf{G}\psi$ in $\mathcal{C}(\varphi)$, ψ is internal.

Example 2. Let $\varphi = \mathbf{G}(\mathbf{F}a \vee (b\,\mathbf{U}\,c))$. Here $\mathcal{C}(\varphi) = \{\varphi, \mathbf{F}a, \mathbf{F}c\}$.

Example 3. Let $\varphi = a\mathbf{U}(b \wedge \mathbf{G}c)$ be an internal subformula of some given formula. $\nabla(\varphi, \varepsilon)$ can take different values depending upon $\varepsilon = (\sigma, \pi)$. Here ex-choice λ does not play a role because the only $\mathbf{U}$ is internal. Note that $\varphi' = \mathbf{F}(b \wedge \mathbf{G}c)$ is in the closure. If $\varphi' \in \alpha$, then $\nabla(\varphi, \varepsilon) = \mathbf{ff}$ because $[\varphi]_\pi$ would be $\mathbf{ff}$ owing to φ being substituted with $\mathbf{ff}$. Let $\varphi' \notin \alpha$. Now if $\mathbf{G}c \in \alpha$ then substituting $\mathbf{tt}$ in place of $\mathbf{G}c$ gives us $a\mathbf{U}b$ whose satisfaction depends upon the truth of a and b as given by σ. So if $\sigma(b) = \mathbf{tt}$ then the $\mathbf{U}$ is immediately satisfied and so $\nabla(\varphi, \varepsilon) = \mathbf{tt}$. If $\sigma(b) = \mathbf{ff}$ then the $\mathbf{U}$ is delayed and hence $\nabla(\varphi, \varepsilon)$ is either $a\mathbf{U}b$ or $\mathbf{ff}$ depending on $\sigma(a) = \mathbf{tt}/\mathbf{ff}$ respectively. If $\mathbf{G}c \notin \alpha$ then truth of b does not matter (as replacing $\mathbf{G}c$ with $\mathbf{ff}$ makes $b \wedge \mathbf{G}c = \mathbf{ff}$) and once again the derivative is $\varphi/\mathbf{ff}$ depending upon $\sigma(a)$.

Checking FG-Predictions in the Presence of Untils and Nexts.

The main idea in being able to check an FG-prediction π was that a correct prediction about an $\mathbf{F}, \mathbf{G}$-subformula also tells us its truth. When we have $\mathbf{U}/\mathbf{X}$s in the mix, we no longer have a prediction available for them, and hence no immediate way to check if some subformula is true. For example when $\mathbf{G}\psi \in \alpha$ we needed to check ψ is true and we did so inductively using the predictions for subformulae in ψ. Now, since ψ can have $\mathbf{U}/\mathbf{X}$ within them it is not clear how we are going to check truth of ψ. In this case we pass ψ to the obligation μ. Similarly when the prediction of $\mathbf{F}\psi$ is changed from β to α we need to check ψ is true so once again we pass ψ to the obligation. So given consecutive FG-predictions π, π' define Ψ as the set

$$\Psi = \{\psi \mid \mathbf{F}\psi \in \beta(\pi) \cap \alpha(\pi') \text{ or } \mathbf{G}\psi \in \alpha(\pi)\} \tag{1}$$

and update the obligation along a transition $(\mu, \pi, n) \xrightarrow{\sigma} (\mu', \pi', n')$ as: $\mu' = \nabla(\mu \wedge (\wedge_{\psi \in \Psi}\psi), \varepsilon)$ where $\varepsilon = (\sigma, \pi, \lambda)$. Now consider the case when the counter is $n > 0$ and need to verify that the nth $\mathbf{F}\psi$ formula in γ is true. In this case we cannot pass on ψ to the obligation because $\mathbf{F}\psi$ may be true because ψ is true at a later point and not now. Since we cannot predict when ψ is going to be true we carry the disjunction of all the derivatives of ψ since the counter was incremented to n. We keep doing it until this "carry" becomes true indicating that ψ became true at some point since we started checking for it. We also increment the counter at that point. This "carry" becomes yet another component ν in the automaton's state. We use $\mathbb{F}(S)$ to denote all $\mathbf{F}\psi$ in set S. Now we are ready to put the pieces together to formally describe the entire construction.

Definition 10 (Construction).

Given a formula $\varphi \in$ LTL over propositions P, let $\mathcal{D}(\varphi)$ be the NBA (Q, δ, I, F) over the alphabet 2^P defined as follows:

- *Q is the set $\mathcal{B}^+(\varphi) \times \mathcal{B}^+(\varphi) \times \Pi(\varphi) \times [n]$ where $n = |\mathbb{F}(\mathcal{C}(\varphi))| + 1$*
- *δ is the set of all transitions $(\mu, \nu, \pi, m) \xrightarrow{\sigma} (\mu', \nu', \pi', m')$ such that*
  - *(a) $\alpha(\pi) \subseteq \alpha(\pi')$ and $\gamma(\pi) = \gamma(\pi')$*
  - *(b) $\mu' = \nabla(\mu \wedge \theta, \varepsilon)$ for some $\lambda \subseteq \Lambda_\varphi$*
    where $\theta = (\wedge_{\psi \in \Psi}\psi)$, Ψ as defined in (1) and $\varepsilon = (\sigma, \pi, \lambda)$

(c) $m' = \begin{cases} (m+1) \, (mod \, |\mathbb{F}(\gamma)| + 1) & \nu = \mathbf{tt} \\ m & \text{otherwise} \end{cases}$

(d) $\nu' = \begin{cases} \psi_{m'} & \nu = \mathbf{tt} \\ \nabla(\nu, \varepsilon) \vee \psi_m & \text{otherwise} \end{cases}$

     where $\{\mathbf{F}\psi_1, .., \mathbf{F}\psi_k\}$ *is an enumeration of* $\mathbb{F}(\gamma)$, $\psi_0 = \mathbf{tt}$ *and* $\varepsilon = (\sigma, \pi)$
■ *I is all states of the form* $(\varphi, \mathbf{tt}, \pi, 0)$
■ *F is all states of the form* $(\mu, \mathbf{tt}, \pi, 0)$ *where* $\beta(\pi) = \emptyset$, $\mu \neq \mathbf{ff}$, μ *is ex-free*

We state the correctness result here and include the proofs in the technical report [9].

Theorem 1. *For* $\varphi \in$ *LTL,* $\mathcal{D}(\varphi)$ *is a limit deterministic automaton such that* $L(\mathcal{D}(\varphi)) = [\![\varphi]\!]$ *and* $\mathcal{D}(\varphi)$ *is of size at most double exponential in* φ.

The number of different formulae in $\mathcal{B}^+(\varphi)$, is at most double exponential in the size of φ, since each can be represented as a collection of subsets of subformulae of φ. $\Pi(\varphi)$ is simply tripartition of $\mathcal{C}(\varphi)$ which is bounded above by $3^{|\varphi|}$. And the counter can take $|\mathbb{F}(\mathcal{C}(\varphi))| + 1$ different values which is $\leq |\varphi|$. The entire state space $\mathcal{B}^+(\varphi) \times \mathcal{B}^+(\varphi) \times \Pi(\varphi) \times [n]$ is upper bounded by the product of these which is clearly doubly exponential.

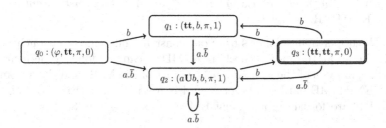

Fig. 3. Our construction for $\varphi = \mathbf{G}(a\mathbf{U}b)$.

We illustrate our construction using $\varphi = \mathbf{G}(a\mathbf{U}b)$ which is a formula outside LTL\GU. The automaton for φ is shown in Fig. 3. First note that the $\mathcal{C}(\varphi) = \{\varphi, \mathbf{F}b\}$. Next, observe that the only interesting FG-prediction is π in which $\alpha = \{\varphi\}$, $\beta = \emptyset$ and $\gamma = \{\mathbf{F}b\}$. This is because any initial state will have $\mu = \varphi$ which forces $\varphi \in \alpha$, and since predictions in α don't change, every reachable state will have $\varphi \in \alpha$ as well. As for $\mathbf{F}b$ note that the corresponding internal until $a\mathbf{U}b$ will become $\mathbf{ff}$ if $\mathbf{F}b$ is in α and thus making the derivative $\mathbf{ff}$ ($a\mathbf{U}b$ is added to the obligation at each step since $\varphi \in \alpha$ and rule **(b)**). Therefore $\mathbf{F}b$ cannot be in α, and it cannot be in β because then it would be eventually in α. So $\mathbf{F}b$ has to be in γ. Now that π is fixed, and given input σ, the obligation μ changes according to rule **(b)** as $\mu' = \nabla(\mu \wedge (a\mathbf{U}b), (\sigma, \pi))$. Similarly the carry ν changes to b if $\nu = \mathbf{tt}$ (as in q_3 to q_1/q_2) and becomes $\nu' = \nabla(\nu, (\sigma, \pi)) \vee b$

otherwise in accordance with rule **(d)**. The initial state is q_0 with $\mu = \varphi$, $\nu = \mathbf{tt}$ and counter $= 0$. The counter is incremented whenever ν becomes $\mathbf{tt}$. It is easy to see that the automaton indeed accepts $\mathbf{G}(a \, \mathbf{U} \, b)$ and is limit deterministic.

4   Efficiency

In this section we state the results regarding the efficiency of our construction for LTL_D. We prove that there are only exponentially many reachable states in $\mathcal{D}(\varphi)$. A state $q = (\mu, \nu, \pi, n)$ of $\mathcal{D}(\varphi)$ is called reachable if there exists a valid finite run of the automaton that ends in q. A μ is said to be reachable if (μ, ν, π, n) is reachable for some choice of ν, π and n. Similarly for ν. We show that the space of reachable μ and ν is only exponentially large in the size of φ. Our approach will be to show that every reachable μ (or ν) can be expressed in a certain way, and we will count the number of different such expressions to obtain an upper bound. The expression for μ and ν relies on them being represented in DNF form and uses the syntactic definition of the derivative given in the technical report [9]. Therefore we state only the main result and its consequence on the model checking complexity here and present the proofs in [9].

Theorem 2. *For $\varphi \in \text{LTL}_\text{D}$ the number of reachable states in the $\mathcal{D}(\varphi)$ is at most exponential in $|\varphi|$.*

Theorem 3. *The model checking problem for MDPs against specification in LTL_D is EXPTIME-complete*

Proof. The upper bound follows from our construction being of exponential size and the fact that the model checking of MDPs can be done by performing a linear time analysis of the synchronous product of the MDP and the automaton [4]. The EXPTIME hardness lower bound is from the fact that the problem is EXPTIME hard for the subfragment $\text{LTL}\backslash GU$ as proved in [8].

5   Expressive Power of LTL_D

In this section we show that LTL_D is semantically more expressive than $\text{LTL}\backslash GU$. We demonstrate that the formula $\varphi_0 = \mathbf{G}(p \vee (q\mathbf{U}r))$ which is expressible in LTL_D, cannot be expressed by any formula in $\text{LTL}\backslash GU$.

Let us fix integers $\ell, k \in \mathbb{N}$. We will use $\text{LTL}_\ell(F, G)$ to denote the subfragment of $\text{LTL}(F,G)$ where formulae have maximum height ℓ. Since $\mathbf{X}$ distributes over all other operators we assume that all the $\mathbf{X}$s are pushed inside. We use $\text{LTL}_{\ell,k}\backslash GU$ to denote the fragment where formulae are built out of $\mathbf{U}$, $\wedge$, $\vee$ and $\text{LTL}_\ell(F, G)$ formulae such that the number of $\mathbf{U}$s used is at most k.

Next, consider the following strings over 2^P where $P = \{p, q, r\}$:

$$u = \{p\}\{p,q\}^\ell\{p\} \quad v = \{q\}\{p,q\}^\ell\{r\} \quad w = \{q\}\{p,q\}^\ell\{p\}$$
$$s_k = (uv)^{k+1}u \qquad \sigma = (uv)^\omega \qquad \eta_k = s_k wv\sigma$$

The observation we make is that σ satisfies φ_0 but η_k does not. We state the main theorem and the corollary here and leave the details in the tech report [9].

Theorem 4. $\forall \varphi \in \text{LTL}_{\ell,k} \backslash GU \quad \sigma \vDash \varphi \implies \eta_k \vDash \varphi$

Corollary 1. φ_0 *is not expressible in* $\text{LTL}_{\ell,k} \backslash GU$. *Also since* ℓ *and* k *are arbitrary,* φ_0 *is not expressible in* $\text{LTL} \backslash GU$.

6 Experimental Results

We present our tool Büchifier (available at [1]) that implements the techniques described in this paper. Büchifier is the first tool to generate LDBA with provable exponential upper bounds for a large class of LTL formulae. The states (μ, ν, π, n) in our automaton described in Definition 10, involve $\mu, \nu \in \mathcal{B}^+(\varphi)$ which are essentially sets of sets of subformulae. We view each subformula as a different proposition. We then interpret the formulae in $\mathcal{B}^+(\varphi)$ as a Boolean function on these propositions. In Büchifier we represent these Boolean functions symbolically using Binary Decision Diagrams (BDD). Our overall construction follows a standard approach where we begin with an initial set of states and keep adding successors to discover the entire reachable set of states. We report the number of states, number of transitions and the number of final states for the limit deterministic automata we construct.

MDP model checkers like PRISM [15], for a long time have used the translation from LTL to deterministic Rabin automata and only recently [20] have started using limit deterministic Büchi automata. As a consequence we compare the performance of our method against Rabinizer 3 [12] (the best known tool for translating LTL to deterministic automata) and ltl2ldba [20] (the only other known tool for translating LTL to LDBA). Rabinizer 3 constructs deterministic Rabin automata with generalized Rabin pairs (DGRA). The experimental results in [5,12] report the size of DGRA using the number of states and number of acceptance pairs of the automata; the size of each Rabin pair is, unfortunately, not reported. Since the size of Rabin pairs influences the efficiency of MDP model checking, we report it here to make a meaningful comparison. We take the size of a Rabin pair to be simply the number of transitions in it. The tool ltl2ldba generates transition-based generalized Büchi automata (TGBA). The experimental results in [20] report the size of the TGBA using number of states and number of acceptance sets, and once again the size of each of these sets is not reported. Since their sizes also effect the model checking procedure we report them here. We take the size of an acceptance set to be simply the number of transitions in it. In Table 1 we report a head to head comparison of Büchifier, Rabinizer 3 and ltl2ldba on various LTL formulae.

1. The first 5 formulae are those considered in [5]; they are from the GR(1) fragment [18] of LTL. These formulae capture Boolean combination of fairness conditions for which generalized Rabin acceptance is particularly well suited. Rabinizer 3 does well on these examples, but Büchifier is not far behind its competitors. The formulae are instantiations of the following templates: $g_0(j) = \wedge_{i=1}^{j}(\mathbf{GF}a_i \Rightarrow \mathbf{GF}b_i)$, $g_1(j) = \wedge_{i=1}^{j}(\mathbf{GF}a_i \Rightarrow \mathbf{GF}a_{i+1})$.

Table 1. A Comparison between the sizes of automata produced by `Büchifier`, `Rabinizer 3` and `ltl2ldba` on various formulae. Column St denotes the number of states, column Tr denotes the number of transitions and column AC denotes the size of the acceptance condition. Entries marked as "–" indicate that the tool failed to construct the automaton and/or the acceptance condition due to the memory limit (1 GB) being exceeded.

	Büchifier			Rabinizer 3			ltl2ldba		
	St	Tr	AC	St	Tr	AC	St	Tr	AC
$g_0(1)$	4	7	2	1	1	3	3	6	2 (1)
$g_0(2)$	12	23	5	1	1	8	5	14	12 (2)
$g_0(3)$	32	63	8	1	1	20	9	36	54 (3)
$g_1(2)$	12	21	5	1	1	8	5	13	11 (2)
$g_1(3)$	31	54	13	1	1	18	9	30	44 (3)
φ_1	5	7	3	5	13	40	7	23	12 (4)
φ_2	26	83	8	12	48	233	36	101	75 (2)
φ_3	13	25	3	16	128	64	21	140	129 (2)
φ_4	17	47	7	2	4	35	9	29	31 (2)
φ_5	36	111	11	12	48	330	41	133	94 (2)
$f_0(1)$	4	7	2	2	4	2	2	4	2 (1)
$f_0(2)$	14	29	5	16	74	26	4	16	16 (2)
$f_0(3)$	44	105	13	–	–	–	8	64	96 (3)
$f_0(4)$	130	369	33	–	–	–	16	256	512 (4)
$f_1(1)$	14	29	5	6	24	10	8	32	12 (1)
$f_1(2)$	130	369	33	–	–	–	64	1024	768 (2)
$f_1(3)$	1050	4801	193	–	–	–	512	32768	36K (3)
$f_2(1)$	1	1	1	2	3	2	1	1	2 (2)
$f_2(2)$	5	7	3	5	13	45	6	21	9 (3)
$f_2(3)$	19	37	7	19	109	847	19	218	28 (4)
$f_2(4)$	65	175	15	167	2529	–	93	6301	75 (5)
$f_3(1)$	2	4	1	3	7	4	1	2	3 (2)
$f_3(2)$	10	20	4	17	91	53	14	62	28 (1)
$f_3(3)$	36	78	12	–	–	–	212	2359	953 (1)
$f_3(4)$	114	288	32	–	–	–	17352	598330	167K (1)
$h(2,1)$	26	54	9	15	49	49	14	44	1 (1)
$h(2,2)$	60	138	21	65	469	469	64	434	1 (1)
$h(2,3)$	182	468	57	315	5119	5119	314	4892	1 (1)
$h(4,1)$	80	146	36	76	250	250	75	229	1 (1)
$h(4,2)$	230	464	96	990	8068	8068	989	7465	1 (1)
$h(4,3)$	908	1994	348	–	–	–	–	–	–
ψ_1	35	62	9	3	6	12	3	6	8 (3)
ψ_2	7	15	3	8	39	53	2	5	18 (3)
ψ_3	29	62	8	29	116	74	62	293	27 (2)
ψ_4	26	92	6	4	11	7	3	8	3 (1)
ψ_5	9	58	1	5	17	9	3	9	3 (1)

2. The next 5 formulae are also from [5] to show how `Rabinizer 3` can effectively handle $\mathbf{X}$s. `Büchifier` has a comparable number of states and much smaller acceptance condition when compared to `Rabinizer 3` and `ltl2ldba` in all these cases. $\varphi_1 = \mathbf{G}(q \vee \mathbf{X}\mathbf{G}p) \wedge \mathbf{G}(r \vee \mathbf{X}\mathbf{G}\neg p)$, $\varphi_2 = (\mathbf{GF}(a \wedge \mathbf{X}^2 b) \vee \mathbf{FG}b) \wedge \mathbf{FG}(c \vee (\mathbf{X}a \wedge \mathbf{X}^2 b))$, $\varphi_3 = \mathbf{GF}(\mathbf{X}^3 a \wedge \mathbf{X}^4 b) \wedge \mathbf{GF}(b \vee \mathbf{X}c) \wedge \mathbf{GF}(c \wedge \mathbf{X}^2 a)$, $\varphi_4 = (\mathbf{GF}a \vee \mathbf{FG}b) \wedge (\mathbf{GF}c \vee \mathbf{FG}(d \vee \mathbf{X}e))$, $\varphi_5 = (\mathbf{GF}(a \wedge \mathbf{X}^2 c) \vee \mathbf{FG}b) \wedge (\mathbf{GF}c \vee \mathbf{FG}(d \vee (\mathbf{X}a \wedge \mathbf{X}^2 b)))$.

3. The next 15 formulae (4 groups) express a variety of natural properties, such as $\mathbf{G}(req \Rightarrow \mathbf{F}ack)$ which says that every request that is received is eventually acknowledged. As shown in the table in many of the cases `Rabinizer 3` runs out of memory (1 GB) and fails to produce an automaton, and `ltl2ldba` fails to scale in comparison with `Büchifier`. The formulae in the table are instantiations of the following templates: $f_0(j) = \mathbf{G}(\wedge_{i=1}^{j}(a_i \Rightarrow \mathbf{F}b_i))$, $f_1(j) = \mathbf{G}(\wedge_{i=1}^{j}(a_i \Rightarrow (\mathbf{F}b_i \wedge \mathbf{F}c_i)))$, $f_2(j) = \mathbf{G}(\vee_{i=1}^{j}(a_i \wedge \mathbf{G}b_i))$, $f_3(j) = \mathbf{G}(\vee_{i=1}^{j}(a_i \wedge \mathbf{F}b_i))$.

4. The next 6 formulae expressible in LTL\$GU$, contain multiple $\mathbf{X}$s and external $\mathbf{U}$s. `Büchifier` constructs smaller automata and is able to scale better than `ltl2ldba` in these cases as well. The formulae are instantiations of: $h(m, n) = (\mathbf{X}^m p) \mathbf{U} (q \vee (\wedge_{i=1}^{n}(a_i \mathbf{U} \mathbf{X}^m b_i)))$.

5. The last few examples are from outside of LTL\$GU$. The first three are in LTL_D while the rest are outside LTL_D. We found that `Büchifier` did better only in a few cases (like ψ_3), this is due to the multiplicative effect that the internal untils have on the size of the automaton. So there is scope for improvement and we believe there are several optimizations that can be done to reduce the size in such cases and leave it for future work. $\psi_1 = \mathbf{FG}((a \wedge \mathbf{X}^2 b \wedge \mathbf{GF}b) \mathbf{U} (\mathbf{G}(\mathbf{X}^2 \neg c \vee \mathbf{X}^2(a \wedge b))))$, $\psi_2 = \mathbf{G}(\mathbf{F}\neg a \wedge \mathbf{F}(b \wedge \mathbf{X}c) \wedge \mathbf{GF}(a \mathbf{U} d))$, $\psi_3 = \mathbf{G}((\mathbf{X}^3 a) \mathbf{U} (b \vee \mathbf{G}c))$, $\psi_4 = \mathbf{G}((a \mathbf{U} b) \vee (c \mathbf{U} d))$, $\psi_5 = \mathbf{G}(a \mathbf{U} (b \mathbf{U} (c \mathbf{U} d)))$.

7   Conclusion

In this paper we presented a translation of formulas in LTL to limit deterministic automata, generalizing the construction from [8]. While the automata resulting from the translation can, in general, be doubly exponential in the size of the original formula, we observe that for formulas in the subfragment LTL_D, the automaton is guaranteed to be only exponential in size. The logic LTL_D is a more expressive fragment than LTL\GU, and thus our results enlarge the fragment of LTL for which small limit deterministic automata can be constructed. One consequence of our results here is a new EXPTIME algorithm for model checking MDPs against LTL_D formulas, improving the previously known upper bound of 2EXPTIME.

Our results in this paper, however, have not fully settled the question of when exponential sized limit deterministic automata can be constructed. We do not believe LTL_D to be the largest class. For example, our construction yields small automata for $\varphi = \mathbf{G}(\vee_i(p_i \mathbf{U} q_i))$, where p_i, q_i are propositions. φ is not expressible in LTL_D. Of course we cannot have an exponential sized construction for full LTL as demonstrated by the double exponential lower bound in [20].

References

1. Büchifier. http://kini2.web.engr.illinois.edu/buchifier/
2. Alur, R., La Torre, S.: Deterministic generators and games for LTL fragments. ACM Trans. Comput. Logic **5**(1), 1–25 (2004)
3. Babiak, T., Blahoudek, F., Křetínský, M., Strejček, J.: Effective translation of LTL to deterministic Rabin automata: beyond the (F,G)-fragment. In: Hung, D., Ogawa, M. (eds.) ATVA 2013. LNCS, vol. 8172, pp. 24–39. Springer, Heidelberg (2013). doi:10.1007/978-3-319-02444-8_4
4. Courcoubetis, C., Yannakakis, M.: The complexity of probabilistic verification. J. ACM **42**(4), 857–907 (1995)
5. Esparza, J., Křetínský, J.: From LTL to deterministic automata: a safraless compositional approach. In: Biere, A., Bloem, R. (eds.) CAV 2014. LNCS, vol. 8559, pp. 192–208. Springer, Cham (2014). doi:10.1007/978-3-319-08867-9_13
6. Hahn, E.M., Li, G., Schewe, S., Turrini, A., Zhang, L.: Lazy probabilistic model checking without determinisation. In: CONCUR, pp. 354–367 (2015)
7. Henzinger, T.A., Piterman, N.: Solving games without determinization. In: Ésik, Z. (ed.) CSL 2006. LNCS, vol. 4207, pp. 395–410. Springer, Heidelberg (2006). doi:10.1007/11874683_26
8. Kini, D., Viswanathan, M.: Limit deterministic and probabilistic automata for LTL\GU. In: Baier, C., Tinelli, C. (eds.) TACAS 2015. LNCS, vol. 9035, pp. 628–642. Springer, Heidelberg (2015). doi:10.1007/978-3-662-46681-0_57
9. Kini, D., Viswanathan, M.: Optimal translation of LTL to limit deterministic automata. Technical report, University of Illinois at Urbana-Champaign (2017). http://hdl.handle.net/2142/95004
10. Klein, J., Baier, C.: Experiments with deterministic ω-automata for formulas of linear temporal logic. Theor. Comput. Sci. **363**(2), 182–195 (2006)
11. Klein, J., Müller, D., Baier, C., Klüppelholz, S.: Are good-for-games automata good for probabilistic model checking? In: Dediu, A.-H., Martín-Vide, C., Sierra-Rodríguez, J.-L., Truthe, B. (eds.) LATA 2014. LNCS, vol. 8370, pp. 453–465. Springer, Cham (2014). doi:10.1007/978-3-319-04921-2_37
12. Komárková, Z., Křetínský, J.: Rabinizer 3: safraless translation of LTL to small deterministic automata. In: Cassez, F., Raskin, J.-F. (eds.) ATVA 2014. LNCS, vol. 8837, pp. 235–241. Springer, Cham (2014). doi:10.1007/978-3-319-11936-6_17
13. Křetínský, J., Esparza, J.: Deterministic automata for the (F,G)-fragment of LTL. In: Madhusudan, P., Seshia, S.A. (eds.) CAV 2012. LNCS, vol. 7358, pp. 7–22. Springer, Heidelberg (2012). doi:10.1007/978-3-642-31424-7_7
14. Křetínský, J., Garza, R.L.: Rabinizer 2: small deterministic automata for LTL\GU. In: Hung, D., Ogawa, M. (eds.) ATVA 2013. LNCS, vol. 8172, pp. 446–450. Springer, Heidelberg (2013). doi:10.1007/978-3-319-02444-8_32
15. Kwiatkowska, M., Norman, G., Parker, D.: PRISM 4.0: verification of probabilistic real-time systems. In: Gopalakrishnan, G., Qadeer, S. (eds.) CAV 2011. LNCS, vol. 6806, pp. 585–591. Springer, Heidelberg (2011). doi:10.1007/978-3-642-22110-1_47
16. Morgenstern, A., Schneider, K.: From LTL to symbolically represented deterministic automata. In: Logozzo, F., Peled, D.A., Zuck, L.D. (eds.) VMCAI 2008. LNCS, vol. 4905, pp. 279–293. Springer, Heidelberg (2008). doi:10.1007/978-3-540-78163-9_24
17. Piterman, N., Pnueli, A., Sa'ar, Y.: Synthesis of reactive(1) designs. In: VMCAI, pp. 279–293 (2006)

18. Piterman, N., Pnueli, A., Sa'ar, Y.: Synthesis of reactive(1) designs. In: Emerson, E.A., Namjoshi, K.S. (eds.) VMCAI 2006. LNCS, vol. 3855, pp. 364–380. Springer, Heidelberg (2005). doi:10.1007/11609773_24
19. Puterman, M.L.: Markov Decision Processes. Wiley, Hoboken (1994)
20. Sickert, S., Esparza, J., Jaax, S., Křetínský, J.: Limit-deterministic Büchi automata for linear temporal logic. In: Chaudhuri, S., Farzan, A. (eds.) CAV 2016. LNCS, vol. 9780, pp. 312–332. Springer, Cham (2016). doi:10.1007/978-3-319-41540-6_17
21. Sickert, S., Křetínský, J.: MoChiBA: probabilistic LTL model checking using limit-deterministic Büchi automata. In: Artho, C., Legay, A., Peled, D. (eds.) ATVA 2016. LNCS, vol. 9938, pp. 130–137. Springer, Cham (2016). doi:10.1007/978-3-319-46520-3_9
22. Vardi, M., Wolper, P., Sistla, A.P.: Reasoning about infinite computation paths. In: FOCS (1983)
23. Vardi, M.Y.: Automatic verification of probabilistic concurrent finite-state programs. In: Proceedings of FOCS, pp. 327–338 (1985)

Quantitative Systems I

Sequential Convex Programming for the Efficient Verification of Parametric MDPs

Murat Cubuktepe[1], Nils Jansen[1(✉)], Sebastian Junges[2], Joost-Pieter Katoen[2], Ivan Papusha[1], Hasan A. Poonawala[1], and Ufuk Topcu[1]

[1] The University of Texas at Austin, Austin, USA
njansen@utexas.edu
[2] RWTH Aachen University, Aachen, Germany

Abstract. Multi-objective verification problems of parametric Markov decision processes under optimality criteria can be naturally expressed as nonlinear programs. We observe that many of these computationally demanding problems belong to the subclass of signomial programs. This insight allows for a sequential optimization algorithm to efficiently compute sound but possibly suboptimal solutions. Each stage of this algorithm solves a geometric programming problem. These geometric programs are obtained by convexifying the nonconvex constraints of the original problem. Direct applications of the encodings as nonlinear programs are model repair and parameter synthesis. We demonstrate the scalability and quality of our approach by well-known benchmarks.

1 Introduction

We study the applicability of *convex optimization* to the formal verification of systems that exhibit randomness or stochastic uncertainties. Such systems are formally represented by so-called parametric Markov models.

In fact, many real-world systems exhibit random behavior and stochastic uncertainties. One major example is in the field of *robotics*, where the presence of measurement noise or input disturbances requires special controller synthesis techniques [39] that achieve robustness of robot actions against uncertainties in the robot model and the environment. On the other hand, formal verification offers methods for rigorously proving or disproving properties about the system behavior, and synthesizing strategies that satisfy these properties. In particular, *model checking* [36] is a well-studied technique that provides guarantees on appropriate behavior for all possible events and scenarios.

Model checking can be applied to systems with stochastic uncertainties, including discrete-time Markov chains (MCs), Markov decision processes

Partly funded by the awards AFRL # FA8650-15-C-2546, DARPA # W911NF-16-1-0001, ARO # W911NF-15-1-0592, ONR # N00014-15-IP-00052, ONR # N00014-16-1-3165, and NSF # 1550212. Also funded by the Excellence Initiative of the German federal and state government and the CDZ project CAP (GZ 1023).

A. Legay and T. Margaria (Eds.): TACAS 2017, Part II, LNCS 10206, pp. 133–150, 2017.
DOI: 10.1007/978-3-662-54580-5_8

(MDPs), and their continuous-time counterparts [31]. Probabilistic model checkers are able to verify reachability properties like "the probability of reaching a set of unsafe states is $\leq 10\%$" and expected costs properties like "the expected cost of reaching a goal state is ≤ 20." A rich set of properties, specified by linear- and branching-time logics, reduces to such properties [31]. Tools like PRISM [15], STORM [29], and iscasMc [22] are probabilistic model checkers capable of handling a wide range of large-scale problems.

Key requirements for applying model checking are a reliable system model and formal specifications of desired or undesired behaviors. As a result, most approaches assume that models of the stochastic uncertainties are precisely given. For example, if a system description includes an environmental disturbance, the mean of that disturbance should be known *before* formal statements are made about expected system behavior. However, the desire to treat many applications where uncertainty measures (e.g., faultiness, reliability, reaction rates, packet loss ratio) are not exactly known at design time gives rise to *parametric* probabilistic models [1,30]. Here, transition probabilities are expressed as functions over system parameters, i.e., *descriptions of uncertainties*. In this setting, *parameter synthesis* addresses the problem of computing parameter instantiations leading to satisfaction of system specifications. More precisely, parameters are mapped to concrete probabilities inducing the resulting *instantiated* model to satisfy specifications. A direct application is *model repair* [13], where a concrete model (without parameters) is changed (repaired) such that specifications *are* satisfied.

Dedicated tools like PARAM [11], PRISM [15], or PROPhESY [25] compute rational functions over parameters that express reachability probabilities or expected costs in a parametric Markov chain (pMC). These optimized tools work with millions of states but are restricted to a few parameters, as the necessary computation of greatest common divisors does not scale well with the number of parameters. Moreover, the resulting functions are inherently *nonlinear* and often of high degree. Evaluation by an SMT solver over nonlinear arithmetic such as Z3 [17] suffers from the fact that the solving procedures are *exponential in the degree of polynomials and the number of variables*.

This paper takes an alternative perspective. We discuss a general nonlinear programming formulation for the verification of parametric Markov decision processes (pMDPs). The powerful modeling capabilities of nonlinear programs (NLPs) enable incorporating multi-objective properties and penalties on the parameters of the pMDP. However, because of their generality, solving NLPs to find a global optimum is difficult. Even feasible solutions (satisfying the constraints) cannot always be computed efficiently [5,37]. In contrast, for the class of NLPs called *convex optimization* problems, efficient methods to compute feasible solutions and global optima even for large-scale problems are available [38].

We therefore propose a novel automated method of utilizing convex optimization for pMDPs. Many NLP problems for pMDPs belong to the class of *signomial programs* (SGPs), a certain class of nonconvex optimization problems. For instance, all benchmarks available at the PARAM–webpage [26] belong to this class. Restricting the general pMDP problem accordingly yields a direct and efficient synthesis method—formulated as an NLP—for a large class of pMDP problems. We list the two main technical results of this paper:

1. We relax nonconvex constraints in SGPs and apply a simple transformation to the parameter functions. The resulting programs are *geometric programs* (GPs) [7], a class of *convex programs*. We show that a solution to the relaxed GP induces feasibility (satisfaction of all specifications) in the original pMDP problem. Note that solving GPs is *polynomial* in the number of variables.
2. Given an initial feasible solution, we use a technique called *sequential convex programming* [7] to improve a signomial objective. This local optimization method for nonconvex problems leverages convex optimization by solving a sequence of convex approximations (GPs) of the original SGP.

Sequential convex programming is known to efficiently find a feasible solution with good, though not necessarily globally optimal, objective values [7,8]. We initialize the sequence with a feasible solution (obtained from the GP) of the original problem and compute a *trust region*. Inside this region, the optimal value of the approximation of the SGP is at least as good as the objective value at the feasible solution of the GP. The optimal solution of the approximation is then the initial point of the next iteration with a new trust region. This procedure is iterated to approximate a local optimum of the original problem.

Utilizing our results, we discuss the concrete problems of parameter synthesis and model repair for multiple specifications for pMDPs. Experimental results with a prototype implementation show the applicability of our optimization methods to benchmarks of up to 10^5 states. As solving GPs is polynomial in the number of variables, our approaches are relatively insensitive to the number of parameters in pMDPs. This is an improvement over state-of-the-art approaches that leverage SMT, which—for our class of problems—scale exponentially in variables and the degree of polynomials. This is substantiated by our experiments.

Related Work. Several approaches exist for pMCs [11,12,23,25] while the number of approaches for pMDPs [12,33] is limited. Ceska *et al.* [21] synthesize rate parameters in stochastic biochemical networks. Multi-objective model checking of non-parametric MDPs [9] is a convex problem [14]. Bortolussi *et al.* [28] developed a Bayesian statistical algorithm for properties on stochastic population models. Convex uncertainties in MDPs without parameter dependencies are discussed in [20]. Parametric probabilistic models are used to rank patches in the repair of software [32] and to compute perturbation bounds [24,34].

2   Preliminaries

A *probability distribution* over a finite or countably infinite set X is a function $\mu \colon X \to [0, 1] \subseteq \mathbb{R}$ with $\sum_{x \in X} \mu(x) = 1$. The set of all distributions on X is denoted by *Distr(X)*.

Definition 1 (Monomial, Posynomial, Signomial). *Let* $V = \{x_1, \ldots, x_n\}$ *be a finite set of strictly positive real-valued* variables. *A* monomial *over* V *is an expression of the form*

$$g = c \cdot x_1^{a_1} \cdots x_n^{a_n} \;,$$

where $c \in \mathbb{R}_{>0}$ *is a positive coefficient, and* $a_i \in \mathbb{R}$ *are exponents for* $1 \leq i \leq n$. *A* posynomial *over* V *is a sum of one or more monomials:*

$$f = \sum_{k=1}^{K} c_k \cdot x_1^{a_{1k}} \cdots x_n^{a_{nk}} \;. \tag{1}$$

If c_k *is allowed to be a negative real number for any* $1 \leq k \leq K$, *then the expression* (1) *is a* signomial. *The sets of all monomials, posynomials, and signomials over* V *are denoted by* Mon_V, Pos_V, *and* Sig_V, *respectively.*

This definition of monomials differs from the standard algebraic definition where exponents are positive integers with no restriction on the coefficient sign. A sum of monomials is then called a *polynomial*. Our definitions are consistent with [7].

Definition 2 (Valuation). *For a set of real-valued variables* V, *a* valuation u *over* V *is a function* $u \colon V \to \mathbb{R}$. *The set of all valuations over* V *is* Val^V.

Applying valuation u to monomial g over V yields a real number $g[u] \in \mathbb{R}$ by replacing each occurrence of variables $x \in V$ in g by $u(x)$; the procedure is analogous for posynomials and signomials using standard arithmetic operations.

Definition 3 (pMDP and pMC). *A* parametric Markov decision process (pMDP) *is a tuple* $\mathcal{M} = (S, s_I, Act, V, \mathcal{P})$ *with a finite set* S *of states, an initial state* $s_I \in S$, *a finite set* Act *of actions, a finite set of real-valued variables* V, *and a transition function* $\mathcal{P} \colon S \times Act \times S \to Sig_V$ *satisfying for all* $s \in S$: $Act(s) \neq \emptyset$, *where* $Act(s) = \{\alpha \in Act \mid \exists s' \in S. \mathcal{P}(s, \alpha, s') \neq 0\}$. *If for all* $s \in S$ *it holds that* $|Act(s)| = 1$, $\mathcal{M}$ *is called a* parametric discrete-time Markov chain (pMC).

$Act(s)$ is the set of *enabled* actions at state s; as $Act(s) \neq \emptyset$, there are no deadlock states. *Costs* are defined using a state–action *cost function* $c \colon S \times Act \to \mathbb{R}_{\geq 0}$.

Remark 1. Largely due to algorithmic reasons, the transition probabilities in the literature [12,25,33] are polynomials or rational functions, i.e., fractions of polynomials. Our restriction to signomials is realistic; *all* benchmarks from the PARAM–webpage [26] contain only signomial transition probabilities.

A pMDP $\mathcal{M}$ is a *Markov decision process (MDP)* if the transition function is a valid probability distribution, i.e., $\mathcal{P} \colon S \times Act \times S \to [0,1]$ and $\sum_{s' \in S} \mathcal{P}(s, \alpha, s') = 1$ for all $s \in S$ s.t. $\alpha \in Act(s)$. Analogously, a Markov chain (MC) is a special class of a pMC; a model is *parameter-free* if all probabilities are constant. Applying a *valuation* u to a pMDP, denoted $\mathcal{M}[u]$, replaces each signomial f in $\mathcal{M}$ by $f[u]$; we call $\mathcal{M}[u]$ the *instantiation* of $\mathcal{M}$ at u. The application of u is to replace the transition function f by the probability $f[u]$. A valuation u is *well-defined* for $\mathcal{M}$ if the replacement yields *probability distributions* at all states; the resulting model $\mathcal{M}[u]$ is an MDP or an MC.

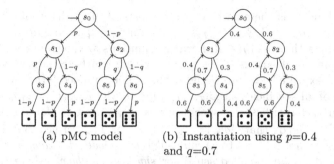

(a) pMC model

(b) Instantiation using $p=0.4$ and $q=0.7$

Fig. 1. A variant of the Knuth–Yao die for unfair coins.

Example 1 (pMC). Consider a variant of the Knuth–Yao model of a die [2], where a six-sided die is simulated by successive coin flips. We alternate flipping two biased coins, which result in *heads* with probabilities defined by the monomials p and q, respectively. Consequently, the probability for *tails* is given by the signomials $1 - p$ and $1 - q$, respectively. The corresponding pMC is depicted in Fig. 1(a); and the *instantiated* MC for $p = 0.4$ and $q = 0.7$ is given in Fig. 1(b). Note that we omit actions, as the model is deterministic.

In order to define a probability measure and expected cost on MDPs, nondeterministic choices are resolved by so-called *schedulers*. For practical reasons we restrict ourselves to *memoryless* schedulers; details can be found in [36].

Definition 4 (Scheduler). *A (randomized) scheduler for an MDP $\mathcal{M}$ is a function $\sigma \colon S \to Distr(Act)$ such that $\sigma(s)(\alpha) > 0$ implies $\alpha \in Act(s)$. The set of all schedulers over $\mathcal{M}$ is denoted by $Sched^{\mathcal{M}}$.*

Applying a scheduler to an MDP yields a so-called *induced Markov chain*.

Definition 5 (Induced MC). *Let MDP $\mathcal{M} = (S, s_I, Act, \mathcal{P})$ and scheduler $\sigma \in Sched^{\mathcal{M}}$. The MC induced by $\mathcal{M}$ and σ is $\mathcal{M}^{\sigma} = (S, s_I, Act, \mathcal{P}^{\sigma})$ where for all $s, s' \in S$,*

$$\mathcal{P}^{\sigma}(s, s') = \sum_{\alpha \in Act(s)} \sigma(s)(\alpha) \cdot \mathcal{P}(s, \alpha, s').$$

We consider *reachability properties* and *expected cost properties*. For MC $\mathcal{D}$ with states S, let $\Pr_s^{\mathcal{D}}(\lozenge T)$ denote the probability of reaching a set of *target states* $T \subseteq S$ from state $s \in S$; simply $\Pr^{\mathcal{D}}(\lozenge T)$ denotes the probability for initial state s_I. We use the standard probability measure as in [36, Chap. 10]. For threshold $\lambda \in [0, 1]$, the *reachability property* asserting that a target state is to be reached with probability at most λ is denoted $\varphi = \mathbb{P}_{\leq \lambda}(\lozenge T)$. The property is satisfied by $\mathcal{D}$, written $\mathcal{D} \models \varphi$, iff $\Pr^{\mathcal{D}}(\lozenge T) \leq \lambda$.

The cost of a path through MC $\mathcal{D}$ until a set of *goal states* $G \subseteq S$ is the sum of action costs visited along the path. The expected cost of a finite path is the product of its probability and its cost. For $\Pr^{\mathcal{D}}(\lozenge G) = 1$, the expected cost of reaching G is the sum of expected costs of all paths leading to G. An expected cost property $EC_{\leq \kappa}(\Diamond G)$ is satisfied if the expected cost of reaching T is bounded by a threshold $\kappa \in \mathbb{R}$. Formal definitions are given in e.g., [36].

If multiple specifications $\varphi_1, \ldots, \varphi_q$ are given, which are either reachability properties or expected cost properties of the aforementioned forms, we write the satisfaction of all specifications $\varphi_1, \ldots, \varphi_q$ for an MC $\mathcal{D}$ as $\mathcal{D} \models \varphi_1 \wedge \ldots \wedge \varphi_q$.

An MDP $\mathcal{M}$ satisfies the specifications $\varphi_1, \ldots, \varphi_q$, iff *for all* schedulers $\sigma \in Sched^{\mathcal{M}}$ it holds that $\mathcal{M}^\sigma \models \varphi_1 \wedge \ldots \wedge \varphi_q$. The verification of multiple specifications is also referred to as *multi-objective model checking* [9,16]. We are also interested in the so-called scheduler *synthesis problem*, where the aim is to find a scheduler σ such that the specifications are satisfied (although other schedulers may not satisfy the specifications).

3   Nonlinear Programming for pMDPs

In this section we formally state a general pMDP parameter synthesis problem and describe how it can be formulated using nonlinear programming.

3.1   Formal Problem Statement

> **Problem 1** Given a pMDP $\mathcal{M} = (S, s_I, Act, V, \mathcal{P})$, specifications $\varphi_1, \ldots, \varphi_q$ that are either probabilistic reachability properties or expected cost properties, and an objective function $f : V \to \mathbb{R}$ over the variables V, compute a well-defined valuation $u \in Val^V$ for $\mathcal{M}$, and a (randomized) scheduler $\sigma \in Sched^{\mathcal{M}}$ such that the following conditions hold:
>
> (a) *Feasibility*: the Markov chain $\mathcal{M}^\sigma[u]$ induced by scheduler σ and instantiated by valuation u satisfies the specifications, i.e., $\mathcal{M}^\sigma[u] \models \varphi_1 \wedge \ldots \wedge \varphi_q$.
> (b) *Optimality*: the objective f is minimized.

Intuitively, we wish to compute a parameter valuation and a scheduler such that all specifications are satisfied, and the objective is globally minimized. We refer to a valuation–scheduler pair (u, σ) that satisfies condition (a), i.e., only guarantees satisfaction of the specifications but does not necessarily minimize the objective f, as a *feasible* solution to the pMDP synthesis problem. If both (a) and (b) are satisfied, the pair is an *optimal* solution to the pMDP synthesis problem.

3.2   Nonlinear Encoding

We now provide an NLP encoding of Problem 1. A general NLP over a set of real-valued variables $\mathcal{V}$ can be written as

$$\text{minimize} \quad f \tag{2}$$
$$\text{subject to}$$
$$\forall i.\, 1 \leq i \leq m \quad g_i \leq 0, \tag{3}$$
$$\forall j.\, 1 \leq i \leq p \quad h_j = 0, \tag{4}$$

where f, g_i, and h_j are arbitrary functions over $\mathcal{V}$, and m and p are the number of inequality and equality constraints of the program respectively. Tools like IPOPT [10] solve small instances of such problems.

Consider a pMDP $\mathcal{M} = (S, s_I, Act, V, \mathcal{P})$ with specifications $\varphi_1 = \mathbb{P}_{\leq\lambda}(\Diamond T)$ and $\varphi_2 = EC_{\leq\kappa}(\Diamond G)$. We will discuss how additional specifications of either type can be encoded. The set $\mathcal{V} = V \cup W$ of variables of the NLP consists of the variables V that occur in the pMDP as well as a set W of additional variables:

- $\{\sigma^{s,\alpha} \mid s \in S, \alpha \in Act(s)\}$, which define the randomized scheduler σ by $\sigma(s)(\alpha) = \sigma^{s,\alpha}$.
- $\{p_s \mid s \in S\}$, where p_s is the probability of reaching the target set $T \subseteq S$ from state s under scheduler σ, and
- $\{c_s \mid s \in S\}$, where c_s is the expected cost to reach $G \subseteq S$ from s under σ.

A valuation over $\mathcal{V}$ consists of a valuation $u \in Val^V$ over the pMDP variables and a valuation $w \in Val^W$ over the additional variables.

$$\text{minimize} \quad f \tag{5}$$
$$\text{subject to}$$
$$p_{s_I} \leq \lambda, \tag{6}$$
$$c_{s_I} \leq \kappa, \tag{7}$$
$$\forall s \in S. \quad \sum_{\alpha \in Act(s)} \sigma^{s,\alpha} = 1, \tag{8}$$
$$\forall s \in S \; \forall \alpha \in Act(s). \quad 0 \leq \sigma^{s,\alpha} \leq 1, \tag{9}$$
$$\forall s \in S \; \forall \alpha \in Act(s). \quad \sum_{s' \in S} \mathcal{P}(s, \alpha, s') = 1, \tag{10}$$
$$\forall s, s' \in S \; \forall \alpha \in Act(s). \quad 0 \leq \mathcal{P}(s, \alpha, s') \leq 1, \tag{11}$$
$$\forall s \in T. \quad p_s = 1, \tag{12}$$
$$\forall s \in S \setminus T. \quad p_s = \sum_{\alpha \in Act(s)} \sigma^{s,\alpha} \cdot \sum_{s' \in S} \mathcal{P}(s, \alpha, s') \cdot p_{s'}, \tag{13}$$
$$\forall s \in G. \quad c_s = 0, \tag{14}$$
$$\forall s \in S \setminus G. \quad c_s = \sum_{\alpha \in Act(s)} \sigma^{s,\alpha} \cdot \left(c(s, \alpha) + \sum_{s' \in S} \mathcal{P}(s, \alpha, s') \cdot c_{s'} \right). \tag{15}$$

The NLP (5)–(15) encodes Problem 1 in the following way. The objective function f in (5) is any real-valued function over the variables $\mathcal{V}$. The constraints (6) and (7) encode the specifications φ_1 and φ_2, respectively. The constraints (8)–(9) ensure that the scheduler obtained is well-defined by requiring that the scheduler variables at each state sum to unity. Similarly, the constraints (10)–(11) ensure that for all states, parameters from V are instantiated such that probabilities sum up to one. (These constraints are included if not all probabilities at a state are constant.) The probability of reaching the target for all states in the target set is set to one using (12). The reachability probabilities in each state depend on the reachability of the successor states and the transition probabilities to those states through (13). Analogously to the reachability probabilities, the cost for each goal state $G \subseteq S$ must be zero, thereby precluding the collection of infinite cost at absorbing states, as enforced by (14). Finally, the expected cost for all states except target states is given by the equation (15), where according to the strategy σ the cost of each action is added to the expected cost of the successors.

We can readily extend the NLP to include more specifications. If another reachability property $\varphi' = \mathbb{P}_{\leq \lambda'}(\lozenge T')$ is given, we add the set of probability variables $\{p'_s \mid s \in S\}$ to W, and duplicate the constraints (12)–(13) accordingly. To ensure satisfaction of φ', we also add the constraint $p'_{s_I} \leq \lambda'$. The procedure is similar for additional expected cost properties. By construction, we have the following result relating the NLP encoding and Problem 1.

Theorem 1. *The NLP* (5)–(15) *is sound and complete with respect to Problem 1.*

We refer to soundness in the sense that each variable assignment that satisfies the constraints induces a scheduler and a valuation of parameters such that a feasible solution of the problem is induced. Moreover, any optimal solution to the NLP induces an optimal solution of the problem. Completeness means that all possible solutions of the problem can be encoded by this NLP; while unsatisfiability means that no such solution exists, making the problem *infeasible*.

Signomial Programs. By Definitions 1 and 3, all constraints in the NLP consist of signomial functions. A special class of NLPs known as *signomial programs* (SGPs) is of the form (2)–(4) where f, g_i and h_j are signomials over $\mathcal{V}$, see Definition 1. Therefore, we observe that the NLP (5)–(15) is an SGP. We will refer to the NLP as an SGP in what follows.

SGPs with equality constraints consisting of functions that are *not affine* are not *convex* in general. In particular, the SGP (5)–(15) is not necessarily convex. Consider a simple pMC only having transition probabilities of the form p and $1 - p$, as in Example 1. The function in the equality constraint (13) of the corresponding SGP encoding is not affine in parameter p and the probability variable p_s for some state $s \in S$. More generally, the equality constraints (10), (13), and (15) involving $\mathcal{P}$ are not necessarily affine, and thus the SGP may not be a convex program [38]. Whereas for convex programs *global optimal solutions* can be found efficiently [38], such guarantees are not given for SGPs. However, we can efficiently obtain local optimal solutions for SGPs in our setting, as shown in the following sections.

4   Convexification

We investigate how to transform the SGP (5)–(15) into a convex program by relaxing equality constraints and a lifting of variables of the SGP. A certain subclass of SGPs called *geometric programs* (GPs) can be transformed into convex programs [7, Sect. 2.5] and solved efficiently. A GP is an SGP of the form (2)–(4) where $f, g_i \in Pos_\mathcal{V}$ and $h_j \in Mon_\mathcal{V}$. We will refer to a constraint with posynomial or monomial function as a posynomial or monomial constraint, respectively.

4.1 Transformation and Relaxation of Equality Constraints

As discussed before, the SGP (5)–(15) is not convex because of the presence of non-affine equality constraints. First observe the following transformation [7]:

$$f \leq h \Longleftrightarrow \frac{f}{h} \leq 1, \tag{16}$$

for $f \in Pos_\mathcal{V}$ and $h \in Mon_\mathcal{V}$. Note that monomials are strictly positive (Definition 1). This *(division-)transformation* of $f \leq h$ yields a *posynomial inequality constraint*.

We *relax* all equality constraints of SGP (5)–(15) that are not monomials to inequalities, then we apply the division-transformation wherever possible. Constraints (6), (7), (8), (10), (13), and (15) are transformed to

$$\frac{p_{s_I}}{\lambda} \leq 1, \tag{17}$$

$$\frac{c_{s_I}}{\kappa} \leq 1, \tag{18}$$

$$\forall s \in S. \quad \sum_{\alpha \in Act(s)} \sigma^{s,\alpha} \leq 1, \tag{19}$$

$$\forall s \in S \, \forall \alpha \in Act(s). \quad \sum_{s' \in S} \mathcal{P}(s, \alpha, s') \leq 1, \tag{20}$$

$$\forall s \in S \setminus T. \quad \frac{\sum\limits_{\alpha \in Act(s)} \sigma^{s,\alpha} \cdot \sum\limits_{s' \in S} \mathcal{P}(s, \alpha, s') \cdot p_{s'}}{p_s} \leq 1, \tag{21}$$

$$\forall s \in S \setminus G. \quad \frac{\sum\limits_{\alpha \in Act(s)} \sigma^{s,\alpha} \cdot \left(c(s, \alpha) + \sum\limits_{s' \in S} \mathcal{P}(s, \alpha, s') \cdot c_{s'} \right)}{c_s} \leq 1. \tag{22}$$

These constraints are not necessarily posynomial inequality constraints because (as in Definition 3) we allow signomial expressions in the transition probability function $\mathcal{P}$. Therefore, replacing (6), (7), (8), (10), (13), and (15) in the SGP with (17)–(22) does not by itself convert the SGP to a GP.

4.2 Convexification by Lifting

The relaxed equality constraints (20)–(22) involving $\mathcal{P}$ are signomial, rather than posynomial, because the parameters enter Problem 1 in signomial form. Specifically, consider the relaxed equality constraint (21) at s_0 in Example 1,

$$\frac{p \cdot p_{s_1} + (1 - p) \cdot p_{s_2}}{p_{s_0}} \leq 1. \tag{23}$$

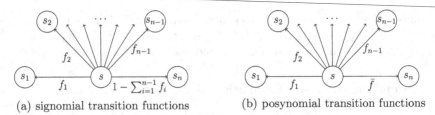

(a) signomial transition functions   (b) posynomial transition functions

Fig. 2. Lifting of signomial transition probability function.

The term $(1 - p) \cdot p_{s_2}$ is signomial in p and p_{s_2}. We *lift* by introducing a new variable $\bar{p} = 1 - p$, and rewrite (23) as a posynomial inequality constraint and an equality constraint in the lifted variables:

$$\frac{p \cdot p_{s_1} + \bar{p} \cdot p_{s_2}}{p_{s_0}} \leq 1, \quad \bar{p} = 1 - p. \tag{24}$$

We relax the (non-monomial) equality constraint to $p + \bar{p} \leq 1$. More generally, we restrict the way parameters occur in $\mathcal{P}$ as follows. Refer to Fig. 2(a). For every state $s \in S$ and every action $\alpha \in Act(s)$ we require that there exists at most one state $\bar{s} \in S$ such that $\mathcal{P}(s, \alpha, \bar{s}) \in Sig_V$ and $\mathcal{P}(s, \alpha, s') \in Pos_V$ for all $s' \in S \setminus \{\bar{s}\}$. In particular, we require that

$$\underbrace{\mathcal{P}(s, \alpha, \bar{s})}_{\in Sig_V} = 1 - \sum_{s' \in S \setminus \{\bar{s}\}} \underbrace{\mathcal{P}(s, \alpha, s')}_{\in Pos_V} .$$

This requirement is met by all benchmarks available at the PARAM–webpage [26]. In general, we lift by introducing a new variable $\bar{p}_{s,\alpha,\bar{s}} = \mathcal{P}(s, \alpha, \bar{s})$ for each such state $s \in S$; refer to Fig. 2(b). We denote this set of *lifting variables* by L. Lifting as explained above then creates a new transition probability function $\bar{\mathcal{P}}$ where for every $s, s' \in S$ and $\alpha \in Act$ we have $\bar{\mathcal{P}}(s, \alpha, s') \in Pos_{V \cup L}$.

We call the set of constraints obtained through transformation, relaxation, and lifting of every constraint of the SGP (6)–(15) as shown above the *convexified constraints*. Any posynomial objective subject to the convexified constraints forms by construction a GP over the pMDP parameters V, the SGP additional variables W, and the lifting variables L.

4.3   Tightening the Constraints

A solution of the GP as obtained in the previous section does not have a direct relation to the original SGP (5)–(15). In particular, a solution to the GP may not have the relaxed constraints satisfied with equality. For (19) and (20), the induced parameter valuation and the scheduler are not well-defined, i.e., the probabilities may not sum to one. We need to relate the relaxed and lifted GP to Problem 1. By defining a *regularization function* F over all parameter and scheduler variables, we ensure that the constraints are satisfied with equality; enforcing well-defined probability distributions.

$$F = \sum_{p \in V} \frac{1}{p} + \sum_{\bar{p} \in L} \frac{1}{\bar{p}} + \sum_{s \in S, \alpha \in Act(s)} \frac{1}{\sigma_{s,\alpha}} . \tag{25}$$

The function F is monotone in all its variables. We discard the original objective f in (5) and form a GP with the regularization objective F (25):

$$\text{minimize} \quad F \tag{26}$$

subject to

$$\frac{p_{s_I}}{\lambda} \leq 1, \tag{27}$$

$$\frac{c_{s_I}}{\kappa} \leq 1, \tag{28}$$

$$\forall s \in S. \quad \sum_{\alpha \in Act(s)} \sigma^{s,\alpha} \leq 1, \tag{29}$$

$$\forall s \in S \, \forall \alpha \in Act(s). \quad \sigma^{s,\alpha} \leq 1, \tag{30}$$

$$\forall s \in S \, \forall \alpha \in Act(s). \quad \sum_{s' \in S} \bar{P}(s, \alpha, s') \leq 1, \tag{31}$$

$$\forall s, s' \in S \, \forall \alpha \in Act(s). \quad \bar{P}(s, \alpha, s') \leq 1, \tag{32}$$

$$\forall s \in T. \quad p_s = 1, \tag{33}$$

$$\forall s \in S \setminus T. \quad \frac{\sum_{\alpha \in Act(s)} \sigma^{s,\alpha} \cdot \sum_{s' \in S} \bar{P}(s, \alpha, s') \cdot p_{s'}}{p_s} \leq 1, \tag{34}$$

$$\forall s \in S \setminus G. \quad \frac{\sum_{\alpha \in Act(s)} \sigma^{s,\alpha} \cdot \left(c(s, \alpha) + \sum_{s' \in S} \bar{P}(s, \alpha, s') \cdot c_{s'} \right)}{c_s} \leq 1. \tag{35}$$

Since the objective F (25) and the inequality constraints (29) and (31) are monotone in V, L, and the scheduler variables, each optimal solution for a feasible problem satisfies them with equality. We obtain a well-defined scheduler σ and a valuation u as in Problem 1. Note that variables from (14) are explicitly excluded from the GP by treating them as constants.

The reachability probability constraints (34) and cost constraints (35) need not be satisfied with equality. However, (34) is equivalent to

$$p_s \geq \sum_{\alpha \in Act(s)} \sigma^{s,\alpha} \cdot \sum_{s' \in S} \bar{P}(s, \alpha, s') \cdot p_{s'}$$

for all $s \in S \setminus T$ and $\alpha \in Act$. The probability variables p_s are assigned upper bounds on the actual probability to reach the target states T under scheduler σ and valuation u. Put differently, the p_s variables cannot be assigned values that are lower than the actual probability; ensuring that σ and u induce satisfaction of the specification given by (27) if the problem is feasible and σ and u are well-defined. An analogous reasoning applies to the expected cost computation (35). A solution consisting of a scheduler or valuation that are not well-defined occurs only if Problem 1 itself is infeasible. Identifying that such a solution has been obtained is easy. These facts allow us to state the main result of this section.

Theorem 2. *A solution of the GP* (26)–(35) *inducing well-defined scheduler* σ *and valuation* u *is a feasible solution to Problem 1.*

Note that the actual probabilities induced by σ and u for the given pMDP $\mathcal{M}$ are given by the MC $\mathcal{M}^\sigma[u]$ induced by σ and instantiated by u. Since all variables are implicitly positive in a GP, no transition probability function will be instantiated to probability zero. The case of a scheduler variable being zero to induce the optimum can be excluded by a previous graph analysis.

5   Sequential Geometric Programming

We showed how to efficiently obtain a feasible solution for Problem 1 by solving GP (26)–(35). We propose a *sequential convex programming* trust-region method to compute a local optimum of the SGP (5)–(15), following [7, Sect. 9.1], solving a sequence of GPs. We obtain each GP by replacing signomial functions in equality constraints of the SGP (5)–(15) with *monomial approximations* of the functions.

Definition 6 (Monomial approximation). *Given a posynomial* $f \in Sig_\mathcal{V}$, *variables* $\mathcal{V} = \{x_1, \ldots, x_n\}$, *and a valuation* $u \in Val^\mathcal{V}$, *a monomial approximation* $\hat{f} \in Mon_\mathcal{V}$ *for* f *near* u *is*

$$\forall i.1 \leq i \leq n \quad \hat{f} = f[u] \prod_{i=1}^{n} \left(\frac{x_i}{u(x_i)} \right)^{a_i}, \quad \text{where } a_i = \frac{u(x_i)}{f[u]} \frac{\partial f}{\partial x_i}[u].$$

Intuitively, we compute a *linearization* $\hat{f}$ of $f \in Sig_\mathcal{V}$ around a fixed valuation u. We enforce the fidelity of monomial approximation $\hat{f}$ of $f \in Sig_\mathcal{V}$ by restricting valuations to remain within a set known as *trust region*. We define the following constraints on the variables $\mathcal{V}$ with $t > 1$ determining the size of the trust region:

$$\forall i.1 \leq i \leq n \quad (1/t) \cdot u(x_i) \leq x_i \leq t \cdot u(x_i) \tag{36}$$

For a given valuation u, we approximate the SGP (5)–(15) to obtain a *local GP* as follows. First, we apply a *lifting* procedure (Sect. 4.2) to the SGP ensuring that all constraints consist of posynomial functions. The thus obtained posynomial inequality constraints are included in the local GP. After replacing posynomials in every equality constraint by their monomial approximations near u, the resulting monomial equality constraints are also included. Finally, we add trust region constraints (36) for scheduler and parameter variables. The objective function is the same as for the SGP. The optimal solution of the local GP is not necessarily a feasible solution to the SGP. Therefore, we first normalize the scheduler and parameter values to obtain well-defined probability distributions. These normalized values are used to compute precise probabilities and expected cost using PRISM. The steps above provide a feasible solution of the SGP.

We use such approximations to obtain a sequence of feasible solutions to the SGP approaching a local optimum of the SGP. First, we compute a feasible solution $u^{(0)}$ for Problem 1 (Sect. 4), forming the initial point of a sequence of solutions $u^{(0)}, \ldots, u^{(N)}, N \in \mathbb{N}$. The solution $u^{(k)}$ for $0 \leq k \leq N$ is obtained from a local GP defined using $u^{(k-1)}$ as explained above.

The parameter t for each iteration k is determined based on its value for the previous iteration, and the ratio of $f\left[u^{(k-1)}\right]$ to $f\left[u^{(k-2)}\right]$, where f is the objective function in (5). The iterations are stopped when $\left|f\left[u^{(k)}\right] - f\left[u^{(k-1)}\right]\right| < \epsilon$. Intuitively, ϵ defines the required improvement on the objective value for each iteration; once there is not enough improvement the process terminates.

6 Applications

We discuss two applications and their restrictions for the general SGP (5)–(15).

Model Repair. For MC $\mathcal{D}$ and specification φ with $\mathcal{D} \not\models \varphi$, the *model repair* problem [13] is to transform $\mathcal{D}$ to $\mathcal{D}'$ such that $\mathcal{D}' \models \varphi$. The transformation involves a change of transition probabilities. Additionally, a cost function measures the change of probabilities. The natural underlying model is a pMC where parameters are added to probabilities. The cost function is minimized subject to constraints that induce satisfaction of φ. In [13], the problem is given as NLP. Heuristic [27] and simulation-based methods [19] (for MDPs) were presented.

Leveraging our results, one can readily encode model repair problems for MDPs, multiple objectives, and restrictions on probability or cost changes directly as NLPs. The encoding as in [13] is handled by our method in Sect. 5 as it involves signomial constraints. We now propose a more efficient approach, which encodes the change of probabilities using monomial functions. Consider an MDP $\mathcal{M} = (S, s_I, Act, \mathcal{P})$ and specifications $\varphi_1, \ldots, \varphi_q$ with $\mathcal{M} \not\models \varphi_1 \wedge \ldots \wedge \varphi_q$. For each probability $\mathcal{P}(s, \alpha, s') = a \in \mathbb{R}$ that may be changed, introduce a parameter p, forming the parameter set V. We define a parametric transition probability function by $\mathcal{P}'(s, \alpha, s') = p \cdot a \in Mon_V$. The quadratic cost function is for instance $f = \sum_{p \in V} p^2 \in Pos_V$. By minimizing the sum of squares of the parameters (with some regularization), the change of probabilities is minimized.

By incorporating these modifications into SGP (5)–(15), our approach is directly applicable. Either we restrict the cost function f to an upper bound, and efficiently solve a feasibility problem (Sect. 4), or we compute a local minimum of the cost function (Sect. 5). In contrast to [13], our approach works for MDPs and has an efficient solution. While [19] uses fast simulation techniques, we can directly incorporate multiple objectives and restrictions on the results while offering an efficient numerical solution of the problem.

Parameter Space Partitioning. For pMDPs, tools like PRISM [15] or PROPh-ESY [25] aim at partitioning the parameter space into regions with respect to a specification. A *parameter region* is given by a convex polytope defined by linear inequalities over the parameters, restricting valuations to a region. Now, for pMDP $\mathcal{M}$ a region is *safe* regarding a specification φ, if no valuation u inside this region and no scheduler σ induce $\mathcal{M}^\sigma[u] \not\models \varphi$. Vice versa, a region is unsafe, if there is no valuation and scheduler such that the specification is satisfied. In [25], this certification is performed using SMT solving. More efficiency is achieved by using an approximation method [33].

Certifying regions to be unsafe is directly possible using our approach. Assume pMDP $\mathcal{M}$, specifications $\varphi_1, \ldots, \varphi_q$, and a region candidate defined by a set of linear inequalities. We incorporate the inequalities in the NLP (5)–(15). If the feasibility problem (Sect. 4) has no solution, the region is unsafe. This yields the *first efficient numerical method* for this problem of which we are aware. Proving that a region is safe is more involved. Given one specification $\varphi = \mathbb{P}_{\leq \lambda}(\Diamond T)$, we maximize the probability to reach T. If this probability is at most λ, the region is safe. For using our method from Sect. 5, one needs domain specific knowledge to show that a local optimum is a global optimum.

7   Experiments

We implemented a prototype using the Python interfaces of the probabilistic model checker STORM [29] and the optimization solver MOSEK [35]. All experiments were run on a 2.6 GHz machine with 32 GB RAM. We used PRISM [15] to correct approximation errors as explained before. We evaluated our approaches using mainly examples from the PARAM–webpage [26] and from PRISM [18]. We considered several parametric instances of the *Bounded Retransmission Protocol* (BRP) [4], *NAND Multiplexing* [6], and the *Consensus* protocol (CONS) [3]. For BRP, we have a pMC and a pMDP version, NAND is a pMC, and CONS is a pMDP. For obtaining feasibility solutions, we compare to the SMT solver Z3 [17]. For additional optimality criteria, there is no comparison to another tool possible as IPOPT [10] already fails for the smallest instances we consider.

Figure 3(a) states for each benchmark instance the number of states (#states) and the number of parameters (#par). We defined two specifications consisting of a expected cost property (EC) and a reachability property ($\mathbb{P}$). For some benchmarks, we also maximized the probability to reach a set of "good states" (*). We list the times taken by MOSEK; for optimality problems we also list the times PRISM took to compute precise probabilities or costs (Sect. 5). For feasibility problems we list the times of Z3. The timeout (*TO*) is 90 min.

We observe that both for feasibility with optimality criteria we can handle most benchmarks of up to 10^5 states within the timeout, while we ran into a timeout for CONS. The number of iterations N in the sequential convex programming is less than 12 for all benchmarks with $\epsilon = 10^{-3}$. As expected, simply solving feasibility problems is faster by at least one order of magnitude. Raising the number of parameters from 2 to 4 for BRP does not cause a major performance hit, contrary to existing tools. For all benchmarks except NAND, Z3 only delivered results for the smallest instances within the timeout.

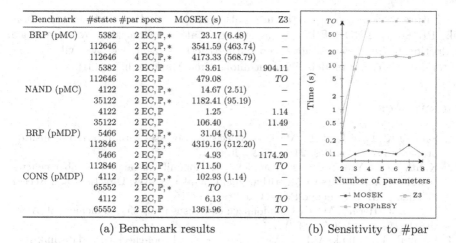

Benchmark	#states	#par specs	MOSEK (s)	Z3
BRP (pMC)	5382	2 EC, $\mathbb{P}$, ∗	23.17 (6.48)	−
	112646	2 EC, $\mathbb{P}$, ∗	3541.59 (463.74)	−
	112646	4 EC, $\mathbb{P}$, ∗	4173.33 (568.79)	−
	5382	2 EC, $\mathbb{P}$	3.61	904.11
	112646	2 EC, $\mathbb{P}$	479.08	TO
NAND (pMC)	4122	2 EC, $\mathbb{P}$, ∗	14.67 (2.51)	−
	35122	2 EC, $\mathbb{P}$, ∗	1182.41 (95.19)	−
	4122	2 EC, $\mathbb{P}$	1.25	1.14
	35122	2 EC, $\mathbb{P}$	106.40	11.49
BRP (pMDP)	5466	2 EC, $\mathbb{P}$, ∗	31.04 (8.11)	−
	112846	2 EC, $\mathbb{P}$, ∗	4319.16 (512.20)	−
	5466	2 EC, $\mathbb{P}$	4.93	1174.20
	112846	2 EC, $\mathbb{P}$	711.50	TO
CONS (pMDP)	4112	2 EC, $\mathbb{P}$, ∗	102.93 (1.14)	−
	65552	2 EC, $\mathbb{P}$, ∗	TO	−
	4112	2 EC, $\mathbb{P}$	6.13	TO
	65552	2 EC, $\mathbb{P}$	1361.96	TO

(a) Benchmark results   (b) Sensitivity to #par

Fig. 3. Experiments.

To demonstrate the insensitivity of our approach to the number of parameters, we considered a pMC of rolling multiple Knuth–Yao dice with 156 states, 522 transitions and considered instances with up to 8 different parameters. The timeout is 100 s. In Fig. 3(b) we compare our encoding in MOSEK for this benchmark to the mere computation of a rational function using PROPhESY [25] and again to Z3. PROPhESY already runs into a timeout for 4 parameters[1]. Z3 needs around 15 s for most of the tests. Using GPs with MOSEK proves far more efficient as it needs less than one second for all instances.

In addition, we test model repair (Sect. 6) on a BRP instance with 17415 states for $\varphi = \mathbb{P}_{\leq 0.9}(\lozenge T)$. The initial parameter instantiation violates φ. We performed model repair towards satisfaction of φ. The probability of reaching T results in 0.79 and the associated cost is 0.013. The computation time is 21.93 s. We compare our result to an implementation of [19], where the probability of reaching T is 0.58 and the associated cost is 0.064. However, the time for the simulation-based method is only 2.4 s, highlighting the expected trade-off between optimality and computation times for the two methods.

Finally, we encode model repair for the small pMC from Example 1 in IPOPT, see [13]. For $\psi = \mathbb{P}_{\leq 0.125}(\lozenge T)$ where T represents the outcome of the die being 2, the initial instantiation induces probability 1/6. With our method, the probability of satisfying ψ is 0.1248 and the cost is 0.0128. With IPOPT, the probability is 0.125 with cost 0.1025, showing that our result is nearly optimal.

8 Conclusion and Future Work

We presented a way to use convex optimization in the field of parameter synthesis for parametric Markov models. Using our results, many NLP encodings of related problems now have a direct and efficient solution.

---

[1] Due to the costly computation of greatest common divisors employed in PROPhESY.

Future work will concern the integration of these methods into mature tools like PRISM or PROPhESY to enable large-scale benchmarking by state space reduction techniques and advanced data structures. Moreover, we will explore extensions to richer models like continuous-time Markov chains [31].

References

1. Satia, J.K., Lave Jr., R.E.: Markovian decision processes with uncertain transition probabilities. Oper. Res. **21**(3), 728–740 (1973)
2. Knuth, D.E., Yao, A.C.: The complexity of nonuniform random number generation. In: Traub, J.F. (ed.) Algorithms and Complexity: New Directions and Recent Results, p. 375. Academic Press, Cambridge (1976)
3. Aspnes, J., Herlihy, M.: Fast randomized consensus using shared memory. J. Algorithms **15**(1), 441–460 (1990)
4. Helmink, L., Sellink, M.P.A., Vaandrager, F.W.: Proof-checking a data link protocol. In: Barendregt, H., Nipkow, T. (eds.) TYPES 1993. LNCS, vol. 806, pp. 127–165. Springer, Heidelberg (1994). doi:10.1007/3-540-58085-9_75
5. Lasserre, J.B.: Global optimization with polynomials and the problem of moments. SIAM J. Optim. **11**(3), 796–817 (2001)
6. Han, J., Jonker, P.: A system architecture solution for unreliable nanoelectronic devices. IEEE Trans. Nanotechnol. **1**, 201–208 (2002)
7. Boyd, S., Kim, S.-J., Vandenberghe, L., Hassibi, A.: A tutorial on geometric programming. Optim. Eng. **8**(1), 67 (2007)
8. Boyd, S.: Sequential convex programming. Lecture Notes (2008)
9. Etessami, K., Kwiatkowska, M., Vardi, M.Y., Yannakakis, M.: Multi-objective model checking of Markov decision processes. LMCS **4**(4), 50–65 (2008)
10. Biegler, L.T., Zavala, V.M.: Large-scale nonlinear programming using IPOPT: an integrating framework for enterprise-wide dynamic optimization. Comput. Chem. Eng. **33**(3), 575–582 (2009)
11. Hahn, E.M., Hermanns, H., Wachter, B., Zhang, L.: PARAM: a model checker for parametric Markov models. In: Touili, T., Cook, B., Jackson, P. (eds.) CAV 2010. LNCS, vol. 6174, pp. 660–664. Springer, Heidelberg (2010). doi:10.1007/978-3-642-14295-6_56
12. Hahn, E.M., Hermanns, H., Zhang, L.: Probabilistic reachability for parametric Markov models. STTT **13**(1), 3–19 (2010)
13. Bartocci, E., Grosu, R., Katsaros, P., Ramakrishnan, C.R., Smolka, S.A.: Model repair for probabilistic systems. In: Abdulla, P.A., Leino, K.R.M. (eds.) TACAS 2011. LNCS, vol. 6605, pp. 326–340. Springer, Heidelberg (2011). doi:10.1007/978-3-642-19835-9_30
14. Forejt, V., Kwiatkowska, M., Norman, G., Parker, D., Qu, H.: Quantitative multi-objective verification for probabilistic systems. In: Abdulla, P.A., Leino, K.R.M. (eds.) TACAS 2011. LNCS, vol. 6605, pp. 112–127. Springer, Heidelberg (2011). doi:10.1007/978-3-642-19835-9_11
15. Kwiatkowska, M., Norman, G., Parker, D.: PRISM 4.0: verification of probabilistic real-time systems. In: Gopalakrishnan, G., Qadeer, S. (eds.) CAV 2011. LNCS, vol. 6806, pp. 585–591. Springer, Heidelberg (2011). doi:10.1007/978-3-642-22110-1_47
16. Forejt, V., Kwiatkowska, M., Parker, D.: Pareto curves for probabilistic model checking. In: Chakraborty, S., Mukund, M. (eds.) ATVA 2012. LNCS, vol. 7561, pp. 317–332. Springer, Heidelberg (2012)

17. Jovanović, D., Moura, L.: Solving non-linear arithmetic. In: Gramlich, B., Miller, D., Sattler, U. (eds.) IJCAR 2012. LNCS (LNAI), vol. 7364, pp. 339–354. Springer, Heidelberg (2012). doi:10.1007/978-3-642-31365-3_27
18. Kwiatkowska, M., Norman, G., Parker, D.: The PRISM benchmark suite. In: QEST, pp. 203–204. IEEE CS (2012)
19. Chen, T., Hahn, E.M., Han, T., Kwiatkowska, M., Qu, H., Zhang, L.: Model repair for Markov decision processes. In: TASE, pp. 85–92. IEEE CS (2013)
20. Puggelli, A., Li, W., Sangiovanni-Vincentelli, A.L., Seshia, S.A.: Polynomial-time verification of PCTL properties of MDPs with convex uncertainties. In: Sharygina, N., Veith, H. (eds.) CAV 2013. LNCS, vol. 8044, pp. 527–542. Springer, Heidelberg (2013). doi:10.1007/978-3-642-39799-8_35
21. Češka, M., Dannenberg, F., Kwiatkowska, M., Paoletti, N.: Precise parameter synthesis for stochastic biochemical systems. In: Mendes, P., Dada, J.O., Smallbone, K. (eds.) CMSB 2014. LNCS, vol. 8859, pp. 86–98. Springer, Heidelberg (2014). doi:10.1007/978-3-319-12982-2_7
22. Hahn, E.M., Li, Y., Schewe, S., Turrini, A., Zhang, L.: ISCASMC: a web-based probabilistic model checker. In: Jones, C., Pihlajasaari, P., Sun, J. (eds.) FM 2014. LNCS, vol. 8442, pp. 312–317. Springer, Heidelberg (2014). doi:10.1007/978-3-319-06410-9_22
23. Jansen, N., Corzilius, F., Volk, M., Wimmer, R., Ábrahám, E., Katoen, J.-P., Becker, B.: Accelerating parametric probabilistic verification. In: Norman, G., Sanders, W. (eds.) QEST 2014. LNCS, vol. 8657, pp. 404–420. Springer, Heidelberg (2014). doi:10.1007/978-3-319-10696-0_31
24. Su, G., Rosenblum, D.S.: Nested reachability approximation for discrete-time Markov chains with univariate parameters. In: Cassez, F., Raskin, J.-F. (eds.) ATVA 2014. LNCS, vol. 8837, pp. 364–379. Springer, Heidelberg (2014). doi:10.1007/978-3-319-11936-6_26
25. Dehnert, C., Junges, S., Jansen, N., Corzilius, F., Volk, M., Bruintjes, H., Katoen, J.-P., Ábrahám, E.: PROPhESY: a PRObabilistic ParamEter SYnthesis tool. In: Kroening, D., Păsăreanu, C.S. (eds.) CAV 2015. LNCS, vol. 9206, pp. 214–231. Springer, Heidelberg (2015). doi:10.1007/978-3-319-21690-4_13
26. PARAM Website (2015). http://depend.cs.uni-sb.de/tools/param/
27. Pathak, S., Ábrahám, E., Jansen, N., Tacchella, A., Katoen, J.-P.: A greedy approach for the efficient repair of stochastic models. In: Havelund, K., Holzmann, G., Joshi, R. (eds.) NFM 2015. LNCS, vol. 9058, pp. 295–309. Springer, Heidelberg (2015). doi:10.1007/978-3-319-17524-9_21
28. Bortolussi, L., Milios, D., Sanguinetti, G.: Smoothed model checking for uncertain continuous-time Markov chains. Inf. Comput. 247, 235–253 (2016)
29. Dehnert, C., Junges, S., Katoen, J.-P., Volk, M.: The probabilistic model checker storm (extended abstract). CoRR, abs/1610.08713 (2016)
30. Delgado, K.V., de Barros, L.N., Dias, D.B., Sanner, S.: Real-time dynamic programming for Markov decision processes with imprecise probabilities. Artif. Intell. 230, 192–223 (2016)
31. Katoen, J.-P.: The probabilistic model checking landscape. In: IEEE Symposium on Logic In Computer Science (LICS). ACM (2016)
32. Long, F., Rinard, M.: Automatic patch generation by learning correct code. In: POPL, pp. 298–312. ACM (2016)
33. Quatmann, T., Dehnert, C., Jansen, N., Junges, S., Katoen, J.-P.: Parameter synthesis for Markov models: faster than ever. In: Artho, C., Legay, A., Peled, D. (eds.) ATVA 2016. LNCS, vol. 9938, pp. 50–67. Springer, Heidelberg (2016). doi:10.1007/978-3-319-46520-3_4

34. Su, G., Rosenblum, D.S., Tamburrelli, G.: Reliability of run-time QOS evaluation using parametric model checking. In: ICSE. ACM (2016, to appear)
35. MOSEK ApS: The MOSEK optimization toolbox for PYTHON. Version 7.1 (Revision 60) (2015)
36. Baier, C., Katoen, J.-P.: Principles of Model Checking. MIT Press, Cambridge (2008)
37. Bertsekas, D.P.: Nonlinear Programming. Athena Scientific, Belmont (1999)
38. Boyd, S., Vandenberghe, L.: Convex Optimization. Cambridge University Press, New York (2004)
39. Thrun, S., Burgard, W., Fox, D.: Probabilistic Robotics. MIT Press, Cambridge (2005)

JANI: Quantitative Model and Tool Interaction

Carlos E. Budde[1], Christian Dehnert[2], Ernst Moritz Hahn[3],
Arnd Hartmanns[4(✉)], Sebastian Junges[2], and Andrea Turrini[3]

[1] Universidad Nacional de Córdoba, Córdoba, Argentina
[2] RWTH Aachen University, Aachen, Germany
[3] State Key Laboratory of Computer Science, Institute of Software,
Chinese Academy of Sciences, Beijing, China
[4] University of Twente, Enschede, The Netherlands
a.hartmanns@utwente.nl

Abstract. The formal analysis of critical systems is supported by a
vast space of modelling formalisms and tools. The variety of incompatible formats and tools however poses a significant challenge to practical
adoption as well as continued research. In this paper, we propose the JANI
model format and tool interaction protocol. The format is a metamodel
based on networks of communicating automata and has been designed
for ease of implementation without sacrificing readability. The purpose
of the protocol is to provide a stable and uniform interface between tools
such as model checkers, transformers, and user interfaces. JANI uses the
JSON data format, inheriting its ease of use and inherent extensibility.
JANI initially targets, but is not limited to, quantitative model checking. Several existing tools now support the verification of JANI models,
and automatic converters from a diverse set of higher-level modelling
languages have been implemented. The ultimate purpose of JANI is to
simplify tool development, encourage research cooperation, and pave the
way towards a future competition in quantitative model checking.

1 Introduction

Significant progress has been made in the area of formal verification to allow the
analysis of ever more realistic, mathematically precise models of performance-,
safety- or economically-critical systems. Such models can be automatically
derived from the program or machine code of an existing implementation, or
they can be constructed in a suitable *modelling language* during the system
design phase. Many such languages, including process algebras like CCS [50]
and CSP [36], lower-level formalisms like reactive modules [2], and high-level
imperative-style languages like PROMELA [37], have been developed. However,
the variety of languages, most of them supported by a single dedicated tool, is
a major obstacle for new users seeking to apply formal methods in their field
of work. Several efforts have been made to standardise modelling languages for
broader use (notably LOTOS [10], an ISO standard), or to develop overarching
formalisms that offer a union of the features of many different specialised languages (a recent example being the CIF language and format [1]). Yet none of

© Springer-Verlag GmbH Germany 2017
A. Legay and T. Margaria (Eds.): TACAS 2017, Part II, LNCS 10206, pp. 151–168, 2017.
DOI: 10.1007/978-3-662-54580-5_9

these efforts appears to have had a lasting impact on practice; of our examples, effectively the only implementation of LOTOS is in the CADP toolset [26], and active CIF support appears restricted to the CIF 3 tool [6].

We argue that the adoption of any standard formalism is hindered by a combination of the proposed standard (a) being complex and difficult to implement, (b) appearing at a time when there are already a number of well-established tools with their own modelling formalisms, and (c) existing in a conflict between supporting many different modelling purposes versus being a succinct way to support a particular technique or type of systems. As most new verification tools are still developed in an academic context, problem a creates work that is at best tangential to the actual research, and problem b means that there is little incentive to implement a new parser in an existing tool since such an effort is unlikely to lead to a publication. We observe that new tools continue to define their own new input language or a new dialect of an existing one as a result.

A New Format. In this paper, we propose jani-model: *another* format for formal models aimed at becoming a common input language for existing and future tools. However, jani-model was created with problems a-c in mind: First of all, it is targeted to the specific field of *quantitative verification* using (extensions of) automata-like probabilistic models such as Markov decision processes (MDP [52]), probabilistic timed automata (PTA [45]), or continuous-time Markov chains (CTMC). This field is much younger than formal methods in general. Consequently, the tooling landscape is at an earlier stage in its evolution. We believe that problem b yet has little relevance there, and that *now* is actually the time where a push for commonality in quantitative verification tools is still possible as well as maximally beneficial. Several tools already support subsets or extensions of the PRISM model checker's [43] language, so a good basis to avoid problem c appears to already exist in this field.

Consequently, the semantic model of the PRISM language—networks of discrete- or continuous-time Markov chains (DTMC or CTMC), MDP or PTA with variables—forms the conceptual basis of jani-model. We have conservatively extended this model to also support Markov automata (MA, [21]) as well as stochastic timed and hybrid automata (STA [9] and SHA [24]). We have also replaced or generalised some concepts to allow more concise and flexible modelling. Notably, we took inspiration from the use of synchronisation vectors in CADP and related tools to compactly-yet-flexibly specify how automata interact; we have added transient variables as seen in RDDL [54] to e.g. allow value passing without having to add state variables; and we have revised the specification of rewards and removed restrictions on global variables.

We could have made these changes and extensions to the textual syntax of the PRISM language, creating a new dialect. However, in our experience, implementing a PRISM language parser is non-trivial and time-consuming. To avoid problem a, jani-model is thus designed to be easy to generate and parse programmatically (while remaining "human-debuggable") without library dependencies. It defines an intentionally small set of core constructs, but its structure allows for easy extensibility. Several advanced features—like support for complex datatypes or recursive functions—are already specified as separate extensions. We do not expect users to create jani-model files manually. Instead, they will be automatically generated from higher-level and domain-specific languages.

A Tool Interaction Protocol. jani-model helps the users as well as the developers of quantitative verification tools. Yet the latter face another obstacle: New techniques often require combining existing approaches implemented by others, or using existing tools for parts of the new analysis. In an academic setting, reimplementation is usually work for little reward, but also squanders the testing and performance tuning effort that went into the original tool. The alternative is to reuse the existing tool through whatever interface it provides: either a command-line interface—usually unstable, changing between tool versions—or an API tied or tailored to one programming language. The same problems apply to benchmarking and verification competitions. To help with interfacing verification tools, we propose the jani-interaction protocol. It defines a clean, flexible, programming language-independent interface to query a tool's capabilities, configure its parameters, perform model transformations, launch verification tasks, and obtain results. Again, we focused on ease of implementation, so jani-interaction is simple to support without dependencies on external libraries or frameworks, and only prescribes a small set of messages with clearly defined extension points.

Tool Support. JANI has been designed in a collaborative effort, and a number of quantitative verification tools implement jani-model and jani-interaction today. They provide connections to existing modelling languages designed for humans as well as a number of analysis techniques with very different capabilities and specialisations based on traditional and statistical model checking. We summarise the current tool support in Sect. 5. We expect the number of JANI implementations to further grow as more input languages are connected and future new verification techniques are implemented for jani-model right from the start.

Related Work. We already mentioned LOTOS as an early standardisation effort, as well as CIF, which covers quantitative aspects such as timed and hybrid, but not probabilistic, behaviour. CIF is a complex specification consisting of a textual and graphical syntax for human use plus an XML representation. It had connections to a variety of tools including those based on MODELICA [25], which itself is also an open specification intended to be supported by tools focusing on continuous system and controller simulation. The HOA format [4] is a tool-independent exchange format for ω-automata designed to represent linear-time properties for or during model checking. ATLANTIF [55] is an intermediate model for real-time systems with data that can be translated to timed automata or Petri nets. In the area of satisfiability-modulo-theories (SMT) solvers, the SMT-LIB standard [5] defines a widely-used data format and tool interface protocol analogous to the pair of jani-model/jani-interaction that we propose for quantitative verification. Boogie 2 [47] is an intermediate language used by static program verification tools. The formats mentioned so far provide concise high-level descriptions of potentially vast state spaces. An alternative is to exchange low-level

```
var ReplyAnalysisEngines = schema({
  "type": "analysis-engines",
  "id": Number.min(1).step(1),
  "engines": Array.of({
    "id": Identifier,
    "metadata": Metadata,
    "?params": Array.of(ParamDef)
  })
});
```

```
{ "type": "analysis-engines",
  "id": 123456,
  "engines": [
    "id": "simengine2"
    "metadata": {
      "name": "FIG",
      "version": {
        "major": 1, "minor": 13
} } ] }
```

Listing 1. js-schema message specification   **Listing 2.** JSON message instance

representations of actual state spaces, representing all the concrete states of the semantics of some high-level model. Examples of such state space-level encodings include CADP's BCG format and MRMC's [41] .tra files. Disadvantages are that the file size explodes with the state space, and all structural information necessary for symbolic (e.g. BDD-based) verification or static analysis is lost.

A number of tools take a reversed approach by providing an interface to plug in different input languages. In the non-quantitative setting, one example is LTSMIN [39] and its PINS interface. However, this is a C/C++ API on the state space level, so every input language needs to provide a complete implementation of its semantics for this tool-specific interface. A prominent tool with a similar approach that uses quantitative models is Möbius [13]. Notably, a command-line interface has recently been added to Möbius' existing graphical and low-level interfaces to improve interoperability [42]. The MODEST TOOLSET [33] also used an internal semantic model similar to that of jani-model that allows it to translate and connect to various external tools, albeit over their command-line interfaces.

The JANI specification can be seen as a *metamodel*. The Eclipse EMF/Ecore platform [19] is popular for building and working with metamodels. We chose to create a standalone specification instead in order to avoid the heavy dependency on Eclipse and to not force a preferred programming language on implementers.

2   JSON and js-schema

jani-model and jani-interaction use the JSON [11] data format to encode their models and messages, respectively. JSON is a textual, language independent format for representing data based on objects, arrays, and a small number of primitives. In contrast to alternatives like XML, it is extremely simple: its entire grammar can be given in just five small syntax diagrams. A generic JSON parser is easy to write, plus native parser libraries are available for many programming languages. The json.org website shows the syntax diagrams and maintains a list of libraries. In contrast to binary encodings, JSON remains human-readable, aiding in debugging. We show an example of the JSON code of an (abbreviated) jani-interaction message in Listing 2. Many of the advantages of JANI can be directly derived from the use of a JSON encoding. We already mentioned the simplicity of implementing a parser, but another important aspect is that a JSON format is

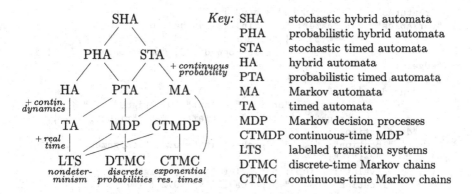

Fig. 1. Model types supported by the jani-model format

inherently extensible as new attributes can be added to objects without breaking an implementation that only reads a previously defined, smaller set of attributes. In addition, both jani-model and jani-interaction contain dedicated versioning and extension mechanisms to cleanly handle situations where future additions may change the semantics of previously defined constructs.

To formally specify what a valid JANI model is, as well as how the messages of the interaction protocol are encoded, we use the js-schema language [51]. js-schema is a lightweight syntax to define object schemas as well as a schema validation library. Compared to the popular alternative of JSON SCHEMA, js-schema specifications are syntactically more similar to the data they describe and thus easier to write and understand. By using an executable schema definition language, we directly obtain a procedure to unambiguously determine whether a given piece of JSON data can represent a JANI object. Some more complex requirements cannot be expressed within js-schema, e.g. when the presence of one attribute is required if and only if another attribute is not present. These additional checks are documented as comments in our js-schema specification for JANI, and they are checked by the reference parser implementation in the MODEST TOOLSET. In Listing 1, we show (part of) the js-schema specification for the `ReplyAnalysisEngines` message type of jani-interaction. The JSON object of Listing fig:json conforms to this schema. An attribute name starting with ? indicates an optional attribute, and in our example, `Identifier`, `Metadata` and `ParamDef` are references to other schemas defined elsewhere within the JANI specification while everything else refers to built-in components of js-schema.

3   The JANI Model Format

The first part of the JANI specification is the jani-model model format. It defines a direct JSON representation of networks of SHA with variables, or special cases thereof. In Fig. 1, we show the automata models supported by jani-model. By providing variables and parallel composition, models with large or infinite state spaces can be represented succinctly. jani-model includes a basic set of variable

```
... "features": [ "derived-operators" ],
    "variables": [ { "name": "i", "initial-value": 0,
                     "type": { "kind": "bounded", "base": "int",
                               "lower-bound": 0, "upper-bound": 7 } } ],
    "edges":
    [ { "location": "loc0",
        "guard": { "op": "∧",
                   "left": { "op": "<", "left": 0, "right": "i" },
                   "right": { "op": "<", "left": "i", "right": 7 } },
        "destinations": [
          { "location": "loc0", "probability": 0.8, "assignments": [
            { "ref": "i",
              "value": { "op": "+", "left": "i", "right": 1 } } ] },
          { "location": "fail", "probability": 0.2 } ] } ], ...
```

Listing 3. Excerpt of a jani-model MDP model

types and expressions with most common operations, and allows the specification of probabilistic and reward-based properties for verification within a model.

The overriding goal of jani-model is simplicity for implementers. The core specification fits on five printed pages. Where expressions over the model's variables are required (such as a guard, the probability of a destination of an edge, or the right-hand side of an assignment), they are represented as expression trees. This is in contrast to other representations of networks of automata, e.g. UPPAAL's [7] XML format, where they are stored as expression strings. Using trees makes it entirely unnecessary to write any kind of expression parsing code to process jani-model models. Listing 3 shows a slightly simplified excerpt of an MDP model with two locations loc0 and fail. It has one edge from loc0 with guard $0 < i \wedge i < 7$ that loops back to loc0 with probability 0.8, incrementing i by 1, and goes to fail with probability 0.2.

An important aspect of the format is its extensibility, which is based on the mentioned use of JSON in combination with an explicit extension mechanism: a model can list a number of *model features* that it makes use of. They are defined separately from the core jani-model specification, and include a derived-operators features, which provides for e.g. max and min operations (which could be represented with comparisons and if-then-else in core jani-model), an arrays and a datatypes feature that specify array types resp. functional-style recursive datatypes (e.g. to define an unbounded linked list type), and a functions feature that allows the definition of (mutually) recursive functions for use in expressions. Feature support will vary between tools; for example, BDD-based model checkers will typically not be able to easily handle unbounded recursive datatypes.

While its syntax is completely different, the semantic concepts of jani-model are based on the PRISM language. However, it is more general in some aspects:

Locations. Automata in jani-model consist of local *variables* and *locations* connected by edges with action labels, guards, rates, probabilistic branches and assignments over the variables. While being natural for an automaton, having both locations and discrete variables is not strictly necessary as one can be encoded using the other. In fact, PRISM only supports the latter, necessitating the use of "program counter" variables to emulate locations if desired. By supporting both, jani-model provides modelling flexibility; if a tool prefers one extreme, an automatic conversion can easily be implemented. Locations provide structural information for e.g. optimisations and static analysis as well as a natural point to store the time progress conditions ("invariants") of TA-based models.

Synchronisation Vectors. A jani-model model consists of a set of automata that execute in parallel. Edges are either performed independently, or two or more automata synchronise on an action label and perform an edge simultaneously. Inspired by CADP's EXP.OPEN tool, jani-model uses *synchronisation vectors* and sets of input-enabled actions as a general specification of synchronisation patterns. As an example, consider three automata. To specify CSP- or PRISM-style multi-way synchronisation on action a, we include the one vector $[a, a, a]$. For CCS-style binary synchronisation between a! and a?, we need the six vectors

$$\{\, [a!, a?, -], [a?, a!, -], [a!, -, a?], [a?, -, a!], [-, a!, a?], [-, a?, a!] \,\}.$$

For UPPAAL-style broadcast synchronisation, we make all automata input-enabled on a? and use the three vectors $\{\, [a!, a?, a?], [a?, a!, a?], [a?, a?, a!] \,\}$. Synchronisation vectors can express all common process-algebraic operations like renaming or hiding, too—they are a concise yet extremely powerful mechanism.

As a further difference to PRISM, jani-model allows assignments to global variables on synchronising edges. Inconsistent concurrent assignments are a modelling error. This small extension removes a major modelling annoyance, but also has important implementation consequences (see Sect. 5 on the STORM tool).

Transient Variables and Assignments. When edges synchronise in a network of automata, the assignments of all participating automata are typically performed all at once, atomically. In jani-model, we additionally allow each assignment to be annotated with an *index*. Assignments with the same index are executed atomically, but sets of assignments with different indices are performed sequentially in the indexed order. In combination with transient variables, which are not part of the state vectors and get reset before and after taking an edge so they do not blow up the state space, this allows e.g. efficient value passing: If two automata synchronise and want to pass a value v, the first one can "send" v by making an assignment $t := v$ to a global transient variable t with index i on its synchronising edge while the second one can "receive" v by making an assignment $l := t$ to the local variable l with index $i' > i$ on its own synchronising edge.

Rewards. Finally, reward structures in jani-model are simply expressions over global (transient or non-transient) variables. Properties indicate whether they are instantaneous or steady-state rewards, or whether to accumulate when edges are taken (edge/transition rewards) or over time in locations (rate rewards). This is again a very simple but expressive way to specify rewards. As an example,

```
{ "op": "Emax", "exp": "i", "accumulate": ["steps"], "step-instant": 6 }
```

asks for the maximum expected reward, computed by accumulating the current value of variable i whenever a transition is taken, after exactly 6 transitions.

4 The JANI Interaction Protocol

The second part of the JANI specification is the jani-interaction tool interaction and automation protocol. Its purpose is to provide a stable interface that allows the reuse of existing implementations from new tools, reduce setup problems by allowing communication between tools running on different machines, and allow for a common integrated graphical user interface for JANI-based verifiers.

jani-interaction is a client-server protocol. A server can support a number of *roles*. We currently define the **analyse** and **transform** roles, which offer access to verification procedures and model transformations, respectively. Roles are the main extension point, allowing new roles to be added in the future. A tool supporting the **analyse** role provides a number of *analysis engines*, which represent the verification algorithms it implements. The protocol then allows analysis tasks to be started, with the server subsequently sending status updates to the client and the client having the ability to cancel the analysis. The jani-interaction specification defines a total of 18 message types, out of which 4 are specific to the **analyse** and 4 are specific to the **transform** role. 5 message types are for task management and used by both roles. The **ReplyAnalysisEngines** message that we showed (in a slightly shortened form) in Listing 1 and 2, for example, is a server-to-client message of the **analyse** role that is sent when the client has queried for the available analysis engines. It includes an array of self-describing parameter definitions; the client can supply values for these parameters to configure the analysis engine when it starts an analysis task. Within the corresponding **StartAnalysisTask** message, the client also submits the model to be analysed. It can be either a jani-model model, which is JSON data and thus included verbatim in the message, or a set of JSON strings with the contents of the model files of any other modelling formalism with a textual representation.

A jani-interaction session consists of the exchange of a number of JSON messages. This can occur in one of two ways: either remotely over the WebSocket network protocol [23], with each message transmitted in one WebSocket text message, or locally by the client starting the server tool and writing its messages into the server's standard input stream, with the server writing its replies onto its standard output stream, one message per line. Using WebSocket communication allows running a tool remotely on a machine that is configured in exactly the way required for the tool to run, and makes it possible to access tools using JavaScript from websites in a browser. Using standard streams is an easier-to-implement alternative for making an existing tool support jani-interaction. We show an example jani-interaction session in Fig. 2.

5 Tool Support

The JANI specification is already supported by a number of quantitative verification tools as outlined in Fig. 3. These tools provide translations from several

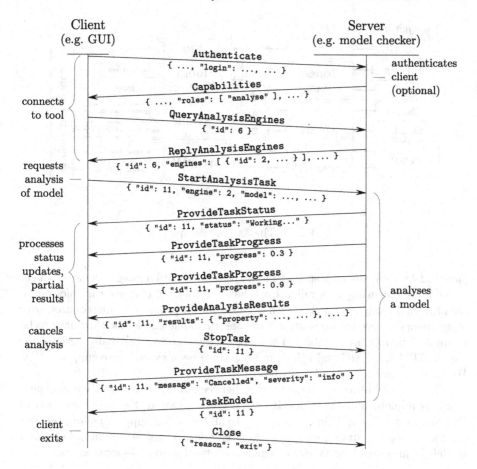

Fig. 2. An example jani-interaction session

higher-level modelling languages to jani-model and, in some cases, vice-versa, thus implementing the functionality of the `transform` role of jani-interaction. Each of them also comes with a set of analysis engines that perform transitional exhaustive or statistical model checking of jani-model models to produce consistent verification results, corresponding to jani-interaction's `analyse` role.

5.1 Modelling Languages

jani-model is designed to be easily machine-readable and we do not expect users to write jani-model files directly. Instead, we provide automated translations from the PRISM language, GSPN, IOSA, MODEST, pGCL and xSADF.

PRISM *language.* The PRISM language is based on reactive modules [2] and used as input language of the PRISM model checker [43]. Variants and subsets are used by other quantitative verification tools, which is why we decided to base

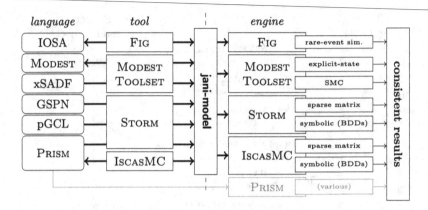

Fig. 3. The JANI landscape

jani-model on its core concepts. A model in the PRISM language consists of a set of modules executing in parallel. Each has a number of discrete variables and a set of probabilistic commands with a guard and a probability distribution over assignments. There are no control flow constructs like e.g. loops; they have to be manually encoded in variables. The PRISM language was originally designed to model DTMC, CTMC and MDP, and has since been extended to support PTA. We show an example of a PRISM model in Fig. 4.

The official bidirectional conversion between the PRISM language and jani-model is implemented in ISCASMC. This gives access to the vast collection of PRISM case studies and benchmarks [44] to all tools that support jani-model, and allows the use of PRISM's model checking engines to analyse jani-model files and models in all input languages for which a conversion to jani-model exists.

GSPN. Petri Nets are a widely-used model for concurrent processes. Generalised stochastic Petri nets (GSPN, [48]) provide *exponentially delayed* transitions in addition to the standard *immediate* transitions. Nondeterminism arising due to the latter has often been resolved by assigning weights, thereby implicitly having discrete probabilistic branching in the model. We show an example GSPN in Fig. 5, which contains two exponentially delayed transitions with rates λ_1 and λ_2. A formal semantics for *every* GSPN, including "confused" ones with actual nondeterminism, in terms of MA has been developed recently [20].

Based on an implementation of this semantics, the STORM tool can translate GSPN given either as a GREATSPN project [3] or in a variant of the ISO-standard PNML [38] format into a jani-model description. Variables describe the markings, and the encoding of nondeterministic and delayed transitions is straightforward. Only weights require a somewhat more involved encoding as expressions.

IOSA. Stochastic automata (SA, [14]) are decision processes in which the occurrence of events is governed by random variables called *clocks*. These can follow arbitrary continuous probability distributions. Input/output SA (I/O SA, [15]) are a variant of networks of SA that guarantee the absence of nondeterminism:

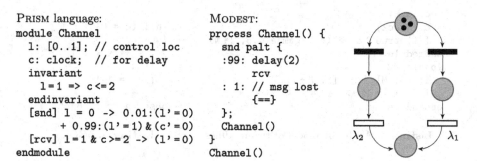

PRISM language:
```
module Channel
  l: [0..1]; // control loc
  c: clock;  // for delay
  invariant
    l=1 => c<=2
  endinvariant
  [snd] l = 0 -> 0.01:(l'=0)
      + 0.99:(l'=1) & (c'=0)
  [rcv] l=1 & c>=2 -> (l'=0)
endmodule
```

MODEST:
```
process Channel() {
  snd palt {
    :99: delay(2)
         rcv
    : 1: // msg lost
         {==}
  };
  Channel()
}
Channel()
```

Fig. 4. A channel PTA model in PRISM and MODEST   **Fig. 5.** A GSPN

Automata must be input-enabled, each output can only be produced by a single automaton in the network, and clocks can only control the timing of outputs. Networks of input/output SA can be modelled in the IOSA language, which is syntactically a variant of the PRISM language. We show an example in Listing 4, where action a is output (!) for M1 and input (?) for M2. Synchronisation is performed in a *broadcast* fashion, meaning an output will synchronise with all matching inputs. This ensures the input-enabledness requirement.

The FIG tool [12] translates IOSA to and from jani-model. In jani-model, the STA model type is used, since I/O SA are a proper subset of STA. When converting from jani-model to IOSA, STA and CTMC models where the synchronisation vectors correspond to broadcast synchronisation are supported. STA are accepted only if the STA clocks are used in a way that can be mapped to SA.

MODEST. The MODEST language is a modelling formalism with a semantics in terms of STA [9], later extended to SHA [29]. It is an expressive, high-level language with features like recursive process calls, do loops, exception handling, and complex datatypes. We show a very small example in Fig. 4. The MODEST TOOLSET implements conversions from MODEST to jani-model and back. In terms of supported model types, MODEST is the most expressive language currently connected to jani-model because everything can be seen as a special case of SHA.

pGCL. Probabilistic programming languages extend standard languages with constructs to sample from random distributions and to condition program runs on observations about (random) data. Such constructs are at the heart of algorithms in machine learning, security, and quantum computing [27]. The operational semantics of probabilistic programs are (possibly infinite) MDP.

One example of a probabilistic programming language is the probabilistic guarded command language (pGCL, [49]) with observe statements [40]. The STORM tool implements a translation from pGCL via program graphs to jani-model. A noticeable feature of the translation is the detection of rewards: In the example pGCL program given in Listing 5, if we omit the observe statement, the variable x can be considered a reward, which then makes the MDP finite and thus amenable to probabilistic model checking.

```
module M1
  c: clock;
  [a!] true @ c -> (c' = gamma(0.5, 2*N));
endmodule
module M2
  i: [0..M];  x: [1..M+1];
  [a?] i <= M -> (i' = x) & (x' = i+1);
endmodule
```

```
while(c = 0)
{
  { x := x + 1 }
  [1/2]
  { c := 1 }
};
observe "x is odd"
```

Listing 4. An IOSA model of two modules   **Listing 5.** pGCL

xSADF. Dataflow formalisms are popular in the study of embedded data processing applications. The recently introduced formalism xSADF [35], an extension of scenario-aware dataflow [56], adds cost annotations (to model, for example, power consumption), nondeterminism, and continuous stochastic execution times. It is equipped with a compositional semantics in terms of STA, which is implemented in the MODEST TOOLSET. Via the latter's support for jani-model, we can now also convert xSADF specifications to jani-model. The resulting models are networks of STA that make use of the `datatypes` and `functions` features to encode the unbounded typed scenario channels of xSADF.

5.2 Analysis Tools

Support for the verification of jani-model models is currently provided by FIG, ISCASMC, the MODEST TOOLSET and STORM, as well as PRISM via ISCASMC's ability to convert jani-model to the PRISM language. We summarise the capabilities and restrictions of the various analysis engines in Table 1. ✓ denotes current support, while ∗ means that an implementation is planned. (1) indicates that only broadcast-based input/output STA that correspond to stochastic automata are supported. (2) marks planned support of the `arrays` feature that will be restricted to fixed-size arrays. The MODEST TOOLSET's support for SHA is via the `prohver` tool [29], indicated by (3), and its statistical model checker only supports deterministic models where marked (4). Concerning supported properties, we consider the broad classes of probabilistic reachability (P), probabilistic computation tree logic (PCTL), the probabilities of linear temporal logic formulas (LTL), any type of expected values or rewards (E) and steady-state measures (S).

FIG. Specialised in rare event simulation, FIG [12] implements novel techniques that allow the use of importance splitting [46] in a fully automated way. Importance splitting speeds up the occurrence of some user-defined rare event in order to better estimate its probability of occurrence.

FIG can be used to study transient and long run behaviour. Transient properties are expressed as $P(\neg stop \cup rare)$, where *stop* and *rare* are propositional formulas describing *simulation truncation* and *rare event occurrence*, respectively. Steady state properties correspond to the CSL expression $S(rare)$. Aside from standard Monte Carlo simulation, an engine based on RESTART-like [57]

Table 1. Support for model types, features and property classes in analysis tools

tool	engine	LTS	DTMC	CTMC	MDP	CTMDP	MA	TA	PTA	STA	SHA	arrays	datatypes	functions	P	PCTL	LTL	E	S
Fig	rare	−	*	✓	−	−	−	−	−	(1)	−	(2)	−	*	✓	−	−	*	✓
IscasMC	sparse	✓	✓	✓	✓	*	*	−	−	−	−	−	−	−	✓	✓	✓	*	*
	BDD	✓	✓	✓	✓	*	*	−	−	−	−	−	−	−	✓	✓	✓	*	*
Modest Toolset	explicit	✓	✓	−	✓	−	−	✓	✓	✓	(3)	✓	✓	✓	✓	*	−	✓	−
	SMC	✓	✓	−	✓	−	(4)	(4)	(4)	(4)	−	✓	✓	✓	✓	−	−	✓	−
Storm	sparse	✓	✓	✓	✓	−	✓	−	−	−	−	*	*	*	✓	✓	−	✓	✓
	BDD	✓	✓	✓	✓	−	*	−	−	−	−	(2)	−	−	✓	✓	−	✓	*
Prism	(various)	✓	✓	✓	✓	−	−	✓	✓	−	−	−	−	−	✓	✓	✓	✓	✓

importance splitting can be used. The importance function needed by the latter can be provided *ad hoc* by the user or computed automatically by the tool.

IscasMC. A Java-based model checker for stochastic systems, IscasMC [31] offers an easy-to-use web interface for the evaluation of Markov chains and decision processes against PCTL, PLTL, and PCTL* specifications. It is particularly efficient in evaluating the probabilities of LTL properties, supporting multiple resolution methods that improve the actual runtime on complex LTL properties [30]. IscasMC provides two analysis engines: one based on an explicit sparse matrix encoding of the state space, and a symbolic one using binary decision diagrams (BDD). IscasMC can be extended with plugins. This permits to support the analysis of other formalisms, like quantum Markov chains [22] and stochastic parity games [32], as well as to use different (multi-terminal) BDD libraries [18] to symbolically represent both the model and the automaton for the LTL formula.

The Modest Toolset. A modular collection of model transformation and analysis tools centred around an internal metamodel of networks of stochastic hybrid systems, which greatly influenced the design of jani-model, the Modest Toolset [33] is an implementation of the multiple-formalism, multiple-solution idea. Its core analysis engines today are the explicit-state model checker mcsta and the statistical model checker (SMC) modes. The former handles MDP, PTA and STA with billions of states via a disk-based approach [34] and efficiently checks time- and reward-bounded properties without unnecessarily unfolding the state space [28]. The latter focuses on detecting spurious nondeterminism on-the-fly during simulation in order to be able to handle not just Markov chains.

Storm. Newly developed as the successor of the probabilistic model checker MRMC [41], Storm [17] works with DTMC, CTMC, MDP and MA models. In addition to its support for jani-model and the Prism language, it can also read files in an explicit state space-level format similar to MRMC's. The analysis of models is backed by different engines that use different representations for the model structure and reachable states, including sparse matrices and BDD. STORM's first aim is to achieve good performance, but special attention is also given to a modular design that enables coherent and easy access to a variety of solvers used by the analysis processes such as linear equation, mixed-integer linear programming, and SMT solvers. STORM also supports parametric DTMC and MDP. As the backend for PROPHESY [16] and using a parameter lifting approach [53], it significantly outperforms other parametric discrete-time verification tools.

Table 2. Comparison of PRISM- and jani-model-based state space generation

model	type	sparse/explicit engines				symbolic engines (BDD)			
			STORM		PRISM		STORM		PRISM
		params	JANI	PRISM		params	JANI	PRISM	
crowds	DTMC	$\langle 20, 5 \rangle$	8.9 s	8.4 s	26.2 s	$\langle 20, 25 \rangle$	9.1 s	9.6 s	9.6 s
cluster	CTMC	250	20.2 s	18.4 s	26.5 s	3000	32.1 s	31.1 s	96.7 s
consensus	MDP	$\langle 6, 4 \rangle$	15.3 s	14.6 s	48.3 s	$\langle 10, 100 \rangle$	24.1 s	25.4 s	27.5 s
CSMA	MDP	$\langle 3, 4 \rangle$	13.8 s	13.1 s	15.4 s	$\langle 4, 4 \rangle$	10.2 s	10.2 s	27.8 s

The PRISM language is known for its ability to compactly represent gigantic models which can be very efficiently handled by BDD-based engines. In STORM, jani-model and PRISM models are currently handled by separate code paths. This provided the opportunity to investigate whether the changes in state space generation code caused by the new concepts of jani-model (in particular to support synchronising assignments to global variables in the BDD-based engine) impact performance. Experiments were run on a quad-core 3.5 GHz Intel Core i7 system with Mac OS X 10.12, using four PRISM benchmark models [44] and their conversions to jani-model. We tested both explicit-state and symbolic engines. Table 2 lists the model construction time of STORM with the jani-model and PRISM files and, for comparison, of PRISM with the PRISM file. The results indicate that allowing for the extra language features in jani-model does not significantly influence the model construction performance; the comparison with PRISM furthermore shows that this is not just due to a naïve implementation of the PRISM code path within STORM.

6   Conclusion

We have proposed the JANI specification for model exchange and tool interaction. The complete specification and a library of models are available at jani-spec.org. The goal of JANI is to reduce the effort required to develop verification tools, especially in an academic setting, and to foster tool interoperation and comparison. Supporting the jani-model format gives access to a large number of existing models (in the format itself and in the various connected languages) for testing and benchmarking at little effort compared to writing a full parser for one of the existing modelling languages, which prioritise being easily human-writeable over being easily machine-readable. While JANI is currently focused on quantitative verification (cf. problem b of Sect. 1), standard labelled transition systems or Kripke structures as used in traditional verification approaches can be represented in jani-model, too, and the jani-interaction protocol can be used with any modelling formalism with a textual representation.

Outlook. As JANI is an ongoing effort, we use the jani-spec.org website to track the growing list of implementing tools and their status (akin to Table 1). Ultimately, we hope that JANI can lead the way towards a more coordinated tool development process in quantitative verification that, together with the previous definition of the PRISM benchmark suite [44], will eventually enable a quantitative model checking competition. Such competitions have been shown to have a strong positive impact on the tooling landscape in affected fields [8].

Acknowledgements. This work is supported by the 3TU project "Big Software on the Run", ANPCyT grant PICT-2012-1823, BMBF-IKT 2020 project 16KIS0138 HODRIAN, CDZ project GZ 1023 (CAP), the CAS Fellowship for International Young Scientists, the CAS/SAFEA International Fellowship Program for Creative Research Teams, the National Natural Science Foundation of China (grants no. 61550110506 and 61650410658), and SeCyT-UNC grant 05/BP12.

References

1. Agut, D.E.N., van Beek, D.A., Rooda, J.E.: Syntax and semantics of the compositional interchange format for hybrid systems. J. Log. Algebr. Program. **82**(1), 1–52 (2013)
2. Alur, R., Henzinger, T.A.: Reactive modules. FMSD **15**(1), 7–48 (1999)
3. Amparore, E.G.: A new greatSPN GUI for GSPN editing and CSL^{TA} model checking. In: Norman, G., Sanders, W. (eds.) QEST 2014. LNCS, vol. 8657, pp. 170–173. Springer, Heidelberg (2014). doi:10.1007/978-3-319-10696-0_13
4. Babiak, T., Blahoudek, F., Duret-Lutz, A., Klein, J., Křetínský, J., Müller, D., Parker, D., Strejček, J.: The Hanoi omega-automata format. In: Kroening, D., Păsăreanu, C.S. (eds.) CAV 2015. LNCS, vol. 9206, pp. 479–486. Springer, Heidelberg (2015). doi:10.1007/978-3-319-21690-4_31
5. Barrett, C., Fontaine, P., Tinelli, C.: The SMT-LIB standard: version 2.5. Technical report, Department of Computer Science, The University of Iowa (2015). www.smt-lib.org
6. van Beek, D.A., Fokkink, W.J., Hendriks, D., Hofkamp, A., Markovski, J., van de Mortel-Fronczak, J.M., Reniers, M.A.: CIF 3: model-based engineering of supervisory controllers. In: Ábrahám, E., Havelund, K. (eds.) TACAS 2014. LNCS, vol. 8413, pp. 575–580. Springer, Heidelberg (2014). doi:10.1007/978-3-642-54862-8_48
7. Behrmann, G., David, A., Larsen, K.G., Håkansson, J., Pettersson, P., Yi, W., Hendriks, M.: UPPAAL 4.0. In: QEST, pp. 125–126. IEEE CS (2006)
8. Beyer, D.: Software verification and verifiable witnesses (report on SV-COMP 2015). In: Baier, C., Tinelli, C. (eds.) TACAS 2015. LNCS, vol. 9035, pp. 401–416. Springer, Heidelberg (2015). doi:10.1007/978-3-662-46681-0_31

9. Bohnenkamp, H.C., D'Argenio, P.R., Hermanns, H., Katoen, J.-P.: MODEST: a compositional modeling formalism for hard and softly timed systems. IEEE TSE **32**(10), 812–830 (2006)
10. Bolognesi, T., Brinksma, E.: Introduction to the ISO specification language LOTOS. Comput. Netw. **14**, 25–59 (1987)
11. Bray, T.: The JavaScript Object Notation (JSON) data interchange format. RFC 7159, RFC Editor, March 2014. rfc-editor.org/rfc/rfc7159.txt
12. Budde, C.E., D'Argenio, P.R., Monti, R.E.: Compositional construction of importance functions in fully automated importance splitting. In: VALUETOOLS, ICST (2016)
13. Courtney, T., Gaonkar, S., Keefe, K., Rozier, E., Sanders, W.H.: Möbius 2.3: an extensible tool for dependability, security, and performance evaluation of large and complex system models. In: DSN, pp. 353–358. IEEE CS (2009)
14. D'Argenio, P.R., Katoen, J.-P.: A theory of stochastic systems part I: stochastic automata. Inf. Comput. **203**(1), 1–38 (2005)
15. D'Argenio, P.R., Lee, M.D., Monti, R.E.: Input/Output stochastic automata - compositionality and determinism. In: Fränzle, M., Markey, N. (eds.) FORMATS 2016. LNCS, vol. 9884, pp. 53–68. Springer, Cham (2016). doi:10.1007/978-3-319-44878-7_4
16. Dehnert, C., Junges, S., Jansen, N., Corzilius, F., Volk, M., Bruintjes, H., Katoen, J.-P., Ábrahám, E.: PROPhESY: a PRObabilistic ParamEter SYnthesis tool. In: Kroening, D., Păsăreanu, C.S. (eds.) CAV 2015. LNCS, vol. 9206, pp. 214–231. Springer, Heidelberg (2015). doi:10.1007/978-3-319-21690-4_13
17. Dehnert, C., Junges, S., Katoen, J.-P., Volk, M.: The probabilistic model checker Storm (extended abstract). CoRR abs/1610.08713 (2016)
18. van Dijk, T., Hahn, E.M., Jansen, D.N., Li, Y., Neele, T., Stoelinga, M., Turrini, A., Zhang, L.: A comparative study of BDD packages for probabilistic symbolic model checking. In: Li, X., Liu, Z., Yi, W. (eds.) SETTA 2015. LNCS, vol. 9409, pp. 35–51. Springer, Heidelberg (2015). doi:10.1007/978-3-319-25942-0_3
19. Eclipse Foundation: Eclipse Modeling Framework (EMF). eclipse.org/modeling/emf. Accessed 27 Jan 2016
20. Eisentraut, C., Hermanns, H., Katoen, J.-P., Zhang, L.: A semantics for every GSPN. In: Colom, J.-M., Desel, J. (eds.) PETRI NETS 2013. LNCS, vol. 7927, pp. 90–109. Springer, Heidelberg (2013). doi:10.1007/978-3-642-38697-8_6
21. Eisentraut, C., Hermanns, H., Zhang, L.: On probabilistic automata in continuous time. In: LICS, pp. 342–351. IEEE CS (2010)
22. Feng, Y., Hahn, E.M., Turrini, A., Zhang, L.: QPMC: a model checker for quantum programs and protocols. In: Bjørner, N., de Boer, F. (eds.) FM 2015. LNCS, vol. 9109, pp. 265–272. Springer, Heidelberg (2015). doi:10.1007/978-3-319-19249-9_17
23. Fette, I., Melnikov, A.: The WebSocket protocol. RFC 6455, RFC Editor, December 2011. rfc-editor.org/rfc/rfc6455.txt
24. Fränzle, M., Hahn, E.M., Hermanns, H., Wolovick, N., Zhang, L.: Measurability and safety verification for stochastic hybrid systems. In: HSCC, pp. 43–52. ACM (2011)
25. Fritzson, P.: Modelica - a cyber-physical modeling language and the OpenModelica environment. In: IWCMC, pp. 1648–1653. IEEE (2011)
26. Garavel, H., Lang, F., Mateescu, R., Serwe, W.: CADP 2011: a toolbox for the construction and analysis of distributed processes. STTT **15**(2), 89–107 (2013)
27. Gordon, A.D., Henzinger, T.A., Nori, A.V., Rajamani, S.K.: Probabilistic programming. In: FOSE, pp. 167–181. ACM (2014)

28. Hahn, E.M., Hartmanns, A.: A comparison of time- and reward-bounded probabilistic model checking techniques. In: Fränzle, M., Kapur, D., Zhan, N. (eds.) SETTA 2016. LNCS, vol. 9984, pp. 85–100. Springer, Heidelberg (2016). doi:10.1007/978-3-319-47677-3_6

29. Hahn, E.M., Hartmanns, A., Hermanns, H., Katoen, J.-P.: A compositional modelling and analysis framework for stochastic hybrid systems. FMSD **43**(2), 191–232 (2013)

30. Hahn, E.M., Li, G., Schewe, S., Turrini, A., Zhang, L.: Lazy probabilistic model checking without determinisation. In: CONCUR, vol. 42. LIPIcs, pp. 354–367. Schloss Dagstuhl - Leibniz-Zentrum fuer Informatik (2015)

31. Hahn, E.M., Li, Y., Schewe, S., Turrini, A., Zhang, L.: ISCASMC: a web-based probabilistic model checker. In: Jones, C., Pihlajasaari, P., Sun, J. (eds.) FM 2014. LNCS, vol. 8442, pp. 312–317. Springer, Heidelberg (2014). doi:10.1007/978-3-319-06410-9_22

32. Hahn, E.M., Schewe, S., Turrini, A., Zhang, L.: A simple algorithm for solving qualitative probabilistic parity games. In: Chaudhuri, S., Farzan, A. (eds.) CAV 2016. LNCS, vol. 9780, pp. 291–311. Springer, Heidelberg (2016). doi:10.1007/978-3-319-41540-6_16

33. Hartmanns, A., Hermanns, H.: The Modest Toolset: an integrated environment for quantitative modelling and verification. In: Ábrahám, E., Havelund, K. (eds.) TACAS 2014. LNCS, vol. 8413, pp. 593–598. Springer, Heidelberg (2014). doi:10.1007/978-3-642-54862-8_51

34. Hartmanns, A., Hermanns, H.: Explicit model checking of very large MDP using partitioning and secondary storage. In: Finkbeiner, B., Pu, G., Zhang, L. (eds.) ATVA 2015. LNCS, vol. 9364, pp. 131–147. Springer, Heidelberg (2015). doi:10.1007/978-3-319-24953-7_10

35. Hartmanns, A., Hermanns, H., Bungert, M.: Flexible support for time and costs in scenario-aware dataflow. In: EMSOFT, pp. 3:1–3:10. ACM (2016)

36. Hoare, C.A.R.: Communicating Sequential Processes. Prentice-Hall, Upper Saddle River (1985)

37. Holzmann, G.J.: The model checker SPIN. IEEE TSE **23**(5), 279–295 (1997)

38. ISO 15909-2:2011. High-level Petri nets – Part 2: Transfer format (2011)

39. Kant, G., Laarman, A., Meijer, J., van de Pol, J., Blom, S., van Dijk, T.: LTSmin: high-performance language-independent model checking. In: Baier, C., Tinelli, C. (eds.) TACAS 2015. LNCS, vol. 9035, pp. 692–707. Springer, Heidelberg (2015). doi:10.1007/978-3-662-46681-0_61

40. Katoen, J.-P., Gretz, F., Jansen, N., Kaminski, B.L., Olmedo, F.: Understanding probabilistic programs. In: Meyer, R., Platzer, A., Wehrheim, H. (eds.) Correct System Design. LNCS, vol. 9360, pp. 15–32. Springer, Heidelberg (2015). doi:10.1007/978-3-319-23506-6_4

41. Katoen, J.-P., Zapreev, I.S., Hahn, E.M., Hermanns, H., Jansen, D.N.: The ins and outs of the probabilistic model checker MRMC. Perform. Eval. **68**(2), 90–104 (2011)

42. Keefe, K., Sanders, W.H.: Möbius shell: a command-line interface for Möbius. In: Joshi, K., Siegle, M., Stoelinga, M., D'Argenio, P.R. (eds.) QEST 2013. LNCS, vol. 8054, pp. 282–285. Springer, Heidelberg (2013). doi:10.1007/978-3-642-40196-1_24

43. Kwiatkowska, M., Norman, G., Parker, D.: PRISM 4.0: verification of probabilistic real-time systems. In: Gopalakrishnan, G., Qadeer, S. (eds.) CAV 2011. LNCS, vol. 6806, pp. 585–591. Springer, Heidelberg (2011). doi:10.1007/978-3-642-22110-1_47

44. Kwiatkowska, M., Norman, G., Parker, D.: The PRISM benchmark suite. In: QEST, pp. 203–204. IEEE CS (2012)

45. Kwiatkowska, M., Norman, G., Segala, R., Sproston, J.: Automatic verification of real-time systems with discrete probability distributions. TCS **282**(1), 101–150 (2002)
46. L'Ecuyer, P., Le Gland, F., Lezaud, P., Tuffin, B.: Splitting techniques. In: Rare Event Simulation using Monte Carlo Methods, pp. 39–61. Wiley, Ltd. (2009)
47. Leino, K.R.M., Rümmer, P.: A polymorphic intermediate verification language: design and logical encoding. In: Esparza, J., Majumdar, R. (eds.) TACAS 2010. LNCS, vol. 6015, pp. 312–327. Springer, Heidelberg (2010). doi:10.1007/978-3-642-12002-2_26
48. Marsan, M.A., Balbo, G., Conte, G., Donatelli, S., Franceschinis, G.: Modelling with Generalized Stochastic Petri Nets, 1st edn. Wiley, New York (1994)
49. McIver, A., Morgan, C.: Abstraction, Refinement and Proof for Probabilistic Systems. Monographs in Computer Science. Springer, New York (2005)
50. Milner, R.: A Calculus of Communicating Systems. LNCS, vol. 92. Springer, Heidelberg (1980)
51. Molnár, G.: js-schema website. molnarg.github.io/js-schema. Accessed 28 Jan 2016
52. Puterman, M.L.: Markov Decision Processes: Discrete Stochastic Dynamic Programming. Wiley, New York (1994)
53. Quatmann, T., Dehnert, C., Jansen, N., Junges, S., Katoen, J.-P.: Parameter synthesis for Markov models: faster than ever. In: Artho, C., Legay, A., Peled, D. (eds.) ATVA 2016. LNCS, vol. 9938, pp. 50–67. Springer, Heidelberg (2016). doi:10.1007/978-3-319-46520-3_4
54. Sanner, S.: Relational dynamic influence diagram language (RDDL): Language description (2010). http://users.cecs.anu.edu.au/~ssanner/IPPC_2011/RDDL.pdf
55. Stöcker, J., Lang, F., Garavel, H.: Parallel processes with real-time and data: the ATLANTIF intermediate format. In: Leuschel, M., Wehrheim, H. (eds.) IFM 2009. LNCS, vol. 5423, pp. 88–102. Springer, Heidelberg (2009). doi:10.1007/978-3-642-00255-7_7
56. Theelen, B.D., Geilen, M., Basten, T., Voeten, J., Gheorghita, S.V., Stuijk, S.: A scenario-aware data flow model for combined long-run average and worst-case performance analysis. In: MEMOCODE, pp. 185–194. IEEE CS (2006)
57. Villén-Altamirano, M., Villén-Altamirano, J.: The rare event simulation method RESTART: efficiency analysis and guidelines for its application. In: Kouvatsos, D.D. (ed.) Network Performance Engineering. LNCS, vol. 5233, pp. 509–547. Springer, Heidelberg (2011). doi:10.1007/978-3-642-02742-0_22

Computing Scores of Forwarding Schemes in Switched Networks with Probabilistic Faults

Guy Avni[1]([⊠]), Shubham Goel[2], Thomas A. Henzinger[1],
and Guillermo Rodriguez-Navas[3]

[1] IST Austria, Klosterneuburg, Austria
guy.avni@ist.ac.at
[2] IIT Bombay, Mumbai, India
[3] Mälardalen University, Västerås, Sweden

Abstract. Time-triggered switched networks are a deterministic communication infrastructure used by real-time distributed embedded systems. Due to the criticality of the applications running over them, developers need to ensure that end-to-end communication is dependable and predictable. Traditional approaches assume static networks that are not flexible to changes caused by reconfigurations or, more importantly, faults, which are dealt with in the application using redundancy. We adopt the concept of handling faults in the switches from non-real-time networks while maintaining the required predictability.

We study a class of forwarding schemes that can handle various types of failures. We consider probabilistic failures. For a given network with a forwarding scheme and a constant ℓ, we compute the *score* of the scheme, namely the probability (induced by faults) that at least ℓ messages arrive on time. We reduce the scoring problem to a reachability problem on a Markov chain with a "product-like" structure. Its special structure allows us to reason about it symbolically, and reduce the scoring problem to #SAT. Our solution is generic and can be adapted to different networks and other contexts. Also, we show the computational complexity of the scoring problem is #P-complete, and we study methods to estimate the score. We evaluate the effectiveness of our techniques with an implementation.

1 Introduction

An increasing number of distributed embedded applications, such as the Internet-of-Things (IoT) or modern Cyber-Physical Systems, must cover wide geographical areas and thus need to be deployed over large-scale switched communication networks. The switches used in such networks are typically fast hardware devices with limited computational power and with a global notion of discrete time. Due

This research was supported in part by the Austrian Science Fund (FWF) under grants S11402-N23 (RiSE/SHiNE) and Z211-N23 (Wittgenstein Award) and by the People Programme (Marie Curie Actions) of the European Union's Seventh Framework Programme FP7/2007-2013/ under REA grant agreement 607727.

© Springer-Verlag GmbH Germany 2017
A. Legay and T. Margaria (Eds.): TACAS 2017, Part II, LNCS 10206, pp. 169–187, 2017.
DOI: 10.1007/978-3-662-54580-5_10

to the criticality of such applications, developers need to ensure that end-to-end communication is dependable and predictable, i.e. messages need to arrive at their destination on time. The weakness of traditional *hard* real-time techniques is that they assume nearly static traffic characteristics and *a priori* knowledge about them. These assumptions do not fit well with setups where highly dynamic traffic and evolving network infrastructure are the rule and not the exception; e.g. see [26]. For this reason, there is a pressing need to combine flexibility and adaptability features with traditional hard real-time methods [11,12,30].

The Time-Triggered (TT) scheduling paradigm has been advocated for real-time communication over switched networks [28]. The switches follow a static *schedule* that prescribes which message is sent through each link at every time slot. The schedule is synthesized offline, and it is repeated cyclically during the system operation [22]. TT-schedules are both predictable and easy to implement using a simple lookup table. Their disadvantage is that they lack *robustness*; even a single fault can cause much damage (in terms of number of lost messages). Error-handling is left to the application designer and is typically solved by statically introducing redundancy [5]. Static allocation of redundancy has its limitations: (i) it adds to the difficulty of finding a TT-schedule, which is a computationally demanding problem even before the addition of redundant messages, and (ii) it reduces the effective utilization of resources.

In contrast, non real-time communication networks typically implement error-recovery functionality within the switches, using some kind of flexible routing, to reduce the impact of crashes. Such an approach is used in *software defined networking* (SDN) [17], which is a booming field in the context of routing in the Internet. Handling crashes has been extensively studied in such networks (c.f., [8,24,33] and references therein), though the goal is different than in real-time networks; a message in their setting should arrive at its destination as long as a path to it exists in the network. Thus, unlike real-time applications, there is no notion of a "deadline" for a message.

In this work we explore the frontier between both worlds. We adopt the concept of programmable switches from SDN to the real-time setting in order to cope with network faults. The challenge is to maintain the predictability requirement, which is the focus of this work. We suggest a class of deterministic routing schemes, which we refer to as *forwarding schemes*, and we show how to predict the behavior of the network when using a particular forwarding scheme. More formally, the input to our problem consists of a network $\mathcal{N}$ that is accompanied with probabilities of failures on edges, a set of messages $\mathcal{M}$ to be routed through $\mathcal{N}$, a (deterministic) forwarding scheme $\mathcal{F}$ that is used to forward the messages in $\mathcal{M}$, a timeout $t \in \mathbb{N}$ on the arrival time of messages, i.e., if a message arrives after time t, it is considered to be lost, and a guarantee $\ell \in \mathbb{N}$ on the number of messages that should arrive. Our goal is to compute the *score* of $\mathcal{F}$, which is defined as the probability (induced by faults) that at least ℓ messages arrive at their destinations on time when forwarding using $\mathcal{F}$.

Our score is a means for predicting the outcome of the network. If the score is too low, a designer can use redundancy techniques to increase it. Also, it is a means to compare forwarding schemes. When constructing a forwarding scheme, be it a TT-schedule or any other scheme, a designer has control on some of the components and others are fixed by the application. For example, in many networks, the size of the switches' queues are fixed to be small, making it impossible to use algorithms that rely on large memories. The choices made by the designer can highly influence the performance of the system on the one hand, and are very hard to predict on the other; especially when faults come into the picture. Our score can be used to compare different forwarding schemes, allowing the designer to evaluate his algorithm of choice. Also, our solution can be used for sensitivity analysis with respect to certain parameters of the network; for example, one can fix the score and ℓ, and find the error probabilities for the channels [4].

A first step towards handling faults in the switches was made in [3]. In their framework, the switches follow a TT-schedule and resort to a forwarding algorithm once a crash occurs. Our forwarding scheme is simpler and allows consideration of richer faults in a clean and elegant manner, which were impossible to handle in [3]'s framework. More importantly, they study adversarial faults whereas we study probabilistic ones, which are a better model for reality while they are considerably more complicated to handle. Using failover paths to allow for flexibility in switched networks was considered in [20,32].

The definition of the class of forwarding schemes requires care. On the one hand, the switches computation power is limited, so forwarding rules in the switches should be specified as propositional rules. But, on the other hand, it is infeasible to manually specify the rules at each switch as the network is large and is subject to frequent changes. So, we are required to use a central symbolic definition of an algorithm. However, while the definition of the central algorithm uses propositional rules, it should allow for variability between the switches and the messages' behavior in them. There are many ways to overcome these challenges, and we suggest one solution, which is simple and robust. Our forwarding scheme consists of three components. The first component is a *forwarding algorithm* that the switches run and is given by means of propositional forwarding rules. The two other components allow variability between the switches, each switch has priorities on messages, and each message has a preference on outgoing edges from each switch. The forwarding rules of the algorithm take these priorities and preferences into consideration. A similar priority-list model is taken in [14]. Our algorithm for computing the score of a scheme is general and can handle various forwarding schemes that are given as propositional rules as we elaborate in Sect. 8.

In order to score a given forwarding scheme, we first reduce the scoring problem to a reachability problem on a certain type of Markov chain, which is constructed in two steps. First, we focus on an individual message m and construct a deterministic automaton $\mathcal{D}_m$ that simulates the forwarding scheme from the perspective of the message. Then, we combine the automata of all the messages into an automaton that simulates their execution simultaneously, and construct a Markov chain $\mathcal{C}$ on top of it by assuming a distribution on input letters (faults). The size of $\mathcal{C}$ is huge and the crux of our approach is reasoning about it symbolically rather than implicitly using PRISM [18] for example. We construct a Boolean formula ψ that simulates the execution of $\mathcal{C}$. The special product-like structure of $\mathcal{C}$ allows us to construct ψ that is proportional in size to the sum of sizes of the $\mathcal{D}_m$ automata rather than the product of their sizes, which is the size of $\mathcal{C}$. There is a one-to-one correspondence between satisfying assignments to ψ and "good outcomes", namely outcomes in which at least ℓ messages arrive on time. We then infer the score of the forwarding scheme from the *weighted* count of satisfying assignments to ψ; the weight of a satisfying assignment is the probability of the crashes in the corresponding execution of the network.

The problem of counting the number of satisfying assignments of a Boolean formula is called #SAT and it has received much attention. The practical developments on this problem are quite remarkable given its computational intractably; even deciding whether a Boolean formula has one solution is an NP-complete problem that was considered impossible to solve practically twenty years ago, *a fortiori* counting the number of solutions of a formula, which is a #P-complete problem and "closer" to PSPACE than to NP. Still, there are tools that calculate an exact solution to the problem [29] and a recent line of work that adapts the rich theory of finding approximate solutions with high probability [16] to practice (see [21] for an overview). Also, extensions of the original problem were studied; strengthening of the formula to SMT rather than SAT [9] and reasoning about assignments with weights, referred to *weighted* #SAT. As mentioned above, our solution requires this second extension. We show that we can alter the formula we construct above to fit in the framework of [7], allowing us to use their reduction and generate an equivalent #SAT instance.

While solving #SAT is becoming more practical, it is still far from solved and it would be surprising if the tools will ever be able to compete with tools for solving SAT, e.g., [10]. Thus, one can question our choice of using such a heavy tool to solve our scoring problem. We show that a heavy tool is essential by showing that scoring a forwarding scheme is #P-complete, by complementing the upper bound above with a reduction in the other direction: from #SAT to scoring a forwarding scheme.

We also study approaches to estimate the score of a forwarding scheme. We run a randomized algorithm that, with high probability, finds a solution that is close to the actual score. Using an approximate counting tool to count the Boolean formula we construct above, performs very poorly as the reduction of [7] constructs an instance which is particularly hard for the approximate counting techniques. Thus, in order to employ the tools to approximately solve #SAT we need to bypass the reduction. We suggest an iterative algorithm that takes advantage of the fact that in practice, the probability of failure is low, so traces with many faults have negligible probability. A second technique we use is a Monte-Carlo simulation, which has been found very useful in reasoning about networks [25] as well as in statistical model checking in tools like PLASMA [15], UPPAAL [19], and PVeSta [1].

We have implemented all our techniques. We show that the exact solution scales to small networks. The solution that relies on approximated counting scales better, but is overshadowed by the Monte-Carlo approach, which scales nicely to moderate networks. We also use the exact solution to evaluate the scores of the Monte-Carlo approach and we find that it is quite accurate. We note that our counting techniques rely on counting tools as black-boxes and, as mentioned above, improving these techniques is an active line of work. We expect these tools to improve over time, which will in turn improve the scalability of our solution.

Due to lack of space some proofs and examples are given in the full version [2].

2   Preliminaries

We model a network as a directed graph $\mathcal{N} = \langle V, E \rangle$. For a vertex $v \in V$, we use $out(v) \subseteq E$ to denote the set of outgoing edges from v, thus $out(v) = \{\langle v, u \rangle \in E\}$. A collection $\mathcal{M}$ of messages are sent through the network. Each message $m \in \mathcal{M}$ has a source and a target vertex, which we refer to as $s(m)$ and $t(m)$, respectively. Time is discrete. There is a global timeout $t \in \mathbb{N}$ and a message meets the timeout if it arrives at its destination by time t.

Forwarding Messages

A *forwarding scheme* is a triple $\mathcal{F} = \langle \mathcal{A}, \{\prec_v\}_{v \in V}, \{\prec_m^v\}_{m \in \mathcal{M}, \, v \in V} \rangle$, where $\mathcal{A}$ is a *forwarding algorithm* that the switches run and we describe the two other components below. For ease of notation, we assume the same number of edges $d \in \mathbb{N}$ exit all the switches in the network and in each switch they are ordered in some manner[1]. Then, our rules forward messages with respect to this order. For example, we can specify a rule that says "forward a message m on the first edge" by writing $\text{FORWARD}(m, e_1)$. The two other components of $\mathcal{F}$ allow variability; each switch $v \in V$ has an order $\prec_v$ on messages, which are priorities on messages, and each message $m \in \mathcal{M}$ has an ordering $\prec_m^v$ on the outgoing edges from v, which are preference on edges.

The propositional rules in $\mathcal{A}$ are of the form $\varphi \to \text{FORWARD}(m, e)$. We refer to φ as the assertion of the rule and its syntax is as follows

$$\varphi ::= m \mid e_i \mid m < m' \mid e_i <_m e_j \mid \varphi \vee \varphi \mid \neg\varphi$$

Note that m and m' refer to specific messages in $\mathcal{M}$ while e_i refers to the i-th exiting edges from a switch. The forwarding at a switch is determined only by the local information it has; the messages in its queue and its outgoing active edges. In other words, switches are not aware of faults in distant parts of the network and this fits well with the philosophy of the simple networks we model.

---

[1] In many settings, messages are grouped into few priorities making "priority ties" common. We assume a total order on message priorities, i.e., there is some arbitrary procedure to break ties.

Intuitively, the algorithm takes as input the messages in the queue as well as the active edges, and the output is the forwarding choices. Accordingly, the semantics of an assertion φ is with respect to a set of messages $M \subseteq \mathcal{M}$ (the messages in the queue) and a set of edges $T \subseteq \{e_1, \ldots, e_d\}$ (the active edges). Consider a rule $\varphi \to \text{FORWARD}(m, e_i)$. We denote by $(M, T) \models_{\prec_v, \{\prec_m^v\}_{m \in \mathcal{M}}} \varphi$ the fact that (M, T) satisfies φ. Then, m is forwarded on the i-th outgoing edge from v, namely e_i. When $\prec_v$ and $\prec_m^v$ are clear from the context, we omit them. The semantics is defined recursively on the structure of φ. For the base cases, we have $(M, T) \models m$ iff $m \in M$, thus m is in v's queue, we have $(M, T) \models e_i$ iff $e_i \in T$, thus e_i is active, we have $(M, T) \models (m < m')$ iff $m \prec_v m'$, thus m' has precedence over m in v, and we have $(M, T) \models (e_i <_m e_j)$ iff $e_i \prec_m^v e_j$, thus m prefers being forwarded on the j-th edge over the i-th edge. The inductive cases are as expected.

The algorithm forwards messages on active links. We think of its output as pairs $O \subseteq \mathcal{M} \times E$, where $\langle m, e \rangle \in O$ implies that the algorithm forwards m on e. We require that the algorithm obey the constraints of the network; at most one message is forwarded on a link, messages are forwarded only on active links, messages originate only from their source switch, they are forwarded only after they are received, and they are not forwarded from their destination.

It is sometimes convenient to use definitions of sets in an algorithm as we illustrate in the examples below. A definition of a set is either a collection of messages or a collection of edges that satisfy an assertion as in the above. We also allow set operations like union, intersection, and difference, for sets over the same types of elements. Later on, when we simulate the execution of the forwarding algorithm as a propositional formula, we use extra variables to simulate these operations.

Example 1. **TT-schedule.** A time-triggered schedule (TT-schedule, for short) assigns messages to edges such that (1) the schedule assigns a message m on a path from its source to target, i.e., it is not possible that m is scheduled on e before it reaches $s(e)$, (2) two messages cannot be sent on the same link at the same time, and (3) all messages must arrive by time t. Given a TT-schedule S, we can construct an equivalent forwarding scheme assuming there is no *redundant waiting*, namely assuming a message m arrives at a switch v at time i and should be forwarded on e at a later time, then, if m stays in v, it is only because e is occupied by a different message. We note that a schedule induces an order on the messages at each vertex, which we use as $\prec_m$, and it induces a path π_m for each message, which induces an order $\prec_m^v$ in which the edges on π_m have the highest preference.

In order to describe the rules of the algorithm (as well as the rules in the following example), we introduce several definition. For $S \subseteq \mathcal{M}$, we define an assertion $\text{priority}(m, S)$ that is satisfied in switches where m has the highest priority out of the messages in S, thus $\text{priority}(m, S) = \bigwedge_{m' \in S}(m' < m)$. Next, we define an assertion $\text{prefers}(m, e_i)$ that is satisfied in vertices where m prefers e_i over all the active edges, thus $\text{prefers}(m, e_i) = \bigwedge_{j \neq i}\left(e_j \to (e_j <_m e_i)\right)$. Finally, we define a set of message $S_{e_i} = \{m \in \mathcal{M} : \text{prefers}(m, e_i)\}$, namely S_{e_i}

at a vertex v contains the messages that are forwarded on i-th outgoing edge from v.

We are ready to describe the algorithm using forwarding rules. For every $m \in \mathcal{M}$ and $i = 1, \ldots, d$, m is forwarded on e_i when (1) m is in the queue, (2) m prefers e_i, (3) e_i is active, and (4) m has the highest priority of the messages in S_{e_i}. The corresponding rule is $m \wedge \mathrm{prefers}(m, e_i) \wedge e_i \wedge \mathrm{priority}(m, S_{e_i}) \rightarrow \mathrm{FORWARD}(m, e_i)$.

Example 2. **Hot-potato.** This algorithm is intended for networks in which the switches' queue size is limited. Intuitively, messages are ordered in decreasing priority and are allowed to choose free edges according to their preferences. So, assume that the set of active outgoing edges of a switch v is $T \subseteq \{e_1, \ldots, e_d\}$, and the message in the queue are $M = \{m_1, \ldots, m_k\}$ ordered in increasing priority, i.e., for $1 \leqslant i < j \leqslant k$, we have $m_j \prec_v m_i$. Then, m_1 chooses its highest priority edge e in T, i.e., for every other edge $e' \in T$, we have $e' \prec_m^v e$. Following m_1, the message m_2 chooses its highest priority edge in $T \setminus \{e\}$, and so forth. If a message is left with no free outgoing edge, it stays in v's queue. The algorithm has a low memory consumption: rather than keeping a message m in the queue till its preferred edge is free, the switch forwards m on a lower-preference edge. Note that unlike the algorithm in Example 1, the hot-potato algorithm has fault tolerant capabilities. The definition of the algorithm using propositional rules can be found in the full version.

Faults and Outcomes

We consider two types of faults. The first type are crashes of edges. We distinguish between two types of crashes: *temporary* and *permanent* crashes in which edges can and cannot recover, respectively. A second type of fault model we consider are faults on sent messages. We consider *omissions* in which a sent message can be lost. We assume the switches detect such omissions, so we model these faults as a sent message that does not reach its destination and re-appears in the sending switch's queue. As we elaborate in Sect. 8, our approach can handle other faults such as "clock glitches", which are common in practice.

The *outcome* of a forwarding scheme $\mathcal{F}$ is a sequence of *snapshots* of the network at each time point. Each snapshot, which we refer to as a *configuration*, includes the positions of all the messages, thus it is a set of $|\mathcal{M}|$ pairs of the form $\langle m, v \rangle$, meaning that m is on vertex v in the configuration. We use $\mathcal{O}$ to denote the set of all outcomes. Each outcome in $\mathcal{O}$ has $t + 1$ configurations, thus $\mathcal{O} \subseteq (\mathcal{M} \times V)^{t+1}$. All outcomes start from the same initial configuration $\{\langle m, s(m) \rangle : m \in \mathcal{M}\}$ in which all messages are at their origin. Consider a configuration C. Defining the next configuration C' in the outcome is done in two steps. In the first step, we run $\mathcal{F}$ in all vertices. Consider a vertex v, let $T \subseteq out(v)$ be a set of active edges. The set of messages in v's queue is $M = \{m : \langle m, v \rangle \in C\}$. Intuitively, we run $\mathcal{F}$ at v with input M and T. The forwarding algorithm keeps some of the messages $S \subseteq M$ in v's queue and forwards others. The messages in S stay in v's queue, thus we have $\langle m, v \rangle \in C'$ for every message

$m \in S$. Recall that the algorithm's output is $O \subseteq (\mathcal{M} \times E)$, where $\langle m, e \rangle \in O$ means that m is forwarded on the link e. In the second step, we allow omissions to occur on the pairs in O. If an omission occurs on $\langle m, \langle v, u \rangle \rangle \in O$, then m returns to the source of the edge and we have $\langle m, v \rangle \in C'$, and otherwise, sending is successful and we have $\langle m, u \rangle \in C'$.

We consider probabilistic failures. For every edge $e \in E$, we assume there is a probability p_{crash}^e that e crashes as well as a probability p_{omit}^e that a forwarded message on e is omitted. Allowing different probabilities for the edges is useful for modeling settings in which the links are of different quality. Note that we allow "ideal" links with probability 0 of failing. Faults occur independently though some dependencies arise from our definitions and we highlight them below. In the temporary-crash model, the probability that e is active at a time i is $1 - p_{crash}^e$. In the permanent-crash model, crashes are dependent. Consider a set of active edges $T \subseteq E$. The probability that the active edges in the next time step are $T' \subseteq T$ is $\prod_{e \in T'} (1 - p_{crash}^e) \cdot \prod_{e \in (T \setminus T')} p_{crash}^e$. We define omissions similarly. Consider a configuration C, active edges T, and let O be the output of the algorithm. The probability that an omission occurs to a pair in $\langle m, e \rangle \in O$ is p_{omit}^e. Here too there is dependency between omissions and crashes: an omission can only occur on an edge that a message is sent on, thus the edge must be active. Such fault probabilities give rise to a probability distribution on $\mathcal{O}$, which we refer to as $\mathcal{D}(\mathcal{O})$.

Definition 1. *Consider $1 \leqslant \ell \leqslant |\mathcal{M}|$. Let G be the set of outcomes in which at least ℓ messages arrive on time. We define $\mathrm{SCORE}(\mathcal{F}) = \mathrm{Pr}_{\pi \sim \mathcal{D}(\mathcal{O})}[\pi \in G]$.*

3 From Computing Scores to Reasoning About Markov Chains

In this section we show how to reduce the problem of finding the score of a forwarding scheme to a reachability problem on a Markov chain. We describe the intuition for the construction and the formal details can be found in the full version. We start with temporary crashes and omissions. A *deterministic automaton* (DFA, for short) is a tuple $\mathcal{D} = \langle \Sigma, Q, \delta, q_0, F \rangle$, where Σ is an alphabet, Q is a set of states, $\delta : Q \times \Sigma \rightarrow Q$ is a transition function, $q_0 \in Q$ is an initial state, and $F \subseteq Q$ is a set of accepting states. We use $|\mathcal{D}|$ to denote the number of states in $\mathcal{D}$. An *automaton frame* is a DFA with no accepting states. A Markov chain is a tuple $\langle Q, \mathcal{P}, q_0 \rangle$, where Q is a set of states, $\mathcal{P} : Q \times Q \rightarrow [0, 1]$ is a probability function such that for every state $q \in Q$, we have $\sum_{e = \langle q, p \rangle \in Q \times Q} \mathcal{P}[e] = 1$, and $q_0 \in Q$ is an initial state. A Markov chain induces a probability distribution on finite paths. The probability of a path $\pi = \pi_1, \ldots, \pi_n$, where $\pi_1 = q_0$ is the product of probabilities of the transitions it traverses, thus $\mathrm{Pr}[\pi] = \prod_{1 \leqslant i < n} \mathrm{Pr}[\langle \pi_i, \pi_{i+1} \rangle]$. For a bound $t \in \mathbb{N}$, we use $\mathrm{Pr}_{\{\pi : |\pi| \leqslant t\}}$ to highlight the fact that we are restricting to the probability space on runs of length at most t.

Consider a network $\mathcal{N} = \langle V, E \rangle$, a set of messages $\mathcal{M}$, a forwarding scheme $\mathcal{F}$, and a message $m \in \mathcal{M}$. We describe an automaton frame $\mathcal{D}_m[\mathcal{N}, \mathcal{M}, \mathcal{F}]$ that simulates the routing of m in $\mathcal{N}$ using $\mathcal{F}$. We have $\mathcal{D}_m[\mathcal{N}, \mathcal{M}, \mathcal{F}] = \langle (2^{\mathcal{M}} \times 2^E) \cup (E \cup \{\bot\}), V \cup E, \delta_m, s(m) \rangle$, where we describe δ_m below. We omit $\mathcal{N}$, $\mathcal{M}$, and

$\mathcal{F}$ when they are clear from the context. Intuitively, the subset of states V model positions in the network and the subset of states E are intermediate states that allow us to model omissions. When $\mathcal{D}_m$ is at state $v \in V$, it models the fact that m is in the switch v. Accordingly, the initial state is $s(m)$ and the transition function δ_m simulates the forwarding scheme $\mathcal{F}$: every outgoing transition τ from a state $v \in V$ corresponds to forwarding rule $\varphi \to \text{FORWARD}(m, e_i)$ for m. The transition τ is labeled by an alphabet letter (M, T), where $M \subseteq \mathcal{M}$ models the messages in v's queue, and $T \subseteq E$ models the active edges. Furthermore, we have $(M, T) \models \varphi$, thus m is forwarded on the i-th edge leaving v. We refer to the state at the end-point of the transition τ as $e \in E$, thus e is the i-th edge leaving v. Recall that e is used to model omission. Accordingly, it has two outgoing transitions: one directs back to v, and the second models a successful transmission and directs to the state that corresponds to the vertex $t(e)$.

Next, given a network $\mathcal{N}$, a set of messages $\mathcal{M}$, and a forwarding scheme $\mathcal{F}$, we construct an automaton-frame DFA $\mathcal{D}[\mathcal{N}, \mathcal{M}, \mathcal{F}]$ that simulates the runs of all the $\mathcal{D}_m$ frames. Consider a guarantee constant $1 \leqslant \ell \leqslant |\mathcal{M}|$. The constant ℓ determines the accepting states of $\mathcal{D}[\mathcal{N}, \mathcal{M}, \mathcal{F}]$: states in which at least ℓ messages arrive on time are accepting. Formally, we have $\mathcal{D}^\ell[\mathcal{N}, \mathcal{M}, \mathcal{F}] = \langle 2^E, V^{|\mathcal{M}|} \cup E^{|\mathcal{M}|}, \delta, q_0^{\mathcal{D}}, F_\ell \rangle$, where we describe the definition of $q_0^{\mathcal{D}}$, δ, and F_ℓ below. We omit $\mathcal{N}$, $\mathcal{M}$, $\mathcal{F}$, and ℓ when they are clear from the context. Recall that $\mathcal{D}$ simulates the execution of the network when routing according to $\mathcal{F}$. A state $\langle v_1, v_2, \ldots, v_{|\mathcal{M}|} \rangle$ in $\mathcal{D}$ represents the fact that, for $1 \leqslant i \leq |\mathcal{M}|$, message m_i is in the switch v_i and its frame is in the corresponding state, and similarly for a state in $E^{|\mathcal{M}|}$. Accordingly, the initial state $q_0^{\mathcal{D}}$ is $\langle s(m_1), \ldots, s(m_{|\mathcal{M}|}) \rangle$ and a state is accepting iff at least ℓ messages arrive at their destination, thus $F_\ell = \{\langle v_1, \ldots, v_{|\mathcal{M}|} \rangle : |\{j : v_j = t(m_j)\}| \geqslant \ell\}$. Recall that the alphabet of a frame $\mathcal{D}_m$ consists of two types of letters; a letter $M \subseteq \mathcal{M}$ models the messages in a switch's queue and a letter $T \subseteq E$ models failures. Since in $\mathcal{D}$, the messages in the queues can be induced by the positions of the frames, the alphabet of the frame $\mathcal{D}$ consists only of the second type of letters. Consider a state $\langle v_1, v_2, \ldots, v_{|\mathcal{M}|} \rangle$ in $\mathcal{D}$ and an input letter $T \subseteq E$. For $1 \leqslant i \leq |\mathcal{M}|$, let $M \subseteq \mathcal{M}$ be the messages at vertex v_i, thus $M = \{m_j : v_j = v_i\}$. Then, the i-th component in the next state of $\mathcal{D}$ is $\delta_{m_i}(v_i, (M, T))$. The definition for states in $E^{|\mathcal{M}|}$ is similar, though here, when an outgoing transition is labeled by a letter $O \subseteq E$, it models the messages that where successfully delivered.

Recall that the letters in $\mathcal{D}[\mathcal{N}, \mathcal{M}, \mathcal{F}]$ model failures. We assume probabilistic failures, thus in order to reason about $\mathcal{N}$ we construct a Markov chain $\mathcal{C}[\mathcal{N}, \mathcal{M}, \mathcal{F}]$ on the structure of $\mathcal{D}[\mathcal{N}, \mathcal{M}, \mathcal{F}]$ by assuming a distribution on input letters. Formally, we have $\mathcal{C}[\mathcal{N}, \mathcal{M}, \mathcal{F}] = \langle V^{|\mathcal{M}|} \cup E^{|\mathcal{M}|}, \mathcal{P}, q_0^{\mathcal{D}} \rangle$, where $\tau = \langle \bar{v}, \bar{e} \rangle \in V^{|\mathcal{M}|} \times E^{|\mathcal{M}|}$ has a positive probability iff there exists $T \subseteq E$ such that $\delta(\bar{v}, T) = \bar{e}$, then $\mathcal{P}[\tau] = \prod_{e \in T} p_e \cdot \prod_{e \notin T} (1 - p_e)$, and the definition of edges from states in $E^{|\mathcal{M}|}$ to $V^{|\mathcal{M}|}$ is similar. We can now specify the score of a forwarding scheme as the probability of reaching F_ℓ in $\mathcal{C}[\mathcal{N}, \mathcal{M}, \mathcal{F}]$.

Theorem 1. *Let $\mathcal{N}$ be a network, $\mathcal{M}$ a set of messages, $\mathcal{F}$ be a forwarding scheme, and $1 \leqslant \ell \leqslant |\mathcal{M}|$ a guarantee. For a timeout $t \in \mathbb{N}$, we have that $\Pr_{\{\pi:|\pi|\leqslant t\}}[\{\pi : \pi \, reaches \, F_\ell\}]$ in $\mathcal{C}[\mathcal{N}, \mathcal{M}, \mathcal{F}]$ equals $\mathrm{SCORE}(\mathcal{F})$.*

The construction above considers temporary crashes. Recall that in permanent crashes, once an edge crashes it does not recover. In order to reason about such crashes, we take a product of $\mathcal{D}$ with $2^{|E|}$. A state that is associated with a set $T \subseteq E$ represents the fact that the edges in $E \setminus T$ have crashed. Thus, input letters from such a state include only edges in T.

4   Computing the Score of a Forwarding Scheme

While Theorem 1 suggests a method to compute the score of a forwarding scheme by solving a reachability problem on the Markov chain $\mathcal{C}$, the size $\mathcal{C}$ is too big for practical purposes. In this section we reason about $\mathcal{C}$ without constructing it implicitly by reducing the scoring problem to #SAT, the problem of counting the number of satisfying assignments of a Boolean formula. We proceed in two steps.

Simulating Executions of $\mathcal{D}$. Recall that the Markov chain $\mathcal{C}$ shares the same structure as an automaton $\mathcal{D}$ whose input alphabet represents faults. We reason about $\mathcal{D}$ by constructing a Boolean formula ψ whose satisfying assignments correspond to accepting runs of length t of $\mathcal{D}$, which correspond in turn to "good outcomes" of the network, i.e., outcomes in which at least ℓ messages arrive on time. The crux of the construction is that the size of ψ is proportional to the sum of sizes of the $\mathcal{D}_m$ automata that compose $\mathcal{D}$ rather than the product of their sizes, which is the size of $\mathcal{D}$. In order to ensure that the run a satisfying assignment simulates, is accepting, we need to verify that at least ℓ messages arrive on time. We show how to simulate a counter using a Boolean formula in the following lemma whose proof can be found in the full version.

Lemma 1. *Consider a set X of $|\mathcal{M}|$ variables, a truth assignment $f : X \to \{\mathtt{tt}, \mathtt{ff}\}$, and a constant $1 \leqslant \ell \leqslant |\mathcal{M}|$. There is a Boolean formula CNT_ℓ over variables $X \cup Y$ such that there is a satisfying assignment to CNT_ℓ that agrees with f on X iff $|\{x \in X : f(x) = \mathtt{tt}\}| \geqslant \ell$. The size of Y is $|\mathcal{M}| \cdot \log\lceil \ell + 1 \rceil$ and CNT_ℓ has linear many constraints in $|X \cup Y|$.*

We proceed to construct the formula ψ.

Theorem 2. *Given a forwarding scheme $\mathcal{F}$ for a network $\mathcal{N}$, a set of messages $\mathcal{M}$, and two constants $t, \ell \in \mathbb{N}$, there is a Boolean formula ψ such that there is a one-to-one correspondence between satisfying assignment to ψ and accepting runs of $\mathcal{D}^\ell[\mathcal{N}, \mathcal{M}, \mathcal{F}]$. The size of ψ is $poly(|\mathcal{N}|, |\mathcal{F}|, |\mathcal{M}|, t, \log \ell)$.*

Proof. We describe the intuition of the construction and the detail can be found in the full version. We use $|\mathcal{M}| \cdot |\mathcal{N}| \cdot t$ variables to simulate the execution of the underlying $|\mathcal{M}|$ frames. A variable of the form $x_{m,v,i}$ represents the fact that message m is on switch v at time i. We model the faults using variables: a variable

$x_{e,i}$ represents the fact that e is active at time i and a variable $x_{e,m,i}$ represents the fact that sending message m on link e at time i was successful. Recall that the transition function of the frames corresponds to the forwarding algorithm, which is given by a set of propositional rules. We simulate these rules using a Boolean formula over the variables. Finally, we add constraints that require that the run starts from the initial state, i.e., $x_{m,s(m),1} = \mathtt{tt}$, and ends in an accepting state, i.e., $|\{m \in \mathcal{M} : x_{m,t(m),t} = \mathtt{tt}\}| \geqslant \ell$. For the later we use the assertion CNT_ℓ that is described in Lemma 1 with $X = \{x_{m,t(m),t} : m \in \mathcal{M}\}$. $\square$

Reasoning About $\mathcal{C}$ Using ψ. Recall that in Theorem 1, we reduce the problem of scoring a forwarding scheme to the problem of finding the probability of reaching the accepting states in $\mathcal{C}$ in t iterations. By Theorem 2 above, a satisfying assignment f to ψ corresponds to such an execution r. We think of f as having a probability, which is $\Pr[r]$. Let $SAT(\psi)$ be the set of satisfying assignments to ψ. We have established the following connection: $\mathrm{SCORE}(\mathcal{F}) = \sum_{f \in SAT(\psi)} \Pr[f]$.

Recall that #SAT is the problem of counting the number of satisfying assignments of a Boolean formula. The counting problem in the right-hand side of the equation above is a *weighted-model counting* (WMC, for short) problem, which generalizes #SAT. The input to WMC is a Boolean formula φ and a weight function w that assigns to each satisfying assignment a weight, and the goal is to calculate $\mathrm{SCORE}(\varphi) = \sum_{f \in SAT(\varphi)} w(f)$. #SAT is a special case in which the weight function is $w \equiv 1$, thus all assignments get weight 1. In order to distinguish between the two problems, we sometimes refer to #SAT as *unweighted model counting* (UMC, for short).

The last step in our solution adjusts ψ to fit in the framework of [7] and use the reduction there from WMC to UMC. Their framework deals with weight functions of a special form: each literal has a probability of getting value true and the literals are independent. So the weight of an assignment is the product of the literals' probabilities. Accordingly, they call this fragment *literal-weighted* WMC. Formally, we have a probability function $\Pr[l]$, for every literal l in ψ. We define $w(f) = \prod_{l:\sigma(l)=\mathtt{tt}} \Pr[l] \cdot \prod_{l:\sigma(l)=\mathtt{ff}} (1 - \Pr[l]))$, and $\mathrm{SCORE}(\psi) = \sum_{f \in SAT(\psi)} w(f)$.

Theorem 3. *Consider the WMC instance $\langle \psi, w \rangle$, where ψ is the Boolean formula obtained in Theorem 2 and, for $f \in SAT(\psi)$ with corresponding execution r, we have $w(f) = \Pr[r]$. There is a literal-weighted WMC $\langle \psi', w' \rangle$ and a factor γ such that $\gamma \cdot \mathrm{SCORE}(\psi') = \mathrm{SCORE}(\psi)$ and ψ' is polynomial in the size of ψ.*

Proof. We prove for temporary crashes and omits and for permanent crashes the proof is similar and can be found in the full version. Recall that there are two types of variables in ψ; variables of the form $x_{m,v,i}$ that simulate the runs of the underlying automata and variables of the form $x_{e,i}$ that represent the fact that a fault occurs in e (crashes for odd i and omissions for even i). Since the automata are deterministic, the values of the first type of variables is determined by the second type of variables. A first attempt to define the weights of the $x_{e,i}$ variables would be to set them to p_{crash}^e and p_{omit}^e, respectively. However, this definition fails as there is dependency between crashes and omits; an omit cannot occur on an edge that crashes. In the following, we introduce new variables to correct the dependencies.

It is convenient to add a variable $fr_{e,i}$ that gets value true when one of the messages is forwarded on e at time i, thus an omission can occur only if $fr_{e,i} = \mathtt{tt}$. Note that it is implicit that $fr_{e,i} = \mathtt{tt}$ only when e does not crash. Let i be even, and recall that $x_{e,i} = \mathtt{tt}$ when e exhibits an omission. The behavior we are expecting is $\Pr[x_{e,i} = \mathtt{tt} | fr_{e,i} = \mathtt{tt}] = p^e_{omit}$ and $\Pr[x_{e,i} = \mathtt{tt} | fr_{e,i} = \mathtt{ff}] = 0$. In order to model this behavior, we multiply the score of ψ' by γ, add two independent variables $a_{e,i}$ and $b_{e,i}$ with respective weights a and b, which we calculate below, and constraints $a_{e,i} = x_{e,i} \wedge fr_{e,i}$ and $b_{e,i} = \neg x_{e,i} \wedge \neg fr_{e,i}$. Recall that $\Pr[x_{e,i} = \mathtt{tt} | fr_{e,i} = \mathtt{tt}]$ should equal p^e_{omit}. In that case, we have $a_{e,i} = \mathtt{tt}$ and $b_{e,i} = \mathtt{ff}$ with probability $a \cdot (1 - b)$. Thus, we have $p^e_{omit} = \gamma \cdot a \cdot (1 - b)$. We do a similar calculation for the three other cases to obtain two other equations: $1 - p^e_{omit} = \gamma \cdot (1 - a) \cdot (1 - b)$ and $1 = \gamma \cdot (1 - a) \cdot b$. Thus, we define $a = p^e_{omit}$, $b = \frac{1}{2 - p^e_{omit}}$, and $\gamma^{-1} = (1 - a) \cdot b$.   □

Finally, we use the reduction from literal-weight WMC to UMC as described in [7], thus we obtain the following.

Theorem 4. *The problem of scoring a forwarding scheme is polynomial-time reducible to #SAT.*

5   Computational Complexity

We study the computational complexity of finding the score of a forwarding scheme. We show that it is #P-complete by showing that it is equivalent to the problem of counting the number of satisfying assignments of a Boolean formula (a.k.a the #SAT problem).

Theorem 5. *The problem of computing the score of a forwarding scheme is #P-Complete.*

Proof. The upper bound follows from Theorem 4. For the lower bound, we reduce #3SAT, the problem of counting the number of satisfying assignments of a 3CNF formula, to the problem of finding the score of a forwarding scheme. Consider an input 3CNF formula $\psi = C_1 \wedge \ldots \wedge C_k$ over a set X of n variables. We construct a network $\mathcal{N}$ with $n + k$ messages, a forwarding scheme $\mathcal{F}$, and $t, \ell \in \mathbb{N}$, such that the number of satisfying assignments to ψ is $(1 - \text{SCORE}(\mathcal{F})) \cdot 2^n$. We describe the intuition of the construction and the details can be found in the full version.

We have two types of messages; *variable messages* of the form m_x, for $x \in X$, and *clause messages* of the form m_C, where C is a clause in ψ. A variable message m_x has two possible paths it can traverse π_x and $\pi_{\neg x}$, where the probability of traversing each path is 0.5. We achieve this by using the hot-potato algorithm of Example 2, using π_x as the first-choice path for m_x and $\pi_{\neg x}$ as the second-choice path, and having the first edge on π_x crash with probability 0.5 and all other edges cannot crash. There is a clear one-to-one correspondence between outcomes and assignments to the variables: an outcome τ corresponds to an assignment $f : X \rightarrow \{\mathtt{tt}, \mathtt{ff}\}$, where $f(x) = \mathtt{tt}$ if m_x traverses π_x in τ and $f(x) = \mathtt{ff}$ if m_x traverses $\pi_{\neg x}$ in τ. Since crashes in times later than 0 do not affect the choice of m_x, we have Pr[outcomes with π_x] = Pr[outcomes with $\pi_{\neg x}$] = 0.5, thus the probability of every assignment is $1/2^n$.

Finally, we associate satisfying assignments with bad outcomes. A bad outcome is an outcome in which no message arrives on time, thus $\ell = 1$. Both paths for the variable messages are longer than the timeout t, so these messages miss the timeout in any case. Each clause message m_C has a unique path π_C and its length is t. Let $l \in \{x, \neg x\}$ be a literal in C. Then, π_C intersects the path π_l in exactly one edge e. The paths are "synchronized" such that if m_x chooses π_l, then both m_x and m_C reach the origin of e at the same time. Since m_x has precedence over m_C, it will traverse e first, making m_C wait at $s(e)$ for one time unit and causing it to miss the timeout (recall that $|\pi_C| = t$). Note that m_C misses the timeout iff one of the literals in it gets value $\mathtt{tt}$. Thus, an outcome in which all clause messages miss the timeout, i.e., a bad outcome, corresponds to a satisfying assignment to ψ, and we are done. □

6   Estimating the Score of a Forwarding Scheme

In this section we relax the requirement of finding an *exact* score and study the problem of estimating the score. We study probabilistic algorithms that with high probability return a score that is close to the exact score.

Iterative Counting Approach. We build on the counting method developed in Sect. 4. A first attempt to estimate the score would be to feed the Boolean formula ψ' we develop there into a tool that approximately solves #SAT. However, this attempt fails as the reduction of [7] from weighted to unweighted counting produces an instance that is particularly hard to solve for such solvers. In order to use the literature on approximate counting, we must develop a different technique. We take advantage of the fact that in practice, the probability of failures is very small. Thus, the executions that include many faults have negligible probability. We find an approximate score of a forwarding scheme in an iterative manner. We start with a score of 0 and uncertainty gap 1, and iteratively improve both. We allow only permanent edge crashes in this approach and we require all edges to have the same probability. In each iteration we allow exactly k crashes. Calculating the probability of all outcomes with k crashes is not hard. The proof of the following lemma can be found in the full version.

Lemma 2. *The probability of all outputs with exactly k crashes is* $\binom{|E|}{k} \cdot (1 - p_{crash})^{(|E|-k) \cdot t} \cdot (1 - (1 - p_{crash})^t)^k$.

We find the probability of the "good outcomes" with k crashes using a counting method, add to the score of the scheme and update the uncertainty gap by deducting the probability of the bad outcomes. We use the weighted counting framework of [6] (which is not weighted-literal WMC). Restricting to k crashes has two advantages, which significantly speed up the counting. First, the solution space is significantly reduced. More importantly, we use the fact that the probabilities of the outcomes do not vary too much. The running time of the method of [6] depends on a given estimation of the ratio between the weight of the maximal weighted satisfying assignment and the minimal weighted one, which the authors refer to as the *tilt*. The proof of the following lemma can be found in the full version.

Lemma 3. $tilt \leqslant (1 - p_{crash})^{k \cdot t}$.

We describe the pseudo code of the approach below.

Input: A network $\mathcal{N} = \langle V, E \rangle$, a set of messages $\mathcal{M}$, a forwarding scheme $\mathcal{F}$, constants $t, \ell \in \mathbb{N}$, the probability of a permanent crash p_{crash}, and $\epsilon > 0$.
Output: An additive ϵ-approximation of SCORE($\mathcal{F}$).
    $uncertainty = 1, score = 0, k = 0$.
    while $uncertainty > \epsilon$ **do**
        $all \leftarrow$ Probability of all outcomes with k crashes.
        $bad \leftarrow$ CALCBADPROB($\mathcal{N}, \mathcal{M}, \mathcal{S}, t, \ell, k$)
        $uncertainty\ \text{--}{=}\ all; \ score\ {+}{=}\ (all - bad); \ k\ {+}{+};$
    return $score$

6.1 A Monte-Carlo Approach

The Monte-Carlo approach is a very simple and well-known approach to reason about reachability in Markov chains. It performs well in practice as we elaborate in Sect. 7. We perform n probabilistic simulations of the execution of the Markov chain $\mathcal{C}$ for $2t$ iterations, where t is the timeout and n is a large number which we choose later. In each simulation, we start from the initial state of $\mathcal{C}$. At each iteration we probabilistically choose an outgoing edge and follow it. If we reach a state in F_ℓ, we list the experiment as 1, and otherwise as 0. We use $y_1, \ldots, y_n$ to refer to the outcomes of the experiments, thus $y_i \in \{0, 1\}$. Let r be the number of successful experiments. We return r/n. We use Hoeffding's inequality to bound the error: $\Pr[\frac{1}{n} \sum_{i=1}^{n} y_i - \text{SCORE}(\mathcal{F}) \geqslant \epsilon] \leqslant e^{-2n\epsilon^2}$. Thus, we choose n so that given requirements on the error and confidence are met.

7 Evaluation

In this section we evaluate the techniques to compute the exact and approximate score of a forwarding scheme. We compare the scalability of these approaches. Our counting techniques rely on black-boxes that count the number of satisfying assignments of a SAT formula. We used sharpSAT [29] to exactly solve #SAT and WeightMC [6] to approximately solve weighted #SAT. Our implementations are in Python and we ran our experiments on a personal computer; an Intel Core i3 quad core 3.40 GHz processor.

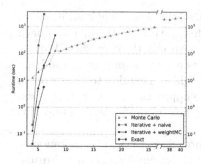

Fig. 1. The running time of the approaches on increasing-sized networks.

Table 1. Comparison of the exact score with the one obtained by the Monte-Carlo approach.

Num. of nodes	Exact	Monte-Carlo	Error
4	0.998	0.998	0.0002
5	0.965	0.963	0.001
6	0.967	0.968	0.0005

Generating a Setting. We evaluate the algorithm on networks that were generated randomly using the library Networkx [13]. We fix the number of vertices, edges, and messages and generate a random directed graph. We consider relatively dense graphs, where the number of edges are approximately 2.5 times the number of vertices. Once we have a graph, we randomly select a source and a target for each message. Recall that a forwarding scheme has three components: the forwarding algorithm, message priorities, and edge priorities for each message.

The forwarding algorithm we use is the "Hot-potato" algorithm, which is described in Example 2 and has some error-handling capabilities. We choose the message priorities arbitrarily, and we choose the edge preference as follows. We follow a common practice in generating TT-schedules in which we restrict messages to be scheduled on few predefined paths from source to target [23, 27]. For each message, we select a "first-choice" path π_m using some simple heuristic like taking the shortest path between $s(m)$ and $t(m)$, and a "fall-back" path from each vertex on π_m to $t(m)$. The collection of fall-back paths form a DAG with one sink $t(m)$. This restriction significantly shrinks the formula ψ that we construct. We assume permanent crashes, and set the probabilities of a crash and an omission uniformly in the network to be 0.01. This is a very high probability for practical uses, but we use it because it is convenient to evaluate the calculation methods with a high probability, and the actual score of the forwarding scheme is less important to us. All results have been averaged over 3–5 runs. Each program times out after 1 h, returning "timeout" if it has not terminated by then.

Execution Time Measurements. We have implemented the exact and estimating approaches that are described in Sects. 4 and 6. The running times are depicted in Fig. 1. We note that it is unfair to compare the exact method to the estimation ones, and we do it nonetheless as it gives context to the results. The sharpSAT tool performs well (even better than the approximation tools) for small instances. But, the jump in running time is sudden and occurs for networks with 7 nodes, where the running time exceeded an hour.

For estimating the score, we have implemented two approaches; an iterative approach and a Monte-Carlo approach. Recall that the crux in the first approach is computing the probability of bad outcomes with exactly k crashes. We use two techniques; the tool weightMC [6] as well as a naive counting method: we iteratively run Z3 [10] to find an assignment and add its negation to the solver so that it is not found again. We combine the naive approach with an optimization that is similar to the one that was shown to be helpful in [3], but we find it is not helpful in our setting.

Finally, we implemented a Monte-Carlo approach in Python using randomization functions from the Numpy library. We ran the simulations on 4 threads, which we found was an optimal number for our working environment. We evaluated the Monte Carlo approach using an error $\epsilon = 0.01$, and a confidence of $\delta = 0.99$.

The leading estimation method is the Monte-Carlo approach, which scales quite well; in reasonable time, it can calculate the score of moderate sized networks and shows a nice linear escalation with the network growth. It is somewhat frustrating that this simple approach beats the approaches that rely on counting hands down as a significant amount of work, both theoretical and in terms of optimizations, has been devoted in them. As mentioned earlier, the research on SAT counting is still new and we expect improvements in the tools, which will in turn help with our scalability.

Evaluating the Approximation. Apart from the theoretical interest in an exact solution, it can serve as a benchmark to evaluate the score the estimation methods output. In Table 1, we compare the scores obtained by the exact solution and by the Monte-Carlo solution and show that the error is well below our required error of 0.01.

8   Discussion

We introduce a class of forwarding schemes that are capable of coping with faults and we reason on the predictability of a forwarding scheme. We study the problem of computing the score of a given a forwarding scheme $\mathcal{F}$ in a network $\mathcal{N}$ subject to probabilistic failures, namely the probability that at least ℓ messages arrive on time when using $\mathcal{F}$ to forward messages in $\mathcal{N}$. We reduce the problem of scoring a forwarding scheme to #SAT, the problem of counting the number of satisfying assignments of a Boolean formula. Our reduction goes through a reachability problem on a succinctly represented Markov chain $\mathcal{C}$. The Boolean formula we construct simulates the executions of $\mathcal{C}$. We considered a class of forwarding schemes that operate in a network with a notion of global time and two types of faults; edge crashes and message omissions. Our solution is general and allows extensions in all three aspects. We can add features to our forwarding scheme such as allowing "message waits" (as was mentioned in Example 1) or even probabilistic behavior of the switches as long as the forwarding scheme is represented by propositional rules in the switches, we can support asynchronous executions of the switches (which requires a careful definition of "timeout"), and we can support other faults like "clock glitches" in which a message arrives at a later time than it is expect to arrive. Our work on reasoning about Markov chains with the "product-like" structure of $\mathcal{C}$ is relevant for other problems in which such structures arise. For example in reasoning about concurrent probabilistic programs [31], where $\mathcal{C}$ simulates the execution of concurrent programs modeled using automata.

Acknowledgments. We thank Kuldeep Meel for his assistance with the tools as well as helpful discussions.

References

1. AlTurki, M., Meseguer, J.: PVeSTA: a parallel statistical model checking and quantitative analysis tool. In: Corradini, A., Klin, B., Cîrstea, C. (eds.) CALCO 2011. LNCS, vol. 6859, pp. 386–392. Springer, Heidelberg (2011). doi:10.1007/978-3-642-22944-2_28
2. Avni, G., Goel, S., Henzinger, T.A., Rodriguez-Navas, G.: Computing scores of forwarding schemes in switched networks with probabilistic faults. coRR, abs/0902.0885 (2017). http://arxiv.org/abs/1701.03519
3. Avni, G., Guha, S., Rodriguez-Navas, G.: Synthesizing time-triggered schedules for switched networks with faulty links. In: Proceedings of the 16th IEEE/ACM International Conference on Embedded Software (2016)
4. Avni, G., Kupferman, O.: Stochastization of weighted automata. In: Italiano, G.F., Pighizzini, G., Sannella, D.T. (eds.) MFCS 2015. LNCS, vol. 9234, pp. 89–102. Springer, Heidelberg (2015). doi:10.1007/978-3-662-48057-1_7
5. Bauer, G., Kopetz, H.: Transparent redundancy in the time-triggered architecture. In: Proceedings International Conference on Dependable Systems and Networks, DSN, pp. 5–13. IEEE (2000)
6. Chakraborty, S., Fremont, D.J., Meel, K.S., Seshia, S.A., Vardi, M.Y.: Distribution-aware sampling and weighted model counting for SAT. In: Proceedings of the 28th Conference on Artificial Intelligence, pp. 1722–1730 (2014)
7. Chakraborty, S., Fried, D., Meel, K.S., Vardi, M.Y.: From weighted to unweighted model counting. In: Proceedings of the 31th International Joint Conference on Artificial Intelligence, pp. 689–695 (2015)
8. Chiesa, M., Gurtov, A.V., Madry, A., Mitrovic, S., Nikolaevskiy, I., Schapira, M., Shenker, S.: On the resiliency of randomized routing against multiple edge failures. In: 43rd International Colloquium on Automata, Languages, and Programming, pp. 134:1–134:15 (2016)
9. Chistikov, D., Dimitrova, R., Majumdar, R.: Approximate counting in SMT and value estimation for probabilistic programs. In: Baier, C., Tinelli, C. (eds.) TACAS 2015. LNCS, vol. 9035, pp. 320–334. Springer, Heidelberg (2015). doi:10.1007/978-3-662-46681-0_26
10. Moura, L., Bjørner, N.: Z3: an efficient SMT solver. In: Ramakrishnan, C.R., Rehof, J. (eds.) TACAS 2008. LNCS, vol. 4963, pp. 337–340. Springer, Heidelberg (2008). doi:10.1007/978-3-540-78800-3_24
11. Ferreira, J., Almeida, L., Fonseca, A., Pedreiras, P., Martins, E., Rodriguez-Navas, G., Rigo, J., Proenza, J.: Combining operational flexibility and dependability in FTT-CAN. IEEE Trans. Industr. Inf. **2**(2), 95–102 (2006)

12. GutiÈrrez, M., Steiner, W., Dobrin, R., Punnekkat, S.: A configuration agent based on the time-triggered paradigm for real-time networks. In: 2015 IEEE World Conference on Factory Communication Systems (WFCS), pp. 1–4, May 2015

13. Hagberg, A.A., Schult, D.A., Swart, P.J.: Exploring network structure, dynamics, and function using NetworkX. In: Proceedings of the 7th Python in Science Conference (SciPy 2008), Pasadena, CA, USA, pp. 11–15, August 2008

14. Harks, T., Peis, B., Schmand, D., Koch, L.V.: Competitive packet routing with priority lists. In: 41st International Symposium on Mathematical Foundations of Computer Science, pp. 49:1–49:14 (2016)

15. Jegourel, C., Legay, A., Sedwards, S.: A platform for high performance statistical model checking – PLASMA. In: Flanagan, C., König, B. (eds.) TACAS 2012. LNCS, vol. 7214, pp. 498–503. Springer, Heidelberg (2012). doi:10.1007/978-3-642-28756-5_37

16. Jerrum, M., Valiant, L.G., Vazirani, V.V.: Random generation of combinatorial structures from a uniform distribution. Theor. Comput. Sci. **43**, 169–188 (1986)

17. Kreutz, D., Ramos, F.M.V., Veríssimo, P.E., Rothenberg, C.E., Azodolmolky, S., Uhlig, S.: Software-defined networking: a comprehensive survey. Proc. IEEE **103**(1), 14–76 (2015)

18. Kwiatkowska, M., Norman, G., Parker, D.: PRISM 4.0: verification of probabilistic real-time systems. In: Gopalakrishnan, G., Qadeer, S. (eds.) CAV 2011. LNCS, vol. 6806, pp. 585–591. Springer, Heidelberg (2011). doi:10.1007/978-3-642-22110-1_47

19. Larsen, K.G., Pettersson, P., Yi, W.: UPPAAL in a Nutshell. STTT **1**(1–2), 134–152 (1997)

20. Liu, V., Halperin, D., Krishnamurthy, A., Anderson, T.: F10: a fault-tolerant engineered network. Presented as Part of the 10th USENIX Symposium on Networked Systems Design and Implementation (NSDI 2013), pp. 399–412 (2013)

21. Meel, K.S., Vardi, M.Y., Chakraborty, S., Fremont, D.J., Seshia, S.A., Fried, D., Ivrii, A., Malik, S.: Constrained sampling and counting: universal hashing meets SAT solving. In: Beyond NP, Papers from the 2016 AAAI Workshop (2016)

22. Pozo, F., Rodriguez-Navas, G., Hansson, H., Steiner, W.: SMT-based synthesis of TTEthernet schedules: a performance study. In: 2015 10th IEEE International Symposium on Industrial Embedded Systems (SIES), pp. 1–4. IEEE (2015)

23. Pozo, F., Steiner, W., Rodriguez-Navas, G., Hansson, H.: A decomposition approach for SMT-based synthesis for time-triggered networks. In: IEEE 20th Conference on Emerging Technologies and Factory Automation (ETFA), pp. 1–8. IEEE (2015)

24. Reitblatt, M., Canini, M., Guha, A., Foster, N.: FatTire: declarative fault tolerance for software-defined networks. In: Proceedings of the Second ACM SIGCOMM Workshop on Hot Topics in Software Defined Networking, pp. 109–114 (2013)

25. Rubinstein, R.Y., Kroese, D.P.: Simulation and the Monte Carlo Method, vol. 707. Wiley, Hoboken (2011)

26. Shreejith, S., Fahmy, S.A., Lukasiewycz, M.: Reconfigurable computing in next-generation automotive networks. IEEE Embed. Syst. Lett. **5**(1), 12–15 (2013)

27. Steiner, W.: An evaluation of SMT-based schedule synthesis for time-triggered multi-hop networks. In: IEEE 31st Real-Time Systems Symposium (RTSS), pp. 375–384. IEEE (2010)

28. Steiner, W., Bonomi, F., Kopetz, H.: Towards synchronous deterministic channels for the internet of things. In: IEEE World Forum on Internet of Things (WF-IoT), pp. 433–436. IEEE (2014)

29. Thurley, M.: sharpSAT – counting models with advanced component caching and implicit BCP. In: Biere, A., Gomes, C.P. (eds.) SAT 2006. LNCS, vol. 4121, pp. 424–429. Springer, Heidelberg (2006). doi:10.1007/11814948_38

30. Valls, M.G., Lopez, I.R., Villar, L.F.: iLAND: an enhanced middleware for real-time reconfiguration of service oriented distributed real-time systems. IEEE Trans. Industr. Inf. $9(1)$, 228–236 (2013)

31. Vardi, M.Y.: Automatic verification of probabilistic concurrent finite-state programs. In: 26th Annual Symposium on Foundations of Computer Science, Portland, pp. 327–338 (1985)

32. Wei, Y., Kim, D.-S.: Exploiting real-time switched ethernet for enhanced network recovery scheme in naval combat system. In: International Conference on Information and Communication Technology Convergence (ICTC), pp. 595–600. IEEE (2014)

33. Yang, B., Liu, J., Shenker, S., Li, J., Zheng, K.: Keep forwarding: towards k-link failure resilient routing. In: 2014 IEEE Conference on Computer Communications, pp. 1617–1625 (2014)

Long-Run Rewards for Markov Automata

Yuliya Butkova[1]([✉]), Ralf Wimmer[2], and Holger Hermanns[1]

[1] Saarland University, Saarbrücken, Germany
{butkova,hermanns}@depend.uni-saarland.de
[2] Albert-Ludwigs-Universität Freiburg, Freiburg im Breisgau, Germany
wimmer@informatik.uni-freiburg.de

Abstract. Markov automata are a powerful formalism for modelling systems which exhibit nondeterminism, probabilistic choices and continuous stochastic timing. We consider the computation of long-run average rewards, the most classical problem in continuous-time Markov model analysis. We propose an algorithm based on value iteration. It improves the state of the art by orders of magnitude. The contribution is rooted in a fresh look on Markov automata, namely by treating them as an efficient encoding of CTMDPs with – in the worst case – exponentially more transitions.

1 Introduction

The need for automated verification is becoming more and more pertinent with the complexity of systems growing day by day. Estimating the expected cost of system maintenance, maximising the expected profit, evaluating the availability of the system in the long run – all these questions can be answered by quantitative model checking.

Quantitative model checking of models such as continuous-time Markov chains (CTMCs) and continuous-time Markov decision processes (CTMDPs) has been studied extensively. Unfortunately, modelling complex systems requires a formalism that admits compositionality, which neither CTMCs nor CTMDPs can offer. The most general compositional formalism available to date are Markov automata [5]. Markov automata can model controllable (via nondeterministic choices) systems running in continuous time that are prone to random phenomena.

Enriching Markov automata with rewards enables the assessment of system performance, dependability and more generally quality of service (QoS) [10]. *State rewards* represent costs that are accumulated over time, for instance, related to energy consumption. Costs associated with executing a certain step or policy, e.g. a deliberate violation of QoS, are modelled by means of *action rewards*.

This work is partly supported by the ERC Advanced Grant 695614 (POWVER), by the German Research Council (DFG) as part of the Cluster of Excellence Brain-Links/BrainTools (EXC 1086) and by the Sino-German Center for Research Promotion as part of the project CAP (GZ 1023).

A. Legay and T. Margaria (Eds.): TACAS 2017, Part II, LNCS 10206, pp. 188–203, 2017.
DOI: 10.1007/978-3-662-54580-5_11

The long-run behaviour of a model is by far the most prominent and most often studied property in the general context of continuous-time Markov models [13,14]. We discuss the corresponding problem for Markov automata with rewards, namely the computation of long-run average reward properties. Thus far, this problem is solved by reducing it to linear programming (LP) [10]. LP solvers, despite the abundance of options as well as numerous techniques improving their efficiency, tend to scale poorly with the size of the model.

In this paper we develop the Bellman equation [1] for long-run average reward properties. This characterisation enables the use of value or policy iteration approaches, which on other Markov models are known to scale considerably better than algorithms based on linear programming. This characterisation is made possible by considering a Markov automaton as a compact representation of a CTMDP with – in the worst case – exponentially more transitions. To arrive there, we do not consider probabilistic states as first-class objects, but rather as auxiliary states that encode the CTMDP's transitions compactly. From this new perspective, the analysis of Markov automata does not require designing new techniques, but lets us adopt those used for CTMDPs. However, a trivial adaptation of CTMDP algorithms to an exponentially larger model obtained from a Markov automaton would obviously induce exponential runtime. We manage to avoid this issue by a dedicated treatment of exponentiality via dynamic programming. As a result, considering the problem from a different angle enables us to design a simple, yet very efficient algorithm. Its building blocks are algorithms that have been known for a long time – relative value iteration for CTMDPs and dynamic programming for classical finite horizon problems.

The original LP-based algorithm is available in the IMCA tool [10]. We have implemented our algorithm in IMCA as well and evaluated both approaches on a number of benchmarks. The runtime of our algorithm for long-run average reward is several orders of magnitude better than the LP-based approach. The latter can outperform our algorithm on small models, but it scales far worse, which makes our algorithm the clearly preferred solution for real-world models.

2   Foundations

Given a finite or countable set S, a *probability distribution* over S is a function $\mu : S \to [0,1]$ such that $\sum_{s \in S} \mu(s) = 1$. We denote the set of all probability distributions over S by $\text{Dist}(S)$. We set $\mu(S') := \sum_{s \in S'} \mu(s)$ for $S' \subseteq S$.

Definition 1. *A (closed) Markov reward automaton (MRA) $\mathcal{M}$ is a tuple $\mathcal{M} = (S, s_0, Act, \hookrightarrow, \rightsquigarrow, r, \rho)$ such that*

- *S is a finite set of states;*
- *$s_0 \in S$ is the initial state;*
- *Act is a finite set of actions;*
- *$\hookrightarrow \subseteq S \times Act \times \text{Dist}(S)$ is a finite probabilistic transition relation;*
- *$\rightsquigarrow \subseteq S \times \mathbb{R}^{\geq 0} \times S$ is a finite Markovian transition relation;*
- *$r : S \times Act \to \mathbb{R}_{\geqslant 0}$ is a transient reward function;*
- *$\rho : S \to \mathbb{R}_{\geqslant 0}$ is a state reward function.*

We often abbreviate $(s, \alpha, \mu) \in \hookrightarrow$ by $s \xrightarrow{\alpha} \mu$ and write $s \xrightarrow{\lambda} s'$ instead of $(s, \lambda, s') \in \rightsquigarrow$. $Act(s) = \{\alpha \in Act \mid \exists \mu \in Dist(S) : s \xrightarrow{\alpha} \mu\}$ denotes the set of actions that are enabled in state $s \in S$. A state s is *probabilistic (Markovian)*, if it has at least one probabilistic transition $s \xrightarrow{\alpha} \mu$ (Markovian transition $s \xrightarrow{\lambda} s'$, resp.). States can be both probabilistic and Markovian. We denote the set of probabilistic states by $PS_{\mathcal{M}}$ and the Markovian states by $MS_{\mathcal{M}}$. To simplify notation, we assume w. l. o. g. that

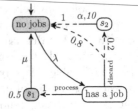

Fig. 1. An example MRA.

actions of probabilistic transitions of a state are pairwise different (this can be achieved by renaming them).

Example 1. Figure 1 shows an example MRA of a lazy server. Grey and white coloring of states indicate the sets $MS_{\mathcal{M}}$, respectively $PS_{\mathcal{M}}$ (their intersection being disjoint here). Transitions labelled as *discard, process* or α are actions enabled in a state. Dashed transitions associated with an action represent the distribution assigned to the action. Purely solid transitions are Markovian. The server has to process jobs, which arrive at rate λ; this is modelled by a Markovian transition with a corresponding rate. Whenever there is a job to process, the server chooses either to *process* or to *discard* it. These decisions are modelled by probabilistic transitions with corresponding actions. A job is processed by the server with rate μ and requires energy. We model energy consumption as a state reward 0.5 for state s_1. Discarding a job doesn't cost any energy, but with a 20% chance leads to a complaint and associated costs. These costs are modelled as an action reward 10 of state s_2 and action α.

For a Markovian state $s \in MS_{\mathcal{M}}$, the value $R(s, s') := \sum_{(s,\lambda,s')\in\rightsquigarrow} \lambda$ is called the *transition rate* from s to s'. The *exit rate* of a Markovian state s is $E(s) := \sum_{s'\in S} R(s, s')$. We require $E(s) < \infty$ for all $s \in MS_{\mathcal{M}}$.

For a probabilistic state s, s.t. $s \xrightarrow{\alpha} \mu$ for some α, the value $\mathbb{P}[s, \alpha, s'] := \mu(s')$. For a Markovian state s with $E(s) > 0$, the branching probability distribution when leaving the state through a Markovian transition is denoted by $\mathbb{P}[s, \cdot] \in Dist(S)$ and defined by $\mathbb{P}[s, s'] := R(s, s')/E(s)$.

The Markovian transitions are governed by an exponential distributions, i.e. the probability of leaving $s \in MS_{\mathcal{M}}$ within $t \geq 0$ time units is given by $1 - e^{-E(s)\cdot t}$, after which the next state is chosen according to $\mathbb{P}[s, \cdot]$.

In this paper we consider *closed* MRA, i.e. probabilistic transitions cannot be delayed by further compositions. Therefore we can make the usual *urgency assumption* that probabilistic transitions happen instantaneously. Whenever the system is in state s with $Act(s) \neq \emptyset$ and an action $\alpha \in Act(s)$ is chosen, the successor s' is selected according to the distribution $\mathbb{P}[s, \alpha, \cdot]$ and the system moves instantaneously from s to s'. The residence time in probabilistic states is therefore always 0. As the execution of a probabilistic transition is instantaneous and because the probability that a Markovian transition is triggered immediately is 0, we can assume that the probabilistic transitions take precedence over the Markovian transitions. We therefore assume $PS_{\mathcal{M}} \cap MS_{\mathcal{M}} = \emptyset$.

Additionally, we make the following non-Zenoness assumption, as in [9]. An MRA is *non-Zeno* iff no *maximal end component* [9] of only probabilistic states is reachable with probability > 0. This excludes models in which there is a chance to get trapped in an infinite number of transitions occurring in finite time.

Paths, Rewards and Schedulers. A *(timed) path* in $\mathcal{M}$ is a finite or infinite sequence $\pi = s_0 \xrightarrow{\alpha_0,t_0} s_1 \xrightarrow{\alpha_1,t_1} \cdots \xrightarrow{\alpha_k,t_k} s_{k+1} \xrightarrow{\alpha_{k+1},t_{k+1}} \cdots$. Here $s_i \xrightarrow{\alpha_i,0} s_{i+1}$ s.t. $\alpha_i \in Act(s_i)$ is a probabilistic transition via action α_i, and $s_i \xrightarrow{\perp,t_i} s_{i+1}$, s.t. $t_i > 0$ and $s_i \overset{\lambda}{\rightsquigarrow} s_{i+1}$, denotes a Markovian transition with sojourn time t_i in state s_i. The set of all finite (infinite) paths of $\mathcal{M}$ is denoted by $Paths^*_{\mathcal{M}}$ ($Paths_{\mathcal{M}}$). An *untimed* path $\pi = s_0 \xrightarrow{\alpha_0} s_1 \xrightarrow{\alpha_1} \cdots \xrightarrow{\alpha_k} s_{k+1} \xrightarrow{\alpha_{k+1}} \cdots$ is a path containing no timing information. We use $\mathrm{prefix}(\pi, t)$ to denote the prefix of path π until time t, i.e. $\mathrm{prefix}(\pi, t) = s_0 \xrightarrow{\alpha_0,t_0} s_1 \xrightarrow{\alpha_1,t_1} \cdots \xrightarrow{\alpha_k,t_k} s_{k+1}$, s.t. $\sum_{i=0}^{k} t_i \leqslant t$ and $\sum_{i=0}^{k+1} t_i > t$. If $\pi = s_0 \xrightarrow{\alpha_0,t_0} s_1 \xrightarrow{\alpha_1,t_1} \cdots \xrightarrow{\alpha_{k-1},t_{k-1}} s_k$ is finite, we define $|\pi| := k$ and $\pi\!\downarrow := s_k$.

Let π be a finite path, we define the *accumulated reward* of π as follows:

$$\mathrm{rew}(\pi) := \sum_{i=0}^{|\pi|-1} \rho(s_i) \cdot t_i + \mathrm{r}(s_i, \alpha_i).$$

For an infinite path π, $\mathrm{rew}(\pi, t) := \mathrm{rew}(\mathrm{prefix}(\pi, t))$ denotes the reward collected until time t. The following two assumptions can be made without restricting reward expressiveness: (i) the state reward of probabilistic states is always 0 (since residence time in probabilistic states is 0); (ii) if $s \in MS_{\mathcal{M}}$ then $\mathrm{r}(s, \cdot) = 0$ (due to the absence of outgoing probabilistic transitions in Markovian states).

In order to resolve the nondeterminism in probabilistic states of an MRA we need the notion of a scheduler. A *scheduler* (or *policy*) $D : Paths^*_{\mathcal{M}} \rightarrow \mathrm{Dist}(\hookrightarrow)$ is a measurable function, s.t. $D(\pi)$ assigns positive probability only to transitions $(\pi\!\downarrow, \alpha, \mu) \in \hookrightarrow$, for some α, μ. The set of all measurable schedulers is denoted by $GM_{\mathcal{M}}$. A *(deterministic) stationary scheduler* is a function $D : PS_{\mathcal{M}} \rightarrow \hookrightarrow$, s.t. $D(s)$ chooses only from transitions $(s, \alpha, \mu) \in \hookrightarrow$, for some α, μ.

An initial state s_0 and a fixed scheduler D induce a stochastic process on $\mathcal{M}$. For a stationary scheduler this process is a continuous-time Markov chain (CTMC). A CTMC is called a *unichain* (*multichain*) if it has only 1 (>1) recurrence class [3] plus possibly some transient states. We say that an MRA $\mathcal{M}$ is a *unichain* if all stationary schedulers induce a unichain CTMC on $\mathcal{M}$, and a *multichain* otherwise.

3   Long-Run Average Reward Property

In this section, we introduce the long-run average reward property on Markov reward automata and discuss the only available algorithm for this problem.

Let $\mathcal{M} = (S, s_0, Act, \hookrightarrow, \rightsquigarrow, \mathrm{r}, \rho)$ be a Markov reward automaton and π an infinite path in $\mathcal{M}$. The random variable $\mathcal{L}_{\mathcal{M}} : Paths_{\mathcal{M}} \rightarrow \mathbb{R}_{\geqslant 0}$ such that

$$\mathcal{L}_{\mathcal{M}}(\pi) := \lim_{t \to \infty} \frac{1}{t} \mathrm{rew}(\pi, t)$$

denotes the long-run average reward over a path π in $\mathcal{M}$. We now define the *optimal expected long-run average reward* on $\mathcal{M}$ with initial state s as follows:

$$\text{aR}^{\text{opt}}_{\mathcal{M}}(s) := \underset{D \in GM_{\mathcal{M}}}{\text{opt}} \ \mathbf{E}_{s,D}[\mathcal{L}_{\mathcal{M}}] = \underset{D \in GM_{\mathcal{M}}}{\text{opt}} \int_{Paths_{\mathcal{M}}} \mathcal{L}_{\mathcal{M}}(\pi) \text{Pr}_{s,D}[d\pi],$$

where $\text{opt} \in \{\sup, \inf\}$. In the following, we use $\text{aR}^{\text{opt}}_{\mathcal{M}}$ instead of $\text{aR}^{\text{opt}}_{\mathcal{M}}(s)$, whenever the value does not depend on the initial state. Furthermore, $\text{aR}^{D}_{\mathcal{M}}(s)$ denotes the long-run average reward gathered when following the policy D.

Guck et al. [10] show that under the assumptions mentioned in Sect. 2 there is always an optimal scheduler for the aR^{opt} problem that is stationary. From now on we therefore consider only stationary schedulers.

Quantification. We will present now the only available solution for the quantification of aR^{opt} [10]. The computation is split into three steps:

1. *Find all maximal end components of $\mathcal{M}$.* A *maximal end component (MEC)* of a MRA can be seen as a maximal sub-MRA whose underlying graph is strongly connected. An MRA may have multiple MECs. The problem of finding all MECs of an MRA is equivalent to decomposing a graph into strongly connected components. This problem admits efficient solutions [4].
2. *Compute $\text{aR}^{\text{opt}}_{\mathcal{M}}$ for each maximal end component.* An optimal scheduler for aR^{opt} on an MEC induces a unichain on this MEC [10]. A solution for unichain MRA is therefore needed for this step. The solution provided by Guck et al. [10] is based on a reduction of the aR^{opt} computation to the solution of a linear optimisation problem. The latter in turn can be solved by any of the available linear programming solvers.
3. *Compute a stochastic shortest path (SSP) problem.* Having the optimal values $\text{aR}^{\text{opt}}_{\mathcal{M}_j}$ for maximal end components $\mathcal{M}_j$, the following holds [9,10]:

$$\text{aR}^{\text{opt}}_{\mathcal{M}}(s) = \sup_{D \in GM} \sum_{j=1}^{k} \text{Pr}_{s,D}[\Diamond \Box S_j] \cdot \text{aR}^{\text{opt}}_{\mathcal{M}_j},$$

where $\text{Pr}_{s,D}[\Diamond \Box S_j]$ denotes the probability to eventually reach and then stay in the MEC $\mathcal{M}_j$ starting from state s and using the scheduler D. S_j is the state space of $\mathcal{M}_j$. The authors reduce this problem to a well-established SSP problem on Markov decision processes [13], that admits efficient solutions, such as value or policy iteration [2].

One can see that steps 1 and 3 of this algorithm admit efficient solutions, while the algorithm for step 2 is based on linear programming. The algorithms for linear programming are, unfortunately, known to not scale well with the size of the problem in the context of Markov decision processes, relative to iterative algorithms based on value or policy iteration. So far, however, no iterative algorithm is known for long-run average rewards on Markov automata. In this work we fill this gap and design an iterative algorithm for the computation of long-run average rewards on MRA.

4 An Iterative Approach to Long-Run Average Rewards

In this section, we present our approach for quantifying the long-run average reward on Markov reward automata. Recall that the original algorithm, described in the previous section, is efficient in all the steps except for step 2 – the computation of the long-run average reward for unichain MRA. We therefore target this specific sub-problem and present our algorithm for unichain MRA. Having an arbitrary MRA $\mathcal{M}$, one can quantify aR^{opt} by applying steps 1 and 3 of the original algorithm and using our solution for unichain MRA for step 2.

Effective Analysis of Unichain MRA. The core of our approach lies in the following observation: a Markov reward automaton can be considered as a compact representation of a possibly exponentially larger continuous-time Markov decision process (CTMDP). This observation enables us to use efficient algorithms available for CTMDPs [13] to compute long-run average rewards. But since that CTMDP, in the worst case, has exponentially more transitions, this naïve approach does not seem promising. We circumvent this problem by means of classical dynamic programming, and thereby arrive at an efficient solution that avoids the construction of the large CTMDP.

For the rest of this section, $\mathcal{M} = (S, s_0, Act, \hookrightarrow, \rightsquigarrow, \mathrm{r}, \rho)$ denotes a unichain Markov reward automaton. Guck et al. [10] show that aR^{opt} for a unichain MRA does not depend on the initial state, i.e. $\forall s, s' : aR_{\mathcal{M}}^{opt}(s) = aR_{\mathcal{M}}^{opt}(s')$. We will therefore refer to this value as $aR_{\mathcal{M}}^{opt}$.

4.1 CTMDP Preserving aR^{opt}

We will now present a transformation from a unichain MRA to a CTMDP that preserves the long-run average reward property.

Definition 2. *A* continuous-time Markov decision process *(CTMDP) is a tuple* $\mathcal{C} = (S, Act, \mathrm{R})$, *where S is a finite set of* states, *Act is a finite set of* actions, *and* $\mathrm{R} : S \times Act \times S \to \mathbb{R}_{\geq 0}$ *is a* rate function.

The set $Act(s) = \{\alpha \in Act \mid \exists s' \in S : \mathrm{R}(s, \alpha, s') > 0\}$ is the set of *enabled actions* in state s. A path in a CTMDP is a finite or infinite sequence $\pi = s_0 \xrightarrow{\alpha_0, t_0} s_1 \xrightarrow{\alpha_1, t_1} \cdots \xrightarrow{\alpha_{k-1}, t_{k-1}} s_k \cdots$, where $\alpha_i \in Act(s_i)$ and t_i denotes the residence time of the system in state s_i. $E(s, \alpha) := \sum_{s' \in S} \mathrm{R}(s, \alpha, s')$ and $\mathbb{P}_{\mathcal{C}}[s, \alpha, s'] := \frac{\mathrm{R}(s, \alpha, s')}{E(s, \alpha)}$. The notions of $Paths_{\mathcal{C}}^*$, $Paths_{\mathcal{C}}$, $\mathrm{prefix}(\pi, t)$, $|\pi|$, $\pi\downarrow$, schedulers and unichain CTMDP are defined analogously to corresponding definitions for an MRA (see Sect. 2).

A *reward structure* on a CTMDP $\mathcal{C}$ is a tuple $(\rho_{\mathcal{C}}, \mathrm{r}_{\mathcal{C}})$, where $\rho_{\mathcal{C}} : S \to \mathbb{R}_{\geq 0}$ and $\mathrm{r}_{\mathcal{C}} : S \times Act \to \mathbb{R}_{\geq 0}$. The reward of a finite path π is defined as follows:

$$\mathrm{rew}_{\mathcal{C}}(\pi) := \sum_{i=0}^{|\pi|-1} \rho_{\mathcal{C}}(s_i) \cdot t_i + \mathrm{r}_{\mathcal{C}}(s_i, \alpha_i)$$

The optimal expected long-run average reward $\mathrm{aR}_{\mathcal{C}}^{\mathrm{opt}}$ of a CTMDP $\mathcal{C}$ is defined analogously to $\mathrm{aR}_{\mathcal{M}}^{\mathrm{opt}}$ on MRA (see Sect. 2). As shown in [13], for a unichain CTMDP $\mathcal{C}$ we have $\forall s, s' \in S : \mathrm{aR}_{\mathcal{C}}^{\mathrm{opt}}(s) = \mathrm{aR}_{\mathcal{C}}^{\mathrm{opt}}(s')$. In the future we will refer to this value as $\mathrm{aR}_{\mathcal{C}}^{\mathrm{opt}}$.

Transformation to Continuous-Time MDP. Let $\mathcal{M}$ be a unichain MRA. We construct the CTMDP $\mathcal{C}_{\mathcal{M}} = (S_{\mathcal{C}}, Act_{\mathcal{C}}, R_{\mathcal{C}})$ with reward structure $(\rho_{\mathcal{C}}, r_{\mathcal{C}})$ as follows:

- $S_{\mathcal{C}} := MS_{\mathcal{M}}$;
- The set $Act_{\mathcal{C}}$ is obtained as follows. Let $s \in MS_{\mathcal{M}}$, then we denote as PS_s the set of all probabilistic states $s' \in PS_{\mathcal{M}}$ reachable from s via the transition relation $\hookrightarrow$. Let A_s be a function $A_s : PS_s \to Act$, s.t. $A_s(s') \in Act(s')$. Then the set of all enabled actions $Act_{\mathcal{C}}(s)$ for state s in $\mathcal{C}_{\mathcal{M}}$ is the set of all possible functions A_s, and $Act_{\mathcal{C}} = \bigcup_{s \in MS_{\mathcal{M}}} Act_{\mathcal{C}}(s)$.
- Next, we define the transition matrix $R_{\mathcal{C}}$. Let $s, s' \in MS_{\mathcal{M}}$, and $\Pi_{PS}(s, A_s, s')$ be the set of all untimed paths in $\mathcal{M}$ from s to s' via only probabilistic states and choosing those actions in the probabilistic states that are defined by A_s. Then $R_{\mathcal{C}}(s, A_s, s') := E(s) \cdot \sum_{\pi \in \Pi_{PS}(s, A_s, s')} \Pr_{\mathcal{M}}[\pi]$, where $\pi = s \xrightarrow{\perp} s_1 \xrightarrow{\alpha_1} \cdots \xrightarrow{\alpha_k} s'$ and $\Pr_{\mathcal{M}}[\pi] = \mathbb{P}[s, s_1] \cdot \mathbb{P}[s_1, \alpha_1, s_2] \cdots \mathbb{P}[s_k, \alpha_k, s']$.
- $\rho_{\mathcal{C}}(s) := \rho(s)$;
- $r_{\mathcal{C}}(s, A_s) := \sum_{s' \in S_{\mathcal{C}}} \sum_{\pi \in \Pi_{PS}(s, A_s, s')} \Pr_{\mathcal{M}}[\pi] \cdot r_{\mathcal{M}}(\pi)$, where $\pi = s \xrightarrow{\perp} s_1 \xrightarrow{\alpha_1} \cdots s_k \xrightarrow{\alpha_k} s'$ and $r_{\mathcal{M}}(\pi) = \sum_{i=1}^{k} r(s_i, A_s(s_i))$. The action reward for state s and action A_s in $\mathcal{C}$ is therefore the expected accumulated action reward over all successors s' (in $\mathcal{C}$) of state s and over all paths from s to s'.

An example of this transformation is depicted in Fig. 2. One can already see that even in small examples the amount of transitions of the CTMDP corresponding to a MRA can grow extremely fast. If every probabilistic successor $s' \in PS_s$ of a state s in $\mathcal{M}$ has 2 enabled actions, the set of enabled actions $Act_{\mathcal{C}}(s)$ of s in $\mathcal{C}_{\mathcal{M}}$ is $2^{|PS_s|}$. This growth is therefore exponential in the worst-case, and the worst case occurs frequently, due to cascades of probabilistic states.

Remark. It is obvious that this transformation if applied to a unichain MRA yields a unichain CTMDP. Moreover, at each state s of the resulting CTMDP the exit rate is the same across all actions enabled. We therefore refer to this exit rate as $E(s)$.

Theorem 1. $\mathrm{aR}_{\mathcal{C}_{\mathcal{M}}}^{\mathrm{opt}} = \mathrm{aR}_{\mathcal{M}}^{\mathrm{opt}}$

4.2   Dealing with Exponentiality

In this section, we will develop a simple yet efficient solution to cope with exponentiality, harvesting the Bellman equation for CTMDPs [13] together with the structure of $\mathcal{M}$. A naïve direct application to $\mathcal{C}_{\mathcal{M}}$ yields:

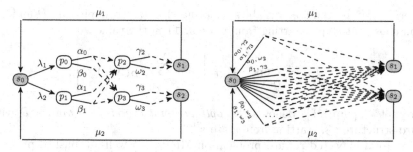

Fig. 2. An example of $\mathcal{M} \to \mathcal{C}_{\mathcal{M}}$ transformation. The MRA $\mathcal{M}$ is depicted on the left and the resulting CTMDP $\mathcal{C}_{\mathcal{M}}$ on the right. In this picture we omitted the probabilities of the probabilistic transitions. If distributions $\mathbb{P}[p_0, \alpha_0, \cdot]$ and $\mathbb{P}[p_0, \alpha_1, \cdot]$ are uniform, then $R_{\mathcal{C}}(s_0, \frac{\alpha_0,\gamma_2}{\alpha_1,\gamma_3}, s_1) = (\lambda_1 + \lambda_2) \cdot \left[\frac{\lambda_1}{\lambda_1 + \lambda_2} (0.5 \cdot 1 + 0.5 \cdot 0) + \frac{\lambda_2}{\lambda_1 + \lambda_2} (1 \cdot 1) \right] = 0.5 \cdot \lambda_1 + \lambda_2$.

Theorem 2 (Bellman equation. Inefficient way). *Let $\mathcal{C}_{\mathcal{M}} = (S_{\mathcal{C}}, Act_{\mathcal{C}}, R_{\mathcal{C}})$ and $(\rho_{\mathcal{C}}, r_{\mathcal{C}})$ be a CTMDP and a reward structure obtained through the above transformation. Let $\mathrm{opt} \in \{\sup, \inf\}$, then there exists a vector $h \in \mathbb{R}^{|S_{\mathcal{C}}|}$ and a unique value $\mathrm{aR}_{\mathcal{M}}^{\mathrm{opt}} \in \mathbb{R}_{\geqslant 0}$ that are a solution to the Bellman equation: $\forall s \in MS_{\mathcal{M}}$:*

$$\frac{\mathrm{aR}_{\mathcal{M}}^{\mathrm{opt}}}{E(s)} + h(s) = \underset{\alpha \in Act(s)}{\mathrm{opt}} \left\{ r_{\mathcal{C}}(s, \alpha) + \frac{\rho_{\mathcal{C}}(s)}{E(s)} + \sum_{s' \in S_{\mathcal{C}}} \mathbb{P}_{\mathcal{C}}[s, \alpha, s'] \cdot h(s') \right\} \quad (1)$$

It is easy to see that the only source of inefficiency in this case is the optimisation operation on the right-hand side, performed over possibly exponentially many actions. Left untreated, this operation in essence is a brute force check of optimality of each action. We will now show how to avoid this problem by working with $\mathcal{M}$ itself and not with $\mathcal{C}_{\mathcal{M}}$. Informally, we will show that the right-hand side optimisation problem on $\mathcal{C}_{\mathcal{M}}$ is nothing more than a *total expected reward* problem on a *discrete-time Markov decision process*. Knowing this, we can apply well-known dynamic programming techniques to solve this problem.

MDPs and Total Expected Reward. We will first need to briefly introduce Markov decision processes and the total expected reward problem.

Definition 3. *A Markov decision process (MDP) is a tuple $\mathcal{D} = (S_{\mathcal{D}}, s_0, Act_{\mathcal{D}}, \mathbb{P}_{\mathcal{D}})$ where $S_{\mathcal{D}}$ is a finite set of states, s_0 is the initial state, $Act_{\mathcal{D}}$ is a finite set of actions, and $\mathbb{P}_{\mathcal{D}} : S_{\mathcal{D}} \times Act_{\mathcal{D}} \to \mathrm{Dist}(S_{\mathcal{D}})$ is a probabilistic transition matrix.*

The definitions of paths, schedulers and other related notions are analogous to those of CTMDP. In contrast to CTMDPs and MRA, MDPs run in discrete time. A reward structure on an MDP is a function $r_{\mathcal{D}} : S_{\mathcal{D}} \times Act_{\mathcal{D}} \to \mathbb{R}_{\geqslant 0}$.

Let X_i^s, Y_i^s be random variables denoting the state occupied by $\mathcal{D}$ and the action chosen at step i starting from state s. Then the value

$$\mathrm{tR}_{\mathcal{D}, \mathrm{r}_{\mathcal{D}}}^{\mathrm{opt}}(s) := \underset{D \in GM_{\mathcal{D}}}{\mathrm{opt}} \; \mathbf{E}_{s, D} \left[\lim_{N \to \infty} \sum_{i=0}^{N-1} \mathrm{r}_{\mathcal{D}}(X_i^s, Y_i^s) \right],$$

where $\mathrm{opt} \in \{\sup, \inf\}$, denotes the *optimal total expected reward* on $\mathcal{D}$ with reward structure $\mathrm{r}_{\mathcal{D}}$, starting from state s [2].

The total expected reward problem on MDPs is a well-established problem that admits policy-iteration and LP-based algorithms [13]. Moreover, for acyclic MDPs it can be computed by the classical finite horizon dynamic programming approach [2], in which each state has to be visited only once. We will present now the iterative scheme that can be used to compute $\mathrm{tR}^{\mathrm{opt}}$ on an acyclic MDP.

A state of an MDP is a *terminal state* if all its outgoing transitions are self-loops with probability 1 and reward 0. We call an MDP *acyclic* if the self-loops of terminal states are its only loops. We say that a non-terminal state s *has maximal depth* i, or $d(s) = i$, if the longest path π from s until a terminal state has length $|\pi| = i$. We define $d(t) := 0$. The following is the iterative scheme to compute the value $\mathrm{tR}^{\mathrm{opt}}$ on $\mathcal{D}$:

$$v_{d(s)}(s) = \begin{cases} 0 & d(s) = 0 \\ \underset{\alpha \in Act}{\mathrm{opt}} \left\{ \mathrm{rew}_{\mathcal{D}}(s, \alpha) + \sum_{s' \in S} \mathbb{P}[s, \alpha, s'] v_{d(s')}(s') \right\} & d(s) > 0 \end{cases} \qquad (2)$$

Theorem 3. $\mathrm{tR}^{\mathrm{opt}}(s) = v_{d(s)}(s)$

Transformation to Discrete-Time MDP. Let $E_{\mathcal{M}}^{\max}$ be the maximal exit rate among all the Markovian states of $\mathcal{M}$ and $\lambda > E_{\mathcal{M}}^{\max}$. We will present now a linear transformation from $\mathcal{M}$ to the *terminal MDP* $\mathcal{D}_{\mathcal{M}}^{\lambda}$:

1. At first we obtain the MDP $\mathcal{D}_{\lambda} = (S, s_0, Act', \mathbb{P}_{\lambda})$ with $Act' = Act \dot{\cup} \{\bot\}$. This MDP contains all probabilistic states of $\mathcal{M}$ and their actions. Additionally, we add the Markovian states by making them probabilistic. In each Markovian state only action $\bot$ is enabled. The probability distribution for this action is obtained by *uniformising* the states. Uniformisation with rate λ fixes the means of the residence times (which are discrete quantities, as opposed to the CTMDP formulation) in all Markovian states s to $\frac{1}{\lambda}$ instead of $\frac{1}{E(s)}$. This is achieved by introducing self-loops [13].

$$\mathbb{P}_{\lambda}[s, \alpha, s'] := \begin{cases} \mathbb{P}[s, \alpha, s'] & \text{for } s \in PS_{\mathcal{M}}, \, \alpha \in Act'(s) \\ \dfrac{R(s, s')}{\lambda} & \text{for } s \in MS_{\mathcal{M}}, \, \alpha = \bot, s' \neq s \\ 1 - \dfrac{E(s) - R(s, s)}{\lambda} & \text{for } s \in MS_{\mathcal{M}}, \, \alpha = \bot, s' = s \end{cases}$$

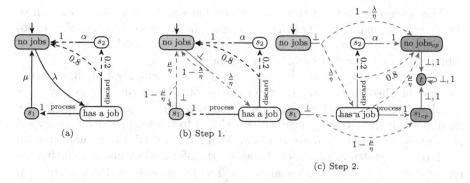

Fig. 3. Transformation to terminal MDP with uniformisation rate η. Figure (a) depicts the original MRA from Fig. 1. The result of the first step of the transformation is shown in figure (b), and the second step is depicted in (c).

2. Next, for each Markovian state, we introduce a copy state and redirect all the transitions leading to Markovian states to these new copy states. Additionally, we introduce a terminal state t, that has only self-loop transitions. Let $\mathcal{D}_\lambda = (S, s_0, Act', \mathbb{P}_\lambda)$ be the MDP obtained in the previous step, then we build $\mathcal{D}^\lambda_{\mathcal{M}} = (S_D, s_0, Act', \mathbb{P}_D)$, where $S_{cp} = \{s_{cp} \mid s \in MS_{\mathcal{M}}\}$, $S_D = S \cup S_{cp} \cup \{t\}$ and

$$\mathbb{P}'_D[s, \alpha, s'] = \begin{cases} \mathbb{P}_\lambda[s, \alpha, p] & \text{for } s' = p_{cp} \in S_{cp} \\ \mathbb{P}_\lambda[s, \alpha, s'] & \text{for } s' \in PS_{\mathcal{M}} \\ 1 & \text{for } s \in S_{cp}, s' = t, \alpha = \perp \\ 1 & \text{for } s, s' = t, \alpha = \perp \end{cases}$$

Figure 3 depicts both steps of the transformation. The resulting MDP is the one that we will use to compute the total expected reward sub-problem.

Efficient Characterisation. We can now present an efficient characterisation of the long-run average reward on unichain MRA.

Let $\mathcal{D}^\lambda_{\mathcal{M}} = (S_D, s_0, Act', \mathbb{P}_D)$ be the terminal MDP for $\mathcal{M}$ and $v : S_D \to \mathbb{R}$. We define the reward structure $\text{rew}_{D,v}$ for $\mathcal{D}^\lambda_{\mathcal{M}}$ as follows:

$$\text{rew}_{D,v}(s, \alpha) := \begin{cases} r(s, \alpha) & \text{for } s \in PS_{\mathcal{M}}, \ \alpha \in Act'(s) \\ \frac{\rho(s)}{\lambda} & \text{for } s \in MS_{\mathcal{M}}, \alpha = \perp \\ v(s) & \text{for } s \in S_{cp}, \quad \alpha = \perp \\ 0 & \text{for } s = t, \qquad \alpha = \perp \end{cases}$$

Theorem 4 (Bellman equation. Efficient way). *There exists a vector* $h \in \mathbb{R}^{|MS_{\mathcal{M}}|}$ *and a unique value* $\text{aR}^{\text{opt}}_{\mathcal{M}} \in \mathbb{R}_{\geqslant 0}$ *that are a solution to the system:*

$$\forall s \in MS_{\mathcal{M}}: \quad \frac{\text{aR}^{\text{opt}}_{\mathcal{M}}}{\lambda} + h(s) = \text{tR}^{\text{opt}}_{\mathcal{D}^\lambda_{\mathcal{M}}, \text{rew}_{D,h}}(s)$$

The difference between this characterisation and the one derived in Theorem 2 is the right-hand side of the equations. The brute force traversal of exponentially many actions of the former is changed to a total expected reward computed over a linear-sized MDP in the latter.

The correctness of the approach is rooted in two facts. First of all, as a consequence of Theorems 1 and 2 the computation of the long-run average reward of an MRA can be reduced to the same problem on a *continuous-time* MDP. By the results of [13] the latter in turn can be reduced to the long-run average reward problem on its *uniformised discrete-time* MDP. This explains the uniformisation of Markovian states in step 1 of the above transformation, and it explains the reward value $\frac{\rho(s)}{\lambda}$ of the Markovian states. The second observation is more technical. For a Markovian state s the right-hand side of Eq. (1) (Theorem 2) is the total expected reward collected when starting from s in the MDP from step 1, and finishing upon encountering a Markovian state for the second time (the first one being s itself). This explains the addition of copy states in step 2 that lead to a terminal state.

The above equation can be solved with many available techniques, e. g. by policy iteration [13]. This will naturally cover cases where the MDP $\mathcal{D}_{\mathcal{M}}^{\lambda}$ has inherited from $\mathcal{M}$ cycles visiting only probabilistic states (without a chance of getting trapped there, since non-Zenoness is assumed). Such a cycle of probabilistic transitions almost never happens in real-world applications and is usually considered a modelling mistake. In fact, we are not aware of any practical example where that case occurs. We therefore treat separately the class of models that have no cycles of this type and call such MRA *PS-acyclic*.

Theorem 5 (Bellman equation for *PS*-acyclic $\mathcal{M}$). *Let $\mathcal{M}$ be a PS-acyclic unichain MRA. Then there exists a vector $h \in \mathbf{R}^{|MS_{\mathcal{M}}|}$ and a unique value $aR_{\mathcal{M}}^{opt} \in \mathbf{R}_{\geqslant 0}$ that are a solution to the Bellman equation:*

$$\forall s \in MS_{\mathcal{M}} : \quad \frac{aR_{\mathcal{M}}^{opt}}{\lambda} + h(s) \quad = \frac{\rho(s)}{\lambda} + \sum_{s' \in PS_{\mathcal{M}}} \frac{R(s,s')}{\lambda} \cdot v_{d(s')}(s')$$

$$+ \sum_{\substack{s' \in MS_{\mathcal{M}} \\ s' \neq s}} \frac{R(s,s')}{\lambda} \cdot h(s') + \left(1 - \frac{E(s) - R(s,s)}{\lambda}\right) \cdot h(s)$$

$$\forall s \in PS_{\mathcal{M}} : \quad v_{d(s)}(s) \quad = \operatorname*{opt}_{\alpha \in Act} \left\{ r(s,\alpha) + \sum_{s' \in MS_{\mathcal{M}}} \mathbb{P}[s,\alpha,s'] \cdot h(s') \right.$$

$$\left. + \sum_{s' \in PS_{\mathcal{M}}} \mathbb{P}[s,\alpha,s'] \cdot v_{d(s')}(s') \right\},$$

where λ is the uniformisation rate used to construct $\mathcal{D}_{\mathcal{M}}^{\lambda}$ and $d(s)$ denotes the depth of state s in $\mathcal{D}_{\mathcal{M}}^{\lambda}$.

Algorithm 1. `RelativeValueIteration`

---

    input   : Unichain MRA $\mathcal{M} = (S, s_0, Act, \hookrightarrow, \rightsquigarrow, \mathrm{r}, \rho)$, opt $\in \{\sup, \inf\}$,
            approximation error $\varepsilon > 0$
    output : $\mathrm{aR}_{\mathcal{M}}^{\varepsilon}$ such that $\|\mathrm{aR}_{\mathcal{M}}^{\varepsilon} - \mathrm{aR}_{\mathcal{M}}^{\mathrm{opt}}\| \leqslant \varepsilon$

1   $\lambda \longleftarrow E_{\mathcal{M}}^{\max} + 1$;
2   $\mathcal{D}_{\mathcal{M}}^{\lambda} \longleftarrow$ terminal MDP obtained as described above;
3   $s^* \longleftarrow$ any Markovian state of $\mathcal{M}$;
4   $v_0 = \overline{0}, v_1 = \overline{1}$;
5   $w_0 = \overline{0}$;

6   **for** $(n = 0; \ sp(v_{n+1} - v_n) < \frac{\varepsilon}{\lambda}; \ n++)$ **do**
7     $\big|$ $v_{n+1} = \texttt{TotalExpectedReward}(\mathcal{D}_{\mathcal{M}}^{\lambda}, \mathrm{rew}_{\mathcal{D}_{\mathcal{M}}^{\lambda}, w_n}, \mathrm{opt})$;
8     $\big|$ $w_{n+1} = v_{n+1} - v_{n+1}(s^*) \cdot e$;   /* e is the vector of ones */
9   **return** $v_{n+1}(s^*) \cdot \lambda$;

4.3 Algorithmic Solution

In order to solve the efficient variant of the Bellman equation, standard value or policy iteration approaches are applicable. In this section, we present the relative value iteration algorithm[1] for this problem (Algorithm 1). This algorithm has two levels of computations: the standard MDP value iteration as an outer loop on Markovian states, and during each iteration of the value iteration we compute the total expected reward on the terminal MDP.

Here $sp(v) := \big| \max_{s \in MS_{\mathcal{M}}} \{v(s)\} - \min_{s \in MS_{\mathcal{M}}} \{v(s)\} \big|$ and `TotalExpectedReward` denotes the function that computes the total expected reward on an MDP.

Theorem 6. *Algorithm 1 computes for all $\varepsilon > 0$ the value $\mathrm{aR}_{\mathcal{M}}^{\varepsilon}$, such that $\|\mathrm{aR}_{\mathcal{M}}^{\varepsilon} - \mathrm{aR}_{\mathcal{M}}^{\mathrm{opt}}\| \leqslant \varepsilon$.*

Remark. Notice that in order to obtain the ε-optimal policy that achieves the value $\mathrm{aR}_{\mathcal{M}}^{\varepsilon}$, one only needs to store the optimising actions, computed during the `TotalExpectedReward` phase.

In case $\mathcal{M}$ is *PS*-acyclic, Theorem 5 applies, and instead of the general algorithm computing the total expected reward (Algorithm 1, line **7**), one can resort to its optimised version, that computes the values (2) as defined in Sect. 4.2.

Remark. Needless to say, the CTMDP for a MRA does not necessarily grow exponentially large. So, an alternative approach would be to first build the CTMDP as described in Sect. 4.1 and then, provided that model is small enough, analyse it with standard algorithms for long-run average reward [13]. Since our approach can directly work on the MRA we did not explore this alternative route.

---

[1] Classical value iteration is also possible, but is known to be numerically unstable.

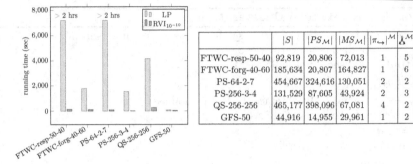

	$|S|$	$|PS_\mathcal{M}|$	$|MS_\mathcal{M}|$	$|\pi_\hookrightarrow|^\mathcal{M}$	$\lambda^\mathcal{M}$
FTWC-resp-50-40	92,819	20,806	72,013	1	5
FTWC-forg-40-60	185,634	20,807	164,827	1	6
PS-64-2-7	454,667	324,616	130,051	2	2
PS-256-3-4	131,529	87,605	43,924	2	3
QS-256-256	465,177	398,096	67,081	4	2
GFS-50	44,916	14,955	29,961	1	2

Fig. 4. Running time comparison of the LP and RVI. The table on the right presents the general data of the models used.

5 Experiments

In this section, we will present the empirical evaluation of the discussed algorithms.

Benchmarks. Our primary interest is to evaluate our approach on real-world examples. We therefore do not consider synthetic benchmarks but rather assess the algorithm on published ones. For this reason the model parameters we can vary is limited. Additionally the degree of variation of some parameters is restricted by the runtime/space requirements of the tool SCOOP [15], used to generate those models. The following is the collection of published benchmark models used to perform the experiments:

PS-S-J-K. The *Polling System* case study [8,16] consists of S servers that process requests of J types, stored in two queues of size K. We enriched this benchmark with rewards denoting maintenance costs. Maintaining a queue yields state reward proportional to its occupancy and processing a request of type j has an action reward dependent on the request type.

QS-K_1-K_2. The *Queuing System* [11] stores requests into two queues of size K_1 and K_2, that are later processed by a server attached to the queue. This model has only state-rewards proportional, which are to the size of the queue.

GFS-N. The *Google File System* [6,7] splits files into chunks, which are maintained by N chunk servers. The system is functioning if it is backed up and for each chunk at least one copy is available. We assign state reward 1 to all the functioning states thus computing the long-run availability of the system.

FTWC-B-N_1-N_2. The *Fault Tolerant Workstation Cluster* [12] models two networks of N_1 and N_2 workstations, interconnected by a switch. The two switches communicate via a backbone. The system is managed by a repairman, his behaviour (B) can be either *responsible, forgetful* or *lazy*. Rewards assigned to states and actions denote the cost of repairs, energy consumption and QoS violation.

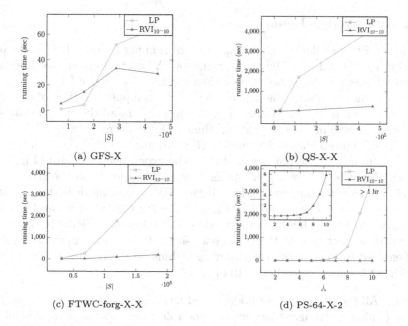

(a) GFS-X

(b) QS-X-X

(c) FTWC-forg-X-X

(d) PS-64-X-2

Fig. 5. Runtime complexity of LP and RVI w.r.t. the increase of the model size.

Implementation/Hardware Aspects. We have implemented our approach as a part of the IMCA/MAMA toolset [8], the only toolset providing quantification of long-run average rewards on MRA. IMCA 1.6 contains the implementation of the aR^{opt} algorithm from [10] that we have discussed in Sect. 3. It uses the SoPlex LP-solver [17] for the solution of linear optimisation problems with the primal and dual feasibility tolerance parameters set to 10^{-6}. All experiments were run on a single core of Intel Core i7-4790 with 8 GB of RAM.

Empirical Evaluation. The space complexity of both the algorithms is polynomial. Therefore, we have used two measures to evaluate the algorithms: running time w.r.t. the increase of precision and model size.

All the models we tested have only one MEC. We will denote the size of this MEC as $|\mathcal{M}|$, and $PS_{\mathcal{M}}$ ($MS_{\mathcal{M}}$) represents the number of probabilistic (Markovian) states of this MEC. We use the symbol $|\pi_{\hookrightarrow}|^{\mathcal{M}}$ to denote the length of the longest path π (in $\mathcal{M}$) that contains only probabilistic states, and $\lambda^{\mathcal{M}}$ stands for the maximal number of enabled actions in probabilistic states of $\mathcal{M}$. RVI$_\varepsilon$

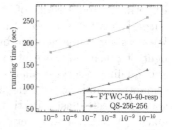

Fig. 6. Observed dependency of RVI on the precision parameter ε in reversed logarithmic x-axis.

denotes that Algorithm 1 ran with precision ε and LP the LP-based algorithm from [9]. We use the symbol "X" whenever the varying parameter of the experiment is a part of the model name, e.g. PS-2-X.

Long-Run Average Reward

Efficiency. Figure 4 depicts the comparison of running times of RVI (with precision 10^{-10}) and LP. The running time of RVI on performed experiments is *several orders of magnitude better* than the running time of LP.

Precision. Figure 6 shows the dependency of the computation time of our approach on the precision parameter ε. We observed in all the experiments significant growth of the computation time with the decrease of ε.

Model size. Figure 5 shows the running time comparison of the two algorithms w.r.t. the increase of the model size. In the experiments shown in Fig. 5a–c, both algorithms show a more or less linear dependency on the state space size. The general observation here is that RVI scales much better with the increase of model size than LP. Figure 5a shows that the LP can be better on smaller models, but on larger models RVI takes over. Figure 5d shows the dependency not only on the state space size but also on the maximal number of enabled actions. In this case both algorithms exhibit quadratic dependency with RVI scaling much better than LP.

Remark. All the models we considered (and all case studies we know of) are *PS*-acyclic (which is stronger than our base non-Zenoness assumption). Therefore, Theorem 5 applies that computes the aR^{opt} value for *PS*-acyclic MRA. The original LP approach we compare with is, however, not optimised for *PS*-acyclicity.

6   Conclusion

We have presented a novel algorithm for long-run expected rewards for Markov automata. It considers the automaton as a compact representation of a possibly exponentially larger CTMDP. We circumvent exponentiality by applying available algorithms for dynamic programming and for total expected rewards on discrete-time MDPs, derived from the Markov automaton using uniformisation. Experiments on a series of case studies have demonstrated that our algorithm outperforms the available LP-based algorithm by several orders of magnitude. We consider this a genuine breakthrough in Markov automata applicability, in light of the importance of long-run evaluations in performance, dependability and quality-of-service analysis, together with the fact that MAs provide the semantic foundation for engineering frameworks such as (dynamic) fault trees, generalised stochastic Petri nets, and the Architecture Analysis & Design Language (AADL). The general approach we developed is particularly efficient if restricted to Markov automata free of cycles of probabilistic states, which are the only models occurring in practice. Whether or not one should consider all models with such loops as instances of Zeno behaviour is an open question. In fact, a profound understanding of all aspects of Zenoness in Markov automata is not yet developed. It is on our research agenda.

References

1. Bellman, R.E.: Dynamic Programming. Princeton University Press, Princeton (1957)
2. Bertsekas, D.P.: Dynamic Programming and Optimal Control, 2nd edn. Athena Scientific, Belmont (2000)
3. Bhattacharya, R.N., Waymire, E.C.: Stochastic Processes with Applications. SIAM, Philadelphia (2009)
4. Chatterjee, K., Henzinger, M.: Faster and dynamic algorithms for maximal end-component decomposition and related graph problems in probabilistic verification. In: Proceedings of SODA, pp. 1318–1336, January 2011
5. Eisentraut, C., Hermanns, H., Zhang, L.: On probabilistic automata in continuous time. In: Proceedings of LICS, pp. 342–351. IEEE CS (2010)
6. Ghemawat, S., Gobioff, H., Leung, S.: The Google file system. In: Scott, M.L., Peterson, L.L. (eds.) Proceedings of SOSP, Bolton Landing, NY, USA, pp. 29–43. ACM, October 2003
7. Guck, D.: Quantitative Analysis of Markov Automata. Master's thesis, RWTH Aachen University, June 2012
8. Guck, D., Hatefi, H., Hermanns, H., Katoen, J.-P., Timmer, M.: Modelling, reduction and analysis of Markov automata. In: Joshi, K., Siegle, M., Stoelinga, M., D'Argenio, P.R. (eds.) QEST 2013. LNCS, vol. 8054, pp. 55–71. Springer, Heidelberg (2013). doi:10.1007/978-3-642-40196-1_5
9. Guck, D., Hatefi, H., Hermanns, H., Katoen, J., Timmer, M.: Analysis of timed and long-run objectives for Markov automata. Log. Methods Comput. Sci. **10**(3) (2014)
10. Guck, D., Timmer, M., Hatefi, H., Ruijters, E., Stoelinga, M.: Modelling and analysis of Markov reward automata. In: Cassez, F., Raskin, J.-F. (eds.) ATVA 2014. LNCS, vol. 8837, pp. 168–184. Springer, Heidelberg (2014). doi:10.1007/978-3-319-11936-6_13
11. Hatefi, H., Hermanns, H.: Model checking algorithms for Markov automata. ECE ASST **53** (2012). http://journal.ub.tu-berlin.de/eceasst/article/view/783
12. Haverkort, B.R., Hermanns, H., Katoen, J.: On the use of model checking techniques for dependability evaluation. In: Proceedings of SRDS, Nürnberg, Germany, pp. 228–237. IEEE CS, October 2000
13. Puterman, M.L.: Markov Decision Processes: Discrete Stochastic Dynamic Programming, 1st edn. Wiley, New York (1994)
14. Stewart, W.J.: Introduction to the Numerical Solution of Markov Chains. Princeton University Press, Princeton (1994)
15. Timmer, M.: SCOOP: a tool for symbolic optimisations of probabilistic processes. In: Proceedings of QEST, Aachen, Germany, pp. 149–150. IEEE CS, September 2011
16. Timmer, M., Pol, J., Stoelinga, M.I.A.: Confluence reduction for Markov automata. In: Braberman, V., Fribourg, L. (eds.) FORMATS 2013. LNCS, vol. 8053, pp. 243–257. Springer, Heidelberg (2013). doi:10.1007/978-3-642-40229-6_17
17. Wunderling, R.: Paralleler und objektorientierter Simplex-Algorithmus. Ph.D. thesis, Berlin Institute of Technology (1996). http://d-nb.info/950219444

SAT and SMT

HiFrog: SMT-based Function Summarization for Software Verification

Leonardo Alt[1(✉)], Sepideh Asadi[1(✉)], Hana Chockler[2(✉)],
Karine Even Mendoza[2(✉)], Grigory Fedyukovich[3(✉)],
Antti E.J. Hyvärinen[1(✉)], and Natasha Sharygina[1(✉)]

[1] Università della Svizzera italiana, Lugano, Switzerland
leonardoaltt@gmail.com, antti.hyvarinen@gmail.com,
{sepideh.asadi,natasha.sharygina}@usi.ch
[2] King's College London, London, UK
{hana.chockler,karine.even_mendoza}@kcl.ac.uk
[3] University of Washington, Seattle, USA
grigory.fedyukovich@gmail.com

Abstract. Function summarization can be used as a means of incremental verification based on the structure of the program. HiFrog is a fully featured function-summarization-based model checker that uses SMT as the modeling and summarization language. The tool supports three encoding precisions through SMT: uninterpreted functions, linear real arithmetics, and propositional logic. In addition the tool allows optimized traversal of reachability properties, counter-example-guided summary refinement, summary compression, and user-provided summaries. We describe the use of the tool through the description of its architecture and a rich set of features. The description is complemented by an experimental evaluation on the practical impact the different SMT precisions have on model-checking.

1 Introduction

Incremental verification addresses the unique opportunities and challenges that arise when a verification task can be performed in an incremental way, as a sequence of smaller closely related tasks. We present an implementation of the incremental verification of software with assertions that uses the insights obtained from a successful verification of earlier assertions. As a fundamental building block in storing the insights we use function summaries known to provide speed-up through localizing and modularizing verification [12,13].

In this paper we describe the HiFrog verification tool that uses Craig interpolation [6] in the context of Bounded Model Checking (BMC) [4] for constructing function summaries. The novelty of the tool is in the unique way it combines function summaries with the expressiveness of satisfiability modulo theories (SMT). The system currently supports verification based on the quantifier-free theories of linear real arithmetics (QF_LRA) and uninterpreted

This work was supported by the SNF projects 153402 and 163001.

A. Legay and T. Margaria (Eds.): TACAS 2017, Part II, LNCS 10206, pp. 207–213, 2017.
DOI: 10.1007/978-3-662-54580-5_12

functions (QF_UF), in addition to propositional logic (QF_BOOL). Compared to our earlier propositional tool FunFrog [13], the SMT summaries are smaller and more efficient in verification. They are also often significantly more human-readable, enabling their easier reuse, as well as injection of summaries provided directly by the user. The difference is due to the propositional summaries being based on correctness proofs over circuit-level representation of arithmetic operations. Theory encoding uses instead directly arithmetic symbols in the summaries. In addition, the tool offers a rich set of features such as verification of recursive programs, different ways of optimizing the summaries with respect to both size and strength, efficient heuristics for removing redundant safety properties, and easy-to-understand witnesses of property violations that can be directly mapped to bugs in the source code.

The paper provides an architectural description of the tool, an introduction to its use, and experimental evidence of its performance. The tool together with a comprehensive demo is available at http://verify.inf.usi.ch/hifrog.

Related Work. Incremental verification is extensively researched in domains such as hardware verification, deductive verification, and model checking. Due to space constraints we provide only a brief review of recent related work. The CPACHECKER tool is able to migrate predicates across program versions [3]. Deductive verification tools such as VIPER and DAFNY offer modular verification [11] and caching the intermediate verification results [9] respectively. CBMC is a symbolic bounded model-checker for C that to a limited extent exploits incremental capabilities of a SAT solver[1], but does not use or output any reusable information like function summaries. Similar to HiFrog, ESBMC also shares the CPROVER infrastructure and is based on an SMT solver. To the best of our knowledge, it does not support incremental verification [5].

2   Tool Overview

HiFrog consists of two main components *SMT encoder* and *interpolating SMT solver*, and the function *summaries* (see Fig. 1). The components are initially configured with the theory and the interpolation algorithms. The tool then processes assertions sequentially using function summaries when possible. The results of a successful assertion verification are stored as interpolated function summaries, and failed verifications trigger a refinement phase or the printing of an error trace. This section details the tool features.

Preprocessing. The source code is parsed and transformed into an intermediate *goto-program* using the GOTO-CC symbolic compiler. The loops are unwound to the pre-determined number of iterations. HiFrog identifies the set of assertions from the source code, reads the user-defined function summaries (if any) in the SMTLIB2-format, and makes them available for the subsequent analysis.

---

[1] http://www.cprover.org.

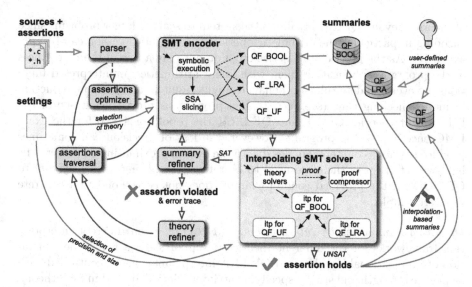

Fig. 1. HiFrog overview. Grey and black arrows connect different modules of the tool (dashed - optional). Blue arrows represent the flow of the input/output data. (Color figure online)

SMT Encoding and Function Summarization. For a given assertion, the goto-program is *symbolically executed* function-per-function resulting in the "modular" Static Single Assignment (SSA) form of the unwound program, i.e., a form where each function has its own isolated SSA-representation. To reduce the size of the SSA form, HiFROG performs *slicing* that keeps only the variables in the SSA form that are syntactically dependent on the variables in the assertion.

When the SSA form is pruned, HiFROG creates the SMT formula in the pre-determined logic (QF_BOOL, QF_UF or QF_LRA). The modularity of the SSA form comes in handy when the function summaries of the chosen logic (either user-defined, interpolation-based, or treated nondeterministically) are available. If this is the case, the call to a function with the available summary is replaced by the summary. The final SMT formula is pushed to an SMT solver to decide its satisfiability.

Due to over-approximating nature of function summaries, the program encoded with the summaries may contain spurious errors. The *summary refiner* identifies and marks summaries directly involved in the detected error, and HiFROG returns to the encoding stage to replace the marked summaries by the precise (up to the pre-determined logic) function representations. Note that due to refinement, HiFROG reveals nested function calls (including recursive ones) which are again replaced by available summaries. For an unsatisfiable SMT formula, HiFROG extracts function summaries using interpolation. The extracted summaries are serialized in a persistent storage so that they are available for other HiFROG runs. For a more detailed description we refer to [13].

Theories. HiFROG supports three different quantifier-free theories in which the program can be modelled: bit-precise QF_BOOL, QF_UF and QF_LRA. The use of theories beyond QF_BOOL allows the system to scale to larger problems since encoding in particular the arithmetic operations using bit-precision can be very expensive. As the precise arithmetics often do not play a role in the correctness of the program, substituting them with linear arithmetics, uninterpreted functions, or even nondeterministic behavior might result in a significant reduction in model-checking time (see Sect. 3). If a property is proved using one of the light-weight theories QF_UF and QF_LRA, the proof holds also for the exact BMC encoding of the program. However, the loss of precision can sometimes produce spurious counterexamples due to the over-approximating encoding. The light-weight theories therefore need to be refined (i.e., using *theory refiner*) to QF_BOOL if the provided counter-example does not correspond to a concrete counterexample.

Obtaining Summaries by Interpolation. HiFROG relies on different interpolation frameworks for the different theories it supports. As a result the generation of propositional, QF_UF and QF_LRA interpolants can be controlled with respect to strength and size by specifying an interpolation algorithm for a theory. For propositional logic we provide the *Labeled Interpolation Systems* [7] including the *Proof-Sensitive* interpolation algorithms [1]. Interpolation for QF_UF is implemented with *duality-based interpolation* [2], and a similar extension is applied to the interpolation algorithm for QF_LRA based on [10]. HiFROG also provides a range of techniques to reduce the size of the generated interpolants through removing redundancies in propositional proofs [12]: the algorithms RecyclePivotsWithIntersection and LowerUnits, structural hashing, and a set of local rewriting rules.

Assertion Optimizer. In addition to incremental verification of a set of assertions, HiFROG supports the basic functionality of classical model checkers to verify all assertions at once. For the cases when the set of assertions is too large, it can be optimized by constructing an *assertion implication relation* and exploiting it to remove redundant assertions [8]. In a nutshell, the assertion optimizer considers pairs of spatially close assertions a_i and a_j and uses the SMT solver to check if a_i conjoined with the code between a_i and a_j implies a_j (if there is any other assertion between a_i and a_j then it is treated as assumption). If the check succeeds then a_j is proven redundant and its verification can be safely skipped.

3   HiFROG Usage

We provide a Linux binary of HiFROG reading as input a C-program, assertions to be verified, a set of parameters and the interpolated or user-defined function summaries in the SMT-LIB2 format. HiFROG exploits the CProver framework and inherits some of its options (e.g., `--unwind` for the loop unrolling, `--show-claims` and `--claim` for managing the assertions checks); the ability for the user to declare and to use a `nondet_TYPE()` function of a specific numerical type (e.g., int, long, double, unsigned, in QF_LRA only) or add a `__CPROVER_assume()` statement to limit the domain to a specific range of values.

HiFROG uses QF_LRA by default but can be switched to QF_UF via the `--logic` option.[2] HiFROG uses a variety of interpolation and proof compression algorithms to control the the precision (with `--itp-uf-algorithm` option for QF_UF, `--itp-lra-algorithm` option for QF_LRA, and `--itp-algorithm` option for propositional interpolation) and the size (with `--reduce-proof`) of summaries. The summary storage is controlled using the `--save-summaries` and `--load-summaries` options. In between verification runs, the summaries contained in the corresponding files for QF_UF and QF_LRA might be edited manually. Note that due to the SMT encoding constraints HiFROG does not allow interchanging summaries between the theories. Finally, HiFROG supports the identification and reporting of redundant assertions with `--claims-opt`, a useful feature for some automatically generated assertions [8].

In the end of each verification run, HiFROG either reports `VERIFICATION SUCCESSFUL` or `VERIFICATION FAILED` accompanied by an error trace. An error trace presents a sequence of steps with a direct reference to the code and the values of variables in these steps. In most cases when QF_UF and QF_LRA introduce a spurious error, HiFROG outputs a warning, and thus the user is advised to use HiFROG with a more precise theory. HiFROG also reports the statistics on the running time and the number of the summary-refinements performed.

Experimental Results. We evaluated HiFROG on a large set of C programs coming from both academic and industrial sources such as SV-COMP. All benchmarks contained multiple assertions to be checked. To demonstrate the advantages of the SMT-based summarization, here we provide data for analysis of benchmarks containing 1086 assertions from which 474 were proven to hold using QF_BOOL (meaning that those properties satisfy the system specifications). Even despite the over-approximating nature of QF_UF and QF_LRA, our experiments witnessed a large amount of properties which were also proven to be correct by employing the light-weight theories of HiFROG (namely, 50.65% and 69.2% of validated properties out of 474 for QF_UF and QF_LRA respectively).

Furthermore, those experiments revealed that model checking using the QF_UF and QF_LRA-based summarization was extremely efficient. Figure 2

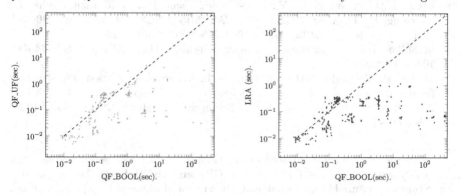

Fig. 2. Running time by QF_BOOL against QF_UF and QF_LRA.

[2] Currently the support for QF_BOOL needs to be specified at compile time.

presents two logarithmic plots for comparison of running times[3] of HiFROG with QF_BOOL to respectively QF_UF and QF_LRA. Each point represents a pair of verification runs of a holding assertion with the two corresponding theories using the interpolation-based summaries. Note that for most of the assertions, the verification with QF_UF and QF_LRA is an order of magnitude faster than the verification with QF_BOOL.

References

1. Alt, L., Fedyukovich, G., Hyvärinen, A.E.J., Sharygina, N.: A proof-sensitive approach for small propositional interpolants. In: Gurfinkel, A., Seshia, S.A. (eds.) VSTTE 2015. LNCS, vol. 9593, pp. 1–18. Springer, Heidelberg (2016). doi:10.1007/978-3-319-29613-5_1
2. Alt, L., Hyvärinen, A.E.J., Sharygina, N.: Duality-based interpolation for quantifier-free equalities and uninterpreted functions (2016). http://www.inf.usi.ch/postdoc/hyvarinen/euf-interpolation.pdf
3. Beyer, D., Löwe, S., Novikov, E., Stahlbauer, A., Wendler, P.: Precision reuse for efficient regression verification. In: ESEC/FSE, pp. 389–399. ACM (2013)
4. Biere, A., Cimatti, A., Clarke, E., Zhu, Y.: Symbolic model checking without BDDs. In: Cleaveland, W.R. (ed.) TACAS 1999. LNCS, vol. 1579, pp. 193–207. Springer, Heidelberg (1999). doi:10.1007/3-540-49059-0_14
5. Cordeiro, L.C., de Lima Filho, E.B.: SMT-based context-bounded model checking for embedded systems: challenges and future trends. ACM SIGSOFT Softw. Eng. Notes **41**(3), 1–6 (2016)
6. Craig, W.: Three uses of the Herbrand-Gentzen theorem in relating model theory and proof theory. J. Symb. Log. **22**(3), 269–285 (1957)
7. D'Silva, V., Kroening, D., Purandare, M., Weissenbacher, G.: Interpolant strength. In: Barthe, G., Hermenegildo, M. (eds.) VMCAI 2010. LNCS, vol. 5944, pp. 129–145. Springer, Heidelberg (2010). doi:10.1007/978-3-642-11319-2_12
8. Fedyukovich, G., D'Iddio, A.C., Hyvärinen, A.E.J., Sharygina, N.: Symbolic detection of assertion dependencies for bounded model checking. In: Egyed, A., Schaefer, I. (eds.) FASE 2015. LNCS, vol. 9033, pp. 186–201. Springer, Heidelberg (2015). doi:10.1007/978-3-662-46675-9_13
9. Leino, K.R.M., Wüstholz, V.: Fine-grained caching of verification results. In: Kroening, D., Păsăreanu, C.S. (eds.) CAV 2015. LNCS, vol. 9206, pp. 380–397. Springer, Heidelberg (2015). doi:10.1007/978-3-319-21690-4_22
10. McMillan, K.L.: An interpolating theorem prover. Theor. Comput. Sci. **345**(1), 101–121 (2005)
11. Müller, P., Schwerhoff, M., Summers, A.J.: Viper: a verification infrastructure for permission-based reasoning. In: Jobstmann, B., Leino, K.R.M. (eds.) VMCAI 2016. LNCS, vol. 9583, pp. 41–62. Springer, Heidelberg (2016). doi:10.1007/978-3-662-49122-5_2

---

[3] The timing results were obtained on an Ubuntu 14.04.1 LTS server running two Intel(R) Xeon(R) E5620 *CPUs* @ 2.40 GHz and 16 GB RAM. We prepared a pre-compiled Linux-binary available at the Virtual Machine at http://verify.inf.usi.ch/hifrog/binary; our benchmarks set is available at http://verify.inf.usi.ch/hifrog/bench and can facilitate the property verification for other researchers.

12. Rollini, S.F., Alt, L., Fedyukovich, G., Hyvärinen, A.E.J., Sharygina, N.: PeRIPLO: a framework for producing effective interpolants in SAT-based software verification. In: McMillan, K., Middeldorp, A., Voronkov, A. (eds.) LPAR 2013. LNCS, vol. 8312, pp. 683–693. Springer, Heidelberg (2013). doi:10.1007/978-3-642-45221-5_45
13. Sery, O., Fedyukovich, G., Sharygina, N.: FunFrog: bounded model checking with interpolation-based function summarization. In: Chakraborty, S., Mukund, M. (eds.) ATVA 2012. LNCS, vol. 7561, pp. 203–207. Springer, Heidelberg (2012). doi:10.1007/978-3-642-33386-6_17

Congruence Closure with Free Variables

Haniel Barbosa[1,2(✉)], Pascal Fontaine[1], and Andrew Reynolds[3]

[1] LORIA–Inria, Université de Lorraine, Nancy, France
{Haniel.Barbosa,Pascal.Fontaine}@inria.fr
[2] Universidade Federal do Rio Grande do Norte, Natal, RN, Brazil
[3] University of Iowa, Iowa City, USA
andrew.j.reynolds@gmail.com

Abstract. Many verification techniques nowadays successfully rely on SMT solvers as back-ends to automatically discharge proof obligations. These solvers generally rely on various instantiation techniques to handle quantifiers. We here show that the major instantiation techniques in SMT solving can be cast in a unifying framework for handling quantified formulas with equality and uninterpreted functions. This framework is based on the problem of E-ground (dis)unification, a variation of the classic rigid E-unification problem. We introduce a sound and complete calculus to solve this problem in practice: Congruence Closure with Free Variables (CCFV). Experimental evaluations of implementations of CCFV in the state-of-the-art solver CVC4 and in the solver veriT exhibit improvements in the former and makes the latter competitive with state-of-the-art solvers in several benchmark libraries stemming from verification efforts.

1 Introduction

SMT solvers [8] are highly efficient at handling large ground formulas with interpreted symbols, but they still struggle with quantified formulas. Pure quantified first-order logic is best handled with *resolution* and *superposition*-based theorem proving [3]. Although there are first attempts to unify such techniques with SMT [13], the main approach used in SMT is still *instantiation*: quantified formulas are reduced to ground ones and refuted with the help of decision procedures for ground formulas. The main instantiation techniques are E-matching based on triggers [12,17,26], finding conflicting instances [24] and model-based quantifier instantiation (MBQI) [19,25]. Each of these techniques contributes to the efficiency of state-of-the-art solvers, yet each one is typically implemented independently.

We introduce the E-ground (dis)unification problem as the cornerstone of a unique framework in which all these techniques can be cast. This problem relates

This work has been partially supported by the ANR/DFG project STU 483/2-1 SMArT ANR-13-IS02-0001 of the Agence Nationale de la Recherche, by the H2020-FETOPEN-2016-2017-CSA project SC^2 (712689), and by the European Research Council (ERC) starting grant Matryoshka (713999).

A. Legay and T. Margaria (Eds.): TACAS 2017, Part II, LNCS 10206, pp. 214–230, 2017.
DOI: 10.1007/978-3-662-54580-5_13

to the classic problem of rigid E-unification and is also NP-complete. Solving E-ground (dis)unification amounts to finding substitutions such that literals containing free variables hold in the context of currently asserted ground literals. Since the instantiation domain of those variables can be bound, a possible way of solving the problem is by first non-deterministically guessing a substitution and checking if it is a solution. The *Congruence Closure with Free Variables* algorithm (CCFV, for short) presented here is a practical decision procedure for this problem based on the classic congruence closure algorithm [21,22]. It is goal-oriented: solutions are constructed incrementally, taking into account the congruence closure of the terms defined by the equalities in the context and the possible assignments to the variables.

We then show how to build on CCFV to implement trigger-based, conflict-based and model-based instantiation. An experimental evaluation of the technique is presented, where our implementations exhibits improvements over state-of-the-art approaches.

1.1 Related Work

Instantiation techniques for SMT have been studied extensively. Heuristic instantiation based on E-matching of selected triggers was introduced by Detlefs et al. [17]. A highly efficient implementation of E-matching was presented by de Moura and Bjørner [12]; it relies on elaborated indexing techniques and generation of machine code for optimizing performance. Rümmer uses triggers alongside a classic tableaux method [26]. Trigger based instantiation unfortunately produces many irrelevant instances. To tackle this issue, a goal-oriented instantiation technique producing only useful instances was introduced by Reynolds et al. [24]. CCFV shares resemblance with this algorithm, the search being based on the structure of terms and a current model coming from the ground solver. The approach here is however more powerful and more general, and somehow subsumes this previous technique. Ge and de Moura's model based quantifier instantiation (MBQI) [19] provides a complete method for first-order logic through successive derivation of conflicting instances to refine a candidate model for the whole formula, including quantifiers. Thus it also allows the solver to find finite models when they exist. Model checking is performed with a separate copy of the ground SMT solver searching for a conflicting instance. Alternative methods for model construction and checking were presented by Reynolds et al. [25]. Both these model based approaches [19,25] allow integration of theories beyond equality, while CCFV for now only handles equality and uninterpreted functions.

Backeman and Rümmer solve the related problem of rigid E-unification through encoding into SAT, using an off-the-shelf SAT solver to compute solutions [5]. Our work is more in line with goal-oriented techniques as those by Goubault [20] and Tiwari et al. [27]; congruence closure algorithms being very efficient at checking solutions, we believe they can also be the core of efficient algorithms to discover them. CCFV differs from those previous techniques notably, since it handles disequalities and since the search for solutions is pruned based on the structure of a ground model and is thus most suitable for an SMT context.

2   Notations and Basic Definitions

We refer to classic notions of many-sorted first-order logic (e.g. by Baader and Nipkow [1] and by Fitting [18]) as the basis for notations in this paper. Only the most relevant are mentioned.

A *first-order language* is a tuple $\mathscr{L} = \langle \mathcal{S}, \mathcal{X}, \mathcal{P}, \mathcal{F}, sort \rangle$ in which $\mathcal{S}, \mathcal{X}, \mathcal{P}$ and $\mathcal{F}$ are disjoint enumerable sets of *sort, variable, predicate* and *function symbols*, respectively, and $sort : \mathcal{X} \cup \mathcal{F} \cup \mathcal{P} \rightarrow \mathcal{S}^+$ is a function assigning sorts, according to the symbols' arities. Nullary functions and predicates are called *constants* and *propositions*, respectively. *Formulas* and *terms* are generated in a well-sorted manner by

$$t ::= x \mid f(t, \ldots, t) \qquad \varphi ::= t \simeq t \mid p(t, \ldots, t) \mid \neg\varphi \mid \varphi \vee \varphi \mid \forall x_1 \ldots x_n.\varphi$$

in which $x, x_1, \ldots, x_n \in \mathcal{X}$, $p \in \mathcal{P}$ and $f \in \mathcal{F}$. The predicate symbol $\simeq$ stands for *equality*. The terms in a formula φ are denoted by $\mathbf{T}(\varphi)$. In a function or predicate application, the symbol being applied is referred as the term's *top symbol*. The *free variables* of a formula φ are denoted by $\mathrm{FV}(\varphi)$. A formula or term is *ground* iff it contains no variables. Whenever convenient, an enumeration of symbols $s_1, \ldots, s_n$ will be represented as $\mathbf{s}$.

A *substitution* σ is a mapping from variables to terms. The application of σ to the formula φ (respectively the term t) is denoted by $\varphi\sigma$ ($t\sigma$). The *domain* of σ is the set $dom(\sigma) = \{x \mid x \in \mathcal{X} \text{ and } x\sigma \neq x\}$, while the *range of* σ is $ran(\sigma) = \{x\sigma \mid x \in dom(\sigma)\}$. A substitution σ is *ground* iff every term in $ran(\sigma)$ is ground and *acyclic* iff, for any variable x, x does not occur in $x\sigma \ldots \sigma$. For an acyclic substitution, $\sigma^\star$ is the fixed point substitution of σ.

Given a set of ground terms $\mathbf{T}$ closed under the subterm relation and a congruence relation $\simeq$ on $\mathbf{T}$, a *congruence* over $\mathbf{T}$ is a subset of $\{s \simeq t \mid s, t \in \mathbf{T}\}$ closed under entailment. The *congruence closure* (CC, for short) of a set of equations E on a set of terms $\mathbf{T}$ is the least congruence on $\mathbf{T}$ containing E. Given a consistent set of equality literals E, two terms t_1, t_2 are said *congruent* iff $E \models t_1 \simeq t_2$ and *disequal* iff $E \models t_1 \not\simeq t_2$. The *congruence class* in $\mathbf{T}$ of a given term is the set of terms in $\mathbf{T}$ congruent to it. The signature of a term is the term itself for a nullary symbol, and $f(c_1, \ldots c_n)$ for a term $f(t_1, \ldots t_n)$ with c_i being the class of t_i. The *signature class* of t is a set $[t]_E$ containing one and only one term in the class of t for each signature. Notice that the signature class of two terms in the same class is the same set of terms, and is a subset of the congruence class. We drop the subscript in $[t]_E$ when E is clear from the context. The *set of signature classes* of E on a set of terms $\mathbf{T}$ is $E^{\mathrm{cc}} = \{[t] \mid t \in \mathbf{T}\}$.

3   *E*-ground (Dis)unification

For simplicity, and without loss of generality, we consider formulas in Skolem form, with all quantified subformulas being quantified clauses; we also assume all atomic formulas are equalities. SMT solvers proceed by enumerating the models for the propositional abstraction of the input formula, i.e. the formula obtained by replacing every atom and quantified subformula by a proposition. Such a model of the propositional abstraction corresponds to a set $E \cup Q$, in which E and Q are conjunctive sets of ground literals and quantified formulas, respectively. If $E \cup Q$ is consistent, all of its models also satisfy the input formula; if not, a new candidate model is derived. The ground SMT solver first checks the satisfiability of E, and, if it is satisfiable, proceeds to reason on the set of quantified formulas Q. Ground instances $\mathcal{I}$ are derived from Q, and subsequently the satisfiability of $E \cup \mathcal{I}$ is checked. This is repeated until either a conflict is found, and a new model for the propositional abstraction must be produced, or no more instantiations are possible. Of course, the whole process might not terminate and the solver might loop indefinitely.

In this approach, a central problem is to determine which instances $\mathcal{I}$ to derive. Section 5 shows that the problem of finding instances via existing instantiation techniques can be reduced to the problem of E-ground (dis)unification.

Definition 1 (E-ground (dis)unification). *Given two finite sets of equality literals E and L, E being ground, the E-ground (dis)unification problem is that of finding substitutions σ such that $E \models L\sigma$.*

E-ground (dis)unification can be recast as the classic problem of (non-simultaneous) rigid E-unification (transformation proof in Appendix B of [6]), i.e. computing substitutions σ such that $E^{eq}\sigma \models s\sigma \simeq t\sigma$, in which E^{eq} is a set of equations and s, t are terms. Rigid E-unification has been studied extensively in the context of automated theorem proving [2,10,15]. In particular, its intrinsic relation with congruence closure has been investigated by Goubault [20] and Tiwari et al. [27], in which variations of the classic procedure are integrated with first-order rewriting techniques and the search for solutions is guided by the structure of the terms. We build on these ideas to develop our method for solving E-ground (dis)unification, as discussed in Sect. 4.

Example 1. Consider the sets $E = \{f(a) \simeq f(b), h(a) \simeq h(c), g(b) \not\simeq h(c)\}$ and $L = \{h(x_1) \simeq h(c), h(x_2) \not\simeq g(x_3), f(x_1) \simeq f(x_3), x_4 \simeq g(x_5)\}$. A solution for their E-ground (dis)unification problem is $\{x_1 \mapsto a, x_2 \mapsto c, x_3 \mapsto b, x_4 \mapsto g(x_5)\}$.

The above example shows that x_5 can be mapped to any term; this E-ground (dis)unification problem has infinitely many solutions. However, here, like in general,[1] the set of all solutions can be finitely represented:

Theorem 1. *Given an E-ground (dis)unification problem, if a substitution σ exists such that $E \models L\sigma$, then there is an acyclic substitution σ' such that $ran(\sigma') \subseteq \mathbf{T}(E \cup L)$, σ'^{*} is ground, and $E \models L\sigma'^{*}$.*

Proof. The proof can be found in Appendix A of [6]. □

---

[1] It is assumed, without loss of generality, that $\mathbf{T}(E \cup L)$ contains at least one ground term of each sort in $E \cup L$.

As a corollary, the problem is in NP: it suffices indeed to guess an acyclic substitution with $ran(\sigma') \subseteq \mathbf{T}(E \cup L)$, and check (polynomially) that it is a solution. The problem is also NP-hard, by reduction of 3-SAT (Appendix C of [6]). As our experiments show, however, a concrete algorithm effective in practice is possible.

4 Congruence Closure with Free Variables

In this section we describe a calculus to find each substitution σ solving an E-ground (dis)unification problem $E \models L\sigma$. This calculus, *Congruence Closure with Free Variables* (CCFV), uses a congruence closure algorithm as a core element to guide the search and build solutions. It proceeds by building a set of equations E_σ such that $E \cup E_\sigma \models L$, in which E_σ corresponds to a solution substitution, built step by step, by decomposing L in a top-down manner into sets of simpler constraints.

Example 2. Considering again E and L as in Example 1, the calculus should find σ such that

$$f(a) \simeq f(b), h(a) \simeq h(c), g(b) \not\simeq h(c)$$
$$\models (h(x_1) \simeq h(c) \wedge h(x_2) \not\simeq g(x_3) \wedge f(x_1) \simeq f(x_3) \wedge x_4 \simeq g(x_5))\, \sigma$$

For L to be entailed by $E \cup E_\sigma$, each of its literals contributes to equations in E_σ in the following manner:

- $h(x_1) \simeq h(c)$: either $x_1 \simeq c$ or $x_1 \simeq a$ belongs to E_σ;
- $h(x_2) \not\simeq g(x_3)$: either $x_2 \simeq c \wedge x_3 \simeq b$ or $x_2 \simeq a \wedge x_3 \simeq b$ belongs to E_σ;
- $f(x_1) \simeq f(x_3)$: either $x_1 \simeq x_3$ or $x_1 \simeq a \wedge x_3 \simeq b$ or $x_1 \simeq b \wedge x_3 \simeq a$ must be in E_σ;
- $x_4 \simeq g(x_5)$: the literal itself must be in E_σ.

One solution is thus $E_\sigma = \{x_1 \simeq a, x_2 \simeq a, x_3 \simeq b, x_4 \simeq g(x_5)\}$, corresponding to the acyclic substitution $\sigma = \{x_1 \mapsto a, x_2 \mapsto a, x_3 \mapsto b, x_4 \mapsto g(x_5)\}$. Notice that, for any ground term $t \in \mathbf{T}(E \cup L)$, $\sigma_g = \sigma \cup \{x_5 \mapsto t\}$ is such that $ran(\sigma_g) \subseteq \mathbf{T}(E \cup L)$, $\sigma_g{}^\star$ is ground, and $E \models L\sigma_g{}^\star$.

4.1 The Calculus

Given an E-ground (dis)unification problem $E \models L\sigma$, the CCFV calculus computes the various possible E_σ corresponding to a coverage of all substitution solutions, i.e. such that $E \cup E_\sigma \models L$. We describe the calculus as a set of rules that operate on states of the form $E_\sigma \Vdash_E C$, in which C is a (disjunctive normal form) formula stemming from the decomposition of L into simpler constraints, and E_σ is a conjunctive set of equalities representing a partial solution. Starting from the initial state $\varnothing \Vdash_E L$, the right side of the state is progressively decomposed, whereas the left side is step by step augmented with new equalities building the candidate solution. Example 2 shows that, for a literal to be entailed by $E \cup E_\sigma$,

Table 1. The CCFV calculus in equational FOL. E is fixed from a problem $E \models L\sigma$.

$$\frac{E_\sigma \Vdash_E x \simeq s \land C}{E_\sigma \cup \{x \simeq s\} \Vdash_E rep(C)} \text{ ASSIGN} \qquad \text{if } x \notin \mathrm{FV}(s)$$

$$\frac{E_\sigma \Vdash_E x \simeq f(u_1, \ldots, u_n) \land C}{E_\sigma \Vdash_E \bigvee_{[t] \in E^{cc}, f(t_1, \ldots, t_n) \in [t]} (x \simeq t \land u_1 \simeq t_1 \land \cdots \land u_n \simeq t_n \land C)} \text{ U\_VAR}$$
$$\text{if } x \in \mathrm{FV}(f(u_1, \ldots, u_n))$$

$$\frac{E_\sigma \Vdash_E f(u_1, \ldots, u_n) \simeq f(s_1, \ldots, s_n) \land C}{E_\sigma \Vdash_E (u_1 \simeq s_1 \land \cdots \land u_n \simeq s_n \land C) \lor \bigvee_{\substack{[t] \in E^{cc}, \\ f(t_1, \ldots, t_n) \in [t], f(t_1', \ldots, t_n') \in [t]}} \begin{pmatrix} u_1 \simeq t_1 \land \cdots \land u_n \simeq t_n \land \\ s_1 \simeq t_1' \land \cdots \land s_n \simeq t_n' \land C \end{pmatrix}} \text{ U\_COMP}$$

$$\frac{E_\sigma \Vdash_E f(u_1, \ldots, u_n) \simeq g(s_1, \ldots, s_m) \land C}{E_\sigma \Vdash_E \bigvee_{\substack{[t] \in E^{cc}, \\ f(t_1, \ldots, t_n) \in [t], g(t_1', \ldots, t_m') \in [t]}} \begin{pmatrix} u_1 \simeq t_1 \land \cdots \land u_n \simeq t_n \land \\ s_1 \simeq t_1' \land \cdots \land s_m \simeq t_m' \land C \end{pmatrix}} \text{ U\_GEN}$$
$$\text{if } f \neq g$$

$$\frac{E_\sigma \Vdash_E x \not\simeq y \land C}{E_\sigma \Vdash_E \bigvee_{[t_1], [t_2] \in E^{cc}, E \models t_1 \not\simeq t_2} (x \simeq t_1 \land y \simeq t_2 \land C)} \text{ R\_VAR}$$

$$\frac{E_\sigma \Vdash_E x \not\simeq f(s_1, \ldots, s_n) \land C}{E_\sigma \Vdash_E \bigvee_{\substack{[t], [t'] \in E^{cc}, \\ E \models t \not\simeq t', f(t_1', \ldots, t_n') \in [t']}} (x \simeq t \land s_1 \simeq t_1' \land \cdots \land s_n \simeq t_n' \land C)} \text{ R\_FAPP}$$

$$\frac{E_\sigma \Vdash_E f(u_1, \ldots, u_n) \not\simeq g(s_1, \ldots, s_m) \land C}{E_\sigma \Vdash_E \bigvee_{\substack{[t], [t'] \in E^{cc}, E \models t \not\simeq t', \\ f(t_1, \ldots, t_n) \in [t], g(t_1', \ldots, t_m') \in [t']}} \begin{pmatrix} u_1 \simeq t_1 \land \cdots \land u_n \simeq t_n \land \\ s_1 \simeq t_1' \land \cdots \land s_m \simeq t_m' \land C \end{pmatrix}} \text{ R\_GEN}$$

$$\frac{E_\sigma \Vdash_E C_1 \lor C_2}{E_\sigma \Vdash_E C_1 \qquad E_\sigma \Vdash_E C_2} \text{ SPLIT} \qquad \frac{E_\sigma \Vdash_E C}{E_\sigma \Vdash_E \top} \text{ YIELD} \quad \text{if } E \cup E_\sigma \models C$$

$$\frac{E_\sigma \Vdash_E C}{E_\sigma \Vdash_E \bot} \text{ FAIL} \quad \begin{array}{l} \text{if no other rule can be applied; or} \\ C \text{ is a conjunction and } E \not\models \ell, \text{ for some ground } \ell \in C \end{array}$$

sometimes several solutions E_σ exist, thus the calculus involves branching. To simplify the presentation, the rules do not apply branching directly, but build disjunctions on the right part of the state, those disjunctions later leading to branching. A branch is closed when its constraint is decomposed into either $\bot$ or $\top$. The latter are branches for which $E \cup E_\sigma \models L$ holds.

The set of CCFV derivation rules is presented in Table 1; t stands for a ground term, x, y for variables, u for non-ground terms, $u_1, \ldots, u_n$ for terms such that at least one is non-ground and $s, s_1, \ldots, s_n$ for terms in general. Rules are applied top-down, the symmetry of equality being used implicitly. Each rule simplifies the constraint of the right hand side of the state, and as a consequence any derivation strategy is terminating (Theorem 2).

When an equality is added to the left hand side of a state $E_\sigma \Vdash_E C$ (rule ASSIGN), the constraint C is normalized with respect to congruence closure to reflect the assignments to variables. That is, all terms in C are representatives of classes in the congruence closure of $E \cup E_\sigma$. We write

$$rep(x) = \begin{cases} \text{some chosen } y \in [x]_{E_\sigma} & \text{if all terms in } [x]_{E_\sigma} \text{ are variables} \\ rep(f(\mathbf{s})) & \text{otherwise, for some } f(\mathbf{s}) \in [x]_{E_\sigma} \end{cases}$$

$$rep(f(s_1, \ldots, s_n)) = \begin{cases} f(s_1, \ldots, s_n) & \text{if } f(s_1, \ldots, s_n) \text{ is ground} \\ f(rep(s_1), \ldots, rep(s_n)) & \text{otherwise} \end{cases}$$

and write $rep(C)$ to denote the result of applying rep on both sides of each literal $s \simeq s'$ or $s \not\simeq s'$ in C. The above definition of rep leaves room for some choice of representative, but soundness and completeness are not impacted by the choice. What actually matters is whether the representative is a variable, a ground term or a non-ground function application. The ASSIGN rule adds equations from the right side of the state into the tentative solution in the left side of the state: it extends E_σ with the mapping for a variable. Because C is replaced by $rep(C)$, one variable (either x, or s if it is a variable) disappears from the right side.

The other rules can be divided into two categories. First are the branching rules (U_VAR through R_GEN), which enumerate all possibilities for deriving the entailment of some literal from C. For example, the rule U_COMP enumerates the possibilities for which a literal of the form $f(u_1, \ldots, u_n) \simeq f(s_1, \ldots, s_n)$ is entailed, which may be either due to syntactic unification, since both terms have the same top symbol, or by matching f-terms occurring in the same signature class of E^{cc}. Second are the structural rules (SPLIT, FAIL and YIELD), which create or close branches. SPLIT creates branches when there are disjunctions in the constraint. FAIL closes a branch when it is no longer possible to build on the current solution to entail the remaining constraints. YIELD closes a branch when all remaining constraints are already entailed by $E \cup E_\sigma$, with E_σ embodying a solution for the given E-ground (dis)unification problem. Theorems 3 and 4 state the correctness of the calculus.

If a branch is closed with YIELD, the respective E_σ defines a substitution $\sigma = \{x \mapsto rep(x) \mid x \in \mathrm{FV}(L)\}$. The set $\mathrm{SOLS}(E_\sigma)$ of all ground solutions extractable from E_σ is composed of substitutions σ_g which extend σ by mapping all variables in $ran(\sigma^\star)$ into ground terms in $\mathbf{T}(E \cup L)$, s.t. each σ_g is acyclic, $\sigma_g^\star$ ground and $E \models L\sigma_g^\star$.

4.2   A Strategy for the Calculus

A possible derivation strategy for CCFV, given an initial state $\varnothing \Vdash_E L$, is to apply the sequence of steps described below at each state $E_\sigma \Vdash_E C$. Let SEL be a function that selects a literal from a conjunction according to some heuristic, such as selecting first literals with less variables or literals whose top symbols have less ground signatures in E^{CC}. The result of SEL is denoted *selected literal*. Since no two rules can be applied on the same literal, the function SEL effectively enforces an order on the application of the rules.

1. *Select branch*: While C is a disjunction, apply SPLIT and consider the leftmost branch, by convention.
2. *Simplify constraint*: Apply the rule for which SEL(C) is amenable.
3. *Discard failure*: If FAIL was applied or a branching rule had the empty disjunction as a result, discard this branch and consider the next open branch.
4. *Mark success*: If all remaining constraints in the branch are entailed by $E \cup E_\sigma$, apply YIELD to mark the successful branch and then consider the next open branch.

A solution σ for the E-ground (dis)unification problem $E \models L\sigma$ can be extracted at each branch terminated by the YIELD rule (Corollary 1).

Example 3. Consider again E and L as in Example 1. The set of signature classes of E is

$$E^{\text{CC}} = \{[a], [b], [c], [f(a), f(b)], [h(a), h(c)], [g(b)]\}$$

Let SEL select the literal in C with the minimum number of variables. The derivation tree produced by CCFV for this problem is shown below. Selected literals are underlined. Disjunctions and the application of SPLIT are kept implicit to simplify the presentation, as is the handling of $x_4 \simeq g(x_5)$. Its entailment does not relate with the other literals in L and it can be handled by an early application of ASSIGN.

$$\dfrac{\varnothing \Vdash_E \underline{h(x_1) \simeq h(c)}, h(x_2) \not\simeq g(x_3), f(x_1) \simeq f(x_3)}{\mathcal{A} \qquad\qquad\qquad \mathcal{B}}\;\text{U\_COMP}$$

with $\mathcal{A}$ being

$$\dfrac{\dfrac{\dfrac{\dfrac{\dfrac{\varnothing \Vdash_E \underline{x_1 \simeq c}, h(x_2) \not\simeq g(x_3),\ f(x_1) \simeq f(x_3)}{\{x_1 \simeq c\} \Vdash_E h(x_2) \not\simeq g(x_3), \underline{f(c) \simeq f(x_3)}}\,\text{ASSIGN}}{\{x_1 \simeq c\} \Vdash_E h(x_2) \not\simeq g(x_3), \underline{x_3 \simeq c}}\,\text{U\_COMP}}{\{x_1 \simeq c, x_3 \simeq c\} \Vdash_E \underline{h(x_2) \not\simeq g(c)}}\,\text{ASSIGN}}{\{x_1 \simeq c, x_3 \simeq c\} \Vdash_E \bot}\,\text{R\_GEN}}{\{x_1 \simeq c, x_3 \simeq c\} \Vdash_E \bot}\,\text{FAIL}$$

and $\mathcal{B}$:

$$\dfrac{\varnothing \Vdash_E \underline{x_1 \simeq a}, h(x_2) \not\simeq g(x_3), f(x_1) \simeq f(x_3)}{\{x_1 \simeq a\} \Vdash_E h(x_2) \not\simeq g(x_3), \underline{f(a) \simeq f(x_3)}}\;\text{ASSIGN}$$

$$\cfrac{}{\{x_1 \simeq a\} \Vdash_E h(x_2) \not\simeq g(x_3), \underline{x_3 \simeq a} \qquad \{x_1 \simeq a\} \Vdash_E h(x_2) \not\simeq g(x_3), \underline{x_3 \simeq b}}\;\text{U\_COMP}$$

$$\dfrac{\dfrac{\{x_1 \simeq a, x_3 \simeq a\} \Vdash_E \underline{h(x_2) \not\simeq g(a)}}{\{x_1 \simeq a, x_3 \simeq a\} \Vdash_E \bot}\,\text{R\_GEN}}{\{x_1 \simeq a, x_3 \simeq a\} \Vdash_E \bot}\,\text{FAIL}$$ (left branch, ASSIGN)

$$\dfrac{\dfrac{\dfrac{\{x_1 \simeq a, x_3 \simeq b\} \Vdash_E \underline{h(x_2) \not\simeq g(b)}}{\{x_1 \simeq a, x_3 \simeq b\} \Vdash_E \underline{x_2 \simeq a}}\,\text{R\_GEN}}{\{x_1 \simeq a, x_2 \simeq a, x_3 \simeq b\} \Vdash_E \top}\,\text{ASSIGN}}{\{x_1 \simeq a, x_2 \simeq a, x_3 \simeq b\} \Vdash_E \top}\,\text{YIELD}$$ (right branch, ASSIGN)

A solution is produced by the rightmost branch of $\mathcal{B}$.

4.3   Correctness of CCFV

Theorem 2 (Termination). *All derivations in* CCFV *are finite.*

Proof (Sketch). The width of any split rule is always finite. It then suffices to show that the depth of the tree is bounded. For simplicity, but without any fundamental effect on the proof, let us assume that all rules but SPLIT apply on conjunctions. Let $d(C)$ be the sum of the depths of all occurrences of variables in the literals of the conjunction C. The ASSIGN rule decreases the number of variables of C. The FAIL and YIELD rules close a branch. All remaining rules from $E_\sigma \Vdash_E C$ to $E'_\sigma \Vdash_E C'_1 \vee \ldots \vee C'_n$ decrease d, i.e. $d(C) > d(C'_1), \ldots, d(C) > d(C'_n)$. At each node, $d(C)$ or the number of variables in C are decreasing, except at the SPLIT steps. Since no branch can contain infinite sequences of SPLIT applications, the depth is always finite. □

Lemma 1. *Given a computed solution E_σ for an E-ground (dis)unification problem $E \models L\sigma$, each $\sigma_g \in \text{SOLS}(E_\sigma)$ is an acyclic substitution such that $ran(\sigma_g) \subseteq \mathbf{T}(E \cup L)$ and $\sigma_g^\star$ is ground.*

Proof (Sketch). The proof can be found in Appendix D of [6]. □

Lemma 2 (Rules capture entailment conditions). *For each rule*

$$\frac{E_\sigma \Vdash_E C}{E'_\sigma \Vdash_E C'} \text{ R}$$

and any ground substitution σ, $E \models (\{C\} \cup E_\sigma)\sigma$ iff $E \models (\{C'\} \cup E'_\sigma)\sigma$.

Proof (Sketch). The proof can be found in Appendix D of [6]. □

Theorem 3 (Soundness). *Whenever a branch is closed with* YIELD, *every $\sigma_g \in \text{SOLS}(E_\sigma)$ is s.t. $E \models L\sigma_g^\star$.*

Proof (Sketch). Consider an arbitrary substitution $\sigma_g \in \text{SOLS}(E_\sigma)$ at the application of YIELD. Lemma 1 ensures that $\sigma_g^\star$ is ground. Thanks to the side condition of the YIELD rule and of the construction of $\sigma_g^\star$, $E \models (\{C\} \cup E_\sigma)\sigma_g^\star$ at the leaf. Then, thanks to Lemma 2, $E \models (\{C\} \cup E_\sigma)\sigma_g^\star$ also holds at the root, in which $C = L$ and $E_\sigma = \emptyset$. Thus $E \models L\sigma_g^\star$. □

Theorem 4 (Completeness). *Let σ be a solution for an E-ground (dis)unification problem $E \models L\sigma$. Then there exists a derivation tree starting on $\emptyset \Vdash_E L$ with at least one branch closed with* YIELD *s.t. $\sigma_g \in \text{SOLS}(E_\sigma)$ and $E \models L\sigma_g^\star$.*

Proof (Sketch). By Theorem 1, there is an acyclic substitution σ_g corresponding to σ such that $ran(\sigma_g) \subseteq \mathbf{T}(E \cup L)$, $\sigma_g^\star$ is ground and $E \models L\sigma_g^\star$. Lemma 2 ensures that all rules in CCFV preserve the entailment conditions according to ground substitutions, therefore there is a branch in the derivation tree starting from $\emptyset \Vdash_E L$ whose leaf is $E_\sigma \Vdash_E \top$ and $\sigma_g \in \text{SOLS}(E_\sigma)$. □

Corollary 1 (CCFV decides E-ground (dis)unification). *Any derivation strategy based on the CCFV calculus is a decision procedure to find all solutions σ for the E-ground (dis)unification problem $E \models L\sigma$.*

5   Relation to Instantiation Techniques

Here we discuss how different instantiation techniques for evaluating a candidate model $E \cup Q$ can be related with E-ground (dis)unification and thus integrated with CCFV.

5.1   Trigger Based Instantiation

The most common instantiation technique in SMT solving is a heuristic one: its search is based solely on E-matching of selected triggers [12,17,26], without further semantic criteria. A *trigger* T for a quantified formula $\forall \mathbf{x}.\psi \in Q$ is a set of terms $f_1(\mathbf{s}_1), \ldots, f_n(\mathbf{s}_n) \in \mathbf{T}(\psi)$ s.t. $\{\mathbf{x}\} \subseteq \mathrm{FV}(f_1(\mathbf{s}_1)) \cup \cdots \cup \mathrm{FV}(f_n(\mathbf{s}_n))$. Instantiations are determined by E-matching all terms in T with terms in $\mathbf{T}(E)$, such that resulting substitutions allow instantiating $\forall \mathbf{x}.\psi$ into ground formulas. Computing such substitutions amounts to solving the E-ground (dis)unification problem

$$E \models (f_1(\mathbf{s}_1) \simeq y_1 \wedge \cdots \wedge f_n(\mathbf{s}_n) \simeq y_n)\,\sigma$$

with the further restriction that σ is acyclic, $ran(\sigma) \subseteq \mathbf{T}(E \cup L)$ and σ is ground. This forces each y_i to be grounded into a term in $\mathbf{T}(E)$, thus enumerating all possibilities for E-matching $f_i(\mathbf{s}_i)$.[2] The desired instantiations are obtained by restricting the found solutions to $\mathbf{x}$.

Example 4. Consider the sets $E = \{f(a) \simeq g(b),\ h(a) \simeq b, f(a) \simeq f(c)\}$ and $Q = \{\forall x.\ f(x) \not\simeq g(h(x))\}$. Triggers from Q are $T_1 = \{f(x)\}$, $T_2 = \{h(x)\}$, $T_3 = \{f(x), g(h(x))\}$ and so on. The instantiations from those triggers are derived from the solutions yielded by CCFV for the respective problems:

- $E \models (f(x) \simeq y)\sigma$, solved by substitutions $\sigma_1 = \{y \mapsto f(a), x \mapsto a\}$ and $\sigma_2 = \{y \mapsto f(c), x \mapsto c\}$
- $E \models (h(x) \simeq y)\sigma$, solved by $\sigma = \{y \mapsto h(a), x \mapsto a\}$
- $E \models (f(x) \simeq y_1 \wedge g(h(x)) \simeq y_2)\sigma$, by $\sigma = \{y_1 \mapsto f(a), y_2 \mapsto g(b), x \mapsto a\}$

Discarding Entailed Instances. Trigger-based instantiation may produce instances which are already entailed by the ground model. Such instances most probably will not contribute to the solving, so they should be discarded. Checking this, however, is not straightforward with pre-processing techniques. CCFV, on the other hand, allows it by simply checking, given an instantiation σ for a quantified formula $\forall \mathbf{x}.\psi$, whether there is a literal $\ell \in \psi$ s.t. $E \cup E_\sigma \models \ell$, with $E_\sigma = \{x \simeq x\sigma \mid x \in dom(\sigma)\}$.

---

[2] For CCFV to generate such solutions it is sufficient to add the side condition to ASSIGN that s is a variable or a ground term and to remove the side condition of U_VAR. This will lead to the application of U_VAR in each $f_i(\mathbf{s}_1) \simeq y_i$.

5.2   Conflict Based Instantiation

A goal-oriented instantiation technique was introduced by Reynolds et al. [24] to provide fewer and more meaningful instances. Quantified formulas are evaluated, independently, in search for *conflicting instances*: for each quantified formula $\forall \mathbf{x}.\psi \in \mathcal{Q}$, only instances $\psi\sigma$ for which $E \cup \psi\sigma$ is unsatisfiable are derived. Such instances force the derivation of a new candidate model $E \cup \mathcal{Q}$ for the formula. Finding a conflicting instance amounts to solving the E-ground (dis)unification problem

$$E \models \neg\psi\sigma, \text{ for some } \forall \mathbf{x}.\psi \in \mathcal{Q}$$

since $\neg\psi$ is a conjunction of equality literals. Differently from the algorithm shown in [24], CCFV finds all conflicting instantiations for a given quantified formula.

Example 5. Let E and $\mathcal{Q}$ be as in Example 4. Applying CCFV in the problem

$$E \models (f(x) \simeq g(h(x)))\, \sigma$$

leads to the sole conflicting instantiation $\sigma = \{x \mapsto a\}$.

Propagating Equalities. As discussed in [24], even when the search for conflicting instances fails it is still possible to "propagate" equalities. Given some $\neg\psi = \ell_1 \wedge \cdots \wedge \ell_n$, let σ be a ground substitution s.t. $E \models \ell_1\sigma \wedge \cdots \wedge \ell_{k-1}\sigma$ and all remaining literals $\ell_k\sigma, \ldots, \ell_n\sigma$ not entailed are ground disequalities with $(\mathbf{T}(\ell_k) \cup \cdots \cup \mathbf{T}(\ell_n)) \subseteq \mathbf{T}(E)$. The instantiation $\forall \mathbf{x}.\psi \rightarrow \psi\sigma$ introduces a disjunction of equalities constraining $\mathbf{T}(E)$. CCFV can generate such propagating substitutions if the side conditions of FAIL and YIELD are relaxed w.r.t. ground disequalities whose terms occur in $\mathbf{T}(E)$ and originally had variables: the former is not applied based on them and the latter is if all other literals are entailed.

Example 6. Consider $E = \{f(a) \simeq t, t' \simeq g(a)\}$ and $\forall x.\ f(x) \not\simeq t \vee f(x) \simeq g(x)$. When applying CCFV in the problem

$$E \models (f(x) \simeq t \wedge f(x) \not\simeq g(x))\, \sigma$$

to entail the first literal a candidate solution $E_\sigma = \{x \simeq a\}$ is produced. The second literal would then be normalized to $f(a) \not\simeq g(a)$, which would lead to the application of FAIL, since it is not entailed by E. However, as it is a disequality whose terms are in $\mathbf{T}(E)$ and originally had variables, the rule applied is YIELD instead. The resulting substitution $\sigma = \{x \mapsto a\}$ leads to propagating the equality $f(a) \simeq g(a)$, which merges two classes previously different in E^{cc}.

5.3   Model Based Instantiation (MBQI)

A complete instantiation technique was introduced by Ge and de Moura [19]. The set E is extended into a total model, each quantified formula is evaluated in this total model, and conflicting instances are generated. The successive rounds of instantiation either lead to unsatisfiability or, when no conflicting instance is generated, to satisfiability with a concrete model. Here we follow the model construction guidelines by Reynolds et al. [25].

A distinguished term e^τ is associated to each sort $\tau \in \mathcal{S}$. For each $f \in \mathcal{F}$ with sort $\langle \tau_1, \ldots, \tau_n, \tau \rangle$ a *default value* ξ_f is defined such that

$$\xi_f = \begin{cases} f(t_1, \ldots, t_n) \in \mathbf{T}(E) & \text{if } [t_1] = [e^{\tau_1}], \ldots, [t_n] = [e^{\tau_n}] \\ \text{some } t \in \mathbf{T}(E) & \text{otherwise} \end{cases}$$

The extension E_{TOT} is built s.t. all fresh ground terms which might be considered when evaluating $\mathcal{Q}$ are in its congruence closure, according to the respective default values; and all terms in $\mathbf{T}(E)$ not asserted equal are explicitly asserted disequal, i.e.

$$E_{\text{TOT}} = E \cup \bigcup\nolimits_{t_1, t_2 \in \mathbf{T}(E)} \{t_1 \not\simeq t_2 \mid E \not\models t_1 \simeq t_2\}$$
$$\bigcup\nolimits_{\forall \mathbf{x}.\psi \in \mathcal{Q}, t \in \mathbf{T}(E)} \left\{ f(\mathbf{s})\sigma \simeq \xi_f \;\middle|\; \begin{array}{l} \sigma = \{\mathbf{x} \mapsto \mathbf{t}\}, f(\mathbf{s}) \in \mathbf{T}(\psi) \text{ and} \\ f(\mathbf{s})\sigma \text{ is not in the CC of } E. \end{array} \right\}$$

As before, finding conflicting instances amounts to solving the E-ground (dis)unification problem

$$E_{\text{TOT}} \models \neg\psi\sigma, \text{ for some } \forall\mathbf{x}.\psi \in \mathcal{Q}$$

Example 7. Let $E = \{f(a) \simeq g(b), h(a) \simeq b\}$, $\mathcal{Q} = \{\forall x.\, f(x) \not\simeq g(x), \forall xy.\, \psi\}$ and $e = a$, with all terms having the same sort. The computed default values of the function symbols are $\xi_f = f(a), \xi_g = a, \xi_h = h(a)$. For simplicity, the extension E_{TOT} is shown explicitly only for $\forall x.\, f(x) \not\simeq g(x)$,

$$E_{\text{TOT}} = E \cup \{a \not\simeq b, a \not\simeq f(a), b \not\simeq f(a)\}$$
$$\cup \{f(b) \simeq f(a), f(f(a)) \simeq f(a), g(a) \simeq a, g(f(a)) \simeq a\} \cup \{\ldots\}$$

Applying CCFV in

$$\{\ldots, f(a) \simeq g(b), f(b) \simeq f(a), \ldots\} \models f(x) \simeq g(x)\sigma$$

leads to a conflicting instance with $\sigma = \{x \mapsto b\}$. Notice that it is not necessary to explicitly build E_{TOT}, which can be quite large. Terms can be defined lazily as they are required by CCFV for building potential solutions.

6   Implementation and Experiments

CCFV has been implemented in the veriT [11] and CVC4 [7] solvers. As is common in SMT solvers, they make use of an E-graph to represent the set of signature classes E^{CC} and efficiently check ground entailment.[3] Indexing techniques for fast

---

[3] Currently the ground congruence closure procedures are not closed under entailment w.r.t. disequalities. E.g. $g(f(a), h(b)) \not\simeq g(f(b), h(a)) \in E$ does not lead to the addition of $a \not\simeq b$ to the data structure. A complete implementation of CCFV requires the ground congruence closure to entail all entailed disequalities.

retrieval of candidates are paramount for a practical procedure, so E^{cc} is indexed by top symbols. Each function symbol points to all their related signatures. They are kept sorted by congruence classes to allow binary search when retrieving all signatures with a given top symbol congruent to a given term. To quickly discard classes without signatures with a given top symbol, bit masks are associated to congruence classes: each symbol is assigned an arbitrary bit, and the mask for the class is the set of all bits of the top symbols. Another important optimization is to minimize E, since the candidate model $E \cup Q$ produced by the SAT solver and guiding the instantiation is generally not minimal. A minimal partial model (a *prime implicant*) for the CNF is computed in linear time [16], and this model is further reduced to circumvent the effect of the CNF transformation, using a process similar to the one described by de Moura and Bjørner [12] for *relevancy*.

During rule application, matching a term $f(\mathbf{u})$ with a ground term $f(\mathbf{t})$ fails unless all the ground arguments are pairwise congruent. Thus after an assignment, if an argument of a term $f(\mathbf{u})$ in a branching constraint becomes ground, it can be checked whether there is a ground term $f(\mathbf{t}) \in \mathbf{T}(E)$ s.t., for every ground argument u_i, $E \models u_i \simeq t_i$. If no such term exists and $f(\mathbf{u})$ is not in a literal amenable for U_COMP, the branch can be *eagerly discarded*. For this technique, a dedicated index for each function symbol f maps tuples of pairs, with a ground term and a position, $\langle (t_1, i_1), \ldots, (t_k, i_k) \rangle$ to all signatures $f(t'_1, \ldots, t'_n)$ in E^{cc} s.t. $E \models t_1 \simeq t'_{i_1}, \ldots, E \models t_k \simeq t'_{i_k}$, i.e. all signatures whose arguments, in the respective positions, are congruent with the given ground terms.

Experiments. Here we evaluate the impact of optimizations and instantiation techniques based on CCFV over previous versions and compare them against the state-of-the-art instantiation based solver Z3 [14]. Different configurations are identified in this section according to which techniques and algorithms they have activated:

t: trigger instantiation through CCFV;
c: conflict based instantiation through CCFV;
e: optimization for eagerly discarding branches with unmatchable applications;
d: discards already entailed trigger based instances (as in Sect. 5.1)

The configuration **verit** refers to the previous version of veriT, which only offered support for quantified formulas through naïve trigger instantiation, without further optimizations. The configuration **cvc** refers to version 1.5 of CVC4, which applies **t** and **c** by default, as well as propagation of equalities. Both implementations of CCFV include efficient term indexing and apply a simple selection heuristic, checking ground and reflexive literals first but otherwise considering the conjunction of constraints as a queue. The evaluation was made on the UF, UFLIA, UFLRA and UFIDL categories of SMT-LIB [9], with 10 495 benchmarks annotated as *unsatisfiable*, mostly stemming for verification and ITP platforms. The categories with bit vectors and non-linear arithmetic are currently not supported by veriT and in those in which uninterpreted functions are not predominant the techniques shown here are not as effective. Our experiments were conducted using machines with 2 CPUs Intel Xeon E5-2630 v3,

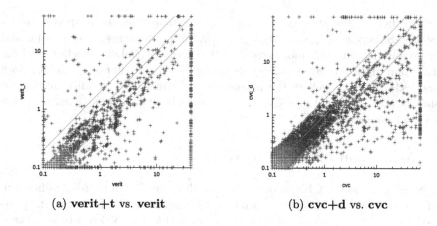

(a) **verit+t** vs. **verit**   (b) **cvc+d** vs. **cvc**

Fig. 1. Improvements in veriT and CVC4

8 cores/CPU, 126 GB RAM, 2x558 GB HDD. The timeout was set for 30 s, since our goal is evaluating SMT solvers as back-ends of verification and ITP platforms, which require fast answers.

Figure 1 exhibits an important impact of CCFV and the techniques and optimizations built on top of it. **verit+t** performs much better than **verit**, solely due to CCFV. **cvc+d** improves significantly over **cvc**, exhibiting the advantage of techniques based on the entailment checking features of CCFV. The comparison between the different configurations of veriT and CVC4 with the SMT solver Z3 (version 4.4.2) is summarized in Table 2, excluding categories whose problems are trivially solved by all systems, which leaves 8 701 problems for consideration. **verit+tc** shows further improvements, solving approximately the same number of problems as Z3, although mostly because of the better performance on the *sledgehammer* benchmarks, containing less theory symbols. It also

Table 2. Instantiation based SMT solvers on SMT-LIB benchmarks

Logic	Class	Z3	cvc+d	cvc+e	cvc	verit+tc	verit+t	verit
UF	grasshopper	418	411	420	415	**430**	418	413
	sledgehammer	1249	1438	**1456**	1428	1265	1134	1066
UFIDL	all	**62**	**62**	**62**	**62**	58	58	58
UFLIA	boogie	**852**	844	834	801	705	660	661
	sexpr	**26**	12	11	11	7	5	5
	grasshopper	341	322	326	319	**357**	340	335
	sledgehammer	1581	1944	**1953**	1929	1783	1620	1569
	simplify	**831**	766	706	705	803	735	690
	simplify2	**2337**	2330	2292	2286	2304	2291	2177
	Total	7697	**8129**	8060	7956	7712	7261	6916

performs best in the *grasshopper* families, stemming from the heap verification tool GRASShopper [23]. Considering the overall performance, both **cvc+d** and **cvc+e** solve significantly more problems than **cvc**, specially in benchmarks from verification platforms, approaching the performance of Z3 in these families. Both these techniques, as well as the propagation of equalities, are fairly important points in the performance of CVC4, so their implementation is a clear direction for improvements in veriT.

7   Conclusion and Future Work

We have introduced CCFV, a decision procedure for E-ground (dis)unification, and shown how the main instantiation techniques of SMT solving may be based on it. Our experimental evaluation shows that CCFV leads to significant improvements in the solvers CVC4 and veriT, making the former surpass the state-of-the-art in instantiation based SMT solving and the latter competitive in several benchmark libraries. The calculus presented is very general, allowing for different strategies and optimizations, as discussed in previous sections.

A direction for improvement is to use *lemma learning* in CCFV, in a similar manner as SAT solvers do. When a branch fails to produce a solution and is discarded, analyzing the literals which led to the conflict can allow *backjump* rather than simple backtracking, thus further reducing the solution search space. The *Complementary Congruence Closure* introduced by Backeman and Rümmer [4] could be extended to perform such an analysis.

Like other main instantiation techniques in SMT, the framework here focuses on the theory of equality only. Extensions to first-order theories such as arithmetic are left for future work. The implementation of MBQI based on CCFV, whose theoretical suitability we outlined, is left for future work as well. Another possible extension of CCFV is to handle rigid E-unification, so it could be applied in techniques such as BREU [5]. This amounts to have non-ground equalities in E, so it is not trivial. It would, however, allow integrating an efficient goal-oriented procedure into E-unification based calculi.

Acknowledgments. We are grateful to David Déharbe for his help with the implementation of CCFV and to Jasmin Blanchette for suggesting textual improvements. Experiments presented in this paper were carried out using the Grid'5000 testbed, supported by a scientific interest group hosted by Inria and including CNRS, RENATER and several universities as well as other organizations (https://www.grid5000.fr).

References

1. Baader, F., Nipkow, T.: Term Rewriting and All That. Cambridge University Press, New York (1998)
2. Baader, F., Snyder, W.: Unification theory. In: Robinson, J.A., Voronkov, A., (eds) Handbook of Automated Reasoning, pp. 445–532. Elsevier and MIT Press (2001)
3. Bachmair, L., Ganzinger, H.: Rewrite-based equational theorem proving with selection and simplification. J. Logic Comput. 4(3), 217–247 (1994)

4. Backeman, P., Rümmer, P.: Efficient algorithms for bounded rigid E-unification. In: Nivelle, H. (ed.) TABLEAUX 2015. LNCS (LNAI), vol. 9323, pp. 70–85. Springer, Heidelberg (2015). doi:10.1007/978-3-319-24312-2_6
5. Backeman, P., Rümmer, P.: Theorem proving with bounded rigid E-unification. In: Felty, A.P., Middeldorp, A. (eds.) CADE 2015. LNCS (LNAI), vol. 9195, pp. 572–587. Springer, Heidelberg (2015). doi:10.1007/978-3-319-21401-6_39
6. Barbosa, H., Fontaine, P., Reynolds, A.: Congruence closure with free variables. Technical report, Inria (2016). https://hal.inria.fr/hal-01442691
7. Barrett, C., Conway, C.L., Deters, M., Hadarean, L., Jovanović, D., King, T., Reynolds, A., Tinelli, C.: CVC4. In: Gopalakrishnan, G., Qadeer, S. (eds.) CAV 2011. LNCS, vol. 6806, pp. 171–177. Springer, Heidelberg (2011). doi:10.1007/978-3-642-22110-1_14
8. Barrett, C., Sebastiani, R., Seshia, S., Tinelli, C.: Satisfiability modulo theories. In: Biere, A., Heule, M.J.H., van Maaren, H., Walsh, T. (eds.) Handbook of Satisfiability. Frontiers in Artificial Intelligence and Applications, vol. 185, pp. 825–885. IOS Press, Amsterdam (2009)
9. Barrett, C., Stump, A., Tinelli, C.: The SML-LIB standard: version 2.0. In: Gupta, A., Kroening, D. (eds) International Workshop on Satisfiability Modulo Theories (SMT) (2010)
10. Beckert, B.: Ridig E-unification. In: Bibel, W., Schimidt, P.H. (eds.) Automated Deduction: A Basis for Applications. Foundations: Calculi and Methods, vol. 1. Kluwer Academic Publishers, Dordrecht (1998)
11. Bouton, T., de Oliveira, D.C.B., Fontaine, P.: veriT: an open, trustable and efficient SMT-solver. In: Schmidt, R.A. (ed.) CADE 2009. LNCS (LNAI), vol. 5663, pp. 151–156. Springer, Heidelberg (2009). doi:10.1007/978-3-642-02959-2_12
12. de Moura, L., Bjørner, N.: Efficient E-matching for SMT solvers. In: Pfenning, F. (ed.) CADE 2007. LNCS (LNAI), vol. 4603, pp. 183–198. Springer, Heidelberg (2007). doi:10.1007/978-3-540-73595-3_13
13. de Moura, L., Bjørner, N.: Engineering DPLL(T) + saturation. In: Armando, A., Baumgartner, P., Dowek, G. (eds.) IJCAR 2008. LNCS (LNAI), vol. 5195, pp. 475–490. Springer, Heidelberg (2008). doi:10.1007/978-3-540-71070-7_40
14. de Moura, L., Bjørner, N.: Z3: an efficient SMT solver. In: Ramakrishnan, C.R., Rehof, J. (eds.) TACAS 2008. LNCS, vol. 4963, pp. 337–340. Springer, Heidelberg (2008). doi:10.1007/978-3-540-78800-3_24
15. Degtyarev, A., Voronkov, A.: Equality reasoning in sequent-based calculi. In: Robinson, J.A., Voronkov, A. (eds.) Handbook of Automated Reasoning, pp. 611–706. Elsevier, Amsterdam (2001)
16. Déharbe, D., Fontaine, P., Le Berre, D., Mazure, B.: Computing prime implicants. In: Formal Methods in Computer-Aided Design (FMCAD), pp. 46–52. IEEE (2013)
17. Detlefs, D., Nelson, G., Saxe, J.B.: Simplify: a theorem prover for program checking. J. ACM **52**(3), 365–473 (2005)
18. Fitting, M.: First-Order Logic and Automated Theorem Proving. Springer, New York (1990)
19. Ge, Y., de Moura, L.: Complete instantiation for quantified formulas in satisfiabiliby modulo theories. In: Bouajjani, A., Maler, O. (eds.) CAV 2009. LNCS, vol. 5643, pp. 306–320. Springer, Heidelberg (2009). doi:10.1007/978-3-642-02658-4_25
20. Goubault, J.: A rule-based algorithm for rigid E-unification. In: Gottlob, G., Leitsch, A., Mundici, D. (eds.) KGC 1993. LNCS, vol. 713, pp. 202–210. Springer, Heidelberg (1993). doi:10.1007/BFb0022569
21. Nelson, G., Oppen, D.C.: Fast decision procedures based on congruence closure. J. ACM **27**(2), 356–364 (1980)

22. Nieuwenhuis, R., Oliveras, A.: Fast congruence closure, extensions. Inf. Comput. **205**(4), 557–580 (2007). Special Issue: 16th International Conference on Rewriting Techniques and Applications

23. Piskac, R., Wies, T., Zufferey, D.: GRASShopper - complete heap verification with mixed specifications. In: Ábrahám, E., Havelund, K. (eds.) TACAS 2014. LNCS, vol. 8413, pp. 124–139. Springer, Heidelberg (2014). doi:10.1007/978-3-642-54862-8_9

24. Reynolds, A., Tinelli, C., de Moura, L.: Finding conflicting instances of quantified formulas in SMT. In: Formal Methods in Computer-Aided Design (FMCAD), pp. 195–202. FMCAD Inc (2014)

25. Reynolds, A., Tinelli, C., Goel, A., Krstić, S., Deters, M., Barrett, C.: Quantifier instantiation techniques for finite model finding in SMT. In: Bonacina, M.P. (ed.) CADE 2013. LNCS (LNAI), vol. 7898, pp. 377–391. Springer, Heidelberg (2013). doi:10.1007/978-3-642-38574-2_26

26. Rümmer, P.: E-matching with free variables. In: Bjørner, N., Voronkov, A. (eds.) LPAR 2012. LNCS, vol. 7180, pp. 359–374. Springer, Heidelberg (2012). doi:10.1007/978-3-642-28717-6_28

27. Tiwari, A., Bachmair, L., Ruess, H.: Rigid E-unification revisited. In: McAllester, D. (ed.) CADE 2000. LNCS (LNAI), vol. 1831, pp. 220–234. Springer, Heidelberg (2000). doi:10.1007/10721959_17

On Optimization Modulo Theories, MaxSMT and Sorting Networks

Roberto Sebastiani and Patrick Trentin$^{(\boxtimes)}$

DISI, University of Trento, Trento, Italy
`patrick.trentin@unitn.it`

Abstract. Optimization Modulo Theories (OMT) is an extension of SMT which allows for finding models that optimize given objectives. (Partial weighted) MaxSMT–or equivalently OMT with Pseudo-Boolean objective functions, OMT+PB– is a very-relevant strict subcase of OMT. We classify existing approaches for MaxSMT or OMT+PB in two groups: MaxSAT-*based* approaches exploit the efficiency of state-of-the-art MaxSAT solvers, but they are specific-purpose and not always applicable; *OMT-based* approaches are general-purpose, but they suffer from intrinsic inefficiencies on MaxSMT/OMT+PB problems.

We identify a major source of such inefficiencies, and we address it by enhancing OMT by means of bidirectional sorting networks. We implemented this idea on top of the OptiMathSAT OMT solver. We run an extensive empirical evaluation on a variety of problems, comparing MaxSAT-based and OMT-based techniques, with and without sorting networks, implemented on top of OptiMathSAT and νZ. The results support the effectiveness of this idea, and provide interesting insights about the different approaches.

1 Introduction

Satisfiability Modulo Theories (SMT) is the problem of deciding the satisfiability of first-order formulas with respect to first-order theories [5,27] (e.g., the theory of linear arithmetic over the rationals, $\mathcal{LRA}$). In the last decade, SMT solvers –powered by very efficient Conflict-Driven-Clause-Learning (CDCL) engines for Boolean Satisfiability [16] combined with a collection of $\mathcal{T}$-Solvers, each one handling a different theory $\mathcal{T}$– have risen to be a pervasive and indispensable tool for dealing with many problems of industrial interest, e.g. formal verification of hardware and software systems, resource planning, temporal reasoning and scheduling of real-time embedded systems.

Optimization Modulo Theories (OMT) is an extension of SMT, which allows for finding models that make a given objective optimum through a combination of SMT and optimization procedures [8,9,11,12,14,15,21,28–31]. Latest advancements in OMT have further broadened its horizon by making it incremental [8,31] and by supporting objectives defined in other theories than linear arithmetic (e.g. Bit-Vectors) [8,9,17]. Moreover, OMT has been extended with the capability of handling multiple objectives at the same time either

© Springer-Verlag GmbH Germany 2017
A. Legay and T. Margaria (Eds.): TACAS 2017, Part II, LNCS 10206, pp. 231–248, 2017.
DOI: 10.1007/978-3-662-54580-5_14

independently (aka boxed optimization) or through their linear, min-max/ max-min, lexicographic or Pareto combination [8,9,31].

We focus on an important strict sub-case of OMT, (partial weighted)[1] MaxSMT –or equivalently OMT with Pseudo-Boolean (PB) objective functions [25], OMT+PB– which is the problem of finding a model for an input formula which both satisfies all *hard* clauses and maximizes the cumulative weight of all *soft* clauses satisfied by the model [11,12,21]. We identify two main approaches which have been adopted in the literature (see related work). One specific-purpose approach, which we call MaxSAT-*based*, is to embed some MaxSAT engine within the SMT solver itself, and use it in combination with dedicated $\mathcal{T}$-*solvers* [3,8,9] or with SMT solvers used as blackboxes [12]. One general-purpose approach, which we call *OMT-based*, is to encode MaxSMT/OMT+PB into general OMT with linear-real-arithmetic cost functions [29].

We compare the two approaches and notice the following facts.

The MaxSAT-based approach can exploit the efficiency of state-of-the-art MaxSAT procedures and solvers. Unfortunately it suffers from some limitations that make it impractical or inapplicable in some cases. First, to the best of our knowledge, available MaxSAT engines deal with integer weights only; some applications, e.g., *(Machine) Learning Modulo Theories, LMT* [34] –a hybrid Machine Learning approach in which OMT is used as an oracle for Support Vector Machines [34]– may require the weight of soft constraints to be high-precision rational values.[2] (In this context, it is preferable not to round the weights associated with soft-clauses since it affects the accuracy of the Machine Learning approach; also multiplying all rational coefficients for their lowest common multiple of the denominators is not practical, because such values tend to become huge.) Second, a MaxSAT engine cannot be directly used when dealing with an OMT problem with multiple-independent objectives that need to be optimized at the same time [15],[3] or when the objective function is given by combinations of PB and arithmetic terms –like, e.g., for Linear Generalized Disjunctive Programming problems [26,29] or LMT problems [34].

The OMT-based approach does not suffer from the above limitations, because it exploits the infinite-precision linear-arithmetic package on the rationals of OMT solvers, and it treats PB functions as any other arithmetic functions. Nevertheless this approach may result in low performances when dealing with MaxSMT/OMT+PB problems.

We analyze the latter fact and identify a major source of inefficiency by noticing that the presence of same-weight soft clauses entails the existence of symmetries in the solution space that may lead to a combinatorial explosion of the partial truth assignments generated by the CDCL engine during the optimization search. To cope with this fact, we introduce and describe a solution

---

[1] Hereafter, when speaking of MaxSAT or MaxSMT, we keep "partial weighted" implicit.

[2] For example, $\frac{1799972218749879}{2251799813685248}$ is a sample weight value from problems in [34].

[3] One could run a MaxSAT-based search separately on each objective, but doing this he/she would loose the benefits of boxed optimization, see [8,15,31].

based on (bidirectional) sorting networks [1, 4, 32]. We implemented this idea within the OPTIMATHSAT OMT solver [30].

We run an empirical evaluation on a large amount of problems comparing MAXSAT-based and OMT-based techniques, with and without sorting networks, implemented on top of OPTIMATHSAT [30] and νZ [9]. The results are summarized as follows.

(a) Comparing MAXSAT-based wrt. OMT-based approaches on problems where the former are applicable, it turns out that the former provide much better performances, in particular when adopting the maximum-resolution [8, 18] MAXSAT engine.

(b) Evaluating the benefits of bidirectional sorting-network encodings, it turns out that they improve significantly the performances of OMT-based approaches, and often also of MAXSAT-based ones.

(c) Comparing νZ and OPTIMATHSAT, it turns out that the former performed better on MAXSAT-based approaches, whilst the latter performed seomtimes equivalently and sometimes significantly better on OMT-based ones, in particular when enhanced by the sorting-network encoding.

Related Work. The idea of MaxSMT and of optimization in SMT was first introduced by Nieuwenhuis & Oliveras [21], who presented a general logical framework of "SMT with progressively stronger theories" (e.g., where the theory is progressively strengthened by every new approximation of the minimum cost), and presented implementations for MaxSMT based on this framework. Cimatti et al. [11] introduced the notion of "Theory of Costs" $\mathcal{C}$ to handle Pseudo-Boolean (PB) cost functions and constraints by an ad-hoc "$\mathcal{C}$-solver" in the standard lazy SMT schema, and implemented a variant of MathSAT tool able to handle SMT with PB constraints and to minimize PB cost functions. Cimatti et al. [12] presented a "modular" approach for MaxSMT, combining a lazy SMT solver with a MaxSAT solver, where the SMT solver is used as an oracle generating $\mathcal{T}$-lemmas that are then learned by the MAXSAT solver so as to progressively narrow the search space toward the optimal solution.

Sebastiani and Tomasi [28, 29] introduced a wider notion of optimization in SMT, namely *Optimization Modulo Theories (OMT) with $\mathcal{LRA}$ cost functions*, OMT($\mathcal{LRA} \cup \mathcal{T}$), which allows for finding models minimizing some $\mathcal{LRA}$ cost term $-\mathcal{T}$ being some (possibly empty) stably-infinite theory s.t. $\mathcal{T}$ and $\mathcal{LRA}$ are signature-disjoint– and presented novel OMT($\mathcal{LRA} \cup \mathcal{T}$) tools which combine standard SMT with LP minimization techniques. ($\mathcal{T}$ can also be a combination of Theories $\bigcup_i \mathcal{T}_i$.) Eventually, OMT($\mathcal{LRA} \cup \mathcal{T}$) has been extended so that to handle costs on the integers, incremental OMT, multi-objective, and lexicographic OMT and Pareto-optimality [8, 9, 14, 15, 30, 31]. To the best of our knowledge only four OMT solvers are currently implemented: BCLT [14], νZ (aka Z3OPT) [8, 9], OPTIMATHSAT [30, 31], and SYMBA [15]. Remarkably, BCLT, νZ and OPTIMATHSAT currently implement also specialized procedures for MaxSMT, leveraging to SMT level state-of-the-art MaxSAT procedures; in addition, νZ features a Pseudo-Boolean $\mathcal{T}$-*solver* which can generate sorting circuits on demand for Pseudo-Boolean inequalities featuring sums with small coefficients when a Pseudo-Boolean inequality is used some times for unit propagation/conflicts [7,9].

Content. The paper is structured as follows. Section 2 briefly reviews the background; Sect. 3 describes the source of inefficiency arising when MAXSMT is encoded in OMT as in [29]; Sect. 4 illustrates a possible solution based on bidirectional sorting networks; in Sect. 5 we provide empirical evidence of the benefits of this approach on two applications of OMT interest. Section 6 provides some conclusions with some considerations on the future work.

2   Background

We assume the reader is familiar with the main theoretical and algorithmic concepts in SAT and SMT solving (see [5,16]). Optimization Modulo Theories (OMT) is an extension of SMT which addresses the problem of finding a model for an input formula φ which is optimal wrt. some objective function obj [21,28]. The basic minimization scheme implemented in state-of-the-art OMT solvers, known as *linear-search* scheme [21,28], requires solving an SMT problem with a solution space that is progressively tightened by means of unit linear constraints in the form $\neg(ub_i \leq obj)$, where ub_i is the value of obj that corresponds to the optimum model of the most-recently found truth assignment μ_i s.t. $\mu_i \models \varphi$. The ub_i value is computed by means of a specialized optimization procedure embedded within the $\mathcal{T}$-*solver* which, taken as input a pair $\langle \mu, obj \rangle$, returns the optimal value ub of obj for such μ. The OMT search terminates when such procedure finds that obj is unbounded or when the SMT search is UNSAT, in which case the latest value of obj (if any) and its associated model M_i is returned as optimal solution value. (Alternatively, binary-search schemes can also be used [28,29].)

An important subcase of OMT is that of MAXSMT, which is a pair $\langle \varphi_h, \varphi_s \rangle$, where φ_h denotes the set of "hard" $\mathcal{T}$-clauses, φ_s is a set of positive-weighted "soft" $\mathcal{T}$-clauses, and the goal is to find the maximum-weight set of $\mathcal{T}$-clauses ψ_s, $\psi_s \subseteq \varphi_s$, s.t. $\varphi_h \cup \psi_s$ is $\mathcal{T}$-satisfiable [3,11,12,21]. As described in [29], MAXSMT $\langle \varphi_h, \varphi_s \rangle$ can be encoded into a general OMT problem with a Pseudo-Boolean objective: first introduce a fresh Boolean variable A_i for each soft-constraint $C_i \in \varphi_s$ as follows

$$\varphi^* \stackrel{\text{def}}{=} \varphi_h \cup \bigcup_{C_i \in \varphi_s} \{(A_i \vee C_i)\}; \quad obj \stackrel{\text{def}}{=} \sum_{C_i \in \varphi_s} w_i A_i \tag{1}$$

and then encode the problem into OMT as a pair $\langle \varphi, obj \rangle$ where φ is defined as

$$\varphi \stackrel{\text{def}}{=} \varphi^* \wedge \bigwedge_i ((\neg A_i \vee (x_i = w_i)) \wedge (A_i \vee (x_i = 0))) \wedge \tag{2}$$

$$\bigwedge_i ((0 \leq x_i) \wedge (x_i \leq w_i)) \wedge \tag{3}$$

$$(obj = \sum_i x_i), \quad x_i, obj \ fresh. \tag{4}$$

Notice that, although redundant from a logical perspective, the constraints in (3) serve the important purpose of allowing early-pruning calls to the $\mathcal{LRA}$-Solver (see [5]) to detect a possible $\mathcal{LRA}$ inconsistency among the current partial truth assignment over variables A_i and linear cuts in the form $\neg(ub \leq obj)$ that are pushed on the formula stack by the OMT solver during the minimization of obj. To this extent, the presence of such constraints improves performance significantly.

3   Problems with OMT-based Approaches

Consider first the case of a MAXSMT-derived OMT problem as in (1) s.t. all weights are identical, that is: let $\langle \varphi, obj \rangle$ be an OMT problem, where $obj = \sum_{i=1}^{n} w \cdot A_i$, where the A_is are Boolean variables, and let μ be a satisfiable truth assignment found by the OMT solver during the minimization of obj. Given $A_T = \{A_i | \mu \models A_i\}$ and $k = |A_T|$, then the upper bound value of obj in μ is $ub = w \cdot k$. As described in [28,29], the OMT solver adds a unit clause in the form $\neg(ub \leq obj)$ in order to (1) remove the current truth assignment μ from the feasible search space and (2) seek for another μ' which improves the current upper-bound value ub. Importantly, the unit clause $\neg(ub \leq obj)$ does not only prune the current truth assignment μ from the feasible search space, but it also makes inconsistent any other (partial) truth assignment μ' which sets exactly k (or more) A_i variables to True. Thus, each new unit clause in this form prunes $\gamma = \binom{n}{k}$ truth assignments from the search space, where γ is the number of possible permutations of μ over the variables A_i. A dual case occurs when some lower-bound unit clause $\neg(obj \leq lb)$ is learned (e.g., in a binary-search step, see [28]).

Unfortunately, the inconsistency of a truth assignment μ' which sets exactly k variables to True wrt. a unit clause $\neg(ub \leq obj)$, where $ub = w \cdot k$, cannot be determined by simple Boolean Constraint Propagation (BCP). In fact, $\neg(ub \leq obj)$ being a $\mathcal{LRA}$ term, the CDCL engine is totally oblivious to this inconsistency until when the $\mathcal{T}$-solver for linear rational arithmetic ($\mathcal{LRA}$-Solver) is invoked, and a conflict clause is generated. Therefore, since the $\mathcal{LRA}$-Solver is much more resource-demanding than BCP and it is invoked less often, it is clear that the performance of an OMT solver can be negatively affected when dealing with this kind of objectives.

Example 1. Figure 1 shows a toy example of OMT search execution over the pair $\langle \varphi, obj \rangle$, where φ is some SMT formula and $obj \stackrel{\text{def}}{=} \sum_{i=1}^{4} A_i$ (i.e., $w_i = 1$ for every i). We assume the problem has been encoded as in (2)–(4), so that the truth assignment $\mu_0 \stackrel{\text{def}}{=} \cup_{i=1}^{4}\{(0 \leq x_i), (x_i \leq 1)\} \cup \{(obj = \sum_{i=1}^{4} x_i)\}$ is immediately generated by BCP, and is part of all truth assignments generated in the search. In the first branch (left) a truth assignment $\mu \stackrel{\text{def}}{=} \mu_0 \cup \{A_1, (x_1 = 1), A_2, (x_2 = 1), \neg A_3, (x_3 = 0), \neg A_4, (x_4 = 0)\}$ is found s.t. $obj = 2$, resulting from the decisions A_1, A_2, $\neg A_3$ and $\neg A_4$. Then the unit clause $\neg(2 \leq obj)$ is learned and the Boolean search is restarted in order to find an improved solution. In the second branch (center) A_1 and A_2 are decided, forcing by BCP the assignment

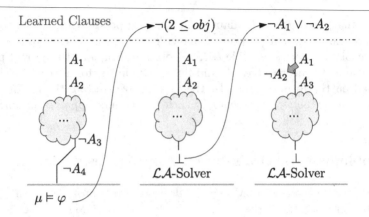

Fig. 1. A simple example of OMT search.

$\mu' \stackrel{\text{def}}{=} \mu_0 \cup \{\neg(2 \leq obj), A_1, (x_1 = 1), A_2, (x_2 = 1)\}$ which is $\mathcal{LRA}$-inconsistent. However, it takes a (possibly-expensive) intermediate call to the $\mathcal{LRA}$-Solver to reveal such an inconsistency.[4] If so, a new conflict clause $\neg A_1 \vee \neg A_2$ is learned, forcing the solver to back-jump and toggle the value of A_2 (right). The search continues with the new decision A_3, which is again $\mathcal{LRA}$ inconsistent, causing a new conflict clause as before, and so on. In this way, the solver might uselessly enumerate and check all the up-to $\binom{4}{2}$ assignments that assign two A_i's to true and are consistent with φ, even though they are intrinsically incompatible with $\neg(2 \leq obj)$. ◇

The performance issue identified with the previous case example can be generalized to any objective obj in which groups of A_i's share the same weights:

$$obj = \tau_1 + \ldots + \tau_m, \tag{5}$$

$$\bigwedge_{j=1}^{m} ((\tau_j = w_j \cdot \sum_{i=1}^{k_j} A_{ji}) \ \wedge \ (0 \leq \tau_j) \wedge (\tau_j \leq w_j \cdot k_j)), \tag{6}$$

where the logically-redundant constraints $(0 \leq \tau_j) \wedge (\tau_j \leq w_j \cdot k_j)$ are added for the same reason as with (3).

4   Combining OMT with Sorting Networks

Notationally, the symbols $\top, \bot, *$ denote respectively "true", "false" and "unassigned". We represent truth assignment as sets (or conjunctions) of literals s.t. a positive [resp. negative] literal denotes the fact that the corresponding atom is assigned to $\top$ [resp. $\bot$]. Given a Boolean formula φ and two truth assignments μ, η on the atoms in φ, "$\langle \varphi, \mu \rangle \vdash_{\text{bcp}} \eta$" denotes the fact that all literals in η are inferred by BCP on φ if all literals in μ are asserted. (Notice that "$\langle \varphi, \mu \rangle \vdash_{\text{bcp}} \eta$" is stronger than "$\varphi \wedge \mu \models \eta$".)

---

[4] The fact that such call is actually performed depends on the early-pruning strategy implemented in the OMT solver; alternatively, a possibly-expensive $\mathcal{T}$-propagation step on the previous $\mathcal{LRA}$-Solver call has a similar effect. (See e.g. [5,27].)

When dealing with MAXSMT and OMT with PB objectives in the form

$$obj = w \cdot \sum_{i=1}^{n} A_i \tag{7}$$

a solution for improving search efficiency is to reduce the dependency on the expensive $\mathcal{LRA}$-Solver by better exploiting BCP with the aid of Boolean *bidirectional sorting networks*.

Definition 1. *Let* $SN[\underline{A}, \underline{B}]$ *be a CNF Boolean formula on n input Boolean variables* $\underline{A} \stackrel{def}{=} \{A_1, \ldots, A_n\}$ *and n output Boolean variables* $\underline{B} \stackrel{def}{=} \{B_1, \ldots, B_n\}$, *possibly involving also auxiliary Boolean variables which are not mentioned.*

We say that $SN[\underline{A}, \underline{B}]$ *is a* **bidirectional sorting network** *if and only if, for every m and k s.t. $n \geq m \geq k \geq 0$ and for every partial truth assignment μ s.t. μ assigns exactly k input variables A_i to $\top$ and $n - m$ variables A_i to $\bot$:*

$$\langle SN[\underline{A}, \underline{B}], \mu \rangle \vdash_{bcp} \{ B_1, \ldots, B_k \}, \tag{8}$$

$$\langle SN[\underline{A}, \underline{B}], \mu \rangle \vdash_{bcp} \{ \neg B_{m+1}, \ldots, \neg B_n \}. \tag{9}$$

$$\langle SN[\underline{A}, \underline{B}], \mu \cup \{ \neg B_{k+1} \} \rangle \vdash_{bcp} \{ \neg A_i \ s.t. \ A_i \ unassigned \ in \ \mu \}, \tag{10}$$

$$\langle SN[\underline{A}, \underline{B}], \mu \cup \{ B_m \} \rangle \vdash_{bcp} \{ A_i \ s.t. \ A_i \ unassigned \ in \ \mu \}. \tag{11}$$

The schema of a bidirectional sorting network is depicted in Fig. 2.

(8)–(9) state that the output values $\underline{B}$ of $SN[\underline{A}, \underline{B}]$ are propagated from the inputs $\underline{A}$ via BCP. (10)–(11) describe how assigning output variables $\underline{B}$ propagates back to input variables $\underline{A}$: (10) states that, when k A_i's are true and B_{k+1} is false, then all other A_i's are forced to be false by BCP; dually, (11) states that, when $n - m$ A_i's are false and B_m is true, then all other A_i's are forced to be true by BCP. (If any of the above BCP assignments conflicts with some previous assignment, a conflict is produced.)

Given an OMT problem $\langle \varphi, obj \rangle$, where obj is as in (7), and a Boolean formula $SN[\underline{A}, \underline{B}]$ encoding a bidirectional sorting network relation as in Definition 1, we extend φ in (2)–(4) as follows:

$$\varphi' = \varphi \wedge SN[\underline{A}, \underline{B}] \wedge \bigwedge_{i=1}^{n} \begin{cases} (\neg B_i \vee (i \cdot w \leq obj)) \wedge \\ (B_i \vee (obj \leq (i-1) \cdot w)) \wedge \\ (\neg (i \cdot w \leq obj) \vee \neg (obj \leq (i-1) \cdot w)) \end{cases} \tag{12}$$

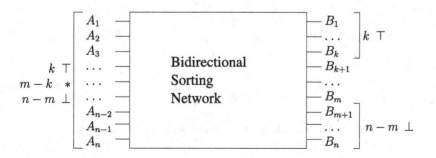

Fig. 2. The basic schema of a bidirectional sorting network.

and optimize *obj* over φ'. Notice here that the third line in Eq. 12 is $\mathcal{LRA}$-valid, but it allows for implying the negation of $(obj \leq (i - 1) \cdot w)$ from $(i \cdot w \leq obj)$ (and vice versa) directly by BCP, without any call to the $\mathcal{LRA}$-Solver.

Consider (8)–(9) and assume that μ assigns k A_is to $\top$ and $n - m$ to $\bot$ as in Definition 1. Then (8) with (12) forces the unit-propagation of $B_1, \ldots, B_k$, and then, among others, of $(k \cdot w \leq obj)$, while (9) with (12) forces the unit-propagation of $\neg B_{m+1}, \ldots, \neg B_n$, and then, among others, of $(obj \leq m \cdot w)$. This automatically restricts the range of *obj* to $[k \cdot w, m \cdot w]$, obtaining the same effect as (2)–(4).

The benefits of the usage of $\mathsf{SN}[\underline{A}, \underline{B}]$ are due to both (10) and (11). When the optimization search finds a new minimum $k \cdot w$ and a unit clause in the form $\neg(k \cdot w \leq obj)$ is learned (see e.g. [28]) and $\neg B_k$ is unit-propagated on (12), then as soon as $k - 1$ A_is are set to True, all the remaining $n - k + 1$ A_is are set to False by BCP (10). A dual case occurs when some lower-bound unit clause $\neg(obj \leq k \cdot w)$ is learned (e.g., in a binary-search step [28]) and B_{k+1} is unit-propagated on (12): as soon as $n - k - 1$ A_is are set to False, then all the remaining $k + 1$ A_is are set to True by BCP (11).

Example 2. Figure 3 considers the same scenario as in Example 1, in which we extend the encoding with a bidirectional sorting-network relation as in (12). The behaviour is identical to that of Example 1 until the assignment μ is generated, the unit clause $\neg(2 \leq obj)$, and the procedure backtracks for the first time (Fig. 3 left). This causes the unit-propagation of $\neg B_2$ on (12). As soon as A_1 is picked as new decision, $\neg A_2, \neg A_3, \neg A_4$ are unit propagated (10), saving up to $\binom{4}{2}$ (expensive) calls to the $\mathcal{LRA}$-Solver (Fig. 3 center). Then $\neg(1 \leq obj)$ is learned, and the search proceeds (Fig. 3 right).   ◇

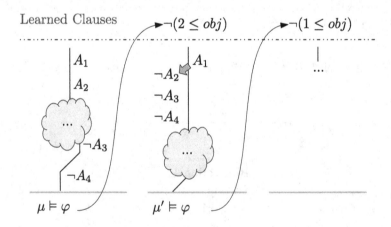

Fig. 3. An example of OMT search with sorting networks.

We generalize this approach to deal with the general objectives as in (5)–(6). In this case a separate sorting circuit is generated for each term τ_j, and constraints in the form

$$\bigwedge_{j=1}^{m} \bigwedge_{i=1}^{k_j} (\neg(w_j \cdot i \leq obj) \rightarrow \neg(w_j \cdot i \leq \tau_j)), \tag{13}$$

are added to ensure that the circuit is activated by BCP.

4.1 Bidirectional Sorting Networks

Unlike the usage of sorting networks in other contexts, which consider only (8) and (10) as relevant properties (e.g. [32]), we are interested in sorting networks which propagate both $\top$ and $\bot$ values in both directions (i.e., which comply with all properties (8)–(11)). To this extent, we have considered two encodings: the sequential counter encoding in [32], which we have extended to comply with all properties (8)–(11), and the cardinality network encoding in [1,4].

Bidirectional Sequential Counter Encoding. The sequential counter encoding $LT_{SEQ}^{n,k}$ for $\leq k(A_1, \ldots, A_n)$ presented in [32] consists of $O(k \cdot n)$ clauses and variables and complies with (8) and (10). The circuit is given by the composition of n sub-circuits, each of which computes $S_i = \sum_{j=1}^{i} A_j$, represented in unary form with the bits $S_{i,j}$, i.e., $S_{i,j} = \top$ if $\sum_{r=1}^{i} A_r \geq j$, so that $B_j \stackrel{\text{def}}{=} S_{n,j}$, $j \in [1 \ldots n]$. The (CNF version of the)[5] following formula is the encoding of $LT_{SEQ}^{n,k}$ presented in [32], with $k \stackrel{\text{def}}{=} n$:

$$(A_1 \rightarrow S_{1,1}) \wedge \bigwedge_{i=2}^{n} \{((A_i \vee S_{i-1,1}) \rightarrow S_{i,1})\} \wedge \tag{14}$$

$$\bigwedge_{i=2}^{n} \{(\neg A_i \vee \neg S_{i-1,n})\} \wedge \bigwedge_{j=2}^{n} \{(\neg S_{1,j})\} \wedge \tag{15}$$

$$\bigwedge_{i,j=2}^{n} \{(((A_i \wedge S_{i-1,j-1}) \vee S_{i-1,j}) \rightarrow S_{i,j})\} \tag{16}$$

Notice that, in order to reduce the size of the encoding, in (14)–(16) only right implications "$\rightarrow$" were used to encode each gate in the Boolean sorting circuit [32], so that (14)–(16) complies with (8) and (10) but not with (9) and (11). To cope with this fact, we have added the following part, which reintroduces the left implications "$\leftarrow$" of the encoding of each gate in (14) and (16), making it compliant also with (9) and (11):

$$(A_1 \leftarrow S_{1,1}) \wedge \bigwedge_{i=2}^{n} \{((A_i \vee S_{i-1,1}) \leftarrow S_{i,1})\} \wedge \tag{17}$$

$$\bigwedge_{i,j=2}^{n} (((A_i \wedge S_{i-1,j-1}) \vee S_{i-1,j}) \leftarrow S_{i,j}). \tag{18}$$

Bidirectional Cardinality Network Encoding. The cardinality network encoding presented in [1,4,13], based on the underlying sorting scheme of the well-known *merge-sort* algorithm, has complexity $O(n \log^2 k)$ in the number of clauses and

---

[5] Here (14)–(18) are written as implications to emphasize the directionality of the encodings.

variables. Due to space limitations, we refer the reader to [1,4] for the encoding of cardinality networks we used in our own work. Notice that, differently than in the previous case, this sorting network propagates both $\top$ and $\bot$ values in both directions (i.e., it complies with all properties (8)–(11) [1,4] and it is thus suitable to be used within OMT without modifications.

Both of the previous encodings are istantiated assuming $k = n$, since the sorting network is generated prior to starting the search. Therefo re, the cardinality network circuit looks more appealing than the sequential counter encoding due to its lower complexity in terms of clauses and variables employed.

5   Experimental Evaluation

We extended OptiMathSAT with a novel internal preprocessing step, which automatically augments the input formula with a sorting network circuit of choice between the bidirectional sequential counter and the cardinality network, as described in Sect. 4. To complete our comparison, we also implemented in OptiMathSAT two MaxSAT-based approaches, the max-resolution approach implemented in νZ [8,18] and (for MaxSMT only) the lemma-lifting approach of [12], using Maxino [2] as external MaxSAT solver.

Here we present an extensive empirical evaluation of various MaxSAT-based and OMT-based techniques in OptiMathSAT [23,30] and νZ [9,22]. Overall, we considered >20,000 OMT problems and run >270,000 job pairs. The problems were produced either by CGM-Tool [10] from optimization of Constrained Goal Models [19,20] (a modeling and automated-reasoning tool for requirement engineering) or by PyLMT [24] from (Machine) Learning Modulo Theories [34]. We partition these problems into two distinct categories. In Sect. 5.1 we analyze problems which are *solvable by* MaxSAT-*based approaches*, like those with PB objective functions or their lexicographic combination, so that to allow both νZ and OptiMathSAT to use their MaxSAT-specific max-resolution engines (plus others). In Sect. 5.2 we analyze problems which *cannot* be solved by MaxSAT-based approaches, because the objective functions involve some non-PB components, forcing to restrict to OMT-based approaches only.

The goal of this empirical evaluation is manyfold:

(i) compare the performance of MaxSAT-based approaches wrt. OMT-based ones, on the kind of OMT problems where the former are applicable;

(ii) evaluate the benefits of sorting-network encodings with OMT-based approaches (and also with MaxSAT-based ones);

(iii) compare the performances of OptiMathSAT with those of νZ.

For goals (i) and (ii) we used the following configurations of OptiMathSAT.

OMT-based: standard, enriched with the bidirectional sequential-counter and cardinality sorting network;

MaxSAT-based: the above-mentioned max-resolution implementation, with and without the cardinality sorting network, and lemma-lifting (for pure MaxSMT only).

For goal (iii) we also used the following configurations of νZ.[6]

OMT-based: standard (encoded as in (2)–(4)).
MAXSAT-based: using alternatively the internal implementations of the max-resolution [8,18] and WMAX [21] procedures.

Each job pair was run on one of two identical Ubuntu Linux machines featuring *8-core Intel-Xeon@2.20 GHz* CPU, 64 GB of ram and kernel 3.8-0-29. Importantly, we verified that all tools/configurations under test agreed on the results on all problems when terminating within the timeout. (The timeout varies with the benchmark sets, see Sects. 5.1 and 5.2.) All benchmarks, as well as our experimental results and all the tools which are necessary to reproduce the results, are available [33].

5.1 Problems Suitable for MaxSAT-Based Approaches

Test Set #1: CGMs with Lexicographic PB Optimization. In our first experiment we consider the set of all problems produced by CGM-TOOL [10] in the experimental evaluation in [19]. They consist of 18996 automatically-generated formulas which encode the problem of computing the lexicographically-optimum realization of a constrained goal model [19], according to a prioritized list of (up to) three objectives $\langle obj_1, obj_2, obj_3 \rangle$. A solution *optimizes lexicographically* $\langle obj_1, \ldots, obj_k \rangle$ if it optimizes obj_1 and, if more than one such obj_1-optimum solutions exists, it also optimizes $obj_2, \ldots$, and so on; both OMT-based and MAXSAT-based techniques handle lexicographic optimization, by optimizing $obj_1, obj_2, \ldots$ in order, fixing the value of each obj_i to its optimum as soon as it is found [8,9,30,31]. In this experiment, we set the timeout at 100 s. The results are reported in Fig. 4 (top and middle).

As far as OPTIMATHSAT (OMT-based) is concerned, extending the input formula with either of the sorting networks increases the number of benchmarks solved within the timeout. Notably, the cardinality network encoding –which has the lowest complexity– scores the best both in terms of number of solved benchmarks and solving time. On the other hand, the sequential counter network is affected by a significant performance hit on a number of benchmarks, as it is witnessed by the left scatter plot in Fig. 4. This not only affects unsatisfiable benchmarks, for which using sorting networks appears to be not beneficial in general, but also satisfiable ones.

A possible strategy for overcoming this performance issue is to reduce the memory footprint determined by the generation of the sorting network circuit.

---

[6] Notice that, unlike OPTIMATHSAT, νZ selects automatically its presumably-best configuration for a given input problem. In particular, when MAXSMT-encodable problems are fed to νZ –like, e.g., those in Sect. 5.1– νZ forces automatically the choice of the MAXSAT-based configuration, allowing the user only the choice of the MAXSAT algorithm. Thus we could not test νZ also with OMT-based configuration for the problems in Sect. 5.1. Alternatively, we should have disguised the input problem, with the risk of affecting the significance or the result.

tool, configuration & encoding	inst.	term.	timeout	time (s.)
OPTIMATHSAT (OMT-based)	18996	16316	2680	48832
OPTIMATHSAT (OMT-based + seq. counter)	18996	16929	2067	90080
OPTIMATHSAT (OMT-based + card. network)	18996	**17191**	1805	39215
OPTIMATHSAT (MAXSAT-based w. maxres)	18996	17933	1063	24369
OPTIMATHSAT (MAXSAT-based w. maxres + seq. counter)	18996	18180	816	49088
OPTIMATHSAT (MAXSAT-based w. maxres + card. netw.)	18996	**18197**	799	26489
νZ (MAXSAT-based w. maxres)	18996	18996	0	1640

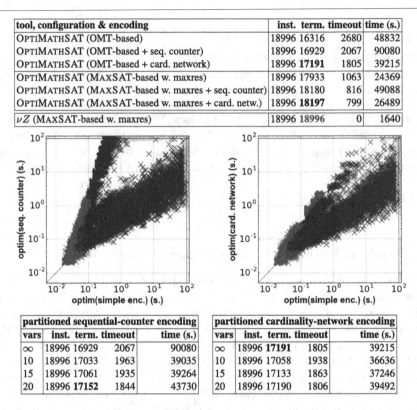

partitioned sequential-counter encoding				
vars	inst.	term.	timeout	time (s.)
∞	18996	16929	2067	90080
10	18996	17033	1963	39035
15	18996	17061	1935	39264
20	18996	**17152**	1844	43730

partitioned cardinality-network encoding				
vars	inst.	term.	timeout	time (s.)
∞	18996	**17191**	1805	39215
10	18996	17058	1938	36636
15	18996	17133	1863	37246
20	18996	17190	1806	39492

Fig. 4. [Top, table] Results of various solvers, configurations and encodings on all the problems encoding CGM optimization with lexicographic PB optimization of [19, 20]. (Values in **boldface** denote the best performance of each category; values in *blue* denote the absolute best performance.) [Middle, scatterplots]. Pairwise comparison on OPTI-MATHSAT (OMT-based) with/out sequential-counter encoding (left) and with/out cardinality-network encoding (right). (*Brown* points denote unsatisfiable benchmarks, *blue* denote satisfiable ones and *green* ones represent timeouts.) [Bottom, tables] Effect of splitting the PB sums into chunks of maximum variable number (no split, 10, 15, 20 variables) with the sequential-counter encoding (left) and the cardinality-network encoding (right). (Color figure online)

This can be easily achieved by splitting each Pseudo-Boolean sum in smaller sized chunks and generating a separate sorting circuit for each splice. The result of applying this enhancement, using chunks of increasing size, is shown in Fig. 4 (bottom). The data suggest that the sequential counter encoding can benefit from this simple heuristic, but it does not reach the performances of the cardinality network, which are not affected by this strategy. (In next experiments this strategy will be no more considered.)

As far as OPTIMATHSAT (MAXSAT-based) is concerned, we notice that it significantly outperforms all OMT-based techniques. Remarkably, extending the input formula with the sorting networks improves the performance also of this configuration.

tool, configuration & encoding	inst.	term.	timeout	time (s.)
OPTIMATHSAT (OMT-based)	2499	1794	705	11178
OPTIMATHSAT (OMT-based + seq. counter)	2499	**2451**	48	18033
OPTIMATHSAT (OMT-based + card. network)	2499	2186	313	10633
OPTIMATHSAT (MAXSAT-based w. maxres)	2499	**2499**	0	**128**
OPTIMATHSAT (MAXSAT-based w. maxres + seq. counter)	2499	2499	0	1638
OPTIMATHSAT (MAXSAT-based w. maxres + card. netw.)	2499	2499	0	257
OPTIMATHSAT (lemma-lifting w. MAXINO)	2499	2497	2	343
νZ (MAXSAT-based w. maxres)	2499	**2499**	0	**119**
νZ (MAXSAT-based w. wmax)	2499	1799	733	10549

Fig. 5. Results of various solvers, configurations and encodings on CGM-encoding problems of [19, 20] with single-objective weight-1.

As far as νZ (MAXSAT-based) is concerned, we notice that when using the max-resolution algorithm it outperforms all other techniques by solving all problems.

Test Set #2: CGMs with Weight-1 PB Optimization. Our second experiment is a variant of the previous one, in which we consider only single-objective optimizations and we fix all weights to 1, so that each problem is encoded as a plain un-weighted MAXSMT problem. We set the timeout to 100 s. The results are reported in Fig. 5.

As far as OPTIMATHSAT (OMT-based) is concerned, extending the input formula with either of the sorting networks increases the number of benchmarks solved within the timeout. Surprisingly, this time the sequential counter network performs significantly better than the cardinality network, despite its bigger size. (We do not have a clear explanation of this fact.)

As far as OPTIMATHSAT (MAXSAT-based) is concerned, we notice that it significantly outperforms all OMT-based techniques, solving all problems. Extending the input formula with the cardinality networks slightly worsens the performances. Also the lemma-lifting techniques outperforms all OMT-based techniques, solving only two problem less than the previous MAXSAT-based techniques.

As far as νZ (MAXSAT-based) is concerned, we notice that using the max-resolution MAXSAT algorithm it is the best scorer, although the differences wrt. OPTIMATHSAT (MAXSAT-based) are negligible, whilst by using the wmax engine the performances decrease drastically.

5.2 Problems Unsuitable for MaxSAT-Based Approaches

Here we present a couple of test sets which cannot be supported by any MAXSAT-based technique in OPTIMATHSAT or νZ and, to the best of our knowledge, no encoding of these problem into MAXSMT has ever been conceived. Thus the solution is restricted to OMT-based techniques. (To this extent, with OptiMathSAT we have used the linear-search strategy rather than the default adaptive linear/binary one to better compare with the linear strategy adopted by νZ.)

Test Set #3: CGMs with Max-Min PB Optimization. In our third experiment we consider another variant of the problems in Test Set #1, in which the three PB/MaxSMT objectives $\langle obj_1, obj_2, obj_3 \rangle$ are subject to a max-min combination: each objective obj_j is normalized so that its range equals $[0, 1]$ (i.e., it is divided by $\sum_i w_{ji}$), then $\bigwedge_{j=1}^{3}(obj_j \leq obj)$ s.t. obj is a fresh $\mathcal{LRA}$ variable is added to the main formula, and the solver is asked to find a solution making obj minimum (see [30]). Notice that max-min optimization guarantees a sort of "fairness" among the objectives $obj_1, \ldots, obj_3$. Since the problem is more complex than the previous ones and the most-efficient MaxSAT-based techniques are not applicable, we increased the timeout to 300 s. The results are shown in Fig. 6. (Unlike with Fig. 4, since the difference in performance between Opti-MathSAT with the two sorting networks is minor, here and in Fig. 7 we have dropped the scatterplot with the sequential-counter encoding and we introduced one comparing with νZ instead.)

Looking at the table and at the scatterplot on the left, we notice that enhancing the OMT-based technique of OptiMathSAT by adding the cardinality networks improves significantly the performances. Also, looking at the table and at the scatterplot on the right, we notice that OMT-based technique of Opti-MathSAT, with the help of sorting networks, performs equivalently or slightly better than that of νZ.

tool, configuration & encoding	inst.	term.	timeout	time (s.)
OptiMathSAT (OMT-based)	2399	2340	59	20841
OptiMathSAT (OMT-based + seq. counter)	2399	2394	5	9511
OptiMathSAT (OMT-based + card. network)	2399	**2395**	4	8275
νZ (OMT-based)	2399	2390	9	8076

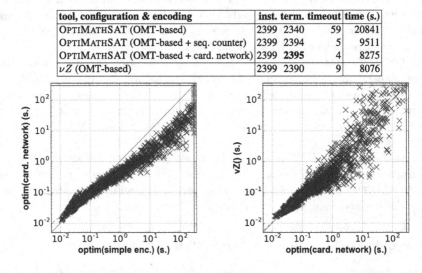

Fig. 6. [Table:] results of various solvers with OMT-based configurations on CGMencoding problems of [19, 20] with max-min objective functions. [Left scatterplot:] Opti-MathSAT + card. network vs. plain OptiMathSAT. [Right scatterplot:] νZ vs. Opti-MathSAT + card. network.

Test Set #4: LMT with Mixed Complex Objective Functions. In our fourth experiment we consider a set of 500 problems taken from PyLMT [24], a tool for Structured Learning Modulo Theories [34] which uses OptiMathSAT as back-end oracle for performing inference in the context of machine learning in hybrid domains. The objective functions *obj* are complex combinations of PB functions in the form:

$$obj \stackrel{\text{def}}{=} \sum_j w_j \cdot B_j + cover - \sum_k w_k \cdot C_k - |K - cover|, \qquad (19)$$

$$s.t. \ cover \stackrel{\text{def}}{=} \sum_i w_i A_i, \qquad (20)$$

A_i, B_j, C_k being Boolean atoms, w_i, v_j, z_k, K being rational constants. We imposed a timeout of 600 s. The results are presented in Fig. 7.

Looking at the table and at the scatterplot on the left, we notice that enhancing the OMT-based technique of OptiMathSAT by adding the cardinality networks improves the performances, although this time the improvement is not dramatic. (We believe this is due that the values of the weights w_i, v_j, z_k, K are very heterogeneous, not many weights share the same value.) Also, looking at the table and at the scatterplot on the right, we notice that OMT-based technique of OptiMathSAT performs significantly better than that of νZ, even without the help of sorting networks.

tool, configuration & encoding	inst.	term.	timeout	time (s.)
OptiMathSAT (OMT-based)	500	421	79	2607
OptiMathSAT (OMT-based + seq. counter)	500	441	59	6381
OptiMathSAT (OMT-based + card. network)	500	**442**	58	6189
νZ (OMT-based)	500	406	94	2120

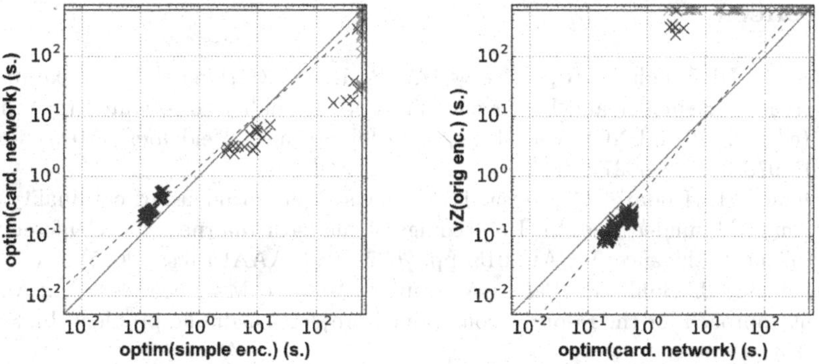

Fig. 7. [Table:] results of various solvers with OMT-based configurations on LMT-encoding problems of [34] with complex objective functions. [Left scatterplot:] OptiMathSAT + card. network vs. plain OptiMathSAT. [Right scatterplot:] νZ vs. OptiMathSAT + card. network.

Discussion. We summarize the results as follows.

(a) When applicable, MAXSAT-based approaches performed much better than OMT-based ones, in particular when adopting Maximum-Resolution as MAXSAT engine.
(b) Bidirectional sorting-network encodings improved significantly the performances of OMT-based approaches, and often also of MAXSAT-based ones.
(c) νZ performed better than OPTIMATHSAT on MAXSAT-based approaches, whilst the latter performed sometimes similarly and sometimes significantly better on OMT-based ones, in particular when enhanced by the sorting-network encodings.

6   Conclusion and Future Work

MAXSMT and OMT with Pseudo-Boolean objective functions are important sub-cases of OMT, for which specialized techniques have been developed over the years, in particular exploiting state-of-the-art MAXSAT procedures. When applicable, these specialized procedures seem to be more efficient than general-purpose OMT. When they are not applicable, OMT-based technique can strongly benefit from the integration with bidirectional sorting networks to deal with PB components of objectives.

OMT is a young technology, with large margins for improvements. Among others, one interesting research direction is that of integrating MAXSAT-based techniques with standard OMT-based ones for efficiently handling complex objectives and constraints, so that to combine the efficiency of the former with the expressivity of the latter.

References

1. Abío, I., Nieuwenhuis, R., Oliveras, A., Rodríguez-Carbonell, E.: A parametric approach for smaller and better encodings of cardinality constraints. In: Schulte, C. (ed.) CP 2013. LNCS, vol. 8124, pp. 80–96. Springer, Heidelberg (2013). doi:10.1007/978-3-642-40627-0_9
2. Alviano, M., Dodaro, C., Ricca, F.: A maxsat algorithm using cardinality constraints of bounded size. In: Proceedings of the 24th International Conference on Artificial Intelligence, IJCAI 2015, pp. 2677–2683. AAAI Press (2015)
3. Ansótegui, C., Bofill, M., Palahí, M., Suy, J., Villaret, M., Theories, S.M.: An efficient approach for the resource-constrained project scheduling problem. In: SARA (2011)
4. Asín, R., Nieuwenhuis, R., Oliveras, A., Rodríguez-Carbonell, E.: Cardinality networks: a theoretical and empirical study. Constraints **16**(2), 195–221 (2011)
5. Barrett, C., Sebastiani, R., Seshia, S.A., Tinelli, C.: Satisfiability modulo theories, Chap. 26, vol. 185, pp. 825–885, Biere et al. [6], February 2009
6. Biere, A., Heule, M.J.H., van Maaren, H., Walsh, T. (eds.): Handbook of Satisfiability, vol. 185. IOS Press, February 2009
7. Bjorner, N.: Personal communication, 02 (2016)

8. Bjorner, N., Phan, A.-D.: νZ - maximal satisfaction with Z3. In: Proceedings of the International Symposium on Symbolic Computation in Software Science, Gammart, Tunisia, December 2014. EasyChair Proceedings in Computing (EPiC). http://www.easychair.org/publications/?page=862275542

9. Bjørner, N., Phan, A.-D., Fleckenstein, L.: νZ - an optimizing SMT solver. In: Baier, C., Tinelli, C. (eds.) TACAS 2015. LNCS, vol. 9035, pp. 194–199. Springer, Heidelberg (2015). doi:10.1007/978-3-662-46681-0_14

10. CGM-Tool. http://www.cgm-tool.eu

11. Cimatti, A., Franzén, A., Griggio, A., Sebastiani, R., Stenico, C.: Satisfiability modulo the theory of costs: foundations and applications. In: Esparza, J., Majumdar, R. (eds.) TACAS 2010. LNCS, vol. 6015, pp. 99–113. Springer, Heidelberg (2010). doi:10.1007/978-3-642-12002-2_8

12. Cimatti, A., Griggio, A., Schaafsma, B.J., Sebastiani, R.: A modular approach to MaxSAT modulo theories. In: Järvisalo, M., Van Gelder, A. (eds.) SAT 2013. LNCS, vol. 7962, pp. 150–165. Springer, Heidelberg (2013). doi:10.1007/978-3-642-39071-5_12

13. Eén, N., Sörensson, N.: Translating pseudo-boolean constraints into SAT. JSAT 2(1–4), 1–26 (2006)

14. Larraz, D., Oliveras, A., Rodríguez-Carbonell, E., Rubio, A.: Minimal-model-guided approaches to solving polynomial constraints and extensions. In: Sinz, C., Egly, U. (eds.) SAT 2014. LNCS, vol. 8561, pp. 333–350. Springer, Heidelberg (2014). doi:10.1007/978-3-319-09284-3_25

15. Li, Y., Albarghouthi, A., Kincad, Z., Gurfinkel, A., Chechik, M.: Symbolic optimization with SMT solvers. In: POPL (2014)

16. Marques-Silva, J.P., Lynce, I., Malik, S.: Conflict-driven clause learning SAT solvers, Chap. 4, vol. 185, pp. 131–153, Biere et al. [6], February 2009

17. Nadel, A., Ryvchin, V.: Bit-vector optimization. In: Chechik, M., Raskin, J.-F. (eds.) TACAS 2016. LNCS, vol. 9636, pp. 851–867. Springer, Heidelberg (2016). doi:10.1007/978-3-662-49674-9_53

18. Narodytska, N., Bacchus, F.: Maximum satisfiability using core-guided maxsat resolution. In: Proceedings of the Twenty-Eighth AAAI Conference on Artificial Intelligence, 27–31 July, Québec City, Québec, Canada, pp. 2717–2723. AAAI Press (2014)

19. Nguyen, C.M., Sebastiani, R., Giorgini, P., Mylopoulos, J.: Multi-object reasoning with constrained goal models. Requirements Eng. 1–37 (2016). http://dx.doi.org/10.1007/s00766-016-0263-5

20. Nguyen, C.M., Sebastiani, R., Giorgini, P., Mylopoulos, J.: Requirements evolution and evolution requirements with constrained goal models. In: Comyn-Wattiau, I., Tanaka, K., Song, I.-Y., Yamamoto, S., Saeki, M. (eds.) ER 2016. LNCS, vol. 9974, pp. 544–552. Springer, Heidelberg (2016). doi:10.1007/978-3-319-46397-1_42

21. Nieuwenhuis, R., Oliveras, A.: On SAT modulo theories and optimization problems. In: Biere, A., Gomes, C.P. (eds.) SAT 2006. LNCS, vol. 4121, pp. 156–169. Springer, Heidelberg (2006). doi:10.1007/11814948_18

22. μZ. http://rise4fun.com/z3opt

23. OptiMathSAT. http://optimathsat.disi.unitn.it

24. PyLMT. http://www.bitbucket.org/stefanoteso/pylmt

25. Roussel, O., Manquinho, V.: Pseudo-boolean and cardinality constraints, Chap. 22, vol. 185, pp. 695–733 Biere et al. [6], February 2009

26. Sawaya, N.W., Grossmann, I.E.: A cutting plane method for solving linear generalized disjunctive programming problems. Comput. Chem. Eng. 29(9), 1891–1913 (2005)

27. Sebastiani, R.: Lazy satisfiability modulo theories. J. Satisf. Boolean Model. Comput. JSAT **3**(3–4), 141–224 (2007)
28. Sebastiani, R., Tomasi, S.: Optimization in SMT with LA(Q) cost functions. In: Gramlich, B., Miller, D., Sattler, U. (eds.) IJCAR 2012. LNCS (LNAI), vol. 7364, pp. 484–498. Springer, Heidelberg (2012). doi:10.1007/978-3-642-31365-3_38
29. Sebastiani, R., Tomasi, S.: Optimization modulo theories with linear rational costs. ACM Trans. Comput. Log. **16**(2), 12 (2015)
30. Sebastiani, R., Trentin, P.: OptiMathSAT: a tool for optimization modulo theories. In: Kroening, D., Păsăreanu, C.S. (eds.) CAV 2015. LNCS, vol. 9206, pp. 447–454. Springer, Heidelberg (2015). doi:10.1007/978-3-319-21690-4_27
31. Sebastiani, R., Trentin, P.: Pushing the envelope of optimization modulo theories with linear-arithmetic cost functions. In: Baier, C., Tinelli, C. (eds.) TACAS 2015. LNCS, vol. 9035, pp. 335–349. Springer, Heidelberg (2015). doi:10.1007/978-3-662-46681-0_27
32. Sinz, C.: Towards an optimal CNF encoding of boolean cardinality constraints. In: Beek, P. (ed.) CP 2005. LNCS, vol. 3709, pp. 827–831. Springer, Heidelberg (2005). doi:10.1007/11564751_73
33. http://disi.unitn.it/trentin/resources/tacas17.tar.gz
34. Teso, S., Sebastiani, R., Passerini, A.: Structured learning modulo theories. Artif. Intell. J. **244**, 166–187 (2015). http://dx.doi.org/10.1016/j.artint.2015.04.002

The Automatic Detection of Token Structures and Invariants Using SAT Checking

Pedro Antonino$^{(\boxtimes)}$, Thomas Gibson-Robinson, and A.W. Roscoe

Department of Computer Science, University of Oxford, Oxford, UK
{pedro.antonino,thomas.gibson-robinson,bill.roscoe}@cs.ox.ac.uk

Abstract. Many distributed systems rely on token structures for their correct operation. Often, these structures make sure that a fixed number of tokens exists at all times, or perhaps that tokens cannot be completely eliminated, to prevent systems from reaching undesired states. In this paper we show how a SAT checker can be used to automatically detect token and similar invariants in distributed systems, and how these invariants can improve the precision of a deadlock-checking framework that is based on local analysis. We demonstrate by a series of practical experiments that this new framework is as efficient as similar incomplete techniques for deadlock-freedom analysis, while handling a different class of systems.

1 Introduction

Many concurrent and distributed systems rely on some token mechanism to avoid reaching undesired states. For these systems, understanding/recognising these token structures often leads to system invariants (i.e. system abstractions) that are sufficiently strong to prove safety properties of the considered system. For instance, token invariants are frequently used to show mutual exclusion properties and deadlock freedom. In this work, motivated by deadlock-freedom analysis, we propose two techniques that can recognise token structures using SAT checking. The first technique detects token structures where the number of tokens is conserved at all times, whereas the second one ensures that at least one token exists in the system at all times.

To demonstrate how these structures can be used in the analysis of safety properties, we combine our detection techniques with the local-analysis framework for deadlock checking presented in [4] to create a more precise, albeit still incomplete, deadlock-checking framework. Incomplete frameworks can be far more scalable than complete ones at the cost of being unable to prove that some deadlock-free systems are deadlock free [6,7,9,10,18,19,24]. The new token framework handles a different class of system than current incomplete techniques for deadlock-freedom analysis. We implement our framework, and detection techniques, in a new mode of the DeadlOx tool [5], called *DeadlOx-VT* (for Virtual Tokens). We reinforce that the core of our framework should be easily adaptable for the verification of other safety properties using other formalisms.

© Springer-Verlag GmbH Germany 2017
A. Legay and T. Margaria (Eds.): TACAS 2017, Part II, LNCS 10206, pp. 249–265, 2017.
DOI: 10.1007/978-3-662-54580-5_15

Outline. Section 2 briefly introduces CSP's operational semantics, which is the formalism upon which our strategy is based. However, this paper can be understood purely in terms of communicating LTSs, and knowledge of CSP is not a prerequisite. Section 3 presents some related invariant generation and incomplete deadlock-freedom-checking techniques. In Sect. 4, we introduce our techniques for automatically detecting token structures. Section 5 presents our new framework for imprecise deadlock-freedom checking. Section 6 presents an experiment conducted to assess the accuracy and efficiency of DeadlOx-VT. Finally, in Sect. 7, we present our concluding remarks.

2   Background

The CSP notation [17,26] models concurrent systems as processes that exchange messages. Here we describe some structures used by the refinement checker FDR3 [15] in implementing CSP's operational semantics. As this paper does not depend on the details of CSP, we do not describe the details of the language or its semantics. These can be found in [26].

FDR3 interprets CSP terms as a *labelled transition system* (LTS).

Definition 1. *A labelled transition system is a 4-tuple* $(S, \Sigma, \Delta, \hat{s})$ *where* S *is a set of states,* Σ *is the alphabet,* $\Delta \subseteq S \times \Sigma \times S$ *is a transition relation, and* $\hat{s} \in S$ *is the starting state.*

FDR3 represents concurrent systems as *supercombinator machines*. A supercombinator machine consists of a set of component LTSs along with a set of rules that describe how components transitions should be combined. We restrict FDR3's usual definition to systems with pairwise communication, as per [5,21].

Definition 2. *A triple-disjoint supercombinator machine is a pair* $(\mathcal{L}, \mathcal{R})$ *where:*

- $\mathcal{L} = \langle L_1, \ldots, L_n \rangle$ *is a sequence of component LTSs;*
- $\mathcal{R}$ *is a set of rules of the form* (e, a) *where:*
  - $e \in (\Sigma \cup \{-\})^n$ *specifies the event that each component must perform, where* $-$ *indicates that the component performs no event.* e *must also be triple-disjoint, that is, at most two components must be involved in a rule.*

$$triple\_disjoint(e) \cong \forall i, j, k \in \{1 \ldots n\} \mid i \neq j \land j \neq k \land i \neq k \bullet$$
$$(e_i = - \lor e_j = - \lor e_k = -)$$

  - $a \in \Sigma$ *is the event the supercombinator performs.*

We say that two components interact/communicate in a supercombinator machine, if a rule in this system requires the participation of these two components. Given a supercombinator machine, a corresponding LTS can be constructed.

Definition 3. *Let* $S = (\langle L_1, \ldots, L_n \rangle, \mathcal{R})$ *be a supercombinator machine where* $L_i = (S_i, \Sigma_i, \Delta_i, \hat{s}_i)$. *The LTS induced by* S *is the tuple* $(S, \Sigma, \Delta, \hat{s})$ *such that:*

- $S = S_1 \times \ldots \times S_n;$
- $\Sigma = \bigcup_{i=1}^{n} \Sigma_i;$
- $\Delta = \{((s_1, \ldots, s_n), a, (s_1', \ldots, s_n')) \mid \exists((e_1, \ldots, e_n), a) \in \mathcal{R} \bullet \forall i \in \{1 \ldots n\} \bullet$
  $(e_i = - \wedge s_i = s_i') \vee (e_i \neq - \wedge (s_i, e_i, s_i') \in \Delta_i)\};$
- $\hat{s} = (\hat{s}_1, \ldots, \hat{s}_n).$

We write $s \xrightarrow{e} s'$ if $(s, e, s') \in \Delta$. There is a path from s to s' with the sequence of events $\langle e_1, \ldots, e_n \rangle \in \Sigma^*$, represented by $s \xrightarrow{\langle e_1, \ldots, e_n \rangle} s'$, if there exist $s_0, \ldots, s_n$ such that $s_0 \xrightarrow{e_1} s_1 \ldots s_{n-1} \xrightarrow{e_n} s_n$, $s_0 = s$ and $s_n = s'$.

From now on, we use *system state* (*component state*) to designate a state in the system's (component's) LTS. Also, for the sake of decidability, we only analyse supercombinator machines with a finite number of components, which are themselves represented by finite LTSs with finite alphabets.

Definition 4. *A LTS* $(S, \Sigma, \Delta, \hat{s})$ *deadlocks in state* s *if and only if the predicate* $deadlock(s) \mathrel{\widehat{=}} reachable(s) \wedge blocked(s)$ *holds, where* $reachable(s) \mathrel{\widehat{=}} \exists t \in \Sigma^* \bullet$ $\hat{s} \xrightarrow{t} s$, *and* $blocked(s) \mathrel{\widehat{=}} \neg \exists s' \in S; e \in \Sigma \bullet s \xrightarrow{e} s'$.

3   Related Work

System invariants are meant to capture compact abstractions of a system's behaviour. For concurrent/distributed systems, invariants are often calculated by combining component invariants using rules that carefully analyse how components interact [5, 8, 13, 20]. Component invariants can be automatically generated using static analysis [5] or by custom-made generation rules [13]. These automatic invariant-generation techniques tend to be either too imprecise to capture token structures in general [5], or too precise so that it captures not only token structures but a much more complex abstraction of the system [13]. Token invariants are commonly used to prove mutual-exclusion properties and deadlock-freedom for Petri nets [1, 23]. However, many systems are more naturally described by formalisms where token structures are not obviously recognisable. We are not aware of any previous use of SAT checkers to calculate token-like invariants.

In the context of deadlock-analysis, we proposed *Pair* [4], a technique that uses local analysis to check deadlock-freedom. It characterises a deadlock by analysing how pairs of components interact using the following projection:

Definition 5. *Let* $S = (\langle L_1, \ldots, L_n \rangle, \mathcal{R})$ *be a supercombinator machine. The pairwise projection* $S_{i,j}$ *of the machine* S *on components* i *and* j *is given by:*

$$S_{i,j} = (\langle L_i, L_j \rangle, \{((e_i, e_j), a) \mid \exists((e_1, \ldots, e_n), a) \in \mathcal{R} \bullet (e_i \neq - \vee e_j \neq -)\})$$

Pair characterises a deadlock as a state of the system that is fully consistent with local reachability and blocking information. We called it a *Pair candidate*.

Definition 6. *Let* $\mathcal{S} = (\langle L_1, \ldots, L_n \rangle, \mathcal{R})$ *be a supercombinator machine, and* $(S, \Sigma, \Delta, \hat{s})$ *its induced LTS. A state* $s = (s_1, \ldots, s_n) \in S$ *is a Pair candidate iff* $pair\_candidate(s)$ *holds, where:*

- *$pair\_candidate(s) \hat{=} pairwise\_reachable(s) \wedge blocked(s)$*
- *$pairwise\_reachable(s) \hat{=} \forall i, j \in \{1 \ldots n\} \mid i \neq j \bullet reachable_{i,j}((s_i, s_j))$*

$reachable_{i,j}$ is the reachable predicate for the pairwise projection $\mathcal{S}_{i,j}$.

The analysis of pairs of components cannot precisely characterise reachability; Pair approximates reachability with $pairwise\_reachable(s)$. This limitation makes this technique unable to show unreachability if that is due to some global property of the system's behaviour.

To cope with this inability, some incomplete frameworks combine the use of local analysis with some system invariants [5,22]. However, these techniques rely on a degree of predicability in how individual components interact. So, they often work well on token *rings* where tokens take a predictable route round the network, but they do not seem to do so on more complex uses of tokens. The following two deadlock-free systems employ a token mechanism where components can dynamically choose which other component to pass a token to; this unpredictability makes these techniques unable to prove them deadlock free.

Running example 1. Let $\mathcal{S} = (\langle L_0, L_1, L_2 \rangle, \mathcal{R})$ be the supercombinator machine with L_0, L_1 and L_2 defined in Fig. 1 and $\mathcal{R}$ the set of rules that require components to synchronise on shared events; e.g. for event $tk_{0,1}$, we have rule $((tk_{0,1}, tk_{0,1}, -), tk_{0,1})$. An arrow with two labels represents two transitions with the same source and target states but with different labels. $\mathcal{S}$ implements a token network where process L_0 has the token initially and event $tk_{i,j}$ represents the passage of a token from L_i to L_j. Both Pair and the techniques in [5] are unable to show (s_1, s_2, s_2) unreachable, so they consider it a deadlock candidate. □

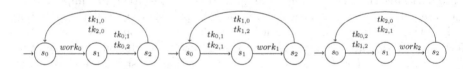

Fig. 1. LTSs of components L_0, L_1, and L_2, respectively.

Running example 2. Let $\mathcal{S} = (\langle L_0, L_1, L_2 \rangle, \mathcal{R})$ be the supercombinator machine with L_0, L_1 and L_2 defined in Fig. 2 and $\mathcal{R}$ the set of rules that requires components to synchronise on shared events except for τ that can be performed independently. Component i can receive a message (i.e. a token) either from component j, via event $tk_{j,i}$, or from its user, via event in_i. If it holds a message, it can pass the message to component j, via event $tk_{i,j}$, or output the message to its user, via out_i. The τ transitions represent an internal (non-deterministic) decision of the component. Neither Pair nor the techniques in [5] can show that the state (s_6, s_6, s_6) is unreachable, so they flag it as a potential deadlock. □

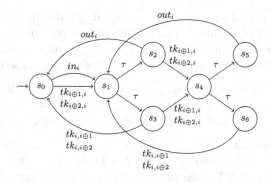

Fig. 2. LTS of component L_i where $\oplus$ represents addition modulo 3.

4 Detecting Token Structures and Invariants Using SAT

Many concurrent systems use some sort of token mechanism to guide interactions between components and avoid undesired behaviours. In this section, we present two techniques that interpret concurrent systems as token networks, trying to understand how *virtual* tokens might flow in these systems. We use "virtual" as tokens are not part of the system itself but rather an element of the abstract token mechanism it employs. Each technique assumes a particular policy that controls how tokens can flow. So, our techniques try to mark in which component states a component holds a token; this marking represents a token flow. This marking is later used to create reachability invariants (i.e. predicates over system states that over-approximate reachability) for the system under analysis.

4.1 Conservative Technique

Each technique proposes a SAT formula $\mathcal{F}$ with a boolean variable $t_{i,s}$ for each state s of each component i such that the values for these variables in a satisfying assignment creates a marking of the component states. The boolean value assigned to $t_{i,s}$ represents whether the component i is holding a virtual token at state s or not. $\mathcal{F}$ is a conjunction of three sub-formulas: *Policy*, *NotAlwaysHoldingToken* and *Participation*.

Policy enforces a token-flow policy; it dictates how tokens are manipulated when components (inter)act (i.e. a system transition takes place). As the system being analysed is triple disjoint, either a component acts on its own (i.e. an individual transition takes place) or a pair of components agrees on a rule and interact (i.e. a pairwise transition takes place). So, this sub-formula relies on constraint $enc_i(s, s')$ to dictate how tokens are to be manipulated by individual transitions, whereas $enc_{i,j}(s, s')$ is its counterpart for pairwise transitions.

The first technique we propose, which we refer to as the *conservative* technique, implements a token-conservation policy. For an individual transition (s, a, s') of component i, $enc_i(s, s')$ is as follows.

$$enc_i(s, s') \mathrel{\widehat{=}} t_{i,s} \leftrightarrow t_{i,s'} \tag{1}$$

For a pairwise transition $(s, a, s') \mathrel{\widehat{=}} ((s_0, s_1), a, (s'_0, s'_1))$ involving components i and j, $enc_{i,j}(s, s')$ is as follows. It allows exchanges of tokens between i and j. It relies on the auxiliary variables max_{src}, min_{src}, max_{tgt}, and min_{tgt} to count the number of tokens in the source s and target s' states, respectively.

$$
\begin{aligned}
enc_{i,j}(s, s') \mathrel{\widehat{=}} \; & max_{src} \leftrightarrow (t_{i,s_0} \vee t_{j,s_1}) \wedge max_{tgt} \leftrightarrow (t_{i,s'_0} \vee t_{j,s'_1}) \\
& \wedge \; min_{src} \leftrightarrow (t_{i,s_0} \wedge t_{j,s_1}) \wedge min_{tgt} \leftrightarrow (t_{i,s'_0} \wedge t_{j,s'_1}) \\
& \wedge \; max_{src} \leftrightarrow max_{tgt} \wedge min_{src} \leftrightarrow min_{tgt}
\end{aligned}
\tag{2}
$$

Policy ensures a token-policy by making sure that for all system transitions either enc_i or $enc_{i,j}$ is enforced, according to whether the transition is individual or pairwise, respectively. Thanks to triple-disjointness, the transitions of system S can be efficiently over-approximated by the examination of components, or rather component projections S_i, and pairs of interacting components, or rather pairwise projections $S_{i,j}$ as per Definition 5.

Definition 7. *Let* $S = (\langle L_1, \ldots, L_n \rangle, \mathcal{R})$ *be a supercombinator machine. The component projection* S_i *of the machine* S *on components* i *is given by:*

$$
S_i = (\langle L_i \rangle, \{((e_i), a) \mid \exists((e_1, \ldots, e_n), a) \in \mathcal{R} \bullet e_i \neq -\})
$$

For a component projection S_i, transitions of its induced LTS that are derived from *pure-individual* rules (i.e. rules that come from individual rules in S) represent possible system transitions, whereas transitions derived from *truncated* rules (i.e. rules that come from pairwise rules of S that involve i and another component of the system) do not. For pairwise projections $S_{i,j}$, only transitions derived from pairwise rules in $S_{i,j}$ represent possible system transitions.

Definition 8. *Let* $S = (\langle L_1, \ldots, L_n \rangle, \mathcal{R})$ *be a supercombinator machine,* Δ_i *the transition relation of the LTS induced by component projection* S_i, $\Delta_{i,j}$ *the transition relation of the LTS induced by pairwise projection* $S_{i,j}$, *and Sync the set of pairs of components interacting, i.e. participating together in a rule, in* S.

$$
Policy \mathrel{\widehat{=}} (\bigwedge_{\substack{i \in \{1 \ldots n\} \\ \wedge (s,a,s') \in \Delta_i \\ \wedge ind_i(s,s')}} enc_i(s, s')) \wedge (\bigwedge_{\substack{(i,j) \in Sync \\ \wedge (s,a,s') \in \Delta_{i,j} \\ \wedge pair_{i,j}(s,s')}} enc_{i,j}(s, s'))
$$

where $ind_i(s, s')$ *holds iff* (s, a, s') *is a transition derived from a pure-individual rule of* S_i *involving component* i, *and* $pair_{i,j}(s, s')$ *holds iff* (s, a, s') *is a transition derived from an pairwise rule of* $S_{i,j}$.

The sub-formulas *NotAlwaysHoldingToken* and *Participation* forbid some trivial markings (i.e. in which tokens do not get exchanged between components) from being valid assignments for our formula. The *NotAlwaysHoldingToken* sub-formula forbids assignments where some component always holds a token, though we do permit components that never hold a token. *Participation* requires the system to hold at least one token initially. To implement *Participation*, we create the participation variables p_i. In a satisfying assignment, the variable p_i states whether component i participates on the token-flow represented by this assignment. These variables play an important role as we present later.

Definition 9. *Let* $\mathcal{S} = (\langle L_1, \ldots, L_n \rangle, \mathcal{R})$ *be a supercombinator machine where* S_i *and* $\hat{s}_i$ *gives the set of states and the starting state of component* L_i, *respectively.*

$$NotAlwaysHoldingToken \mathrel{\hat{=}} \bigwedge_{i \in \{1 \ldots n\}} (\bigvee_{s \in S_i} \neg t_{i,s})$$

$$Participation \mathrel{\hat{=}} \bigwedge_{i \in \{1 \ldots n\}} (p_i \leftrightarrow (\bigvee_{s \in S_i} t_{i,s})) \wedge \bigvee_{i \in \{1 \ldots n\}} t_{i,\hat{s}_i}$$

For the conservative technique, we end up with the following formula:

Definition 10. *For the supercombinator machine* $\mathcal{S}$,

$$\mathcal{F} \mathrel{\hat{=}} Policy \wedge NotAlwaysHoldingToken \wedge Participation$$

where Policy uses enc_i *and* $enc_{i,j}$ *as defined in* (1) *and* (2), *respectively.*

This technique uses function FINDMARKINGS in Algorithm 1 to systematically find markings for different parts of the systems. For this algorithm, we use the function SOLVE to solve SAT formulas. It returns whether the formula is satisfiable and updates the global field $\mathcal{A}$ with a satisfying assignment. When SOLVE is called for an unsatisfiable formula, $\mathcal{A}$ is not updated. We use $\mathcal{A}(var)$ to denote the value assigned to variable var on the satisfying assignment $\mathcal{A}$.

The call to SOLVE in FINDMARKINGS tries to find a marking for some subsystem (i.e. a subset of components) of the system $\mathcal{S}$. Note that the *Participation* clause only requires some subsystem of $\mathcal{S}$ to participate in a token-flow. If a marking is found, it is minimised by MINIMISE. The minimal marking is, then, recorded by EXTRACTMARKING. We modify our formula at the end of each iteration to ensure that in the next iteration we look for a marking for a different subsystem; this also guarantees that our function terminates.

MINIMISE iteratively minimises the subsystem currently marked (i.e. the components that participate in the token-flow associated with the current satisfying assignment in $\mathcal{A}$), making sure a component in this subsystem holds a token initially, until a minimal subsystem is found. It begins with the subsystem marked by FINDMARKINGS, and at each iteration, it tries to mark a strictly smaller subsystem. Finally, EXTRACTMARKING records in the global fields *partitions* and *marking* the subsystem marked and the marking itself.

The proposed minimisation attempts to more finely capture the behaviour of systems. Small(er) subsystems imply that we know more precisely where tokens are confined, and so, we have a better understanding on how tokens can move around. For instance, we can better identify illegal behaviours such as a token that has moved between two confined subsystems.

We use the information recorded in *partitions* and *marking* to create reachability invariants. As we enforce the preservation of the number of tokens for any system transition, all reachable states must have the same number of tokens. So, we can calculate the number of tokens at the initial state and use it to enforce this *sum invariant*; we systematically enforce it for each subsystem in *partitions*.

Algorithm 1. Algorithm to find conservative token-structures

```
1: function FINDMARKINGS(S)
2:     partitions := ∅; marking := ∅
3:     Construct F for S
4:     while SOLVE(F) do
5:         MINIMISE(F)
6:         EXTRACTMARKING(A)
7:         F := F ∧ (        ⋀        ¬p_i)
                       i∈{1...n}∧A(p_i)
8:     end while
9: end function

10: function MINIMISE(F)
11:     repeat
12:         F := F ∧ (  ⋁   ¬p_i) ∧ (  ⋁   t_{i,ŝ_i}) ∧ (  ⋀   ¬p_i)
                     i∈{1...n}        i∈{1...n}           i∈{1...n}
                     ∧A(p_i)          ∧A(p_i)            ∧¬A(p_i)
13:     until not SOLVE(F)
14: end function

15: function EXTRACTMARKING(A)
16:     partitions := partitions ∪ {{i | i ∈ {1...n} ∧ A(p_i)}}
17:     marking := marking ∪ {(i, s, A(t_{i,s})) | i ∈ {1...n} ∧ s ∈ S_i ∧ A(p_i)}
18: end function
```

Definition 11. *Let $\mathcal{S} = (\langle L_1, \ldots, L_n \rangle, \mathcal{R})$ be a supercombinator machine where $\hat{s}_i$ is the starting state for L_i, partitions and marking the sets recorded after the execution of* FINDMARKINGS*(S) in Algorithm 1, and marking(i,s) yields 1 if the state s of component i is assigned to true, and 0 otherwise. The reachability invariant $reach_C(s)$ is as follows:*

$$reach_C(s) \,\hat{=}\, \forall sub \in partitions \bullet N(sub) = Tks(sub, s)$$

where $N(sub) \,\hat{=}\, \sum_{i \in sub} marking(i, \hat{s}_i)$, *and* $Tks(sub, s) \,\hat{=}\, \sum_{i \in sub} marking(i, s_i)$.

This technique should be particularly useful when applied to systems that implement a token-conservation mechanism to avoid reaching undesired states. We illustrate the application of this technique with Running Example 1.

Running example 1. FINDMARKINGS($\mathcal{S}$) can result in *partitions* $= \{\{0, 1, 2\}\}$ and *marking* $= \{(0, s_0), (0, s_1), (1, s_1), (1, s_2), (2, s_1), (2, s_2)\}$; for conciseness, we represent a marking by the states that are assigned to true, so the missing states are assigned to false. With this information, we create the invariant $reach_C(s) \,\hat{=}\, Tks(\{0, 1, 2\}, s) = 1$. As we have that $Tks(\{0, 1, 2\}, (s_1, s_2, s_2)) = 3$, we have that this technique is able to prove that (s_1, s_2, s_2) is unreachable. This reachability invariant can show that this system can never be either filled with tokens, as in (s_1, s_2, s_2), or empty, as in (s_2, s_0, s_0). As these are the two cases in which this system is blocked, this technique can prove that $\mathcal{S}$ is deadlock-free.

In this example, $\mathcal{S}$ is a token network with three components and a single token, initially held by L_0. This technique can, in fact, show that similar systems with N components and n (where $0 < n < N$) tokens are deadlock-free.   □

4.2   Existential Technique

We term our second approach the *existential technique*. It enforces a token-flow policy where tokens can be created and destroyed but not eliminated altogether. We implement this new policy using the following definitions for enc_i and $enc_{i,j}$. For an individual transition (s, a, s') of component i, we define $enc_i(s, s')$ as follows. It says that such transitions can create but not destroy tokens.

$$enc_i(s, s') \mathrel{\widehat{=}} t_{i,s} \rightarrow t_{i,s'} \tag{3}$$

For a pairwise transition $(s, a, s') \mathrel{\widehat{=}} ((s_0, s_1), a, (s_0', s_1'))$ involving components i and j, i and j can create or destroy tokens, provided that whenever a token is destroyed one of i and j continues to hold one. Thus the only way a token can be destroyed is in a pairwise transition where both parties hold a token before and only one after. The auxiliary variables $hastk_{src}$ and $hastk_{tgt}$ represent whether a component holds a token in the source s and target s' states, respectively.

$$enc_{i,j}(s, s') \mathrel{\widehat{=}} hastk_{src} \leftrightarrow (t_{i,s_0} \vee t_{j,s_1}) \wedge hastk_{tgt} \leftrightarrow (t_{i,s_0'} \vee t_{j,s_1'}) \tag{4}$$
$$\wedge \, hastk_{src} \leftrightarrow hastk_{tgt}$$

So, for this technique, we have the following SAT formula:

Definition 12. *For the supercombinator machine $\mathcal{S}$,*

$$\mathcal{F} \mathrel{\widehat{=}} Policy \wedge NotAlwaysHoldingToken \wedge Participation$$

where Policy uses enc_i and $enc_{i,j}$ as defined in (3) and (4), respectively.

The existential technique uses FINDMARKINGS presented in Algorithm 2 to systematically find markings. It works exactly like the one presented for the conservative technique except that it does a second minimisation step, carried out by FURTHERMINIMISE. The functions MINIMISE and EXTRACTMARKING are as described in Algorithm 1.

While MINIMISE tries to minimise the subsystem being marked, FURTHER-MINIMISE tries to minimise the timespan in which components hold a token. Given the minimal assignment found by MINIMISE, it tries to reduce the number of component states where tokens are held[1]. This second minimisation is an attempt to prevent the creation of spurious tokens; for instance, the creation of unnecessary tokens by individual transitions. Again, markings and subsystems marked are recorded in the global fields *marking* and *partitions*.

---

[1] Setting the polarity of SAT variables, so that the solver first decides to assign variables to *false*, can substantially speed this minimisation process.

Algorithm 2. Algorithm to find existential token-structures

```
1: function FINDMARKINGS(S)
2:     partitions := ∅; marking := ∅
3:     Construct F for S
4:     while SOLVE(F) do
5:         MINIMISE(F)
6:         FURTHERMINIMISE(F)
7:         EXTRACTMARKING(A)
8:         F := F ∧ (      ⋀        ¬p_i)
                    i∈{1...n}∧A(p_i)
9:     end while
10: end function

11: function FURTHERMINIMISE(F)
12:     repeat
13:         F := F ∧ (        ⋁        ¬t_{i,s}) ∧ (        ⋀        ¬t_{i,s})
                      i∈{1...n}∧A(p_i)               i∈{1...n}∧A(p_i)
                      ∧s∈S_i∧A(t_{i,s})             ∧s∈S_i∧¬A(t_{i,s})
14:     until not SOLVE(F)
15: end function
```

The information in *partitions* and *marking* is, once again, used to create reachability invariants. Note that our token-flow policy allows tokens to be destroyed as long as tokens are not completely annihilated from the system. So, as this technique guarantees that at least a token exists initially, a token should exists at all times. The reachability invariant that we propose enforce this *existential property* for each subsystem in *partitions*.

Definition 13. *Let* $S = (\langle L_1, \ldots, L_n \rangle, \mathcal{R})$ *be a supercombinator machine where* $\hat{s}_i$ *is the starting state for* L_i, *partitions and marking the sets recorded after the execution of* FINDMARKINGS*(S) in Algorithm 2, and marking*(i, s) *yields* 1 *if the state* s *of component* i *is assigned to true, and* 0 *otherwise. Also,* $Tks(sub, s) \mathrel{\hat{=}} \sum_{i \in sub} marking(i, s_i)$. *The reachability invariant* $reach_E(s)$ *is as follows:*

$$reach_E(s) \mathrel{\hat{=}} \forall sub \in partitions \bullet Tks(sub, s) \geq 1$$

This technique should be particularly useful when applied to systems where tokens represent property of components and the fact that at least one component always has this property (i.e. a token) prevents the system from reaching a "bad" state. We illustrate the application this technique with Running Example 2.

Running example 2. Applying FINDMARKINGS to S can result in *partitions* = $\{\{0, 1, 2\}\}$ and

$$marking = \{(0, s_0), (0, s_1), (0, s_2), (0, s_3), (1, s_0), (1, s_1),$$
$$(1, s_2), (1, s_3), (2, s_0), (2, s_1), (2, s_2), (2, s_3)\}$$

With this information, we create invariant $reach_E(s) \mathbin{\widehat{=}} Tks(\{0,1,2\}, s) \geq 1$. For this examples, we can interpret tokens as marking states in which the component is *not* full, and the invariant being that all components cannot be full at the same time. As we have that $Tks(\{0,1,2\}, (s_6, s_6, s_6)) = 0$, this technique is able to prove that (s_6, s_6, s_6) is unreachable. As this state is the only one in which the system is blocked, this technique can prove that S is deadlock-free. In this example, S is a token network with three components, each of them has a two-slot buffer to store messages. This technique can, in fact, show that similar systems with $N \geq 3$ components with b-slot buffers, where $b \geq 2$, are deadlock-free. $\square$

5 Checking Deadlock-Freedom

In this section we combine Pair, a technique proposed in [4], with the new reachability tests presented in Sect. 4. In this new framework, a potential deadlock is a pair candidate that meets our new reachability invariants.

Definition 14. *Let S be a supercombinator machine and $(S, \Sigma, \Delta, \hat{s})$ its induced LTS. A state $s \in S$ is a deadlock candidate iff deadlock_candidate(s) holds, where deadlock_candidate(s) $\mathbin{\widehat{=}}$ pair_candidate(s) $\wedge$ reach$_C(s) \wedge$ reach$_E(s)$.*

Since our reachability tests over-approximate reachability and every deadlock is also a Pair candidate [4], every deadlock must also be a deadlock candidate. So, a system free of deadlock candidates has to be deadlock free (see proof in [3]).

Theorem 1. *If a supercombinator machine is deadlock-candidate free, then it must also be deadlock free.*

Our new characterisation is clearly more precise than the Pair one, but it remains imprecise: a blocked state can be unreachable and yet meet our two reachability invariants. Nevertheless, by conjoining these new reachability tests, we tighten the state space analysed. Observe that it only takes one failed test to consider a state unreachable. Furthermore, we note that the techniques presented in Sect. 4 might generate different reachability invariants for the same system. This means that we might have different outcomes when verifying systems with this deadlock-checking technique. We illustrate the unpredictability and incompleteness of our method with the following example.

Example 1. Let $S = (\langle L_1, L_2, L_3 \rangle, \mathcal{R})$ be the supercombinator machine such that L_1, L_2 and L_3 are described in Fig. 3 and $\mathcal{R}$ requires components to synchronise on shared events. The states (p_0, q_0, r_1) and (p_1, q_1, r_2) are blocked but not reachable, so neither of them represents a deadlock. Let us consider *partitions* = $\{1, 2, 3\}$, *marking* = $\{p_1, q_1, r_0, r_2\}$ and *marking'* = $\{p_0, q_0, r_0, r_1\}$. For S, the conservative technique cannot find any markings, while the existential technique might compute either *partition* and *marking* or *partition* and *marking'*. If it computes *marking*, then (p_0, q_0, r_1) is proved unreachable but not (p_1, q_1, r_2). In case *marking'* is computed, (p_1, q_1, r_2) is proved unreachable but not (p_0, q_0, r_1). As it cannot use *marking* and *marking'* simultaneously, it cannot show that S is deadlock free. It could with a slightly modification in our techniques. $\square$

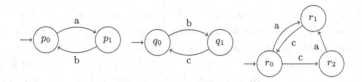

Fig. 3. LTSs of components L_1, L_2 and L_3, respectively.

5.1 Implementation

We built upon [4] to create an efficient implementation for our framework. So, we encode the search for a deadlock candidate as a satisfiability problem to be later checked by a SAT solver. For the remainder of this section, let $S = (\langle L_1, \ldots, L_n \rangle, \mathcal{R})$, where $L_i = (S_i, \Sigma_i, \Delta_i, \hat{s}_i)$, be a supercombinator machine, and $(S, \Sigma, \Delta, \hat{s})$ its induced LTS.

In our propositional encoding, $st_{i,s}$ is the boolean variable representing the state s of component i. The assignment $st_{i,s} = true$ indicates this component state belongs to a deadlock candidate, whereas $st_{i,s} = false$ means it does not. Our formula $\mathcal{DC} \cong PC \wedge Reach_C \wedge Reach_E$ is a conjunction of three sub-formulas, each of them captures a predicate of our deadlock characterisation. The combination of component states assigned to true in a satisfying assignment of $\mathcal{DC}$ forms a deadlock candidate.

The first sub-formula PC captures the pair-candidate characterisation; we reuse the propositional formula that is presented in [4]. The component states assigned to true in a satisfying assignment for PC form a Pair candidate.

$Reach_C$ and $Reach_E$ capture the reachability invariants $reach_C$ and $reach_E$, respectively. To encode $Reach_x$ where x in $\{C, E\}$, we encode the markings with $Marking_x$ and the associated cardinality constraints with $Cardinality_x$. In the following, we assume $partitions_C$ and $marking_C$ were generated by our conservative technique, and $partitions_E$ and $marking_E$ by the existential one.

$Marking_x$, where x is C or E, uses a boolean variable tk_x^i for each component i (tk_x^i conveys whether component i holds a token) to encode the information recorded in $marking_x$, i.e. in which states components hold tokens.

$$Marking_x \cong \bigwedge_{i \in \{1 \ldots n\} \wedge s \in S_i} st_{i,s} \rightarrow \begin{cases} tk_x^i & \text{if } (i, s, true) \in marking_x \\ \neg tk_x^i & \text{if } (i, s, false) \in marking_x \end{cases}$$

The cardinality constraint $Cardinality_C$ uses the variables tk_C^i to make sure that, in a satisfying assignment, subsystems in $partitions_C$ have their expected number of tokens. Let sub be a subsystem in $partitions_C$, $\overline{tk}_C^{sub}$ the vector of variables tk_C^i such that $i \in sub$, $\overline{x}^{sub}$ a vector of fresh boolean variable of size $|sub|$, and $N_C^{sub} = \sum_{i \in sub} marking_C(i, \hat{s}_i)$ the number of tokens confined in sub. Constraint $Sort(\overline{tk}_C^{sub}, \overline{x}^{sub})$ makes sure that $\overline{x}^{sub}$ is the result of sorting the values assigned to $\overline{tk}_C^{sub}$, i.e. true values come first. We use odd-even-merging sorting networks [12] to implement this sorting; they tend to provide a better compromise between the size of the encoding and the efficiency in which these constraints are checked [14]. Intuitively, $\overline{tk}_C^{sub}$ is a unary-unordered representation of the number of tokens being held by components in sub, whereas $\overline{x}^{sub}$ gives its unary-ordered representation. Constraint $Eq(\overline{x}^{sub}, N_C^{sub})$ ensures that $\overline{x}^{sub}$ is the unary-ordered representation of number N_C^{sub}.

$$Cardinality_C \; \hat{=} \bigwedge_{sub \in partitions_C} Sort(\overline{tk}_C^{sub}, \overline{x}_{sub}) \wedge Eq(\overline{x}_{sub}, N_C^{sub})$$

For instance, if in a satisfying assignment we have $\overline{tk}_C^{sub} = (true, false, true)$ (i.e. 101, a unary-unordered representation of 2), $Sort$ makes sure that $\overline{x}^{sub} = (true, true, false)$ (i.e. 110, *the* unary-ordered representation of 2).

The cardinality constraint $Cardinality_E$ uses the variables tk_E^i to ensure that, in a satisfying assignment, subsystems in *partitions* have at least one token. The "at least one token is being held" restriction is a trivial case of a cardinality constraint that can be implemented without need to sorting networks.

$$Cardinality_E \; \hat{=} \bigwedge_{sub \in partitions_E} (\bigvee_{i \in sub} tk_E^i)$$

6   Practical Evaluation

We here evaluate our framework. FDR3's ability to analyse CSP and generate supercombinator machines is exploited in generating our SAT encoding, which is then checked by the Glucose 4.0 solver [11]. Our framework, implemented as the new DeadlOx-VT mode in the DeadlOx tool [5], detects both types of structures and combine them to prove deadlock-freedom[2]. Our tool and the models used in this section are available at [2]. For this experiment, we checked deadlock freedom for some CSP benchmark problems. The experiment was conducted on a dedicated machine with a quad-core Intel Core i5-4300U CPU @ 1.90GHz, and 8GB of RAM. We compare our prototype against: CSDD and FSDD (which are implemented in Martin's Deadlock Checker tool [22]); the original DeadlOx mode [5]; FDR3's built-in deadlock freedom assertion (FDR3) [15], and its combination with partial order reduction (FDR3p) [16] or compression techniques (FDR3c) [25]. We point out that only FDR3's techniques take advantage of the multicore setting.

We analyse 12 systems that are deadlock free, triple disjoint and cannot be proved deadlock-free by pure local analysis. We evaluate systems that cannot be proved deadlock free by pure local analysis as we want to evaluate how well incomplete techniques can leverage global invariants. Out of these systems, 10

---

[2] Note that the conditions for the conservative technique imply those for the existential one. So, a system that has a conservative invariant must have a existential one as well. We plan to improve our tool by, first, detecting conservative structures, and then only in case the invariants derived from these structures are not strong enough to prove deadlock-freedom, we would search for existential structures.

Table 1. Benchmark efficiency comparison. N is a parameter that is used to alter the size of the system. We measure in seconds the time taken to check deadlock freedom for each system. * means that the method took longer than 300 s. - means that the method is unable to prove deadlock freedom. + means that no efficient compression technique could be found. For the DeadlOx-VT, we present the total time taken to verify deadlock freedom in column DF, whereas columns Co and Ex present the time taken for token-structure detection by the conservative and existential techniques, respectively, and x means that a token structure has not been detected. There was no significant difference between the time taken by successful and failed detections of token structures.

	N	Incomplete						Complete		
		DeadlOx	DeadlOx-VT			CSDD	FSDD	FDR3c	FDR3p	FDR3
			DF	Co	Ex					
DDB	5	0.14	-	x	0.02	-	-	0.31	0.18	0.15
	10	1.61	-	x	0.47	-	-	*	*	*
	20	57.75	-	x	19.13	-	-	*	*	*
Mat	10	3.68	-	0.05	0.05	0.17	-	15.52	0.29	*
	20	48.19	-	0.37	0.30	0.59	-	*	22.43	*
	30	*	-	1.97	1.14	2.08	-	*	*	*
Ring	500	0.80	1.34	x	0.22	-	0.86	0.64	*	*
	1000	2.38	4.47	x	0.50	-	2.63	1.49	*	*
	1500	5.02	9.83	x	0.88	-	5.93	6.68	*	*
Sched	500	0.55	0.82	0.19	0.23	0.45	-	3.05	103.26	*
	1000	1.29	2.23	0.55	0.73	0.84	-	8.72	*	*
	1500	2.29	4.76	1.31	1.62	1.30	-	20.06	*	*
Tk	50	0.78	1.08	0.22	0.21	-	-	+	45.62	11.85
	100	5.84	7.40	1.43	1.35	-	-	+	*	*
	200	66.44	76.11	11.23	11.84	-	-	+	*	*
Tk2	50	0.75	1.05	0.21	0.21	-	-	+	*	*
	100	5.71	7.56	1.40	1.46	-	-	+	*	*
	200	63.74	79.13	12.62	12.91	-	-	+	*	*
Tck	100	-	0.48	0.09	0.09	-	-	20.56	2.30	1.30
	200	-	1.16	0.22	0.18	-	-	209.96	23.84	9.24
	500	-	4.85	0.67	0.58	-	-	*	*	177.07
Tck2	100	-	0.55	0.09	0.09	-	-	20.66	*	*
	200	-	1.24	0.21	0.22	-	-	209.96	*	*
	500	-	5.03	0.66	0.54	-	-	*	*	*
RC	30	-	18.81	4.59	4.50	-	-	+	*	5.65
	40	-	79.52	19.00	18.61	-	-	+	*	36.05
	50	-	241.36	54.97	54.69	-	-	+	*	134.58
RC2	30	-	19.08	4.66	4.52	-	-	+	*	*
	40	-	79.95	19.05	19.15	-	-	+	*	*
	50	-	243.39	55.88	55.58	-	-	+	*	*
RE	25	-	0.80	x	0.21	-	-	+	*	*
	50	-	5.21	x	1.42	-	-	+	*	*
	100	-	38.86	x	10.64	-	-	+	*	*
RE10	30	-	20.18	x	5.94	-	-	+	*	*
	40	-	44.93	x	13.09	-	-	+	*	*
	50	-	87.53	x	26.30	-	-	+	*	*

can be proved deadlock free by DeadlOx-VT, 6 by DeadlOx, 2 by CSDD, and 1 by FSDD. The systems that we evaluated are: a distributed database (DDB), a matrix multiplication system (Mat), a non-fillable ring system (Ring), Milner's scheduler (Sched), a token ring system with a single token (Tk), a token ring system with $N/2$ tokens (Tk2), a train track system with two trains (Tck), a train track system with $2N$ trains (Tck2), and four routing networks: RC and RC2 implement a conservative token mechanism with two and $N/2$ tokens intially, respectively, whereas RE and RE10 implement an existential token structure with components that have two-slot and 10-slot buffers, respectively. Table 1 presents the results that we obtain for them.

Our results attest that DeadlOx-VT is able to handle a class of systems that is different from the one tackled by the original DeadlOx, while faring similarly in terms of analysis time. Comparing to the complete approaches, incomplete frameworks are consistently faster than the best complete approach, which is the combination of FDR3's deadlock assertion with compression techniques, while being able to prove deadlock freedom for almost all benchmark problems. The effective use of compression techniques, however, requires a careful and skilful application of those, whereas our method is fully automatic.

The token structures discovered in the Mat example are interesting because we did not anticipate them. Considering these structures, it seems no single one can prove deadlock freedom for this example. However, we have established that a combination of them can. We will comment on this is a subsequent paper.

7 Conclusion

Motivated by deadlock analysis, we have demonstrated that token structures of concurrent systems, sometimes too subtle to be obviously recognisable as such, can be recognised by SAT checkers and used to prove safety properties of the system concerned. We have identified two types of token structures: the first one makes sure that tokens are conserved, and the second one ensures at least one token is present in the system at all times. While we have interpreted these structures as token mechanisms, there might be other views to them. For instance, as we discussed in the application of our existential technique to Running Example 2, tokens can be seen as the component property "component is not full". Our token-structure-detection techniques are combined to create a useful framework for deadlock-freedom analysis that improves on the precision of current incomplete locally-based frameworks, as confirmed by our experiments. These experiments have also demonstrated that, for the systems analysed, the SAT calculations used to detect token structures can be carried out efficiently.

There is nothing CSP-specific in our methods, other than that we have a systems described as a network of pairwise-interacting LTSs. So, the ideas in this paper should transfer easily to any formalism where systems are described as such. DeadlOx-VT uses FDR3 to obtain supercombinator machines from systems described using CSP, but an analogous tool could be created for other notations by replacing its use of FDR3 to generate such machines.

This work begs a number of questions. What other uses, besides deadlock-checking, do the types of invariant we have identified have? What other sorts of invariants are there where partitioning of component states can be efficiently calculated? An obvious one is to handle token systems where nodes can have more than one token, or where there are multiple tokens with different properties. We will aim to answer these questions in future research.

Acknowledgments. The first author is a CAPES Foundation scholarship holder (Process no: 13201/13-1). The second and third authors are partially sponsored by DARPA under agreement number FA8750-12-2-0247 and EPSRC under agreement number EP/N022777.

References

1. Agerwala, T., Choed-Amphai, Y.-C.: A synthesis rule for concurrent systems. In: 15th Conference on Design Automation, pp. 305–311. IEEE (1978)
2. Antonino, P., Gibson-Robinson, T., Roscoe, A.W.: Experiment package (2016). http://www.cs.ox.ac.uk/people/pedro.antonino/pkg-vt.zip
3. Antonino, P., Gibson-Robinson, T., Roscoe, A.W.: The automatic detection of token structures and invariants using SAT checking. Technical report, University of Oxford (2016). http://www.cs.ox.ac.uk/people/pedro.antonino/techreport-vt.pdf
4. Antonino, P., Gibson-Robinson, T., Roscoe, A.W.: Efficient deadlock-freedom checking using local analysis and SAT solving. In: Ábrahám, E., Huisman, M. (eds.) IFM 2016. LNCS, vol. 9681, pp. 345–360. Springer, Heidelberg (2016). doi:10.1007/978-3-319-33693-0_22
5. Antonino, P., Gibson-Robinson, T., Roscoe, A.W.: Tighter reachability criteria for deadlock-freedom analysis. In: Fitzgerald, J., Heitmeyer, C., Gnesi, S., Philippou, A. (eds.) FM 2016. LNCS, vol. 9995, pp. 43–59. Springer, Heidelberg (2016). doi:10.1007/978-3-319-48989-6_3
6. Antonino, P.R.G., Oliveira, M.M., Sampaio, A.C.A., Kristensen, K.E., Bryans, J.W.: Leadership election: an industrial SoS application of compositional deadlock verification. In: Badger, J.M., Rozier, K.Y. (eds.) NFM 2014. LNCS, vol. 8430, pp. 31–45. Springer, Heidelberg (2014). doi:10.1007/978-3-319-06200-6_3
7. Antonino, P., Sampaio, A., Woodcock, J.: A refinement based strategy for local deadlock analysis of networks of CSP processes. In: Jones, C., Pihlajasaari, P., Sun, J. (eds.) FM 2014. LNCS, vol. 8442, pp. 62–77. Springer, Heidelberg (2014). doi:10.1007/978-3-319-06410-9_5
8. Apt, K.R., Francez, N., de Roever, W.P.: A proof system for communicating sequential processes. ACM Trans. Program. Lang. Syst. (TOPLAS) **2**(3), 359–385 (1980)
9. Attie, P.C., Bensalem, S., Bozga, M., Jaber, M., Sifakis, J., Zaraket, F.A.: An abstract framework for deadlock prevention in BIP. In: Beyer, D., Boreale, M. (eds.) FMOODS/FORTE -2013. LNCS, vol. 7892, pp. 161–177. Springer, Heidelberg (2013). doi:10.1007/978-3-642-38592-6_12
10. Attie, P.C., Chockler, H.: Efficiently verifiable conditions for deadlock-freedom of large concurrent programs. In: Cousot, R. (ed.) VMCAI 2005. LNCS, vol. 3385, pp. 465–481. Springer, Heidelberg (2005). doi:10.1007/978-3-540-30579-8_30
11. Audemard, G., Simon, L.: Predicting learnt clauses quality in modern SAT solvers. In: IJCAI 2009, San Francisco, CA, USA, pp. 399–404 (2009)

12. Batcher, K.E.: Sorting networks and their applications. In: Proceedings of the April 30-May 2, Spring Joint Computer Conference, AFIPS 1968 (Spring), pp. 307–314. ACM, New York (1968)

13. Bensalem, S., Lakhnech, Y.: Automatic generation of invariants. Form. Methods Syst. Des. **15**(1), 75–92 (1999)

14. Eén, N., Sörensson, N.: Translating pseudo-boolean constraints into SAT. JSAT **2**(1–4), 1–26 (2006)

15. Gibson-Robinson, T., Armstrong, P., Boulgakov, A., Roscoe, A.W.: FDR3 — a modern refinement checker for CSP. In: Ábrahám, E., Havelund, K. (eds.) TACAS 2014. LNCS, vol. 8413, pp. 187–201. Springer, Heidelberg (2014). doi:10.1007/978-3-642-54862-8_13

16. Gibson-Robinson, T., Hansen, H., Roscoe, A.W., Wang, X.: Practical partial order reduction for CSP. In: Havelund, K., Holzmann, G., Joshi, R. (eds.) NFM 2015. LNCS, vol. 9058, pp. 188–203. Springer, Heidelberg (2015). doi:10.1007/978-3-319-17524-9_14

17. Hoare, C.A.R.: Communicating Sequential Processes. Prentice-Hall, Upper Saddle River (1985)

18. Jezequel, L., Lime, D.: Lazy reachability analysis in distributed systems. In: 27th International Conference on Concurrency Theory, CONCUR 2016, 23-26 August 2016, Quebec City, Canada, pp. 17:1–17:14 (2016)

19. Lambertz, C., Majster-Cederbaum, M.: Analyzing component-based systems on the basis of architectural constraints. In: Arbab, F., Sirjani, M. (eds.) FSEN 2011. LNCS, vol. 7141, pp. 64–79. Springer, Heidelberg (2012). doi:10.1007/978-3-642-29320-7_5

20. Lamport, L.: Proving the correctness of multiprocess programs. IEEE Trans. Softw. Eng. **2**, 125–143 (1977)

21. Martin, J.M.R.: The design and construction of deadlock-free concurrent systems. Ph.D. thesis, University of Buckingham (1996)

22. Martin, J.M.R., Jassim, S.A.: An efficient technique for deadlock analysis of large scale process networks. In: Fitzgerald, J., Jones, C.B., Lucas, P. (eds.) FME 1997. LNCS, vol. 1313, pp. 418–441. Springer, Heidelberg (1997). doi:10.1007/3-540-63533-5_22

23. Murata, T.: Petri nets: properties, analysis and applications. Proc. IEEE **77**(4), 541–580 (1989)

24. Oliveira, M.V.M., Antonino, P., Ramos, R., Sampaio, A., Mota, A., Roscoe, A.W.: Rigorous development of component-based systems using component metadata and patterns. Formal Aspects Comput. **28**, 937–1004 (2016)

25. Roscoe, A.W., Gardiner, P.H.B., Goldsmith, M.H., Hulance, J.R., Jackson, D.M., Scattergood, J.B.: Hierarchical compression for model-checking CSP or how to check 10^{20} dining philosophers for deadlock. In: Brinksma, E., Cleaveland, W.R., Larsen, K.G., Margaria, T., Steffen, B. (eds.) TACAS 1995. LNCS, vol. 1019, pp. 133–152. Springer, Heidelberg (1995). doi:10.1007/3-540-60630-0_7

26. Roscoe, A.W.: Understanding Concurrent Systems. Springer, Heidelberg (2010)

Quantitative Systems II

Maximizing the Conditional Expected Reward for Reaching the Goal

Christel Baier[⊠], Joachim Klein[⊠], Sascha Klüppelholz[⊠],
and Sascha Wunderlich[⊠]

Institute for Theoretical Computer Science, Technische Universität Dresden,
Dresden, Germany
{christel.baier,joachim.klein,sascha.klueppelholz,
sascha.wunderlich}@tu-dresden.de

Abstract. The paper addresses the problem of computing maximal conditional expected accumulated rewards until reaching a target state (briefly called *maximal conditional expectations*) in finite-state Markov decision processes where the condition is given as a reachability constraint. Conditional expectations of this type can, e.g., stand for the maximal expected termination time of probabilistic programs with nondeterminism, under the condition that the program eventually terminates, or for the worst-case expected penalty to be paid, assuming that at least three deadlines are missed. The main results of the paper are (i) a polynomial-time algorithm to check the finiteness of maximal conditional expectations, (ii) PSPACE-completeness for the threshold problem in acyclic Markov decision processes where the task is to check whether the maximal conditional expectation exceeds a given threshold, (iii) a pseudo-polynomial-time algorithm for the threshold problem in the general (cyclic) case, and (iv) an exponential-time algorithm for computing the maximal conditional expectation and an optimal scheduler.

1 Introduction

Stochastic shortest (or longest) path problems are a prominent class of optimization problems where the task is to find a policy for traversing a probabilistic graph structure such that the expected value of the generated paths satisfying a certain objective is minimal (or maximal). In the classical setting (see e.g. [15,22,25,29]), the underlying graph structure is given by a finite-state Markov decision process (MDP), i.e., a state-transition graph with nondeterministic choices between several actions for each of its non-terminal states, probability distributions specifying the probabilities for the successor states for each state-action pair and a reward function that assigns rational values to the state-action pairs. The stochastic shortest (longest) path problem asks to find a scheduler, i.e., a function that resolves the nondeterministic choices, possibly in a

---

The authors are supported by the DFG through the collaborative research centre HAEC (SFB 912), the Excellence Initiative by the German Federal and State Governments (cluster of excellence cfAED), the Research Training Group QuantLA (GRK 1763), and the DFG-project BA-1679/11-1.

A. Legay and T. Margaria (Eds.): TACAS 2017, Part II, LNCS 10206, pp. 269–285, 2017.
DOI: 10.1007/978-3-662-54580-5_16

history-dependent way, which minimizes (maximizes) the expected accumulated reward until reaching a goal state. To ensure the existence of the expectation for given schedulers, one often assumes that the given MDP is contracting, i.e., the goal is reached almost surely under all schedulers, in which case the optimal expected accumulated reward is achieved by a memoryless deterministic scheduler that optimizes the expectation from each state and is computable using a linear program with one variable per state (see e.g. [25]). The contraction assumption can be relaxed by requiring the existence of at least one scheduler that reaches the goal almost surely and taking the extremum over all those schedulers [15,16,22]. These algorithms and corresponding value or policy iteration approaches have been implemented in various tools and used in many application areas.

The restriction to schedulers that reach the goal almost surely, however, limits the applicability and significance of the results. First, the known algorithms for computing extremal expected accumulated rewards are not applicable for models where the probability for never visiting a goal state is positive under each scheduler. Second, statements about the expected rewards for schedulers that reach the goal with probability 1 are not sufficient to draw any conclusion for the best- or worst-case behavior, if there exist schedulers that miss the goal with positive probability. This motivates the consideration of *conditional stochastic path problems* where the task is to compute the optimal expected accumulated reward until reaching a goal state, under the condition that a goal state will indeed be reached and where the extrema are taken over all schedulers that reach the goal with positive probability. More precisely, we address here a slightly more general problem where we are given two sets F and G of states in an MDP $\mathcal{M}$ with non-negative integer rewards and ask for the maximal expected accumulated reward until reaching F, under the condition that G will be visited (denoted $\mathbb{E}^{\max}_{\mathcal{M},s_{init}}(\Phi F | \Diamond G)$ where s_{init} is the initial state of $\mathcal{M}$). Computation schemes for conditional expectations of this type can, e.g., be used to answer the following questions (assuming the underlying model is a finite-state MDP):

(Q1) What is the maximal termination time of a probabilistic and nondeterministic program, under the condition that the program indeed terminates?

(Q2) What are the maximal expected costs of the repair mechanisms that are triggered in cases where a specific failure scenario occurs, under the condition that the failure scenario indeed occurs?

(Q3) What is the maximal energy consumption, under the condition that all jobs of a given list will be successfully executed within one hour?

The relevance of question (Q1) and related problems becomes clear from the work [14,20,23,24,26] on the semantics of probabilistic programs where no guarantees for almost-sure termination can be given. Question (Q2) is natural for a worst-case analysis of resilient systems or other types of systems where conditional probabilities serve to provide performance guarantees on the protocols triggered in exceptional cases that appear with positive, but low probability. Question (Q3) is typical when the task is to study the trade-off between cost and utility functions (see e.g. [9]). Given the work on anonymity and related notions for information leakage using conditional probabilities in MDP-like models [7,21] or

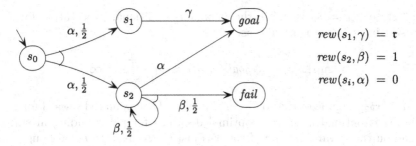

Fig. 1. MDP $\mathcal{M}[\mathfrak{r}]$ for Example 1.1

the formalization of posterior vulnerability as an expectation [4], the concept of conditional accumulated excepted rewards might also be useful to specify the degree of protection of secret data or to study the trade-off between privacy and utility, e.g., using gain functions [3,5]. Other areas where conditional expectations play a crucial role are risk management where the conditional value-at-risk is used to formalize the expected loss under the assumption that very large losses occur [2,32] or regression analysis where conditional expectations serve to predict the relation between random variables [31].

Example 1.1. To illustrate the challenges for designing algorithms to compute maximal conditional expectations we regard the MDP $\mathcal{M}[\mathfrak{r}]$ shown in Fig. 1. The reward of the state-action pair (s_1, γ) is given by a reward parameter $\mathfrak{r} \in \mathbb{N}$. Let $s_{init} = s_0$ be the initial state and $F = G = \{goal\}$. The only nondeterministic choice is in state s_2, while states s_0 and s_1 behave purely probabilistic and *goal* and *fail* are trap states. Given a scheduler $\mathfrak{S}$, we write $\mathbb{CE}^{\mathfrak{S}}$ for the conditional expectation $\mathbb{E}^{\mathfrak{S}}_{\mathcal{M}[\mathfrak{r}], s_0}(\diamondsuit goal | \diamondsuit goal)$. (See also Sect. 2 for our notations.) For the two memoryless schedulers that choose α resp. β in state s_2 we have:

$$\mathbb{CE}^{\alpha} = \frac{\frac{1}{2} \cdot \mathfrak{r} + \frac{1}{2} \cdot 0}{\frac{1}{2} + \frac{1}{2}} = \frac{\mathfrak{r}}{2} \quad \text{and} \quad \mathbb{CE}^{\beta} = \frac{\frac{1}{2} \cdot \mathfrak{r} + 0}{\frac{1}{2} + 0} = \mathfrak{r}$$

We now regard the schedulers $\mathfrak{S}_n$ for $n = 1, 2, \ldots$ that choose β for the first n visits of s_2 and action α for the $(n+1)$-st visit of s_2. Then:

$$\mathbb{CE}^{\mathfrak{S}_n} = \frac{\frac{1}{2} \cdot \mathfrak{r} + \frac{1}{2} \cdot \frac{1}{2^n} \cdot n}{\frac{1}{2} + \frac{1}{2} \cdot \frac{1}{2^n}} = \mathfrak{r} + \frac{n - \mathfrak{r}}{2^n + 1}$$

Thus, $\mathbb{CE}^{\mathfrak{S}_n} > \mathbb{CE}^{\beta}$ iff $n > \mathfrak{r}$, and the maximum is achieved for $n = \mathfrak{r}+2$.

This example illustrates three phenomena that distinguish conditional and unconditional expected accumulated rewards and make reasoning about maximal conditional expectations harder than about unconditional ones. First, optimal schedulers for $\mathcal{M}[\mathfrak{r}]$ need a counter for the number of visits in state s_2. Hence, memoryless schedulers are not powerful enough to maximize the conditional expectation. Second, while the maximal conditional expectation for $\mathcal{M}[\mathfrak{r}]$ with initial state $s_{init} = s_0$ is finite, the maximal conditional expectation for $\mathcal{M}[\mathfrak{r}]$ with starting state s_2 is infinite as:

$$\sup_{n\in\mathbb{N}} \mathbb{E}^{\mathfrak{S}_n}_{\mathcal{M}[\mathfrak{r}],s_2}(\oplus goal\,|\Diamond goal) = \sup_{n\in\mathbb{N}} \frac{\frac{n}{2^n}}{\frac{1}{2^n}} = \infty$$

Third, as $\mathfrak{S}_2$ maximizes the conditional expected accumulated reward for $\mathfrak{r} = 0$, while $\mathfrak{S}_3$ is optimal for $\mathfrak{r} = 1$, optimal decisions for paths ending in state s_2 depend on the reward value r of the γ-transition from state s_1, although state s_1 is not reachable from s_2. Thus, optimal decisions for a path π do not only depend on the past (given by π) and possible future (given by the sub-MDP that is reachable from π's last state), but require global reasoning.   ∎

The main results of this paper are the following theorems. We write $\mathbb{CE}^{max}$ for the maximal conditional expectation, i.e., the supremum of the conditional expectations $\mathbb{E}^{\mathfrak{S}}_{\mathcal{M},s_{init}}(\oplus F\,|\Diamond G)$, when ranging over all schedulers $\mathfrak{S}$ where $\Pr^{\mathfrak{S}}_{\mathcal{M},s_{init}}(\Diamond G)$ is positive and $\Pr^{\mathfrak{S}}_{\mathcal{M},s_{init}}(\Diamond F\,|\Diamond G) = 1$. (See also Sect. 2 for our notations.)

Theorem 1 (Checking finiteness and upper bound). *There is a polynomial-time algorithm that checks if $\mathbb{CE}^{max}$ is finite. If so, an upper bound $\mathbb{CE}^{ub}$ for $\mathbb{CE}^{max}$ is computable in pseudo-polynomial time for the general case and in polynomial time if $F = G$ and $\Pr^{min}_{\mathcal{M},s}(\Diamond G) > 0$ for all states s with $s \models \exists\Diamond G$.*

The threshold problem asks whether the maximal conditional expectation exceeds or misses a given rational threshold ϑ.

Theorem 2 (Threshold problem). *The problem "does $\mathbb{CE}^{max} \bowtie \vartheta$ hold?" (where $\bowtie\, \in \{>, \geq, <, \leq\}$) is PSPACE-hard and solvable in exponential (even pseudo-polynomial) time. It is PSPACE-complete for acyclic MDPs.*

For the computation of an optimal scheduler, we suggest an iterative scheduler-improvement algorithm that interleaves calls of the threshold algorithm with linear programming techniques to handle zero-reward actions. This yields:

Theorem 3 (Computing optimal schedulers). *The value $\mathbb{CE}^{max}$ and an optimal scheduler $\mathfrak{S}$ are computable in exponential time.*

Algorithms for checking finiteness and computing an upper bound (Theorem 1) will be sketched in Sect. 3. Section 4 presents a pseudo-polynomial threshold algorithm and a polynomially space-bounded algorithm for acyclic MDPs (Theorem 2) as well as an exponential-time computation scheme for the construction of an optimal scheduler (Theorem 3). Further details, soundness proofs and a proof for the PSPACE-hardness as stated in Theorem 2 can be found in [13]. The general feasibility of the algorithms will be shown by experimental studies with a prototypical implementation (for details, see Appendix K of [13]).

Related Work. Although conditional expectations appear rather naturally in many applications and despite the large amount of publications on variants of stochastic path problems and other forms of expectations in MDPs (see e.g. [18,30]), we are not aware that they have been addressed in the context of MDPs. Computation schemes for extremal conditional probabilities $\Pr^{\max}(\varphi|\psi)$ or $\Pr^{\min}(\varphi|\psi)$ where both the objective φ and the assumption ψ are path properties specified in some temporal logic have been studied in [6,8,11]. For reachability properties φ and ψ, the algorithm of [6,8] has exponential time complexity, while the algorithm of [11] runs in polynomial time. Although the approach of [11] is not applicable for calculating maximal conditional expectations (see Appendix B of [13]), it can be used to compute an upper bound for $\mathbb{CE}^{\max}$ (see Sect. 3). Conditional expected rewards in Markov chains can be computed using the rescaling technique of [11] for finite Markov chains or the approximation techniques of [1,19] for certain classes of infinite-state Markov chains. The conditional weakest precondition operator of [26] yields a technique to compute conditional expected rewards for purely probabilistic programs (without non-determinism).

2   Preliminaries

We briefly summarize our notations used for Markov decision processes. Further details can be found in textbooks, see e.g. [25,29] or Chapter 10 in [10].

A *Markov decision process* (MDP) is a tuple $\mathcal{M} = (S, Act, P, s_{init}, rew)$ where S is a finite set of states, Act a finite set of actions, $s_{init} \in S$ the initial state, $P : S \times Act \times S \rightarrow [0,1] \cap \mathbb{Q}$ is the transition probability function and $rew : S \times Act \rightarrow \mathbb{N}$ the reward function. We require that $\sum_{s' \in S} P(s, \alpha, s') \in \{0,1\}$ for all $(s, \alpha) \in S \times Act$. We write $Act(s)$ for the set of actions that are enabled in s, i.e., $\alpha \in Act(s)$ iff $P(s, \alpha, \cdot)$ is not the null function. State s is called a *trap* if $Act(s) = \varnothing$. The paths of $\mathcal{M}$ are finite or infinite sequences $s_0 \alpha_0 s_1 \alpha_1 s_2 \alpha_2 \ldots$ where states and actions alternate such that $P(s_i, \alpha_i, s_{i+1}) > 0$ for all $i \geqslant 0$. A path π is called *maximal* if it is either infinite or finite and its last state is a trap. If $\pi = s_0 \alpha_0 s_1 \alpha_1 s_2 \alpha_2 \ldots \alpha_{k-1} s_k$ is finite then $rew(\pi) = rew(s_0, \alpha_0) + rew(s_1, \alpha_1) + \ldots + rew(s_{k-1}, \alpha_{k-1})$ denotes the accumulated reward and $first(\pi) = s_0$, $last(\pi) = s_k$ its first resp. last state. The *size* of $\mathcal{M}$, denoted $size(\mathcal{M})$, is the sum of the number of states plus the total sum of the logarithmic lengths of the non-zero probability values $P(s, \alpha, s')$ and the reward values $rew(s, \alpha)$.[1]

An *end component* of $\mathcal{M}$ is a strongly connected sub-MDP. End components can be formalized as pairs $\mathcal{E} = (E, \mathfrak{A})$ where E is a nonempty subset of S and $\mathfrak{A}$ a function that assigns to each state $s \in E$ a nonempty subset of $Act(s)$ such that the graph induced by $\mathcal{E}$ is strongly connected.

A *(randomized) scheduler* for $\mathcal{M}$, often also called policy or adversary, is a function $\mathfrak{S}$ that assigns to each finite path π where $last(\pi)$ is not a trap a

---

[1]   The logarithmic length of an integer n is the number of bits required for a representation of n as a binary number. The logarithmic length of a rational number a/b is defined as the sum of the logarithmic lengths of its numerator a and its denominator b, assuming that a and b are coprime integers and b is positive.

probability distribution over $Act(last(\pi))$. $\mathfrak{S}$ is called memoryless if $\mathfrak{S}(\pi) = \mathfrak{S}(\pi')$ for all finite paths π, π' with $last(\pi) = last(\pi')$, in which case $\mathfrak{S}$ can be viewed as a function that assigns to each non-trap state s a distribution over $Act(s)$. $\mathfrak{S}$ is called deterministic if $\mathfrak{S}(\pi)$ is a Dirac distribution for each path π, in which case $\mathfrak{S}$ can be viewed as a function that assigns an action to each finite path π where $last(\pi)$ is not a trap. We write $\Pr^{\mathfrak{S}}_{\mathcal{M},s}$ or briefly $\Pr^{\mathfrak{S}}_s$ to denote the probability measure induced by $\mathfrak{S}$ and s. Given a measurable set ψ of maximal paths, then $\Pr^{\min}_{\mathcal{M},s}(\psi) = \inf_{\mathfrak{S}} \Pr^{\mathfrak{S}}_{\mathcal{M},s}(\psi)$ and $\Pr^{\max}_{\mathcal{M},s}(\psi) = \sup_{\mathfrak{S}} \Pr^{\mathfrak{S}}_{\mathcal{M},s}(\psi)$. We will use LTL-like notations to specify measurable sets of maximal paths. For these it is well-known that optimal deterministic schedulers exists. If ψ is a reachability condition then even optimal deterministic memoryless schedulers exist.

Let $\varnothing \neq F \subseteq S$. For a comparison operator $\bowtie \in \{=, >, \geqslant, <, \leqslant\}$ and $r \in \mathbb{N}$, $\lozenge^{\bowtie r} F$ denotes the event "reaching F along some finite path π with $rew(\pi) \bowtie r$". The notation $\spadesuit F$ will be used for the random variable that assigns to each maximal path ς in $\mathcal{M}$ the reward $rew(\pi)$ of the shortest prefix π of ς where $last(\pi) \in F$. If $\varsigma \not\models \lozenge F$ then $(\spadesuit F)(\varsigma) = \infty$. If $s \in S$ then $\mathbb{E}^{\mathfrak{S}}_{\mathcal{M},s}(\spadesuit F)$ denotes the expectation of $\spadesuit F$ in $\mathcal{M}$ with starting state s under $\mathfrak{S}$, which is infinite if $\Pr^{\mathfrak{S}}_{\mathcal{M},s}(\lozenge F) < 1$. $\mathbb{E}^{\max}_{\mathcal{M},s}(\spadesuit F) \in \mathbb{R} \cup \{\pm\infty\}$ stands for $\sup_{\mathfrak{S}} \mathbb{E}^{\mathfrak{S}}_{\mathcal{M},s}(\spadesuit F)$ where the supremum is taken over all schedulers $\mathfrak{S}$ with $\Pr^{\mathfrak{S}}_{\mathcal{M},s}(\lozenge F) = 1$. Let ψ be a measurable set of maximal paths. $\mathbb{E}^{\mathfrak{S}}_{\mathcal{M},s}(\spadesuit F | \psi)$ stands for the expectation of $\spadesuit F$ w.r.t. the conditional probability measure $\Pr^{\mathfrak{S}}_{\mathcal{M},s}(\cdot | \psi)$ given by $\Pr^{\mathfrak{S}}_{\mathcal{M},s}(\varphi | \psi) = \Pr^{\mathfrak{S}}_{\mathcal{M},s}(\varphi \wedge \psi) / \Pr^{\mathfrak{S}}_{\mathcal{M},s}(\psi)$. $\mathbb{E}^{\max}_{\mathcal{M},s}(\spadesuit F | \psi)$ is the supremum of $\mathbb{E}^{\mathfrak{S}}_{\mathcal{M},s}(\spadesuit F | \psi)$ where $\Pr^{\mathfrak{S}}_{\mathcal{M},s}(\psi) > 0$ and $\Pr^{\mathfrak{S}}_{\mathcal{M},s}(\lozenge F | \psi) = 1$, and $\Pr^{\max}_{\mathcal{M},s}(\varphi | \psi) = \sup_{\mathfrak{S}} \Pr^{\mathfrak{S}}_{\mathcal{M},s}(\varphi | \psi)$ where $\mathfrak{S}$ ranges over all schedulers with $\Pr^{\mathfrak{S}}_{\mathcal{M},s}(\psi) > 0$ and $\sup \varnothing = -\infty$.

For the remainder of this paper, we suppose that two nonempty subsets F and G of S are given such that $\Pr^{\max}_{\mathcal{M},s}(\lozenge F | \lozenge G) = 1$. The task addressed in this paper is to compute the maximal conditional expectation given by:

$$\mathbb{CE}^{\max}_{\mathcal{M},s} \stackrel{\text{def}}{=} \sup_{\mathfrak{S}} \mathbb{CE}^{\mathfrak{S}}_{\mathcal{M},s} \in \mathbb{R} \cup \{\infty\} \quad \text{where} \quad \mathbb{CE}^{\mathfrak{S}}_{\mathcal{M},s} = \mathbb{E}^{\mathfrak{S}}_{\mathcal{M},s}(\spadesuit F | \lozenge G)$$

Here, $\mathfrak{S}$ ranges over all schedulers $\mathfrak{S}$ with $\Pr^{\mathfrak{S}}_{\mathcal{M},s}(\lozenge G) > 0$ and $\Pr^{\mathfrak{S}}_{\mathcal{M},s}(\lozenge F | \lozenge G) = 1$. If $\mathcal{M}$ and its initial state are clear from the context, we often simply write $\mathbb{CE}^{\max}$ resp. $\mathbb{CE}^{\mathfrak{S}}$. We assume that all states in $\mathcal{M}$ are reachable from s_{init} and $s_{init} \notin F \cup G$ (as $\mathbb{CE}^{\max} = 0$ if $s \in F$ and $\mathbb{CE}^{\max} = \mathbb{E}^{\max}_{\mathcal{M},s_{init}}(\spadesuit F)$ if $s \in G \setminus F$).

3   Finiteness and Upper Bound

Checking Finiteness. We sketch a polynomially time-bounded algorithm that takes as input an MDP $\mathcal{M} = (S, Act, P, s_{init}, rew)$ with two distinguished subsets F and G of S such that $\Pr^{\max}_{\mathcal{M},s_{init}}(\lozenge F | \lozenge G) = 1$. If $\mathbb{CE}^{\max} = \mathbb{E}^{\max}_{\mathcal{M},s_{init}}(\spadesuit F | \lozenge G) = \infty$ then the output is "no". Otherwise, the output is an MDP $\hat{\mathcal{M}} = (\hat{S}, \hat{Act}, \hat{P}, \hat{s}_{init}, \hat{rew})$ with two trap states $goal$ and $fail$ such that:

(1) $\mathbb{E}^{\max}_{\mathcal{M}, \hat{s}_{init}}(\diamondsuit\!\!\!\!\!\!\diamond\, F | \diamondsuit G) = \mathbb{E}^{\max}_{\hat{\mathcal{M}}, \hat{s}_{init}}(\diamondsuit\!\!\!\!\!\!\diamond\, goal | \diamondsuit goal)$,

(2) $\hat{s} \models \exists\diamondsuit goal$ and $\Pr^{\min}_{\hat{\mathcal{M}}, \hat{s}}(\diamondsuit(goal \vee fail)) = 1$ for all states $\hat{s} \in \hat{S} \setminus \{fail\}$, and

(3) $\hat{\mathcal{M}}$ does not have critical schedulers where a scheduler $\mathfrak{U}$ for $\hat{\mathcal{M}}$ is said to be critical iff $\Pr^{\mathfrak{U}}_{\hat{\mathcal{M}}, \hat{s}_{init}}(\diamondsuit fail) = 1$ and there is a reachable positive $\mathfrak{U}$-cycle.[2]

We provide here the main ideas of the algorithms and refer to Appendix C of [13] for the details. The algorithm first transforms $\mathcal{M}$ into an MDP $\tilde{\mathcal{M}}$ that permits to assume $F = G = goal$. Intuitively, $\tilde{\mathcal{M}}$ simulates $\mathcal{M}$, while operating in four modes: "normal mode", "after G", "after F" and "goal". $\tilde{\mathcal{M}}$ starts in normal mode where it behaves as $\mathcal{M}$ as long as neither F nor G have been visited. If a $G \setminus F$-state has been reached in normal mode then $\tilde{\mathcal{M}}$ switches to the mode "after G". Likewise, as soon as an $F \setminus G$-state has been reached in normal mode then $\tilde{\mathcal{M}}$ switches to the mode "after F". $\tilde{\mathcal{M}}$ enters the goal mode (consisting of a single trap state $goal$) as soon as a path fragment containing a state in F and a state in G has been generated. This is the case if $\mathcal{M}$ visits an F-state in mode "after G" or a G-state in mode "after F", or a state in $F \cap G$ in the normal mode. The rewards in the normal mode and in mode "after G" are precisely as in $\mathcal{M}$, while the rewards are 0 in all other cases. We then remove all states $\tilde{s}$ in the "after G" mode with $\Pr^{\max}_{\tilde{\mathcal{M}}, \tilde{s}}(\diamondsuit goal) < 1$, collapse all states $\tilde{s}$ in $\tilde{\mathcal{M}}$ with $\tilde{s} \not\models \exists\diamondsuit goal$ into a single trap state called $fail$ and add zero-reward transitions to $fail$ from all states $\tilde{s}$ that are not in the "after G" mode and $\Pr^{\max}_{\tilde{\mathcal{M}}, \tilde{s}}(\diamondsuit goal) = 0$.

Using techniques as in the unconditional case [22] we can check whether $\tilde{\mathcal{M}}$ has positive end components, i.e., end components with at least one state-action pair (s, α) with $rew(s, \alpha) > 0$. If so, then $\mathbb{E}^{\max}_{\mathcal{M}, \hat{s}_{init}}(\diamondsuit\!\!\!\!\!\!\diamond\, F | \diamondsuit G) = \infty$. Otherwise, we collapse each maximal end component of $\tilde{\mathcal{M}}$ into a single state.

Let $\hat{\mathcal{M}}$ denote the resulting MDP. It satisfies (1) and (2). Property (3) holds iff $\mathbb{E}^{\max}_{\hat{\mathcal{M}}, \hat{s}_{init}}(\diamondsuit\!\!\!\!\!\!\diamond\, goal | \diamondsuit goal) < \infty$. This condition can be checked in polynomial time using a graph analysis in the sub-MDP of $\hat{\mathcal{M}}$ consisting of the states $\hat{s}$ with $\Pr^{\min}_{\hat{\mathcal{M}}, \hat{s}}(\diamondsuit goal) = 0$ (see Appendix C of [13]).

Computing an Upper Bound. Due to the transformation used for checking finiteness of the maximal conditional expectation, we can now suppose that $\mathcal{M} = \hat{\mathcal{M}}$, $F = G = \{goal\}$ and that (2) and (3) hold. We now present a technique to compute an upper bound $\mathbb{CE}^{ub}$ for $\mathbb{CE}^{\max}$. The upper bound will be used later to determine a saturation point from which on optimal schedulers behave memoryless (see Sect. 4).

We consider the MDP $\mathcal{M}'$ simulating $\mathcal{M}$, while operating in two modes. In its first mode, $\mathcal{M}'$ attaches the reward accumulated so far to the states. More precisely, the states of $\mathcal{M}'$ in its first mode have the form $\langle s, r \rangle \in S \times \mathbb{N}$ where $0 \leqslant r \leqslant R$ and $R = \sum_{s \in S'} \max\{rew_{\mathcal{M}'}(s, \alpha) : \alpha \in Act_{\mathcal{M}'}(s)\}$. The initial state of $\mathcal{M}'$ is $s'_{init} = \langle s_{init}, 0 \rangle$. The reward for the state-action pairs $(\langle s, r \rangle, \alpha)$ where $r + rew(s, \alpha) \leqslant R$ is 0. If $\mathcal{M}'$ fires an action α in state $\langle s, r \rangle$ where

---

[2] The latter means a $\mathfrak{U}$-path $\pi = s_0 \alpha_0 s_1 \alpha_1 \ldots \alpha_{k-1} s_k$ where $s_0 = \hat{s}_{init}$ and $s_i = s_k$ for some $i \in \{0, 1, \ldots, k-1\}$ such that $r\hat{e}w(s_j, \alpha_j) > 0$ for some $j \in \{i, \ldots, k-1\}$.

$r' \stackrel{\text{def}}{=} r + rew(s, \alpha) > R$ then it switches to the second mode, while earning reward r'. In its second mode $\mathcal{M}'$ behaves as $\mathcal{M}$ without additional annotations of the states and earning the same rewards as $\mathcal{M}$. From the states $\langle goal, r \rangle$, $\mathcal{M}'$ moves to $goal$ with probability 1 and reward r. There is a one-to-one correspondence between the schedulers for $\mathcal{M}$ and $\mathcal{M}'$ and the switch from $\mathcal{M}$ to $\mathcal{M}'$ does not affect the probabilities and the accumulated rewards until reaching $goal$.

Let $\mathcal{N}$ denote the MDP resulting from $\mathcal{M}'$ by adding reset-transitions from $fail$ (as a state of the second mode) and the copies $\langle fail, r \rangle$ in the first mode to the initial state s'_{init}. The reward of all reset transitions is 0. The reset-mechanism has been taken from [11] where it has been introduced as a technique to compute maximal conditional probabilities for reachability properties. Intuitively, $\mathcal{N}$ "discards" all paths of $\mathcal{M}'$ that eventually enter $fail$ and "redistributes" their probabilities to the paths that eventually enter the goal state. In this way, $\mathcal{N}$ mimics the conditional probability measures $\Pr^{\mathfrak{S}}_{\mathcal{M}', s'_{init}}(\, \cdot \, | \Diamond goal) = \Pr^{\mathfrak{S}}_{\mathcal{M}, s_{init}}(\, \cdot \, | \Diamond goal)$ for prefix-independent path properties. Paths π from s_{init} to $goal$ in $\mathcal{M}$ are simulated in $\mathcal{N}$ by paths of the form $\varrho = \xi_1; \ldots \xi_k; \pi$ where ξ_i is a cycle in $\mathcal{N}$ with $first(\xi_i) = s'_{init}$ and ξ_i's last transition is a reset-transition from some fail-state to s'_{init}. Thus, $rew(\pi) \leqslant rew_{\mathcal{N}}(\varrho)$. The distinction between the first and second mode together with property (3) ensure that the new reset-transitions do not generate positive end components in $\mathcal{N}$. By the results of [22], the maximal unconditional expected accumulated reward in $\mathcal{N}$ is finite and we have:

$$\mathbb{E}^{\max}_{\mathcal{M}, s_{init}}(\oplus goal | \Diamond goal) = \mathbb{E}^{\max}_{\mathcal{M}', s'_{init}}(\oplus goal | \Diamond goal) \leqslant \mathbb{E}^{\max}_{\mathcal{N}, s'_{init}}(\oplus goal)$$

Hence, we can deal with $\mathbb{CE}^{\mathrm{ub}} = \mathbb{E}^{\max}_{\mathcal{N}, s'_{init}}(\oplus goal)$, which is computable in time polynomial in the size of $\mathcal{N}$ by the algorithm proposed in [22]. As $size(\mathcal{N}) = \Theta(R \cdot size(\mathcal{M}))$ we obtain a pseudo-polynomial time bound for the general case. If, however, $\Pr^{\min}_{\mathcal{M}, s}(\Diamond goal) > 0$ for all states $s \in S \setminus \{fail\}$ then there is no need for the detour via $\mathcal{M}'$ and we can apply the reset-transformation $\mathcal{M} \rightsquigarrow \mathcal{N}$ by adding a reset-transition from $fail$ to s_{init} with reward 0, in which case the upper bound $\mathbb{CE}^{\mathrm{ub}} = \mathbb{E}^{\max}_{\mathcal{N}, s_{init}}(\oplus goal)$ is obtained in time polynomial in the size of $\mathcal{M}$. For details we refer to Appendix C of [13].

4   Threshold Algorithm and Computing Optimal Schedulers

In what follows, we suppose that $\mathcal{M} = (S, Act, P, s_{init}, rew)$ is an MDP with two trap states $goal$ and $fail$ such that $s \models \exists \Diamond goal$ for all states $s \in S \setminus \{fail\}$ and $\min_{s \in S} \Pr^{\min}_{\mathcal{M}, s}(\Diamond(goal \vee fail)) = 1$ and $\mathbb{CE}^{\max} = \mathbb{E}^{\max}_{\mathcal{M}, s_{init}}(\oplus goal | \Diamond goal) < \infty$.

A scheduler $\mathfrak{S}$ is said to be $reward$-$based$ if $\mathfrak{S}(\pi) = \mathfrak{S}(\pi')$ for all finite paths π, π' with $(last(\pi), rew(\pi)) = (last(\pi'), rew(\pi'))$. Thus, deterministic reward-based schedulers can be seen as functions $\mathfrak{S} : S \times \mathbb{N} \to Act$. We show in Appendix D of [13] that $\mathbb{CE}^{\max}$ equals the supremum of the values $\mathbb{CE}^{\mathfrak{S}}$, when ranging over all deterministic reward-based schedulers $\mathfrak{S}$ with $\Pr^{\mathfrak{S}}_{\mathcal{M}, s_{init}}(\Diamond goal) > 0$.

The basis of our algorithms are the following two observations. First, there exists a saturation point $\wp \in \mathbb{N}$ such that the optimal decision for all paths π with $rew(\pi) \geqslant \wp$ is to maximize the probability for reaching the goal state (see Proposition 4.1 below). The second observation is a technical statement that will be used at several places. Let $\rho, \theta, \zeta, r, x, y, z, p \in \mathbb{R}$ with $0 \leqslant p, x, y, z \leqslant 1, p > 0$, $y > z$ and $x + z > 0$ and let

$$A = \frac{\rho + p(ry + \theta)}{x + py}, \quad B = \frac{\rho + p(rz + \zeta)}{x + pz} \quad \text{and} \quad C = \max\{A, B\}$$

Then:

$$A \geqslant B \quad \text{iff} \quad r + \frac{\theta - \zeta}{y - z} \geqslant C \quad \text{iff} \quad \theta - (C - r)y \geqslant \zeta - (C - r)z \qquad (\dagger)$$

and the analogous statement for $>$ rather than $\geqslant$. For details, see Appendix G of [13]. We will apply this observation in different nuances. To give an idea how to apply statement ($\dagger$), suppose $A = \mathbb{CE}^{\mathfrak{T}}$ and $B = \mathbb{CE}^{\mathfrak{U}}$ where $\mathfrak{T}$ and $\mathfrak{U}$ are reward-based schedulers that agree for all paths ϱ that do not have a prefix π with $rew(\pi) = r$ where $last(\pi)$ is a non-trap state, in which case x denotes the probability for reaching $goal$ from s_{init} along such a path ϱ and ρ stands for the corresponding partial expectation, while p denotes the probability of the paths π from s_{init} to some non-trap state with $rew(\pi) = r$. The crucial observation is that $r + (\theta - \zeta)/(y - z)$ does not depend on x, ρ, p. Thus, if $r + (\theta - \zeta)/(y - z) \geqslant \mathbb{CE}^{ub}$ for some upper bound $\mathbb{CE}^{ub}$ of $\mathbb{CE}^{max}$ then ($\dagger$) allows to conclude that $\mathfrak{T}$'s decisions for the state-reward pairs (s, r) are better than $\mathfrak{U}$, independent of x, ρ and p.

Let $R \in \mathbb{N}$ and $\mathfrak{S}, \mathfrak{T}$ be reward-based schedulers. The *residual* scheduler $\mathfrak{S} \upharpoonright R$ is given by $(\mathfrak{S} \upharpoonright R)(s, r) = \mathfrak{S}(s, R + r)$. $\mathfrak{S} \triangleleft_R \mathfrak{T}$ denotes the unique scheduler that agrees with $\mathfrak{S}$ for all state-reward pairs (s, r) where $r < R$ and $(\mathfrak{S} \triangleleft_R \mathfrak{T}) \upharpoonright R = \mathfrak{T}$. We write $\mathbb{E}^{\mathfrak{S}}_{\mathcal{M}, s}$ for the *partial expectation*

$$\mathbb{E}^{\mathfrak{S}}_{\mathcal{M}, s} = \sum_{r=0}^{\infty} \Pr^{\mathfrak{S}}_{\mathcal{M}, s}(\lozenge^{=r} goal) \cdot r$$

Thus, $\mathbb{E}^{\mathfrak{T}}_{\mathcal{M}, s} = \mathbb{E}^{\mathfrak{T}}_{\mathcal{M}, s}(\lozenge goal)$ if $\Pr^{\mathfrak{T}}_{\mathcal{M}, s}(\lozenge goal) = 1$, while $\mathbb{E}^{\mathfrak{T}}_{\mathcal{M}, s} < \infty = \mathbb{E}^{\mathfrak{T}}_{\mathcal{M}, s}(\lozenge goal)$ if $\Pr^{\mathfrak{T}}_{\mathcal{M}, s}(\lozenge goal) < 1$.

Proposition 4.1. *There exists a natural number $\wp$ (called saturation point of $\mathcal{M}$) and a deterministic memoryless scheduler $\mathfrak{M}$ such that:*

(a) $\mathbb{CE}^{\mathfrak{T}} \leqslant \mathbb{CE}^{\mathfrak{T} \triangleleft_{\wp} \mathfrak{M}}$ *for each scheduler $\mathfrak{T}$ with $\Pr^{\mathfrak{T}}_{\mathcal{M}, s_{init}}(\lozenge goal) > 0$, and*

(b) $\mathbb{CE}^{\mathfrak{S}} = \mathbb{CE}^{max}$ *for some deterministic reward-based scheduler $\mathfrak{S}$ such that $\Pr^{\mathfrak{S}}_{\mathcal{M}, s_{init}}(\lozenge goal) > 0$ and $\mathfrak{S} \upharpoonright \wp = \mathfrak{M}$.*

The proof of Proposition 4.1 (see Appendices E and F of [13]) is constructive and yields a polynomial-time algorithm for generating a scheduler $\mathfrak{M}$ as in Proposition 4.1 and a pseudo-polynomial algorithm for the computation of a saturation point $\wp$.

Scheduler $\mathfrak{M}$ maximizes the probability to reach *goal* from each state. If there are two or more such schedulers, then $\mathfrak{M}$ is one where the conditional expected accumulated reward until reaching goal is maximal under all schedulers $\mathfrak{U}$ with $\mathrm{Pr}^{\mathfrak{U}}_{\mathcal{M},s}(\lozenge goal) = \mathrm{Pr}^{\max}_{\mathcal{M},s}(\lozenge goal)$ for all states s. Such a scheduler $\mathfrak{M}$ is computable in polynomial time using linear programming techniques. (See Appendix E of [13].)

The idea for the computation of the saturation point is to compute the threshold $\wp$ above which the scheduler $\mathfrak{M}$ becomes optimal. For this we rely on statement (†) where θ/y stands for the conditional expectation under $\mathfrak{M}$, ζ/z for the conditional expectation under an arbitrary scheduler $\mathfrak{S}$ and $C = \mathbb{CE}^{\mathrm{ub}}$ is an upper bound of $\mathbb{CE}^{\max}$ (see Theorem 1), while $r = \wp$ is the wanted value. More precisely, for $s \in S$, let $\theta_s = \mathrm{E}^{\mathfrak{M}}_{\mathcal{M},s}$, $y_s = \mathrm{Pr}^{\mathfrak{M}}_{\mathcal{M},s}(\lozenge goal) = \mathrm{Pr}^{\max}_{\mathcal{M},s}(\lozenge goal)$. To compute a saturation point we determine the smallest value $\wp \in \mathbb{N}$ such that

$$\theta_s - (\mathbb{CE}^{\mathrm{ub}} - \wp) \cdot y_s = \max_{\mathfrak{S}} \left(\mathrm{E}^{\mathfrak{S}}_{\mathcal{M},s} - (\mathbb{CE}^{\mathrm{ub}} - \wp) \cdot \mathrm{Pr}^{\mathfrak{S}}_{\mathcal{M},s}(\lozenge goal) \right)$$

for all states s where $\mathfrak{S}$ ranges over all schedulers for $\mathcal{M}$. In Appendix F of [13] we show that instead of the maximum over all schedulers $\mathfrak{S}$ it suffices to take the local maximum over all "one-step-variants" of $\mathfrak{M}$. That is, a saturation point is obtained by $\wp = \max\{\lceil \mathbb{CE}^{\mathrm{ub}} - D \rceil, 0\}$ where

$$D = \min \left\{ (\theta_s - \theta_{s,\alpha})/(y_s - y_{s,\alpha}) : s \in S, \alpha \in Act(s), y_{s,\alpha} < y_s \right\}$$

and $y_{s,\alpha} = \sum_{t \in S} P(s,\alpha,t) \cdot y_t$ and $\theta_{s,\alpha} = rew(s,\alpha) \cdot y_{s,\alpha} + \sum_{t \in S} P(s,\alpha,t) \cdot \theta_t$.

Example 4.2. The so obtained saturation point for the MDP $\mathcal{M}[\mathfrak{r}]$ in Fig. 1 is $\wp = \lceil \mathbb{CE}^{\mathrm{ub}} + 1 \rceil$. Note that only state $s = s_2$ behaves nondeterministically, and $\mathfrak{M}(s) = \alpha$, $y_s = y_{s,\alpha} = 1$, $\theta_s = \theta_{s,\alpha} = 0$, while $y_{s,\beta} = \theta_{s,\beta} = \frac{1}{2}$. This yields $D = (0 - \frac{1}{2})/(1 - \frac{1}{2}) = -1$. Thus, $\wp \geq \mathfrak{r} + 2$ as $\mathbb{CE}^{\mathrm{ub}} \geq \mathbb{CE}^{\max} > \mathfrak{r}$. ∎

The logarithmic length of $\wp$ is polynomial in the size of $\mathcal{M}$. Thus, the value (i.e., the length of an unary encoding) of $\wp$ can be exponential in $size(\mathcal{M})$. This is unavoidable as there are families $(\mathcal{M}_k)_{k \in \mathbb{N}}$ of MDPs where the size of $\mathcal{M}_k$ is in $\mathcal{O}(k)$, while 2^k is a lower bound for the smallest saturation point of $\mathcal{M}_k$. This, for instance, applies to the MDPs $\mathcal{M}_k = \mathcal{M}[2^k]$ where $\mathcal{M}[\mathfrak{r}]$ is as in Fig. 1. Recall from Example 1.1 that the scheduler $\mathfrak{S}_{\mathfrak{r}+2}$ that selects β by the first $\mathfrak{r}+2$ visits of s and α for the $(\mathfrak{r}+3)$-rd visit of s is optimal for $\mathcal{M}[\mathfrak{r}]$. Hence, the smallest saturation point for $\mathcal{M}[2^k]$ is $2^k + 2$.

Threshold Algorithm. The input of the threshold algorithm is an MDP $\mathcal{M}$ as above and a non-negative rational number ϑ. The task is to generate a deterministic reward-based scheduler $\mathfrak{S}$ with $\mathfrak{S} \uparrow \wp = \mathfrak{M}$ (where $\mathfrak{M}$ and $\wp$ are as in Proposition 4.1) such that $\mathbb{CE}^{\mathfrak{S}} > \vartheta$ if $\mathbb{CE}^{\max} > \vartheta$, and $\mathbb{CE}^{\mathfrak{S}} = \vartheta$ if $\mathbb{CE}^{\max} = \vartheta$. If $\mathbb{CE}^{\max} < \vartheta$ then the output of the threshold algorithm is "no".[3]

---

[3] The threshold algorithm solves all four variants of the threshold problem. E.g., $\mathbb{CE}^{\max} \leq \vartheta$ iff $\mathbb{CE}^{\mathfrak{S}} = \vartheta$, while $\mathbb{CE}^{\max} < \vartheta$ iff the threshold algorithm returns "no".

The algorithm operates level-wise and determines *feasible* actions $action(s, r)$ for all non-trap states s and $r = \wp-1, \wp-2, \ldots, 0$, using the decisions $action(\cdot, i)$ for the levels $i \in \{r+1, \ldots, \wp\}$ that have been treated before and linear programming techniques to treat zero-reward loops. In this context, feasibility is understood with respect to the following condition: If $\mathbb{CE}^{\max} \trianglerighteq \vartheta$ where $\trianglerighteq \in \{>, \geqslant\}$ then there exists a reward-based scheduler $\mathfrak{S}$ with $\mathbb{CE}^{\mathfrak{S}} \trianglerighteq \vartheta$ and $\mathfrak{S}(s, R) = action(s, \min\{\wp, R\})$ for all $R \geqslant r$.

The algorithm stores for each state-reward pair (s, r) the probabilities $y_{s,r}$ to reach *goal* from s and the corresponding partial expectation $\theta_{s,r}$ for the scheduler given by the decisions in the action table. The values for $r = \wp$ are given by $action(s, \wp) = \mathfrak{M}(s)$, $y_{s,\wp} = \Pr_{\mathcal{M},s}^{\mathfrak{M}}(\Diamond goal)$ and $\theta_{s,\wp} = \mathrm{E}_{\mathcal{M},s}^{\mathfrak{M}}$. The candidates for the decisions at level $r < \wp$ are given by the deterministic memoryless schedulers $\mathfrak{P}$ for $\mathcal{M}$. We write $\mathfrak{P}_+$ for the reward-based scheduler given by $\mathfrak{P}_+(s, 0) = \mathfrak{P}(s)$ and $\mathfrak{P}_+(s, i) = action(s, \min\{\wp, r+i\})$ for $i \geqslant 1$. Let $y_{s,r,\mathfrak{P}} = \Pr_{\mathcal{M},s}^{\mathfrak{P}_+}(\Diamond goal)$ and $\theta_{s,r,\mathfrak{P}} = \mathrm{E}_{\mathcal{M},s}^{\mathfrak{P}_+}$ be the corresponding partial expectation.

To determine feasible actions for level r, the threshold algorithm makes use of a variant of (†) stating that if $\theta - (\vartheta-r)y \geqslant \zeta - (\vartheta-r)z$ and $\mathsf{B} \trianglerighteq \vartheta$ then $\mathsf{A} \trianglerighteq \vartheta$, where A and B are as in (†) and the requirement $y > z$ is dropped. Thus, the aim of the threshold algorithm is to compute a deterministic memoryless scheduler $\mathfrak{P}^*$ for $\mathcal{M}$ such that the following condition $(*)$ holds:

$$\theta_{s,r,\mathfrak{P}^*} - (\vartheta-r) \cdot y_{s,r,\mathfrak{P}^*} = \max_{\mathfrak{P}} \left(\theta_{s,r,\mathfrak{P}} - (\vartheta-r) \cdot y_{s,r,\mathfrak{P}} \right) \qquad (*)$$

Such a scheduler $\mathfrak{P}^*$ is computable in time polynomial in the size of $\mathcal{M}$ (without the explicit consideration of all schedulers $\mathfrak{P}$ and their extensions $\mathfrak{P}_+$) using the following linear program with one variable x_s for each state. The objective is to minimize $\sum_{s \in S} x_s$ subject to the following conditions:

(1) If $s \in S \setminus \{goal, fail\}$ then for each action $\alpha \in Act(s)$ with $rew(s, \alpha) = 0$:

$$x_s \geqslant \sum_{t \in S} P(s, \alpha, t) \cdot x_t$$

(2) If $s \in S \setminus \{goal, fail\}$ then for each action $\alpha \in Act(s)$ with $rew(s, \alpha) > 0$:

$$x_s \geqslant \sum_{t \in S} P(s, \alpha, t) \cdot \left(\theta_{t,R} + rew(s, \alpha) \cdot y_{t,R} - (\vartheta-r) \cdot y_{t,R} \right)$$

where $R = \min\{\wp, r+rew(s, \alpha)\}$

(3) For the trap states: $x_{goal} = r - \vartheta$ and $x_{fail} = 0$.

This linear program has a unique solution $(x_s^*)_{s \in S}$. Let $Act^*(s)$ denote the set of actions $\alpha \in Act(s)$ such that the following constraints (E1) and (E2) hold:

(E1) If $rew(s, \alpha) = 0$ then: $x_s^* = \sum_{t \in S} P(s, \alpha, t) \cdot x_t^*$

(E2) If $rew(s, \alpha) > 0$ and $R = \min\{\wp, r+rew(s, \alpha)\}$ then:

$$x_s^* = \sum_{t \in S} P(s, \alpha, t) \cdot \left(\theta_{t,R} + rew(s, \alpha) \cdot y_{t,R} - (\vartheta-r) \cdot y_{t,R} \right)$$

Let $\mathcal{M}^* = \mathcal{M}^*_{r,\vartheta}$ denote the MDP with state space S induced by the state-action pairs (s, α) with $\alpha \in Act^*(s)$ where the positive-reward actions are redirected to the trap states. Formally, for $s, t \in S$, $\alpha \in Act^*(s)$ we let $P_{\mathcal{M}^*}(s, \alpha, t) = P(s, \alpha, t)$ if $rew(s, \alpha) = 0$ and $P_{\mathcal{M}^*}(s, \alpha, goal) = \sum_{t \in S} P(s, \alpha, t) \cdot y_{t,R}$ and $P_{\mathcal{M}^*}(s, \alpha, fail) = 1 - P_{\mathcal{M}^*}(s, \alpha, goal)$ if $rew(s, \alpha) > 0$ and $R = \min\{\wp, r + rew(s, \alpha)\}$. The reward structure of $\mathcal{M}^*$ is irrelevant for our purposes.

A scheduler $\mathfrak{P}^*$ satisfying $(*)$ is obtained by computing a memoryless deterministic scheduler for $\mathcal{M}^*$ with $\Pr^{\mathfrak{P}^*}_{\mathcal{M}^*,s}(\lozenge goal) = \Pr^{\max}_{\mathcal{M}^*,s}(\lozenge goal)$ for all states s. This scheduler $\mathfrak{P}^*$ indeed provides feasible decisions for level r, i.e., if $\mathbb{CE}^{\max} \unrhd \vartheta$ where $\unrhd \in \{>, \geqslant\}$ then there exists a reward-based scheduler $\mathfrak{S}$ with $\mathbb{CE}^{\mathfrak{S}} \unrhd \vartheta$, $\mathfrak{S}(s, r) = \mathfrak{P}^*(s)$ and $\mathfrak{S}(s, R) = action(s, \min\{\wp, R\})$ for all $R > r$.

The threshold algorithm then puts $action(s, r) = \mathfrak{P}^*(s)$ and computes the values $y_{s,r}$ and $\theta_{s,r}$ as follows. Let T denote the set of states $s \in S \setminus \{goal, fail\}$ where $rew(s, \mathfrak{P}^*(s)) > 0$. For $s \in T$, the values $y_{s,r} = y_{s,r,\mathfrak{P}^*}$ and $\theta_{s,r} = \theta_{s,r,\mathfrak{P}^*}$ can be derived directly from the results obtained for the previously treated levels $r+1, \ldots, \wp$ as we have:

$$y_{s,r} = \sum_{t \in S} P(s, \alpha, t) \cdot y_{t,R} \quad \text{and} \quad \theta_{s,r} = rew(s, \alpha) \cdot y_{s,r} + \sum_{t \in S} P(s, \alpha, t) \cdot \theta_{t,R}$$

where $\alpha = \mathfrak{P}^*(s)$ and $R = \min\{\wp, r + rew(s, \alpha)\}$. For the states $s \in S \setminus T$:

$$y_{s,r} = \sum_{t \in T} \Pr^{\mathfrak{P}^*}_{\mathcal{M},s}(\neg T \, \mathsf{U} \, t) \cdot y_{t,r} \quad \text{and} \quad \theta_{s,r} = \sum_{t \in T} \Pr^{\mathfrak{P}^*}_{\mathcal{M},s}(\neg T \, \mathsf{U} \, t) \cdot \theta_{t,r}$$

Having treated the last level $r = 0$, the output of the algorithm is as follows. Let $\mathfrak{S}$ be the scheduler given by the action table $action(\cdot)$. For the conditional expectation we have $\mathbb{CE}^{\mathfrak{S}} = \theta_{s_{init},0}/y_{s_{init},0}$ if $y_{s_{init},0} > 0$. If $y_{s_{init},0} = 0$ or $\theta_{s_{init},0}/y_{s_{init},0} < \vartheta$ then the algorithm returns the answer "no". Otherwise, the algorithm returns $\mathfrak{S}$, in which case $\mathbb{CE}^{\mathfrak{S}} > \vartheta$ or $\mathbb{CE}^{\mathfrak{S}} = \vartheta = \mathbb{CE}^{\max}$. Proofs for the soundness and the pseudo-polynomial time complexity are provided in Appendix G of [13].

Example 4.3. For the MDP $\mathcal{M}[\mathfrak{r}]$ in Example 1.1, scheduler $\mathfrak{M}$ selects action α for state $s = s_2$. Thus, $action(s, \wp) = \alpha$ for the computed saturation point $\wp \geqslant \mathfrak{r} + 2$ (see Example 4.2). The threshold algorithm for each positive rational threshold ϑ computes for each level $r = \wp - 1, \wp - 2, \ldots, 1, 0$ where $action(s, r + 1) = \alpha$, the value $x^*_s = \max\{r - \vartheta, \frac{1}{2} + \frac{1}{2}(r - \vartheta)\}$ and the action set $Act^*(s) = \{\alpha\}$ if $r > \vartheta + 1$, $Act^*(s) = \{\alpha, \beta\}$ if $r = \vartheta + 1$ and $Act^*(s) = \{\beta\}$ if $r < \vartheta + 1$. Thus, if $n = \min\{\wp, \lceil \vartheta + 1 \rceil\}$ then $action(s, r) = \alpha$, $y_{s,r} = 1$, $\theta_{s,r} = 0$ for $r \in \{n, \ldots, \wp\}$, while $action(s, n-k) = \beta$, $y_{s,n-k} = 1/2^k$, $\theta_{s,n-k} = k/2^k$ for $k = 1, \ldots, n$. That is, the threshold algorithm computes the scheduler $\mathfrak{S}_n$ that selects β for the first n visits of s and α for the $(n+1)$-st visit of s. Thus, if $\mathfrak{r} \leqslant \vartheta < \mathfrak{r} + 1$ then $n = \mathfrak{r} + 2$, in which case the computed scheduler $\mathfrak{S}_n$ is optimal (see Example 1.1). The returned answer depends on whether $\vartheta \leqslant \mathbb{CE}^{\max}$. If, for instance, $\vartheta = \frac{\mathfrak{r}}{2}$ and $\mathfrak{r} > 0$ is even then the threshold algorithm returns the scheduler $\mathfrak{S}_n$ where $n = \frac{\mathfrak{r}}{2} + 1$, whose conditional expectation is $\mathfrak{r} - (\frac{\mathfrak{r}}{2} - 1)/(2^{\frac{\mathfrak{r}}{2}+1} + 1) > \frac{\mathfrak{r}}{2} = \vartheta$. ∎

MDPs Without Zero-Reward Cycles and Acyclic MDPs. If $\mathcal{M}$ does not contain zero-reward cycles then there is no need for the linear program. Instead we can use a topological sorting of the states in the graph of the sub-MDP consisting of zero-reward actions and determine a scheduler $\mathfrak{P}^*$ satisfying (*) directly. For acyclic MDPs, there is even no need for a saturation point. We can explore $\mathcal{M}$ using a recursive procedure and determine feasible decisions for each reachable state-reward pair (s, r) on the basis of (*). This yields a polynomially space-bounded algorithm to decide whether $\mathbb{CE}^{\max} \trianglerighteq \vartheta$ in acyclic MDPs. (See Appendix I of [13].)

Construction of an Optimal Scheduler. Let *ThresAlgo*$[\vartheta]$ denote the scheduler that is generated by calling the threshold algorithm for the threshold value ϑ. A simple approach is to apply the threshold algorithm iteratively:

let $\mathfrak{S}$ be the scheduler $\mathfrak{M}$ as in Proposition 4.1;
REPEAT $\vartheta := \mathbb{CE}^{\mathfrak{S}}$; $\mathfrak{S} := $ *ThresAlgo*$[\vartheta]$ UNTIL $\vartheta = \mathbb{CE}^{\mathfrak{S}}$;
return ϑ and $\mathfrak{S}$

The above algorithm generates a sequence of deterministic reward-based schedulers that are memoryless from $\wp$ on with strictly increasing conditional expectations. The number of such schedulers is bounded by $md^{\wp}$ where md denotes the number of memoryless deterministic schedulers for $\mathcal{M}$. Hence, the algorithm terminates and correctly returns $\mathbb{CE}^{\max}$ and an optimal scheduler. As md can be exponential in the number of states, this simple algorithm has double-exponential time complexity.

To obtain a (single) exponential-time algorithm, we seek for better (larger, but still promising) threshold values than the conditional expectation of the current scheduler. We propose an algorithm that operates level-wise and freezes optimal decisions for levels $r = \wp, \wp-1, \wp-2, \ldots, 1, 0$. The algorithm maintains and successively improves a left-closed and right-open interval $I = [A, B[$ with $\mathbb{CE}^{\max} \in I$ and $\mathbb{CE}^{\mathfrak{S}} \in I$ for the current scheduler $\mathfrak{S}$.

Initialization. The algorithm starts with the scheduler $\mathfrak{S} = $ *ThresAlgo*$[\mathbb{CE}^{\mathfrak{M}}]$ where $\mathfrak{M}$ is as above. If $\mathbb{CE}^{\mathfrak{S}} = \mathbb{CE}^{\mathfrak{M}}$ then the algorithm immediately terminates. Suppose now that $\mathbb{CE}^{\mathfrak{S}} > \mathbb{CE}^{\mathfrak{M}}$. The initial interval is $I = [A, B[$ where $A = \mathbb{CE}^{\mathfrak{S}}$ and $B = \mathbb{CE}^{\mathrm{ub}}+1$ where $\mathbb{CE}^{\mathrm{ub}}$ is as in Theorem 1.

Level-wise Scheduler Improvement. The algorithm successively determines optimal decisions for the levels $r = \wp-1, \wp-2, \ldots, 1, 0$. The treatment of level r consists of a sequence of scheduler-improvement steps where at the same time the interval I is replaced with proper sub-intervals. The current scheduler $\mathfrak{S}$ has been obtained by the last successful run of the threshold algorithm, i.e., it has the form $\mathfrak{S} = $ *ThresAlgo*$[\vartheta]$ where $\mathbb{CE}^{\mathfrak{S}} > \vartheta$. Besides the decisions of $\mathfrak{S}$ (i.e., the actions $\mathfrak{S}(s, R)$ for all state-reward pairs (s, R) where $s \in S \setminus \{goal, fail\}$ and $R \in \{0, 1, \ldots, \wp\}$), the algorithm also stores the values $y_{s,R}$ and $\theta_{s,R}$ that have been computed in the threshold algorithm.[4] For the

---

[4] As the decisions of the already treated levels are optimal, the values $y_{s,R}$ and $\theta_{s,R}$ for $R \in \{r+1, \ldots, \wp\}$ can be reused in the calls of the threshold algorithms. That is, the calls of the threshold algorithm that are invoked in the scheduler-improvement steps at level r can skip levels $\wp, \wp-1, \ldots, r+1$ and only need to process levels $r, r-1, \ldots, 1, 0$.

current level r, the algorithm also computes for each state $s \in S \setminus \{goal, fail\}$ and each action $\alpha \in Act(s)$ the values $y_{s,r,\alpha} = \sum_{t \in S} P(s, \alpha, t) \cdot y_{t,R}$ and $\theta_{s,r,\alpha} = rew(s, \alpha) \cdot y_{s,r,\alpha} + \sum_{t \in S} P(s, \alpha, t) \cdot \theta_{t,R}$ where $R = \min\{\wp, r + rew(s, \alpha)\}$.

Scheduler-improvement Step. Let r be the current level, $I = [A, B[$ the current interval and $\mathfrak{S}$ the current scheduler with $\mathbb{CE}^{\max} \in I$. At the beginning of the scheduler-improvement step we have $\mathbb{CE}^{\mathfrak{S}} = A$. Let

$$\mathcal{I}_{\mathfrak{S},r} = \left\{ r + \frac{\theta_{s,r} - \theta_{s,r,\alpha}}{y_{s,r} - y_{s,r,\alpha}} \ : \ s \in S \setminus \{goal, fail\}, \ \alpha \in Act(s), \ y_{s,r} > y_{s,r,\alpha} \right\}$$

$$\mathcal{I}_{\mathfrak{S},r}^{\uparrow} = \{ d \in \mathcal{I}_{\mathfrak{S},r} \ : \ d \geqslant \mathbb{CE}^{\mathfrak{S}} \} \qquad \mathcal{I}_{\mathfrak{S},r}^{B} = \{ d \in \mathcal{I}_{\mathfrak{S},r} \ : \ d < B \}$$

Intuitively, the values in $d \in \mathcal{I}_{\mathfrak{S},r}^{B}$ are the "most promising" threshold values, as according to statement (†) these are the points where the decision of the current scheduler $\mathfrak{S}$ for some state-reward pair (s, r) can be improved, provided that $\mathbb{CE}^{\max} > d$. (Note that the values in $\mathcal{I}_{\mathfrak{S},r} \setminus \mathcal{I}_{\mathfrak{S},r}^{B}$ can be discarded as $\mathbb{CE}^{\max} < B$.)

The algorithm proceeds as follows. If $\mathcal{I}_{\mathfrak{S},r}^{B} = \varnothing$ then no further improvements at level r are possible as the function $\mathfrak{P}^* = \mathfrak{S}(\cdot, r)$ satisfies $(*)$ for the (still unknown) value $\vartheta = \mathbb{CE}^{\max}$. See Appendix H of [13]. In this case:

- If $r = 0$ then the algorithm terminates with the answer $\mathbb{CE}^{\max} = \mathbb{CE}^{\mathfrak{S}}$ and $\mathfrak{S}$ as an optimal scheduler.
- If $r > 0$ then the algorithm goes to the next level $r-1$ and performs the scheduler-improvement step for $\mathfrak{S}$ at level $r-1$.

Suppose now that $\mathcal{I}_{\mathfrak{S},r}^{B}$ is nonempty. Let $\mathcal{K} = \mathcal{I}_{\mathfrak{S},r}^{\uparrow} \cup \{\mathbb{CE}^{\mathfrak{S}}\}$. The algorithm seeks for the largest value $\vartheta' \in \mathcal{K} \cap I$ such that $\mathbb{CE}^{\max} \geqslant \vartheta'$. More precisely, it successively calls the threshold algorithm for the threshold value $\vartheta' = \max(\mathcal{K} \cap I)$ and performs the following steps for the generated scheduler $\mathfrak{S}' = ThresAlgo[\vartheta']$:

- If the result of the threshold algorithm is "no" and $\Pr_{\mathcal{M}, s_{init}}^{\mathfrak{S}'}(\Diamond goal)$ is positive (in which case $\mathbb{CE}^{\mathfrak{S}'} \leqslant \mathbb{CE}^{\max} < \vartheta'$), then:
  - If $\mathbb{CE}^{\mathfrak{S}'} \leqslant A$ then the algorithm refines I by putting $B := \vartheta'$.
  - If $\mathbb{CE}^{\mathfrak{S}'} > A$ then the algorithm refines I by putting $A := \mathbb{CE}^{\mathfrak{S}'}$, $B := \vartheta'$ and adds $\mathbb{CE}^{\mathfrak{S}'}$ to $\mathcal{K}$ (Note that then $\mathbb{CE}^{\mathfrak{S}'} \in \mathcal{K} \cap I$, while $\mathbb{CE}^{\mathfrak{S}} \in \mathcal{K} \setminus I$.)
- Suppose now that $\mathbb{CE}^{\mathfrak{S}'} \geqslant \vartheta'$. The algorithm terminates if $\mathbb{CE}^{\mathfrak{S}'} = \vartheta'$, in which case $\mathfrak{S}'$ is optimal. Otherwise, i.e., if $\mathbb{CE}^{\mathfrak{S}'} > \vartheta'$, then the algorithm aborts the loop by putting $\mathcal{K} := \varnothing$, refines the interval I by putting $A := \mathbb{CE}^{\mathfrak{S}'}$, updates the current scheduler by setting $\mathfrak{S} := \mathfrak{S}'$ and performs the next scheduler-improvement step.

The soundness proof and complexity analysis can be found in Appendix H of [13], where (among others) we show that the scheduler-improvement step for schedulers $\mathfrak{S}$ with $\mathbb{CE}^{\mathfrak{S}} < \mathbb{CE}^{\max}$ terminates with some scheduler $\mathfrak{S}'$ such that $\mathbb{CE}^{\mathfrak{S}} < \mathbb{CE}^{\mathfrak{S}'}$. The total number of calls of the threshold algorithm is in $\mathcal{O}(\wp \cdot md \cdot |S| \cdot |Act|)$. This yields an exponential time bound as stated in Theorem 3.

Example 4.4. We regard again the MDP $\mathcal{M}[\mathfrak{r}]$ of Example 1.1 where we suppose $\mathfrak{r}$ is positive and even. The algorithm first computes $\mathbb{CE}^{ub}$ (see Sect. 3), a saturation point $\wp \geqslant \mathfrak{r}+2$ (see Example 4.2), the scheduler $\mathfrak{M}$, its conditional expectation $\mathbb{CE}^{\mathfrak{M}} = \frac{\mathfrak{r}}{2}$ and the scheduler $\mathfrak{S} = ThresAlgo[\frac{\mathfrak{r}}{2}]$. The initial interval is $I = [A, B[$ where $A = \mathbb{CE}^{\mathfrak{S}} = \mathfrak{r} - (\frac{\mathfrak{r}}{2}-1)/(2^{\frac{\mathfrak{r}}{2}+1}+1)$ (see Example 4.3) and $B = \mathbb{CE}^{ub}+1$. The scheduler improvement step for $\mathfrak{S}$ at levels $r = \wp-1, \ldots, \mathfrak{r}+1$ determines the set $\mathcal{I}_{\mathfrak{S},r} = \{r-1\}$ and calls the threshold algorithm for $\vartheta' = r-1$. These calls are not successful for $r = \wp-1, \ldots, \mathfrak{r}+2$. That is, the scheduler $\mathfrak{S}$ remains unchanged and the upper bound B is successively improved to $r-1$. At level $r = \mathfrak{r}+1$, the threshold algorithm is called for $\vartheta' = \mathfrak{r}$, which yields the optimal scheduler $\mathfrak{S}' = ThresAlgo[\vartheta']$ (see Example 4.3).   ∎

Implementation and Experiments. We have implemented the algorithms presented in this paper as a prototypical extension of the model checker PRISM [27,28] and carried out initial experiments to demonstrate the general feasibility of our approach (see https://wwwtcs.inf.tu-dresden.de/ALGI/PUB/TACAS17/ and Appendix K of [13] for details).

5   Conclusion

Although the switch to conditional expectations appears rather natural to escape from the limitations of known solutions for unconditional extremal expected accumulated rewards, to the best of our knowledge computation schemes for conditional expected accumulated rewards have not been addressed before. Our results show that new techniques are needed to compute maximal conditional expectations, as optimal schedulers might need memory and local reasoning in terms of the past and possible future is not sufficient (Example 1.1). The key observations for our algorithms are the existence of a saturation point $\wp$ for the reward that has been accumulated so far, from which on optimal schedulers can behave memoryless, and a linear correlation between optimal decisions for all state-reward pairs (s, r) of the same reward level r (see (∗) and the linear program used in the threshold algorithm). The difficulty to reason about conditional expectations is also reflected in the achieved complexity-theoretic results stating that all variants of the threshold problem lie between PSPACE and EXPTIME. While PSPACE-completeness has been established for acyclic MDPs (Appendix I of [13]), the precise complexity for cyclic MDPs is still open. In contrast, optimal schedulers for unconditional expected accumulated rewards as well as for conditional reachability probabilities are computable in polynomial time [11,22].

Using standard automata-based approaches, our method can easily be generalized to compute maximal conditional expected rewards for regular co-safety conditions (rather than reachability conditions $\Diamond G$) and/or where the accumulation of rewards is "controlled" by a deterministic finite automaton as in the logics considered in [12,17] (rather than $\Diamond F$). In this paper, we restricted to MDPs with non-negative integer rewards. Non-negative rational rewards can be treated by multiplying all reward values with their least common multiple (Appendix J.1 of [13]). In the case of acyclic MDPs, our methods are even applicable if the MDP has negative and positive rational rewards (Appendix J.2 of [13]). By swapping the sign of all rewards, this yields a technique to compute minimal conditional expectations in acyclic MDPs. We expect that minimal conditional expectations in cyclic MDPs with non-negative rewards can be computed using similar algorithms as we suggested for maximal conditional expectations. This as well as MDPs with negative and positive rewards will be addressed in future work.

References

1. Abdulla, P.A., Henda, N.B., Mayr, R.: Decisive Markov chains. Logical Methods Comput. Sci. **3**(4) (2007)
2. Acerbi, C., Tasche, D.: Expected shortfall: a natural coherent alternative to value at risk. Econ. notes **31**(2), 379–388 (2002)
3. Alvim, M.S., Andrés, M.E., Chatzikokolakis, K., Degano, P., Palamidessi, C.: On the information leakage of differentially-private mechanisms. J. Comput. Secur. **23**(4), 427–469 (2015)
4. Alvim, M.S., Chatzikokolakis, K., McIver, A., Morgan, C., Palamidessi, C., Smith, G.: Axioms for information leakage. In: Proceedings of Computer Security Foundations Symposium (CSF), pp. 77–92. IEEE Computer Society (2016)
5. Alvim, M.S., Chatzikokolakis, K., Palamidessi, C., Smith, G.: Measuring information leakage using generalized gain functions. In: Proceedings of Computer Security Foundations Symposium (CSF), pp. 265–279. IEEE Computer Society (2012)
6. Andrés, M.E.: Quantitative Analysis of Information Leakage in Probabilistic and Nondeterministic Systems. Ph.D. thesis, UB Nijmegen (2011)
7. Andrés, M.E., Palamidessi, C., van Rossum, P., Sokolova, A.: Information hiding in probabilistic concurrent systems. Theoret. Comput. Sci. **412**(28), 3072–3089 (2011)
8. Andrés, M.E., van Rossum, P.: Conditional probabilities over probabilistic and nondeterministic systems. In: Ramakrishnan, C.R., Rehof, J. (eds.) TACAS 2008. LNCS, vol. 4963, pp. 157–172. Springer, Heidelberg (2008). doi:10.1007/978-3-540-78800-3_12
9. Baier, C., Dubslaff, C., Klein, J., Klüppelholz, S., Wunderlich, S.: Probabilistic model checking for energy-utility analysis. In: Breugel, F., Kashefi, E., Palamidessi, C., Rutten, J. (eds.) Horizons of the Mind. A Tribute to Prakash Panangaden. LNCS, vol. 8464, pp. 96–123. Springer, Heidelberg (2014). doi:10.1007/978-3-319-06880-0_5
10. Baier, C., Katoen, J.-P.: Principles of Model Checking. MIT Press, Cambridge (2008)
11. Baier, C., Klein, J., Klüppelholz, S., Märcker, S.: Computing conditional probabilities in Markovian models efficiently. In: Ábrahám, E., Havelund, K. (eds.) TACAS 2014. LNCS, vol. 8413, pp. 515–530. Springer, Heidelberg (2014). doi:10.1007/978-3-642-54862-8_43
12. Baier, C., Klein, J., Klüppelholz, S., Wunderlich, S.: Weight monitoring with linear temporal logic: complexity and decidability. In: Proceedings of Computer Science Logic/Logic in Computer Science (CSL-LICS), pp. 11:1–11:10. ACM (2014)
13. Baier, C., Klein, J., Klüppelholz, S. Wunderlich, S.: Maximizing the conditional expected reward for reaching the goal (extended version). arXiv:1701.05389 (2017)
14. Barthe, G., Espitau, T., Ferrer Fioriti, L.M., Hsu, J.: Synthesizing probabilistic invariants via Doob's decomposition. In: Chaudhuri, S., Farzan, A. (eds.) CAV 2016. LNCS, vol. 9779, pp. 43–61. Springer, Heidelberg (2016). doi:10.1007/978-3-319-41528-4_3

15. Bertsekas, D.P., Tsitsiklis, J.N.: An analysis of stochastic shortest path problems. Math. Oper. Res. **16**(3), 580–595 (1991)
16. Bertsekas, D.P., Yu, H.: Stochastic path problems under weak conditions. Technical report, M.I.T. Cambridge, Report LIDS 2909 (2016)
17. Boker, U., Chatterjee, K., Henzinger, T.A., Kupferman, O.: Temporal specifications with accumulative values. In: Proceedings of Logic in Computer Science (LICS), pp. 43–52. IEEE Computer Society (2011)
18. Brázdil, T., Brozek, V., Chatterjee, K., Forejt, V., Kucera, A.: Two views on multiple mean-payoff objectives in Markov decision processes. Logical Methods Comput. Sci. **10**(1) (2014)
19. Brázdil, T., Kučera, A.: Computing the expected accumulated reward and gain for a subclass of infinite Markov Chains. In: Sarukkai, S., Sen, S. (eds.) FSTTCS 2005. LNCS, vol. 3821, pp. 372–383. Springer, Heidelberg (2005). doi:10.1007/11590156_30
20. Chatterjee, K., Fu, H., Goharshady, A.K.: Termination analysis of probabilistic programs through Positivstellensatz's. In: Chaudhuri, S., Farzan, A. (eds.) CAV 2016. LNCS, vol. 9779, pp. 3–22. Springer, Heidelberg (2016). doi:10.1007/978-3-319-41528-4_1
21. Chatzikokolakis, K., Palamidessi, C., Braun, C.: Compositional methods for information-hiding. Math. Struct. Comput. Sci. **26**(6), 908–932 (2016)
22. Alfaro, L.: Computing minimum and maximum reachability times in probabilistic systems. In: Baeten, J.C.M., Mauw, S. (eds.) CONCUR 1999. LNCS, vol. 1664, pp. 66–81. Springer, Heidelberg (1999). doi:10.1007/3-540-48320-9_7
23. Gretz, F., Katoen, J., McIver, A.: Operational versus weakest pre-expectation semantics for the probabilistic guarded command language. Perform. Eval. **73**, 110–132 (2014)
24. Jansen, N., Kaminski, B.L., Katoen, J., Olmedo, F., Gretz, F., McIver, A.: Conditioning in probabilistic programming. In: Proceedings of Mathematical Foundations of Programming Semantics (MFPS), Electronic Notes Theoretical Computer Science, vol. 319, pp. 199–216 (2015)
25. Kallenberg, L.: Markov Decision Processes. Lecture Notes. University of Leiden, Leiden (2011)
26. Katoen, J.-P., Gretz, F., Jansen, N., Kaminski, B.L., Olmedo, F.: Understanding probabilistic programs. In: Meyer, R., Platzer, A., Wehrheim, H. (eds.) Correct System Design. LNCS, vol. 9360, pp. 15–32. Springer, Heidelberg (2015). doi:10.1007/978-3-319-23506-6_4
27. Kwiatkowska, M., Norman, G., Parker, D.: PRISM 4.0: verification of probabilistic real-time systems. In: Gopalakrishnan, G., Qadeer, S. (eds.) CAV 2011. LNCS, vol. 6806, pp. 585–591. Springer, Heidelberg (2011). doi:10.1007/978-3-642-22110-1_47
28. PRISM model checker. http://www.prismmodelchecker.org/
29. Puterman, M.L.: Markov Decision Processes: Discrete Stochastic Dynamic Programming. Wiley, New York (1994)
30. Randour, M., Raskin, J.-F., Sankur, O.: Variations on the stochastic shortest path problem. In: D'Souza, D., Lal, A., Larsen, K.G. (eds.) VMCAI 2015. LNCS, vol. 8931, pp. 1–18. Springer, Heidelberg (2015). doi:10.1007/978-3-662-46081-8_1
31. Seber, G., Lee, A.: Linear Regression Analysis. Wiley Series in Probability and Statistics. Wiley, New York (2003)
32. Uryasev, S.: Conditional value-at-risk: optimization algorithms and applications. In Proceedings of Computational Intelligence and Financial Engineering (CIFEr), pp. 49–57. IEEE (2000)

ARES: Adaptive Receding-Horizon Synthesis of Optimal Plans

Anna Lukina[1]([✉]), Lukas Esterle[1], Christian Hirsch[1], Ezio Bartocci[1], Junxing Yang[2], Ashish Tiwari[3], Scott A. Smolka[2], and Radu Grosu[1,2]

[1] Cyber-Physical Systems Group, Technische Universität Wien, Vienna, Austria
anna.lukina@tuwien.ac.at
[2] Department of Computer Science, Stony Brook University, New York, USA
[3] SRI International, Menlo Park, USA

Abstract. We introduce ARES, an efficient approximation algorithm for generating optimal plans (action sequences) that take an initial state of a Markov Decision Process (MDP) to a state whose cost is below a specified (convergence) threshold. ARES uses Particle Swarm Optimization, with *adaptive sizing* for both the receding horizon and the particle swarm. Inspired by Importance Splitting, the length of the horizon and the number of particles are chosen such that at least one particle reaches a *next-level* state, that is, a state where the cost decreases by a required delta from the previous-level state. The level relation on states and the plans constructed by ARES implicitly define a Lyapunov function and an optimal policy, respectively, both of which could be explicitly generated by applying ARES to all states of the MDP, up to some topological equivalence relation. We also assess the effectiveness of ARES by statistically evaluating its rate of success in generating optimal plans. The ARES algorithm resulted from our desire to clarify if flying in V-formation is a flocking policy that optimizes energy conservation, clear view, and velocity alignment. That is, we were interested to see if one could find optimal plans that bring a flock from an arbitrary initial state to a state exhibiting a single connected V-formation. For flocks with 7 birds, ARES is able to generate a plan that leads to a V-formation in 95% of the 8,000 random initial configurations within 63 s, on average. ARES can also be easily customized into a model-predictive controller (MPC) with an adaptive receding horizon and statistical guarantees of convergence. To the best of our knowledge, our adaptive-sizing approach is the first to provide *convergence guarantees* in receding-horizon techniques.

1 Introduction

Flocking or swarming in groups of social animals (birds, fish, ants, bees, etc.) that results in a particular global formation is an emergent collective behavior that continues to fascinate researchers [1,7]. One would like to know if such a formation serves a higher purpose, and, if so, what that purpose is.

One well-studied flight-formation behavior is *V-formation*. Most of the work in this area has concentrated on devising simple dynamical rules that,

© Springer-Verlag GmbH Germany 2017
A. Legay and T. Margaria (Eds.): TACAS 2017, Part II, LNCS 10206, pp. 286–302, 2017.
DOI: 10.1007/978-3-662-54580-5_17

when followed by each bird, eventually stabilize the flock to the desired V-formation [11,12,26]. This approach, however, does not shed very much light on the overall purpose of this emergent behavior.

In previous work [35,36], we hypothesized that flying in V-formation is nothing but an optimal policy for a flocking-based Markov Decision Process (MDP) $\mathcal{M}$. States of $\mathcal{M}$, at discrete time t, are of the form $(\boldsymbol{x}_i(t), \boldsymbol{v}_i(t))$, $1 \leqslant i \leqslant N$, where $\boldsymbol{x}_i(t)$ and $\boldsymbol{v}_i(t)$ are N-vectors (for an N-bird flock) of 2-dimensional positions and velocities, respectively. $\mathcal{M}$'s transition relation, shown here for bird i is simply and generically given by

$$\boldsymbol{x}_i(t+1) = \boldsymbol{x}_i(t) + \boldsymbol{v}_i(t+1),$$
$$\boldsymbol{v}_i(t+1) = \boldsymbol{v}_i(t) + \boldsymbol{a}_i(t),$$

where $\boldsymbol{a}_i(t)$ is an action, a 2-dimensional acceleration in this case, that bird i can take at time t. $\mathcal{M}$'s cost function reflects the energy-conservation, velocity-alignment and clear-view benefits enjoyed by a state of $\mathcal{M}$ (see Sect. 2).

In this paper, we not only confirm this hypothesis, but we also devise a very general *adaptive, receding-horizon synthesis algorithm* (ARES) that, given an MDP and one of its initial states, generates an optimal plan (action sequence) taking that state to a state whose cost is below a desired threshold. In fact, ARES implicitly defines an *optimal, online-policy, synthesis algorithm* that could be used in practice if plan generation can be performed in real-time.

ARES makes repeated use of Particle Swarm Optimization (PSO) [23] to effectively generate a plan. This was in principle unnecessary, as one could generate an optimal plan by calling PSO only once, with a maximum plan-length horizon. Such an approach, however, is in most cases impractical, as every unfolding of the MDP adds a number of new dimensions to the search space. Consequently, to obtain an adequate coverage of this space, one needs a very large number of particles, a number that is either going to exhaust available memory or require a prohibitive amount of time to find an optimal plan.

A simple solution to this problem would be to use a short horizon, typically of size two or three. This is indeed the current practice in Model Predictive Control (MPC) [13]. This approach, however, has at least three major drawbacks. First, and most importantly, it does not guarantee convergence and optimality, as one may oscillate or become stuck in a local optimum. Second, in some of the steps, the window size is unnecessarily large thereby negatively impacting performance. Third, in other steps, the window size may be not large enough to guide the optimizer out of a local minimum (see Fig. 1 (left)). One would therefore like to find the proper window size adaptively, but the question is how one can do it.

Inspired by Importance Splitting (IS), a sequential Monte-Carlo technique for estimating the probability of rare events, we introduce the notion of a *level-based horizon* (see Fig. 1 (right)). Level ℓ_0 is the cost of the initial state, and level ℓ_m is the desired threshold. By using a state function, asymptotically converging to the desired threshold, we can determine a sequence of levels, ensuring convergence of ARES towards the desired optimal state(s) having a cost below $\ell_m = \varphi$.

The levels serve two purposes. First, they implicitly define a Lyapunov function, which guarantees convergence. If desired, this function can be explicitly

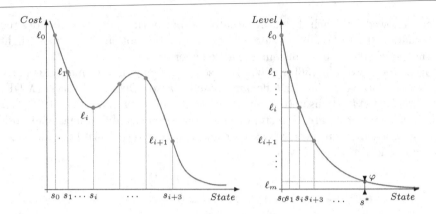

Fig. 1. Left: If state s_0 has cost ℓ_0, and its successor-state s_1 has cost less than ℓ_1, then a horizon of length 1 is appropriate. However, if s_i has a local-minimum cost ℓ_i, one has to pass over the cost ridge in order to reach level ℓ_{i+1}, and therefore ARES has to adaptively increase the horizon to 3. Right: The cost of the initial state defines ℓ_0 and the given threshold φ defines ℓ_m. By choosing m equal segments on an asymptotically converging (Lyapunov) function (where the number m is empirically determined), one obtains on the vertical cost-axis the levels required for ARES to converge.

generated for all states, up to some topological equivalence. Second, the levels help PSO overcome local minima (see Fig. 1 (left)). If reaching a next level requires PSO to temporarily pass over a state-cost ridge, ARES incrementally increases the size of the horizon, up to a maximum length.

Another idea imported from IS is to maintain n clones of the initial state at a time, and run PSO on each of them (see Fig. 3). This allows us to call PSO for each clone and desired horizon, with a very small number of particles per clone. Clones that do not reach the next level are discarded, and the successful ones are resampled. The number of particles is increased if no clone reaches a next level, for all horizons chosen. Once this happens, we reset the horizon to one, and repeat the process. In this way, we adaptively focus our resources on escaping from local minima. At the last level, we choose the optimal particle (a V-formation in case of flocking) and traverse its predecessors to find a plan.

We assess the rate of success in generating optimal plans in form of an (ε, δ)-approximation scheme, for a desired error margin ε, and confidence ratio $1-\delta$. Moreover, we can use the state-action pairs generated during the assessment (and possibly some additional new plans) to construct an explicit (tabled) optimal policy, modulo some topological equivalence. Given enough memory, one can use this policy in real time, as it only requires a table look-up.

To experimentally validate our approach, we have applied ARES to the problem of V-formation in bird flocking (with a deterministic MDP). The cost function to be optimized is defined as a weighted sum of the (flock-wide) clear-view, velocity-alignment, and upwash-benefit metrics. Clear view and velocity alignment are more or less obvious goals. Upwash optimizes energy savings. By flapping its wings, a bird generates a trailing upwash region off its wing tips; by using this upwash, a bird flying in this region (left or right) can save energy. Note that by requiring that at most one bird does not feel its effect, upwash can be used to define an analog version of a connected graph.

We ran ARES on 8,000 initial states chosen uniformly and at random, such that they are packed closely enough to feel upwash, but not too close to collide. We succeeded to generate a V-formation 95% of the time, with an error margin of 0.05 and a confidence ratio of 0.99. These error margin and confidence ratio dramatically improve if we consider all generated states and the fact that each state within a plan is independent from the states in all other plans.

The rest of this paper is organized as follows. Section 2 reviews our work on bird flocking and V-formation, and defines the manner in which we measure the cost of a flock (formation). Section 3 revisits the swarm optimization algorithm used in this paper, and Sect. 4 examines the main characteristics of importance splitting. Section 5 states the definition of the problem we are trying to solve. Section 6 introduces ARES, our adaptive receding-horizon synthesis algorithm for optimal plans, and discusses how we can extend this algorithm to explicitly generate policies. Section 7 measures the efficiency of ARES in terms of an (ε, δ)-approximation scheme. Section 8 compares our algorithm to related work, and Sect. 9 draws our conclusions and discusses future work.

2   V-Formation MDP

We represent a flock of birds as a dynamically evolving system. Every bird in our model [16] moves in 2-dimensional space performing acceleration actions determined by a global controller. Let $\boldsymbol{x}_i(t), \boldsymbol{v}_i(t)$ and $\boldsymbol{a}_i(t)$ be 2-dimensional vectors of positions, velocities, and accelerations, respectively, of bird i at time t, where $i \in \{1, \ldots, b\}$, for a fixed b. The discrete-time behavior of bird i is then

$$\boldsymbol{x}_i(t+1) = \boldsymbol{x}_i(t) + \boldsymbol{v}_i(t+1),$$
$$\boldsymbol{v}_i(t+1) = \boldsymbol{v}_i(t) + \boldsymbol{a}_i(t). \tag{1}$$

The controller detects the positions and velocities of all birds through sensors, and uses this information to compute an optimal acceleration for the entire flock. A bird uses its own component of the solution to update its velocity and position.

We extend this discrete-time dynamical model to a (deterministic) MDP by adding a cost (fitness) function[1] based on the following metrics inspired by [35]:

- *Clear View (CV)*. A bird's visual field is a cone with angle θ that can be blocked by the wings of other birds. We define the clear-view metric by accumulating the percentage of a bird's visual field that is blocked by other birds. Figure 2 (left) illustrates the calculation of the clear-view metric. The optimal value in a V-formation is $CV^* = 0$, as all birds have a clear view.
- *Velocity Matching (VM)*. The accumulated differences between the velocity of each bird and all other birds, summed up over all birds in the flock defines

---

[1] A classic MDP [28] is obtained by adding sensor/actuator or wind-gust noise, which are the case we are addressing in the follow-up work.

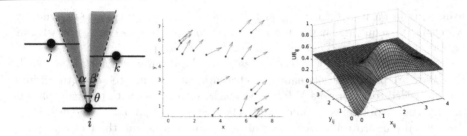

Fig. 2. Illustration of the clear view (CV), velocity matching (VM), and upwash benefit (UB) metrics. Left: Bird i's view is partially blocked by birds j and k. Hence, its clear view is $CV = (\alpha + \beta)/\theta$. Middle: A flock and its unaligned bird velocities results in a velocity-matching metric $VM = 6.2805$. In contrast, $VM = 0$ when the velocities of all birds are aligned. Right: Illustration of the (right-wing) upwash benefit bird i receives from bird j depending on how it is positioned behind bird j. Note that bird j's downwash region is directly behind it.

VM. Figure 2 (middle) depicts the values of VM in a velocity-unmatched flock. The optimal value in a V-formation is $VM^* = 0$, as all birds will have the same velocity (thus maintaining the V-formation).

- *Upwash Benefit (UB)*. The trailing upwash is generated near the wingtips of a bird, while downwash is generated near the center of a bird. We accumulate all birds' upwash benefits using a Gaussian-like model of the upwash and downwash region, as shown in Fig. 2 (right) for the right wing. The maximum upwash a bird can obtain has an upper bound of 1. For bird i with UB_i, we use $1 - UB_i$ as its upwash-benefit metric, because the optimization algorithm performs minimization of the fitness metrics. The optimal value in a V-formation is $UB^* = 1$, as the leader does not receive any upwash.

Finding smooth and continuous formulations of the fitness metrics is a key element of solving optimization problems. The PSO algorithm has a very low probability of finding an optimal solution if the fitness metric is not well-designed.

Let $c(t) = \{c_i(t)\}_{i=1}^b = \{x_i(t), v_i(t)\}_{i=1}^b \in \mathbb{R}$ be a flock configuration at timestep t. Given the above metrics, the overall fitness (cost) metric J is of a sum-of-squares combination of VM, CV, and UB defined as follows:

$$J(c(t), a^h(t), h) = (CV(c_a^h(t)) - CV^*)^2 + (VM(c_a^h(t)) - VM^*)^2$$
$$+ (UB(c_a^h(t)) - UB^*)^2, \qquad (2)$$

where h is the receding prediction horizon (RPH), $a^h(t) \in \mathbb{R}$ is a sequence of accelerations of length h, and $c_a^h(t)$ is the configuration reached after applying $a^h(t)$ to $c(t)$. Formally, we have

$$c_a^h(t) = \{x_a^h(t), v_a^h(t)\} = \{x(t) + \sum_{\tau=1}^{h(t)} v(t + \tau), v(t) + \sum_{\tau=1}^{h(t)} a^\tau(t)\}, \qquad (3)$$

where $a^\tau(t)$ is the τth acceleration of $a^h(t)$. A novelty of this paper is that, as described in Sect. 6, we allow RPH $h(t)$ to be *adaptive* in nature.

The fitness function J has an optimal value of 0 in a perfect V-formation. The main goal of ARES is to compute the sequence of acceleration actions that lead the flock from a random initial configuration towards a controlled V-formation characterized by optimal fitness in order to conserve energy during flight including optimal combination of a clear visual field along with visibility of lateral neighbors. Similar to the centralized version of the approach given in [35], ARES performs a single flock-wide minimization of J at each time-step t to obtain an optimal plan of length h of acceleration actions:

$$\mathbf{opt}-\boldsymbol{a}^h(t) = \{\mathbf{opt}-\boldsymbol{a}_i^h(t)\}_{i=1}^b = \underset{\boldsymbol{a}^h(t)}{\arg\min}\, J(\boldsymbol{c}(t), \boldsymbol{a}^h(t), h). \tag{4}$$

The optimization is subject to the following constraints on the maximum velocities and accelerations: $\|\boldsymbol{v}_i(t)\| \leqslant \boldsymbol{v}_{max}, \|\boldsymbol{a}_i^h(t)\| \leqslant \rho\|\boldsymbol{v}_i(t)\| \,\forall\, i \in \{1,\dots,b\}$, where $\boldsymbol{v}_{max}$ is a constant and $\rho \in (0,1)$. The above constraints prevent us from using mixed-integer programming, we might, however, compare our solution to other continuous optimization techniques in the future. The initial positions and velocities of each bird are selected at random within certain ranges, and limited such that the distance between any two birds is greater than a (collision) constant d_{min}, and small enough for all birds, except for at most one, to feel the UB. In the following sections, we demonstrate how to generate optimal plans taking the initial state to a stable state with optimal fitness.

3   Particle Swarm Optimization

Particle Swarm Optimization (PSO) is a randomized approximation algorithm for computing the value of a parameter minimizing a possibly nonlinear cost (fitness) function. Interestingly, PSO itself is inspired by bird flocking [23]. Hence, PSO assumes that it works with a flock of birds.

Note, however, that in our running example, these birds are "acceleration birds" (or particles), and not the actual birds in the flock. Each bird has the same goal, finding food (reward), but none of them knows the location of the food. However, every bird knows the distance (horizon) to the food location. PSO works by moving each bird preferentially toward the bird closest to food.

ARES uses Matlab-Toolbox `particleswarm`, which performs the classical version of PSO. This PSO creates a swarm of particles, of size say p, uniformly at random within a given bound on their positions and velocities. Note that in our example, each particle represents itself a flock of bird-acceleration sequences $\{\boldsymbol{a}_i^h\}_{i=1}^b$, where h is the current length of the receding horizon. PSO further chooses a neighborhood of a random size for each particle j, $j = \{1,\dots,p\}$, and computes the fitness of each particle. Based on the fitness values, PSO stores two vectors for j: its so-far personal-best position $\mathbf{x}_P^j(t)$, and its fittest neighbor's position $\mathbf{x}_G^j(t)$. The positions and velocities of each particle j in the particle swarm $1 \leqslant j \leqslant p$ are updated according to the following rule:

$$\mathbf{v}^j(t+1) = \omega \cdot \mathbf{v}^j(t) + y_1 \cdot \mathbf{u_1}(t+1) \otimes (\mathbf{x}_P^j(t) - \mathbf{x}^j(t))$$
$$+ y_2 \cdot \mathbf{u_2}(t+1) \otimes (\mathbf{x}_G^j(t) - \mathbf{x}^j(t)), \tag{5}$$

where ω is *inertia weight*, which determines the trade-off between global and local exploration of the swarm (the value of ω is proportional to the exploration range); y_1 and y_2 are *self adjustment* and *social adjustment*, respectively; $\mathbf{u_1}, \mathbf{u_2} \in \text{Uniform}(0,1)$ are randomization factors; and $\otimes$ is the vector dot product, that is, $\forall$ random vector $\mathbf{z}$: $(\mathbf{z}_1, \ldots, \mathbf{z}_b) \otimes (\mathbf{x}_1^j, \ldots, \mathbf{x}_b^j) = (\mathbf{z}_1 \mathbf{x}_1^j, \ldots, \mathbf{z}_b \mathbf{x}_b^j)$.

If the fitness value for $\mathbf{x}^j(t+1) = \mathbf{x}^j(t) + \mathbf{v}^j(t+1)$ is lower than the one for $\mathbf{x}_P^j(t)$, then $\mathbf{x}^j(t+1)$ is assigned to $\mathbf{x}_P^j(t+1)$. The particle with the best fitness over the whole swarm becomes a global best for the next iteration. The procedure is repeated until the number of iterations reaches its maximum, the time elapses, or the minimum criteria is satisfied. For our bird-flock example we obtain in this way the best acceleration.

4 Importance Splitting

Importance Splitting (IS) is a sequential Monte-Carlo approximation technique for estimating the probability of rare events in a Markov process [21]. The algorithm uses a sequence $S_0, S_1, S_2, \ldots, S_m$ of sets of states (of increasing "importance") such that S_0 is the set of initial states and S_m is the set of states defining the rare event. The probability p, computed as $\mathbf{P}(S_m \mid S_0)$ of reaching S_m from the initial set of states S_0, is assumed to be extremely low (thus, a rare event), and one desires to estimate this probability [15]. Random sampling approaches, such as the additive-error approximation algorithm described in Sect. 7, are bound to fail (are intractable) in this case, as they would require an enormous number of samples to estimate p with low-variance.

Importance splitting is a way of decomposing the estimation of p. In IS, the sequence $S_0, S_1, \ldots$ of sets of states is defined so that the conditional probabilities $p_i = \mathbf{P}(S_i \mid S_{i-1})$ of going from one level, S_{i-1}, to the next one, S_i, are considerably larger than p, and essentially equal to one another. The resulting probability of the rare event is then calculated as the product $p = \prod_{i=1}^{k} p_i$ of the intermediate probabilities. The levels can be defined adaptively [22].

To estimate p_i, IS uses a swarm of particles of size N, with a given initial distribution over the states of the stochastic process. During stage i of the algorithm, each particle starts at level S_{i-1} and traverses the states of the stochastic process, checking if it reaches S_i. If, at the end of the stage, the particle fails to reach S_i, the particle is discarded. Suppose that K_i particles survive. In this case, $p_i = K_i/N$. Before starting the next stage, the surviving particles are resampled, such that IS once again has N particles. Whereas IS is used for estimating probability of a rare event in a Markov process, we use it here for synthesizing a plan for a *controllable* Markov process, by combining it with ideas from controller synthesis (receding-horizon control) and nonlinear optimization (PSO).

5 Problem Definition

Definition 1. *A **Markov decision process (MDP)** $\mathcal{M}$ is a sequential decision problem that consists of a set of states S (with an initial state s_0), a set of actions A, a transition model T, and a cost function J. An MDP is **deterministic** if for each state and action, $T : S \times A \rightarrow S$ specifies a unique state.*

Definition 2. *The **optimal plan synthesis problem** for an MDP $\mathcal{M}$, an arbitrary initial state s_0 of $\mathcal{M}$, and a threshold φ is to synthesize a sequence of actions $\boldsymbol{a}^i$ of length $1 \leqslant i \leqslant m$ taking s_0 to a state s^* such that cost $J(s^*) \leqslant \varphi$.*

Section 6 presents our adaptive receding-horizon synthesis algorithm (ARES) for the optimal plan synthesis problem. In our flocking example (Sect. 2), ARES is used to synthesize a sequence of acceleration-actions bringing an arbitrary bird flock s_0 to an optimal state of V-formation s^*. We assume that we can easily extend such an optimal plan to maintain the cost of successor states below φ ad infinitum (optimal stability).

6 The ARES Algorithm for Plan Synthesis

As mentioned in Sect. 1, one could in principle solve the optimization problem defined in Sect. 5 by calling the PSO only once, with a horizon h in $\mathcal{M}$ equaling the maximum length m allowed for a plan. This approach, however, tends to explode the search space, and is therefore in most cases intractable. Indeed, preliminary experiments with this technique applied to our running example could not generate any convergent plan.

A more tractable approach is to make repeated calls to PSO with a small horizon length h. The question is how small h can be. *The current practice in model-predictive control (MPC) is to use a fixed h, $1 \leqslant h \leqslant 3$* (see the outer loop of Fig. 3, where resampling and conditional branches are disregarded). Unfortunately, this forces the selection of *locally-optimal plans* (of size less than three) in each call, and there is *no guarantee of convergence* when joining them together. In fact, in our running example, we were able to find plans leading to a V-formation in only 45% of the time for 10,000 random initial flocks.

Inspired by IS (see Figs. 1 (right) and 3), we introduce the notion of a *level-based horizon*, where level ℓ_0 equals the cost of the initial state, and level ℓ_m equals the threshold φ. Intuitively, by using an asymptotic cost-convergence function ranging from ℓ_0 to ℓ_m, and dividing its graph in m equal segments, we can determine on the vertical axis a sequence of levels ensuring convergence.

The asymptotic function ARES implements is essentially $\ell_i = \ell_0 \, (m - i)/m$, but specifically tuned for each particle. Formally, if particle k has previously reached level equaling $J_k(s_{i-1})$, then its next target level is within the distance $\Delta_k = J_k(s_{i-1})/(m - i + 1)$. In Fig. 3, after passing the thresholds assigned to them, values of the cost function in the current state s_i are sorted in ascending order $\{\widehat{J}_k\}_{k=1}^n$. The lowest cost $\widehat{J}_1$ should be apart from the previous level ℓ_{i-1} at least on its Δ_1 for the algorithm to proceed to the next level $\ell_i := \widehat{J}_1$.

The levels serve two purposes. First, they implicitly define a Lyapunov function, which guarantees convergence. If desired, this function can be explicitly generated for all states, up to some topological equivalence. Second, the levels ℓ_i help PSO overcome local minima (see Fig. 1 (left)). If reaching a next level requires PSO to temporarily pass over a state-cost ridge, then ARES incrementally increases the size of the horizon h, up to a maximum size h_{max}. For particle

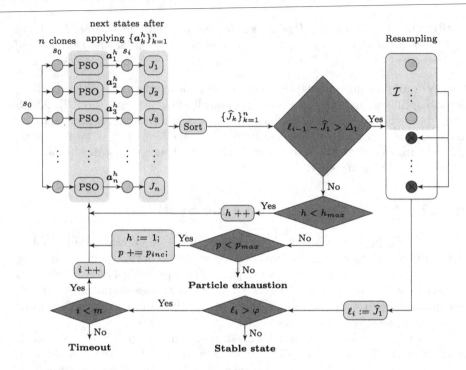

Fig. 3. Graphical representation of ARES.

k, passing the thresholds Δ_k means that it reaches a new level, and the definition of Δ_k ensures a smooth degradation of its threshold.

Another idea imported from IS and shown in Fig. 3, is to maintain n clones $\{\mathcal{M}_k\}_{k=1}^n$ of the MDP $\mathcal{M}$ (and its initial state) at any time t, and run PSO, for a horizon h, on each h-unfolding $\mathcal{M}_k^h$ of them. This results in an action sequence a_k^h of length h (see Algorithm 1). This approach allows us to call PSO for each clone and desired horizon, with a very small number of particles p per clone.

Algorithm 1. Simulate $(\mathcal{M}, h, i, \{\Delta_k, J_k(s_{i-1})\}_{k=1}^n)$

---

1 **foreach** $\mathcal{M}_k \in \mathcal{M}$ **do**
2      $[a_k^h, \mathcal{M}_k^h] \leftarrow$ particleswarm$(\mathcal{M}_k, p, h)$; // *use PSO in order to determine best next action for the MDP $\mathcal{M}_k$ with RPH h*
3      $J_k(s_i) \leftarrow$ Cost$(\mathcal{M}_k^h, a_k^h, h)$; // *calculate cost function if applying the sequence of optimal actions of length h*
4   **if** $J_k(s_{i-1}) - J_k(s_i) > \Delta_k$ **then**
5        $\Delta_k \leftarrow J_k(s_i)/(m-i)$; // *new level-threshold*
6   **end**
7 **end**

Algorithm 2. Resample $(\{\mathcal{M}_k^h, J_k(s_i)\}_{k=1}^n)$

---

1   $\mathcal{I} \leftarrow$ Sort ascending $\mathcal{M}_k^h$ by their current costs; // *find indexes of MDPs whose*
    costs are below the median among all the clones
2   **for** $k = 1$ **to** n **do**
3   **if** $k \notin \mathcal{I}$ **then**
4 | Sample r uniformly at random from $\mathcal{I}$; $\mathcal{M}_k \leftarrow \mathcal{M}_r^h$;
5   **else**
6 | $\mathcal{M}_k \leftarrow \mathcal{M}_k^h$; // *Keep more successful MDPs unchanged*
7   **end**
8   **end**

To check which particles have overcome their associated thresholds, we sort the particles according to their current cost, and split them in two sets: the successful set, having the indexes $\mathcal{I}$ and whose costs are lower than the median among all clones; and the unsuccessful set with indexes in $\{1, \ldots, n\} \setminus \mathcal{I}$, which are discarded. The unsuccessful ones are further replenished, by sampling uniformly at random from the successful set $\mathcal{I}$ (see Algorithm 2).

The number of particles is increased $p = p + p_{inc}$ if no clone reaches a next level, for all horizons chosen. Once this happens, we reset the horizon to one, and repeat the process. In this way, we adaptively focus our resources on escaping from local minima. From the last level, we choose the state s^* with the minimal cost, and traverse all of its predecessor states to find an optimal plan comprised of actions $\{a^i\}_{1 \leqslant i \leqslant m}$ that led MDP $\mathcal{M}$ to the optimal state s^*. In our running example, we select a flock in V-formation, and traverse all its predecessor flocks. The overall procedure of ARES is shown in Algorithm 3.

Proposition 1 (Optimality and Minimality). *(1) Let $\mathcal{M}$ be an MDP. For any initial state s_0 of $\mathcal{M}$, ARES is able to solve the optimal-plan synthesis problem for $\mathcal{M}$ and s_0. (2) An optimal choice of m in function Δ_k, for some particle k, ensures that ARES also generates the shortest optimal plan.*

Proof (Sketch). (1) The dynamic-threshold function Δ_k ensures that the initial cost in s_0 is continuously decreased until it falls below φ. Moreover, for an appropriate number of clones, by adaptively determining the horizon and the number of particles needed to overcome Δ_k, ARES always converges, with probability 1, to an optimal state, given enough time and memory. (2) This follows from convergence property (1), and from the fact that ARES always gives preference to the shortest horizon while trying to overcome Δ_k.

The optimality referred to in the title of the paper is in the sense of (1). One, however, can do even better than (1), in the sense of (2), by empirically determining parameter m in the dynamic-threshold function Δ_k. Also note that ARES is an *approximation algorithm*. As a consequence, it might return non-minimal plans. Even in these circumstances, however, the plans will still lead to an optimal state. This is a V-formation in our flocking example.

Algorithm 3. ARES

Input : $\mathcal{M}, \varphi, p_{start}, p_{inc}, p_{max}, h_{max}, m, n$
Output: $\{a^i\}_{1 \leqslant i \leqslant m}$ // *synthesized optimal plans*

1 Initialize $\ell_0 \leftarrow \inf$; $\{J_k(s_0)\}_{k=1}^n \leftarrow \inf$; $p \leftarrow p_{start}$; $i \leftarrow 1$; $h \leftarrow 1$; $\Delta_k \leftarrow 0$;
2 **while** $(\ell_i > \varphi) \vee (i < m)$ **do**
3   // *find and apply best actions with RPH h*
4      $[\{a_k^h, J_k(s_i), \mathcal{M}_k^h\}_{k=1}^n] \leftarrow$ Simulate$(\mathcal{M}, h, i, \{\Delta_k, J_k(s_{i-1})\}_{k=1}^n)$;
    $\widehat{J}_1 \leftarrow sort(J_1(s_i), \ldots, J_n(s_i))$; // *find minimum cost among all the clones*
5   **if** $\ell_{i-1} - \widehat{J}_1 > \Delta_1$ **then**
6          $\ell_i \leftarrow \widehat{J}_1$; // *new level has been reached*
7          $i \leftarrow i+1$; $h \leftarrow 1$; $p \leftarrow p_{start}$; // *reset adaptive parameters*
8          $\{\mathcal{M}_k\}_{k=1}^n \leftarrow$ Resample$(\{\mathcal{M}_k^h, J_k(s_i)\}_{k=1}^n)$;
9   **else**
10   **if** $h < h_{max}$ **then**
11             $h \leftarrow h+1$; // *improve time exploration*
12   **else**
13   **if** $p < p_{max}$ **then**
14                 $h \leftarrow 1$; $p \leftarrow p + p_{inc}$; // *improve space exploration*
15   **else**
16   break;
17   **end**
18   **end**
19   **end**
20 **end**
21 Take a clone in the state with minimum cost $\ell_i = J(s_i^*) \leqslant \varphi$ at the last level i;
22 **foreach** i **do**
23     $\{s_{i-1}^*, a^i\} \leftarrow Pre(s_i^*)$; // *find predecessor and corresponding action*
24 **end**

---

7   Experimental Results

To assess the performance of our approach, we developed a simple simulation environment in Matlab. All experiments were run on an Intel Core i7-5820K CPU with 3.30 GHz and with 32 GB RAM available.

We performed numerous experiments with a varying number of birds. Unless stated otherwise, results refer to 8,000 experiments with 7 birds with the following parameters: $p_{start} = 10$, $p_{inc} = 5$, $p_{max} = 40$, $\ell_{max} = 20$, $h_{max} = 5$, $\varphi = 10^{-3}$, and $n = 20$. The initial configurations were generated independently uniformly at random subject to the following constraints:

1. Position constraints: $\forall i \in \{1, \ldots, 7\}$. $\boldsymbol{x}_i(0) \in [0, 3] \times [0, 3]$.
2. Velocity constraints: $\forall i \in \{1, \ldots, 7\}$. $\boldsymbol{v}_i(0) \in [0.25, 0.75] \times [0.25, 0.75]$.

Table 1 gives an overview of the results with respect to the 8,000 experiments we performed with 7 birds for a maximum of 20 levels. The average fitness across all experiments is at 0.0282 with a standard deviation of 0.1654. We

Table 1. Overview of the results for 8,000 experiments with 7 birds

No. experiments	Successful				Total			
	7573				8000			
	Min	Max	Avg	Std	Min	Max	Avg	Std
Cost, J	$2.88 \cdot 10^{-7}$	$9 \cdot 10^{-4}$	$4 \cdot 10^{-4}$	$3 \cdot 10^{-4}$	$2.88 \cdot 10^{-7}$	1.4840	0.0282	0.1607
Time, t	23.14 s	310.83 s	63.55 s	22.81 s	23.14 s	661.46 s	64.85 s	28.05 s
Plan length, i	7	20	12.80	2.39	7	20	13.13	2.71
RPH, h	1	5	1.40	0.15	1	5	1.27	0.17

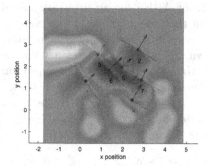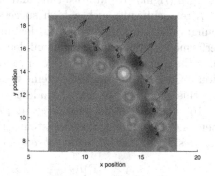

Fig. 4. Left: Example of an arbitrary initial configuration of 7 birds. Right: The V-formation obtained by applying the plan generated by ARES. In the figures, we show the wings of the birds, bird orientations, bird speeds (as scaled arrows), upwash regions in yellow, and downwash regions in dark blue. (Color figure online)

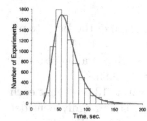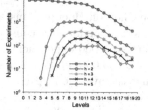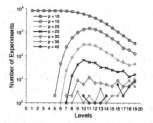

Fig. 5. Left: Distribution of execution times for 8,000 runs. Middle: Statistics of increasing RPH h. Right: Particles of PSO p for 8,000 experiments

achieved a success rate of 94.66% with fitness threshold $\varphi = 10^{-3}$. The average fitness is higher than the threshold due to comparably high fitness of unsuccessful experiments. When increasing the bound for the maximal plan length m to 30 we achieved a 98.4% success rate in 1,000 experiments at the expense of a slightly longer average execution time.

The left plot in Fig. 5 depicts the resulting distribution of execution times for 8,000 runs of our algorithm, where it is clear that, excluding only a few outliers from the histogram, an arbitrary configuration of birds (Fig. 4 (left)) reaches

Table 2. Average duration for 100 experiments with various number of birds

No. of birds	3	5	7	9
Avg. duration	4.58 s	18.92 s	64.85 s	269.33 s

V-formation (Fig. 4 (right)) in around 1 min. The execution time rises with the number of birds as shown in Table 2.

In Fig. 5, we illustrate for how many experiments the algorithm had to increase RPH h (Fig. 5 (middle)) and the number of particles used by PSO p (Fig. 5 (right)) to improve time and space exploration, respectively.

After achieving such a high success rate of ARES for an arbitrary initial configuration, we would like to demonstrate that the number of experiments performed is sufficient for high confidence in our results. This requires us to determine the appropriate number N of random variables $Z_1, ... Z_N$ necessary for the Monte-Carlo approximation scheme we apply to assess efficiency of our approach. For this purpose, we use the additive approximation algorithm as discussed in [16]. If the sample mean $\mu_Z = (Z_1 + ... + Z_N)/N$ is expected to be large, then one can exploit the Bernstein's inequality and fix N to $\Upsilon \propto ln(1/\delta)/\varepsilon^2$. This results in an *additive* or *absolute-error (ε, δ)-approximation scheme*:

$$\mathbf{P}[\mu_Z - \varepsilon \leq \widetilde{\mu}_Z \leq \mu_Z + \varepsilon] \geq 1 - \delta,$$

where $\widetilde{\mu}_Z$ approximates μ_Z with absolute error ε and probability $1 - \delta$.

In particular, we are interested in Z being a Bernoulli random variable:

$$Z = \begin{cases} 1, \text{ if } J(\boldsymbol{c}(t), \boldsymbol{a}(t), h(t)) \leqslant \varphi, \\ 0, \text{ otherwise.} \end{cases}$$

Therefore, we can use the Chernoff-Hoeffding instantiation of the Bernstein's inequality, and further fix the proportionality constant to $\Upsilon = 4 \, ln(2/\delta)/\varepsilon^2$, as in [19]. Hence, for our performed 8,000 experiments, we achieve a success rate of 95% with absolute error of $\varepsilon = 0.05$ and confidence ratio 0.99.

Moreover, considering that the average length of a plan is 13, and that each state in a plan is independent from all other plans, we can roughly consider that our above estimation generated 80,000 independent states. For the same confidence ratio of 0.99 we then obtain an approximation error $\varepsilon = 0.016$, and for a confidence ratio of 0.999, we obtain an approximation error $\varepsilon = 0.019$.

8 Related Work

Organized flight in flocks of birds can be categorized in *cluster flocking* and *line formation* [18]. In cluster flocking the individual birds in a large flock seem to be uncoordinated in general. However, the flock moves, turns, and wheels as if it were one organism. In 1987 Reynolds [27] defined his three famous rules describing separation, alignment, and cohesion for individual birds in order to have them flock together. This work has been great inspiration for research in the area of collective behavior and self-organization.

In contrast, line formation flight requires the individual birds to fly in a very specific formation. Line formation has two main benefits for the long-distance migrating birds. First, exploiting the generated uplift by birds flying in front, trailing birds are able to conserve energy [9,24,34]. Second, in a staggered formation, all birds have a clear view in front as well as a view on their neighbors [1]. While there has been quite some effort to keep a certain formation for multiple entities when traveling together [10,14,30], only little work deals with a task of achieving this extremely important formation from a random starting configuration [6]. The convergence of bird flocking into V-formation has been also analyzed with the use of combinatorial techniques [7].

Compared to previous work, in [5] this question is addressed without using any behavioral rules but as problem of *optimal control*. In [35] a cost function was proposed that reflects all major features of V-formation, namely, *Clear View* (CV), *Velocity Matching* (VM), and *Upwash Benefit* (UB). The technique of MPC is used to achieve V-formation starting from an arbitrary initial configuration of n birds. MPC solves the task by minimizing a functional defined as squared distance from the optimal values of CV, VM, and UB, subject to constraints on input and output. The approach is to choose an optimal *velocity adjustment*, as a control input, at each time-step applied to the velocity of each bird by predicting model behavior several time-steps ahead.

The controller synthesis problem has been widely studied [33]. The most popular and natural technique is Dynamic Programming (DP) [4] that improves the approximation of the functional at each iteration, eventually converging to the optimal one given a fixed asymptotic error. Compared to DP, which considers all the possible states of the system and might suffer from state-space explosion in case of environmental uncertainties, approximate algorithms [2,3,17,25,31,32] take into account only the paths leading to desired target. One of the most efficient ones is Particle Swarm Optimization (PSO) [23] that has been adopted for finding the next best step of MPC in [35]. Although it is a very powerful optimization technique, it has not yet been possible to achieve a high success rate in solving the considered flocking problem. Sequential Monte-Carlo methods proved to be efficient in tackling the question of control for linear stochastic systems [8], in particular, Importance Splitting (IS) [22]. The approach we propose is, however, the first attempt to combine adaptive IS, PSO, and receding-horizon technique for *synthesis of optimal plans for controllable systems*. We use MPC to synthesize a plan, but use IS to determine the intermediate fitness-based waypoints. We use PSO to solve the multi-step optimization problem generated by MPC, but choose the planning horizon and the number of particles adaptively. These choices are governed by the difficulty to reach the next level.

9   Conclusion and Future Work

In this paper, we have presented ARES, a very general adaptive, receding-horizon synthesis algorithm for MDP-based optimal plans. Additionally, ARES can be readily converted into a model-predictive controller with an adaptive receding horizon and statistical guarantees of convergence. We also conducted a very thorough performance analysis of ARES based on the problem of V-formation in a flock of birds. For flocks of 7 birds, with high confidence ARES is able to generate an optimal plan leading to a V-formation in 95% of the 8,000 random initial configurations we considered, with an average execution time of only 63 s per plan.

The execution time of the ARES algorithm can be improved even further. First, we currently do not parallelize our implementation of the PSO algorithm. Recent work [20,29,37] has shown how Graphic Processing Units (GPUs) are very efficient at accelerating PSO computation. Modern GPUs, by providing thousands of cores, are well-suited for implementing PSO as they enable execution of a very large number of particles in parallel. Together with the parallelization of the fitness function calculation, this should significantly speed up our simulations and improve accuracy of the optimization procedure.

Second, we are currently using a static approach to decide how to increase our prediction horizon and the number of particles used in PSO. Specifically, we first increase the prediction horizon from 1 to 5, while keeping the number of particles unchanged at 10; if this fails to find a solution with fitness $\widehat{J_1}$ satisfying $\ell_{i-1} - \widehat{J_1} > \Delta_1$, we then increase the number of particles by 5. Based on our results, we speculate that in the initial stages, increasing the prediction horizon is more beneficial (leading rapidly to the appearance of cost-effective formations), whereas in the later stages, increasing the number of particles is more helpful. As future work, we will use machine-learning approaches to decide on the value of above parameters at runtime given the current level and state of the MDP, as well as study the impact of different level decomposition. Moreover, in our approach, we calculate the number of clones for resampling based on the current state. An alternative approach would rely on statistics built up over multiple levels along with the rank in the sorted list to chose configurations for resampling.

Finally, we are currently using our approach to generate plans for a flock to go from an initial configuration to a final V-formation. Our eventual goal is to achieve formation flight for a robotic swarm of (bird-like) drones. A real-world example is parcel-delivering drones that follow the same route to their destinations. Letting them fly together for a while could save energy and increase flight time. To achieve this goal, we first need to investigate the wind dynamics of multi-rotor drones. Then, the fitness function needs to be adopted to the new wind dynamics. Lastly, a decentralized approach of this method needs to be implemented and tested on the drone firmware, as well as various attacking modes are to be analyzed for proving the resilience of the approach.

Acknowledgments. The first author and the last author would like to thank Jan Křetínský for very valuable feedback. This work was partially supported by the Doctoral Program Logical Methods in Computer Science and the Austrian National Research Network RiSE/SHiNE (S11405-N23 and S11412-N23) project funded by the Austrian Science Fund (FWF) project W1255-N23, the EU ICT COST Action IC1402 ARVI, the Fclose (Federated Cloud Security) project funded by UnivPM, and National Science Foundation grant CCF 1423296.

References

1. Bajec, I.L., Heppner, F.H.: Organized flight in birds. Anim. Behav. **78**(4), 777–789 (2009)
2. Bartocci, E., Bortolussi, L., Brázdil, T., Milios, D., Sanguinetti, G.: Policy learning for time-bounded reachability in continuous-time Markov decision processes via doubly-stochastic gradient ascent. In: Agha, G., Houdt, B. (eds.) QEST 2016. LNCS, vol. 9826, pp. 244–259. Springer, Heidelberg (2016). doi:10.1007/978-3-319-43425-4_17
3. Baxter, J., Bartlett, P.L., Weaver, L.: Experiments with infinite-horizon, policy-gradient estimation. J. Artif. Int. Res. **15**(1), 351–381 (2011)
4. Bellman, R.: Dynamic Programming. Princeton University Press, Princeton (1957)
5. Camacho, E.F., Alba, C.B.: Model Predictive Control. Advanced Textbooks in Control and Signal Processing. Springer, Heidelberg (2007)
6. Cattivelli, F.S., Sayed, A.H.: Modeling bird flight formations using diffusion adaptation. IEEE Trans. Signal Process. **59**(5), 2038–2051 (2011)
7. Chazelle, B.: The convergence of bird flocking. J. ACM **61**(4), 21:1–21:35 (2014)
8. Chen, Y., Wu, B., Lai, T.L.: Fast Particle Filters and Their Applications to Adaptive Control in Change-Point ARX Models and Robotics. INTECH Open Access Publisher (2009)
9. Cutts, C., Speakman, J.: Energy savings in formation flight of pink-footed geese. J. Exp. Biol. **189**(1), 251–261 (1994)
10. Dang, A.D., Horn, J.: Formation control of autonomous robots following desired formation during tracking a moving target. In: Proceedings of the International Conference on Cybernetics, pp. 160–165. IEEE (2015)
11. Dimock, G., Selig, M.: The aerodynamic benefits of self-organization in bird flocks. Urbana **51**, 1–9 (2003)
12. Flake, G.W.: The Computational Beauty of Nature: Computer Explorations of Fractals, Chaos, Complex Systems, and Adaptation. MIT Press, Cambridge (1998)
13. García, C.E., Prett, D.M., Morari, M.: Model predictive control: theory and practice – a survey. Automatica **25**(3), 335–348 (1989)
14. Gennaro, M.C.D., Iannelli, L., Vasca, F.: Formation control and collision avoidance in mobile agent systems. In: Proceedings of the International Symposium on Control and Automation Intelligent Control, pp. 796–801. IEEE (2005)
15. Glasserman, P., Heidelberger, P., Shahabuddin, P., Zajic, T.: Multilevel splitting for estimating rare event probabilities. Oper. Res. **47**(4), 585–600 (1999)
16. Grosu, R., Peled, D., Ramakrishnan, C.R., Smolka, S.A., Stoller, S.D., Yang, J.: Using statistical model checking for measuring systems. In: Margaria, T., Steffen, B. (eds.) ISoLA 2014. LNCS, vol. 8803, pp. 223–238. Springer, Heidelberg (2014). doi:10.1007/978-3-662-45231-8_16
17. Henriques, D., Martins, J.G., Zuliani, P., Platzer, A., Clarke, E.M.: Statistical model checking for Markov decision processes. In: Proceedings of QEST 2012: The Ninth International Conference on Quantitative Evaluation of Systems, QEST 2012, pp. 84–93. IEEE Computer Society (2012)
18. Heppner, F.H.: Avian flight formations. Bird-Banding **45**(2), 160–169 (1974)
19. Hérault, T., Lassaigne, R., Magniette, F., Peyronnet, S.: Approximate probabilistic model checking. In: Steffen, B., Levi, G. (eds.) VMCAI 2004. LNCS, vol. 2937, pp. 73–84. Springer, Heidelberg (2004). doi:10.1007/978-3-540-24622-0_8
20. Hung, Y., Wang, W.: Accelerating parallel particle swarm optimization via GPU. Optim. Methods Softw. **27**(1), 33–51 (2012)

21. Kahn, H., Harris, T.E.: Estimation of particle transmission by random sampling. Natl. Bur. Stand. Appl. Math. Ser. **12**, 27–30 (1951)
22. Kalajdzic, K., Jegourel, C., Lukina, A., Bartocci, E., Legay, A., Smolka, S.A., Grosu, R.: Feedback control for statistical model checking of cyber-physical systems. In: Margaria, T., Steffen, B. (eds.) ISoLA 2016. LNCS, vol. 9952, pp. 46–61. Springer, Heidelberg (2016). doi:10.1007/978-3-319-47166-2_4
23. Kennedy, J., Eberhart, R.: Particle swarm optimization. In: Proceedings of 1995 IEEE International Conference on Neural Networks, pp. 1942–1948 (1995)
24. Lissaman, P., Shollenberger, C.A.: Formation flight of birds. Science **168**(3934), 1003–1005 (1970)
25. Mannor, S., Rubinstein, R.Y., Gat, Y.: The cross entropy method for fast policy search. In: ICML, pp. 512–519 (2003)
26. Nathan, A., Barbosa, V.C.: V-like formations in flocks of artificial birds. Artif. Life **14**(2), 179–188 (2008)
27. Reynolds, C.W.: Flocks, herds and schools: a distributed behavioral model. SIGGRAPH Comput. Graph. **21**(4), 25–34 (1987)
28. Russell, S., Norvig, P.: Artificial Intelligence: A Modern Approach, 3rd edn. Prentice-Hall, Upper Saddle River (2010)
29. Rymut, B., Kwolek, B., Krzeszowski, T.: GPU-accelerated human motion tracking using particle filter combined with PSO. In: Blanc-Talon, J., Kasinski, A., Philips, W., Popescu, D., Scheunders, P. (eds.) ACIVS 2013. LNCS, vol. 8192, pp. 426–437. Springer, Heidelberg (2013). doi:10.1007/978-3-319-02895-8_38
30. Seiler, P., Pant, A., Hedrick, K.: Analysis of bird formations. In: Proceedings of the Conference on Decision and Control, vol. 1, pp. 118–123. IEEE (2002)
31. Stulp, F., Sigaud, O.: Path integral policy improvement with covariance matrix adaptation. arXiv preprint arXiv:1206.4621 (2012)
32. Stulp, F., Sigaud, O.: Policy improvement methods: between black-box optimization and episodic reinforcement learning (2012). http://hal.upmc.fr/hal-00738463/
33. Verfaillie, G., Pralet, C., Vidal, V., Teichteil, F., Infantes, G., Lesire, C.: Synthesis of plans or policies for controlling dynamic systems. AerospaceLab (4), 1–12 (2012)
34. Weimerskirch, H., Martin, J., Clerquin, Y., Alexandre, P., Jiraskova, S.: Energy saving in flight formation. Nature **413**(6857), 697–698 (2001)
35. Yang, J., Grosu, R., Smolka, S.A., Tiwari, A.: Love thy neighbor: V-formation as a problem of model predictive control. In: LIPIcs-Leibniz International Proceedings in Informatics, vol. 59. Schloss Dagstuhl-Leibniz-Zentrum fuer Informatik (2016)
36. Yang, J., Grosu, R., Smolka, S.A., Tiwari, A.: V-formation as optimal control. In: Proceedings of the Biological Distributed Algorithms Workshop 2016 (2016)
37. Zhou, Y., Tan, Y.: GPU-based parallel particle swarm optimization. In: Proceedings of the Congress on Evolutionary Computation, pp. 1493–1500. IEEE (2009)

FlyFast: A Mean Field Model Checker

Diego Latella[1], Michele Loreti[2,3][✉], and Mieke Massink[1]

[1] Consiglio Nazionale delle Ricerche - Istituto di Scienza e Tecnologie
dell'Informazione 'A. Faedo', CNR, Pisa, Italy
{diego.latella,mieke.massink}@isti.cnr.it
[2] Università di Firenze, Florence, Italy
michele.loreti@unifi.it
[3] IMT Alti Studi, Lucca, Italy

Abstract. We present FlyFast, a recently introduced on-the-fly *mean field* model checker for the verification of time-dependent probabilistic properties of individual objects in the context of large populations. An example of its use is illustrated analysing a push-pull gossip protocol. Such protocols form the basis on top of which many smart collective adaptive systems are built. Typical properties are the replication of a fresh data element throughout a network, the coverage of the network, and the time to convergence.

Keywords: Mean field model checking · Collective Adaptive Systems · Discrete time markov chains · Self-organisation · Gossip protocols

1 Introduction

FlyFast is a, first of its kind, *on-the-fly mean field* probabilistic model checker. Its purpose is the automatic verification of bounded PCTL (Probabilistic Computation Tree Logic) properties of a *selected individual* in the context of systems that consist of a *large number* of (similar, but) independent, *interacting objects*. Typical examples of such systems are large scale Collective Adaptive Systems (CAS) and distributed algorithms for sharing data in a distributed network, such as gossip protocols. Following the mean field approach proposed in [7], an on-the-fly mean field model checking algorithm was developed and proven correct in [4,6]. Models that can be analysed by FlyFast are time-synchronous DTMC-based population models in which each object performs a probabilistic step in each discrete time unit, moving between its local states and possibly returning to the same state. Objects interact in an indirect way, via the global state of the system. In fact, the evolution of the global system is specified by the *local* transition probabilities of an object. The latter are the same for each object in the population (i.e. one abstracts from their identity) and may depend on the distribution of local states of all objects in the system, i.e. its occupancy

---

Research partially funded by the EU project QUANTICOL (nr. 600708).

A. Legay and T. Margaria (Eds.): TACAS 2017, Part II, LNCS 10206, pp. 303–309, 2017.
DOI: 10.1007/978-3-662-54580-5_18

measure vector[1]. When the number of objects is large (at least several hundreds) the overall behaviour, in terms of its occupancy measure vector, can be approximated by the deterministic solution of a difference equation, which is called the 'mean field' [7]. This iterative approach to obtain the occupancy measure vector has shown to combine very well with an on-the-fly probabilistic model checking approach [6]. The latter is parametric w.r.t. the semantics interpretation of the model specification language and in FlyFast it is instantiated on a mean-field population semantics. The algorithm consists of two phases, an expansion phase and a computation phase. Both phases are linear in the number of states and transitions of the expansion of the initial state of the selected object and occupancy measure vector [6] for the time bounded fragment of PCTL. FlyFast has been applied on a.o. bike sharing [6], client-server systems and computer worm epidemic models [5].

FlyFast is provided within the jSAM (java StochAstic Model Checker) framework which is an open source Eclipse plugin[2] integrating a set of tools for stochastic analysis of concurrent and distributed systems specified using process algebras. We illustrate the use of FlyFast using a push-pull gossip protocol as a running example [1,2]. Gossip protocols provide a scalable, simple, robust and fully decentralised communication mechanism for the spreading of information in large-scale networks where nodes periodically contact each other in a random fashion, exchanging part of their local information. They also form the basis for higher level interaction between nodes in large CAS. Besides mean field model checking procedures, FlyFast also provides two kinds of stochastic simulation procedures: one based on standard individual probabilistic simulation and one based on fast simulation [7]. The latter uses a mean-field approximation to simulate the behaviour of a single object in a large population.

2   Gossip Protocol

As a running example we consider the gossip shuffle protocol of [1,2] that we briefly recall in the following. In particular, as in [1], we analyse the dissemination of a generic data item d in a *fully connected network* in which the nodes execute the shuffling protocol. We consider the discrete time variant of this protocol with a maximal delay between two subsequent gossips of a node denoted by G_{max}. Following the mean field approximation technique [1,2,7] the behaviour of an individual node is based on its local state and the current occupancy measure vector.

Figure 1 shows the states and transitions of a single node where $G_{max} = 3$ due to space limitations. The red states, $D0$ and $O0$, denote states in which the gossip node is active, i.e. it can initiate an exchange of local information with a passive node; in $D0$ (resp. $O0$) the node has (resp. does not have) the

---

[1] More specifically, the occupancy measure vector consists of a number of elements equal to the number of local states of an object, providing, for each state, the fraction of objects in the total population that are currently in that state.

[2] http://quanticol.github.io/jSAM/.

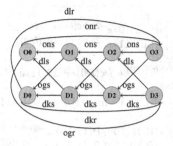

Fig. 1. Push-pull gossip model of individual gossip node with rounds of length 3 (i.e. $g_{max} = 3$). Active states are red, passive ones blue. (Color figure online)

data element in its local store. The blue states denote states in which the node is passive and can be contacted by an active node. The D/O convention w.r.t. having the data element applies also to the passive nodes. For further details of the model the reader is referred to [1,2].

3   The FlyFast Population Modelling Language

The modelling language of FlyFast consists of basic constructs to describe the probabilistic behaviour of an individual object, such as constants, states, action probabilities and transitions. The constants in the gossip model are the total number of nodes N, the number of different data elements in the system n, the size of the cache c and the number of data elements exchanged between two shuffling nodes s. Their definition is shown in Fig. 2. Furthermore, the action probabilities make use of a number of conditional probabilities, expressed in terms of the constants n, c and s. For example, P_01_10 stands for P(01|10) and denotes the conditional probability that after a shuffle the active node looses the data element, whereas the passive node acquires it (the '01' part of P_01_10) given that before the shuffle the active node had the data element and the passive one did not (the '10' part of P_01_10, see [1,2] for details).

Action probabilities are defined as shown in Fig. 3. The action labels are those of Fig. 1. For example, the action dlr ('has **d**, **l**ooses it and **r**esets gossip delay') labels the transition from the active state in which the object has the d-element ($D0$) to the passive state without d in which the clock is reset to G_{max}, i.e. $O3$

const N $= 2500$	**const** P_01_10 $= \frac{s}{c} * \frac{n-c}{n-s}$	**const** P_11_10 $=$ P_11_01
const n $= 500$	**const** P_10_01 $=$ P_01_10	**const** P_01_11 $= \frac{s}{c} * \frac{c-s}{c} * \frac{n-c}{n-s}$
const c $= 100$	**const** P_01_01 $= \frac{c-s}{c}$	**const** P_10_11 $=$ P_01_11
const s $= 50$	**const** P_10_10 $=$ P_01_01	**const** P_11_11 $= 1 - 2 * \frac{s}{c} * \frac{c-s}{c} * \frac{n-c}{n-s}$
	const P_11_01 $= \frac{s}{c} * \frac{c-s}{n-s}$	**const** P_00_00 $= 1$

Fig. 2. Constants of the FlyFast Gossip model.

action dlr :
$(\mathrm{frc}(O1)+\mathrm{frc}(O2)+\mathrm{frc}(O3))*\mathrm{P\_01\_10}*e^{-2*(\mathrm{frc}(O0)+\mathrm{frc}(D0))}+$
$(\mathrm{frc}(D1)+\mathrm{frc}(D2)+\mathrm{frc}(D3))*\mathrm{P\_01\_11}*e^{-2*(\mathrm{frc}(O0)+\mathrm{frc}(D0))}$
action dls :
$\mathrm{frc}(O0)*\mathrm{P\_10\_01}*e^{-2*(\mathrm{frc}(O0)+\mathrm{frc}(D0))}+ \mathrm{frc}(D0)*\mathrm{P\_10\_11}*e^{-2*(\mathrm{frc}(O0)+\mathrm{frc}(D0))}$
action dkr :
$(\mathrm{frc}(O1)+\mathrm{frc}(O2)+\mathrm{frc}(O3)+\mathrm{frc}(D1)+\mathrm{frc}(D2)+\mathrm{frc}(D3))*(1-e^{-2*(\mathrm{frc}(O0)+\mathrm{frc}(D0))})+$
$(\mathrm{frc}(O0)+\mathrm{frc}(D0))+$
$(\mathrm{frc}(O1)+\mathrm{frc}(O2)+\mathrm{frc}(O3))*(\mathrm{P\_10\_10}+\mathrm{P\_11\_10})*e^{-2*(\mathrm{frc}(O0)+\mathrm{frc}(D0))}+$
$(\mathrm{frc}(D1)+\mathrm{frc}(D2)+\mathrm{frc}(D3))*(\mathrm{P\_10\_11}+\mathrm{P\_11\_11})*e^{-2*(\mathrm{frc}(O0)+\mathrm{frc}(D0))}$
action dks :
$(\mathrm{frc}(O0)+\mathrm{frc}(D0))*(1-e^{-2*(\mathrm{frc}(O0)+\mathrm{frc}(D0))})+(1-(\mathrm{frc}(O0)+\mathrm{frc}(D0)))+$
$\mathrm{frc}(O0)*(\mathrm{P\_01\_01}+\mathrm{P\_11\_01})*e^{-2*(\mathrm{frc}(O0)+\mathrm{frc}(D0))}+$
$\mathrm{frc}(D0)*(\mathrm{P\_01\_11}+\mathrm{P\_11\_11})*e^{-2*(\mathrm{frc}(O0)+\mathrm{frc}(D0))}$
action ogr : $(\mathrm{frc}(D1)+\mathrm{frc}(D2)+\mathrm{frc}(D3))*(\mathrm{P\_10\_01}+\mathrm{P\_11\_01})*e^{-2*(\mathrm{frc}(O0)+\mathrm{frc}(D0))}$
action ons :
$(\mathrm{frc}(O0)+\mathrm{frc}(D0))*(1-e^{-2*(\mathrm{frc}(O0)+\mathrm{frc}(D0))})+(1-(\mathrm{frc}(O0)+\mathrm{frc}(D0)))+$
$\mathrm{frc}(O0)*\mathrm{P\_00\_00}*e^{-2*(\mathrm{frc}(O0)+\mathrm{frc}(D0))}+ \mathrm{frc}(D0)*\mathrm{P\_10\_10}*e^{-2*(\mathrm{frc}(O0)+\mathrm{frc}(D0))}$
action onr :
$(\mathrm{frc}(O1)+\mathrm{frc}(O2)+\mathrm{frc}(O3)+\mathrm{frc}(D1)+\mathrm{frc}(D2)+\mathrm{frc}(D3))*(1-e^{-2*(\mathrm{frc}(O0)+\mathrm{frc}(D0))})+$
$(\mathrm{frc}(O0)+\mathrm{frc}(D0))+$
$(\mathrm{frc}(O1)+\mathrm{frc}(O2)+\mathrm{frc}(O3))*\mathrm{P\_00\_00}*e^{-2*(\mathrm{frc}(O0)+\mathrm{frc}(D0))}+$
$(\mathrm{frc}(D1)+\mathrm{frc}(D2)+\mathrm{frc}(D3))*\mathrm{P\_01\_01}*e^{-2*(\mathrm{frc}(O0)+\mathrm{frc}(D0))}$
action ogs : $\mathrm{frc}(D0)*(\mathrm{P\_01\_10}+\mathrm{P\_11\_10})*e^{-2*(\mathrm{frc}(O0)+\mathrm{frc}(D0))}$

Fig. 3. Actions and their probabilities in the FlyFast Gossip model

state D0 {dlr.O3 + dkr.D3}	**state O0** {ogr.D3 + onr.O3}
state D1 {dls.O0 + dks.D0}	**state O1** {ogs.D0 + ons.O0}
state D2 {dls.O1 + dks.D1}	**state O2** {ogs.D1 + ons.O1}
state D3 {dls.O2 + dks.D2}	**state O3** {ogs.D2 + ons.O2}
system mainO0 = <O0[1],O0[(N/4)-1],O1[N/4], ..., O3[N/4],D0[1]>	

Fig. 4. States and initial configuration of the FlyFast Gossip model.

in this case. The probability of action dlr depends on the occupancy measure via the quantities $\mathrm{frc}(Xi)$, with $X \in \{O, D\}$ and $i \in \{0,\ldots,3\}$, which denote the *fraction* of objects that are in state Xi. The expression $e^{-2*(\mathrm{frc}(O0)+\mathrm{frc}(D0))}$ denotes the probability that no 'collision' occurs in the communication between two nodes, such as two active nodes that contact each other. Finally, Fig. 4 shows the definition of the states and transitions of a single node as in Fig. 1, and the non-empty elements of the initial occupancy measure vector mainO0. By default, the first element of the vector is the object selected for FlyFast analysis. We refer to [1] for further details of the model.

4   FlyFast Properties and Verification

The FlyFast syntax of bounded PCTL formulas is:

$$\Phi ::= \text{ap} \mid !\Phi \mid \Phi|\Phi \mid \Phi\&\Phi \mid P\{\bowtie p\}[\varphi] \qquad \text{with } \varphi ::= X\,\Phi \mid \Phi\,U_{\leq}\,k\,\Phi$$

where $\bowtie \in \{<, \leq, >, \geq\}$ and ap an atomic proposition, !, |,& the usual Boolean operators, P the probabilistic path quantifier, X and U the next and until operators. These bounded PCTL formulas are interpreted over *state labelled* DTMCs in which the states consist of pairs where the first element is the local state of the selected object and the second element the limit occupancy measure vector [7]. The formal semantics can be found in [6]. FlyFast uses memoization to speed up the computation of series of path formulas where the time-bound is a parameter. For example, for a model extended in the obvious way to one in which $G_{max} = 9$, Fig. 5 shows the probability that the selected node has seen the data element within time $t \in \{0, \ldots, 3000\}$:

$$\text{isTrue } U \leq t \text{ hasD } \textit{where } \text{ hasD} = \text{inD0} \mid \ldots \mid \text{inD9}$$

Since all nodes have the same probabilistic behaviour, this probability corresponds to the fraction of the network that has seen the data-element within time t (i.e. the coverage and convergence). This parametric analysis required 16,997 ms on an iMAC, 2,66 GHz ICi5, with 8 GB memory (same for *any* population size $N \geq 2500$!). The results in [1] show close correspondence to those obtained[3] with FlyFast for an initial state defined as system main in Fig. 4 but for $G_{max} = 9$. Figure 6 shows an example of a parametric *nested* path formula expressing, for time-bounds $t \in \{0, \ldots, 1000\}$, the probability to reach a state in which the probability to get the data element within 20 steps is greater than 0.1. The jump in the graph at $t = 700$ can be explained by the crossing of a threshold

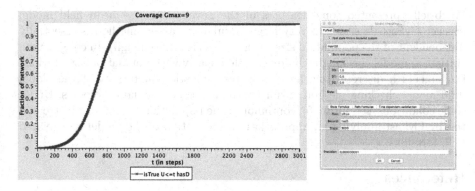

Fig. 5. Network coverage for a model with $G_{max} = 9$, $N = 2500$, $n = 500$, $s = 100$ and $c = 50$.

---

[3] Note that there is no need to extend the model with additional states that represent the fact that a node 'has seen' the data element, as was the case in [1].

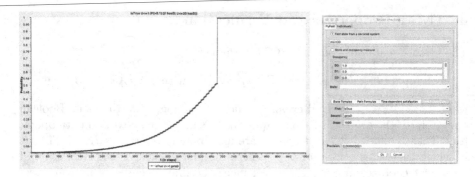

Fig. 6. Nested time-dependent probability for $G_{max} = 9$, $N = 2500$, $n = 500$, $s = 100$ and $c = 50$.

in the distribution of the data element in the network w.r.t. the bounds used in the formula[4].

$$\text{isTrue U} \leq t \; (\text{P}\{> 0.1\}[!\text{hasD U} \leq 20 \; \text{hasD}])$$

Also *time-dependent* probabilities of (non-parametric) path formulas can be analysed. For example we may wish to make sure that in the model the probability to leave active state $O0$ in the next step is equal to 1 at any time of interest, given that such transitions model clock-ticks in this gossip model. As this probability depends on the limit occupancy measure, this may not be given for granted. However, analysis of the path formula $O0 \; \text{U} \leq 1(D9 \mid O9)$, at different times $0, \dots, 3000$, shows that the probability is indeed 1. Results can be visualised with the graph view in the Eclipse plugin, as in Figs. 5 and 6, or exported for customised visualisation via Gnuplot, Octave or Matlab.

5   Related Work and Conclusions

We briefly presented some features of the novel on-the-fly mean field model checker FlyFast. It scales to very large populations as the method is essentially independent of the population size (as long as it is large enough). In comparison, statistical model checking techniques scale linearly with population size. FlyFast implements a discrete time, on-the-fly probabilistic counterpart of the global fluid model checking method [3] for continuous time population models. Under some conditions, set out in [5], continuous time population models can be treated too by FlyFast applying an appropriate discretisation of the model and related CSL formulas.

References

1. Bakhshi, R.: Gossiping models - formal analysis of epidemic protocols. Ph.D. thesis, Vrije Universiteit Amsterdam, January 2011. http://www.cs.vu.nl/en/Images/Gossiping_Models_van_Rena_Bakhshi_tcm210-256906.pdf

---

[4] Model checking time: 14,720 ms.

2. Bakhshi, R., Cloth, L., Fokkink, W., Haverkort, B.R.: Mean-field framework for performance evaluation of push-pull gossip protocols. Perform. Eval. **68**(2), 157–179 (2011)
3. Bortolussi, L., Hillston, J.: Model checking single agent behaviours by fluid approximation. Inf. Comput. **242**, 183–226 (2015)
4. Latella, D., Loreti, M., Massink, M.: On-the-fly fast mean-field model-checking. In: Abadi, M., Lluch Lafuente, A. (eds.) TGC 2013. LNCS, vol. 8358, pp. 297–314. Springer, Heidelberg (2014)
5. Latella, D., Loreti, M., Massink, M.: On-the-fly fluid model checking via discrete time population models. In: Beltrán, M., Knottenbelt, W., Bradley, J. (eds.) EPEW 2015. LNCS, vol. 9272, pp. 193–207. Springer, Heidelberg (2015)
6. Latella, D., Loreti, M., Massink, M.: On-the-fly PCTL fast mean-field approximated model-checking for self-organising coordination. Sci. Comput. Program. **110**, 23–50 (2015)
7. Le Boudec, J., McDonald, D.D., Mundinger, J.: A generic mean field convergence result for systems of interacting objects. In: Fourth International Conference on the Quantitative Evaluation of Systems (QEST 2007), pp. 3–18. IEEE Computer Society (2007)

ERODE: A Tool for the Evaluation and Reduction of Ordinary Differential Equations

Luca Cardelli[1], Mirco Tribastone[2], Max Tschaikowski[2],
and Andrea Vandin[2(✉)]

[1] Microsoft Research & University of Oxford, Oxford, UK
[2] IMT School for Advanced Studies Lucca, Lucca, Italy
andrea.vandin@imtlucca.it

Abstract. We present *ERODE*, a multi-platform tool for the solution and exact reduction of systems of ordinary differential equations (ODEs). *ERODE* supports two recently introduced, complementary, equivalence relations over ODE variables: *forward differential equivalence* yields a self-consistent aggregate system where each ODE gives the cumulative dynamics of the sum of the original variables in the respective equivalence class. *Backward differential equivalence* identifies variables that have identical solutions whenever starting from the same initial conditions. As back-end *ERODE* uses the well-known Z3 SMT solver to compute the largest equivalence that refines a given initial partition of ODE variables. In the special case of ODEs with polynomial derivatives of degree at most two (covering affine systems and elementary chemical reaction networks), it implements a more efficient partition-refinement algorithm in the style of Paige and Tarjan. *ERODE* comes with a rich development environment based on the Eclipse plug-in framework offering: (i) seamless project management; (ii) a fully-featured text editor; and (iii) importing-exporting capabilities.

1 Introduction

Ordinary differential equations (ODEs) have gained momentum in computer science due to the interest in formal methods for computational biology [14,20,35] and for their capability of accurately approximating large-scale Markovian models [5,24,30,37,39]. This has led to a number of results concerning the important, cross-disciplinary, and longstanding problem of reducing the size of ODE systems (e.g., [2,27,32]) using techniques such as abstract interpretation [13,18] and bisimulation [9,12,19,26,38].

Our contribution borrows ideas from programming languages and concurrency theory to recast the ODE reduction problem into finding an appropriate equivalence relation over ODE variables [9,11,12]. Two equivalence relations are presented in [12] for a class of nonlinear systems that covers multivariate rational derivatives and minimum/maximum operators. *Forward differential equivalence* (FDE) identifies a partition of the ODE variables for which a self-consistent aggregate ODE system can be provided which preserves the sums

© Springer-Verlag GmbH Germany 2017
A. Legay and T. Margaria (Eds.): TACAS 2017, Part II, LNCS 10206, pp. 310–328, 2017.
DOI: 10.1007/978-3-662-54580-5_19

of variables within each block. Variables related by a *backward differential equivalence* (BDE) have the same solution whenever initialized equally. The largest differential equivalence that refines a given input partition is computed via an SMT encoding, using Z3 [15] as a back-end.

ODEs with derivatives that are multivariate polynomials of degree at most two are an important sub-class, covering notable models such as affine systems and *elementary* chemical reaction networks (CRNs) with mass-action semantics (where each reaction has at most two reagents). For this class, in [9] we presented the notions of *forward bisimulation* (FB) and *backward bisimulation* (BB). FB is a sufficient condition for FDE; BB, instead, coincides with BDE for this class of ODEs. The main advantage in using these bisimulations is that the more expensive, symbolic checks through SMT are replaced by "syntactic" ones on a *reaction network*, a finitary structure similar to a CRN which encodes the ODE system. This has led in [11] to an efficient partition-refinement algorithm with polynomial space and time complexity. The bisimulations can be seen as liftings of equivalences and minimization algorithms for continuous-time Markov chains (CTMCs). Indeed the well-known notions of CTMC ordinary and exact lumpability [7] correspond to FB and BB, respectively, when the ODEs represent the CTMC's Kolmogorov equations; and, in this case, the complexity of our partition-refinement algorithm collapses to those of the best-performing ones for CTMC minimization [16,41]. As a consequence of this connection, FDE and BDE are not comparable in general.

This paper presents *ERODE* (https://sysma.imtlucca.it/tools/erode/), a fully-featured multi-platform tool implementing the reduction techniques from [9,11,12]. The tool distinguishes itself from the prototypes accompanying [9,11,12] in that: (i) It is not a command-line prototype but a mature tool with a modern integrated development environment; (ii) It collects all the techniques of our framework for ODE reduction in a unified coherent environment; (iii) It offers a language, and an editor, to express the entire class of ODEs supported by the reduction techniques, while the prototypes could reduce only CRNs; (iv) It implements an ODE workflow consisting of numerical solution and graphical visualization of results; (v) It offers importing/exporting facilities for other formats like biochemical models for the well-known tools BioNetGen [4] and Microsoft GEC [21], or ODEs defined in MATLAB.

Paper Outline. Section 2 reviews the reduction techniques from [9,11,12]; Sect. 3.1 describes *ERODE*'s architecture, while Sect. 3.2 details its functionalities by discussing the components of an *ERODE* specification. *ERODE*'s capabilities are further stated using a collection of large examples in Sect. 4. Finally, Sect. 5 concludes.

2 Theory Overview

The theory behind the techniques implemented in *ERODE* has been presented in [9,11,12], while a tutorial-like unifying presentation can be found in [43]. This section provides an overview that emphasizes relevant aspects for explaining *ERODE*'s performance.

$$A_u \xrightarrow{r_1} A_p$$

$$A_p \xrightarrow{r_2} A_u$$

$$A_u + B \xrightarrow{r_3} A_u B$$

$$A_u B \xrightarrow{r_4} A_u + B$$

$$A_p + B \xrightarrow{r_3} A_p B$$

$$A_p B \xrightarrow{r_4} A_p + B$$

(a)

$$[\dot{A_u}] = -r_1[A_u] + r_2[A_p] - r_3[A_u][B] + r_4[A_u B]$$

$$[\dot{A_p}] = \ \ r_1[A_u] - r_2[A_p] - r_3[A_p][B] + r_4[A_p B]$$

$$[\dot{B}] = -r_3[A_u][B] + r_4[A_u B] - r_3[A_p][B] + r_4[A_p B]$$

$$[\dot{A_u B}] = \ \ r_3[A_u][B] - r_4[A_u B]$$

$$[\dot{A_p B}] = \ \ r_3[A_p][B] - r_4[A_p B]$$

(b)

Fig. 1. CRN model (a) and underlying ODEs (b) of an idealized biochemical interaction.

Illustrating Example. Let us consider an idealized biochemical interaction between molecules A and B; A can be in two states, u (unphosphorylated) and p (phosphorylated) and can bind/unbind with B. This results in a network with five *species*, denoted by A_u, A_p, B, $A_u B$, and $A_p B$. The dynamics of the system is described in Fig. 1(a) through a CRN with six reactions, where r_1, r_2, r_3 and r_4, are the kinetic constants. By applying the well-known law of mass action, each species is associated with one ODE variable which models the evolution of its concentration as a function of time, with reactions that fire at a speed proportional to their rate times the concentrations of their reagents. For example, $A_u + B \xrightarrow{r_3} A_u B$ fires at speed $r_3[A_u][B]$, where $[\cdot]$ denotes the current concentration of a species. Consequently, this term appears with negative sign in the ODEs of its *reagents* (A_u and B), and with positive sign in the ODE of its *product*, $A_u B$. The resulting ODEs for our sample system are shown in Fig. 1(b), where the 'dot' operator denotes the (time) derivative. The model is completed by an *initial condition* which assigns the initial concentration $[X](0)$ to each species X in the network.[1]

Differential Equivalences. It can be shown that $\{\{[A_u], [A_p]\}, \{[B]\}, \{[A_u B], [A_p B]\}\}$ is an FDE for our running example. Indeed, exploiting basic properties one can write self-consistent ODEs for the sums of species in each equivalence class:

$$[\dot{A_u}] + [\dot{A_p}] = -r_3([A_u] + [A_p])[B] + r_4([A_u B] + [A_p B]),$$

$$[\dot{B}] = -r_3([A_u] + [A_p])[B] + r_4([A_u B] + [A_p B]),$$

$$[\dot{A_u B}] + [\dot{A_p B}] = r_3([A_u] + [A_p])[B] - r_4([A_u B] + [A_p B]). \qquad (1)$$

By the change of variables $[A] = [A_u] + [A_p]$ and $[AB] = [A_u B] + [A_p B]$, we get:

$$[\dot{A}] = -r_3[A][B] + r_4[AB], \quad [\dot{B}] = -r_3[A][B] + r_4[AB], \quad [\dot{AB}] = r_3[A][B] - r_4[AB]$$

This *quotient* ODE model essentially disregards the phosphorilation status of the A molecule. Setting the initial condition $[A](0) = [A_u](0) + [A_p](0)$ and $[AB](0) = $

---

[1] Throughout the paper we will work with *autonomous* ODE systems, which are not dependent on time. Also, we will use the terms 'variable' and 'species' interchangeably.

$[A_uB](0) + [A_pB](0)$ yields that the solution satisfies $[A](t) = [A_u](t) + [A_p](t)$ and $[AB](t) = [A_uB](t) + [A_pB](t)$ at all time points t.

Backward differential equivalence (BDE) equates variables that have the same solutions at all time points, if initialized equally. It can be shown that $\{\{[A_u], [A_p]\}, \{[B]\}, \{[A_uB], [A_pB]\}\}$ is also a BDE if $r_1 = r_2$. In this case, we obtain a quotient ODE by keeping only one variable (and equation) per equivalence class, say $[A_u]$, $[B]$ and $[A_uB]$, and rewriting every occurrence of $[A_p]$ and $[A_pB]$ as $[A_u]$ and $[A_uB]$, respectively:

$$[\dot{A_u}] = -2r_1[A_u] - r_3[A_u][B] + r_4[A_uB]$$
$$[\dot{B}] = -2r_3[A_u][B] + 2r_4[A_uB]$$
$$[\dot{A_uB}] = r_3[A_u][B] - r_4[A_uB]$$

Both FDE and BDE yield a reduced model that can be exactly related to the original one. BDE is lossless, because every variable in the same equivalence class has the same solution, but it is subject to the constraint that variables in the same block be initialized equally. Instead, with FDE one cannot recover the individual solution of an original variable in general, but no constraint is imposed on the initial conditions.

Symbolic Minimization Algorithms. In [12], establishing that a given partition is a differential equivalence amounts to checking the equality of the functions representing their derivatives. This is encoded in (quantifier-free) first-order logic formulae over the nonlinear theory of the reals. The problem is decidable for a large class of ODEs (and Z3 implements a decision procedure [28]). Such a class is identified by the IDOL language of [12], covering polynomials of any degree, rational expressions, minima and maxima. This captures affine systems, CRNs with mass-action or Hill kinetics [44], and the deterministic *fluid* semantics of process algebra [24, 37].

A partition of ODE variables is a BDE if any assignment with equal values in any equivalence class has equal derivatives within each equivalence class. Thus, $\{\{[A_u], [A_p]\}, \{[B], [A_uB], [A_pB]\}\}$ is a BDE if and only if the following formula is *valid* (i.e. true for all assignments to the real variables $[A_u]$, $[A_p]$, $[B]$, $[A_uB]$, and $[A_pB]$):

$$[A_u] = [A_p] \wedge [B] = [A_uB] = [A_pB] \implies$$
$$f_{[A_u]} = f_{[A_p]} \wedge f_{[B]} = f_{[A_uB]} = f_{[A_pB]} \quad (2)$$

where $f_{[\cdot]}$ stands for the derivative assigned to the corresponding species in Fig. 1(b). As usual, the SMT solver will check the satisfiability of its negation.

To automatically find differential equivalences of an ODE model, the SMT checks are embedded in a partition-refinement algorithm that computes the largest differential equivalence which refines a given input partition of variables. In particular, a current partition is refined at each step using the *witness* returned by the SMT solver, i.e. a variable assignment that falsifies the hypothesis that the current partition is a differential equivalence. The algorithm terminates when no witness is found, guaranteeing that the current partition is a differential equivalence. Let us fix the rates $r_1 = r_2 = 1$, $r_3 = 3$ and $r_4 = 4$. Then, $\{\{[A_u], [A_p]\}, \{[B], [A_uB], [A_pB]\}\}$ is not a BDE for our running example. Indeed, the assignment $\{[A_u] = 1, [A_p] = 1, [B] = 2, [A_uB] = 2, [A_pB] = 2\}$ is a witness for the negation of Eq. 2, since we get $f_{[A_u]} = 2$, $f_{[A_p]} = 2$, $f_{[B]} = 4$, $f_{[A_uB]} = -2$ and $f_{[A_pB]} = -2$ under this assignment. This information is then used to refine the current partition by splitting its blocks into sub-blocks of variables that have the same computation of derivative, obtaining $\{\{[A_u], [A_p]\}, \{[B]\}, \{[A_uB], [A_pB]\}\}$. No witness can be generated for this partition, ensuring that it is a BDE.

The FDE case is more involved, as discussed in [12]. Considering our running example, we have that $\{\{[A_u], [A_p]\}, \{[B], [A_uB], [A_pB]\}\}$ is an FDE if and only if

$$(f_{[A_u]} + f_{[A_p]} = \hat{f}_{[A_u]} + \hat{f}_{[A_p]}) \wedge (f_{[B]} + f_{[A_uB]} + f_{[A_pB]} = \hat{f}_{[B]} + \hat{f}_{[A_uB]} + \hat{f}_{[A_pB]}) \quad (3)$$

is *valid*, where each $\hat{f}_{[\cdot]}$ is obtained from the corresponding derivative $f_{[\cdot]}$ by replacing each variable with the sum of the variables in its block divided by the size of the block. For example, each occurrence of the term $r_4[A_uB]$ is replaced by $r_4 \frac{[B]+[A_uB]+[A_uB]}{3}$. It can be shown that the partition is not an FDE, because a witness falsifying Eq. 3 can be found by the SMT solver. However, differently from the BDE case, Eq. 3 does not compare single derivatives, but sums of derivatives, hence it cannot be used to decide how to refine the partition. For this, a "binary" characterization of FDE performs SMT checks on each pair of species in the same block of a partition to decide if they have to be split into different sub-blocks.

We remark that the algorithms allow the preservation of user-defined observables. For instance, a variable of interest can be put in an initial singleton block when reducing with FDE. Similarly, in order to meet the constraints on BDE, one can build an initial partition *consistent* with the initial conditions of the original model (that is, two variables are in the same initial block if their initial conditions are the same).

Syntax-Driven Minimisation. A reaction network (RN) differs from an elementary CRN in that the kinetic constants may be negative. This gives rise to an ODE system with derivatives that are multivariate polynomials of degree at most two [11]. FB and BB are equivalence relations over variables/species in the Larsen-Skou style of probabilistic bisimulation [31]. They are defined in terms of quantities computed by inspecting the set of reactions [31]. In order to check if a given partition of species $\mathcal{H}$ is an FB one computes the *ρ-reaction rate* of a species X, and the *cumulative ρ-production rate* by X of the species in a block $H \in \mathcal{H}$, defined respectively as:

$$\mathbf{crr}[X, \rho] := (\rho(X) + 1) \sum_{X + \rho \xrightarrow{\alpha} \pi \in R} \alpha, \quad \mathbf{pr}[X, H, \rho] := (\rho(X) + 1) \sum_{X + \rho \xrightarrow{\alpha} \pi \in R} \alpha \cdot \pi(H)$$

where ρ and π are multisets of species, and $\rho(X)$ and $\pi(H)$ denote the multiplicity of X in ρ, and the cumulative multiplicity of species from H in ρ, respectively. We note that ρ is the *reagent partner* of X, which can be either $\emptyset$ for unary reactions, or a species for binary ones. Intuitively, $\mathbf{crr}[X, \rho]$ quantifies the decrease of X's concentration due to reactions where X has partner ρ, while $\mathbf{pr}[X, H, \rho]$ quantifies the increase of its concentration gained by the species in H. In particular, $\mathcal{H}$ is an FB if for any pair of species X, Y in the same block of $\mathcal{H}$ it holds that $\mathbf{crr}[X, \rho] = \mathbf{crr}[Y, \rho]$ and $\mathbf{pr}[X, H, \rho] = \mathbf{pr}[Y, H, \rho]$ for all blocks H of $\mathcal{H}$, and all reagent partners ρ. BB is defined similarly. We refer to [9] for a detailed presentation of FB and BB.

The bisimulation style enabled in [11] the adaptation of Paige and Tarjan's coarsest refinement problem [33] to compute the largest FB/BB. This is done by generalizing algorithms for Markov chain lumping [16,41], obtaining algorithms with $\mathcal{O}(m \cdot n \cdot \log n)$ and $\mathcal{O}(m \cdot n)$ time and space complexity, respectively, with m being the number of monomials appearing in the underlying ODE system, and n the number of ODE variables.

Let us fix $r_1 = 1$, $r_2 = 2$, $r_3 = 3$ and $r_4 = 4$ in our running example. Then, $\{\{A_u, A_p\}, \{B, A_uB, A_pB\}\}$ is not an FB. The algorithm from [11] proceeds in two steps.

In the first step, $\mathbf{crr}[X, \rho]$ is computed for each species X and partner ρ. This information is used to refine the input partition, obtaining $\{\{A_u\}, \{A_p\}, \{B\}, \{A_uB, A_pB\}\}$. The first block is split because we have $\mathbf{crr}[A_u, \emptyset] = r_1$ and $\mathbf{crr}[A_u, \emptyset] = r_2$. Similarly, B is singled out because $\mathbf{crr}[B, \emptyset] = 0$, while $\mathbf{crr}[A_uB, \emptyset] = \mathbf{crr}[A_pB, \emptyset] = r_4$.

In the second step, the algorithm iteratively refines the current partition by selecting one of its blocks, H_{sp}, as a *splitter* in the current iteration: $\mathbf{pr}[X, H_{sp}, \rho]$ is computed for each X and ρ. This can be done efficiently by considering only reactions with species of H_{sp} in their products. Let us assume that $\{A_u\}$ is the splitter used in the first iteration. Only two reactions have A_u in their products, leading to the computation of $\mathbf{pr}[A_p, \{A_u\}, \emptyset] = r_2$ and $\mathbf{pr}[A_uB, \{A_u\}, \emptyset] = r_4$. Any other production rate of $\{A_u\}$, like $\mathbf{pr}[A_pB, \{A_u\}, \emptyset]$, has value 0. This information is used to refine the partition, obtaining $\{\{A_u\}, \{A_p\}, \{B\}, \{A_uB\}, \{A_pB\}\}$. No further refinement is possible in the following iterations, hence the partition, which is an FB, is returned.

3   ERODE

ERODE is an application based on the Eclipse framework for Windows, Mac OS and Linux. It does not require any installation process, and it is available, together with a manual and sample models, at http://sysma.imtlucca.it/tools/erode.

3.1   Architecture

Figure 2 provides a pictorial representation of the architecture of *ERODE*. It is organized in the presentation layer, with the graphical user interface, and the

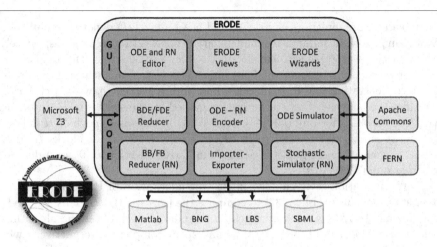

Fig. 2. *ERODE*'s architecture.

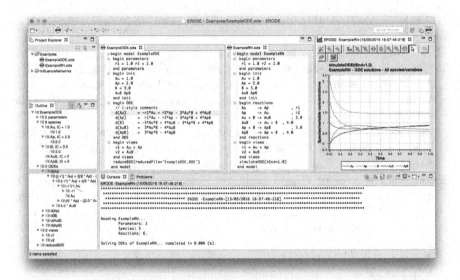

Fig. 3. A screenshot of *ERODE*.

core layer. The main components of the GUI layer are depicted in the screenshot of *ERODE* in Fig. 3, including a fully-featured text editor based on the *xText* framework which supports syntax highlighting, content assist, error detection and fix suggestions (top-middle of Fig. 3). This layer also offers a number of views, including a *project explorer* to navigate among different *ERODE* files (top-left of Fig. 3); an *outline* to navigate the parts of the currently open *ERODE* file (bottom-left of Fig. 3); a *plot view* to display ODE solutions (top-right of Fig. 3); and a *console view* to display diagnostic information like warnings and model reduction statistics (bottom-right of Fig. 3). Finally, the GUI layer offers a number of wizards for: (i) updating *ERODE* to the latest distribution; (ii) creating new *ERODE* files and projects; and (iii) importing models provided in third-party languages.

The core layer implements the minimization algorithms and related data structures for FDE, BDE, FB and BB (not detailed here because already addressed in [11,12,43]). A wrapper to Z3 via Java bindings is included for FDE/BDE reduction. The core layer also provides functionalities to encode an RN specification in its corresponding explicit ODE (or IDOL) format, and vice versa, as well as export/import functionalities for third-party languages. Finally, this layer provides support for numerical ODE solvers, using the Apache Commons Maths library [3]. When the input is a CRN (i.e. an RN with only positive rates) it can also be interpreted as a CTMC, following an established approach [22]. Using the *FERN* library [17], *ERODE* features CTMC simulation.

3.2 Language

This section details *ERODE*'s features by discussing the parts composing an *ERODE* file. We do this referring to the two alternative specification formats of our running example from Fig. 1, expressed in *ERODE* in Listings 1 and 2 There are six components of an *ERODE* specification: (i) parameter specification; (ii) declaration of variables and (optional) initial conditions; (iii) initial partition of variables; (iv) ODE system, either in plain format or as an RN; (v) observables, called *views*, tracked by the numerical solver; (vi) commands for ODE numerical solution, reduction, and exporting into other formats.

```
begin model ExampleODE
 begin parameters
  r1 = 1.0
  r2 = 2.0
 end parameters
 begin init
  Au = 1.0 Ap = 2.0 B = 3.0
  AuB = 0 ApB = 0
 end init
 begin partition
  {Au,Ap}, {AuB}, {B,ApB}
 end partition
 begin ODE
  // C-style comments
  d(Au)  = -r1*Au + r2*Ap - 3*Au*B + 4*AuB
  d(Ap)  =  r1*Au - r2*Ap - 3*Ap*B + 4*ApB
  d(B)   = -3*Au*B + 4*AuB - 3*Ap*B + 4*ApB
  d(AuB) =  3*Au*B - 4*AuB
  d(ApB) =  3*Ap*B - 4*ApB
 end ODE
 begin views
  v1 = Au + Ap
  v2 = AuB
 end views
 reduceBDE(reducedFile="ExampleODE_BDE.ode")
end model
```

Listing 1. Direct ODE specification.

```
begin model ExampleRN
 begin parameters
  r1 = 1.0
  r2 = 2.0
 end parameters
 begin init
  Au = 1.0 Ap = 2.0 B = 3.0
  AuB ApB
 end init
 begin partition
  {Au,Ap}, {AuB}
 end partition
 begin reactions
  Au      -> Ap      , r1
  Ap      -> Au      , r2
  Au + B  -> AuB     , 3.0
  AuB     -> Au + B  , 4.0
  Ap + B  -> ApB     , 3.0
  ApB     -> Ap + B  , 4.0
 end reactions
 begin views
  v1 = Au + Ap
  v2 = AuB
 end views
 simulateODE(tEnd=1.0)
end model
```

Listing 2. Reaction network.

Parameter Specification. An *ERODE* specification might start with an optional list of parameters enclosed in the **parameters** block, each is specified as:

$$\texttt{<parameter> = expression}$$

where **expression** is an arithmetic expression involving parameter names and reals through the following operators: +, -, *, / ^ abs, min, and max. Parameters can be used to specify values of initial conditions, kinetic rates, or views.

Variable Declaration. The mandatory **init** block defines all ODE variables of the model, each specified as:

$$\texttt{<variable> [= expression]}$$

where **expression** is an arithmetic expression as above that evaluates to the initial condition assigned to the variable (defaulting to zero if not specified).

Initial Partition of Variables. Optionally, a partition of variables can be specified in the **partition** block. This can then be used as the initial partition of the partition-refinement algorithms, as described later. (The user is required to specify only the partition blocks of interest, while all variables not mentioned explicitly are assigned to an implicit additional block.) For instance, Listings 1 and 2 represent the same initial partition {{Au,Ap},{AuB},{B,ApB}}.

ODE Definition. In the direct declaration format (Listing 1) the derivatives are specified within the **ODE** block. Each equation is specified as:

$$\texttt{d(<variable>) = derivative}$$

where **derivative** is an arithmetic expression, possibly containing also ODE variables. This allows to express ODEs belonging to IDOL [12].

In the reaction network format (Listing 2), the ODEs are inferred from reactions of the form:

$$\texttt{reagents -> products, rate}$$

where **reagents** and **products** are two multisets of variables. The multiplicity of a variable in a multiset can be defined through the + operator or with the * operator in the obvious way; that is, A + A is equivalent to 2*A. If rate is a variable-free expression that evaluates to a real number (as in all reactions of Listing 2), then the reaction represents a dynamics akin to the law of mass action, discussed in Sect. 2. In addition, *ERODE* supports more general arithmetical expressions for rates through the **arbitrary** keyword. In this case, the reaction firing rate is explicit. For instance, the two following reactions are equivalent:

```
Au + B    ->   AuB, arbitrary   3.0*Au*B        Au + B   ->   AuB, 3.0
```

Views. Views are the observations of interest. As for ODEs, each view can be specified as an arithmetic expression involving variables, parameters and reals. In Listings 1 and 2 the intent is to collect the total concentration of the A-molecules, regardless of their phosphorylation state (view v1), and the concentration of the species AuB (view v2).

For a CRN specification, views can also contain terms of form var(s1) and covar(s1,s2), to compute the variance of the variable s1 and the covariance of s1 and s2, respectively. To do so, *ERODE* implements the so-called *linear noise approximation* (e.g., [6]) to be able to study approximations of higher order moments of the concentrations of species in a CRN.

ODE Solution. The ODEs can be numerically solved using the command:

```
simulateODE(tEnd=<value>,   steps=<value>,   csvFile=<filename>)
```

It numerically integrates the ODE system starting from the specified initial conditions up to time point tEnd, interpolating the results at steps equally spaced time points. Two plots are generated, one for the trace of each ODE variable and one for the trace of each specified view, respectively. If the optional argument csvFile is present, the plots are exported into a comma-separated values format.

Conversion Options. An explicit ODE specification can be converted in the RN format (and vice versa) using

```
write(fileOut=fileName,format=<ODE|RN|MA-RN>)
```

If format is set to ODE, then the target file will be in explicit ODE format, while with RN an RN with possibly arbitrary rates will be generated. If the *ERODE* input to be exported is an explicit ODE with derivatives given by multivariate polynomials of degree at most two, the MA-RN will use the encoding of [11] to output a mass-action RN.

Export to Third-Party Languages. The command:

```
export<format> (fileOut=fileName)
```

exports *ERODE* files into four different target third-party languages:

Matlab: a Matlab function representing an ODE system (extension .m).
BNG: a CRN generated with the well-established tool BioNetGen version 2.2.5-stable [4] (extension .net). This is available for CRN specifications only.
LBS: format of the Microsoft's tool GEC [21] (extension .lbs), available for CRN specifications only.
SBML: the well-known SBML interchange format (http://sbml.org) (extension .sbml).

Reduction Commands. All ODE reduction commands share the common signature

```
reduce<kind> (prePartition=<NO|IC|USER>,    reducedFile=<name>)
```

where `kind` can be FDE, BDE, FB, or BB. The ODE input format affects which reduction options are available. For an ODE system defined directly, only FDE and BDE are enabled. FB and BB are additionally available for RNs representing polynomial ODE systems of degree at most two [11]. This is imposed by having reagents multisets of size at most two in each reaction and restricting to mass-action type rate expressions.

The option `prePartition` defines the initial partition for the minimization algorithm. The maximal aggregation is obtained with the NO option. If it is set to IC, the initial partition is built according to the constraints given by the initial conditions: variables are in the same initial block whenever their initial conditions are equal. If the option is set to USER, then the partition specified in the `partition` block will be used.

If `reducedFile` is present, then a reduced model will be generated according to the computed partition following the model-to-model transformation from [9] (for FB and BB) and [12] (for FDE and BDE). This will have the same format as the input, and will contain one variable for each equivalence class. The name of the variable is given by the first variable name in that block, according to a lexicographical order.

Considering our running example, no reduction is found running `reduceFDE` on Listing 1 if pre-partitioning is set to USER. Instead, when it is set to NO we find the FDE $\{\{A_u, A_p\}, \{B\}, \{A_u B, A_p B\}\}$ discussed in Sect. 2, implying that it is the maximal one of the model. The output file for the case without pre-partitioning is provided in Listing 3, which also shows that the association between the original ODE variables and those in the reduced model is maintained by annotating the output file with comments alongside the new variables.[2] This information can be useful for visually inspecting the reduced model in order to gain insights into the physical interpretation of the reduction [9]. Finally, we note that each reduced species has initial concentration equal to the sum of those in the corresponding block.

In Sect. 2 we have shown that the partition $\{\{A_u, A_p\}, \{B\}, \{A_u B, A_p B\}\}$ is also a BDE provided that $r_1 = r_2$. However, this reduction is not found if running `reduceBDE` with pre-partitioning set to IC, as it violates the initial conditions for Au and Ap. Instead, if the pre-partitioning is disabled, then the above partition is the coarsest refinement, but the user is warned about the inconsistency with the initial conditions. The BDE reduction without pre-partitioning for r1=r2=1.0 is given in Listing 4. The initial condition for the ODE of each representative is equal to that of the corresponding original variable.

---

[2] Here output files have been typographically adjusted to improve presentation.

```
begin model ExampleODE_FDE
 begin parameters
  r1 = 1.0
  r2 = 2.0
 end parameters
 begin init
  Au  = 1.0 + 2.0
  B   = 3.0
  AuB
 end init
 begin ODE
  d(Au)  = - 3*Au*B + 4*AuB
  d(B)   = - 3*Au*B + 4*AuB
  d(AuB) =   3*Au*B - 4*AuB
 end ODE
 //Comments associated to the
    species
 //Au:  Block {Au, Ap}
 //B:   Block {B}
 //AuB: Block {AuB, ApB}
end model
```

Listing 3. FDE reduction.

```
begin model ExampleODE_BDE
 begin parameters
  r1 = 1.0
  r2 = 1.0
 end parameters
 begin init
  Au  = 1.0
  B   = 3.0
  AuB
 end init
 begin ODE
  d(Au)  = - 3*Au*B + 4*AuB
  d(B)   = - 6*Au*B + 8*AuB
  d(AuB) =   3*Au*B - 4*AuB
 end ODE
 //Comments associated to the
    species
 //Au:  Block {Au, Ap}
 //B:   Block {B}
 //AuB: Block {AuB, ApB}
end model
```

Listing 4. BDE reduction.

The model of Listing 2 is not reduced by FB, independently on the pre-partitioning choice. This is consistent with FB being only a sufficient condition for FDE (although it is effective on many meaningful models from the literature, as discussed in [11]). The result of the BB reduction is instead provided in the right inset. As for BDE, we considered the case r1=1.0 and r2=1.0 without pre-partitioning. It can be shown that the underlying ODEs of the reduced model correspond to those of Listing 4, as expected. (The placeholder species SINK is created to rule out reactions that have no products.)

```
begin parameters
 r1 = 1.0   r2 = 1.0
end parameters
begin init
 Au = 1.0   B = 3.0   AuB
 SINK
end init
begin reactions
 Au -> 2*Au , r2
 Au -> SINK , r1
 Au + B -> Au , 3.0
 Au + B -> AuB , 3.0
 AuB -> Au + B , 4.0
 AuB -> B + AuB , 4.0
end reactions
//Comments associated to the species
//Au:  Block {Au, Ap}
//B:   Block {B}
//AuB: Block {AuB, ApB}
end model
```

4   Evaluation

Prototypal versions of *ERODE*'s reduction algorithms have been evaluated in [9, 11, 12, 43] against a number of models from the literature. The main outcomes of these analyses are: (i) Our reduction techniques are effective, as we found reductions in many large-scale models that enjoy substantial speed-ups for the numerical ODE solution [9, 11]; (ii) Our forward and backward notions are not comparable in general, as there are models which can be reduced by the former but not by the latter, and vice versa [9]; (iii) In some cases, observables of interest specified by the modeller can be used to automatically generate initial partitions that lead to forward reductions preserving them [43]; (iv) FDE and BDE are less efficient than FB and BB, but are more general and lead to better reductions in the forward case [12]. (v) FB and BB correspond to the notions of ordinary and exact CTMC lumpability [7], respectively [11]; in particular FB has been validated in [11] against the ordinary CTMC lumping algorithm [16] implemented in MRMC [29].

With *ERODE* we could confirm all these previously reported results. In this section, we carry out a systematic evaluation of *ERODE*'s capabilities in terms of scalability as a function of: the input model size (Sect. 4.1), its degree of non-linearity (Sect. 4.2), and its degree of aggregability (Sect. 4.3). For this, we considered a collection of synthetic benchmarks to be able to gain full control on the model parameters to be changed for performing these studies.

All experiments were run on a 3.2 GHz Intel Core i5 machine with 16 GB of RAM. In order to avoid interferences, each single model was tested on a fresh Java Virtual Machine, with assigned 10 GB of RAM. For each reduction we used initial partitions with one block only containing all variables. Information on how to replicate the experiments is available at http://sysma.imtlucca.it/tools/erode/benchmarks.

4.1   Scalability

We begin by studying the scalability of the partition-refinement algorithms in terms of the model size. Such an assessment has been conducted already in [12] for BDE/FDE, where it has been shown that BDE can handle models up to 786,432 reactions and 65,538 species, while FDE handled up to 8,620 reactions and 745 species. For larger models Z3 issued out-of-memory errors. Here we confirm these figures when using *ERODE*.

Instead, to study the scalability of FB and BB, we consider a number of random RNs underlying degree-two polynomials. The set-up is as follows. First, we fixed 7 different configurations with increasing number of reactions and species (columns $|R|$ and $|S|$ of Table 1, respectively). For each configuration, we generated five random RNs, each having 70% unary reactions in the form $A \to B$, leading to degree-one monomials in the ODEs for species A and B, and 30%

Table 1. FB and BB reductions for random RNs with 30% of binary reactions.

Configuration		FB reduction (s)			BB reduction (s)		
$\|R\|$	$\|S\|$	Min	Avg	Max	Min	Avg	Max
1.00E+6	1.00E+5	2.34E+0	**2.35E+0**	2.38E+0	4.98E+0	**5.40E+0**	6.17E+0
5.00E+6	5.00E+5	1.95E+1	**1.96E+1**	1.98E+1	3.91E+1	**3.96E+1**	3.98E+1
1.00E+7	1.00E+6	3.89E+1	**3.91E+1**	3.92E+1	9.59E+1	**9.77E+1**	9.95E+1
1.50E+7	1.50E+6	9.62E+1	**9.71E+1**	9.86E+1	1.67E+2	**1.68E+2**	1.69E+2
2.00E+7	2.00E+6	1.58E+2	**1.59E+2**	1.62E+2	3.30E+2	**3.31E+2**	3.33E+2
2.50E+7	2.50E+6	3.42E+2	**3.46E+2**	3.52E+2	8.72E+2	**8.92E+2**	9.24E+2
3.00E+7	3.00E+6	Out of memory			Out of memory		

binary reactions in the form $A + B \to C$, leading to degree-two monomials for A, B, and C. (Here the percentage of binary reactions was fixed arbitrarily — it will be studied in more detail in the next subsection.) The species involved in each reaction were sampled uniformly (with re-insertion), while the kinetic rates were drawn uniformly from the interval [1;10,000]. We ensured that none of the RNs could be reduced in order to stress the algorithm by forcing it to evaluate the maximum number of partition-refinement iterations. To reduce noise, the measurements for each RN were repeated three times, for a total of 15 experiments per configuration.

Table 1 summarizes the results. The columns *Min*, *Avg* and *Max* provide, respectively, the minimum, average, and maximum reduction times obtained per configuration. FB and BB reductions succeeded for models up to 25,000,000 reactions and 2,50,0000 species, requiring about 5 and 15 min, respectively. Larger RNs led to out-of-memory errors. The first and sixth row show that an increment of factor 25 in both the number of species and reactions leads to about two order of magnitude larger runtimes, consistently with the algorithms' complexities (Sect. 2). Finally, we note that BB reductions were performed twice as slow as the corresponding FB ones This is consistent with [11], which shows that for BB the inner loops of the partition-refinement algorithm execute about twice as many instructions as for FB (see Algorithms 4 and 5 from [11]).

4.2 Degree of Nonlinearity

We now study how the reduction runtimes are affected by the nonlinearity in the model, here measured as the percentage of monomials of degree greater than one in the ODE.

For FB and BB we fixed a configuration with $|R| = 3{,}500{,}000$, and $|S| = 250{,}000$, similarly to the largest CRN in [9,11], and considered models with increasing percentage of binary reactions. For each percentage, we generated five RNs similarly to Sect. 4.1. Table 2 gives the reduction runtimes. We note an increase in the runtimes as a function of the percentage of binary reactions. This is consistent with the time complexity of FB and BB (Sect. 2). In fact, RNs

Table 2. Reductions of random elementary RNs with varying ratio of binary reactions.

Percentage of binary reactions					
0%	20%	40%	60%	80%	100%
Syntactic reductions $\|R\|$=3.50E+6 and $\|S\|$=2.50E+5					
FB (s) 6.40E+0	1.31E+1	1.58E+1	2.03E+1	2.18E+1	2.65E+1
BB (s) 1.51E+1	2.53E+1	3.06E+1	3.61E+1	4.44E+1	4.98E+1
Symbolic reductions $\|R\|$=1.50E+3 and $\|S\|$=2.50E+2					
FDE (s) —	2.81E+2	3.63E+2	4.86E+2	1.06E+3	2.50E+3
BDE (s) 2.87E–1	2.89E–1	2.90E–1	2.92E–1	2.95E–1	2.96E–1

with higher ratio of binary reactions have more monomials in the underlying ODEs (see Sect. 4.1). However we note that in practice the runtimes at worst only quadruplicates respect to the linear case (column 0%).

Table 2 also reports the evaluation for FDE/BDE considering RNs of size $|R|$ = 1,500 and $|S|$ = 250. We note that BDE requires much less time than FDE, as expected from the discussion in Sect. 2. In addition, we find that the BDE runtimes are essentially not affected. The same does not hold for FDE: incrementing the percentage of binary reactions by 20 leads to an increment of factor between 1.3 and 2.3 in the runtimes. The different impact on the performance of BDE and FDE can be explained by the algebraic transformations required by FDE to compute the $\hat{f}_{[\cdot]}$ terms shown in Eq. (3). Consider for example a partition $\mathcal{H}$ and a species X belonging to a block H of $\mathcal{H}$. Then, terms of form X^2 are substituted with terms of form $(\sum_{Y \in H} Y)^2/|H|^2$, with an explosion in the number of monomials appearing in the derivatives. We do not provide the FDE runtime for the 0% case, because it can be shown that, akin to CTMC lumpability, partitions with one block only are FDE for RNs with unary reagents and products only.

We further study the behavior of FDE/BDE as a function of the maximum degree of the polynomials. For this, we constructed RNs with 60% unary reactions and 40% n-ary reactions (leading to degree n monomials in the underlying ODEs), with n = 20, 40, 60, 80, 100. The RNs have size $|R| = 1,500$, $|S| = 250$, as in the last rows of Table 2. The runtimes, averaged over 5 random RNs, are given in the bottom inset. The BDE runtime for n = 20 is five times that of the corresponding one for degree-two polynomials (third column of Table 2), and it further increases of factor 20 for n = 100. FDE succeeded for up to n = 40, despite the discussed highly demanding algebraic manipulations required, while Z3 returned "unknown" for larger values of n, suggesting an out of memory error.

	Maximum degree of the polynomial n				
	20	40	60	80	100
BDE (s)	1.46E+0	8.30E+0	9.881E+0	1.42E+1	3.34E+1
FDE (s)	7.00E+2	2.00E+3	–	"unknown"	–

4.3 Number of Iterations vs Runtime

Finally, we study how the number of performed iterations of the partition-refinement algorithms affects the runtime. For FB and BB this is done using variants of model M1 of [9,11], with 3,538,944 reactions and 262,146 species. It is the largest of a family of synthetic benchmarks used in [36] to study the scalability of a network-free simulator for CRNs. It models an idealized binding/unbiding interaction between two molecules, A and B, which can take place through A's nine *binding sites*. Symmetries in the model are introduced through the assumption that such binding sites are equivalent, in the sense that the rate of binding/unbinding does not depend on the identity of the binding site.

Table 3(a) studies increasingly less symmetric variants of the model, obtained by changing the binding/unbinding rates of each site; the first column shows

Table 3. Reductions for variants of M1 of [9,11] by decreasing binding sites' symmetries.

	FB reduction			BB reduction		
Sym.	Red. (s)	Iter.	$|\mathcal{H}|$	Red. (s)	Iter.	$|\mathcal{H}|$
9	3.61E+0	223	222	7.60E+0	224	222
8	3.96E+0	663	662	8.12E+0	664	662
7	4.18E+0	1,923	1,922	8.63E+0	1,924	1,922
6	4.51E+0	5,379	5,378	8.73E+0	5,380	5,378
5	4.51E+0	14,339	14,338	8.77E+0	14,340	14,338
4	4.71E+0	35,849	35,842	8.97E+0	35,844	35,842
3	5.29E+0	81,959	81,922	9.58E+0	81,924	81,922
2	5.56E+0	163,910	163,842	9.71E+0	163,845	163,842
0	6.29E+0	262,147	262,146	1.12E+1	262,157	262,146

(a) 9 binding sites, $|R|$=3,538,944, $|S|$=262,146

	FDE reduction			BDE reduction		
Sym.	Red.(s)	Iter.	$|\mathcal{H}|$	Red.(s)	Iter.	$|\mathcal{H}|$
4	1.39E+2	13,284	37	4.10E-1	42	37
3	2.66E+2	38,355	82	6.00E-1	81	82
2	3.52E+2	50,517	162	7.75E-1	113	162
0	2.54E+2	37,022	258	2.22E-1	9	258

(b) 4 binding sites, $|R|$=1,536, $|S|$=258

the number of equivalent sites in the model. The columns *Red.* provide the runtimes of our algorithms. Columns *Iter.* and $|\mathcal{H}|$ show the number of iterations performed and the blocks for the coarsest partitions obtained. Decreasing the number of symmetric binding sites by one leads to an increment of factor between 2 and 3 in the number of iterations and blocks in the partitions. Instead, the runtime increases only slightly: the number of iterations between the first and the last experiment are separated by three orders of magnitude while their respective runtimes at most only double for both FB and BB. This can be explained by the fact that, at each iteration, one block of the current partition is chosen as a potential *splitter*. Therefore only the reactions that have species belonging to the splitter in their products will be inspected. As a result, the smaller is the current splitter, the fewer reactions are scanned in the iteration. More importantly, as discussed in detail in [11], the FB/BB algorithms follow Paige and Tarjan's approach of *ignoring the largest sub-part* [33]. This means that, whenever a block is split, one of its sub-blocks with maximal size will not be further used as splitter. This guarantees that each species will appear in at most $\log |S|$ splitters, with S being the species in the model.

Table 3(b) reports a similar analysis for FDE and BDE. We use a simplification of M1 where A has only four binding sites, obtaining 1,536 reactions and 258 species, to which both FDE and BDE can be successfully applied. The table has the same structure of Table 3(a), however here *Iter.* counts the number of performed SMT checks. The table also shows that our symbolic algorithms are strongly affected by the number of performed iterations: the nature of the FDE/BDE algorithms does not allow for advanced optimizations like those discussed for FB/BB. Lastly, it is interesting to note that the number of necessary iterations decreases in the case when no reduction is found (last row of Table 3(b)). Here, the computation of the largest BDE required nine SMT checks: the SMT solver was able to split the initial block in 250 blocks in the first iteration, then one new block has been created in the following eight iterations until reaching the final partition with one block per species. For FDE, instead, 37,022 SMT checks were necessary. We note that this is relatively close to the number of binary comparisons among 258 elements, i.e. $\binom{258}{2} = 33153$, as expected from the discussion in Sect. 2.

5   Conclusion

We presented *ERODE*, a tool for the analysis and reduction of ODEs. The main novelty is in the implementation of partition-refinement algorithms that compute the largest equivalence over ODE variables that refine an initial partition, using both syntactic criteria as well as symbolic SMT ones. However, currently *ERODE* does not support algorithms required when the modeler is interested in equivalences that satisfy constraints that are not expressible as initial partitions. An example is the notion of emulation used for model comparison between two CRNs [8], where each BDE partition block must contain at least one species of the *source* CRN, and exactly one of the *target*. We plan to integrate *ERODE* with the algorithm for computing all the BDEs of a CRN from [10].

ERODE is concerned with exact aggregations. These may be too strong in some cases, as small perturbations in the parameters might prevent reductions for ODE variables with nearby trajectories in practice. This motivated the development of approximate notions of equivalence [1,23,34,42]. Preliminary work is treated in [25,40]. However these approaches lack an algorithm for automatic reduction, and they provide error bounds that tend to grow fast with time. In the future we aim at tackling these two issues.

Acknowledgments. This work was partially supported by the EU project QUANTI-COL, 600708. L. Cardelli is partially funded by a Royal Society Research Professorship.

References

1. Aldini, A., Bravetti, M., Gorrieri, R.: A process-algebraic approach for the analysis of probabilistic noninterference. JCS **12**(2), 191–245 (2004)
2. Aoki, M.: Control of large-scale dynamic systems by aggregation. IEEE Trans. Autom. Control **13**(3), 246–253 (1968)
3. Apache Commons Mathematics Library. http://commons.apache.org/proper/commons-math/
4. Blinov, M.L., Faeder, J.R., Goldstein, B., Hlavacek, W.S.: Bionetgen: software for rule-based modeling of signal transduction based on the interactions of molecular domains. Bioinformatics **20**(17), 3289–3291 (2004)
5. Bortolussi, L., Hillston, J., Latella, D., Massink, M.: Continuous approximation of collective system behaviour: a tutorial. Perform. Eval. **70**(5), 317–349 (2013)
6. Bortolussi, L., Lanciani, R.: Model checking Markov population models by central limit approximation. In: Joshi, K., Siegle, M., Stoelinga, M., D'Argenio, P.R. (eds.) QEST 2013. LNCS, vol. 8054, pp. 123–138. Springer, Heidelberg (2013). doi:10.1007/978-3-642-40196-1_9
7. Buchholz, P.: Exact and ordinary lumpability in finite Markov Chains. J. Appl. Probab. **31**(1), 59–75 (1994)

8. Cardelli, L.: Morphisms of reaction networks that couple structure to function. BMC Syst. Biol. **8**(1), 84 (2014)

9. Cardelli, L., Tribastone, M., Tschaikowski, M., Vandin, A.: Forward and backward bisimulations for chemical reaction networks. In: CONCUR (2015)

10. Cardelli, L., Tribastone, M., Tschaikowski, M., Vandin, A.: Comparing chemical reaction networks: a categorical and algorithmic perspective. In: LICS (2016)

11. Cardelli, L., Tribastone, M., Tschaikowski, M., Vandin, A.: Efficient syntax-driven lumping of differential equations. In: Chechik, M., Raskin, J.-F. (eds.) TACAS 2016. LNCS, vol. 9636, pp. 93–111. Springer, Heidelberg (2016). doi:10.1007/978-3-662-49674-9_6

12. Cardelli, L., Tribastone, M., Tschaikowski, M., Vandin, A.: Symbolic computation of differential equivalences. In: POPL (2016)

13. Danos, V., Feret, J., Fontana, W., Harmer, R., Krivine, J.: Abstracting the differential semantics of rule-based models: exact and automated model reduction. In: LICS, pp. 362–381 (2010)

14. Danos, V., Laneve, C.: Formal molecular biology. Theoret. Comput. Sci. **325**(1), 69–110 (2004)

15. Moura, L., Bjørner, N.: Z3: an efficient SMT solver. In: Ramakrishnan, C.R., Rehof, J. (eds.) TACAS 2008. LNCS, vol. 4963, pp. 337–340. Springer, Heidelberg (2008). doi:10.1007/978-3-540-78800-3_24

16. Derisavi, S., Hermanns, H., Sanders, W.H.: Optimal state-space lumping in Markov chains. Inf. Process. Lett. **87**(6), 309–315 (2003)

17. Erhard, F., Friedel, C.C., Zimmer, R.: FERN - a Java framework for stochastic simulation and evaluation of reaction networks. BMC Bioinform. **9**(1), 356 (2008)

18. Feret, J., Danos, V., Krivine, J., Harmer, R., Fontana, W.: Internal coarse-graining of molecular systems. Proc. Nat. Acad. Sci. **106**(16), 6453–6458 (2009)

19. Feret, J., Henzinger, T., Koeppl, H., Petrov, T.: Lumpability abstractions of rule-based systems. Theoret. Comput. Sci. **431**, 137–164 (2012)

20. Fisher, J., Henzinger, T.A.: Executable cell biology. Nat. Biotechnol. **25**(11), 1239–1249 (2007)

21. Microsoft GEC. http://research.microsoft.com/en-us/projects/gec/

22. Gillespie, D.T.: Exact stochastic simulation of coupled chemical reactions. J. Phys. Chem. **81**(25), 2340–2361 (1977)

23. Gupta, V., Jagadeesan, R., Panangaden, P.: Approximate reasoning for real-time probabilistic processes. Log. Methods Comput. Sci. **2**(1), 1–23 (2006)

24. Hayden, R.A., Bradley, J.T.: A fluid analysis framework for a Markovian process algebra. Theor. Comput. Sci. **411**(22–24), 2260–2297 (2010)

25. Iacobelli, G., Tribastone, M.: Lumpability of fluid models with heterogeneous agent types. In: DSN, pp. 1–11 (2013)

26. Iacobelli, G., Tribastone, M., Vandin, A.: Differential bisimulation for a Markovian process algebra. In: Italiano, G.F., Pighizzini, G., Sannella, D.T. (eds.) MFCS 2015. LNCS, vol. 9234, pp. 293–306. Springer, Heidelberg (2015). doi:10.1007/978-3-662-48057-1_23

27. Iwasa, Y., Andreasen, V., Levin, S.: Aggregation in model ecosystems. I. Perfect aggregation. Ecol. Model. **37**(3–4), 287–302 (1987)

28. Jovanović, D., Moura, L.: Solving non-linear arithmetic. In: Gramlich, B., Miller, D., Sattler, U. (eds.) IJCAR 2012. LNCS (LNAI), vol. 7364, pp. 339–354. Springer, Heidelberg (2012). doi:10.1007/978-3-642-31365-3_27

29. Katoen, J.-P., Khattri, M., Zapreev, I.S.: A Markov reward model checker. In: QEST, pp. 243–244 (2005)

30. Kowal, M., Tschaikowski, M., Tribastone, M., Schaefer, I.: Scaling size and parameter spaces in variability-aware software performance models. In: ASE (2015)
31. Larsen, K.G., Skou, A.: Bisimulation through probabilistic testing. Inf. Comput. **94**(1), 1–28 (1991)
32. Li, G., Rabitz, H.: A general analysis of exact lumping in chemical kinetics. Chem. Eng. Sci. **44**(6), 1413–1430 (1989)
33. Paige, R., Tarjan, R.: Three partition refinement algorithms. SIAM J. Comput. **16**(6), 973–989 (1987)
34. Pierro, A., Hankin, C., Wiklicky, H.: Quantitative relations and approximate process equivalences. In: Amadio, R., Lugiez, D. (eds.) CONCUR 2003. LNCS, vol. 2761, pp. 508–522. Springer, Heidelberg (2003). doi:10.1007/978-3-540-45187-7_33
35. Regev, A., Shapiro, E.: Cellular abstractions: cells as computation. Nature **419**(6905), 343–343 (2002)
36. Sneddon, M.W., Faeder, J.R., Emonet, T.: Efficient modeling, simulation and coarse-graining of biological complexity with NFsim. Nat. Methods **8**(2), 177–183 (2011)
37. Tribastone, M., Gilmore, S., Hillston, J.: Scalable differential analysis of process algebra models. IEEE Trans. Softw. Eng. **38**(1), 205–219 (2012)
38. Tschaikowski, M., Tribastone, M.: Exact fluid lumpability for markovian process algebra. In: Koutny, M., Ulidowski, I. (eds.) CONCUR 2012. LNCS, vol. 7454, pp. 380–394. Springer, Heidelberg (2012). doi:10.1007/978-3-642-32940-1_27
39. Tschaikowski, M., Tribastone, M.: A unified framework for differential aggregations in Markovian process algebra. J. Log. Algebr. Meth. Program. **84**(2), 238–258 (2015)
40. Tschaikowski, M., Tribastone, M.: Approximate reduction of heterogenous nonlinear models with differential hulls. IEEE Trans. Autom. Control **61**, 1099–1104 (2016)
41. Valmari, A., Franceschinis, G.: Simple $O(m \log n)$ time Markov chain lumping. In: Esparza, J., Majumdar, R. (eds.) TACAS 2010. LNCS, vol. 6015, pp. 38–52. Springer, Heidelberg (2010). doi:10.1007/978-3-642-12002-2_4
42. van Breugel, F., Worrell, J.: Approximating, computing behavioural distances in probabilistic transition systems. Theoret. Comput. Sci. **360**(1–3), 373–385 (2006)
43. Vandin, A., Tribastone, M.: Quantitative abstractions for collective adaptive systems. In: Bernardo, M., Nicola, R., Hillston, J. (eds.) SFM 2016. LNCS, vol. 9700, pp. 202–232. Springer, Heidelberg (2016). doi:10.1007/978-3-319-34096-8_7
44. Voit, E.O.: Biochemical systems theory: a review. ISRN Biomath. **2013**, 53 (2013)

SV COMP

Software Verification with Validation of Results
(Report on SV-COMP 2017)

Dirk Beyer

LMU Munich, Munich, Germany

Abstract. This report describes the 2017 Competition on Software Verification (SV-COMP), the 6th edition of the annual thorough comparative evaluation of fully-automatic software verifiers. The goal is to reflect the current state of the art in software verification in terms of effectiveness and efficiency. The major achievement of the 6th edition of SV-COMP is that the verification results were validated in most categories. The verifiers have to produce verification witnesses, which contain hints that a validator can later use to reproduce the verification result. The answer of a verifier counts only if the validator confirms the verification result. SV-COMP uses two independent, publicly available witness validators. For 2017, a new category structure was introduced that now orders the verification tasks according to the property to verify on the top level, and by the type of programs (e.g., which kind of data types are used) on a second level. The categories *Overflows* and *Termination* were heavily extended, and the category *SoftwareSystems* now contains also verification tasks from the software system BUSYBOX. The competition used 8 908 verification tasks that each consisted of a C program and a property (reachability, memory safety, termination). SV-COMP 2017 had 32 participating verification systems from 12 countries.

1 Introduction

Software verification is an increasingly important research area, and the annual Competition on Software Verification (SV-COMP)[1] is the showcase of the state of the art in the area, in particular, of the effectiveness and efficiency that is currently achieved by tool implementations of the most recent ideas, concepts, and algorithms for fully-automatic verification. Every year, the SV-COMP project consists of two parts: (1) The collection of verification tasks and their partition into categories has to take place before the actual experiments start, and requires quality-assurance work on the source code in order to ensure a high-quality evaluation. It is important that the SV-COMP verification tasks reflect what the research and development community considers interesting and challenging for evaluating the effectivity (soundness and completeness) and efficiency (performance) of state-of-the-art verification tools. (2) The actual experiments of the comparative evaluation of the relevant tool implementations is performed

---

[1] https://sv-comp.sosy-lab.org

© Springer-Verlag GmbH Germany 2017
A. Legay and T. Margaria (Eds.): TACAS 2017, Part II, LNCS 10206, pp. 331–349, 2017.
DOI: 10.1007/978-3-662-54580-5_20

by the organizer of SV-COMP. Since SV-COMP shall stimulate and showcase new technology, it is necessary to explore and define standards for a reliable and reproducible execution of such a competition: we use BENCHEXEC [10], a modern framework for reliable benchmarking and resource measurement, to run the experiments, and verification witnesses [7,8] to validate the verification results.

As for every edition, this SV-COMP report describes the (updated) rules and definitions, presents the competition results, and discusses other interesting facts about the execution of the competition experiments. Also, we need to measure the success of SV-COMP by evaluating whether the main objectives of the competition are achieved (list taken from [5]):

1. provide an overview of the state of the art in software-verification technology and increase visibility of the most recent software verifiers,
2. establish a repository of software-verification tasks that is publicly available for free use as standard benchmark suite for evaluating verification software,
3. establish standards that make it possible to compare different verification tools, including a property language and formats for the results, and
4. accelerate the transfer of new verification technology to industrial practice.

As for (1), there were 32 participating software systems from 12 countries, representing a broad spectrum of technology (cf. Table 4). SV-COMP is considered an important event in the research community, and increasingly also in industry. This year, SV-COMP for the first time had two participating verification systems from industry. As for (2), the total set of verification tasks increased in size from 6 661 to 8 908. Still, SV-COMP has an ongoing focus on collecting and constructing verification tasks to ensure even more diversity. Compared to the last years, the level and amount of quality-assurance activities from the SV-COMP community increased significantly, as witnessed by the issue tracker[2] and by the pull requests[3] in the GitHub project. As for (3), the largest step forward was to apply an extension of the standard witness language as a common, exchangeable format to correctness witnesses as well this year (violation witnesses have been used before). This means, if a verifier reports FALSE (claims to know an error path through the program that violates the specification), then it produces a violation witness; if a verifier reports TRUE (claims to know a proof of correctness), then it produces a correctness witness. The two points of the SV-COMP scoring schema for correct answers TRUE are assigned only if the correctness witness was confirmed by a witness validator, i.e., a proof of correctness could be reconstructed by a different tool. As for (4), we continuously received positive feedback from industry.

Related Competitions. It is well-understood that competitions are an important evaluation method, and there are other competitions in the field of software verification: RERS[4] [20] and VerifyThis[5] [22]. While SV-COMP performs replicable

---

[2] https://github.com/sosy-lab/sv-benchmarks/issues?q=is:issue
[3] https://github.com/sosy-lab/sv-benchmarks/pulls?q=is:pr
[4] http://rers-challenge.org
[5] http://etaps2016.verifythis.org

experiments in a *controlled* environment (dedicated resources, resource limits), the RERS Challenges give more room for exploring combinations of interactive with automatic approaches without limits on the resources, and the VerifyThis Competition focuses on evaluating approaches and ideas rather than on *fully-automatic* verification. The termination competition termCOMP[6] [16] concentrates on termination but considers a broader range of systems, including logic and functional programs. A more comprehensive list of other competitions is provided in the report on SV-COMP 2014 [4].

2   Procedure

The overall competition organization did not change in comparison to the past editions [2–6]. SV-COMP is an open competition, where all verification tasks are known before the submission of the participating verifiers, which is necessary due to the complexity of the language C. During the *benchmark submission* phase, new verification tasks were collected and classified, during the *training* phase, the teams inspected the verification tasks and trained their verifiers (also, the verification tasks received fixes and quality improvement), and during the *evaluation* phase, verification runs were preformed with all competition candidates, and the system descriptions were reviewed by the competition jury. The participants received the results of their verifier directly via e-mail, and after a few days of inspection, the results were publicly announced on the competition web site. The *Competition Jury* consisted again of the chair and one member of each participating team. Team representatives of the jury are listed in Table 3.

3   Definitions, Formats, and Rules

Verification Task. The definition of verification task was not changed (taken from [4]). A verification task consists of a C program and a property. A verification run is a non-interactive execution of a competition candidate (verifier) on a single verification task, in order to check whether the following statement is correct: "The program satisfies the property." The result of a verification run is a triple (ANSWER, WITNESS, TIME). ANSWER is one of the following outcomes:

TRUE: The property is satisfied (no path exists that violates the property), and a correctness witness is produced that contains hints to reconstruct the proof.

FALSE: The property is violated (there exists a path that violates the property), and a violation witness is produced that contains hints to replay the error path to the property violation.

UNKNOWN: The tool cannot decide the problem, or terminates abnormally, or exhausts the computing resources time or memory (the competition candidate does not succeed in computing an answer TRUE or FALSE).

---

[6] http://termination-portal.org/wiki/Termination_Competition

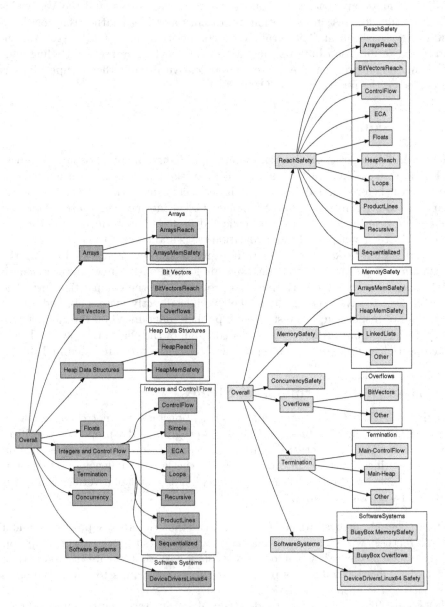

Fig. 1. Categories; left: SV-COMP 2016; right: SV-COMP 2017; category *Falsification* contains all verification tasks of *Overall* without *Termination*

Table 1. Properties used in SV-COMP 2017 (cf. [5] for more details)

Formula	Interpretation
G ! call(foo())	A call to function foo is not reachable on any finite execution
G valid-free	All memory deallocations are valid (counterexample: invalid free). More precisely: There exists no finite execution of the program on which an invalid memory deallocation occurs
G valid-deref	All pointer dereferences are valid (counterexample: invalid dereference). More precisely: There exists no finite execution of the program on which an invalid pointer dereference occurs
G valid-memtrack	All allocated memory is tracked, i.e., pointed to or deallocated (counterexample: memory leak). More precisely: There exists no finite execution of the program on which the program lost track of some previously allocated memory
F end	All program executions are finite and end on proposition **end**, which marks all program exits (counterexample: infinite loop). More precisely: There exists no execution of the program on which the program never terminates

The component WITNESS [7,8] was this year for the first time mandatory for *both* answers TRUE or FALSE; a few categories were excluded from validation if the validators did not sufficiently support a certain kind of program or property. We used the two publicly available witness validators CPACHECKER and UAUTOMIZER. TIME is measured as consumed CPU time until the verifier terminates, including the consumed CPU time of all processes that the verifier started [10]. If TIME is equal to or larger than the time limit (15 min), then the verifier is terminated and the ANSWER is set to 'timeout' (and interpreted as UNKNOWN).

Categories. The collection of verification tasks is partitioned into categories. A major update was done on the structure of the categories, in order to support various extensions that were planned for SV-COMP 2017. For example, the categories *Overflows* and *Termination* were considerably extended (*Overflows* from 12 to 328 and *Termination* from 631 to 1 437 verification tasks). Figure 1 shows the previous structure of main and sub-categories on the left, and the new structure is shown on the right. The guideline is to have main categories that correspond to different properties and sub-categories that reflect the type of program. The goal of the category *SoftwareSystems* is to complement the other categories (which sometimes contain small and constructed examples to show certain verification features) by large and complicated verification tasks from real software systems (further structured according to system and property to verify). The category assignment was proposed and implemented by the competition chair, and approved by the competition jury. SV-COMP 2017 has a total of eight categories for which award plaques are handed out, including the six main categories, category *Overall*, which contains the union of all categories,

Table 2. Scoring schema for SV-COMP 2017

Reported result	Points	Description
UNKNOWN	0	Failure to compute verification result
FALSE correct	+1	Violation of property in program was correctly found
FALSE incorrect	−16	Violation reported but property holds (false alarm)
TRUE correct	+2	Correct program reported to satisfy property
TRUE correct unconfirmed	+1	Correct program reported to satisfy property, but the witness was not confirmed by a validator
TRUE incorrect	−32	Incorrect program reported as correct (wrong proof)

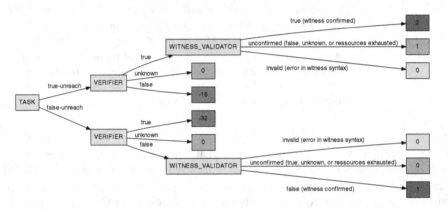

Fig. 2. Visualization of the scoring schema for the reachability property

and category *Falsification*. Category *Falsification* consists of all verification tasks with safety properties, and any answers TRUE are not counted for the score (the goal of this category is to show bug-hunting capabilities of verifiers that are not able to construct correctness proofs). The categories are described in more detail on the competition web site.[7]

Properties and Their Format. For the definition of the properties and the property format, we refer to the previous competition report [5]. All specifications are available in the main directory of the benchmark repository. Table 1 lists the properties and their syntax as overview.

Evaluation by Scores and Run Time. The scoring schema of SV-COMP 2017 is similar to the previous scoring schema, except that results with answer TRUE are now assigned two points only if the witness was confirmed by a validator, and one point is assigned if the answer matches the expected result but the witness was not confirmed. Table 2 provides the overview and Fig. 2 visually illustrates the score assignment for one property. The ranking is decided based on the sum of points (normalized for meta categories) and for equal sum of points according to success run time, which is the total CPU time over all verification

---

[7] https://sv-comp.sosy-lab.org/2017/benchmarks.php

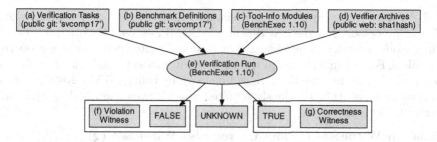

Fig. 3. Setup: SV-COMP components that support reproducibility

tasks for which the verifier reported a correct verification result. *Opt-out from Categories* and *Score Normalization for Meta Categories* was done as described previously [3] (page 597).

4 Reproducibility

It is important that the SV-COMP experiments can be independently replicated, and that the results can be reproduced. Therefore, all major components that are used for the competition need to be publicly available. Figure 3 gives an overview over the components that contribute to the reproducible setup of SV-COMP.

Repositories for Verification Tasks (a), Benchmark Definitions (b), and Tool-Information Modules (c). The previous competition report [6] describes how replicability is ensured by making all essential ingredients available in public archives. The verification tasks (a) are available via the tag 'svcomp17' in a public Git repository.[8] The benchmark definitions (b) define for each verifier (i) on which verification tasks the verifier is to be executed (each verifier can choose which categories to participate in) and (ii) which parameters need to be passed to the verifier (there are global parameters that are specified for all categories, and there are specific parameters such as the bit architecture). The benchmark definitions are available via the tag 'svcomp17' in another public Git repository.[9] The tool-information modules (c) ensure, for each verifier respectively, that the command line to execute the verifier is correctly assembled (including source and property file as well as the options) from the parts specified in the benchmark definition (b), and that the results of the verifier are correctly interpreted and translated into the uniform SV-COMP result (TRUE, FALSE(p), UNKNOWN). The tool-info modules that were used for SV-COMP 2017 are available in BENCHEXEC 1.10.[10]

Reliable Assignment and Controlling of Computing Resources (e). We use BENCHEXEC[11] [10] to satisfy the requirements for scientifically valid experimentation, such as (i) accurate measurement and reliable enforcement of limits

---

[8] https://github.com/sosy-lab/sv-benchmarks/tree/svcomp17/c

[9] https://github.com/sosy-lab/sv-comp/tree/svcomp17/benchmark-defs

[10] https://github.com/sosy-lab/benchexec/tree/1.10/benchexec/tools

[11] https://github.com/sosy-lab/benchexec

for CPU time and memory, and (ii) reliable termination of processes (including all child processes). For the first time in SV-COMP, we used BENCHEXEC's container mode, in order to make sure that read and write operations are properly controlled. For example, it was previously not automatically and reliably enforced that tools do not increase the assigned memory by using a RAM disk. This and some other issues that previously required manual inspection and analysis are now systematically solved.

Violation Witnesses (f) and Correctness Witnesses (g). In SV-COMP, each verification run (if applicable) is followed by a validation run that checks whether the witness adheres to the exchange format and can be confirmed. The resource limits for the witness validators were 2 processing units (one physical CPU core with hyper-threading), 7 GB memory, and 10% of the verification time (i.e., 1.5 min) for violation witnesses and 100% (15 min) for correctness witnesses. The purpose of the tighter resource limits is to avoid delegating all verification work to the validator. This witness-based validation process ensures a higher quality of assignment of scores, compared to without witnesses: if a verifier claims a found bug but is not able to provide a witness, then the verifier does not get the full score. The witness format and the validation process is explained on the witness-format web page[12]. The version of the exchange format that was used for SV-COMP 2017 has the tag 'svcomp17'. More details on witness validation is given in two related research articles [7,8].

Verifier Archives (d). Due to legal issues we do not re-distribute the verifiers on the competition web site, but list for each verifier a URL to an archive that the participants promised to keep publicly available, together with the SHA1 hash of the archive that was used in SV-COMP. An overview table is provided on the systems-description page of the competition web site[13]. For replicating experiments, the archive can be downloaded and verified against the given SHA1 hash. Each archive contains all parts that are needed to execute the verifier (statically-linked executables and all components that are required in a certain version, or for which no standard Ubuntu package is available). The archives are also supposed to contain a license that permits use in SV-COMP, replicating the SV-COMP experiments, that all data that the verifier produces as output are property of the person that executes the verifier, and that the results obtained from the verifier can be published without any restriction.

5   Results and Discussion

For the sixth time, the competition experiments represent the state of the art in fully-automatic software-verification tools. The report shows the improvements of the last year, in terms of effectiveness (number of verification tasks that can

---

[12] https://github.com/sosy-lab/sv-witnesses/tree/svcomp17
[13] https://sv-comp.sosy-lab.org/2017/systems.php

Table 3. Competition candidates with tool references and representing jury members

Participant	Ref.	Jury member	Affiliation
2LS	[34]	Peter Schrammel	U. of Sussex, UK
APROVE	[19]	Jera Hensel	RWTH Aachen, Germany
BLAST	[35]	Vadim Mutilin	ISP RAS, Russia
CBMC	[26]	Michael Tautschnig	Queen Mary, UK
CEAGLE		Guang Chen	Tsinghua U., China
CIVL	[37]	Stephen Siegel	U. of Delaware, USA
CONSEQUENCE		Anand Yeolekar	TCS, India
CPA-BAM-BNB	[1]	Pavel Andrianov	ISP RAS, Russia
CPA-KIND	[9]	Matthias Dangl	U. of Passau, Germany
CPA-SEQ	[14]	Karlheinz Friedberger	U. of Passau, Germany
DEPTHK	[33]	Herbert O. Rocha	Federal U. of Roraima, Brazil
ESBMC	[28]	Lucas Cordeiro	U. of Oxford, UK
ESBMC-FALSI	[28]	Bernd Fischer	Stellenbosch U., ZA
ESBMC-INCR	[28]	Denis Nicole	U. of Southampton, UK
ESBMC-KIND	[15]	Mikhail Ramalho	U. of Southampton, UK
FORESTER	[21]	Martin Hruska	Brno U. of Technology, Czechia
HIPTNT+	[27]	Ton Chanh Le	National U. of Singapore, Singapore
LAZY-CSEQ	[23]	Omar Inverso	Gran Sasso Science Institute, Italy
LAZY-CSEQ-ABS	[30]	Bernd Fischer	Stellenbosch U., ZA
LAZY-CSEQ-SWARM		Truc Nguyen Lam	U. of Southampton, UK
MU-CSEQ	[36]	Salvatore La Torre	U. of Salerno, Italy
PREDATORHP	[25]	Tomas Vojnar	Brno U. of Technology, Czechia
SKINK	[11]	Franck Cassez	Macquarie U. at Sydney, Australia
SMACK	[32]	Zvonimir Rakamarić	U. of Utah, USA
SYMBIOTIC	[12]	Jan Strejček	Masaryk U., Czechia
SYMDIVINE	[24]	Jiří Barnat	Masaryk U., Czechia
UAUTOMIZER	[18]	Matthias Heizmann	U. of Freiburg, Germany
UKOJAK	[31]	Daniel Dietsch	U. of Freiburg, Germany
UL-CSEQ	[29]	Gennaro Parlato	U. of Southampton, UK
UTAIPAN	[17]	Marius Greitschus	U. of Freiburg, Germany
VERIABS	[13]	Priyanka Darke	TCS, India
YOGAR-CBMC		Liangze Yin	National U. of Defense Techn., China

be solved, correctness of the results, as accumulated in the score) and efficiency (resource consumption in terms of CPU time). The results that are presented in this article were inspected and approved by the participating teams.

Participating Verifiers. Table 3 provides an overview of the participating competition candidates and Table 4 lists the features and technologies that are used in the verification tools.

Table 4. Technologies and features that the competition candidates offer

Participant	CEGAR	Predicate Abstraction	Symbolic Execution	Bounded Model Checking	k-Induction	Property-Directed Reach.	Explicit-Value Analysis	Numeric. Interval Analysis	Shape Analysis	Separation Logic	Bit-Precise Analysis	ARG-Based Analysis	Lazy Abstraction	Interpolation	Automata-Based Analysis	Concurrency Support	Ranking Functions
2LS				✓	✓		✓				✓						✓
APROVE			✓				✓	✓			✓						✓
BLAST	✓	✓					✓					✓	✓	✓			
CBMC				✓							✓					✓	
CEAGLE	✓	✓		✓							✓	✓	✓				
CIVL			✓	✓				✓								✓	
CONSEQUENCE				✓							✓					✓	
CPA-BAM-BNB	✓	✓					✓				✓	✓	✓	✓			
CPA-KIND	✓	✓		✓	✓			✓			✓	✓	✓				
CPA-SEQ	✓	✓		✓	✓		✓	✓	✓		✓	✓	✓	✓		✓	✓
DEPTHK				✓	✓						✓					✓	
ESBMC				✓							✓					✓	
ESBMC-FALSI				✓							✓					✓	
ESBMC-INCR				✓							✓					✓	
ESBMC-KIND				✓	✓						✓					✓	
FORESTER	✓								✓						✓		
HIPTNT+									✓	✓							✓
LAZY-CSEQ				✓							✓					✓	
LAZY-CSEQ-ABS				✓			✓				✓					✓	
LAZY-CSEQ-SWARM				✓							✓					✓	
MU-CSEQ				✓							✓					✓	
PREDATORHP									✓								
SKINK	✓						✓							✓	✓	✓	
SMACK	✓			✓		✓					✓		✓			✓	
SYMBIOTIC			✓								✓						
SYMDIVINE			✓				✓				✓				✓	✓	
UAUTOMIZER	✓	✓									✓		✓	✓	✓		✓
UKOJAK	✓	✓									✓		✓	✓			
UL-CSEQ	✓	✓										✓	✓	✓		✓	
UTAIPAN	✓	✓									✓		✓	✓	✓		
VERIABS				✓	✓			✓									
YOGAR-CBMC	✓			✓							✓		✓			✓	

Table 5. Quantitative overview over all results; empty cells mark opt-outs

Participant	ReachSafety 4696 points 2897 tasks	MemSafety 541 points 328 tasks	ConcurrencySafety 1293 points 1047 tasks	Overflows 533 points 328 tasks	Termination 2513 points 1437 tasks	SoftwareSystems 5520 points 2871 tasks	FalsificationOverall 2908 points 7471 tasks	Overall 14553 points 8908 tasks
2LS	1038	-918	0	310	624	720	-4330	-1204
APROVE					1492			
BLAST						866		
CBMC	2154	219	1135	230		37	2554	4766
CEAGLE	2170	138		12		352	343	1972
CIVL			1251					
CONSEQUENCE			794					
CPA-BAM-BNB						975	-735	
CPA-KIND	2156	0	0	101	0	778	232	1963
CPA-SEQ	2862	88	1020	101	974	1011	1302	5296
DEPTHK	1552	27	548	85	-307	254	976	1894
ESBMC	1125	-85	601	105	0	301	184	1674
ESBMC-FALSI	583	-65	552	106	0	-17	1269	1261
ESBMC-INCR	1810	80	756	187	0	0	1482	3209
ESBMC-KIND	1940	191	654	304	0	334	1610	4335
FORESTER								
HIPTNT+					835			
LAZY-CSEQ			1226					
LAZY-CSEQ-ABS			1293					
LAZY-CSEQ-SWARM			1293					
MU-CSEQ			1179					
PREDATORHP		319						
SKINK			-102					
SMACK	3432	150	1208	417	0	1695	1154	6917
SYMBIOTIC	2063	304	0	281	0	-7079	-2698	42
SYMDIVINE			389					
UAUTOMIZER	2372	308	0	372	2184	1055	982	7099
UKOJAK	1564	268	0	356	0	410	900	3837
UL-CSEQ			1177					
UTAIPAN	1894	296	0	365	0	1067	918	4511
VERIABS								
YOGAR-CBMC			1293					

Table 6. Overview of the top-three verifiers for each category (CPU time in h, rounded to two significant digits)

Rank	Participant	Score	CPU Time	Solved Tasks	False Alarms	Wrong Proofs
ReachSafety						
1	SMACK	**3432**	100	1 543		
2	CPA-Seq	2862	39	1 874	5	
3	U Automizer	2372	27	1 344		
MemSafety						
1	PredatorHP	**319**	.82	219		
2	U Automizer	308	1.9	145		
3	Symbiotic	304	.080	233		
ConcurrencySafety						
1	Yogar-CBMC	**1293**	.35	1 047		
2	Lazy-CSeq-Abs	1293	2.1	1 047		
3	Lazy-CSeq-Swarm	1293	3.2	1 047		
Overflows						
1	SMACK	**417**	18	271		1
2	U Automizer	372	.83	273		
3	U Taipan	365	.85	270		
Termination						
1	U Automizer	**2184**	8.3	1 272		
2	AProVE	1492	3.6	520		
3	CPA-Seq	974	14	821	4	
SoftwareSystems						
1	SMACK	**1695**	20	1 391	2	
2	U Taipan	1067	18	1 567	7	4
3	U Automizer	1055	19	1 568	7	4
FalsificationOverall						
1	CBMC	**2554**	8.1	1 817		
2	ESBMC-kind	1610	27	1 341	20	
3	ESBMC-incr	1482	32	1 400	25	
Overall						
1	U Automizer	**7099**	57	4 602	7	4
2	SMACK	6917	180	4 463	12	2
3	CPA-Seq	5296	81	5 393	29	

Computing Resources. The resource limits were the same as last year [6]: Each verification run was limited to 8 processing units (cores), 15 GB of memory, and 15 min of CPU time. The witness validation was limited to 2 processing units, 7 GB of memory, and 1.5 min of CPU time for violation witnesses and 15 min of CPU time for correctness witnesses. The machines for running the experiments were different from last year, because we now had 168 machines available and each verification run could be executed on a completely unloaded,

Table 7. Necessary effort to compute results FALSE versus TRUE (measurement values rounded to two significant digits)

Result	TRUE		FALSE	
	CPU time (avg. in s)	CPU energy (avg. in J)	CPU time (avg. in s)	CPU energy (avg. in J)
UAUTOMIZER	46	450	42	420
SMACK	210	2 200	51	580
CPA-SEQ	65	650	39	320

dedicated machine, in order to achieve precise measurements. Each machine had one Intel Xeon E3-1230 v5 CPU, with 8 processing units each, a frequency of 3.4 GHz 33 GB of RAM, and a GNU/Linux operating system (x86_64-linux, Ubuntu 16.04 with Linux kernel 4.4).

One complete verification execution of the competition consisted of 421 benchmarks (each verifier on each selected category according to the opt-outs), summing up to 170 417 verification runs. Witness validation required 678 benchmarks (combinations of verifier, category with witness validation, and two validators) summing up to 232 916 validation runs. The consumed total CPU time for one complete competition run for verification required a total of 490 days of CPU time. Each tool was executed several times, in order to make sure no installation issues occur during the execution. We used BENCHEXEC [10] to measure and control computing resources (CPU time, memory, CPU energy) and VERIFIERCLOUD[14] to distribute, install, run, and clean-up verification runs, and to collect the results.

Quantitative Results. Table 5 presents the quantitative overview over all tools and all categories (FORESTER participated only in subcategory *ReachSafety-Heap*, *MemSafety-Heap*, and *MemSafety-LinkedLists*; VERIABS participated only in some subcategories of *ReachSafety*). The head row mentions the category, the maximal score for the category, and the number of verification tasks. The tools are listed in alphabetical order; every table row lists the scores of one verifier for each category. We indicate the top-three candidates by formatting their scores in bold face and in larger font size. An empty table cell means that the verifier opted-out from the respective category. There was one category for which the winner was decided based on the run time: in category *ConcurrencySafety*, all top-three verifiers achieved the maximum score of 1293 points, but the run time differed. More information (including interactive tables, quantile plots for every category, and also the raw data in XML format) is available on the competition web-site.[15]

Table 6 reports the top-three verifiers for each category. The run time (column 'CPU Time') refers to successfully solved verification tasks (column 'Solved Tasks'). The columns 'False Alarms' and 'Wrong Proofs' report the number of

---

[14] https://vcloud.sosy-lab.org/
[15] https://sv-comp.sosy-lab.org/2017/results/

verification tasks for which the verifier reported wrong results: reporting an error path but the property holds (incorrect FALSE) and claiming that the program fulfills the property although it actually contains a bug (incorrect TRUE), respectively.

Discussion of Scoring Schema and Normalization. The verification community considers it more difficult to compute correctness proofs compared to computing error paths: according to Table 2, an answer TRUE yields 2 points (confirmed witness) and 1 point (unconfirmed witness), while an answer FALSE yields 1 point (confirmed witness). This can have consequences on the final ranking, as discussed in the report on the last SV-COMP edition [6].

Assigning a higher score value to results TRUE (compared to results FALSE) seems justified by the CPU time and energy that the verifiers need to compute the result. Table 7 shows actual numbers on this: the first column lists the three best verifiers of category *Overall*, the second and third columns report the average CPU time and average CPU energy for results TRUE, and the forth and fifth columns for results FALSE. The average is taken over all verification tasks; the CPU time is reported in seconds and the CPU energy in Joule (BENCHEXEC reads and accumulates the energy measurements of Intel CPUs). Especially for the verifier SMACK, the effort to compute results TRUE is significantly higher compared to the effort to compute results FALSE: 210 s versus 51 s of average CPU time per verification task and 2 200 J versus 580 J of average CPU energy.

A similar consideration was made on the score normalization. The community considers the value of each category equal, which has the consequence that solving a verification task in a large category (many, often similar verification tasks) has less value than solving a verification task in a small category (only a few verification tasks) [3]. The values for category *Overall* in Table 6 illustrate the purpose of the score normalization: CPA-SEQ solved 5 393 tasks, which is 791 solved tasks more than the winner UAUTOMIZER could solve (4 602). So why did CPA-SEQ not win the category? Because UAUTOMIZER is better in the intuitive sense of 'overall': it solved tasks more diversely, the 'overall' value of the verification work is higher. Thus, UAUTOMIZER received 7 099 points and CPA-SEQ received 5 296 points. Similarly, in category *SoftwareSystems*, UAUTOMIZER solved 177 more tasks than SMACK; the tasks that UAUTOMIZER solved were considered of less value (i.e., from large categories). SMACK was able to solve considerably more verification tasks in the seemingly difficult BUSYBOX categories. In these cases, the score normalization correctly maps the community's intuition.

Score-Based Quantile Functions for Quality Assessment. We use score-based quantile functions [3] because these visualizations make it easier to understand the results of the comparative evaluation. The web-site (see footnote 15) includes such a plot for each category; as example, we show the plot for category *Overall* (all verification tasks) in Fig. 4. A total of 15 verifiers participated in category *Overall*, for which the quantile plot shows the overall performance over all categories (scores for meta categories are normalized [3]). A more detailed

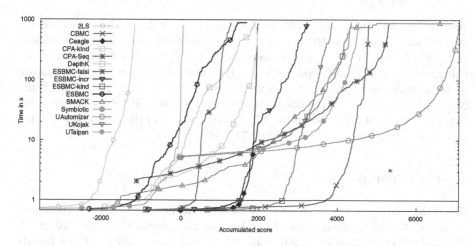

Fig. 4. Quantile functions for category *Overall*. Each quantile function illustrates the quantile (*x*-coordinate) of the scores obtained by correct verification runs below a certain run time (*y*-coordinate). More details were given previously [3]. A logarithmic scale is used for the time range from 1 s to 1000 s, and a linear scale is used for the time range between 0 s and 1 s.

Table 8. Confirmation rate of witnesses

Result	TRUE			FALSE		
	Total	Confirmed	Unconfirmed	Total	Confirmed	Unconfirmed
UAUTOMIZER	3 558	3 481	77	1 173	1 121	52
SMACK	2 947	2 695	252	1 929	1 768	161
CPA-SEQ	3 357	3 078	279	2 342	2 315	27

discussion of score-based quantile plots, including examples of what interesting insights one can obtain from the plots, is provided in previous competition reports [3,6].

Correctness of Results. Out of those verifiers that participated in all categories, UKOJAK is the only verifier that did not report any wrong result, CBMC did not report any false alarm, and CEAGLE, CPA-KIND, CPA-SEQ, and ESBMC-FALSI did not report any wrong proof.

Verifiable Witnesses. For SV-COMP, it is not sufficient to answer with just TRUE or FALSE: each answer must be accompanied by a verification witness. For correctness witnesses, an unconfirmed answer TRUE was still accepted, but was assigned only 1 point instead of 2 (cf. Table 2). All verifiers in categories that required witness validation support the common exchange format for violation and correctness witnesses. We used the two independently developed witness validators that are integrated in CPACHECKER and UAUTOMIZER [7,8].

It is interesting to see that the majority of witnesses that the top-three verifiers produced can be confirmed by the witness-validation process (more than 90%). Table 8 shows the confirmed versus unconfirmed result: the first column lists the three best verifiers of category *Overall*, the three columns for result TRUE reports the total, confirmed, and unconfirmed number of verification tasks for which the verifier answered with TRUE, respectively, and the three columns for result FALSE reports the total, confirmed, and unconfirmed number of verification tasks for which the verifier answered with FALSE, respectively. More information (for all verifiers) is given in the detailed tables on the competition web-site (see footnote 15), cf. also the report on the demo category for correctness witnesses from SV-COMP 2016 [6].

6   Conclusion

SV-COMP 2017, the 6th edition of the Competition on Software Verification, attracted 32 participating teams from 12 countries (number of teams 2012: 10, 2013: 11, 2014: 15, 2015: 22, 2016: 35). SV-COMP continues to be the broadest overview of the state of the art in automatic software verification. For the first time in verification history, proof hints (stored in an exchangeable witness) from verifiers were used on a large scale to help a different tool (validator) to validate whether it can, given the proof hints, reproduce a correctness proof. Given the results (cf. Table 8), this approach is successful. The two points for the results TRUE were counted only if the correctness witness was confirmed; for unconfirmed results TRUE, only 1 point was assigned. The number of verification tasks was increased from 6 661 to 8 908. The partitioning of the verification tasks into categories was considerably restructured; the categories *Overflows*, *MemSafety*, and *Termination* were extended and structured using sub-categories; many verification tasks from the software system BUSYBOX were added to the category *SoftwareSystems*. As before, the large jury and the organizer made sure that the competition follows the high quality standards of the TACAS conference, in particular with respect to the important principles of fairness, community support, and transparency.

References

1. Andrianov, P., Mutilin, V., Friedberger, K., Mandrykin, M., Volkov, A.: CPA-BAM-BNB: Block-abstraction memorization and region-based memory models for predicate abstractions (competition contribution). In: Legay, A., Margaria, T. (eds.) TACAS 2017, Part II. LNCS, vol. 10206, pp. 355–359. Springer, Heidelberg (2017)
2. Beyer, D.: Competition on software verification (SV-COMP). In: Flanagan, C., König, B. (eds.) TACAS 2012. LNCS, vol. 7214, pp. 504–524. Springer, Heidelberg (2012)
3. Beyer, D.: Second competition on software verification. In: Piterman, N., Smolka, S.A. (eds.) TACAS 2013. LNCS, vol. 7795, pp. 594–609. Springer, Heidelberg (2013)
4. Beyer, D.: Status report on software verification. In: Ábrahám, E., Havelund, K. (eds.) TACAS 2014. LNCS, vol. 8413, pp. 373–388. Springer, Heidelberg (2014)

5. Beyer, D.: Software verification and verifiable witnesses. In: Baier, C., Tinelli, C. (eds.) TACAS 2015. LNCS, vol. 9035, pp. 401–416. Springer, Heidelberg (2015)
6. Beyer, D.: Reliable and reproducible competition results with BENCHEXEC and witnesses (report on SV-COMP 2016). In: Chechik, M., Raskin, J.-F. (eds.) TACAS 2016. LNCS, vol. 9636, pp. 887–904. Springer, Heidelberg (2016)
7. Beyer, D., Dangl, M., Dietsch, D., Heizmann, M.: Correctness witnesses: Exchanging verification results between verifiers. In: FSE, pp. 326–337. ACM (2016)
8. Beyer, D., Dangl, M., Dietsch, D., Heizmann, M., Stahlbauer, A.: Witness validation and stepwise testification across software verifiers. In: FSE, pp. 721–733. ACM (2015)
9. Beyer, D., Dangl, M., Wendler, P.: Boosting k-induction with continuously-refined invariants. In: Kröning, D., Păsăreanu, C.S. (eds.) CAV 2015. LNCS, vol. 9206, pp. 622–640. Springer, Cham (2015)
10. Beyer, D., Löwe, S., Wendler, P.: Benchmarking and resource measurement. In: Fischer, B., Geldenhuys, J. (eds.) SPIN 2015. LNCS, vol. 9232, pp. 160–178. Springer, Cham (2015)
11. Cassez, F., Sloane, T., Roberts, M., Pigram, M., Aledo, P.G.D., Suvanpong, P.: SKINK 2.0: Static analysis of LLVM intermediate representation (competition contribution). In: Legay, A., Margaria, T. (eds.) TACAS 2017, Part II. LNCS, vol. 10206, pp. 380–384. Springer, Heidelberg (2017)
12. Chalupa, M., Vitovská, M., Jonáš, M., Slaby, J., Strejček, J.: SYMBIOTIC 4: Beyond reachability (competition contribution). In: Legay, A., Margaria, T. (eds.) TACAS 2017, Part II. LNCS, vol. 10206, pp. 385–389. Springer, Heidelberg (2017)
13. Chimdyalwar, B., Darke, P., Chauhan, A., Shah, P., Kumar, S., Venkatesh, R.: VERIABS: Verification by abstraction (competition contribution). In: Legay, A., Margaria, T. (eds.) TACAS 2017, Part II. LNCS, vol. 10206, pp. 404–408. Springer, Heidelberg (2017)
14. Dangl, M., Löwe, S., Wendler, P.: CPACHECKER with support for recursive programs and floating-point arithmetic. In: Baier, C., Tinelli, C. (eds.) TACAS 2015. LNCS, vol. 9035, pp. 423–425. Springer, Heidelberg (2015)
15. Gadelha, M.Y.R., Ismail, H.I., Cordeiro, L.C.: Handling loops in bounded model checking of C programs via k-induction. STTT 19(1), 97–114 (2017)
16. Giesl, J., Mesnard, F., Rubio, A., Thiemann, R., Waldmann, J.: Termination competition (termCOMP 2015). In: Felty, A.P., Middeldorp, A. (eds.) CADE 2015. LNCS (LNAI), vol. 9195, pp. 105–108. Springer, Cham (2015)
17. Greitschus, M., Dietsch, D., Heizmann, M., Nutz, A., Schätzle, C., Schilling, C., Schüssele, F., Podelski, A.: ULTIMATE TAIPAN: Trace abstraction and abstract interpretation (competition contribution). In: Legay, A., Margaria, T. (eds.) TACAS 2017, Part II. LNCS, vol. 10206, pp. 399–403. Springer, Heidelberg (2017)
18. Heizmann, M., Chen, Y.-W., Dietsch, D., Greitschus, M., Musa, B., Nutz, A., Schätzle, C., Schilling, C., Schüssele, F., Podelski, A.: ULTIMATE AUTOMIZER with an on-demand construction of Floyd-Hoare automata (competition contribution). In: Legay, A., Margaria, T. (eds.) TACAS 2017, Part II. LNCS, vol. 10206, pp. 394–398. Springer, Heidelberg (2017)
19. Hensel, J., Emrich, F., Frohn, F., Stroeder, T., Giesl, J.: APROVE: Proving and disproving termination of memory-manipulating C programs (competition contribution). In: Legay, A., Margaria, T. (eds.) TACAS 2017, Part II. LNCS, vol. 10206, pp. 350–354. Springer, Heidelberg (2017)

20. Howar, F., Isberner, M., Merten, M., Steffen, B., Beyer, D.: The RERS grey-box challenge 2012: Analysis of event-condition-action systems. In: Margaria, T., Steffen, B. (eds.) ISoLA 2012. LNCS, vol. 7609, pp. 608–614. Springer, Heidelberg (2012)

21. Hruska, M., Holik, L., Vojnar, T., Lengal, O., Rogalewicz, A., Simacek, J.: FORESTER: From heap shapes to automata predicates (competition contribution). In: Legay, A., Margaria, T. (eds.) TACAS 2017, Part II. LNCS, vol. 10206, pp. 365–369. Springer, Heidelberg (2017)

22. Huisman, M., Klebanov, V., Monahan, R.: VerifyThis 2012: A program verification competition. STTT **17**(6), 647–657 (2015)

23. Inverso, O., Nguyen, T.L., Fischer, B., La Torre, S., Parlato, G.: LAZY-CSEQ: A context-bounded model checking tool for multi-threaded C programs. In: ASE, pp. 807–812. IEEE (2015)

24. Jonáš, M., Mrázek, J., Štill, V., Barnat, J., Lauko, H.: Optimizing and caching SMT queries in SYMDIVINE (competition contribution). In: Legay, A., Margaria, T. (eds.) TACAS 2017, Part II. LNCS, vol. 10206, pp. 390–393. Springer, Heidelberg (2017)

25. Kotoun, M., Peringer, P., Šoková, V., Vojnar, T.: Optimized PREDATORHP and the SV-COMP heap and memory-safety benchmark (competition contribution). In: Chechik, M., Raskin, J.-F. (eds.) TACAS 2016. LNCS, vol. 9636, pp. 942–945. Springer, Heidelberg (2016)

26. Kröning, D., Tautschnig, M.: CBMC: C bounded model checker (competition contribution). In: Ábrahám, E., Havelund, K. (eds.) TACAS 2014. LNCS, vol. 8413, pp. 389–391. Springer, Heidelberg (2014)

27. Le, T.C., Ta, Q.-T., Chin, W.-N.: HIPTNT+: A termination and non-termination analyzer by second-order abduction (competition contribution). In: Legay, A., Margaria, T. (eds.) TACAS 2017, Part II. LNCS, vol. 10206, pp. 370–374. Springer, Heidelberg (2017)

28. Morse, J., Ramalho, M., Cordeiro, L., Nicole, D., Fischer, B.: ESBMC 1.22 (competition contribution). In: Ábrahám, E., Havelund, K. (eds.) TACAS 2014. LNCS, vol. 8413, pp. 405–407. Springer, Heidelberg (2014)

29. Nguyen, T.L., Fischer, B., La Torre, S., Parlato, G.: Lazy sequentialization for the safety verification of unbounded concurrent programs. In: Artho, C., Legay, A., Peled, D. (eds.) ATVA 2016. LNCS, vol. 9938, pp. 174–191. Springer, Cham (2016)

30. Nguyen, T.L., Inverso, O., Fischer, B., La Torre, S., Parlato, G.: LAZY-CSEQ 2.0: Combining lazy sequentialization with abstract interpretation (competition contribution). In: Legay, A., Margaria, T. (eds.) TACAS 2017, Part II. LNCS, vol. 10206, pp. 375–379. Springer, Heidelberg (2017)

31. Nutz, A., Dietsch, D., Mohamed, M.M., Podelski, A.: ULTIMATE KOJAK with memory-safety checks (competition contribution). In: Baier, C., Tinelli, C. (eds.) TACAS 2015. LNCS, vol. 9035, pp. 458–460. Springer, Heidelberg (2015)

32. Rakamarić, Z., Emmi, M.: SMACK: Decoupling source language details from verifier implementations. In: Biere, A., Bloem, R. (eds.) CAV 2014. LNCS, vol. 8559, pp. 106–113. Springer, Cham (2014)

33. Rocha, W., Rocha, H.O., Ismail, H., Cordeiro, L., Fischer, B.: DEPTHK: A k-induction verifier based on invariant inference for C programs (competition contribution). In: Legay, A., Margaria, T. (eds.) TACAS 2017, Part II. LNCS, vol. 10206, pp. 360–364. Springer, Heidelberg (2017)

34. Schrammel, P., Kröning, D.: 2LS for program analysis (competition contribution). In: Chechik, M., Raskin, J.-F. (eds.) TACAS 2016. LNCS, vol. 9636, pp. 905–907. Springer, Heidelberg (2016)
35. Shved, P., Mandrykin, M., Mutilin, V.: Predicate analysis with BLAST 2.7 (competition contribution). In: Flanagan, C., König, B. (eds.) TACAS 2012. LNCS, vol. 7214, pp. 525–527. Springer, Heidelberg (2012)
36. Tomasco, E., Nguyen, T.L., Inverso, O., Fischer, B., La Torre, S., Parlato, G.: MU-CSEQ 0.4: Individual memory location unwindings (competition contribution). In: Chechik, M., Raskin, J.-F. (eds.) TACAS 2016. LNCS, vol. 9636, pp. 938–941. Springer, Heidelberg (2016)
37. Zheng, M., Edenhofner, J.G., Luo, Z., Gerrard, M.J., Rogers, M.S., Dwyer, M.B., Siegel, S.F.: CIVL: Applying a general concurrency verification framework to C/P threads programs (competition contribution). In: Chechik, M., Raskin, J.-F. (eds.) TACAS 2016. LNCS, vol. 9636, pp. 908–911. Springer, Heidelberg (2016)

AProVE: Proving and Disproving Termination of Memory-Manipulating C Programs
(Competition Contribution)

Jera Hensel, Frank Emrich, Florian Frohn, Thomas Ströder,
and Jürgen Giesl$^{(\boxtimes)}$

LuFG Informatik 2, RWTH Aachen University, Aachen, Germany
{hensel,florian.frohn,stroeder,giesl}@informatik.rwth-aachen.de,
frank.emrich@rwth-aachen.de

Abstract. AProVE is a system for automatic termination and complexity analysis of C, Java, Haskell, Prolog, and several forms of rewrite systems. The new contributions in this version of AProVE are its capabilities to prove non-termination of C programs and to handle recursive C programs, even if these programs use pointer arithmetic combined with direct memory accesses. Moreover, in addition to mathematical integers, AProVE can now also handle fixed-width bitvector integers.

1 Verification Approach and Software Architecture

The focus of AProVE's analysis for C programs lies on the connection between memory addresses and their contents. To this end, AProVE employs symbolic execution and abstraction to obtain a finite *symbolic execution graph* from a C program. This graph over-approximates all possible program executions and models memory addresses and contents explicitly. However, all reasoning required to construct this graph is reduced to first-order SMT solving on integers. During the construction of the graph, AProVE proves that the original program does not expose undefined behavior. For proving termination, the strongly connected components (SCCs) of the graph are transformed to integer transition systems (ITSs). Standard techniques can be used to analyze termination of these ITSs and in case of success, this implies termination of the original program. For more information on AProVE's approach to prove termination of C programs, we refer to [15]. Moreover, AProVE's modular architecture allows to use the same backend to prove termination for several programming languages (cf. the figure on the next page). An overview on the use of AProVE for different languages is found in [10].

The approach of [15] is powerful for *termination* of C, but we need several adaptions for *non-termination*, as both the symbolic execution graph and the resulting ITSs are over-approximations. So in general, non-termination of an ITS does not imply non-termination of the original program. However, there are many program instructions that are modeled precisely

---

Supported by DFG grant GI 274/6-1.

J. Hensel—Jury member.

A. Legay and T. Margaria (Eds.): TACAS 2017, Part II, LNCS 10206, pp. 350–354, 2017.
DOI: 10.1007/978-3-662-54580-5_21

in the graph and in the resulting ITSs. Therefore, to prove non-termination of the program, it suffices to find a non-terminating lasso of the graph that does not contain any proper over-approximation. Here, a lasso

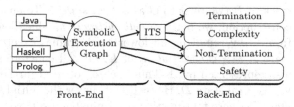

is an SCC together with a path from the root of the graph to the SCC. AProVE's back-end does not consider that evaluation of ITSs may only begin with designated "start terms" (in order to exclude spurious symbolic execution paths). Thus, to prove non-termination of the resulting ITS, we use the tool T2 [4] which takes such start terms into account. Moreover, we heuristically add conditions to the ITS rules which restrict the possible values of the variables (i.e., they yield an under-approximation of the ITS). Then, non-termination of the under-approximated ITS implies non-termination of the program.

In addition, we implemented an alternative approach for non-termination which uses our over-approximation of the program to detect *candidates* for non-terminating executions. Afterwards, one still has to prove that the candidate corresponds to an actual execution of the program. To this end, we build SMT formulas for the cycles in the symbolic execution graph. They encode that those program variables and memory contents which influence the control flow are not changed when traversing the cycle. A model M_1 of such a formula φ_1 corresponds to actual values where a loop in the program is not left. Then, this model needs to be traced back to the initial state of the graph. For this, the path from the initial state to the cycle is transformed into an SMT formula φ_2, where the values in the cycle are chosen according to the model M_1. A model of φ_2 yields concrete input values for the initial state that lead to a non-terminating execution. This approach is based on a previous technique in AProVE for proving non-termination of Java programs [3]. Since both our approaches to prove non-termination are orthogonal in power, these approaches are run in parallel in AProVE.

We also extended our graph construction of [15] to support recursive programs. To this end, we adapted our techniques developed for recursive Java programs [2] to handle explicit (de)allocation of memory and pointer arithmetic. (Compared to [2], a particular challenge is to infer and exploit information about memory that is not reachable from program variables.) The nodes of the symbolic execution graph are *abstract states*, which represent sets of concrete program states.

To prove termination of a function f, we start with a state A whose program position is at f's initial instruction. If A evaluates to a state B where f is called recursively, this yields a next state C where a new stack frame at f's initial instruction is added on top of the stack of B (we refer to C as a "*call state*"). To ensure termination of the graph construction, we perform *call abstraction*, which leads to a state D that results from C by removing all lower stack frames except the top one. Our previous state A is a *generalization* of D, i.e., all concrete states represented by D are also represented by A. Thus, we do not need further symbolic execution for the less general state D. However, whenever the initial state A evaluates to a *return state* R where the function f terminates, we have to take into account that the call of f in state C might lead to such a return state. Thus, for every pair of a call state C and a return state R of f, we construct an *intersection* state I which represents those states that result from C after completely executing the call of f in its topmost stack frame. With this extension, the symbolic execution graph construction of [15] can now also deal with recursion.

Finally, while up to now we assumed the program variables to range over mathematical integers $\mathbb{Z}$, we now developed an extension which also allows to handle fixed-width bitvector integers, cf. [11]. So our technique for termination analysis of C programs now covers both byte-accurate pointer arithmetic and bit-precise modeling of integers. To this end, we express relations between bitvectors by corresponding relations on $\mathbb{Z}$. In this way, we can use standard SMT solving over $\mathbb{Z}$ for all steps needed to construct the symbolic execution graph. Moreover, this allows us to obtain ITSs over $\mathbb{Z}$ from these graphs, and to use standard approaches for termination analysis of these ITSs.

2   Strengths and Weaknesses

Our approach is particularly powerful when the control flow depends on relations between addresses and memory contents. In addition, AProVE also proves absence of undefined behavior while many other termination analyzers just *assume* memory safety when analyzing C programs. AProVE's participation at former editions of *SV-COMP* and at the annual *Termination Competition*[1] shows the applicability of our approach to termination analysis of real-world programming languages: AProVE won most categories related to termination of C, Java, Haskell, Prolog, and to termination or runtime complexity of rewriting.

The downside of our approach is that it often takes long to construct symbolic execution graphs and that AProVE cannot give any meaningful answer before this construction is finished. Thus, AProVE's runtime is often higher than that of other tools. Moreover, our approach is currently limited to programs operating on integers and pointers (including arrays) but without struct types. For struct types, a main challenge for future work is to extend our approach to handle recursive data types in combination with explicit low-level pointer arithmetic.

3   Setup and Configuration

Since the setup of AProVE has not changed much during the last years, this section is mainly a recapitulation of the corresponding section in [14]. AProVE is

---

[1] http://www.termination-portal.org/wiki/Termination_Competition.

developed in the *"Programming Languages and Verification"* group headed by Jürgen Giesl at RWTH Aachen University. On the website [1], AProVE can be obtained as a command-line tool or as a plug-in for the popular Eclipse software development environment [8]. In this way, AProVE can already be applied during program construction. Moreover, AProVE can be accessed directly via a web interface as well. The website [1] also contains a list of external tools used by AProVE and a list of present and past contributors.

The particular version for analyzing C programs according to the *SV-COMP* format can be downloaded from the following URL. AProVE only participates in the category *"Termination"*. Thus, in this version of AProVE, we disabled some checks for memory safety, since it was agreed that only memory safe programs will be included in the termination category of *SV-COMP*.

http://aprove.informatik.rwth-aachen.de/eval/Pointer/AProVE2017.zip

All files from this archive must be extracted into one folder. AProVE is implemented in Java and needs a Java 8 Runtime Environment. To avoid handling the intricacies of C, we analyze programs in the intermediate representation of the LLVM compilation framework [12] and AProVE requires the Clang compiler [5] (version ≥ 3.5) to translate C to LLVM. To solve the search problems in the back-end, AProVE uses T2 and it applies the satisfiability checkers Z3 [6], Yices [7], and MiniSAT [9] in parallel (our archive contains all these tools). As a dependency of T2, Mono [13] (version ≥ 4.0) needs to be installed. Extending the path environment is necessary so that AProVE can find these programs. AProVE can be invoked using the wrapper script `aprove.py` in the BenchExec tool.

References

1. AProVE. http://aprove.informatik.rwth-aachen.de/
2. Brockschmidt, M., Otto, C., Giesl, J.: Modular termination proofs of recursive Java Bytecode programs by term rewriting. In: Schmidt-Schauß, M. (ed.) RTA 2011. LIPIcs, vol. 10, pp. 155–170. Dagstuhl Publishing (2011). doi:10.4230/LIPIcs.RTA.2011.155
3. Brockschmidt, M., Ströder, T., Otto, C., Giesl, J.: Automated detection of non-termination and NullPointerExceptions for Java Bytecode. In: Beckert, B., Damiani, F., Gurov, D. (eds.) FoVeOOS 2011. LNCS, vol. 7421, pp. 123–141. Springer, Heidelberg (2012). doi:10.1007/978-3-642-31762-0_9
4. Brockschmidt, M., Cook, B., Ishtiaq, S., Khlaaf, H., Piterman, N.: T2: temporal property verification. In: Chechik, M., Raskin, J.-F. (eds.) TACAS 2016. LNCS, vol. 9636, pp. 387–393. Springer, Heidelberg (2016). doi:10.1007/978-3-662-49674-9_22
5. Clang. http://clang.llvm.org
6. de Moura, L., Bjørner, N.: Z3: an efficient SMT solver. In: Ramakrishnan, C.R., Rehof, J. (eds.) TACAS 2008. LNCS, vol. 4963, pp. 337–340. Springer, Heidelberg (2008). doi:10.1007/978-3-540-78800-3_24
7. Dutertre, B., de Moura, L.: The Yices SMT solver, 2006. Tool paper at http://yices.csl.sri.com/tool-paper.pdf
8. Eclipse. http://www.eclipse.org/

9. Eén, N., Sörensson, N.: An extensible SAT-solver. In: Giunchiglia, E., Tacchella, A. (eds.) SAT 2003. LNCS, vol. 2919, pp. 502–518. Springer, Heidelberg (2004). doi:10.1007/978-3-540-24605-3_37

10. Giesl, J., Aschermann, C., Brockschmidt, M., Emmes, F., Frohn, F., Fuhs, C., Otto, C., Plücker, M., Schneider-Kamp, P., Ströder, T., Swiderski, S., Thiemann, R.: Analyzing program termination and complexity automatically with AProVE. J. Autom. Reason. **58**(1), 3–31 (2017)

11. Hensel, J., Giesl, J., Frohn, F., Ströder, T.: Proving termination of programs with bitvector arithmetic by symbolic execution. In: De Nicola, R., Kühn, E. (eds.) SEFM 2016. LNCS, vol. 9763, pp. 234–252. Springer, Heidelberg (2016). doi:10.1007/978-3-319-41591-8_16

12. Lattner, C., Adve, V.S.: LLVM: a compilation framework for lifelong program analysis and transformation. In: CGO 2004, pp. 55–88. IEEE (2004). doi:10.1109/CGO.2004.1281665

13. Mono. http://www.mono-project.com/

14. Ströder, T., Aschermann, C., Frohn, F., Hensel, J., Giesl, J.: AProVE: termination and memory safety of C programs (competition contribution). In: Baier, C., Tinelli, C. (eds.) TACAS 2015. LNCS, vol. 9035, pp. 417–419. Springer, Heidelberg (2015). doi:10.1007/978-3-662-46681-0_32

15. Ströder, T., Giesl, J., Brockschmidt, M., Frohn, F., Fuhs, C., Hensel, J., Schneider-Kamp, P., Aschermann, C.: Automatically proving termination and memory safety for programs with pointer arithmetic. J. Autom. Reason. **58**(1), 33–65 (2017)

CPA-BAM-BnB: Block-Abstraction Memoization and Region-Based Memory Models for Predicate Abstractions
(Competition Contribution)

Pavel Andrianov[1]($\boxtimes$), Karlheinz Friedberger[2], Mikhail Mandrykin[1], Vadim Mutilin[1], and Anton Volkov[1]

[1] Institute for System Programming of the Russian Academy of Sciences, Moscow, Russia
andrianov@ispras.ru
[2] University of Passau, Passau, Germany

Abstract. Our submission to SV-COMP'17 is based on the software verification framework CPACHECKER. Combined with value analysis and predicate analysis we use the concept of block-abstraction memoization with optimization and several fixes relative to the version of SV-COMP'16. A novelty of our approach is usage of BnB memory model for predicate analysis, which efficiently divides the accessed memory into memory regions and thus leads to smaller formulas.

1 Software Architecture

The framework CPACHECKER can be used for software verification. Following the concept of CONFIGURABLE PROGRAM ANALYSIS (CPA) [1], each abstract domain is implemented in its own CPA, e.g., common tasks like tracking the program location or the call stack are implemented in their own CPAs. The CPAs in the framework can be combined to build an efficient and more precise approach like value analysis or predicate analysis. A configurable algorithm like CEGAR uses the CPAs to verify reachability and memory-safety properties.

CPACHECKER is a JAVA program that uses the Eclipse CDT[1] to parse C source code, and the JavaSMT library[2] [2] to query SMT solvers like SMTInterpol[3], for deciding the satisfiability of formulas and generating interpolants.

2 Verification Approach

Our configuration uses two orthogonal approaches, block-abstraction memoization (BAM) and BnB memory model, to speedup the analysis. These approaches are explained in the following.

The research was supported by RFBR grant 15-01-03934.

[1] https://eclipse.org/cdt.
[2] https://github.com/sosy-lab/java-smt.
[3] https://ultimate.informatik.uni-freiburg.de/smtinterpol.

A. Legay and T. Margaria (Eds.): TACAS 2017, Part II, LNCS 10206, pp. 355–359, 2017.
DOI: 10.1007/978-3-662-54580-5_22

2.1 Block-Abstraction Memoization with Value Analysis and Predicate Analysis

BAM [3,4] implements modular verification by dividing the program into blocks and analyzing them separately. The block size matches function calls, i.e., a block starts at a function entry and ends at the corresponding function exit. The analysis uses a cache to reuse block abstractions, such that whenever a block that has been already analyzed is visited again, the stored result from the cache is applied. BAM uses a nested analysis to track variables and assignments. In our configuration BAM executes value analysis and predicate analysis in a parallel manner, because this was found to be a very effective approach for finding bugs and verifying programs with BAM. Figure 1 shows the control flow of our approach. After finding a counterexample path, two precise counterexample checks are applied, one for each analysis. For a spurious path we apply a refinement, for a feasible path we report a violation witness.

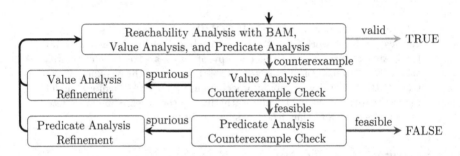

Fig. 1. Control flow for BAM with value analysis and predicate analysis

2.2 Modeling Memory with Memory Regions

BnB is a memory model based on ideas of Bornat and Burstall [5,6]. The model is implemented into the predicate analysis, which uses uninterpreted functions for mapping memory locations to memory values. An uninterpreted function f is a mathematical function, i.e. it satisfies the axiom $\forall a.\forall b.(a = b \Rightarrow f(a) = f(b))$.

In a program a memory location is represented by an lvalue expression, e.g., a pointer dereference $*p$. Assignments to lvalues change the memory state and are modeled by introducing a new uninterpreted function having the new memory value for the changed memory location and the same memory values for the unchanged ones. For example, if we have an assignment for a pointer dereference $*p = expr$, we model it by introducing a new function f_{new} with $f_{new}(p) = formula(expr)$. At the same time we should add retention conditions stating equality of memory values for the unchanged memory locations of this assignment. As far as we may not know the memory location for an lvalue expression during analysis, the retention conditions C are represented as a conjunction of disjunctions for each memory location a:

$$C := \bigwedge_{a \in \{A_1,\dots,A_N\}} \left(p = a \lor f_{new}(a) = f_{old}(a) \right),$$

where p is an lvalue expression, $A_1, \ldots, A_N$ are memory locations, $A_i \neq A_j$ for $i \neq j$, and f_{old} and f_{new} are uninterpreted functions for old and new memory states. The complexity of C highly depends on the number of memory locations.

To reduce the formula complexity we introduce memory regions representing disjoint sets of memory locations, i.e., a pointer associated with one memory region never references a memory location in another region. For each memory region R with $R \subseteq \{A_1, \ldots, A_N\}$ we introduce a separate uninterpreted function f^R. For each lvalue expression we associate a memory region R, such that an assignment to it changes only the memory locations from the associated region. Hence in retention conditions C' we consider only addresses a^R from a corresponding region R:

$$C' := \bigwedge_{a^R \in R} \left(p = a^R \vee f_{new}^R(a^R) = f_{old}^R(a^R) \right).$$

The retention conditions C' are less complex than C, because only a subset R of memory locations is used to construct the formula instead of all possible ones.

The previous implementation of the memory model [7] used *type regions* with an assumption that every memory location is always accessed with the same type. For this year we implemented *BnB regions*, which divide structure types into separate memory regions by field names. For each structure field we introduce a region defined by its name and structure type if we never take the memory address of that field. In that case we assume that the field is always accessed using field access expressions. Otherwise, if a memory address was taken, then somewhere in a program we may access this field with a pointer to a field type, thus we place such fields to a common memory region defined by the field type.

3   Strengths and Weaknesses

The contributed configuration is optimized for large programs where we need to ignore many irrelevant details. BAM is effective for the programs consisting of many functions, so that we can reuse block abstractions and have little overhead of BAM itself.

The BnB memory model benefits from separation of memory into memory regions for different fields. We have made experiments on 2795 tasks from the category *DeviceDriversLinux64* and the ratio *number of not addressed fields/number of fields* was 77%. According to the BnB memory model the majority of fields can be placed into separate regions. Thus the number of disjunctions in the resulting formulas becomes smaller. We have compared the results to the tool without BnB memory model. The CPU time was almost the same. With BnB memory model it proves 6 tasks more, but finds 5 less false, thus gets a little more points. In practice the BnB memory model may work slower if the program contains pointers for which memory was not allocated with standard memory allocation functions. In this case the analysis may prove more paths to be unreachable, thus requiring more refinements.

As far as BnB separates different fields into disjoint regions it knows that an assignment to one field does not change the other memory regions even if the pointer does not point to properly allocated memory.

Consider the following example:

```
p = not_malloc();
p->f = a;                // write access
q->g = b; p->h = c;      // updates of other fields
if (p->f != a) __VERIFIER_error();
```

The assignments to q->g and p->h do not change p->f and we can be sure that it still contains value a.

4   Setup and Configuration

We submit CPACHECKER in version 1.6.1-svcomp17-bam-bnb build from revision ldv-bam:23987 for participation in the categories *DeviceDriversLinux64* and *Falsification*. The tool requires a Java 8 runtime environment and is available at: http://linuxtesting.org/downloads/CPAchecker-1.6.1-svcomp17-bam-bnb-unix.tar.bz2

CPACHECKER has to be executed with the following command line:

```
scripts/cpa.sh -sv-comp17-bam-bnb -heap 10000m -spec prop.prp program.i
```

5   Project and Contributors

The CPACHECKER project is open-source and developed by an international research group from Ludwig-Maximilian University of Munich, University of Passau, and Institute for System Programming of the Russian Academy of Sciences. We thank all contributors for their work. More information about the project (including a list of bugs in the Linux kernel found by LDV[4] with CPACHECKER) can be accessed at https://cpachecker.sosy-lab.org.

References

1. Beyer, D., Henzinger, T.A., Théoduloz, G.: Configurable software verification: concretizing the convergence of model checking and program analysis. In: Damm, W., Hermanns, H. (eds.) CAV 2007. LNCS, vol. 4590, pp. 504–518. Springer, Heidelberg (2007). doi:10.1007/978-3-540-73368-3_51
2. Karpenkov, E.G., Friedberger, K., Beyer, D.: JavaSMT: a unified interface for SMT solvers in java. In: Blazy, S., Chechik, M. (eds.) VSTTE 2016. LNCS, vol. 9971, pp. 139–148. Springer, Heidelberg (2016). doi:10.1007/978-3-319-48869-1_11
3. Wonisch, D., Wehrheim, H.: Predicate analysis with block-abstraction memoization. In: Aoki, T., Taguchi, K. (eds.) ICFEM 2012. LNCS, vol. 7635, pp. 332–347. Springer, Heidelberg (2012). doi:10.1007/978-3-642-34281-3_24

---

[4] http://linuxtesting.org/ldv.

4. Friedberger, K.: CPA-BAM: block-abstraction memoization with value analysis and predicate analysis. In: Chechik, M., Raskin, J.-F. (eds.) TACAS 2016. LNCS, vol. 9636, pp. 912–915. Springer, Heidelberg (2016). doi:10.1007/978-3-662-49674-9_58
5. Bornat, R.: Proving pointer programs in Hoare logic. In: Backhouse, R., Oliveira, J.N. (eds.) MPC 2000. LNCS, vol. 1837, pp. 102–126. Springer, Heidelberg (2000). doi:10.1007/10722010_8
6. Burstall, R.M.: Some techniques for proving correctness of programs which alter data structures. Mach. Intell. **7**, 23–50 (1972)
7. Löwe, S., Mandrykin, M., Wendler, P.: CPACHECKER with sequential combination of explicit-value analyses and predicate analyses. In: Ábrahám, E., Havelund, K. (eds.) TACAS 2014. LNCS, vol. 8413, pp. 392–394. Springer, Heidelberg (2014). doi:10.1007/978-3-642-54862-8_27

DepthK: A k-Induction Verifier
Based on Invariant Inference for C Programs
(Competition Contribution)

Williame Rocha[1], Herbert Rocha[2(✉)], Hussama Ismail[1], Lucas Cordeiro[1,3],
and Bernd Fischer[4]

[1] Electronic and Information Research Center,
Federal University of Amazonas, Manaus, Brazil
[2] Department of Computer Science, Federal University of Roraima, Boa Vista, Brazil
herberthb12@gmail.com
[3] Department of Computer Science, University of Oxford, Oxford, UK
[4] Division of Computer Science,
University of Stellenbosch, Stellenbosch, South Africa

Abstract. DepthK is a software verification tool that employs a proof by induction algorithm that combines k-induction with invariant inference. In order to efficiently and effectively verify and falsify safety properties in C programs, DepthK infers program invariants using polyhedral constraints. Experimental results show that our approach can handle a wide variety of safety properties in several intricate verification tasks.

1 Overview

DepthK is a software verification tool that employs bounded model checking (BMC) and k-induction based on program invariants, which are automatically generated using polyhedral constraints. DepthK uses ESBMC, a context-bounded symbolic model checker that verifies single- and multi-threaded C programs [1,2], as its main verification engine. More specifically, it uses ESBMC either to find property violations up to a given bound k or to prove correctness by using the k-induction schema [3–5]. However, in contrast to the "plain" ESBMC, DepthK first infers program invariants using polyhedral constraints. It can use the PAGAI [8] (employed in the SVCOMP'17) and PIPS tools [9,10] to infer these invariants. DepthK also integrates the witness checkers CPAchecker [6] (employed in the SVCOMP'17) and Ultimate Automizer [7] for checking verification results.

DepthK pre-processes the C program to classify (bounded and unbounded) loops by tracking variables in the loop header. Based on that categorization, DepthK verifies the C program using either plain BMC or k-induction, together with invariant inference and witness checking. The k-induction uses an iterative deepening approach and checks, for each step k up to a maximum value, three different cases, called base case, forward condition, and inductive step, respectively. Intuitively, in the base case, DepthK searches for a counterexample of

© Springer-Verlag GmbH Germany 2017
A. Legay and T. Margaria (Eds.): TACAS 2017, Part II, LNCS 10206, pp. 360–364, 2017.
DOI: 10.1007/978-3-662-54580-5_23

the safety property ϕ with up to k iterations of the loop. The forward condition checks whether loops have been fully unrolled and whether ϕ holds in all states reachable within k iterations. The inductive step verifies that if ϕ is valid for k iterations, then ϕ will also be valid for the next iteration. In order to improve the effectiveness of the k-induction algorithm, DepthK tries to infer invariants that prune the state space and strengthen the induction hypothesis.

2 Verification Approach

DepthK extends ESBMC to falsify or prove correctness of a given (safety) property for any depth without manual annotation of loops with invariants. In our preliminary experiments, the integration of the inferred program invariants, in the form of polyhedral constraints, with the k-induction algorithm allows DepthK to solve more verification tasks than plain ESBMC.

Figure 1 shows an overview of the DepthK tool, with the k-induction algorithm, invariant generation, and witness validation components. The tool's inputs are a C program P (without invariants) and a safety property ϕ. It returns *TRUE* (if there is no path that violates the safety property), *FALSE* (if there exists a path that violates the safety property), or *UNKNOWN* otherwise.

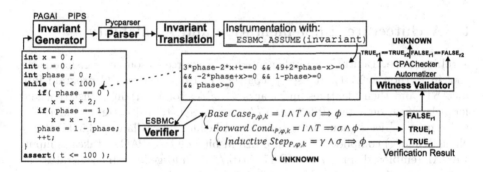

Fig. 1. Flow of the proposed method.

DepthK infers program invariants using the PAGAI and PIPS tools, which are both inter-procedural source-to-source transformation tools for C programs and rely on a polyhedral abstraction of the program behavior. PAGAI applies source code analysis to infer invariants for each control-flow point of a C program using the LLVM infrastructure (see http://llvm.org), focusing on path distinction inside the control-flow graph, while avoiding a systematic exponential path enumeration [8]. PIPS performs a two-step analysis [9]. (1) Each program instruction is associated to an affine transformer, representing its underlying transfer function. This is a bottom-up procedure, starting from elementary instructions, then working on compound statements and up to function definitions. (2) Polyhedral invariants are propagated along with instructions, using the previously computed transformers.

In DepthK, PAGAI and PIPS receive as input the program to be analyzed and generate as output C code that contains invariants written as comments around instructions. These invariants are then translated into assume statements, to constrain all possible values of those variables related to the invariants. DepthK needs to perform this step since PAGAI and PIPS generate invariants represented as mathematical expressions, which are not accepted by the syntax of C programs.

DepthK also checks the results provided by the ESBMC k-induction algorithm. In particular, DepthK checks the results related to the forward condition and inductive step using the witness validators. This re-checking procedure is needed due to the inclusion of invariants, which over-approximates the analyzed program; otherwise, the invariants could result in incorrect exploration of the states sets.

Additionally, DepthK also checks the result provided by the base case of the ESBMC k-induction algorithm, using CPAchecker (as default) or Ultimate Automizer as witness checkers via a *graphml* file. DepthK executes this step due to limitations in the memory model adopted by ESBMC [11]. We observed that the use of witness checkers has significantly improved DepthK's results, given that we are able to decrease the number of wrong proofs and false alarms by an order of magnitude.

3   Architecture, Implementation and Availability

Architecture. DepthK is implemented as a source-to-source transformation tool in Python (v2.7.1). It uses pycparser (v2.10) to parse a C program into an AST, and then identifies and tracks variables for invariant translation and loop classification. Ctags (v5.8, http://sourceforge.net/projects/ctags) identifies C language objects found in C source and header files. Clang (v3.5.0, http://clang.llvm.org) compiles a C file into LLVM bitcode that PAGAI takes as input. PAGAI (employed for SVCOMP'17, http://pagai.forge.imag.fr) generates the program invariants. It uses Uncrustify (v0.60, http://uncrustify.sourceforge.net) as a source code beautifier. ESBMC (v3.1) is employed as k-induction verifier, and CPAchecker (v1.3.10) as witness validator. In the current submission, DepthK uses Z3 (v4.0, https://z3.codeplex.com) as SMT solver in ESBMC's k-induction schema. DepthK participates in all categories of SVCOMP'17.

Availability and Installation. DepthK is freely available under the GPL license. The competition candidate DepthK v3 (for a 64-bit Linux environment) can be downloaded from https://github.com/hbgit/depthk/archive/depthk_v3. tar.gz. It must be installed as a Python script; it also requires the installation of pycparser, Uncrustify, Ctags, Clang, and open-jdk-7-jre (http://openjdk.java. net/install/). The verifiers ESBMC and CPAchecker, and the invariant generator PAGAI are included with the DepthK distribution.

User Interface. DepthK is invoked via a command-line (as in the depthk.py module for BenchExec) as follows: `./depthk-wrapper.sh -c propertyFile.prp` `file.i` DepthK accepts the property file and the verification task and provides as result: *TRUE + Witness, FALSE + Witness, or UNKNOWN*. For each error-path or correctness witness, a file that contains the witness proof is generated in the DepthK root-path *graphml* folder; this file contains the same verification task name with the extension `graphml`.

4 Strengths and Weaknesses of the Approach

The strength of the tool lies in the combination of the proof by induction algorithm with the program invariants inference to specify pre- and post-conditions, and witness validation to check the verification results of the k-induction algorithm. DepthK uses CPAchecker as a witness validator to confirm the verification results, which leads to improvements in DepthK to avoid false alarms and wrong proof. However, DepthK is in the initial development and there are still limitations on the structure of the programs and the inference of strong program invariants to prove properties. In particular, in the preliminary experiments with SV-COMP benchmarks, we observed that PAGAI/PIPS tool could not generate strong invariants for the k-induction algorithm, either due to a weak transformer or due to invariants that are not convex. All incorrect answers produced by our tool in the competition are due to bugs in its implementation.

Results. DepthK has proven to be a noticeable improvement over "plain" ESBMC. In particular, it outperforms all ESBMC versions in the sub-categories *ReachSafety-BitVectors*, *ReachSafety-Heap*, *ReachSafety-Loops*, and *MemSafety-Arrays*. It also outperforms CPA-kInd, which implements a similar approach to DepthK, in the sub-categories *ReachSafety-Heap*, *ReachSafety-Recursive*, *Overflows-BitVectors*, as well as in the category *FalsificationOverall*. In total, DepthK produced 1091 confirmed correct true results and 1056 confirmed correct false results, with a further 467 unconfirmed results. It also produced 20 incorrect true results and 32 incorrect false results, mostly due to limitations in ESBMC's memory model.

5 Software Project and Contributors

DepthK is an open-source project, mainly developed by members of the software verification group from Federal University of Roraima and Federal University of Amazonas. The script, source code, and self-contained binaries for 64-bit Linux environments are available at https://github.com/hbgit/depthk/; versions for other operating systems are available on request. The current development of DepthK is funded by the Amazonas State Research Funding Agency (FAPEAM).

References

1. Cordeiro, L., Fischer, B.: Verifying multi-threaded software using SMT-based context-bounded model checking. In: ICSE, pp. 331–340 (2011)
2. Cordeiro, L., Fischer, B., Marques-Silva, J.: SMT-based bounded model checking for embedded ANSI-C software. In: ASE, pp. 137–148 (2009)
3. Morse, J., Cordeiro, L., Nicole, D., Fischer, B.: Handling unbounded loops with ESBMC 1.20. In: Piterman, N., Smolka, S.A. (eds.) TACAS 2013. LNCS, vol. 7795, pp. 619–622. Springer, Heidelberg (2013). doi:10.1007/978-3-642-36742-7_47
4. Gadelha, M.Y.R., Ismail, H.I., Cordeiro, L.C.: Handling loops in bounded model checking of C programs via k-induction. STTT (to appear)
5. Rocha, H., Ismail, H., Cordeiro, L.C., Barreto, R.S.: Model checking embedded C software using k-induction and invariants. In: SBESC, pp. 90–95 (2015)
6. Beyer, D., Keremoglu, M.E.: CPACHECKER: a tool for configurable software verification. In: Gopalakrishnan, G., Qadeer, S. (eds.) CAV 2011. LNCS, vol. 6806, pp. 184–190. Springer, Heidelberg (2011). doi:10.1007/978-3-642-22110-1_16
7. Heizmann, M., Dietsch, D., Greitschus, M., Leike, J., Musa, B., Schätzle, C., Podelski, A.: Ultimate automizer with two-track proofs. In: Chechik, M., Raskin, J.-F. (eds.) TACAS 2016. LNCS, vol. 9636, pp. 950–953. Springer, Heidelberg (2016). doi:10.1007/978-3-662-49674-9_68
8. Henry, J., Monniaux, D., Moy, M.: PAGAI: a path sensitive static analyser. Electron. Notes Theor. Comput. Sci. **289**, 15–25 (2012)
9. PIPS: Automatic parallelizer and code transformation framework (2013). http://pips4u.org
10. Maisonneuve, V., Hermant, O., Irigoin, F.: Computing invariants with transformers: experimental scalability and accuracy. In: NSAD, vol. 307, pp. 17–31 (2014)
11. Morse, J., Ramalho, M., Cordeiro, L., Nicole, D., Fischer, B.: ESBMC 1.22 - (competition contribution). In: Ábrahám, E., Havelund, K. (eds.) TACAS 2014. LNCS, vol. 8413, pp. 405–407. Springer, Heidelberg (2014). doi:10.1007/978-3-642-54862-8_31

FORESTER: From Heap Shapes to Automata Predicates
(Competition Contribution)

Lukáš Holík, Martin Hruška[(✉)], Ondřej Lengál, Adam Rogalewicz,
Jiří Šimáček, and Tomáš Vojnar

FIT, Brno University of Technology, IT4Innovations Centre of Excellence,
Brno, Czech Republic
ihruska@fit.vutbr.cz

Abstract. This paper describes the participation of FORESTER in
the SV-COMP 2017 competition on software verification. We briefly
present the verification procedure used by FORESTER, the architecture
of FORESTER, and changes in FORESTER done since the previous year
of SV-COMP, in particular the fully-automatically refinable abstraction
for hierarchical forest automata.

1 Verification Approach

FORESTER implements an automated shape analysis that uses forest automata
(FAs) to represent sets of reachable shapes of the heap of the analysed program.
In particular, heap configurations are viewed as (directed) graphs, decomposed
into tuples of trees, and sets of such decompositions are encoded by FAs that
themselves have the form of tuples of tree automata (TAs). The tree decomposition is based on detecting the so-called *cut-points* of the heap graphs, which are
nodes either pointed by a variable or having more than one incoming edge. The
tree decomposition is then obtained by cutting a heap graph at the cut-points
and redirecting each incoming edge of a cut-point to a new leaf node labelled by
a reference to the tree with the cut-point as the root.

In order to allow for representing data structures with an unbounded number
of cut-points, a notion of *hierarchical FAs* (HFAs) is introduced. An example of a
structure for whose representation plain FAs are insufficient and HFAs are needed
is the doubly-linked list (DLL). Indeed, each internal DLL node is a cut-point
since it is pointed to by its predecessor and successor nodes. An HFA can use
other HFAs, called *nested HFAs* or *boxes*, as symbols of its alphabet. Boxes can
represent (repeating) sub-graphs of heap graphs, possibly encapsulating (hiding)
an unbounded number of cut-points. A special *folding* operation is then used to
pack a part of an HFA into a box and add the box to the alphabet of the resulting
HFA. On the contrary, when an analysed program accesses a part of a heap folded
into a box, the box is *unfolded* by plugging its content back to the wrapping HFA.
A more detailed description of these operations can be found in [1,2].

M. Hruška —Jury member.

A. Legay and T. Margaria (Eds.): TACAS 2017, Part II, LNCS 10206, pp. 365–369, 2017.
DOI: 10.1007/978-3-662-54580-5_24

The verification procedure implemented in FORESTER symbolically executes the program in the abstract domain of HFAs. At loop points, HFAs are abstracted, implementing the idea of *abstract regular model checking* [3]. The abstraction is applied component-wise, i.e., to individual TAs, collapsing some of their states, which over-approximates the set of reachable heap configurations. The abstraction speeds up the reachability analysis and enables termination on infinite state spaces, but can also yield spurious counterexamples. To recognize them, FORESTER was, in the previous SV-COMP [8], modified to run backwards (not using any abstraction) along a suspected error trace. Together with using predicate language abstraction of TAs—which collapses TA states intersecting with the same predicate languages, and which can be refined by adding more predicate languages—a *counterexample-guided abstraction refinement* (CEGAR) [6] loop is obtained.

The backward run is performed over a trace consisting of micro-instructions used by FORESTER. The trace leads from the beginning of the analysed program to a line where the given specification was found broken. FORESTER then precisely reverts all micro-instructions along the trace starting from its end. For example, when a new state of an FA was created in the forward run, FORESTER removes it in the backward run. The abstraction is reverted by intersecting FAs from the forward and backward run. If the intersection is empty, FORESTER reports a spurious counterexample, derives new predicates to refine the abstraction, and restarts the analysis. The new predicate languages are encoded by TAs selected from the FA obtained in the backward run at the point where the empty intersection with the forward run was detected. Otherwise, if the backward run reaches the beginning of the trace, the counterexample is reported as real.

For SV-COMP 2017, we extended the backward run and predicate language abstraction from plain FAs (done in [8]) to HFAs, which requires one to take into account boxes. In particular, if the original algorithms were used, it may happen that some subgraphs would be folded into a box in the forward run, while they would not be folded into this box in the backward run, meaning that the general structure of the FAs would be different. The intersection operation (which does not consider the semantics of boxes) would then determine that languages of the corresponding HFAs do not intersect. This would significantly decrease the precision of the operation. One option how to address this issue and increase the precision would be to modify the intersection operation to take into account the semantics of boxes and make it try to unfold them on the fly. We take a different approach, which enables us to successfully a larger class of programs.

Our way of dealing with the issue is to keep the HFAs obtained during the backward run *compatible* with the HFAs in the forward run. The compatibility intuitively means that the two HFAs partition the same heaps in the same way, in other words, if a heap is accepted by both HFAs, it is decomposed into the same components and the same boxes in both HFAs. When compatibility is enforced, we can (i) avoid inner inspection of boxes during the intersection operation, (ii) enable precise reversion of micro-instructions, and, as a side-effect, (iii) use a simple standard TA intersection operation performed component-wise on the HFAs. To maintain the HFAs in the backward compatible, we needed to significantly alter instructions used therein (previously, no structural constraints were imposed on the FAs; in order to deal with their different interconnection structure, a more complex intersection operation was needed).

The operations that are the most challenging to revert in the backward run are the following: folding (which is, in fact, performed together with abstraction in a loop of the form fold, abstract, fold, abstract, and so on until a fixpoint is reached), unfolding, and normalization. The normalization removes cut-points that are no longer needed, glues together TAs that stop being separated by cut-points, and orders component TAs in an FA in order to transforms the given HFA into a so-called *canonicity-respecting form* needed for testing inclusion. The reversion of folding then needs to guarantee that the sub-graphs in the folded box will appear in the correct components after the operation (taking into account that folding can be done multiple times during a single abstraction). On the other hand, the reversion of unfolding needs to guarantee that the unfolded box will be folded back into a box within the correct component. Lastly, the reversion of normalization needs to cut and re-order components into correct places. A more precise description of the described methods can be found in [7].

2   Tool Architecture

FORESTER is implemented in C++11 as a GCC plugin using the Code Listener framework [4]. The representation of a program obtained through Code Listener is translated into FORESTER's own internal microcode, which is symbolically executed. FORESTER uses the VATA library [5] for representation and manipulation with *nondeterministic TAs* (NTAs). VATA contains an optimized implementation of efficient algorithms for dealing with TAs, including operations such as state reduction of NTAs and testing their language inclusion, which is a crucial operation in FORESTER for determining whether an execution branch has reached a fixpoint.

3   Strengths and Weaknesses

One of the most important features of Forester is that it is sound (wrt the intermediate code obtained from GCC, which may have already removed some possible behaviours of the original code; e.g., GCC already fixes the order of evaluation of a function's parameters), i.e., if it answers *TRUE*, there is indeed no bug in the program. Moreover, due to the recent improvements in FORESTER regarding counterexample-based abstraction refinement [7], the number of false positives (i.e., wrong answers *FALSE*) on the benchmark of SV-COMP 2017 is significantly reduced. Concretely, the new version gets no false positives, which gives us approximately 40% more points than we would have obtained with the version of FORESTER from SV-COMP 2016, in particular on examples that contain DLLs and need to perform abstraction refinement. FORESTER can also output *UNKNOWN* if it establishes that it cannot give a correct answer.

This happens when the tool exceeds the time given by the SV-COMP rules—e.g., when searching for a shape invariant not expressible using HFAs—or upon detection of an unsupported feature of C. FORESTER specialises almost exclusively in pointer manipulations and inference of complex shape properties of pointer structures. It does not implement advanced syntactic features such as function pointers, heavily used in the LDV benchmark, but also more basic features such as arrays, unions, recursion, arithmetic, or bit operations.

The formalism of HFAs allows FORESTER to represent in a quite precise way the invariant of rather complex data structures, such as skip lists of 2 or 3 levels, various flavours of nested lists, or trees with parent and root pointers. The used representation is, moreover, quite compact, and kept small via simulation-based reduction of NTAs.

4   Tool Setup, Configuration, and Witnesses

The distribution of FORESTER for SV-COMP 2017 is available from the web page of FORESTER[1] from the link highlighted as the SV-COMP 2017 binary version. The tool is provided in the form of a shared object library libfa.so together with a Python wrapper sv_comp_run.py. The file README-FORESTER-SVCOMP-2017 describes the dependencies of FORESTER and parameters of the Python script.

The sv_comp_run.py script is run as follows:

```
sv_comp_run.py [--help] <source>
    --properties <prp> --trace <trace>
```

where <trace> is the output file for a (violation/correctness) witness, <prp> is the path to the property file, and <source> is the verified program. When FORESTER is run within the BenchExec framework, most of the parameters are set automatically by its BenchExec wrapper script. The only exception is the parameter --trace, which must be defined manually in an option node of the XML input file of BenchExec.

The format of a violation witness is an automaton, represented using GraphML (an XML schema), that represents a buggy trace through the program, while the format of a correctness witness is (again) a GraphML automaton whose states correspond to loop points in the program, and are further annotated (using an XML node with the key automaton) by a representation of the set of FAs over-approximating the set of reachable program configurations at the given state. FORESTER participates only in the MemSafety-Heap and ReachSafety-Heap categories and opts out from the rest.

5   Software Project and Contributors

FORESTER has been under development at Brno University of Technology since 2010. FORESTER and the VATA library are both licensed under GPLv3.

---

[1] http://www.fit.vutbr.cz/research/groups/verifit/tools/forester.

The source code of FORESTER is available at https://github.com/martinhruska/forester/. The authors of this paper are currently the only people involved in its development.

Acknowledgement. Supported by the Czech Science Foundation (project 17-12465S), the BUT FIT project FIT-S-17-4014, and the IT4IXS: IT4Innovations Excellence in Science project (LQ1602). Martin Hruška is a holder of the Brno Ph.D. Talent Scholarship, funded by the Brno City Municipality.

References

1. Habermehl, P., Holík, L., Rogalewicz, A., Šimáček, J., Vojnar, T.: Forest automata for verification of heap manipulation. Formal Methods Syst. Des. **41**(1), 83–106 (2012)
2. Holík, L., Lengál, O., Rogalewicz, A., Šimáček, J., Vojnar, T.: Fully automated shape analysis based on forest automata. In: Sharygina, N., Veith, H. (eds.) CAV 2013. LNCS, vol. 8044, pp. 740–755. Springer, Heidelberg (2013). doi:10.1007/978-3-642-39799-8_52
3. Bouajjani, A., Habermehl, P., Rogalewicz, A., Vojnar, T.: Abstract regular (tree) model checking. STTT **14**(2), 167–191 (2012)
4. Dudka, K., Peringer, P., Vojnar, T.: An easy to use infrastructure for building static analysis tools. In: Moreno-Díaz, R., Pichler, F., Quesada-Arencibia, A. (eds.) EURO-CAST 2011. LNCS, vol. 6927, pp. 527–534. Springer, Heidelberg (2012). doi:10.1007/978-3-642-27549-4_68
5. Lengál, O., Šimáček, J., Vojnar, T.: VATA: a library for efficient manipulation of non-deterministic tree automata. In: Flanagan, C., König, B. (eds.) TACAS 2012. LNCS, vol. 7214, pp. 79–94. Springer, Heidelberg (2012). doi:10.1007/978-3-642-28756-5_7
6. Clarke, E., Grumberg, O., Jha, S., Lu, Y., Veith, H.: Counterexample-guided abstraction refinement. In: Emerson, E.A., Sistla, A.P. (eds.) CAV 2000. LNCS, vol. 1855, pp. 154–169. Springer, Heidelberg (2000). doi:10.1007/10722167_15
7. Holík, L., Hruška, M., Lengál, O., Rogalewicz, A., Vojnar, T.: Counterexample validation and interpolation-based refinement for forest automata. In: Bouajjani, A., Monniaux, D. (eds.) VMCAI 2017. LNCS, vol. 10145, pp. 288–309. Springer, Cham (2017). doi:10.1007/978-3-319-52234-0_16
8. Holík, L., Hruška, M., Lengál, O., Rogalewicz, A., Šimáček, J., Vojnar, T.: Run Forester, Run Backwards!. In: Chechik, M., Raskin, J.-F. (eds.) TACAS 2016. LNCS, vol. 9636, pp. 923–926. Springer, Heidelberg (2016). doi:10.1007/978-3-662-49674-9_61

HipTNT+: A Termination and Non-termination Analyzer by Second-Order Abduction
(Competition Contribution)

Ton Chanh Le$^{(\boxtimes)}$, Quang-Trung Ta, and Wei-Ngan Chin

School of Computing, National University of Singapore, Singapore, Singapore
{chanhle,taqt,chinwn}@comp.nus.edu.sg

Abstract. HipTNT+ is a modular termination and non-termination analyzer for imperative programs. For each given method, the analyzer first annotates it with an initial specification with second-order unknown predicates and then incrementally derives richer known specifications with case analysis. Subsequently, the final inference result indicates either (conditional) termination, non-termination, or unknown. During the proving process, new conditions for the case analysis are abductively inferred from the failure of both termination and non-termination proof, which aim to separate the terminating and non-terminating behaviors for each method. This paper introduces the verification approach and the structure of HipTNT+, and instructs how to set up and use the system.

1 Overview

HipTNT+ is an automated verification and inference system for the termination and non-termination properties of imperative programs [2,3]. The system is built upon the HIP/SLEEK toolset [1], a separation logic-based platform for automatically proving and inferring functional correctness of heap-manipulating programs. The development of HipTNT+ follows an incremental process, in which a verifier with an appropriate specification logic for reasoning about both program termination and non-termination is first developed, prior to augmenting it with specification inference capability. In our approach, the outcomes of inference mechanism are represented by an enriched specification logic, that can be optionally re-verified by the verifier constructed in the earlier phase. This development methodology is helpful for debugging a new inference mechanism that is being implemented. In contrast, the other analyzers simply represent their outcomes in some internal forms, without automated re-scrutiny.

2 Verification Approach

HipTNT+ has been developed based on two technical innovations proposed by Le et al., that are *(i)* a unified resource-based specification logic [2],

---

T.C. Le—Jury member.

© Springer-Verlag GmbH Germany 2017
A. Legay and T. Margaria (Eds.): TACAS 2017, Part II, LNCS 10206, pp. 370–374, 2017.
DOI: 10.1007/978-3-662-54580-5_25

and *(ii)* an abductive specification inference mechanism [3] for reasoning about both program termination and non-termination *at the same time*. These approaches analyze the program terminating and non-terminating behaviors on a per-method basis, thus providing a modular, reusable and scalable proving technique for these program properties.

2.1 Termination Verification via Resource Reasoning

To specify and verify the termination and non-termination of a program, Le et al. [2] propose a unified specification logic with three temporal predicates Term M, Loop, and MayLoop, denoting definite termination (with a lexicographic ing function M), definite non-termination and possible (unknown) non-termination, respectively. The formal semantics of these predicates can be uniformly defined using a *resource capacity* predicate LC(L, U) with a lower bound L and an upper bound U on the execution length, as follows:

$$\text{Term } M \triangleq \text{LC}(0, f(M)) \quad \text{Loop} \triangleq \text{LC}(\infty, \infty) \quad \text{MayLoop} \triangleq \text{LC}(0, \infty)$$

where f is an order-embedding from a finite list of non-negative expressions into naturals.

Intuitively, a program terminates if its execution length has a finite upper bound. On the other hand, a non-terminating program has an infinite lower bound on the execution length. Verification conditions involving these temporal predicates can be discharged in terms of resource reasoning via a resource consumption entailment $\vdash_t$. Given the current program state ρ with an execution resource θ_a and a code fragment that requires a resource θ_c to execute, the entailment $\rho \wedge \theta_a \vdash_t \theta_c \blacktriangleright \theta_r$ checks if the required resource θ_c can be met (or subsumed) by the current resource θ_a. If succeeded, the entailment returns the (largest) remaining execution resource, denoted by the residue θ_r, after θ_c is consumed in θ_a.

2.2 From Verification to Inference

To infer the termination specification of each method in a program, Le et al. [3] first enhance the proposed specification logic by a pair of *second-order* temporal pre-predicate, for precondition, and post-predicate, for postcondition, to capture the unknown status of (non-)termination properties. They then extend the resource entailment procedure to handle entailments with these unknown temporal predicates, and employs a Hoare-style forward verification to collect a set of relational assumptions on them.

From these relational assumptions, a comprehensive summary of both termination and non-termination behaviors of each program's method is incrementally constructed. Specifically, the pre-assumptions collected when proving preconditions at method calls guide the overall inference process and can be used to infer ing functions when proving termination. The post-assumptions collected when proving postconditions contain information about the reachability or unreachability of the method's exits. Therefore, they can be used *(i)* to determine base-case scenarios with obvious termination property, *(ii)* to prove inductive unreachability for a definite non-termination, and *(iii)* to derive new conditions for further case-split via an abductive inference from the failure proofs of definite termination and non-termination. Note that the ranking functions and the abductive conditions can be inferred by the constraint-based synthesis technique via Farkas' lemma.

The derived summary of the method's termination and non-termination characteristics is represented in the high-level specification logic, so that it can be reused in the inference of the remaining methods higher-up in the calling hierarchy. This enables better modularity and reuse for the proving process.

3   Software Architecture

As illustrated in Fig. 1, HipTNT+ has been built on top of the HIP/SLEEK platform, so that it can exploit the infrastructure of HIP/SLEEK, such as the front-end components, the Hoare-style verification, and the SMT solver's interface. Note that the annotated specifications are optional; when they are not given, the system automatically inserts a second-order specification for each method of the input program to trigger the inference process.

For reasoning about termination and non-termination, the core of HipTNT+ is made up of two main components:

- A prover for the resource-based termination logic. This prover implements the resource consumption entailment $\vdash_t$ to discharge verification conditions involving the temporal constraints. Moreover, it also generates a set of relational assumptions on the unknown temporal predicates as the input of the termination inference system.
- An abductive inference system for termination and non-termination analysis. This component implements the search procedure to simultaneously analyze the termination and non-termination behaviors of a program from a given set of relational assumptions, via case analysis with abductive inference.

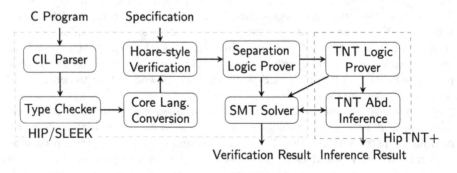

Fig. 1. Structure of HipTNT+

4   Strengths and Weaknesses

The incorporation of HipTNT+ in a verification toolset like HIP/SLEEK allows us to gradually evolve our termination analyzer with new capabilities. For example, HipTNT+ can analyze heap-based programs with ease because they are natively supported by HIP/SLEEK via separation logic. However, it is also our main weakness as we have to wait for the support from HIP/SLEEK to handle string-manipulating programs or programs with function pointers in the SV-COMP benchmarks.

5   Tool Setup and Configuration

Download and Installation. The competition submission of the HipTNT+ system is at version 2.0. A zip bundle containing a wrapper script and self-contained binaries of HipTNT+ v2.0 can be freely downloaded from http://loris-5.d2.comp.nus.edu.sg/hiptnt/plus/hiptnt_svcomp17.zip. The bundle also provides for your convenience executables of all needed third party provers, i.e., Omega Calculator[1] and Z3[2] provers.

To run the system, the wrapper script hiptnt.sh can be invoked via a command-line interface as follows: ./hiptnt.sh file.c. Note that the current working directory must be the one that contains this wrapper. The system outputs the verification results, i.e., TRUE, FALSE + *Witness*, or UNKNOWN, to the console. A witness represents a counterexample to termination, indicating a feasible path of method call locations to a definite non-termination condition with Loop.

Participation Statement. HipTNT+ participates in the Termination category.

6   Software Project and Contributors

HipTNT+ is maintained by Ton Chanh Le, a member of the Software Verification research group, led by Wei-Ngan Chin, at the National University of Singapore. HipTNT+ is freely available for academic and non-commercial use at http://loris-5.d2.comp.nus.edu.sg/hiptnt/plus/. For third party provers, i.e., Omega Calculator and Z3, their original licensing requirements apply. Our thanks go to all contributors of the core verification system HIP/SLEEK. The full description of the system can be found at http://loris-5.d2.comp.nus.edu.sg/hip/, it is also where all of its contributors are listed.

Acknowledgement. Ton Chanh and Wei-Ngan are partially supported by the MoE Tier-2 grant MOE2013-T2-2-146.

---

[1] http://www.cs.umd.edu/projects/omega/.
[2] https://github.com/Z3Prover/z3.

References

1. Chin, W., David, C., Nguyen, H.H., Qin, S.: Automated verification of shape, size and bag properties via user-defined predicates in separation logic. Sci. Comput. Program. **77**(9), 1006–1036 (2012)
2. Le, T.C., Gherghina, C., Hobor, A., Chin, W.-N.: A resource-based logic for termination and non-termination proofs. In: Merz, S., Pang, J. (eds.) ICFEM 2014. LNCS, vol. 8829, pp. 267–283. Springer, Cham (2014). doi:10.1007/978-3-319-11737-9_18
3. Le, T.C., Qin, S., Chin, W.: Termination and non-termination specification inference. In: PLDI, pp. 489–498 (2015)

Lazy-CSeq 2.0: Combining Lazy Sequentialization with Abstract Interpretation
(Competition Contribution)

Truc L. Nguyen[1], Omar Inverso[4], Bernd Fischer[2], Salvatore La Torre[3], and Gennaro Parlato[1(✉)]

[1] Electronics and Computer Science, University of Southampton,
Southampton, UK
gennaro@ecs.soton.ac.uk
[2] Division of Computer Science, Stellenbosch University, Stellenbosch, South Africa
[3] Dipartimento di Informatica, Università degli Studi di Salerno, Fisciano, Italy
[4] Gran Sasso Science Institute, L'Aquila, Italy

Abstract. Lazy sequentialization has emerged as one of the most effective techniques to find bugs in concurrent programs. However, the size of the shared global and thread-local state still poses a problem for further scaling. We therefore use abstract interpretation to minimize the representation of the concurrent program's state variables. More specifically, we run the Frama-C abstract interpretation tool over the sequentialized program output by Lazy-CSeq to compute over-approximating intervals for all (original) state variables and then exploit CBMC's bitvector support to reduce the number of bits required to represent these in the sequentialized program. We demonstrate that this leads to substantial performance gains on complex instances.

1 Verification Approach

Overview. In recent editions of the software verification competition [1,5,9,10], as well as in complex industrial case studies [11], sequentialization has proven to be a very effective program verification approach expecially for bug-hunting purposes. However, the size of the shared global and thread-local state still poses a problem for further scaling. In an experiment [11], we manually reduced the size of the state variables to the minimum required to find the bug (three bits in the case of safestack), which lead to a 20x speed-up. This clearly indicates the potential benefits of such a reduction.

Here, we automate this reduction and integrate abstract interpretation into the lazy sequentialization described in [6], in order to minimize the representation of the concurrent program's state variables, and to scale up sequentialization to more complex concurrent verification tasks. This integration of abstract interpretation is the main novelty of Lazy-CSeq 2.0 over previous versions [5,8].

Partially supported by EPSRC EP/M008991/1, INDAM-GNCS 2016, and MIUR-FARB 2014–2016 grants.

© Springer-Verlag GmbH Germany 2017
A. Legay and T. Margaria (Eds.): TACAS 2017, Part II, LNCS 10206, pp. 375–379, 2017.
DOI: 10.1007/978-3-662-54580-5_26

More specifically, we use abstract interpretation to over-approximate the intervals of all variables of the sequentialized program P' corresponding to a given a concurrent program P. Then, we replace in P' the original state variables from P with bitvectors of sizes sufficient to safely represent them; these bitvectors are often much smaller than the original data types. Finally, the resulting sequential program P'' is verified using an off-the-shelf verification backend for sequential programs. In Lazy-CSeq 2.0, we rely on Frama-C [2] as abstract interpretation framework for the interval analysis and CBMC [3] as sequential verification backend with native support for bitvectors.

In more detail, we first transform the input concurrent program P into a bounded concurrent program by inlining the functions and unwinding the loops up to a given depth. Then, we sequentialize this program by bounding the number of rounds of thread executions; in each round all threads are executed at most once and always in the same order [6]. The resulting non-deterministic sequential program P' simulates all computations that P can execute in the given number of round-robin schedules and loop unwinding depth. Program flattening guarantees that in P' there is a bounded number of threads, that each statement is executed at most once, and that all jumps are forward. P' consists of a main driver function and a simulation function for each thread instance (including the original `main`) identified during the unrolling phase.

Data Structures. P' stores and maintains, for each thread, a flag denoting whether the thread is active, the thread's original arguments, and the program location at which the previous context switch has happened. In addition, Lazy-CSeq 2.0 also maintains, for each thread, the length of each round. An important optimization is that all variables in P' that refer to program locations (i.e., the context switch locations, the round lengths, and the current program counters) are now kept separate for each thread, which allows us to use bitvectors with different sizes as data types, and so to reduce the memory overhead introduced by the translation. Further, as mentioned above, the original state variables of P are represented in P'' using bitvectors of a possibly more compact size, safely over-approximated using abstraction-based interval analysis.

Main Driver. The main function of P' consists of two phases. The first phase simply guesses all round lengths, and ensures that the guesses are smaller than the corresponding thread sizes. In our experience this leads to simpler verification conditions than the original approach, where the individual run lengths were guessed right before the corresponding sequentialized thread functions were called. The second phase consists of a sequence of small code snippets, one for each thread and each round, that (if the thread's active flag is on) set the next context switch point, call the sequentialized thread function with the original arguments, and store the context switch point for the next round.

Thread Translation. Within the simulation function for each thread instance, each statement is guarded by a check whether its location is before the stored location or after the guessed next context switch. In the former case, the statement has already been executed in a previous round, and the simulation jumps ahead one hop; in the latter case, the statement will be executed in a future round, and the simulation jumps to the thread's exit. Each jump target (corresponding either directly to a goto label or indirectly to a branch of an if statement) is also guarded by an additional check to ensure that the jump does not jump over the context switch.

2   Software Architecture

Lazy-CSeq 2.0 is implemented as a source-to-source transformation tool in Python (v2.7.9) within the CSeq framework [4,7], which consists of independent modules that can be configured and composed easily. In particular, it is implemented as CSeq configuration of about twenty modules, which include (i) the frontend processing module, which is based on the pycparser (v2.14, http://github.com/eliben/pycparser); (ii) simple transformation modules to rewrite the input program in steps into a progressively simplified syntax; (iii) translators for program flattening to produce a bounded program [6]; (iv) two modules implementing the sequentialization algorithm and that produce a backend-independent sequentialized file [6]; (v) wrappers for the abstract interpretation backend and for transforming the program's state variables into bitvectors of compact size, exploiting the over-approximated intervals; (vi) a standard program instrumentation to adapt the sequentialized file for a specific backend; and (vii) wrappers for backend invocation and user report generation or counterexample translation.

Due to CSeq's source-to-source translation architecture, we can use Frama-C as a black box. We simply run it over the sequentialized program and extract, for each state variable, the intervals estimated at the end of P'. Since these over-approximate the size requried to hold the variables' values at any given program point, the bitvector transformation can simply compute bitvector sizes from the upper bounds of these intervals.

3   Tool Setup and Configuration

Availability and Installation. Lazy-CSeq 2.0 can be downloaded from http://users.ecs.soton.ac.uk/gp4/cseq/lazy-cseq-2.0-svcomp17.tar.gz. It can be installed as global Python script. It requires installation of the pycparser, CBMC (v5.6), and Frama-C (Aluminium version); CBMC must be installed in the same directory as the Python script. For convenience, our archive contains the required CBMC and Frama-C versions. The wrapper script for the tool on the BenchExec repository is lazycseqabs.py.

Call. Lazy-CSeq 2.0 only participates in the concurrency category. It should be called in the installation directory using a wrapper script as follows:

```
lazy-cseq-abs.py -i<file> --spec<specfile> --witness<logfile>.
```

Note that Lazy-CSeq 2.0 produces a witness in a CBMC-like textual format, since there is no witness format for concurrent programs. The wrapper script bundles up translation and verification and calls Lazy-CSeq 2.0 six times, with different parameters and bounds. As soon as it detects a reachable error condition within the given bounds, it reports FALSE and terminates; otherwise it continues with the next set of parameters otherwise. If the last invocation reports no reachable error conditions, the script returns TRUE.

4 Strengths and Weaknesses

Since Lazy-CSeq 2.0 is not a full verification tool but only a concurrency pre-processor, we only competed in the Concurrency category.

Lazy sequentialization has already proven to be effective, especially in a bug-hunting setting, in recent editions of the software verification competition. The strength of this year's approach is in the compact bitblasting induced by the combined use of abstract interpretation's interval analysis and bitvector support. This can indeed provide significant analysis speedups on complex problems. In particular, interval analysis turns out to be quite lightweight yet quite accurate even on such problems, perhaps due to the particularly simple structure of the sequentialized programs. In practice, the interval analysis requires only a few hundreds of milliseconds to a few seconds, and overall verification times can improve by tens of seconds.

The intervals of the program's state variables are safely over-approximated, to minimize the number of bits needed for their representation while avoiding overflow problems. This enabled us to correctly solve all benchmarks.

On the other hand, one possible weakness of our approach is that a judicious choice of bounding parameters is essential, because it is ultimately based on bounded model-checking. This is not really a problem in the competition setting, where fine-tuning of the parameters is possible during the training phase.

References

1. Beyer, D.: Reliable and reproducible competition results with benchexec and witnesses (Report on SV-COMP 2016). In: Chechik, M., Raskin, J.-F. (eds.) TACAS 2016. LNCS, vol. 9636, pp. 887–904. Springer, Heidelberg (2016). doi:10.1007/978-3-662-49674-9_55
2. Canet, G., Cuoq, P., Monate, B.: A value analysis for C programs. In: SCAM, pp. 123–124 (2009)
3. Clarke, E., Kroening, D., Lerda, F.: A tool for checking ANSI-C programs. In: Jensen, K., Podelski, A. (eds.) TACAS 2004. LNCS, vol. 2988, pp. 168–176. Springer, Heidelberg (2004). doi:10.1007/978-3-540-24730-2_15
4. Fischer, B., Inverso, O., Parlato, G.: CSeq: a concurrency pre-processor for sequential C verification tools. In: ASE, pp. 710–713 (2013)
5. Inverso, O., Tomasco, E., Fischer, B., La Torre, S., Parlato, G.: Lazy-CSeq: a lazy sequentialization tool for C. In: Ábrahám, E., Havelund, K. (eds.) TACAS 2014. LNCS, vol. 8413, pp. 398–401. Springer, Heidelberg (2014). doi:10.1007/978-3-642-54862-8_29

6. Inverso, O., Tomasco, E., Fischer, B., La Torre, S., Parlato, G.: Bounded model checking of multi-threaded C programs via lazy sequentialization. In: Biere, A., Bloem, R. (eds.) CAV 2014. LNCS, vol. 8559, pp. 585–602. Springer, Heidelberg (2014). doi:10.1007/978-3-319-08867-9_39
7. Inverso, O., Nguyen, T.L., Fischer, B., La Torre, S., Parlato, G.: Lazy-CSeq: a context-bounded model checking tool for multi-threaded C-programs. In: ASE, pp. 807–812 (2015)
8. Nguyen, T.L., Fischer, B., La Torre, S., Parlato, G.: Lazy sequentialization for the safety verification of unbounded concurrent programs. In: Artho, C., Legay, A., Peled, D. (eds.) ATVA 2016. LNCS, vol. 9938, pp. 174–191. Springer, Heidelberg (2016). doi:10.1007/978-3-319-46520-3_12
9. Tomasco, E., Inverso, O., Fischer, B., La Torre, S., Parlato, G.: Verifying concurrent programs by memory unwinding. In: Baier, C., Tinelli, C. (eds.) TACAS 2015. LNCS, vol. 9035, pp. 551–565. Springer, Heidelberg (2015). doi:10.1007/978-3-662-46681-0_52
10. Tomasco, E., Nguyen, T.L., Inverso, O., Fischer, B., La Torre, S., Parlato, G.: MU-CSeq 0.4: individual memory location unwindings. In: Chechik, M., Raskin, J.-F. (eds.) TACAS 2016. LNCS, vol. 9636, pp. 938–941. Springer, Heidelberg (2016). doi:10.1007/978-3-662-49674-9_65
11. Tomasco, E., Nguyen, T.L., Inverso, O., Fischer, B., La Torre, S., Parlato, G.: Lazy sequentialization for TSO and PSO via shared memory abstractions. In: FMCAD, pp. 193–200 (2016)

Skink: Static Analysis of Programs in LLVM Intermediate Representation

(Competition Contribution)

Franck Cassez[✉], Anthony M. Sloane, Matthew Roberts, Matthew Pigram, Pongsak Suvanpong, and Pablo Gonzalez de Aledo

Macquarie University, Sydney, Australia
franck.cassez@mq.edu.au

Abstract. SKINK is a static analysis tool that analyses the LLVM intermediate representation (LLVM-IR) of a program source code. The analysis consists of checking whether there is a feasible execution that can reach a designated error block in the LLVM-IR. The result of a program analysis is "correct" if the error block is not reachable, "incorrect" if the error block is reachable, or "inconclusive" if the status of the program could not be determined. In this paper, we introduce SKINK 2.0 to analyse single and multi-threaded C programs.

1 Overview

SKINK is a static analysis tool that analyses the LLVM intermediate representation (LLVM-IR) of a source program. For instance, SKINK can analyse C/C++ programs using the LLVM-IR as generated by the CLANG compiler. The objective of the static analysis is to check whether a program is correct w.r.t. a given specification. For C/C++ programs, the specification is provided via `assert(condition)` statements in the C program. The aim of the analysis is to determine whether a condition can be violated. In the SV-COMP setting, `assert` calls `__VERIFIER_error` if the condition is false.

The LLVM-IR representation consists of a collection of *functions* made up of *blocks*. A block represents a sequence of simple instructions (e.g., `store`, `load`, function calls) and ends with a terminating instruction such as a branch that points to the next block(s). The LLVM-IR we analyse contains a designated "error" block that corresponds to a call to `__VERIFIER_error`. A (feasible) program trace (execution) that contains the error block is an *error trace*. A program is incorrect if and only if it can generate an error trace.

2 Verification Approach

SKINK's strategy to determine whether an error trace exists uses the iterative *refinement of the trace abstraction* algorithm of Heizmann [1,2]. First the LLVM-IR of a source program is mapped to a control flow graph (CFG) which is a

© Springer-Verlag GmbH Germany 2017
A. Legay and T. Margaria (Eds.): TACAS 2017, Part II, LNCS 10206, pp. 380–384, 2017.
DOI: 10.1007/978-3-662-54580-5_27

finite labeled automaton. The labels are the "basic blocks" and the "choices" (branching) of the LLVM-IR. In the automaton the labels are letters and do not carry any special meaning.

The (regular) language accepted by the CFG is the set of traces *leading to an error block*. These traces are *abstract error traces*: the CFG does not give any semantics to the labels, and it is not guaranteed that any such trace is actually *feasible* in the concrete program.

Checking whether a program is correct reduces to determining whether an abstract error trace is *feasible* or equivalently whether the language of the CFG contains a *feasible* abstract error trace. To determine whether a trace is feasible, we take into account the semantics of the instructions of the basic blocks. This is achieved by encoding a trace of the CFG as a logical statement and checking whether this statement is satisfiable or not. If satisfiable, a feasible error trace has been found and the program is incorrect. Otherwise, if a trace t is spurious, an *interpolant automaton* can be computed that accepts t and other traces that are infeasible for the same reason as t [1,2]. In the latter case, we can *refine* the CFG and look for an error trace in the language of the CFG minus the language accepted by the interpolant automaton. When this iterative refinement process stops[1] either no error traces remain and the program is correct or a feasible error trace is discovered and the program is incorrect.

This algorithm can also be used for checking *concurrent* programs using the *product of the CFGs* in each thread. This is in general not very effective as the number of interleavings grows exponentially in the number of threads. The algorithm implemented in SKINK 2.0 to analyse multi-threaded C programs extends our previous work that showed how to combine trace abstraction refinement and *partial-order reduction* [3].[2] In SKINK 2.0 we have combined trace abstraction refinement with state-of-the-art *dynamic partial order reduction* techniques [4].

3   Software Architecture

SKINK 2.0 is developed in SCALA and can directly analyse LLVM-IR programs. SKINK 2.0 is currently able to analyse programs in C (via CLANG) but it is trivially expandable to any language that can be compiled to LLVM-IR.

Front-end: SKINK's front-end is written using our SBT-RATS parser generator [5][3] and our KIAMA SCALA library for language processing [6].[4] We have developed a Scala-LLVM parser that can read LLVM-IR and build an abstract syntax tree (AST). Semantic analysis is performed on the AST to recover information such as variable types. SKINK 2.0 constructs CFGs for functions from the AST using the KIAMA attribute grammar methods.

---

[1] It may never stop and in this case the analysis is inconclusive.

[2] The implementation introduced in [3] has nothing in common with SKINK; it was limited to analysing programs written in a custom input language (but not C) and implemented static partial-order reductions algorithms.

[3] https://bitbucket.org/inkytonik/sbt-rats.

[4] https://bitbucket.org/inkytonik/kiama.

Middle-end: Our SCALA library AUTOMAT[5] provides the automata-theoretic operations (union, intersection, DFS, partial order reduction) that are needed in the refinement algorithm. This is used to obtain candidate abstract error traces (via a test for language emptiness) and to construct the refinements (difference between two regular languages). On top of the automata-based refinement algorithm, SKINK 2.0 provides two core functionalities. The first is the encoding of an abstract error trace into an SSA form and eventually a logical formula; this logical formula is satisfiable if and only if the trace is feasible. Satisfiability is determined by an SMT-solver (see *Back-end* section below). The second is the computation of an *interpolant automaton* which is based on an annotation of an infeasible trace with *invariants*.

Back-end: To check whether a (symbolic) abstract error trace is feasible we use a SCALA abstraction over the SMTLIB standard for common languages and interfaces for SMT solvers. Our library MQ-SCALA-SMTLIB[6] provides this abstraction. MQ-SCALA-SMTLIB was also developed using SBT-RATS and KIAMA.

We support most of the SMT-solvers (including Z3[7], SMTINTERPOL [8] and CVC4[9]) via a common SCALA abstract interface. As a result we can choose which solver to use at run time, and we may use multiple and different solvers during the same program analysis. In the current implementation, SKINK 2.0, we mostly use Z3, SMTInterpol and CVC4, depending on the theories and operations we need (linear integer arithmetic, arrays, bitvectors, interpolants) and on the SV-COMP categories to analyse.

4   Strengths and Weaknesses

SKINK 2.0 does not support the full LLVM-IR assembly language and our front-end parser may fail to parse some LLVM-IR input. Another limitation of SKINK 2.0 is that we use the LLVM *inlining* capability (`opt -inline`) to obtain a single CFG for each LLVM-IR. This may fail preventing the subsequent program analysis. These limitations should be overcome in the next months by extending our front-end Scala-LLVM parser and implementing our modular analysis technique [7]. We may assume unbounded integers in the analysis and this may result in false negatives due to overflow/underflow errors (in our tests it happened once in the ControlFlow category).

On the positive side, SKINK 2.0 can analyse programs that can be compiled into LLVM-IR which makes it usable on a variety of languages including C/C++, Objective C and Swift. A major strength of SKINK 2.0 is that it can discover loop invariants (interpolants) and is able to establish program correctness.

---

[5] https://bitbucket.org/franck44/automat.

[6] https://bitbucket.org/franck44/mq-scala-smtlib.

[7] https://github.com/Z3Prover/z3.

[8] https://ultimate.informatik.uni-freiburg.de/smtinterpol/.

[9] http://cvc4.cs.nyu.edu/web/.

Our abstract SCALA solver library MQ-SCALA-SMTLIB provides access to a number of theories (Arrays, BitVectors) and solver capabiltities (generate interpolants). SKINK 2.0 is, to the best of our knowledge, the only tool that combines trace abstraction refinement with a version (source-DPOR) of the optimal state-of-the-art *dynamic partial order reduction* algorithm [4]. This enables us to efficiently verify some programs in the Concurrency benchmarks category.

5   Set up and Configuration

Participation Statement: SKINK opts-out from all categories except *Integer and Control Flow, Concurrency* and *BitVectors.*

Set up and Configuration: SKINK 2.0 is available from http://science.mq.edu. au/~fcassez/sw/skinkv2.0.tgz. The archive includes all dependencies needed to run it on Ubuntu Xenial Xerus 64-bit (16.04.1). skink.sh is the simplest and the recommended way to run this SKINK 2.0 distribution[10]. skink.sh should be passed the C file on which analysis is to be performed. It will place along that file the verification output (.verif) and the witness file (.graphml) as appropriate.

6   Software Project and Contributors

SKINK 2.0 is developed by F. Cassez, A. M. Sloane, M. Roberts, M. Pigram, P. Gonzalez, P. Suvanpong at the Department of Computing, Macquarie University. The libraries used in SKINK 2.0 are open-source software. More information can be found at http://science.mq.edu.au/~fcassez/software-verif.html.

References

1. Heizmann, M., Hoenicke, J., Podelski, A.: Refinement of trace abstraction. In: Palsberg, J., Su, Z. (eds.) SAS 2009. LNCS, vol. 5673, pp. 69–85. Springer, Heidelberg (2009). doi:10.1007/978-3-642-03237-0_7
2. Heizmann, M., Hoenicke, J., Podelski, A.: Software model checking for people who love automata. In: Sharygina, N., Veith, H. (eds.) CAV 2013. LNCS, vol. 8044, pp. 36–52. Springer, Heidelberg (2013). doi:10.1007/978-3-642-39799-8_2
3. Cassez, F., Ziegler, F.: Verification of concurrent programs using trace abstraction refinement. In: Davis, M., Fehnker, A., McIver, A., Voronkov, A. (eds.) LPAR 2015. LNCS, vol. 9450, pp. 233–248. Springer, Heidelberg (2015). doi:10.1007/978-3-662-48899-7_17
4. Abdulla, P.A., Aronis, S., Jonsson, B., Sagonas, K.F.: Optimal dynamic partial order reduction. In: Jagannathan, S., Sewell, P. (eds.) POPL 2014, San Diego, CA, USA, 20–21 January 2014, pp. 373–384. ACM (2014)
5. Sloane, A.M., Cassez, F., Buckley, S.: The sbt-rats parser generator plugin for ala (tool paper). In: SCALA 2016, pp. 110–113. ACM, New York (2016)

---

[10] The required Scala run-time and libraries are bundled into the skink.jar file.

6. Sloane, A.M.: Lightweight language processing in Kiama. In: Fernandes, J.M., Lämmel, R., Visser, J., Saraiva, J. (eds.) GTTSE 2009. LNCS, vol. 6491, pp. 408–425. Springer, Heidelberg (2011). doi:10.1007/978-3-642-18023-1_12
7. Cassez, F., Müller, C., Burnett, K.: Summary-based inter-procedural analysis via modular trace refinement. In: FSTTCS 2014, LIPIcs, vol. 29, pp. 545–556. Schloss Dagstuhl - Leibniz-Zentrum fuer Informatik (2014)

Symbiotic 4: Beyond Reachability
(Competition Contribution)

Marek Chalupa[✉], Martina Vitovská, Martin Jonáš, Jiri Slaby,
and Jan Strejček

Faculty of Informatics, Masaryk University, Brno, Czech Republic
xchalup4@fi.muni.cz

Abstract. The fourth version of SYMBIOTIC brings a brand new instrumentation part, which can now instrument the analyzed program with
code pieces checking various specification properties. As a consequence,
SYMBIOTIC 4 participates for the first time also in categories focused on
memory safety. Further, we have ported both SYMBIOTIC and KLEE to
LLVM 3.8 and added new features to the slicer which is now modular and
easily extensible.

1 Verification Approach and Software Architecture

SYMBIOTIC implements the approach of [6] combining instrumentation, slicing,
and symbolic execution [4] to detect errors in C programs. While all the previous
releases [2,5,7] focus on checking reachability of an error location, SYMBIOTIC
4 can check any property definable by a finite state machine. For example, the
finite state machine of Fig. 1 describes the double free error. Intuitively, for every
allocated block of memory we create a copy of the state machine that tracks its
current status. An error state is reached if the block is deallocated twice. Hence,
the instrumentation reduces property checking to unreachability checking as the
program violates the property iff the error state is reachable.

Creation and tracking of the state machine is performed by code instrumented
to the original program. In fact, the brand new instrumentation implemented
in SYMBIOTIC works more generally. It gets a JSON file with instrumentation
rules. Every rule specifies a function call to be inserted before (or after) each
occurrence of a given sequence of instructions. Bodies of called functions are then
defined in a separate file written in C. Each instrumentation rule can be refined
using an output of a specified static analysis. For example, a code checking NULL
dereference does not have to be instrumented to locations where a suitable static
analysis guarantees that the corresponding pointer cannot be NULL.

For SV-COMP 2017, we have prepared instrumentation rules for checking
memory safety properties. For *overflow* property, we let CLANG sanitizer to

---

The research was supported by The Czech Science Foundation, grant GA15-17564S.

A. Legay and T. Margaria (Eds.): TACAS 2017, Part II, LNCS 10206, pp. 385–389, 2017.
DOI: 10.1007/978-3-662-54580-5_28

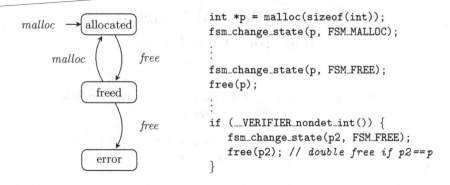

Fig. 1. State machine describing double free and a code example with instrumented function calls (red). (Color figure online)

instrument the program. We do not support checking *termination* property as it cannot be simply translated to reachability analysis.

The workflow of SYMBIOTIC 4 is illustrated by Fig. 2. As the first step, we check that the verified property is not *termination*. Then we translate the analyzed C program to the LLVM bitcode by CLANG. Next, we check that the bitcode contains no calls to pthread_create as neither our slicer, nor KLEE can process concurrent programs. If the check is successful, we proceed to the instrumentation of the bitcode. The instrumentation step has two phases. In the first phase, we insert instructions that tell the symbolic executor to treat all memory as symbolic, which allows us to correctly handle uninitialized variables. In the second phase, we perform a static analysis of the bitcode and instrument it as described above. We currently use a points-to analysis when instrumenting *memory safety* properties to insert property-checking functions only to the locations where the analysis itself does not guarantee that the property holds. The inserted functions call __VERIFIER_error whenever the property is violated. Definitions of the inserted property-checking functions as well as definitions of __VERIFIER_* functions are then linked to the bitcode. Parts of the produced code that have no effect on reaching __VERIFIER_error call sites are consequently removed by slicing. Moreover, code optimizations provided by LLVM are used before and after slicing. Before the bitcode is symbolically executed by KLEE [1], we check that it does not contain instructions related to the *floating point arithmetic* not supported by KLEE, e.g. __isnan or __inf. We use our fork of KLEE that produces an error witness when a property violation is detected. If KLEE reports that __VERIFIER_error is unreachable, we return true and a trivial correctness witness unless KLEE warns about not exploring the whole state space. This can happen for example due to limitted support of floating point instructions. In such cases, we return unknown.

The slicer has undergone significant changes. Points-to analyses and reaching definitions analysis (needed to build dependency graphs for slicing [3]) were redesigned into a more general modular framework: SYMBIOTIC now supports

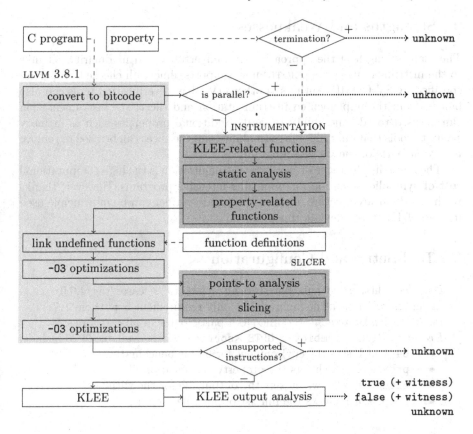

Fig. 2. Workflow of SYMBIOTIC 4. Dashed lines represent verification inputs, solid lines LLVM bitcode and control flow, and dotted lines represent outputs.

more types of analyses that share a common interface and are therefore interchangeable. In particular, the current version of SYMBIOTIC supports both flow-sensitive and flow-insensitive points-to analyses and for both of these analyses, field-sensitive and field-insensitive variants are available. Further, points-to analyses can now precisely handle a larger subset of LLVM including `memset` and `memcpy` LLVM's intrinsic calls. We have also implemented additional optimizations based on the information about strongly connected components of the program's control flow graph to speed up the analyses. Note that the redesigned analyses are not firmly integrated into the slicer and can therefore be reused by external tools.

The last significant change in SYMBIOTIC 4 is that all components have been ported to LLVM 3.8, including the symbolic executor KLEE. Finally, we got rid of separate Perl and bash scripts in favor of a concise modular implementation in Python.

2 Strengths and Weaknesses

The main strength of the approach is its universality and modularity. Thanks to the instrumentation, SYMBIOTIC now supports almost all checked properties specified by SV-COMP. Authors of other LLVM-based verification tools can also benefit from the implemented instrumentation and slicer: the instrumentation can be used to add the ability to verify additional properties such as memory safety to tools that only support reachability and the slicer can be used to remove irrelevant parts of the verified program.

The main disadvantage of the current configuration is the high computational cost of symbolic execution for branching-intensive programs. However, thanks to the modular architecture, a suitable software verifier can be in principle used instead of KLEE to alleviate this problem.

3 Tool Setup and Configuration

- *Download:* https://github.com/staticafi/symbiotic/releases/tag/4.0.0
- *Installation:* Unpack the archive. The only requirement is python 2.7.
- *Participation Statement:* SYMBIOTIC 4 participates in all categories.
- *Execution:* Run ./symbiotic OPTS <source>, where available OPTS include:
  - --64, which sets the environment for 64-bit benchmarks,
  - --prp=file, which sets the property specification file to use,
  - --witness=file, which sets the output file for the witness,
  - --help, which shows the full list of possible options.

4 Software Project and Contributors

SYMBIOTIC 4 has been developed by M. Chalupa, M. Vitovská, and J. Slaby with support of M. Jonáš and under supervision of J. Strejček. The tool and its components are available under GNU GPLv2 and MIT Licenses. The project is hosted by the Faculty of Informatics, Masaryk University. LLVM, KLEE, STP, and MiniSat are also available under open-source licenses. The project web page is: https://github.com/staticafi/symbiotic

References

1. Cadar, C., Dunbar, D., Engler, D.: KLEE: unassisted and automatic generation of high-coverage tests for complex systems programs. In: OSDI, pp. 209–224. USENIX Association (2008)
2. Chalupa, M., Jonáš, M., Slaby, J., Strejček, J., Vitovská, M.: Symbiotic 3: new slicer and error-witness generation. In: Chechik, M., Raskin, J.-F. (eds.) TACAS 2016. LNCS, vol. 9636, pp. 946–949. Springer, Heidelberg (2016). doi:10.1007/978-3-662-49674-9_67
3. Horwitz, S., Reps, T.W., Binkley, D.: Interprocedural slicing using dependence graphs. ACM Trans. Program. Lang. Syst. 12(1), 26–60 (1990)

4. King, J.C.: Symbolic execution and program testing. Commun. ACM **19**(7), 385–394 (1976)
5. Slaby, J., Strejček, J.: Symbiotic 2: more precise slicing. In: Ábrahám, E., Havelund, K. (eds.) TACAS 2014. LNCS, vol. 8413, pp. 415–417. Springer, Heidelberg (2014). doi:10.1007/978-3-642-54862-8_34
6. Slabý, J., Strejček, J., Trtík, M.: Checking properties described by state machines: on synergy of instrumentation, slicing, and symbolic execution. In: Stoelinga, M., Pinger, R. (eds.) FMICS 2012. LNCS, vol. 7437, pp. 207–221. Springer, Heidelberg (2012). doi:10.1007/978-3-642-32469-7_14
7. Slaby, J., Strejček, J., Trtík, M.: Symbiotic: synergy of instrumentation, slicing, and symbolic execution. In: Piterman, N., Smolka, S.A. (eds.) TACAS 2013. LNCS, vol. 7795, pp. 630–632. Springer, Heidelberg (2013). doi:10.1007/978-3-642-36742-7_50

Optimizing and Caching SMT Queries in SymDIVINE

(Competition Contribution)

Jan Mrázek[✉], Martin Jonáš, Vladimír Štill, Henrich Lauko, and Jiří Barnat

Faculty of Informatics, Masaryk University, Brno, Czech Republic
jan.mrazek@mail.muni.cz

Abstract. This paper presents a new version of the tool SymDIVINE, a model-checker for concurrent C/C++ programs. SymDIVINE uses a control-explicit data-symbolic approach to model checking, which allows for the bit-precise verification of programs with inputs, by representing data part of a program state by a first-order bit-vector formula. The new version of the tool employs a refined representation of symbolic states, which allows for efficient caching of SMT queries. Moreover, the new version employs additional simplifications of first-order bit-vector formulas, such as elimination of unconstrained variables from quantified formulas. All changes are documented in detail in the paper.

1 Verification Approach and Software Architecture

SymDIVINE is a model checker that primarily aims for verification of parallel C and C++ programs. In contrast to explicit-state model checker [2], SymDIVINE represents data values symbolically and can therefore handle programs with inputs, which would otherwise cause state-space explosion due to the number of possible input values. In particular, SymDIVINE uses the control-explicit data-symbolic (CEDS) approach to model checking in which control-flow of the program is represented explicitly and values of data structures are represented symbolically [1, 7].

We now describe the approach in more detail. In a CEDS model checker, each generated state is a triple that contains a control part (program counter for each thread), explicit data storage, and symbolic data storage. The explicit data storage keeps values of constants and of variables whose values are uniquely determined. The symbolic data storage represents a set of possible values of program variables by a first-order formula in the theory of bit-vectors. To generate the state space, SymDIVINE explores all possible evaluations of the program and tracks the effect of program instructions on the explicit values and on the formula representing the symbolic values. To avoid exploring infeasible paths, an SMT solver is used to check satisfiability of the formula representing the data

This work has been partially supported by Czech Science Foundation grant No. 15-08772S.

A. Legay and T. Margaria (Eds.): TACAS 2017, Part II, LNCS 10206, pp. 390–393, 2017.
DOI: 10.1007/978-3-662-54580-5_29

values. The current version of SymDIVINE relies on the SMT solver Z3 [6]. For purposes of the competition we used version 4.4.1. Additionally, in order to avoid generating unnecessary thread interleavings, SymDIVINE collapses steps invisible to other threads into a single transition using the τ-reduction algorithm [3].

In addition to verification of safety properties, SymDIVINE also supports verification of properties specified in LTL. To check such properties, SymDIVINE uses standard LTL model checking algorithms based on detection of accepting cycles in the product of the program with the Büchi automaton. However, in order to detect accepting cycles, SymDIVINE has to be able to test states for equality. The equality of states is represented as a quantified bit-vector formula, which is handed to an SMT solver [1]. Use of the state equality test can also reduce the state space, as the same state is represented and explored only once. On the other hand, the equality test requires potentially expensive quantified SMT reasoning.

To increase performance of SymDIVINE, we added several optimizations in the latest version. The first one, state slicing, is a new method of state representation. In this representation, the symbolic part of the state is represented by multiple independent formulas that describe sets of variables that do not affect each other. This allows for more efficient emptiness and equality tests as query results can be cached and smaller queries (related only to the changed program variables) can be issued. Moreover, the issued queries are usually smaller and can, in many cases, be handled by internal SymDIVINE optimizations, like checking for the syntactic equality of formulas, without the need to query the SMT solver. The motivation for state slicing comes from the observation regarding the verified LLVM bitcode. As the LLVM bitcode is in the single static assignment (SSA) form, individual instructions usually affect only a few variables. These local changes are often independent of the rest of the state. This is not just the case for concurrent programs, but also for sequential programs containing repeated function calls or non-trivial loops. We have also implemented caching, which can leverage the decomposition of the issued SMT queries to independent parts.

The second optimization is the integration of formula simplifications based on elimination of unconstrained variables [4,5] (i.e. variables that occur only once in the formula) from quantified bit-vector formulas. The effectivity of such simplifications also follows from the SSA form of LLVM: the formulas generated by SymDIVINE often contain many unconstrained variables. Although the elimination of unconstrained variables in quantifier-free formulas is provided by standard SMT solvers, we have extended the approach to quantified formulas, which is necessary for equality queries generated by SymDIVINE. Therefore, we have implemented our own elimination of unconstrained variables from quantified bit-vector formulas in SymDIVINE.

From the implementation point of view, SymDIVINE can be seen as three components – an LLVM interpreter, a state representation and an exploration algorithm. The algorithm uses the interpreter to produce successors of each state and uses emptiness and equality tests provided by the state representation to detect empty (unreachable) or already visited states. An overview of this architecture can be seen in Fig. 1. In the picture, the SMT *store* refers to

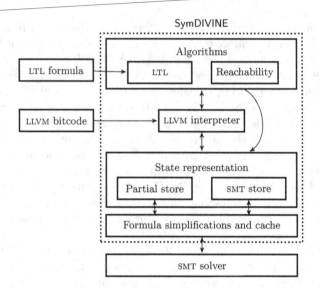

Fig. 1. High-level overview of the SymDIVINE architecture. Nested boxes correspond to interfaces and their concrete implementations.

the original storage of states and the *partial store* refers to the newly implemented storage using state slicing. Both storages are available and users can use whichever they prefer. The entire tool is written in C++ and leverages the LLVM framework. Thanks to the well-defined interface, each of the three main components is easily interchangeable.

2   Strengths and Weaknesses

The main strength of the approach is its universality: although it is aimed at parallel programs, SymDIVINE is applicable to all competition categories except termination, heap manipulation and overflows. SymDIVINE can also verify programs in multiple programming languages, as it uses the LLVM bitcode as the input format.

SymDIVINE is also precise: it can find every race condition in the program regardless of the necessary number of context switches, and thanks to the symbolic representation in the bit-vector theory, the verification is also bit-precise. Moreover, unlike symbolic execution or bounded model checkers, SymDIVINE also handles programs with infinite behaviour provided that their state space is finite. The usage of the LLVM infrastructure allows to precisely capture compiler optimizations and architecture-specific issues such as the bit width of variables.

On the other hand, the approach does not deal well with loops with number of iterations dependent on an input. In the worst-case scenario, SymDIVINE unrolls the cycle completely, resulting in an enormous state space. SymDIVINE also cannot handle programs that spawn an infinite number of threads or allocate memory from the heap. Support for other SMT solvers is not currently implemented in SymDIVINE.

3   Tool Setup and Configuration

In order to run SymDIVINE, `libboost-graph`, Z3 and `clang-3.5` have to be installed. If LTL model checking is requested, `ltl2tgba` is also required.

A prebuilt package of the tool (version 0.5) can be downloaded from a GitHub release[1]. The archive contains binaries for SymDIVINE and also a run script that eases the process of verification by automatically compiling C/C++ files to the LLVM bitcode. To verify a C program, run `run_symdivine <symdivine_dir> [options] <benchmark>`, where `<symdivine_dir>` is a directory in which the SymDIVINE executable is located. All available options can be listed by using the switch `--help`. We decided to opt-out from categories Arrays, BitVectors, Heap Data Structures and Floats. The tool should be run with options `--fix_volatile --fix_inline --silent -Os`.

4   Software Project and Contributors

SymDIVINE source code can be found on GitHub[2] under the MIT License. The tool is developed at the Faculty of Informatics, Masaryk University, and includes contributions by the authors of this paper, Petr Bauch, and Vojtěch Havel.

References

1. Barnat, J., Bauch, P., Havel, V.: Model checking parallel programs with inputs. In: PDP, pp. 756–759 (2014)
2. Barnat, J., Brim, L., Havel, V., Havlíček, J., Kriho, J., Lenčo, M., Ročkai, P., Štill, V., Weiser, J.: DiVinE 3.0 - an explicit-state model checker for multithreaded C & C++ programs. In: Sharygina, N., Veith, H. (eds.) CAV 2013. LNCS, vol. 8044, pp. 863–868. Springer, Heidelberg (2013). doi:10.1007/978-3-642-39799-8_60
3. Barnat, J., Brim, L., Ročkai, P.: Towards LTL model checking of unmodified thread-based C & C++ programs. In: Goodloe, A.E., Person, S. (eds.) NFM 2012. LNCS, vol. 7226, pp. 252–266. Springer, Heidelberg (2012). doi:10.1007/978-3-642-28891-3_25
4. Brummayer, R.: Efficient SMT solving for bit vectors and the extensional theory of arrays. Ph.D. thesis, Johannes Kepler University of Linz (2010)
5. Bruttomesso, R.: RTL verification: from SAT to SMT(BV). Ph.D. thesis, University of Trento (2008)
6. Moura, L., Bjørner, N.: Z3: an efficient SMT solver. In: Ramakrishnan, C.R., Rehof, J. (eds.) TACAS 2008. LNCS, vol. 4963, pp. 337–340. Springer, Heidelberg (2008). doi:10.1007/978-3-540-78800-3_24
7. Mrázek, J., Bauch, P., Lauko, H., Barnat, J.: SymDIVINE: tool for control-explicit data-symbolic state space exploration. In: Bošnački, D., Wijs, A. (eds.) SPIN 2016. LNCS, vol. 9641, pp. 208–213. Springer, Cham (2016). doi:10.1007/978-3-319-32582-8_14

---

[1] https://github.com/yaqwsx/SymDIVINE/releases/download/v0.5/symdivine.zip.
[2] https://github.com/yaqwsx/SymDIVINE.

Ultimate Automizer with an On-Demand Construction of Floyd-Hoare Automata
(Competition Contribution)

Matthias Heizmann[(✉)], Yu-Wen Chen, Daniel Dietsch, Marius Greitschus,
Alexander Nutz, Betim Musa, Claus Schätzle, Christian Schilling,
Frank Schüssele, and Andreas Podelski

University of Freiburg, Freiburg, Germany
heizmann@informatik.uni-freiburg.de

Abstract. ULTIMATE AUTOMIZER is a software verifier that implements
an automata-based approach for the verification of safety and liveness
properties. A central new feature that speeded up the abstraction refinement of the tool is an on-demand construction of *Floyd-Hoare automata*.

1 Verification Approach

ULTIMATE AUTOMIZER is a software verifier of the ULTIMATE program analysis framework[1]. The tool implements the automata-theoretic verification approach [3,4] that is outlined in Fig. 1 and is able to analyze reachability of error
functions, memory safety, absence of overflows and termination. In this section,
we briefly explain the overall algorithm and discuss a feature that speeded up the
tool significantly, namely the on-demand construction of Floyd-Hoare automata,
in detail.

1   $\mathcal{A}_0^{\mathsf{abs}} :=$ constructCFA()
2   **for** $i = 0, 1, 2, \ldots$
3   **if** $(\mathcal{A}_i^{\mathsf{abs}} = \emptyset)$
4   **return** property holds
5   take error trace $\pi_i \in \mathcal{A}_i^{\mathsf{abs}}$
6   **if** $(\pi_i$ is feasible$)$
7   **return** property violated
8   construct automaton $\mathcal{A}_i^{\mathsf{fh}}$ s.t.
      $\pi_i \in \mathcal{A}_i^{\mathsf{fh}}$ and $\mathcal{A}_i^{\mathsf{fh}}$ accepts
      only infeasible traces
9   $\mathcal{A}_{i+1}^{\mathsf{abs}} := \mathcal{A}_i^{\mathsf{abs}} \backslash \mathcal{A}_i^{\mathsf{fh}}$

Fig. 1. Overall verification algorithm

We initially construct an automaton,
called control flow automaton (CFA),
that resembles the control flow graph
and whose acceptance condition reflects
the property that is checked. E.g., for
reachability problems, the *error location*
of the program is the accepting state of
the CFA. The alphabet Σ of the CFA
consists of all program statements that
occur in the control flow graph. We call
a word over the alphabet Σ a *trace* and
a word that is accepted by the CFA an
error trace. The input program violates
the given property if and only if there
exists a feasible error trace, i.e., an error

---

[1] https://ultimate.informatik.uni-freiburg.de.

© Springer-Verlag GmbH Germany 2017
A. Legay and T. Margaria (Eds.): TACAS 2017, Part II, LNCS 10206, pp. 394–398, 2017.
DOI: 10.1007/978-3-662-54580-5_30

trace that corresponds to a real program execution. In our algorithm we construct automata $\mathcal{A}_i^{\text{abs}}$ that overapproximate the set of feasible error traces. Our initial abstraction $\mathcal{A}_0^{\text{abs}}$ is the CFA. All subsequent abstractions $\mathcal{A}_i^{\text{abs}}$ are constructed in a CEGAR-style refinement loop (depicted in Fig. 1).

A central step of this algorithm is the construction of the automaton $\mathcal{A}_i^{\text{fh}}$ in line 8. This automaton defines the set of (spurious) error traces that are eliminated in the current iteration. If this automaton accepts only few traces, the overall algorithm is more likely to diverge. For soundness, we require that $\mathcal{A}_i^{\text{fh}}$ does not accept any feasible error trace. To account for that we construct $\mathcal{A}_i^{\text{fh}}$ as a Floyd-Hoare automaton [4] which is a kind of automaton over the alphabet of program statements that accepts only infeasible traces. More details on the construction are given below.

Construction of Difference. In line 9 of the algorithm we construct a new abstraction for the set of feasible error traces. This new abstraction is an automaton $\mathcal{A}_{i+1}^{\text{abs}}$ whose set of traces is the set-theoretic difference of the traces from the old abstraction $\mathcal{A}_i^{\text{abs}}$ and the traces from the Floyd-Hoare automaton $\mathcal{A}_i^{\text{fh}}$. The automaton $\mathcal{A}_i^{\text{fh}}$ is deterministic and total. We construct $\mathcal{A}_{i+1}^{\text{abs}}$ as the product automaton of $\mathcal{A}_i^{\text{abs}}$ and $\mathcal{A}_i^{\text{fh}}$ where a state of the product is accepting iff its first component is accepting and the second component is not accepting. In our implementation, we construct this product incrementally. We start with the initial state of the product and construct successively all reachable states and transitions. This allows us to construct the Floyd-Hoare automaton $\mathcal{A}_i^{\text{fh}}$ on-demand as we explain next.

On-Demand Construction of Floyd-Hoare Automata . The input for the construction is a set of predicates Pred. We obtain this set by computing sequences of interpolants along infeasible error traces. Conceptually, the Floyd-Hoare automaton $\mathcal{A}_i^{\text{fh}}$ is the automaton (defined in Fig. 2) whose states are the input predicates and all conjunctions of the input predicates. By construction, this automaton accepts only infeasible traces.

$$\mathcal{A}_i^{\text{fh}} := (\Sigma, Q, \delta, q_0, Q_{\text{fin}})$$
$$Q := \{\textstyle\bigwedge P \mid P \in 2^{\text{Pred}}\}$$
$$\delta(\varphi, \mathbf{s}) := \textstyle\bigwedge\{p \in \text{Pred} \mid \text{Hoare triple}$$
$$\{\varphi\}\mathbf{s}\{p\} \text{ is valid}\}$$
$$q_0 := \text{true}$$
$$Q_{\text{fin}} := \{\text{false}\}$$

Fig. 2. Definition of Floyd-Hoare automaton for i-th iteration

Usually, the automaton $\mathcal{A}_i^{\text{abs}}$ is very sparse and hence only few transitions of $\mathcal{A}_i^{\text{fh}}$ contribute to the difference operation (line 9). Since we construct the reachable state-space of the difference incrementally, we can construct the Floyd-Hoare automaton $\mathcal{A}_i^{\text{fh}}$ on-demand. At the beginning, we construct only the initial state. Whenever the difference operation asks for successors of a state φ under a symbol $\mathbf{s}$, we check if this transition was already added. If not, we compute the successor state and add transition and successor state if necessary. The successor state is the conjunction of all input predicates $p \in \text{Pred}$ such that the Hoare triple $\{\varphi\}\mathbf{s}\{p\}$ is valid.

Checking Hoare Triples Using a Cache and Unified Predicates. We can check Hoare triples using an SMT solver. However, these calls to an SMT solver can be costly and we try to reduce their number as follows. First, we keep a cache in which we store for each Hoare triple that has been checked so far whether it was valid or not. In order to have only one representative for logically equivalent predicates, we unify all predicates and all conjunctions of predicates that were constructed as states of the Floyd-Hoare automaton $\mathcal{A}_i^{\text{fh}}$. In this unification process, we check for all pairs of formulas φ, ψ whether the implications $\varphi \models \psi$ and $\psi \models \varphi$ hold and store the results. If we now have to check the validity of a Hoare triple, we first check if one of the rules depicted in Fig. 3 is applicable. Only if none of these rules is applicable we use an SMT solver for the Hoare triple check.

$$\frac{\begin{array}{c}\varphi \models \varphi' \\ \psi' \models \psi \\ \{\varphi'\}st\{\psi'\} \text{ is valid}\end{array}}{\{\varphi\}st\{\psi\} \text{ is valid}} \; \text{ImplPos} \qquad \frac{\begin{array}{c}\varphi \models \psi \\ \mathsf{vars}(\varphi) \cap \mathsf{write}(st) = \emptyset\end{array}}{\{\varphi\}st\{\psi\} \text{ is valid}} \; \text{DataPos}$$

$$\frac{\begin{array}{c}\varphi' \models \varphi \\ \psi \models \psi' \\ \{\varphi'\}st\{\psi'\} \text{ is not valid}\end{array}}{\{\varphi\}st\{\psi\} \text{ is not valid}} \; \text{ImplNeg} \qquad \frac{\begin{array}{c}\varphi \not\models \psi \\ \mathsf{vars}(\varphi) \cap \mathsf{read}(st) = \emptyset \\ \mathsf{vars}(\psi) \cap \mathsf{read}(st) = \emptyset \\ \mathsf{vars}(\psi) \cap \mathsf{write}(st) = \emptyset\end{array}}{\{\varphi\}st\{\psi\} \text{ is not valid}} \; \text{DataNeg}$$

Fig. 3. Rules that allow us to infer validity of Hoare triples without calling an SMT solver. The set $\mathsf{vars}(\varphi)$ contains all variables that occur in the formula φ, the sets $\mathsf{read}(st)$ and $\mathsf{write}(st)$ contain all variables that are read (resp. written) by the statement st.

2   Software Architecture

ULTIMATE AUTOMIZER uses several SMT solvers. For the unification of predicates, the simplification of formulas and the Hoare triple checks we use Z3[2] because this solver can handle several SMT theories in combination with quantifiers. For the analysis of error traces we use CVC4[3], MathSAT[4], SMTInterpol[5], and Z3. These solvers each provide interpolants or unsatisfiable cores, which both can be used by ULTIMATE to extract predicates from infeasible traces. Furthermore, ULTIMATE AUTOMIZER uses several components of the ULTIMATE program analysis framework. The termination analysis is performed by the BÜCHI AUTOMIZER [5] component. This component requires

---

[2] https://github.com/Z3Prover.
[3] https://cvc4.cs.nyu.edu.
[4] http://mathsat.fbk.eu.
[5] https://ultimate.informatik.uni-freiburg.de/smtinterpol/.

ranking functions [6] and nontermination arguments [7] which are provided by LASSORANKER[6]. LASSORANKER uses SMTInterpol for the synthesis of ranking functions and Z3 for the synthesis of nontermination arguments. For our inter-procedural analysis, we use nested word automata; in the termination analysis these automata have a Büchi acceptance condition. Data structures and algo-rithms for these automata are provided by the AUTOMATA LIBRARY. ULTIMATE also provides support for violation witnesses [2] and correctness witnesses [1]. Our competition candidate is able to produce and to validate both kinds of witnesses[7].

3   Tool Setup and Configuration

A zip archive that contains the tool and all above mentioned SMT solvers is available at the website of ULTIMATE AUTOMIZER[8]. The tool can be started by the following command,

```
./Ultimate.py prop.prp inputfile 32bit|64bit simple|precise
```

where `Ultimate.py` is a Python script, `prop.prp` the SV-COMP property file, and `inputfile` a C program. The other parameters determine the architecture and the memory model, respectively.

4   Software Project

The ULTIMATE program analysis framework is mainly developed at the Uni-versity of Freiburg and received contributions from more than 50 people. The framework is written in Java and the source code is available on Github[9].

References

1. Beyer, D., Dangl, M., Dietsch, D., Heizmann, M.: Correctness witnesses: exchanging verification results between verifiers. In: FSE. ACM (2016)
2. Beyer, D., Dangl, M., Dietsch, D., Heizmann, M., Stahlbauer, A.: Witness validation and stepwise testification across software verifiers. In: ESEC/FSE, pp. 721–733. ACM (2015)
3. Heizmann, M., Hoenicke, J., Podelski, A.: Nested interpolants. In: Hermenegildo, M.V., Palsberg, J. (eds.) POPL, pp. 471–482. ACM, New York (2010)
4. Heizmann, M., Hoenicke, J., Podelski, A.: Software model checking for people who love automata. In: Sharygina, N., Veith, H. (eds.) CAV 2013. LNCS, vol. 8044, pp. 36–52. Springer, Heidelberg (2013). doi:10.1007/978-3-642-39799-8_2

---

[6] https://ultimate.informatik.uni-freiburg.de/LassoRanker/.

[7] https://github.com/sosy-lab/sv-witnesses.

[8] https://ultimate.informatik.uni-freiburg.de/automizer/.

[9] https://github.com/ultimate-pa.

5. Heizmann, M., Hoenicke, J., Podelski, A.: Termination analysis by learning terminating programs. In: Biere, A., Bloem, R. (eds.) CAV 2014. LNCS, vol. 8559, pp. 797–813. Springer, Cham (2014). doi:10.1007/978-3-319-08867-9_53
6. Leike, J., Heizmann, M.: Ranking templates for linear loops. In: Ábrahám, E., Havelund, K. (eds.) TACAS 2014. LNCS, vol. 8413, pp. 172–186. Springer, Heidelberg (2014). doi:10.1007/978-3-642-54862-8_12
7. Leike, J., Heizmann, M.: Geometric nontermination arguments. CoRR, abs/1609.05207 (2016)

Ultimate Taipan: Trace Abstraction and Abstract Interpretation
(Competition Contribution)

Marius Greitschus[(✉)], Daniel Dietsch, Matthias Heizmann, Alexander Nutz,
Claus Schätzle, Christian Schilling, Frank Schüssele, and Andreas Podelski

University of Freiburg, Freiburg im Breisgau, Germany
greitsch@informatik.uni-freiburg.de

Abstract. ULTIMATE TAIPAN is a software model checker for C programs. It is based on a CEGAR variant, trace abstraction [7], where program abstractions, counterexample selection and abstraction refinement are based on automata. ULTIMATE TAIPAN constructs path programs from counterexamples and computes fixpoints for those path programs using abstract interpretation. If the fixpoints are strong enough to prove the path program to be correct, they are guaranteed to be loop invariants for the path program. If they are not strong enough, ULTIMATE TAIPAN uses an interpolating SMT solver to obtain state assertions from the original counterexample, thus guaranteeing progress.

1 Verification Approach

ULTIMATE TAIPAN unifies the strengths of trace abstraction [7] and abstract interpretation [5]. Trace abstraction follows a counterexample-guided abstraction refinement (CEGAR) [4] approach for verifying programs. The initial abstraction is a program automaton constructed from the control flow graph (CFG) of the program. In the program automaton, accepting locations, called *error locations*, represent the violations of reachability properties of the program. Thus, the language accepted by the program automaton corresponds to all sequences of statements, i.e., to all *traces*, that lead to an error location. In each iteration, a trace τ is chosen from the current program automaton and analyzed for feasibility. If τ is feasible, it represents a concrete counterexample to the correctness of the program, as the error location is reachable. If τ is infeasible, a proof for its infeasibility is constructed. The proof is again encoded as an automaton, whose language consists of infeasible traces. Next, this automaton is *generalized* by adding transitions such that it accepts all traces of the program which are infeasible for the same reason as τ. This generalized automaton is then removed from the current program automaton by computing the automata-theoretic difference and the next iteration of trace abstraction starts. If the program automaton represents the empty language, i.e., if there are no traces of the program automaton left to analyze, the program is proven to be correct, because no error location is reachable.

A. Legay and T. Margaria (Eds.): TACAS 2017, Part II, LNCS 10206, pp. 399–403, 2017.
DOI: 10.1007/978-3-662-54580-5_31

The efficiency of this approach relies on the reasons for infeasibility of a trace. If the analyzed trace contains statements that are part of a loop, these reasons should ideally form an inductive loop invariant. If this is not the case, the trace abstraction algorithm *diverges*, i.e., the loop is unrolled until all traces of the loop have been excluded, either by discovering a suitable loop invariant, or by complete unrolling.

In ULTIMATE TAIPAN, we combat divergence by analyzing *path programs* [2] instead of traces [6]. A path program is a projection of the original program to the trace, i.e., a program in which only those statements occur that also occur in the trace. Hence, the path program may contain loops if the trace contains statements which are part of a loop. After choosing a trace of the program automaton, we construct a path program from the trace and use abstract interpretation to compute fixpoints for each path program location. If the fixpoint for an error location is *false*, this error location is unreachable and the computed fixpoints provide the proof of infeasibility for the whole path program, including the initially chosen trace. The advantage is that we are guaranteed to obtain inductive loop invariants if our abstract interpreter can prove the path program. In the case where abstract interpretation is not strong enough to prove infeasibility of the path program, we fall back on the classical analysis of single traces.

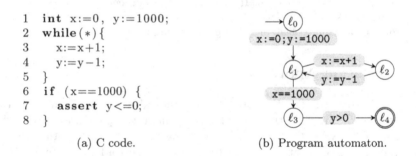

```
1   int x:=0, y:=1000;
2   while (*) {
3       x:=x+1;
4       y:=y-1;
5   }
6   if (x==1000) {
7       assert y<=0;
8   }
```

(a) C code.   (b) Program automaton.

Fig. 1. Example C code and its corresponding program automaton. The location ℓ_0 of the automaton is the initial location, ℓ_4 is the error location.

Example. Consider the program and its corresponding program automaton in Fig. 1. In the program automaton, the violation of the assertion in line 7 is encoded by the accepting error location ℓ_4. ULTIMATE TAIPAN analyzes this program by first picking a counterexample trace starting in the initial location and ending in location ℓ_4, e.g. $\tau_1 = $ `x:=0;y:=1000` `x==1000` `y>0`. This trace is infeasible because the first and the second statement contradict each other. A state assertion capturing this fact is, e.g., $x = 0$. In the next step, an automaton recognizing all traces that are infeasible because of this fact is constructed and subtracted from the current program automaton.

In the next iteration, ULTIMATE TAIPAN's algorithm picks the trace $\tau_2 = $ `x:=0;y:=1000` `x:=x+1` `y:=y-1` `x==1000` `y>0`. Like τ_1, τ_2 is infeasible. The statements `x:=0`, `x:=x+1`, and `x==1000` contradict each other. This time, the analysis of this single trace uses $x = 1$ as state assertion. If the algorithm continued in this fashion, it would need to unroll the loop completely, because the inductive loop invariant, which has to relate the variables x and y, would not be discovered. The reason for this is that the analysis of a single trace uses an interpolating SMT solver that favors "easier" and more concise state assertions over the relational one.

Hence, ULTIMATE TAIPAN uses a different method to extract state assertions. When analyzing τ_2, which contains statements that are part of a loop body, ULTIMATE TAIPAN constructs a path program from the trace and analyzes this path program with an abstract interpreter. Note that the path program corresponding to τ_2 is coincidentally the same as the program automaton. When using a relational abstract domain, e.g. octagons, in abstract interpretation, the state assertion $x \geq 0 \land y \leq 1000 \land x + y = 1000$ is found, which is an inductive loop invariant and thus suitable to prove unreachability of the error location in the path program. Therefore, when the path program is excluded from the program automaton, the resulting program automaton becomes empty and the program is proven to be safe.

2 Strengths and Weaknesses

ULTIMATE TAIPAN uses an abstract interpreter for proving infeasibility of traces containing loops. By not analyzing the whole program but a smaller path program, the imprecision that typically comes with abstract interpretation is mitigated and allows ULTIMATE TAIPAN to find inductive loop invariants in many cases. Because ULTIMATE TAIPAN needs to compensate for cases where the used abstract domain is not able to infer a proof of the path program, an interpolating SMT solver is still required. The combination of proofs obtained by the SMT solver with the proofs obtained from the abstract interpreter, e.g. during generation of correctness witnesses for the whole program, is expensive. In our current version, the computed fixpoints contain information about all variables in the path program, which leads to large SMT formulas.

3 Software Project

ULTIMATE TAIPAN is implemented on top of the program analysis framework ULTIMATE[1]. Nearly all components except the refinement algorithm and the abstract interpretation engine were already provided by ULTIMATE. We developed a new abstract interpretation plugin and integrated the refinement algorithm in the CEGAR loop of ULTIMATE AUTOMIZER. ULTIMATE provided the parsing back end and the verification condition generation as well as the construction of the control flow graph, the various automata operations, internal data structures for logic, the SMT solver SMTInterpol [3], and an interface to external SMT solvers compatible with the SMT-LIBv2 or v2.5

---

[1] https://ultimate.informatik.uni-freiburg.de.

format. Like ULTIMATE, ULTIMATE TAIPAN is written in Java and the source code is available on GitHub[2]. ULTIMATE TAIPAN is licensed under LGPLv3[3].

4   Tool Setup and Configuration

ULTIMATE TAIPAN's website[4] provides a zip archive containing the competition submission. This archive contains an executable version of ULTIMATE TAIPAN for Linux platforms as well as the necessary theorem provers Z3[5] and CVC4[6]. ULTIMATE TAIPAN itself only requires a current Java installation ($\geq$JRE 1.8).

The archive also contains a Python script, `Ultimate.py`, which maps the SV-COMP interface to ULTIMATE's command line interface and automatically selects the correct settings and the correct toolchain for ULTIMATE TAIPAN. This script requires a working Python 2.7 installation. In the SV-COMP scenario, the input to the script is a C program `input`, a property file `prop.prp`, the architecture setting `32bit` or `64bit`, and the memory model (either `simple` or `precise`) that should be assumed for the input file. ULTIMATE TAIPAN can be invoked with the following command.

```
./Ultimate.py prop.prp input 32bit|64bit simple|precise
```

The output of ULTIMATE TAIPAN is written to the file `Ultimate.log` and the result is written to `stdout`. When using the B<small>ENCH</small>E<small>XEC</small>[7] benchmarking framework to evaluate ULTIMATE TAIPAN, the output will automatically be translated by the tool-info module `ultimatetaipan.py` contained in B<small>ENCH</small>E<small>XEC</small>.

If the checked property does not hold, a human readable counterexample is stored in the file `UltimateCounterExample.errorpath` and a violation witness [1] is written to `witness.graphml`.

References

1. Beyer, D., Dangl, M., Dietsch, D., Heizmann, M., Stahlbauer, A.: Witness validation and stepwise testification across software verifiers. In: ESEC/FSE 2015, pp. 721–733 (2015)
2. Beyer, D., Henzinger, T.A., Majumdar, R., Rybalchenko, A.: Path invariants. In: PLDI 2007, pp. 300–309 (2007)
3. Christ, J., Hoenicke, J.: Cutting the mix. In: Kroening, D., Păsăreanu, C.S. (eds.) CAV 2015. LNCS, vol. 9207, pp. 37–52. Springer, Heidelberg (2015). doi:10.1007/978-3-319-21668-3_3
4. Clarke, E.M., Grumberg, O., Peled, D.A.: Model Checking. MIT Press, Cambridge (1999)

---

[2] https://github.com/ultimate-pa/ultimate/.
[3] https://www.gnu.org/licenses/lgpl-3.0.en.html.
[4] https://ultimate.informatik.uni-freiburg.de/taipan.
[5] https://github.com/Z3Prover/z3.
[6] https://cvc4.cs.nyu.edu/.
[7] https://github.com/sosy-lab/benchexec.

5. Cousot, P., Cousot, R.: Abstract interpretation: a unified lattice model for static analysis of programs by construction or approximation of fixpoints. In: POPL 1977, pp. 238–252 (1977)
6. Greitschus, M., Dietsch, D., Podelski, A.: Refining Trace Abstraction using Abstract Interpretation. arXiv:1702.02369 [cs.LO] (2017)
7. Heizmann, M., Hoenicke, J., Podelski, A.: Software model checking for people who love automata. In: Sharygina, N., Veith, H. (eds.) CAV 2013. LNCS, vol. 8044, pp. 36–52. Springer, Heidelberg (2013). doi:10.1007/978-3-642-39799-8_2

VeriAbs: Verification by Abstraction (Competition Contribution)

Bharti Chimdyalwar, Priyanka Darke$^{(\boxtimes)}$, Avriti Chauhan, Punit Shah, Shrawan Kumar, and R. Venkatesh

Tata Research Development and Design Center, Pune, India
{bharti.c,priyanka.darke,avriti.chauhan,shah.punit,shrawan.kumar,
r.venky}@tcs.com

Abstract. VeriAbs verifies C programs by transforming them to abstract programs. The transformation replaces loops in the original code by abstract loops of small known bounds. Bounded model checkers can then be used to prove properties over such programs. To perform such a transformation, VeriAbs implements (i) a static value analysis to compute loop invariants, (ii) abstract acceleration and output abstraction for numerical loops, (iii) a novel array witness selection for loops that iterate over arrays, and (iv) an iterative refinement using an enhanced k-induction technique. To find errors, VeriAbs computes bounds of the original loops and then checks for errors within those bounds. VeriAbs can thus prove properties and find errors using bounded model checking. It uses the C Bounded Model Checker (CBMC) version 5.4 with MiniSat version 2.2.

1 Verification Approach

Bounded model checking [3] verifies programs up to a finite execution length. Hence it can find errors effectively but not prove properties. To overcome this limitation, we present a tool called VeriAbs that implements a loop abstraction technique to transform a source C program to an abstract program called a *target*. By this, loops in the source are replaced with abstract loops of small known bounds in the target. Due to the known bounds of the abstract loops, the target has a finite execution length and bounded model checking can then prove properties over this program. The following two techniques are applied to abstract loops in the source:

Numerical Loop Abstraction. VeriAbs abstracts a loop by over-approximating the values of numerical variables modified by that loop [5]. The variables modified by a loop are called *output variables* and are classified as (i) *input-output (IO)* - variables that are read and modified in the loop body, and (ii) *pure output (PO)* - variables that are modified but never read in the loop body. We explain the abstraction of outputs as follows.

P. Darke—Jury member.

© Springer-Verlag GmbH Germany 2017
A. Legay and T. Margaria (Eds.): TACAS 2017, Part II, LNCS 10206, pp. 404–408, 2017.
DOI: 10.1007/978-3-662-54580-5_32

The IO variables are abstracted using *abstract acceleration* [5] which captures the effect of several loop iterations. It comprises of assignments to all IO variables using closed form expressions, like those computed for recurrence relations. This generates an abstraction of the IO variables at the start of a non-deterministically chosen k^{th} iteration of the loop. VeriAbs then executes the loop body to generate an abstraction of the IO variables at the end of the kth iteration. A pure output on the other hand cannot be accelerated, as it is never read in the loop body but only *modified* through assignments. So to abstract one pure output, VeriAbs non-deterministically selects and executes an iteration that assigns to the pure output. Before executing this iteration VeriAbs applies abstract acceleration to the IO variables. Executing the loop body in this manner abstracts the pure output because all variables controlling the execution of the assignment to the pure output or read in the assignment to the pure output were abstracted using acceleration. So to abstract all outputs of a loop, VeriAbs applies abstract acceleration followed by loop body execution, then repeats this as many times as the number of pure outputs. This generates an abstract loop of a known small bound.

To improve precision, VeriAbs applies induction whenever the input property lies within the loop [5]. The base case of the induction consists of the original loop body with the property check; and the induction step consists of the abstract loop assuming the property holds (the induction hypothesis), followed by the original loop body with the property check. VeriAbs extends this to incremental k-induction in order to refine the abstraction as explained in Sect. 1.1. VeriAbs for the first time implements k-induction wherein the induction hypothesis is generated using numerical loop abstraction. This technique can lead to a better precision than others which only assign non-deterministic values to the outputs in the hypothesis. VeriAbs also generates loop invariants using a light weight value analysis [8]. These invariants are further strengthened by loop abstraction and k-induction.

Array Loop Abstraction. The abstraction differs for loops that process arrays of large or unknown sizes [9]. In such cases, the abstraction over-approximates the behavior of the original program by substituting the loop with an abstract loop that executes over a small non-deterministically chosen sequence of array elements. We call this chosen sequence as a *witness sequence* of the original loop. The witness sequence guides the abstract loop to execute iterations that correspond to specific iterations of the original loop. This abstraction ensures that if the program is incorrect, the abstract program will also be incorrect and the same will be demonstrated by some witness sequence. The size of witness sequence depends on the input property and loop body characteristics.

1.1 Verification Process

VeriAbs accepts C code with user defined properties and outputs its verification result as successful (if all properties hold), failure (if any property fails), or unknown (if any property is unresolved). For this, VeriAbs first transforms the source to generate a target with abstract arrays and loops of known small bounds.

Since the target is an over-approximation of the source, if the property holds in the target, it holds in the source as well. VeriAbs verifies the input property using the following steps:

- *Step 1*: It passes the target to a bounded model checker while ensuring that each loop in the target is unrolled up to its known small bound. So if the model checker proves the property, VeriAbs reports the verification status as successful. If it generates a counter example due to over-approximation, *Step 2* is executed.
- *Step 2*: In this step, VeriAbs computes bounds of loops which have a constant number of iterations in the source. For this it uses a light weight value analysis [8]. Then the source along with these bounds are passed to the bounded model checker while ensuring that the model checker is inconclusive if any loop is not unrolled up to its maximum bound. Accordingly, VeriAbs reports the verification status if the model checker is able to (in)validate the property. If the model checker is inconclusive due to loops of unknown or infinite bounds, *Step 3* is executed.
- *Step 3*: In this step, VeriAbs iteratively refines the target by incrementally applying k-induction to the loops in which the input property lies. k-induction implemented by VeriAbs consists of k base cases of the original loop followed by the induction step as explained in Sect. 1. In each refinement iteration, VeriAbs generates a target with an incremented value of k starting from 2. It then passes this abstraction to the bounded model checker while ensuring that each abstract loop is unrolled up to its known bound. Thus VeriAbs reports the verification status as successful if the model checker proves the property. Otherwise it continues to refine the target till the property is proved or k reaches a threshold value of 150 (chosen heuristically) and the property remains unresolved.

VeriAbs generates safety witnesses from the target, and violation witnesses from the source using an off-the-shelf witness generator.

2   Software Architecture

Figure 1 shows the architecture of VeriAbs. It implements a static analysis in Java to perform loop and array abstraction, compute loop bounds, and generate

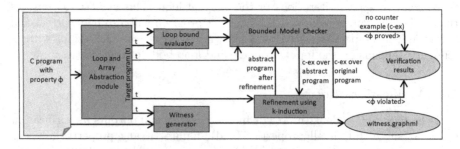

Fig. 1. The architecture of VeriAbs

target code. It uses a program analysis framework called PRISM [7] to implement this analysis. It implements iterative refinement in Java and Perl. It uses the C Bounded Model Checker (CBMC) version 5.4 [4] with a SAT solver, MINISAT version 2.2 [6]. It uses CPAchecker version 1.6.1 [2] for generating witnesses in the graphml format.

3   Strengths and Weaknesses

The main strength of VeriAbs is that it is sound. All transformations implemented by the tool are abstractions and hence if the tool reports that a property holds then it indeed holds. Another key strength is that it transforms all loops in a program to abstract loops with a known finite number of iterations, enabling the use of bounded model checkers for property proving. The main weakness of the tool is that it does not implement a refinement process that is well suited to find errors. VeriAbs uses bounded model checkers directly to find errors by unrolling loops a small finite number of times.

4   Tool Setup and Configuration

The VeriAbs executable for SV-COMP 2017 is available for download at the URL http://115.113.148.49/VeriAbs.htm. To install the tool, download the archive, extract its contents, and follow the installation instructions in VeriAbs/INSTALL.txt. To execute VeriAbs, the user needs to specify the property file of the respective verification category using the property-file option. The witness is generated in the current working directory as witness.graphml. A sample command is as follows:

```
VeriAbs/scripts/veriabs --property-file ALL.prp example.c
```

VeriAbs executes CBMC with the unwinding-assertions option to ensure soundness. It is participating in the Arrays, ControlFlow, ECA, Loops, Product-Lines, Recursive and Sequentialized sub-categories of the ReachSafety category.

5   Software Project and Contributors

VeriAbs and the PRISM program analysis framework are maintained by TCS Research [1]. VeriAbs has been developed by Bharti Chimdyalwar, Priyanka Darke, Avriti Chauhan and Punit Shah under the guidance of R Venkatesh and Shrawan Kumar. We would like to thank graduate and under-graduate interns who have contributed to the development of the numerical loop abstraction module in VeriAbs.

References

1. TCS Research. http://www.tcs.com/research/Pages/default.aspx
2. Beyer, D., Erkan Keremoglu, M.: CPAchecker: a tool for configurable software verification. CoRR, abs/0902.0019 (2009)

3. Biere, A., Cimatti, A., Clarke, E., Zhu, Y.: Symbolic model checking without BDDs. In: Cleaveland, W.R. (ed.) TACAS 1999. LNCS, vol. 1579, pp. 193–207. Springer, Heidelberg (1999). doi:10.1007/3-540-49059-0_14

4. Clarke, E., Kroening, D., Lerda, F.: A tool for checking ANSI-C programs. In: Jensen, K., Podelski, A. (eds.) TACAS 2004. LNCS, vol. 2988, pp. 168–176. Springer, Heidelberg (2004). doi:10.1007/978-3-540-24730-2_15

5. Darke, P., Chimdyalwar, B., Venkatesh, R., Shrotri, U., Metta, R.: Over-approximating loops to prove properties using bounded model checking. In: DATE 2015, Grenoble, France, 9–13 March 2015, pp. 1407–1412. IEEE (2015)

6. Eén, N., Sörensson, N.: An extensible SAT-solver. In: Giunchiglia, E., Tacchella, A. (eds.) SAT 2003. LNCS, vol. 2919, pp. 502–518. Springer, Heidelberg (2004). doi:10. 1007/978-3-540-24605-3_37

7. Khare, S., Saraswat, S., Kumar, S.: Static program analysis of large embedded code base: an experience. In: ISEC, pp. 99–102. ACM (2011)

8. Kumar, S., Chimdyalwar, B., Shrotri, U.: Precise range analysis on large industry code. In: ESEC/FSE 2013, pp. 675–678 (2013)

9. Kumar, S., Sanyal, A., Venkatesh, R., Shah, P.: Property checking array programs using witness sequences. TCS Internal Technical report (2016)

Author Index

Printed in the United States
By Bookmasters